LIVERPOOL

D0274430

Love and Eroticism

edited by
Mike Featherstone

SAGE Publications
London · Thousand Oaks

LIVERPOOL JMU LIBRARY

3 1111 00784 6197

Love & Eroticism is simultaneously published as Volume 15,
Numbers 3–4 of *Theory, Culture & Society*.

© Theory, Culture & Society 1999

First published 1999

All rights reserved. No part of this publication may be reproduced,
stored in a retrieval system, transmitted or utilized in any form or by
any means, electronic, mechanical, photocopying, recording or
otherwise, without permission in writing from the Publishers.

Published in association with *Theory, Culture & Society, Nottingham
Trent University*

 SAGE Publications Ltd
6 Bonhill Street
London EC2A 4PU

SAGE Publications Inc
2455 Teller Road
Thousand Oaks, California 91320

SAGE Publications India Pvt Ltd
32, M-Block Market
Greater Kailash – I
New Delhi 110 048

British Library Cataloguing in Publication data

A catalogue record for this book is available from the British Library

ISBN 0 7619 6251 4
ISBN 0 7619 6252 2 (pbk)

Library of Congress catalog record available

Typeset by Type Study, Scarborough, UK.
Printed in Great Britain by The Alden Press, Oxford.

Contents

Love and Eroticism
An Introduction

Mike Featherstone

ACCORDING TO OCTAVIO PAZ (1996: 7), when we speak of love and eroticism we cannot but be aware of their association with the absent third term, sexuality. Paz, the Mexican poet and Nobel Prize winner, argues that sexuality is clearly the primordial source with eroticism and love the derivative forms. The need to reproduce sexually is something we share with other animal species, along with most plant species as well. Yet, as Paz reminds us, animals always copulate in the same way, whereas human beings have woven around this act a wide range of practices, institutions, rites and representations. Eroticism is this infinite variety of forms based upon constant invention, elaboration, taming and regulation of the sexual impulse. Sexuality, then, makes eroticism possible, but eroticism transcends reproduction through its capacity to elaborate sexual experience and invent a separate realm of associated pleasures. Or, as Zygmunt Bauman succinctly puts it in his contribution to the volume, eroticism is the 'cultural processing' of sex.

While erotic attraction to another person is universal and appears in all societies, love on the other hand is usually seen as culturally and historically specific. Of course, as Paz (1996: 26) reminds us, the 'amatory feeling', the mysterious and passionate attraction towards a particular person, is something which is more exceptional, but nevertheless it too can be found in all societies and historical periods. This amatory feeling, according to Paz, requires two contradictory conditions: in the first place, the mysterious attraction that the lovers experience is perceived as an involuntary force that can overcome the reason and will; yet, on the other hand, the other person must be freely chosen and must themselves be in a position to decide otherwise. While this amatory sentiment is the rudimentary form of love, love itself goes further: as Paz (1996: 26) puts it, 'love goes

■ *Theory, Culture & Society* 1998 (SAGE, London, Thousand Oaks and New Delhi),
Vol. 15(3–4): 1–18
[0263-2764(199808/11)15:3–4;1–18;006056]

beyond the desired body and seeks the soul in the body and the body in the soul. The whole person.' This is a point emphasized by Maria Esther Maciel in her contribution, which focuses on Paz's book *The Double Flame: Essays on Love and Eroticism* (1996).

This movement from the amatory sentiment to love itself, in which the beloved becomes seen as the necessary missing part essential to complete one's being and the pursuit of the relationship becomes an overwhelming life project, is enhanced with the development of a philosophy of love. The latter arises only with the presence of a particular set of social, intellectual and moral circumstances. Sometimes the idea of love can become a powerful ideology which dominates a society. Then, as Paz (1996: 28) reminds us 'we find ourselves in the presence of a way of life, an art of living and dying, an ethic, an aesthetic, and an etiquette. A *courtesy*, to use the medieval term.' Important here are the ways in which a culture of love emerged within court societies and became a privileged body of knowledge and practice of a small group of men and women. Yet we should be aware that this form of courtly love emerged not only in Europe but in the Islamic world, India and East Asia too. The Chinese novel *Dream of the Red Chamber* by Ts'ao Hsúeh-ch'in and the Japanese novel *The Tale of Genji* by Murasaki Shikubu both describe love affairs in the courtly aristocratic world (Paz, 1996: 29ff). Both books point to the close relationship between a high courtly culture and a philosophy of love – something which is absent from many accounts of the history of love.[1]

There are two aspects of the court society which are particularly relevant to the emergence of love as a way of life and as a powerful cultural image: the role of cultural specialists who made and circulated representations of love and the growth of the power of women. Love, then, should not just be seen as a practice, a physical relationship between two people, the history of love is also the history of a literary genre. The literature on love generally developed in close interplay with the philosophy of each era. As Paz (1996: 126) reminds us, all the great changes in love correspond to shifts in literary movements, which both reflected on the different forms love could take and converted them into high ideals.

The growth of romantic love in 12th-century France was, therefore, made possible through the development of Provençal poetry which offered an image and ideal of courtly love worthy of imitation. Hence the Provençal poets were responsible for the formation of the Western code of love: they invented love as a way of life alongside the invention of lyric poetry. Important here was the transition from chivalrous poetry written by noblemen for aristocratic women of their own strata to romantic lyric poetry written and performed by non-aristocratic professional poets who wandered from castle to castle. The poetry was not constructed to be read, but to be heard, with poems accompanied by music performed in the castle of the great lord. The subject of the poems was generally love between a man and a woman, and the poems were spoken in the vernacular form and not Latin, so that the ladies of the court could understand. The relative shift in the balance of power between the sexes among the aristocracy which permittec women to have greater freedom was hence accompanied by the emergence of a group of troubadours who were wandering poets, who furthered the shift by presenting the man as the slave of his lady in their poems.[2] The poets were almost always inferior in social rank to the ladies and love was frequently presented as a mysterious exaltation, both physical and spiritual, a state of bliss derived from purified desire. The longing for the lady was all the more poignant given the social differential and physical separation from the beloved which was both experienced and also something that could only begin to be adequately expressed in poetry.[3] For Paz (1996: 64) the emergence of love is inseparable from the rise in status of woman; as he remarks 'There is no love without feminine freedom.' Love, then, depends upon the capacity of the woman not only to attract, but to choose and reject, to become seen as a person in her own right, albeit that this ideal, along with that of courtesy, was limited to the upper strata. In terms of the predominant form of arranged marriages, love relationships were daring and dangerous transgressions.

The movement towards the fully developed court society, such as the Versailles of Louis XIV described by Norbert Elias (1983), in the 'gilded cage' of court life with its elaborate ceremonies and rituals, cultivation of formal conversation and good manners, provided a closed world replete with artifice, spying and intense rivalries in which the yearning for romantic relationships with social inferiors became a strong counter-ideal. As Elias (1983: 214ff; see also Featherstone, 1995: 26) reminds us, the sociogenesis of the romantic sentiment can be found not only in the middle classes, but in the court society, where aristocrats who were subjected to the incessant self-control and calculation of court life developed a nostalgia for the simpler life, not only manifest in a longing for country life, but in a longing for the more expressive and spontaneous relationships of romantic love with trusted social inferiors. A literature developed around these romantic themes. In the subsequent years, love relationships and the trials and sufferings of those involved in them became subjected to an endless elaborate set of representations not only in literature and the arts, but increasingly in Western popular cultural forms too.

At the same time, in the Western tradition, there is a good deal of attention paid to the dangers of love, to the irrationality of attraction, to the impossibility of sustaining love and the eventual price to be paid in the disruption of social relationships. In her article in this collection, Mary Evans argues that while there has been a fascination with romantic love in the West, love has generally had a bad press from novelists, with women being as critical as men. Jane Austen, for example, is seen as the most profound and articulate critic of romantic love. She was strongly opposed to the 'young, heated fancy', the expectation of love and romance which people assumed was necessary for marriage. Austen is for detached reason and judgement against the cultivation of passionate feelings. Romantic love is seen as trapping women in false expectations and crippling demands. The

tory of love in post-Enlightenment Europe, Evans tells us,
ested one. On the one hand, love has often been regarded as
irrational, with men and the socially powerful perceiving
ig. On the other hand, for women and the less powerful the
...eve the recognition of love has been linked to the project of
tne domestication of men and the achievement of female autonomy and
citizenship. The paradox is that love has at the same time been a weapon of
the powerless and a vehicle of oppression.

For women, romantic attraction has meant that they have increased
their capacity to exercise choice. It has also been a way to undermine the
emotional stability of men. Nevertheless, Evans reminds us that the ardour
of the pursuit increases the aggression and violence between the sexes.
Cultures like ours which condone romance are also beset with the consequences of the misreadings of romantic intentions. The problem is that by
falling in love we expect that the other person will make good the intimacies
experienced in childhood which were lost in adult life. In the end Evans's
verdict is a sober one: 'Far from giving individuals a guide to the expression
and articulation of emotional feelings, romance distorts and limits the
possibilities of human relationships.'

A more sanguine view of this process is provided by Elisabeth Beck-
Gernsheim in her contribution entitled 'On the Way to a Post-Familial
Family'. She sees the history of the family as involving a process of
individualization. This entails women progressively moving out of the
dependence of the private sphere (in what is referred to as the 'halved
modernity' of the 19th century, which still contains some survivals of feudal
institutions [see Beck, 1993; Beck and Beck-Gernsheim, 1995]) to a
situation of greater state support against the market in the second half of
the 20th century which has increased the scope for individual action,
particularly for women ('reflexive modernity'). In this second phase women
are able to see themselves more as individuals and enjoy greater autonomy
and the capacity to construct their own life projects ('do-it-yourself biographies'). This of course also opens up a vast market for advice books,
magazines, counselling and therapy on how to build, undo and reconstruct
relationships, bodies, selves and sex lives (the consumer culture market is
discussed later). The class dimensions of this process of individualization,
and the potential reversals among specific groups (among the expanding
underclass or in fundamentalist groups such as the Patriots, the 'Pure Love
Movement' and the 'Born Again Virgins of America', in the USA [see the
discussion in Cindy Patton's contribution]), also need inscribing into the
same social space. Aspects which suggest a more complex set of social and
cultural power struggles are at work and not just the logic of reflexive
modernization.

The process of individualization has also been linked to the differentiation of the family by Georg Simmel in his essay 'On the Sociology of
the Family', which appears for the first time in English translation in this
collection. Simmel draws attention to the part played by love in this process.

Love is associated with the transition to individual choice of partners and hence an improvement in the status of women. As David Frisby reminds us in his Introduction to the translation, for Simmel love was something both within everyday experience, in the I–You relationship, yet it created a third entity, a phenomenon totally beyond it, something which was 'more-than-life'. This double aspect of the process is also captured by Beck-Gernsheim. On the one hand she points to the increasing fragmentation and complexities of family life, in terms of the difficulties of coordinating the increasingly unstable and irregular tempos of family members, who have their own individual biographies to construct and priorities to negotiate, as they increasingly seek to live their own lives. Yet she also suggests that this increasing complexity does not diminish the quest for love and intimacy. Rather, individualization may drive men and women apart,[4] but it also fosters a longing for the opposite, the world of intimacy, security and closeness, the 'normal chaos' of love (see Beck and Beck-Gernsheim, 1995: 34ff; Sennett, 1998).

As Charles Lindholm mentions in his contribution, a number of sociologists such as Weber, Simmel, Parsons, Habermas and Luhmann have investigated the connection between romantic love and modernization. Yet this attention to modernity contains the danger that the pre-modern is confined to the homogeneous category of tradition, which continues to retain its Enlightenment resonance as a blame-word. Lindholm suggests that it is possible to find correspondences between Western romantic love in 'simpler' societies. Anthropologists, for example, suggest that the Ojibwa of the northern Great Lakes live in a society of extreme competitive individualism with mobility of residence and a lack of stable authority structures and social hierarchy. In this social climate of distrust romantic love is associated with marriage and the couple idealized as a refuge against a hostile world.

One of the most interesting sociological accounts of love is provided by Niklas Luhmann (1986), who suggests that amid the constant information flows and impersonality of the modern world, romantic love stands out as an important means of symbolic exchange (see Bertilsson, 1986). Luhmann argues that love gains significance in the transition from the feudal to the market society. In pre-modern societies love was restricted to certain groups and was highly delimited in terms of who could love whom, when and where (as, for example, in the case of court society). With the rise of industrial society passionate love became extended throughout the population. The literature on love of the 18th and 19th centuries (confessions, novels, pornography) became socially important by helping to provide 'codes' between men and women, especially in the increasingly urbanized world of strangers. In effect, the growing predominance of passionate love had the function of encouraging strangers to meet and converse. A parallel market to the economic market, the market of free emotions started to develop. A market which saw the new ideology of love increasingly extend its scope across the social space to undermine the 'restrictive practices' of class, religion and ethnicity. The growing democratization of love in the 18th century also saw love as increasingly linked to sexuality and both becoming central to marriage.[5]

Yet if love and sexuality came together in the 18th century, a number of commentators see them as becoming increasingly separated in the late 20th century. Eva Illouz reminds us that the growing medical discourse in the 18th century began this process of disentanglement. Michel Foucault (1981) has, of course, discussed in detail the processes whereby medical and therapeutic discourses emerged to investigate and monitor the sexual body as part of an extension of 'bio-power'. Arguing for an increased separation of love and sex in the late 20th century, Illouz remarks that love at first sight is no longer credible as it is seen as merely a pretence for sexual desire. Increasingly, sex becomes a key component of intimacy, hence the romantic narrative of love has lost its cultural motivation. Love has become flattened out in the search for intensities of sensation and feelings. She argues that 'Postmodern romance has seen the collapse of overarching, life-long romantic narrative, which it has compressed into the briefer and repeatable form of the affair.'

In contrast to the single-minded *grand amour*, the affair legitimated sex for its own sake and fitted in well with the post-Second World War consumer culture with its quest for novelty and pleasurable experiences. Since the 1960s, Illouz alleges that there has also been a democratization of the affair with both sexes participating on a more equal basis. Affairs increasingly reflect the consumer culture balance between lifestyle choice and consumer rationality, the sort of calculating hedonism associated with the new middle class (see Featherstone, 1991). As Illouz puts it, 'Affairs characterize the romantic experience of those professional and new cultural intermediaries, located in large urban centres, who are most proficient at switching between sexual pleasure and forms of economic rationality.' According to Illouz, the model of romantic love as an intense and spontaneous feeling has lost its power as members of this group are able to switch skilfully between consumer hedonism, sexual experimentation and calculating rationality. The overexposure and disenchantment of romantic passion in the mass media and consumer culture, along with emotional and value pluralism and the therapeutic ethos, have generated a deep-seated suspicion of the possibility of lasting love (see Illouz, 1997). Illouz opens her piece with the remark of La Rochefoucauld that 'most people would not have fallen in love if they had not heard about it', only to conclude her article with the wry reverse comment that under the postmodern condition 'many people doubt they are in love, precisely because they have heard about it in excess'.

This theme is taken further in Cas Wouters's contribution, a detailed analysis of self-help manuals and women's magazines since the 1960s. He argues that in the past there was a lust-dominated sexuality for men and a romantic love or relationship-dominated sexuality for women. The balance between love and sex has shifted for women, especially since the 1960s, with notions of passivity replaced by a higher expectation of active sexual

pleasure. More specifically, Wouters sees a series of swings betv
of increasing equality between the sexes, such as the 1960s anɾ
phases of greater concern with intimacy and love, such as tɦ
1990s. He relates these swings to broader social changes. In the 1ყ6ʋ_ ̣
1970s entire groups were socially rising and there was strong pressure from
below against old authoritarian relations. This phase is more egalitarian
with individual desires and interests given more importance and legitimation. In the 1980s and 1990s there is increasing pressure from above and the
project of collective emancipation recedes. This is a phase of accommodation and resignation with a greater longing for enduring intimacy. The
balance of power between the sexes shifts with each phase. For example, in
the first phase men will often use the 'gender strategy' of appealing to a
woman's *old* identity underneath, whereas women will seek to appeal to a
man's *new* identity. Hence, Wouters reminds us, sex and love no longer can
be seen as given facts but as 'talents to be exploited'. A process which
requires more skilful and flexible emotional management from both
partners, as they attempt to balance the longing for more intimate romantic
relationships with the longing for easier sexual relationships without lasting
ties.

Zygmunt Bauman, in his contribution 'On the Postmodern Uses of
Sex', draws attention to the way in which bodily pleasures have become
central to contemporary consumer culture. For Bauman there has been a
move away from a surveillance and disciplinary order where norms of health
were imposed on populations, to the quest for sensation. Fitness, not health
has become the object for bodies. Fitness, he tells us, has no upper limit,
because it has to do with lived experience and sensations which can't be
objectively measured or validated intersubjectively. The aim is to maximize
bodily pleasures, yet the inability to establish norms and limits leads to
greater anxieties. Bauman goes on to remark that today sexual delights are
the most sought-after pleasurable sensations. A good contemporary example
here would be the publicity surrounding the new drug for male impotence,
Viagra, which is already the fastest-selling prescription drug in history
since its launch in March 1998. The key point here is not that there are
massive numbers of impotent men suddenly coming forward, rather Viagra
is being marketed and publicized, despite medical establishment dis-
claimers, as an aphrodisiac to boost people's sex lives – predominantly
aimed at men, but women as well.[6] Hence, as Bauman remarks, 'postmodern
sex is about orgasm', with the ultimate experience seen as still to come in
the future, something achievable with the help of drugs, gadgets, training
and counselling. Sex, then, is inevitably a source of anxiety because of the
premonition of failure, given the limitations of the ageing body and the
inevitability of death.

Bauman's focus is primarily on what has been referred to as the 'inner
body', the consumer culture emphasis upon training and maintaining the
body at peak fitness to enjoy the full range of sensations available. Yet as
has been argued previously, within consumer culture the inner body should

be seen as conjoined to the outer body, appearance (Featherstone, 1982; Hepworth and Featherstone, 1982). The achievement of fitness then is not just to work on tuning the body as the vehicle for maximizing pleasurable sensations, but also to enhance physical appearance: to achieve a slimmer, firmer, healthier, more active, energetic and sexy-looking body. This has of course its own particular logic and reflexivity, as spelt out in consumer culture slogans such as 'if you look good you feel good – and vice versa'. In a world of strangers the look of the body becomes an important passport to participate in the symbolic exchange and market of free emotions which Luhmann (1986) speaks of in which public life is seen as both a sphere of communication and excitement. This participation may be purely on the level of sexual attraction and erotic desire, but it also contains the promise of something more: the passionate affair and even love.

'Love is born the moment one sees a beautiful person. Even though desire is universal and spurs everyone on, each desires something different.'[7] So remarks Diotima in Plato's *Symposium* (quoted in Paz, 1996: 35). Yet Octavio Paz disputes whether Diotima was really speaking of love, for him she is talking about erotic attraction. For there to be love we need a philosophy of love with its emphasis upon fidelity in the love relationship. A fidelity conceives itself as a higher authority than mundane social bonds which can lead to adultery, suicide and death. This type of love, associated with the worship of women and celebrated in the stories of Tristan and Isolde, Lancelot and Guinevere, the love Dante feels for Beatrice described in *La Vita Nuova*, often has tragic consequences. It is an aspect of love which has been likened to a religious conversion, in which we are pulled out of the mundane everyday world into an enchanted life (see Alberoni, 1983) – something which has a clear physical aspect: the body alters its appearance and functioning and goes through a state of shock.

As Andrew Travers informs us in his contribution to this collection 'The Nazi Eye Code of Falling in Love', our cultural assumption is that a woman in love cannot help employing a particular eye code. It is assumed that if her love is pure and intense her eyes will shine as if she is lit up from within. Travers argues that the eye code of falling in love 'always carries a Nazi virus . . . because as Tolstoy reveals, it involves the surrender of reason to a cruel mysticism'. He suggests a parallel between Anna Karenin/ Vronsky and Hitler/Goebbels. In the same way that Goebbels was immediately converted through experiencing the presence of Hitler while gazing at the Führer when he was speaking at a rally, so the eyes of a woman in love affect her lover.[8] Yet the price of such powerful emotional experiences is that they end in tragedy, as was the case with Anna Karenin. Tolstoy increasingly distanced himself from this form of embodied passionate love in favour of a more sober religious love, to the extent that towards the end of his life in his short story 'The Kreutzer Sonata', he denounced all passion as a terrible evil. Travers also argues that we often fail to appreciate the complexity of the eye code: in this context he is critical of notions such as the male gaze (Mulvey, 1975), for its lack of sensitivity to the range of gazes employed by both men and women (see also Gamman and Marshment, 1988). This point is also made by Mike Hepworth in his contribution 'Love, Gender and Morality', in which he discusses Stephen Kern's book *The Eyes of Love* (1996). While some influential feminists, art historians and critics have focused attention on the woman as an object of the male gaze in Victorian paintings, following Kern he argues that although the male gaze in paintings is more erotically direct, the female gaze expresses a greater tension between sexual desire and love, with the latter seen as the longing for a reciprocal, enduring and moral union of two persons. The female gaze is less subservient to the male expression of sexual desire, or lust, than is often suggested in art history, reflecting a more mature knowledge of worldly reality along with the tension between hope and experience.

In his contribution 'On the Elementary Forms of the Socioerotic Life', Sasha Weitman argues that there is a distinctive socioerotic realm, which provides a range of opportunities to get away from everyday life. Erotic reality is seen as set off in time (evenings, nights, weekends, vacations) and space (home, bedrooms, hotel, beach, car) from everyday life. It is a sphere in which the body is central, in which partners seek to reduce themselves to their bodies, to enjoy pleasure and sensation; in disrobing they effectively discard their social roles. Weitman argues that:

> there exists a distinctive realm in interpersonal affairs, the socioerotic, that this realm entails a variety of rituals, occasions and relations, ranging from perfunctory social contacts (greetings, openings and closings) at one end, to elaborate social ceremonials and erotic sexuality at the other; that this realm is governed by its own distinctive logic, formulable in terms of laws and rules, that these generate and sustain distinctive practices (socioerotic rites) and experiences (socioerotic emotions) all of which involve the body, revolve around the experience of pleasures and consist of various and sundry rites of inclusion; finally, that it is these practices and attendant experiences that constitute the social bonds that tie people to one another. . . .

Weitman sees the socioerotic realm as indispensable for social life, as it provides modes of social inclusion, the rites and rituals which provide solidarity and closeness which bind people together. Echoing Durkheim, Weitman emphasizes the emotional excitement and bonding that can be generated when people come together in close embodied proximity. A form of bonding which generates its own set of rites and rituals, a scaled-down version of the sacred, which acts as a 'battery' to be charged up and sustains people when they return to the routine colourless world of everyday life (see Featherstone, 1991: ch. 8).

Important in Weitman's analysis is the fact that he draws attention to the spatial and temporal parameters of the erotic realm. On one level it is useful to distinguish the socioerotic realm from the wider field of everyday life. Yet it is also important to see this as a process involving different moments and phases. Initially there is a process of differentiation, in which the erotic realm becomes separated and the subject of elaboration, codification and intellectualization. Later stages of the process contain the possibility of de-differentiation, or merging back together of the erotic and everyday life. Yet as we shall see, if we refer to the process of the eroticization of everyday life as a parallel process to the aestheticization of everyday life, then we need to account for not just the long-term historical temporality, but the specific spaces (e.g. the city) and times (e.g. 'free time') where these processes take place. We also need to be aware, following Georg Simmel (1997), of the capacity of erotic interludes, such as the affair, to take on a peculiarly aestheticized form and temporality. The love affair can, under certain conditions, like the adventure, not only fall out of the usual continuity of everyday life, but also attain a vividness and sense of narrative continuity and aesthetic unity that make a piece of life seem like a dream or a work of art.[9] Indeed it is also possible for some individuals to seek to live their lives as an erotic adventure, to the extent that the swings between erotic immersion and dream-like involvement and instantiation seem to dominate the whole of life, and are not seen as merely an episodic break from it. In this sense the erotic can aspire to be a form of inner-worldly salvation and a life-order (see Featherstone, 1995: 59ff).

In his famous '*Zwischenbetrachtung*' essay Max Weber (1948) refers to the differentiation of the cultural sphere into separate aesthetic, intellectual and erotic life-orders. For Weber, the aesthetic, intellectual and erotic spheres were unable to repair the loss of ethical totality and capacity to provide a meaningful ordered life, as was the case with Protestantism (see Featherstone, 1995: 38ff). His negative view of aesthetics and erotics was based upon the assumption that the preoccupation with forms and immersion is the irrational force of sexual life, 'the only and the ineradicable link to animality' (Weber, 1948: 347), deflected attention away from the ethic of brotherliness. This concomitantly reduced ethics to aesthetics, with the consistency of conduct central to ethics becoming merely a matter of transitory taste and style, or the quest for sensation. Yet Weber was to alter his opinion about the erotic sphere later in his life through his involvement with Else Jaffe and Otto Gross. Else and Otto began a passionate love affair in 1907 and we have the first translations of some of their love letters in this collection. The letters are introduced by Sam Whimster, who draws a contrast between Max Weber and Otto Gross. Else wanted to bring the two men together, but they were diametrically opposed in temperament, lifestyle and intellectual beliefs (see Whimster, 1989; Green, 1976). Weber was distrustful of the blend of psychoanalysis, *Lebensphilosophie* and bohemianism which Gross advocated and saw it as a threat to science and civilization, which necessarily depended upon sublimation. Weber made visits in 1913 and 1914 to the countercultural communes that Gross and his followers had set up in Ascona in Switzerland, but although he was to admit that eroticism could represent a valid alternative to both ethical values and routinized everyday life in its capacity to offer an inner-worldly form of salvation, in terms of his own life-practice he maintained a restrained detachment.

Otto Gross, as Elizabeth Wilson argues, can be located within a bohemian tradition of love and eroticism. Certainly his advocacy and practice of an erotic and anarchistic lifestyle made Gross a precursor of Wilhelm Reich, R.D. Laing and others who were to be taken up by the 1960s counterculture. Elizabeth Wilson charts the history of Bohemian ideologies of love which can be traced back to the French literary culture of the 1830s. Here we think of the novels of Gautier and Balzac and the poetry of Baudelaire which explored love and death in relation to marginality, transgression and homosexuality. The Bohemia that grew up in Paris had a characteristic flouting of conventional bourgeois morality, taste and sexual mores. Baudelaire saw a new more virile type of womanhood as emerging in the city: lesbians, woman labourers and prostitutes. The *flâneur* can be seen as a feminine form of impotent wandering, a form of perpetual deferral rather than mastery which was part of a process of feminizing men. In the second half of the 19th century we find a more commercialized image of the Bohemian as some of the characteristic inversions of Bohemia became transformed into operas: Puccini's *La Bohème* and Bizet's *Carmen* being the most notable examples.

The figure of Carmen, as Pels and Crebas (1991) suggest, is particularly interesting in the way she is often presented as a transgressive *femme fatale*, someone who seems to both confirm the romantic myth and deny it. Bizet's opera was taken from Prosper Mérimée's novella *Carmen*, published in 1845. Mérimée's *Carmen* shows strong similarities to a story he had published a year earlier, *Arsène Guillot*, about a young Parisienne cocotte who is maintained by her lovers, which reveals Mérimée's sympathies for the Bohemian way of life. The novel *Carmen* is set in the exotic world of gypsies in Spain, yet there is a strong connection in the common usage of the term Bohemian to mean gypsy, vagabond, wanderer: hence its association with the marginal urban subcultural figures. The Bohemians were seen to resemble gypsies in a number of characteristics: their preference for the open spaces of the city to the home; their wandering from lodging to lodging to escape debts; their preference for casual lovers and relationships (Pels and Crebas, 1991: 356). Indeed, in many ways the figure of Carmen represents a projection of Bohemian free love and individualistic values combined with an idealized romantic version of gypsy life. What is interesting about the figure of Carmen is the way in which it has subsequently become a powerful cultural image and modern myth. Within consumer culture Carmen-inspired fashions reappear periodically along with the Carmen-look on covers of women's magazines. The Carmen image challenged the possessiveness and passivity associated with more traditional feminine ideals of love; instead, Carmen stands for a more active and individualistic ideal of non-exclusive love.

The Bohemian tradition, once transgressive and scandalous, with the value it placed upon romantic passion as the key to relations between the sexes, as Elizabeth Wilson reminds us, has been adopted more widely throughout Western society. This process goes back a long way and was apparent, for example, in the commercialization of Greenwich Village which was taking place by the end of the First World War. This is also a central theme of Daniel Bell's *The Cultural Contradictions of Capitalism* (1976). The decline of Bohemia has been associated with the take-up and diffusion within consumer culture of many of its central assumptions such as transgression, excess, the triumph of feeling and sensation. Sharon Zukin (1988) also argues that Bohemia and the artistic lifestyle have become saleable commodities. The new middle classes now seek to live and spend their leisure time amid the 'staged authenticity' and ambience of the aestheticized public and private spaces in 'heritage' Bohemias such as Greenwich Village.

Henning Bech in his contribution to this collection on 'Citysex' seeks to bring together two aspects of social and cultural life which are usually held apart. Sex is absent from most studies of urbanization and the city, and the city is absent from most studies of sexuality. Yet, he argues, the city is thoroughly sexualized and modern sexuality is essentially urban. For Bech, the modern city has been supplemented over the last 50 years by the telecity, the telemediated city, and modern sexuality must be understood in relation to this world of strangers we see when viewing television. The telecity feeds back into urban everyday life to heighten the mixture of fantasy and reality, the anticipation of the seemingly ever present possibility of chance sexual encounters, generated perhaps by the glance of someone in the crowd, or the glimpse of a face on an advertising poster. This is a long way from the purposive rational activity of someone actively pursuing a specifically sexual goal, rather it works within a world of civil inattentiveness, and swings between routine bored surveillance and momentary flashes of deeper involvement.

Bech's argument here recalls the world of the *flâneur* in mid-19th-century Paris described by Walter Benjamin (1973). The distracted stroller passing through the urban spaces is subjected to a constant flow of new sensations and half-formed experiences, coupled with the momentary jolt from a face in the crowd, perhaps the experience of 'love at last sight' Baudelaire spoke of. This is the city which has been aestheticized through the ornamented surfaces of the urban fabric: the buildings, the street lamps, advertising hoardings, posters, handbills and countless other detritus of the urban consumer culture landscape. For Benjamin, they performed an allegorical function, summoning up half-remembered memories and associations, which flash into the mind only to be lost under the weight of the ever changing urban scene (Benjamin, 1973, 1982; Buck-Morss, 1989; Buci-Glucksmann, 1994; Featherstone, 1991: ch. 5). It is a world in which commodities and objects develop an anorganic sexual quality: they take their place in a landscape of fetishized and sexualized objects (van Reijen, 1988). Hence the excitement at the possibility of sexualized encounters Bech speaks of takes place against the backcloth of an urbanized sexual landscape in which many of the objects in the city fabric are already sexualized, already doubly-seen.[10]

Bech remarks how motion and movement are important in urban sexuality: in playing 'the game of the eye'. While cruising one enters a world of exposure to the gaze of others, while simultaneously decoding the gaze and body movements of others too. This world of possibilities not only exists in fictional accounts and urban legends of sex between strangers, there are observed documented accounts of sexual encounters on trains, in taxis and discos. Contemporary pornography plays off this world of omnipresent potential sexuality, in which the possibility of the sexual adventure lurks in every public place. Bech argues that there is a widespread awareness of the sexualized dimension of the city and people realize they have a choice in terms of how far they want to participate and the extent to which they seek to sexualize their own body surface. The associations of fetishized garments such as the Brando leather jacket or the female leg in a black stocking are evident. In this urban sexual landscape the modern male homosexual has become a prototypical figure. Certain city districts, especially in global cities, become refurbished as 'gay villages', which city authorities, after overcoming their initial ambivalence, are often quick to 'theme' and package as part of the general cultural ambience, something increasingly seen as a marketable component of the city image.

The greater visibility of gay culture in urban public space raises issues about the legal parameters of sexuality in public. As Leslie Moran (forthcoming) argues, the public–private distinction is central to gay politics, given the criminalization of genital intimacy between men in public. The emergence of 'queer' as a new form of oppositional gender politics has accompanied the attempts to contest the confinement of genital intimacy to private space, something which is seen as reproducing public space as a heterocentric realm. These issues are central to notions of sexual citizenship, as Jeffrey Weeks shows in his contribution. To speak of citizenship is to speak of the public sphere, of the rights and responsibilities associated with full membership of a community. There has been a process of gradual extension of notions of citizenship from political to economic and social rights, designed to end various class, gender and other exclusions operative in public life, education and employment. Sexual citizenship can be understood as an extension of this process in terms of control over one's own body, one's access to relationships, representations, public space and choice of identity and gender experiences. Historically sexuality has been separated from the public sphere, with sexual conduct seen as an intensely private matter. Sexual citizenship seeks to achieve an intertwining of the public and the private. According to Weeks, it gained its impetus with the shift of the lesbian/gay movement from a concern with transgression, the attack on existing traditions and institutions along with an attempt to invent and reinvent new forms of sexual identities, to the concern with citizenship, the assumption that without full citizenship the pursuit of difference can never find a proper home. Increasingly, Weeks argues, love and partnerships are seen as a matter of choice and there is a greater quest for fulfilment through experimental forms of living. Identities are seen as projects, something to be constructed and performed, as Weeks puts it:

> In this new world of infinite possibility, but also of ever-present uncertainty, we need pioneers, voyagers, experimenters with the self and with relationships. This would-be sexual citizen, I suggest, represents that spirit of searching and adventure.

Cindy Patton, in her contribution on 'Locating Affect in Nationalism after AIDS', suggests that this is far from being the whole picture. While she agrees that the trajectory in gay politics has moved from calls to smash the family and love in the 1970s to a more nuanced concern to reclaim the family, to construct 'families we choose', and a greater concern with compassion and 'alternative love', as part of a move towards responsible sexual citizenship, this trend has also to be set alongside the search for political love. Following the work of Benedict Anderson (1991), she argues that there has been a tendency to neglect the affect for nation, the way which love for country and sacrifice have been central to citizenship. The emphasis on the responsible duty-bound homosexual citizens in the wake of the AIDS crisis of the 1980s and 1990s occludes the resurgence of conservative ideas on love and sex. Internet websites have been one outlet for the Pure Love Movement, which is strongly against cultural relativism and multiculturalism. The movement through linking together the body, nation and religion aims to bring about 'a new sexual revolution, a national movement for purity'.

A related point is made by Laura Rival, Don Slater and Danny Miller in 'Sex and Sociality', where they contest the 'hyper-existentialist manifesto', in which the individual is seen as becoming an artist of his/her life able to construct their self and gender in a creative way. In his study of Internet Relay Chat, Don Slater found little evidence of transgressions, quest for danger or release from the social bond. Rather, on-line sex chat and the exchange of 'sexpics' were contained within tight normative constraints. People used sexpic trading and sexchat to provide 'a sensually-coated ambience' to eroticize everyday life, an aphrodisiac for their normal relationships. For Rival, Slater and Miller, too much of the discussion of sex and gender is merely from academics attempting to work through the liberationist potential of modernity to the neglect of mundane sexuality, the ways in which for many people sexuality is an integral part of normative and moral orders. Apart from what they characterize as the social constructionism of Michel Foucault and Judith Butler, a further target here is the poststructuralist appropriation of the writings of Bataille with their celebration of transgression.

The writings of Bataille and the Surrealists on love, the erotic and sacrifice are the subject of the contribution by Michael Richardson. Surrealism, which developed in the interwar years, should be seen as diametrically opposed to the licentiousness of artistic Bohemia. Its basic rule was passionate love, preferably faithful. In the resistance to the absorption of love into sexuality and celebration of pure love, there is an element of moral puritanism. Sex was seen as just a commodity consumer object, whereas love was seen as the irruption of desire into ordinary existence which could lead to the transformation of our being. Love entails the passionate vision of the other, the giving of oneself unconditionally which was necessarily transgressive. For Bataille, love promises a way out of our suffering, our isolation and separateness. The erotic impulse takes us outside of ourselves and propels us into a realm of terror and dissociation where we sacrifice the gift of our identities. The erotic provides a glimpse of the realm beyond existence, it bring us into contact with death. As Richardson remarks:

> In confronting our own identity with that of another in eroticism we are also confronting what both affirms and destroys us. As an affirmation of life, sexuality is thus in complicity with death.

As Art Frank in his contribution entitled 'Bodies, Sex and Death', a discussion of books by Gary Fisher and Gillian Rose, reminds us, love and sex are bound up with death. He quotes Gillian Rose's remark 'Love-making is never simply pleasure'. It is a process of self-creation, the genesis of experience, too. This sense of self-creation is captured by Octavio Paz's (1996: 5) remark that 'the relationship of poetry to language resembles that of eroticism to sexuality'. Eroticism embodies the capacity for invention, to meander and side-step the linear purposiveness of those who seek to order social life. He goes on to tell us that 'poetry places communication in brackets in the same way that eroticism brackets reproduction' (Paz, 1996: 6). It is, therefore, really not surprising that those interested in culture should find it significant.

Notes

This issue of *Theory, Culture & Society* has been a long time in the making. It originated when a number of articles on love and eroticism were by chance submitted to *TCS* at the same time. Initially the collection was planned as a special section, but partly through the efforts and encouragement of Sasha Weitman it just grew and grew. I would like to thank a number of people who have helped with this issue in a variety of ways: Zygmunt Bauman, Ana Zahira Bassit, Roy Boyne, Roger Bromley, Neal Curtis, Mike Hepworth, Richard Johnson, Scott Lash, Bernard McGuirk, Wendy Paterson, Chris Rojek, Bryan S. Turner and Else Vieira.

1. Paz (1996: 29) finds this to be the case with one of the most influential books on the history of love – Denis de Rougemont's *Love in the Western World* (1983). De Rougemont links the rise of romantic love to the West and in particular the Troubadours of south-west France in the 12th century. Paz is especially critical of de Rougemont's link between the Provençal poets and the rise of the Cathar heresy, a popular religious movement which was eventually put down through the

combined efforts of the King of France and the Pope. Paz also suggests that there is a further important distinction between the East and the West. In the East love was conceived within a religious tradition, whereas in the West love developed alongside a critical philosophy. At the same time Western love was influenced by conceptions of love developed by the Persians and Arabs, which shared with Christianity and monotheistic religions the notions of the eternal soul and the person.

2. Paz (1996: 72) tells us that the Provençal poets were influenced by the poetry of Muslim Spain, not only in adopting the popular Arabic-Andalusian forms, but also in their emphasis on the custom of the Arab emirs in declaring themselves the slaves of their beloveds.

3. Norbert Elias (1987: 298–300) recounts a similar situation in Ancient Rome in which the balance of power shifted between patrician men and women in the second and first century BC, as women gradually gained the right to accumulate their own property and even divorce their husbands. He refers to the capacity of great ladies to attract the attentions of younger socially inferior men who developed a similar form of emotional control and longing, accompanied by love poetry, which were later to emerge in the courtly love tradition of the troubadours and in court societies in general.

4. It is now estimated that 25 percent of people in the UK live in single households.

5. For an interesting analysis of the 18th century as a turning point in the history of erotica see Wagner (1988) who also explores the link between pornography and medicine.

6. See, for example, the page spread in the popular British tabloid newspaper, *The Mirror*, 15 May 1998, where in an article 'Sex Drug Made Me Ravish My Man 5 Times in a Night: A Woman's View of the Viagra Effect', 37-year-old reporter Annie Williams described her experiences in using the drug as an aphrodisiac. In the USA the 63-year-old female partner of an American millionaire is suing Viagra for $2 million, on the grounds that their relationship broke up after her husband's impotence was treated and his sexual potency restored by the drug. Allegedly he left her in hot pursuit of younger sexual partners (T. Varadarajan ' Sex Drug Turns Aged Tycoon into Errant Stud', *The Times* 30 May 1998: 1).

7. For a discussion of beauty see Marwick (1988) and Pacteau (1994). Female beauty is associated with sexual attraction, something which has become extensively represented within consumer culture in the 20th century, which holds out the promise that beauty, like charisma, can be manufactured through fashion, cosmetics, body maintenance and health regimes. From the 1920s Hollywood popularized new standards of beauty and sexiness with the beauty secrets of the stars marketed to ordinary women (see discussion of 'the Hollywood ideal' in Featherstone, 1982; Hepworth and Featherstone, 1982).

8. For a discussion of the power of Hitler as a public orator and the manufacturing of the charismatic persona he projected see Stern (1990). Speer was also fascinated with Hitler's eyes. His smile was also the subject of a good deal of analysis. Norbert Elias (1994: 46) recounts how in 1932 or 1933 he disguised himself as an aristocrat and attended a Hitler rally.

9. For an account of the way in which the French tradition of conducting a love affair developed into an art form, researched from the letters, diaries and memoirs of famous French writers, see Hofstadter (1996).

10. For an interesting collection of photographs of the urban consumer landscape which incorporate the advertisement and other photographs to bring out this doubly-seen dream-world quality, see Greg Leach *Twice Told Tales* (1992).

References

Alberoni, F. (1983) *Falling in Love*. New York: Random House.

Anderson, B. (1991) *Imagined Communities*, rev. edn. London: Verso.

Beck, U. (1993) *Risk Society*. London: Sage.

Beck, U. and E. Beck-Gernsheim (1995) *The Normal Chaos of Love*. Cambridge: Polity.

Bell, D. (1976) *The Cultural Contradictions of Capitalism*. London: Heinemann.

Benjamin, W. (1973) *Charles Baudelaire*. London: New Left Books.

Benjamin, W. (1982) *Das Passagen-Werk*, 2 vols. Frankfurt: Suhrkamp.

Bertilsson, M. (1986) 'Love's Labour Lost? A Sociological View', *Theory, Culture & Society* 3(2): 19–35. Reprinted in M. Featherstone, M. Hepworth and B.S. Turner (eds) *The Body: Social Process and Cultural Theory*. London: Sage, 1991.

Buci-Glucksmann, C. (1994) *Baroque Reason: The Aesthetics of Modernity*. London: Sage.

Buck-Morss, S. (1989) *The Dialectic of Seeing: Walter Benjamin and the Arcades Project*. Cambridge, MA: MIT Press.

de Rougemont, D. (1983) *Love in the Western World*. Princeton, NJ: Princeton University Press.

Elias, N. (1983) *The Court Society*. Oxford: Blackwell.

Elias, N. (1987) 'The Changing Balance of Power between the Sexes – A Process-Sociological Study: The Example of the Ancient Roman State', *Theory, Culture & Society* 4(2–3): 287–316.

Elias, N. (1994) *Reflections on a Life*. Cambridge: Polity.

Featherstone, M. (1982) 'The Body in Consumer Culture', *Theory, Culture & Society* 1(2): 18–33. Reprinted in M. Featherstone, M. Hepworth and B.S. Turner (eds) *The Body*. London: Sage, 1991.

Featherstone, M. (1991) *Postmodernism and Consumer Culture*. London: Sage.

Featherstone, M. (1995) *Undoing Culture: Globalization, Postmodernism and Identity*. London: Sage.

Foucault, M. (1981) *The History of Sexuality, Volume 1: Introduction*. Harmondsworth: Penguin.

Gamman, L. and M. Marshment (1988) *The Female Gaze*. London: The Women's Press.

Green, M. (1976) *The Von Richthoven Sisters*. New York: Basic Books.

Hepworth, M. and M. Featherstone (1982) *Surviving Middle Age*. Oxford: Blackwell.

Hofstadter, D. (1996) *The Love Affair as a Work of Art*. New York: Farrar, Straus and Giroux.

Illouz, E. (1997) *Consuming the Romantic Utopia*. Berkeley: University of California Press.

Kern, S. (1996) *The Eyes of Love: The Gaze in English and French Paintings and Novels 1840–1900*. London: Reaktion Books.

Leach, G. (1992) *Twice Told Tales*. Manchester.

Luhmann, N. (1986) *Love as Passion: the Codification of Intimacy*. Cambridge, MA: Harvard University Press.

Marwick, A. (1988) *Beauty in History*. London: Thames and Hudson.

Moran, L. (forthcoming) 'Law Made Flesh: Homosexual Acts', *Body & Society* 5 (1999).

Mulvey, L. (1975) 'Visual Pleasure and Narrative Cinema', *Screen* 16(3).

Pacteau, F. (1994) *The Symptom of Beauty*. London: Reaktion Books.

Paz, O. (1996) *The Double Flame: Essays on Love and Eroticism*. London: Haverill.

Pels, D. and A. Crebas (1991) 'Carmen – Or the Invention of a New Feminine Myth', in M. Featherstone, M. Hepworth and B.S. Turner (eds) *The Body*. London: Sage, 1991. (Originally in *Theory, Culture & Society* 4, 1987.)

Sennett, R. (1998) 'Growth and Failure: The New Political Economy and its Culture', in M. Featherstone and S. Lash (eds) *Spaces of Culture*. London: Sage.

Simmel, G. (1997) 'The Adventure', in D. Frisby and M. Featherstone (eds) *Simmel on Culture*. London: Sage.

Stern, J. P. (1990) *Hitler, the Führer and the People*, rev. edn. London: Fontana.

Van Reijen, W. (1988) '*The Dialectic of Enlightenment* Read as Allegory', *Theory, Culture & Society* Special Issue on Postmodernism 5(2–3): 409–29.

Wagner, P. (1988) *Eros Revived: Erotica of the Enlightenment in England and America*. London: Secker and Warburg.

Weber, Max (1948) 'Religious Rejections of the World and their Directions', in H. H. Gerth and C. Wright Mills (eds) *From Max Weber*. London: Routledge.

Whimster, S. (1989) 'Heidelberg Man: Recent Literature on Max Weber', *Theory, Culture & Society* 6(3): 451–69.

Zukin, S. (1988) *Loft Living*. London: Radius.

Mike Featherstone is Professor of Sociology and Communications at Nottingham Trent University. His latest publications include *Undoing Culture: Globalization, Postmodernism and Identity* (Sage, 1995), *Simmel on Culture* (edited with David Frisby, Sage, 1997) and *Spaces of Culture* (edited with Scott Lash, Sage, 1999).

On Postmodern Uses of Sex

Zygmunt Bauman

I N HIS BEAUTIFUL book-long essay *La llama doble – Amor y erotismo*, published in 1993, the great Mexican thinker Octavio Paz explores the complex interaction between sex, eroticism and love – three close relatives yet so unlike each other that each needs a separate language to account for its own existence. The central metaphor of the book, most fittingly, is one of fire: above the primordial fire of sex, lit by nature long before the first stirrings of humanity, rises the red flame of eroticism, above which quivers and shivers the delicate blue flame of love. There would be no flame without fire; yet there is more, much more, to the red and blue flames, and to each one of them, than there is in the fire from which they arise.

Sex, eroticism and love are linked yet separate. They can hardly exist without each other, and yet their existence is spent in the ongoing war of independence. The boundaries between them are hotly contested – alternatively, but often simultaneously, the sites of defensive battles and of invasions. Sometimes the logic of war demands that the cross-border dependencies are denied or suppressed; sometimes the invading armies cross the boundary in force with the intention of overpowering and colonizing the territory. Torn between such contradictory impulses, the three areas are notorious for the unclarity of their frontiers and the three discourses that serve (or perhaps produce) them are known to be confused and inhospitable to pedantry and precision.

Sex, so Octavio Paz reminds us, is the least human of the three. Indeed, sex is natural, not a cultural product: we share it with a large part of non-human species. In its natural form untainted by culture sex is always the same; as Theodore Zeldin (1994: 86ff) observed, 'there has been more progress in cooking than in sex'. It is but the erotic sublimation of sex, fantasy and sex-substitutes, that are infinitely variable. All '*history of sex*' is therefore the history of the *cultural manipulation* of sex. It began with the birth of eroticism – through the cultural trick of separating sexual *experience*

■ *Theory, Culture & Society* 1998 (SAGE, London, Thousand Oaks and New Delhi),
Vol. 15(3–4): 19–33
[0263-2764(199808/11)15:3–4;19–33;006057]

(in the sense of *Erlebnis*, not *Erfahrung*), and especially the *pleasure* associated with that experience, from reproduction, that primary function of sex and its raison d'etre. Nature, we may say, is taking no chances and for that reason it cannot but be wasteful; it showers its targets with bullets so that at least one bullet will hit the bull's eye. Sex is no exception; sexually reproducing species are as a rule supplied with quantities of sexual energy and capacity for sexual encounters far in excess of what reproduction proper would require. And so eroticism is not just a purely cultural feat and in no way is it an act of violence committed on nature, an 'unnatural' act; nature virtually tempted human wits into the invention, lavish as nature is in turning out huge, redundant and untapped volumes of sexual energy and desire. That surplus is a standing invitation to cultural inventiveness. Yet the uses to which that reproductively redundant and wasted excess may be put is a cultural creation.

Eroticism is about recycling that waste. It depends on filling the sexual act with a surplus value – over and above its reproductive function. Human beings would not be erotic creatures were they not first sexual beings; sexuality is the only soil in which the cultural seeds of eroticism may be sown and grow – but this soil has limited fertility. Eroticism begins from reproduction, but it transcends it from the start; reproduction, its life-giving force, soon turns into a constraint. To freely manipulate, to process at will the surplus capacity for sexuality, eroticism must be 'replanted' into other soils of greater potency and additional nutritional power; culture must emancipate sexual delight from reproduction, its primary utilitarian application. Hence the reproductive function of sex is simultaneously the indispensable condition and a thorn in the flesh of eroticism; there is an unbreakable link, but also a constant tension between the two – that tension being as incurable as the link is unbreakable.

Theoretically speaking, there are several tension-management strategies. They were all tried, and the 'history of sex' may be told in terms of the focus shifting from one strategy to another, different strategies gaining temporary cultural dominance in various historical eras. The choice, however, is limited. By and large it is confined to the redeployment of cultural forces either on the sex/eroticism or eroticism/love frontier, and certain combinations between the troop movements in both territories.

Greatly simplifying, we may say that throughout the modern era two cultural strategies vied with each other for domination. One – officially promoted and supported by the legislative powers of the state and ideological powers of the Church and the School, was the strategy of reinforcing the limits imposed by the reproductive functions of sex upon the freedom of erotic imagination – relegating the unmanageable surplus of sexual energy to culturally suppressed and socially degraded spheres of pornography, prostitution and illicit – extramarital – liaisons. The other – always carrying a tinge of dissent and rebelliousness – was the romantic strategy of cutting the ties linking eroticism to sex and tying it instead to love.

In the first strategy, eroticism had to justify itself in terms of its sexual (reproductive) utility, with the third element – love – being a welcome, yet supernumerary, embellishment. Sex was 'culturally silent' – it had no language of its own, no language recognized as public vernacular and a means of public communication. Mid-19th-century intercourse, as Stephen Kern (1992) noted, was by comparison with 20th-century sex 'deadly serious' and 'abruptly over'; it was 'abruptly over' since 'the post-coital interlude was particularly embarrassing, because eyes opened, lights came on, and couples were obliged to look at one another or else away and begin to speak or else endure a nerve-breaking silence'. In the second strategy, love was accorded the sole legitimizing power, and eroticism was cast in the image of a handmaiden of love, while its link with sexuality was either frowned upon or reduced to the role of a non-essential, even if pleasurable, attribute. In both strategies, eroticism sought anchorage in something other than itself – either in sex or in love; both strategies were variants of the policy of alliance, and the potential allies were sought beyond the borders of eroticism. Both strategies assumed that the cultural manipulation and redeployment of surplus sexual energy needed a functional justification, not being able to stand on its own and be 'its own purpose' or a value in its own right. Both strategies stemmed as well from the tacit assumption that, left to itself, human erotic inventiveness would easily run out of control, playing havoc with the delicate tissue of human relations; it needs therefore outside, authoritative and resourceful powers to contain it within acceptable limits and stave off its potentially destructive potential.

Seen against that background, the late modern or postmodern rendition of eroticism appears unprecedented – a genuine breakthrough and novelty. It enters alliance with neither sexual reproduction nor love, claiming independence from both neighbours and flatly refusing all responsibility for the impact it may make on their fate; it proudly and boldly proclaims itself to be its only, and sufficient, reason and purpose. As Marc C. Taylor and Esa Saarinen (1994) put it, with a wonderful epigrammatic precision, 'desire does not desire satisfaction. To the contrary, desire desires desire.' When (seldom, and in a whisper) voiced before, such claims were classified as the heresy of libertinism and exiled to the Devil's Island of sexual disorder and perversion. Now the self-sufficiency of eroticism, the freedom to seek sexual delights for their own sake, has risen to the level of cultural norm, changing places with its critics, now assigned to the *Kunstkammer* of cultural oddities and relics of extinct species. Nowadays eroticism has acquired substance it was never before able to carry on its own shoulders, but also an unheard-of lightness and volatility. Being an eroticism 'with no strings attached', untied, unbridled, let loose – the postmodern eroticism is free to enter and leave any association of convenience, but also an easy prey to forces eager to exploit its seductive powers.

It has become the folklore of social science to lay the responsibility for the 'erotic revolution' at the door of the 'market forces' (an address all the more convenient for the mystery surrounding its notoriously elusive resident). Eager to fill the void left by the Divine Providence and laws of progress, scientifically oriented study of changing human behaviour seeks a candidate for the vacant position of 'main determinant' – and 'market forces' are no worse, and in many respects better, than the others. I for once am not particularly worried by the void staying empty and the position remaining unfilled. 'Market forces' can be blamed, at the utmost, for exploiting without scruples the resources already at hand, and for exploiting them while being guided solely by their commercial potential and oblivious to all other, including the culturally devastating or morally iniquitous, aspects of the matter. Charging them with the powers to conjure up the resources themselves would be like accepting the alchemist's authorship of the gold found in the test-tube: an exercise in magical rather than scientific reasoning (though, frankly, the difference between the two within social studies is far from unambiguous). It takes more than the greed for profit, free competition and the refinement of the advertising media to accomplish a cultural revolution of a scale and depth equal to that of the emancipation of eroticism from sexual reproduction and love. To be redeployed as an economic factor, eroticism must have been first culturally processed and given a form fit for a would-be commodity.

So let me leave aside the 'commercial' uses of eroticism, not really surprising in a society in which the care for whatever is seen as a human need is increasingly mediatized by the commodity market – and concentrate instead on the somewhat less obvious, and certainly less fully described and much too little discussed links between the erotic revolution and other aspects of the emergent postmodern culture. Among such aspects, two in particular seem to be directly relevant to our topic.

The first is the collapse of the 'panoptic' model of securing and perpetuating social order. That model, as you know, has been described in detail by Michel Foucault, in reference to Jeremy Bentham's idea of the universal solution to all tasks requiring the instilling of discipline and so obtaining the desirable sort of conduct from a great number of people. That solution, according to Bentham, was *seeing without being seen*, a surreptitious surveillance with its objects made aware that they might be closely scrutinized at every moment yet having no way of knowing when they are indeed under observation. Foucault used Bentham's idea as a paradigm of the order-making activity of modern powers. Factories, workhouses, prisons, schools, hospitals, asylums or barracks, whatever their manifest functions, were also throughout the modern era manufacturers of order; in this lay their latent, yet arguably their paramount social function. Among all the panoptical institutions two were decisive for the performance of that latter function due to their vast catchment area. The two panoptical institutions in question were industrial factories and conscript armies. Most male members of society could reasonably be expected to pass through their disciplining treadmill and acquire the habits that would guarantee their obedience to the order-constituting rules (and later to enforce those habits on the female members in their capacity of the 'heads of families'). Yet in order to perform their role such panoptical institutions needed men capable of undertaking industrial work and army duties – able to endure the hardships of industrial work and army life. Industrial invalidity and disqualification from army service meant exclusion from panoptical control and drill. Ability to work and to fight became therefore the measure of the 'norm', while inability was tantamount to social abnormality, deviation from the norm, alternatively subjected to medical or penological treatment. Modern medicine gave that norm the name of 'health'. A 'healthy man' was a person capable of a certain amount of physical exertion, required by productive work and/or military exploits; the norm guiding the assessment of the state of health and the infinite variety of possible abnormalities was therefore 'objectively measurable'. It could be easily set as a target; hitting or missing the target could be defined with considerable precision.

Contemporary society needs neither mass industrial labour nor mass (conscript) armies. The era when factories and troops were the decisive order-sustaining institution is (at least in our part of the world) over. But so is, as well, panoptical power as the main vehicle of social integration, and normative regulation as the major strategy of order-maintenance. The great majority of people – men as well as women – are today integrated through seduction rather than policing, advertising rather than indoctrinating, need-creation rather than normative regulation. Most of us are socially and culturally trained and shaped as sensation-seekers and gatherers, rather than producers and soldiers. Constant openness to new sensations and greed for ever new experience, always stronger and deeper than before, is a condition sine qua non of being amenable to seduction. It is not 'health', with its connotation of a steady state, of an immobile target on which all properly trained bodies converge – but 'fitness', implying being always on the move or ready to move, capacity for imbibing and digesting ever greater volumes of stimuli, flexibility and resistance to all closure, that grasps the quality expected from the experience-collector, the quality she or he must indeed possess to seek and absorb sensations. And if the mark of 'disease' was incapacity for factory or army life, the mark of 'unfitness' is the lack of *élan vital, ennui, acedia,* inability to feel strongly, lack of energy, stamina, interest in what the colourful life has to offer, desire and desire to desire....

'Fitness' as a definition of a desirable bodily state, however, presents problems of which the norm of 'health' was free.

First – 'health' is a norm, and norms are clearly delineated from above and below alike. 'Fitness' has perhaps its lower, though rather blurred and murky threshold, but cannot, by definition, have an upper limit; 'fitness' is, after all, about the constant ability to move further on, to rise to ever higher levels of experience. Hence 'fitness' will never acquire the comforting exactitude and precision of a norm. 'Fitness' is a never-to-be-reached horizon looming forever in the future, a spur to unstoppable efforts, none of which can be seen as fully satisfactory, let alone the ultimate. Pursuit of fitness, its little triumphs notwithstanding, is shot through with incurable anxiety and is an inexhaustible source of self-reproach and self-indignation.

Second – since it is solely about the *Erlebnis*, the subjectively lived-through sensations, fitness cannot be intersubjectively compared nor objectively measured; it can hardly even be reported in interpersonally meaningful terms and so confronted with other subjects' experience. Much as counsel is needed to make up for that immanent un-graspability of evidence, there is possibly an ultimate limit to the counsellors' intervention; name-giving and quotations of statistical averages will stop short of breaking open the loneliness of the sensation-seeker. As we know from Ludwig Wittgenstein, there is no such thing as private language, but one would need nothing less than a private language to express sensations – that most thoroughly and uncompromisingly private ingredient of the *Lebenswelt*. This is, indeed, a Catch 22 – demanding no less than the squaring of a circle.

One way or the other, since certainty can be only an interpersonal, social achievement, the fitness-seekers can never be sure how far they got and how far they still need to go. Third – in the game called fitness, the player is simultaneously the fiddle and the fiddler. It is the bodily pleasurable, exciting or thrilling sensations which a fit person seeks – but the sensations-collector *is that body* and, at the same time, that body's owner, guardian, *trainer and director*. The two roles are inherently incompatible. The first requires total immersion and self-abandonment, the second calls for a distance and sober judgement. Reconciliation of the two demands is a tall order – if attainable at all, which is doubtful. Added to the two previously signalled troubles, that additional worry makes the plight of the fitness-seeker an agony of which our health-conscious ancestors had no inkling. All three troubles daily generate a great deal of anxiety; what is more, however, that anxiety – the specifically *postmodern* affliction – is unlikely ever to be cured and stopped. It is also diffuse, as Jean Baudrillard pointed out; and diffuse, unfocused anxieties admit no specific remedies. . . .

Sexual delight is arguably the topmost of pleasurable sensations; indeed, a pattern by which all other pleasures tend to be measured and of which they are, by common consent, but pale reflections at best, inferior or counterfeit imitations at worst. Whatever has been said above about the sensation-gathering life strategy in general, applies in a magnified measure to the specifically postmodern rendition of eroticism, that 'cultural processing' of sex. All the contradictions inherent to the life of a sensation-collector in general hit sexual life with concentrated power – but there is an extra difficulty arising from the inborn monotonous inflexibility of sex (sex, let us remember, being a phenomenon of nature and not of culture, leaves little room for the inventiveness typical of culture). In its postmodern rendition, sexual activity is focused narrowly on its orgasmic effect; for all practical intents and purposes, postmodern sex *is about orgasm*. Its paramount task is to supply ever stronger, infinitely variable, preferably novel and unprecedented *Erlebnisse*; little can be done however in this field and so the ultimate sexual experience remains forever a task ahead and no actual sexual experience is truly satisfying, none makes further training, instruction, counsel, recipe, drug or gadget unnecessary.

There is another aspect of the relation between the present-day erotic revolution and the wider postmodern cultural transformations which I wish now to bring to your attention.

Sex, as we know, is nature's evolutionary solution to the issue of continuity, durability of life forms; it sets mortality of every individual living organism against immortality of the species. Only humans know that this is the case; only humans know that they are bound to die, and only humans may imagine the perpetuity of humankind; only for them does the transient existence of the body run its course in the shadow of the perpetuity of humanity as a whole. Such knowledge has tremendous consequences; it is by no means fanciful to suppose that it lies behind the notorious dynamics of human cultural inventions which all, as a rule, are contraptions meant to render the duration of social forms immune to the transience and inborn perishability of human individual lives; or, rather, the ingenious workshops where durability is continually produced out of the transient – where the fragile, time-bound existence of human bodies is reforged into the solid perpetuity of humanity.

Sex lies at the heart of that alchemy. Sex is the material substratum of that cultural production of immortality and the pattern or supreme metaphor for the effort to transcend individual mortality and stretch human existence beyond the life-span of individual humans. Sex is involved – centrally and inextricably – in the greatest feat and the most awe-inspiring of cultural miracles: that of conjuring up immortality out of mortality, the interminable out of the temporal, the imperishable out of the evanescent. The enigma of that logic-defying miracle, that mind-boggling puzzle of the most vulnerable and abstruse accomplishment of culture saturates every sexual act: the communion of two mortal beings is lived through as the birth of immortality.... With the advent of human awareness of mortality sex loses its innocence irretrievably.

Located on the other side of eroticism, love is the emotional/intellectual superstructure which culture built upon the sexual differences and their sexual reunion, thereby investing sex with rich and infinitely expandable meaning which protects and reinforces its power to recast mortality into immortality. Love is a cultural replica or a refined likeness of that overcoming of the opposition between the transience of sexual bodies and the durability of their reproduction, which is matter-of-factly accomplished in the sexual act. Like sex itself, love is therefore burdened with ambiguity, residing as it does on the thin line dividing the natural from the supernatural, the familiar present and the enigmatic, impenetrable future. Love of another mortal person is one of the principal cultural ventures into immortality; it is, we may say, a spiritual mirror held to the sexually created biological eternity. Like sex, love is a source of incurable anxiety, though perhaps an anxiety deeper still for being soaked through with the premonition of failure. In love, the hope and the promise of 'eternal love' is invested here in the body which is anything but eternal; the eternity of love and of the beloved is culture's saving lie, helping to assimilate what in fact defies comprehension. A mortal person is loved as if he or she were immortal, and is loved by a mortal person in a way accessible only to eternal beings.

We have noted before that a most prominent mark of the postmodern erotic revolution is cutting the ties connecting eroticism on one side to sex (in its essential reproductive function) and on the other to love. Precautions are taken in the postmodern culture to secure the emancipation of erotically inspired activity from the constraints imposed biologically by the reproductive potential of sex and culturally by love's demands of eternal and strictly selective, in fact exclusive, loyalty. Eroticism has thereby been set free of both links tying it to the production of immortality, physical or spiritual. But in this spectacular liberation it was not alone; it followed the much more universal trends which affect in equal measure arts, politics, life strategies and virtually every other area of culture.

It is a general feature of postmodern condition that it flattens time and condenses the perception of the infinitely expendable flow of time into the experience (*Erlebnis*) of *Jetztzeit*, or slices it into a series of self-sustained episodes, each to be lived through as an intense experience of the fleeting moment and cut off as thoroughly as possible from both its past and its future consequences. Politics of movements is being replaced with the politics of campaigns, aimed at instant results and unconcerned with their long-term repercussions; concern with lasting (everlasting!) fame gives way to the desire for notoriety; historical duration is identified with instant (and in principle effaceable) recording; works of art, once meant to last 'beyond the grave', are replaced with deliberately short-lived happenings and once-off installations; identities of a kind meant to be built diligently and to last for life's duration are exchanged for identity kits fit for immediate assembly and equally instant dismantling. The new postmodern version of immortality is meant to be lived instantly and enjoyed here and now; no longer it is a hostage to the merciless and uncontrollable flow of objective time.

The postmodern 'deconstruction of immortality' – the tendency to cut off the present from both past and future – is paralleled by tearing eroticism apart from both sexual reproduction and love. This offers erotic imagination and practice, like the rest of postmodern life-politics, a freedom of experimentation which they never enjoyed before. Postmodern eroticism is free-floating; it can enter chemical reaction with virtually any other substance, feed and draw juices from any other human emotion or activity. It has become an unattached signifier capable of being wedded semiotically to virtually unlimited numbers of signifieds, but also a signified ready to be represented by any of the available signifiers. Only in such a liberated and detached version may eroticism sail freely under the banner of pleasure-seeking, undaunted and undiverted from its pursuits by any other than aesthetic, that is *Erlebnis*-oriented, concerns. It is free now to establish and negotiate its own rules as it goes, but this freedom is its fate which eroticism can neither change nor ignore. The void created by the absence of external constraints, by the retreat or neutral disinterestedness of legislating powers, must be filled or at least an attempt must be made to fill it. The newly acquired underdetermination is the basis of an exhilaratingly vast freedom but also the cause of extreme uncertainty and anxiety. No authoritative solutions to go by, everything to be negotiated anew and ad hoc. . . .

Eroticism, in other words, has become a sort of a Jack-of-all-trades desperately seeking a secure abode and steady job yet fearing the prospect of finding them. . . . This circumstance makes it available for new kinds of social uses, sharply different from the ones known from most of modern history. Two in particular need to be briefly discussed here.

The first is the deployment of eroticism in the postmodern construction of identity. The second is the role played by eroticism in servicing the network of interpersonal bonds on the one hand, the separatist battles of individualization on the other.

Identity ceased to be the 'given', the product of the 'Divine chain of being', and became instead a 'problem' and an individual task with the dawn of modern times. In this respect there is no difference between the 'classic' modernity and its postmodern phase. What is new is the nature of the problem and the way the resulting tasks are tackled. In its classic modern form, the problem of identity consisted, for most men and women, in the need to *acquire* their social definitions, to build them using their own efforts and resources, out of performances and appropriations, rather than inherited properties. The task was to be approached through setting a target – a model of identity desired – and then doggedly sticking throughout one's life to the itinerary determined by the target set. At the sunset of the classic era of modernity, Jean-Paul Sartre summed up that time-honoured experience in his concept of the 'life project', which does not so much express as create the 'essence' of the human individual. Identities of postmodern men and women remain, like the identities of their ancestors, human-made. But no longer do they need to be meticulously designed, carefully built and rock-solid. Their most coveted virtue is *flexibility*: all structures should be light and mobile so that they can be rearranged at short notice, one-way streets should be avoided, no commitment should be strongly binding enough to cramp free movement. Solidity is an anathema as is all permanence – now the sign of dangerous maladjustment to the rapidly and unpredictably changing world, to the surprise opportunities it holds and the speed with which it transforms yesterday's assets into today's liabilities.

Eroticism cut free from its reproductive and amorous constraints fits the bill very well; it is as if it were made to measure for the multiple, flexible, evanescent identities of postmodern men and women. Sex free of reproductive consequences and stubborn, lingering love attachments can be securely enclosed in the frame of an episode, as it will engrave no deep grooves on the constantly re-groomed face being thus insured against limiting the freedom of further experimentation. Free-floating eroticism is therefore eminently suitable for the task of tending to the kind of identity which, like all other postmodern cultural products, is (in George Steiner's memorable words) calculated for 'maximal impact and instant obsolescence'.

Free-floating eroticism stands as well behind what Anthony Giddens has dubbed 'plastic sex'. A hundred years or so ago, when eroticism was tightly wrapped around sexual reproduction, given no right to independent existence and denied having its own *telos*, men and women were culturally expected and pressed to live up to the fairly precise standards of maleness and feminity, organized around their respective roles in reproductive sex and protected by the requirement of the lasting attachment of partners. That was the era of norm, and the boundary between the normal and the abnormal was clearly drawn and closely guarded. The difference between sex and its 'perversion' left little to the imagination. This has not got to be the case, and is not, now – when but a small parcel of the vast erotic territory is dedicated to the reproductive aspects of sex and the territory as a whole allows for free movement and has but a few long-lease residences. For males and females alike, the way their sexuality is erotically exploited bears no direct relation to their reproductive role and there is no reason why it should be limited to the experience obtainable through the performance of that role. Much richer sensual fruits of sexuality can be harvested through experimenting as well with other than straightforwardly heterosexual activities. As in so many other areas, so too in sexuality the realm once thought to be ruled by nature alone is invaded and colonized by cultural troops; the gender aspect of identity, like all other aspects, is not *given* once and for all – it has to be *chosen*, and may be discarded if it is deemed unsatisfactory or not satisfying enough. This aspect, like all other constituents of postmodern identity, is therefore permanently underdetermined, incomplete, open to change, and so a realm of uncertainty and an inexhaustible source of anxiety and soul-searching, as well as fear that some precious kinds of sensation have been missed and the pleasure-giving potential of the body has not been squeezed to the last drop.

Let me say now a few words about the role assigned to eroticism in the weaving and unstitching of the tissue of interpersonal relations.

In his 'Introduction' to *The History of Sexuality* Michel Foucault (1990: 40–4, 103–7) argued convincingly that in all its manifestations, whether those known since time immemorial or such as have been discovered or named for the first time, sex served the articulation of new – modern – mechanisms of power and social control. The medical and educational discourses of the 19th century construed, among other notions, also the phenomenon of infantile sexuality, later to be turned by Freud, ex post facto, into the cornerstone of psychoanalysis. The central role in this articulation was played by the panic contrived around the child's proclivity to masturbate – perceived simultaneously as a natural inclination and a disease, a vice impossible to uproot and a danger of an incalculably damaging potential. It was the task of parents and teachers to defend children against this danger – but in order to make the protection effective, it was necessary to spy the affliction in every change of demeanour, every gesture and facial expression, to order strictly the whole of the children's lives to make the morbid practice impossible. Around the never-ending struggle against the threat of masturbation a whole system was constructed of parental, medical and pedagogical invigilation and surveillance. In Foucault's words, 'control of infantile sexuality hoped to reach it through a simultaneous propagation of its own power and of the object on which it was brought to bear'. The indomitable and merciless parental control needed to be justified in terms of the universality and resilience of the infantile vice, and so the vice must have been shown – by the universality and resilience of the controlling practices – to be itself universal and resilient.

> Wherever there was the chance [that the temptation] may appear, devices of surveillance were installed; traps were laid for compelling admissions; inexhaustible and corrective discourses were imposed; parents and teachers were alerted, and left with the suspicion that all children are guilty, and with fear of being themselves at fault if their suspicions were not sufficiently strong; they were kept in readiness in the face of this recurrent danger; their conduct was prescribed and their pedagogy recodified; an entire medico-sexual regime took hold of the family milieu. The child 'vice' was not so much an enemy as a support. . . .
>
> More than the old taboos, this form of power demanded constant, attentive and curious presences for its exercise; it presupposed proximities; it proceeded through examination and insistent observation; it required an exchange of discourses, through questions that extorted admissions, and confidences that went beyond the questions that were asked. It implied a physical proximity and an interplay of intense sensations. . . . The power which thus took charge of sexuality set about contacting bodies, caressing them with its eyes, intensifying areas, electrifying surfaces, dramatizing troubled moments. It wrapped the sexual body in its embrace.

The manifest or latent, awakened or dormant sexuality of the child used to be a powerful instrument in the articulation of modern family relationships. It provided the reason and the impetus for the comprehensive and obtrusive parental interference with children's lives; it called the parents to be constantly 'in touch', to keep children constantly within the parental sight, to engage in intimate conversations, encourage confessions and require confidence and secret-sharing.

Today, on the contrary, the sexuality of children is becoming an equally powerful factor in loosening human bonds and thus liberating the individual power of choice, and particularly in the matter of parents–children separation and 'keeping distance'. Today's fears emanate from the sexual desire of the parents, not of the children; it is not in what children do on their own impulse, but in what they do or may do at the behest of their parents, that we are inclined to suspect sexual undertones; it is what parents like to do with (and to) their children that frightens and calls for vigilance – only this is a kind of vigilance which advises caution, parental withdrawal and reticence. Children are now perceived mainly as sexual *objects* and potential victims of their parents as sexual *subjects*; and since the parents are by nature stronger than their children and placed in the position of power, parental sexuality may easily lead to the abuse of that power in the

LIVERPOOL
JOHN MOORES UNIVERSITY
AVRIL ROBARTS LRC
TEL. 0151 231 4022

service of the parents' sexual instincts. The spectre of sex, therefore, also haunts family homes. To exorcize it, one needs to keep children at a distance – and above all abstain from intimacy and overt, tangible manifestations of parental love. . . .

Some time ago Great Britain witnessed a virtual epidemic of the 'sexual exploitation of children'. In a widely publicized campaign, social workers, in cooperation with doctors and teachers, charged dozens of parents (mainly fathers, but also a growing number of mothers) with incestuous assaults against their children; child victims were forcibly removed from parental homes, while readers of the popular press were treated to blood-curdling stories about the dens of debauchery into which family bedrooms and bathrooms have been turned. Newspapers brought news about sexual abuse of the infantile wards in one care home or borstal after another.

Only a few of the publicly discussed cases were brought to trial. In some cases the accused parents managed to prove their innocence and get their children back. But what happened, had happened. Parental tenderness lost its innocence. It has been brought to public awareness that children are always and everywhere sexual objects, that there is a potentially explosive sexual underside in any act of parental love, that every caress has its erotic aspect and every loving gesture may hide a sexual advance. As Suzanne Moore (1995) noted, an NSPCC survey reported that 'one in six of us was a victim of "sexual interference" as a child', while according to a Barnardo's report 'six out of 10 women and a quarter of men "experience some kind of sexual assault or interference before they are 18"'. Suzanne Moore agrees that 'sexual abuse is far more widespread than we are prepared to accept', but she points out nevertheless that 'the word abuse is now so over-used that almost any situation can be constructed as abusive'. In the once unproblematic area of parental love and care an abyss of ambivalence has been revealed. Nothing is clear and obvious any more, everything is shot through with ambiguity – and from things ambiguous one is advised to steer clear.

In one of the widely publicized cases 3-year-old Amy was found in school making plasticine sausage- or snake-like objects (which the teacher identified as penises) and talked of things that 'squirt white stuff'. The parents' explanation that the mysterious object squirting white stuff was a nasal spray against congestion, while the sausage-like things were images of Amy's favourite jelly sweets, did not help. Amy's name was placed on the list of 'children at risk', and her parents went into battle to clear their names. As Rosie Waterhouse (1995) comments on this and other cases:

> Hugging, kissing, bathing, even sleeping with your children – are these natural patterns of parental behaviour or are they inappropriate, over-sexualised acts of abuse?
>
> And what are normal childish pastimes? When children draw pictures of witches and snakes, does this mean they are symbols of frightening,

abusive events? These are fundamental questions with which teachers, social workers and other professionals involved in caring for children frequently have to grapple.

Maureen Freely (1997) has recently vividly described the panic that haunts the postmodern family homes as the result:

> If you're a man, you are likely to think twice about going over to a sobbing, lost child and offering your help. You'll be reluctant to grab a 13-year-old daughter's hand when crossing a dangerous intersection, and ... you will balk at taking film containing pictures of naked children of any age into Boots. If *Pretty Baby* came out today, it would most certainly be picketed. If *Lolita* were published for the first time in 1997, no one would dare call it classic.

Parent–child relationships are not the only ones which are presently undergoing a thorough check-up and are in the process of being re-assessed and renegotiated in the times of the postmodern erotic revolution. All other kinds of human relations are – keenly, vigilantly, obsessively, sometimes in a panic-stricken fashion – being purified of even the palest of sexual undertones which stand the slightest chance of condensing those relations into permanence. Sexual undertones are suspected and sniffed out in every emotion reaching beyond the meagre inventory of feelings permitted in the framework of mismeeting (or quasi-encounter, fleeting encounter, incon-sequential encounter – see the chapter 'Forms of Togetherness' in *Life in Fragments*, Bauman, 1996), in every offer of friendship and every manifes-tation of a deeper-than-average interest in another person. A casual remark on the beauty or charm of a workmate is likely to be censured as sexual provocation, and an offer of a cup of coffee as sexual harassment. The spectre of sex now haunts company offices and college seminar rooms; there is a threat involved in every smile, gaze, form of address. The overall outcome is the rapid emaciation of human relations, stripping them of intimacy and emotionality, and the wilting of the desire to enter them and keep them alive. But not just companies and colleges are affected.

In one country after another, the courts legalize the concept of 'marital rape'; sexual services are no longer marital rights and duties, and insisting on them can be classified as a punishable crime. Since it is notoriously difficult to interpret one's partner's conduct 'objectively', unambiguously, as either consent or refusal (particularly if the partners share the bed each night), and since to define the event as a rape calls for the decision of one partner only, virtually every sexual act can be with a modicum of good (or rather ill) will presented as an act of rape (which certain radical feminist writers were quick to proclaim the 'truth of the male sex as such'). Sexual partners need to remember on every occasion, therefore, that discretion is the better part of valour. The ostensible obviousness and unproblematic character of marital rights, which was once meant to encourage the partners to prefer marital sex over sex outside marriage, allegedly a more risky affair, is now more and more often perceived as a trap; as a result, the reasons for associating the satisfaction of erotic desire with marriage become less and less evident or convincing – particularly when satisfaction without strings attached is so easy to obtain elsewhere.

The weakening of bonds is an important condition of successful social production of sensation-gatherers who happen as well to be fully fledged, effective consumers. If once upon a time, at the threshold of the modern era, the separation of business from household allowed the first to submit to the stern and unemotional demands of competition and remain deaf to all other, notably moral, norms and values – the present-day separation of eroticism from other interhuman relations allows it to submit without qualification to the aesthetic criteria of strong experience and sensual gratification. But there are huge costs to be paid for this gain. In the time of the re-evaluation of all values and the revision of historically shaped habits no norm of human conduct can be taken for granted, and none is likely to stay uncontested for long. All pursuit of delight is therefore shot through with fear; habitual social skills are looked upon with suspicion, while the new ones, particularly such as are commonly accepted, are in short supply and slow in coming. To make the plight of postmodern men and women worse still, the few rules of thumb which emerge from the confusion add more fog of their own because of their seemingly insoluble contradictions. Postmodern culture eulogizes the delights of sex and encourages the investment of every nook and cranny of the *Lebenswelt* with erotic significance. It prompts the postmodern sensation-seeker to develop in full the potential of the sexual subject. On the other hand, though, the same culture explicitly forbids treating another sensation-seeker as a sex object. The trouble is, however, that in every erotic encounter we are subjects as well as objects of desire and – as every lover knows only too well – no erotic encounter is conceivable without the partners assuming both roles, or, better still, merging them into one. Contradictory cultural signals covertly undermine what they overtly praise and encourage. This is a situation pregnant with psychic neuroses all the more grave for the fact that it is no longer clear what the 'norm' is and therefore what kind of 'conformity to the norm' could heal them.

References

Bauman, Z. (1996) *Life in Fragments*. Oxford: Blackwell.

Foucault, Michel (1990) *The History of Sexuality*, vol. 1. London: Penguin.

Freely, Maureen (1997) 'Let Girls Be Girls', *Independent on Sunday* 2 March.

Giddens, Anthony (1992) *The Transformation of Intimacy: Sexuality, Love and Eroticism in Modern Societies*. Cambridge: Polity Press.

Kern, Stephen (1992) *The Culture of Love: Victorians to Moderns*. Cambridge, MA: Harvard University Press.

Moore, Suzanne (1995) 'For the Good of the Kids – and Us', *Guardian* 15 June.

Paz, Octavio (1993) *La llama doble – Amor y erotismo*. Polish translation, *Podwójny Płomien*. Kraków: Wydawnictwo Literackie, 1996.

Taylor, Marc C. and Esa Saarinen (1994) *Imagologies: Media Philosophy*. London: Routledge.

Waterhouse, Rosie (1995) 'So what is Child Abuse?', *Independent on Sunday* 23 July.

Zeldin, Theodore (1994) *An Intimate History of Humanity*. New York: Harper-Collins.

Zygmunt Bauman is Emeritus Professor of Sociology at the University of Leeds. His latest publications include *Globalization: The Human Consequences* (Polity Press, 1998) and *Work, Consumerism and the New Poor* (Open University Press, 1998).

The Sexual Citizen

Jeffrey Weeks

The Sexual Citizen: Who or What?

I OFFER for your consideration a new phenomenon in the erotic firmament, the sexual citizen. Who or what is he, she or it? The sexual citizen, I want to argue, could be male or female, young or old, black or white, rich or poor, straight or gay: could be anyone, in fact, but for one key characteristic. The sexual citizen exists – or, perhaps better, wants to come into being – because of the new primacy given to sexual subjectivity in the contemporary world. The claim to a new form of belonging, which is what citizenship is ultimately about, arises from and reflects the remaking of the self and the multiplicity and diversity of possible identities that characterize the late, or post-, modern world. The would-be sexual citizen, despite obvious traceable precursors in a complex past, is a new presence because of ever accelerating transformations of everyday life, and the social and political implications that flow from this. Which is why the sexual citizen deserves more serious attention than s/he has previously received: this new personage is a harbinger of a new politics of intimacy and everyday life.

We are now very conscious that the idea of sexuality as a separate continent of either experience or knowledge is itself a historical invention, with traceable conditions of existence (Foucault, 1979; Weeks, 1985). It is a contingent, culturally specific, often unstable linkage of related, but separable, elements: bodily potentials, desires, practices, concepts and beliefs, identities, institutional forms. It is highly gendered, but notoriously malleable. It may have hegemonic patterns, but these patterns in turn are usually defined by excluded others, and marked by variations shaped by culturally and materially defined differences: class, age, ethnicity, nationality, geography. The erotic is neither a thing in itself, nor predominantly (if at all) a natural phenomenon, neither something that can be detached from the body, nor cut off from the mind. It is more than an empty space, but less

■ *Theory, Culture & Society* 1998 (SAGE, London, Thousand Oaks and New Delhi),
  Vol. 15(3–4): 35–52
  [0263-2764(199808/11)15:3–4;35–52;006058]

than an all-encompassing imperative. It has become a land of possibility where need, pleasure, commitment and passion can be explored (see Blasius, 1994).

The would-be sexual citizen must live these complexities as circumstances and social location permit. On the surface at least, the idea of the sexual citizen is a contradiction in terms. The sexual is traditionally a focus of our most intimate personal life, an arena of pleasure and pain, love and violence, power and resistance, sequestered away, in theory at least, from the public gaze (Giddens, 1992). Historically, of course, the separation of sexuality from the public sphere has only intensified our interest in it, yet we still tend to regard the erotic as an arena of intensely private and personal experience, however noisy the public resonances. Citizenship, on the other hand, if it means anything, must be about involvement in a wider society (Marshall, 1950). The citizen operates in the public sphere, carrying rights and entitlements but also responsibilities to fellow citizens and to the community which defines citizenship. The sexual citizen, therefore, is a hybrid being, breaching the public/private divide which Western culture has long held to be essential.

Yet this intermingling of the personal and public is precisely what makes the idea of the sexual citizen so contemporary. Even 30 years or so ago, no one would have said, for example, 'I am gay/lesbian', or 'sado-masochist', or 'transgendered', or 'queer', or anything like that as a defining characteristic of personhood and of social involvement and presence. Today, at least in the metropolitan heartlands of Western societies, it is commonplace for many previously marginalized people – those belonging to sexual minorities – to define themselves both in terms of personal and collective identities by their sexual attributes, and to claim recognition, rights and respect as a consequence. The emergence of the sexual citizen therefore, I would argue, tells us a great deal about the impact of ever accelerating social change and the transformation of the sexual world, and about new possibilities of the self and identity.

I have argued elsewhere (Weeks, 1995) that the new sexual movements of the past generation, particularly feminism and the lesbian and gay movement, have had two characteristic elements: a moment of transgression, and a moment of citizenship. The moment of transgression is characterized by the constant invention and reinvention of new senses of the self, and new challenges to the inherited institutions and traditions that hitherto had excluded these new subjects: the moment when the non-heterosexual comes out as lesbian or gay, rejecting the negative stereotypes; when the housewife joins a consciousness-raising group and redefines herself as a feminist, when the cross-dresser proclaims him or herself as transgendered, when the marginally different or the apparently normatively ordinary becomes 'queer'. The characteristic form of expression is subversive of traditional ways of being: the zaps of the 1960s and 1970s, the public demonstrations, the camaraderie of collective political action, the new forms of self expression – the men dressed as nuns, the mythologized bra burning of feminists, the women in leather on motorbikes in the vanguard of lesbian and gay pride marches, the kiss-ins in public spaces in capital cities. Even as I write, the British newspapers are full of stories of a queer disruption of the Archbishop of Canterbury's Easter sermon, with activists seizing the pulpit calling for lesbian and gay equality, to the dismay of tabloids, the broadsheet leader writers, liberal opinion and feminist columnists alike (*Guardian*, 13 April 1998). The aim of such carnivalesque displays, whether conscious or not, is to challenge the status quo and various forms of social exclusion by exotic manifestations of difference. Yet contained within these movements is also a claim to inclusion, to the acceptance of diversity, and a recognition of and respect for alternative ways of being, to a broadening of the definition of belonging. This is the moment of citizenship: the claim to equal protection of the law, to equal rights in employment, parenting, social status, access to welfare provision, and partnership rights, or even marriage, for same-sex couples (Donovan et al., forthcoming).

Although these tend to be different moments in the discourse of sexual politics, they are, I would suggest, both necessary to each other. Without the transgressive moment, the claims of the hitherto excluded would barely be noticed in the apparently rigid and complacent structures of old and well entrenched societies. Transgression appears necessary to face the status quo with its inadequacies, to hold a mirror up to its prejudices and fears (and unsurprisingly, such transgressive moments tend to cause outrage and controversy: such is their purpose; rightly or wrongly they assume that nothing succeeds like excess). But without the claim to full citizenship, difference can never find a proper home. The sexual citizen then makes a claim to transcend the limits of the personal sphere by going public, but the going public is, in a necessary but nevertheless paradoxical move, about protecting the possibilities of private life and private choice in a more inclusive society.

Putting Sexuality into Citizenship

People do not go around saying 'I want to be a sexual citizen'. It is not an identity which people aspire to, nor is it an explicit project which people usually group around. Nevertheless the concept is a useful metaphor, condensing a range of cultural and political practices that embrace a whole set of new challenges and possibilities. Sexual, or what Ken Plummer prefers to call intimate, citizenship is about:

> the *control (or not) over* one's body, feelings, relationships: *access (or not) to* representations, relationships, public spaces, etc; and *socially grounded choices (or not) about* identities, gender experiences. (Plummer, 1995: 151; emphasis in original)

The idea of sexual or intimate citizenship is a sensitizing concept (Plummer, 1997), which alerts us to new concerns, hitherto marginalized in public discourse: with the body, its possibilities, needs and pleasures; with new sexualized identities; and with the forces that inhibit their free, consensual development in a democratic polity committed to full and equal citizenship (for overviews of the debates see Evans, 1993, 1995; Waites, 1996; Richardson, 1998). It has a positive content, in the articulation of new claims to rights and 'sexual justice' (Kaplan, 1997). But it also offers a sharp critique of traditional discourses on citizenship, and on the occlusions and hesitations of contemporary debates.

Most discussion on citizenship has tended until recently to follow Marshall (1950) and concentrate on three particular phases: the civil or legal, the political and the social. Contemporary critiques and developments of the idea of citizenship have demonstrated the lacunae in Marshall's teleology: by broadening the scope (Andrews, 1991; Turner, 1993; Stevenson, 1998); uncovering the gendered nature of the concept (Walby, 1994; Lister, 1996, 1997; *Feminist Review*, 1997); and laying bare its national and racialized dimensions (Anthias and Yuval-Davis, 1992). It is now apparent that the citizenship discourse embraces a multiplicity of interlocked strands which reveal the dense interconnections of class, gender – and sexuality.

The concepts of civil and political citizenship have their origin in the Greek city-states and a particular moment of importance in the transformations of the late 18th century – the American and French Revolutions and their aftermath. They have been concerned with equality under the law and with claims to equal political participation, still of central concern, and far from achieved in many parts of the world. For the question of political citizenship raises powerful and disruptive questions about who should be citizens. We know that the ancient Greek ideal was about male participation in the public sphere and relied on the exclusion of women as well as children and slaves. The 18th-century revolutions were scarcely more welcoming. From the 19th century, however, women struggled for equal political citizenship through the suffrage campaigns which in turn raised unsettling questions about the nature of the similarities and differences between men and women. But it was not until the 20th century that women's full equality under the law and in the political sphere was recognized in Western countries; and it is still contested elsewhere in the world today (for a recent overview see Stepan, 1998).

But by the late 19th century a new emphasis was clearly emerging, the idea of social and economic citizenship, represented by the trade union struggles, the emergence of new labour movements and various collective struggles against poverty. The idea of economic emancipation as the key to wider social change has been a dominating one during this century, and has been a major element in the rise of the notion of social citizenship. Social citizenship is theoretically about the ending of exclusion based on class, poverty, of achieving a society where everyone's worth is recognized and people are prevented from falling into the traps of complete destitution and internal exile. The post-war welfare states can be seen as an attempt to bring together notions of political equality, economic rights and protections and social inclusion to achieve a better life for all, what we have become accustomed to see as the social democratic settlement. Yet until very recently labour movements throughout the West, despite their universalistic aspirations, have tended to be male-dominated, based on assumptions about the split between work and home, men's spheres and women's spheres, differential pay and work opportunities, and the devaluation of work in the home. Again, despite the egalitarian assumptions of the welfare states of the post-war world, built into them were many of the patriarchal assumptions of the labour movements and of the wider society. In Britain, for instance, there is no doubt that the post-Beveridge welfare state, as constructed by the Labour governments after 1945, assumed a working husband, a functioning family and women's sphere as the home. And despite all the attempts over the years, these assumptions are still writ large in the entitlements of the welfare state (Turner, 1993; Lister, 1996, 1997).

The notion of sexual or intimate citizenship, then, is an attempt to remedy the limitations of earlier notions of citizenship, to make the concept more comprehensive. But it simultaneously requires us to accommodate different analytical categories: not only class, not even just gender and race, but also the impact of the heterosexual/homosexual binarism (Sedgwick, 1990), the institutionalization of heterosexuality (Richardson, 1996, 1998), and the question of equity and justice for emergent 'sexual minorities', of whom the lesbian and gay communities are the most vocal, organized and challenging (Herman, 1994; Wilson, 1995; Rayside, 1998). The idea of sexual citizenship has many features in common with other claims to citizenship. It is about enfranchisement, about inclusion, about belonging, about equity and justice, about rights balanced by new responsibilities. What is different about it is that it is bringing to the fore issues and struggles that were only implicit or silenced in earlier notions of citizenship. On one level, as already suggested, these are old issues newly re-articulated in the concept of sexual citizenship. But the idea of sexual citizenship goes much further than this. It is an attempt to put on the agenda issues that have only fully come to the fore since the 1960s, and have now moved from the margins to the centre of our concerns because of very powerful cultural and social changes (see, for examples, the essays in Weeks and Holland, 1996).

In the rest of this article I want to explore the concept of the sexual citizen more closely by looking at three interrelated themes which seem to me to be central to these wider shifts: (1) the democratization of relationships; (2) the emergence of new subjectivities; and (3) the development of new narratives or 'stories' about personal life.

One possible criticism of what I am going to say is that I will be dealing with issues which do not directly relate to most people's experience. The majority of people on a global scale still have to struggle with getting their daily bread, against the exigencies of extreme poverty, famine, drought, war, authoritarian governments, corruption and violence. Compared to these questions, concerns about sexuality and the body and a sense of self may seem fairly trivial when most people have to struggle just to survive, the worries of the *bien pensant* educated middle class rather than the preoccupations of the embattled majority. Rorty (1998) has recently lamented the culturalist turn of the American left, of which sexual politics can be seen as a critical part, which neglects the needs of the population for incremental social reform. But acknowledging the continuing reality of exploitation and domination, both in the South as well as in the heartlands of contemporary society, should not lead us to neglect trying to understand new fissures, new tensions, new struggles and the emergence of new forms of politics in the affluent countries of the North. Struggles for sexual rights have not emerged fully armed from the heads of postmodern intellectuals. They have a grassroots energy behind them.

In examining the concept of sexual citizenship, and related issues about the transformation of the self, the emergence of new identities and new collective struggles, I am not claiming that the old agenda has been completely achieved, or that there are not continuing inequalities, injustices, violence and fear. I am not pretending that power in its old negative exclusive form has disappeared. I do claim, however, that the issues raised by the sexual politics of the last 30 years tell us something very profound about the changing nature of Western societies. Not everything happens at the same pace in every country or culture or part of the world. There are different rhythms in different societies, depending on local traditions, specific histories, the contingent balance of power, different legal, religious and customary ways of doing things. But there are major forces on a global scale, I want to argue, which are transforming relationships and opening up new possibilities that are affecting people in the emerging economies as well as becoming focal concerns of people in the metropolitan countries.

We could argue about the nature of globalization, but I don't think there is any doubt that we are living in a world of profound and rapid change. Global influences have specific local manifestations, and those local manifestations inflect and change some of the global influences. But unless we understand this dialectic between the global and the local, between the universal and the particular, we will be unable to understand why issues around sexuality have become so important for so many people, and how they fit in to a developing life politics concerned with how we should live (Giddens, 1994; Plummer, 1995).

The Democratization of Relationships

The first theme is what can best be characterized as a long-term tendency towards the democratization of relationships. The claim to sexual citizenship is in part at least the combination of various cultural shifts which are together working to undermine traditional hierarchical relationships. There are several elements to this. I will concentrate on three: detraditionalization; egalitarianism; and autonomy.

Detraditionalization

Throughout the Western world we are witnessing a radical unsettling of traditional forms and values (for a summary argument see Giddens, 1994;

Beck and Beck-Gernsheim, 1995). Rapid economic, social and cultural changes on a global scale are undermining many of the traditional bastions of legitimate authority: the churches, customary ways of life, state forms, with the so-called crisis of the family at the epicentre of these transformations. There has been a profound destabilization in the balance of relationships that the family is supposed to represent. The traditional ordered distinctions and balances between men and women have been radically challenged by both material and cultural changes, not least the impact of feminism. The binary divide between homosexuality and heterosexuality, which was codified in the 19th century and has come to be regarded as the very definition of natural in the 20th century, has been significantly challenged by the public emergence of vocal lesbian and gay movements and collective identities. In the wake of these movements a more radical sexual fringe has emerged, 'queering' sexuality in new ways (Evans, 1993; Plummer, 1995; Weeks, 1985). As Cooper (1995: 68–9) points out, the emergence out of the shadows of pathologization of sexual minorities poses inherent problems for concepts of citizenship, and unsettles our ordered erotic categories. Boundaries dissolve, and new ones have to be hastily assembled. The relationship between adults and children has become particularly fraught, the subject of constant negotiation and renegotiation, as a whole series of moral panics and public controversies ranging from the fear of video violence to the now perceived endemic threat of paedophilia underlines. The emergence of 'the paedophile', especially, indicates the limit case for any claim to sexual citizenship.

At the same time the balance between what has traditionally been conceived of as a neat division between private life and public life is being constantly rethought. As mentioned earlier, what was hitherto regarded as the most intimate sphere has now become a major topic of public concern. Contrariwise, what we had always regarded as the legitimate sphere of public concern – the quality of life, the nature of public services, safety on the streets – has in many Western countries as a result of radical right policies increasingly been subject to privatization. While many of the functions of the family have become the object of public concern, governments desperate to save on public expenditure have made various, although often haphazard, attempts to thrust back responsibility, for caring for the old for example or the sick, back on to the family (Weeks, 1995).

The family as we have come to know it in ideology and practice is no longer what it was. We need not recreate the myth of a golden past to recognize many of the symptoms of breakdown in traditional ordering of domestic life. The divorce figures, the incidence of single parenting, the delay of marriage, the rise of cohabitation, rapid rise of single households, the emergence of new patterns of intimacy, for example lesbian and gay 'families of choice', all these are indices of profound change. The pessimists regard these with the deepest gloom. Francis Fukuyama (1997), the prophet of the 'end of history', has recently spoken of the 'Great Disruption' produced by these changes The meliorists, represented by communitarians such as Etzioni (1995), look forward to the bolstering of family life, even if in new forms. The optimists among us see new opportunities particularly in the search for a new balance between autonomy and mutuality (see Giddens, 1992; Beck and Beck-Gernsheim, 1995; Weeks et al., 1999). But whatever the ethical stance we take, there can be no doubt of the massive, and certainly irreversible, shifts in the inherited patterns of intimate life. And whatever the difficulties, and continuing patterns of inequality, violence and struggle, it has often been women who have been in the vanguard of these changes. In Britain, for example, most divorces are initiated by women (though whether this is a flight to freedom or an enforced escape from oppression is contested: see Jamieson, 1998).

Egalitarianism

These changes are aspects of what Anthony Giddens (1992) has called 'the transformation of intimacy', a long-term shift towards the ideal of the democratic egalitarian relationship between men and women, men and men, women and women. I am not going to argue that the ideal is a reality in all or perhaps even a majority of relationships. The empirical evidence underlines the intransigence of inherited inequalities between men and women, as young people reproduce the sexual brutalities and struggles that optimists hoped had long disappeared, and older ones slip complacently into conventional patterns (Holland et al., 1998; Jamieson, 1998). Yet the same evidence reveals an unprecedented acknowledgement of the merits of companionate and more equal relationships, even as we fail to achieve them. The real point is that the egalitarian relationship has become a measure by which everyone has to judge their own individual lives. At the centre of this ideal is the fundamental belief that love relationships and partnerships should be a matter of personal choice and not of arrangement or tradition. And the reasons for choice are quite clear: personal attraction, sexual desire, mutual trust and compatibility. Although the ideal may still be lifelong commitments, a new contingency has entered relationships, which is why there is frequently a sense of uncertainty and anxiety in intimate life. People stay together only so long as the relationship fulfils the needs of the partners. This is what Giddens (1992) calls the pure relationship, based on confluent love, which implies an openness to the other which is dependent on equality and mutual trust.

This in turn implies that commitments must be based on negotiation between consenting partners, not on tradition or lineage. Ties of obligation, based on blood relationship, are increasingly being displaced by ideas of commitments that have to be worked out day-by-day, week-by-week. As Finch and Mason (1993) have argued with regard to kinship relationships in contemporary Britain, people still feel bound by ties of commitment to blood relatives, but these are subject all the time to negotiation. In research I have recently conducted with colleagues[1] on non-heterosexual families of choice in Britain (see Weeks et al., 1998, 1999), it has become clear, among self-defined non-heterosexual people at least, that the language of obligation and duty is being displaced by a language of negotiated commitment and mutual responsibility:

> Responsibility is something I decide to do and I keep to it; obligation is when I feel I have to. . . (F01)

> . . . duty is something that is imposed on you . . . if you feel responsible for someone, I mean, being a parent, you're responsible for your children, then you do that because you feel you want to, not because somebody else feels you ought to. . . . (M44)

> I have a duty to care for my mother. And I feel I have a duty to care for Charlie, but only because that's what we've chosen. . . . (M03)

This need not, should not, mean a minimization of commitment. On the contrary, because relationships are developed on the basis of choice rather than ascription, they are potentially stronger because they are freely chosen. Our research suggests that new patterns of relationships are no less strong in caring for children or the vulnerable whether young or old. Commitments to mutual care, responsibility and respect are at the heart of these elective relationships. My point is, however, that these represent a significant shift away from the sorts of duties and obligations that tied people together in the past.

I am not arguing that these patterns are universal. There is strong evidence that the achievement of egalitarian relationships is in fact more likely outside heterosexual relationships (Giddens, 1992; Dunne, 1997; Jamieson, 1998). As one of the participants in our research put it:

> [in heterosexual relationships] there is an essential power imbalance that there are certain roles, which are backed up by economics and backed by sanctions. And also . . . men and women are socialized differently in terms of what . . . heterosexual relationships are. (F34)

The inherited inequalities between the genders are constantly reproduced in the intimate as well as other spheres, as much research as well as our day-to-day experience underlines. But the urge to equality is now, I suggest, at the centre of increasing numbers of relationships, however inadequately it may be realized.

Autonomy

These new patterns may be seen as expressions of a new form of democratic autonomy, the quest for individual fulfilment in the context of freely chosen egalitarian relationships, as the emerging norm of individual lives. We are here on quite difficult ground. There is no doubt that the economic and cultural changes of the past 20 or 30 years have tended to exalt the individual over the collective. The sweep of economic liberalism throughout most Western countries since the 1970s has elevated individual self-expression and material well-being and undermined many of the traditional sources of solidarity such as the trade unions and other collective forms. The paradox of the 1980s in countries like Britain and the USA was that an extreme economic individualism coincided with attempts at social authoritarianism: at restoring traditional values, the traditional family, tightening the barriers against radical change (Weeks, 1995). The 1990s have demonstrated, however, that the triumph of economic individualism has tended to undermine the social authoritarianism, and given rise to a new libertarianism where potentially anything goes. It is one of the more interesting sights of the death agonies of conservatism in Britain that many right-wing thinkers who ten years ago would have been in the vanguard of social authoritarianism are now justifying the decriminalization of drugs, lesbian and gay marriages and forms of sexual hedonism. The idea of individual freedom cannot be confined to one sphere; it interpenetrates all, dissolving traditional bonds and producing a new 'moral fluency' with incalculable consequences (see Mulgan, 1997).

But anything-goes libertarianism is not the only possibility. The principles of democratic autonomy suggest the need both for individual fulfilment and for mutual involvement, and there are many examples one could cite of this being worked through. I will give one example, but an example which I think throws light on the whole transformation of relationships that is taking place: the HIV/AIDS crisis. As we know, the first manifestations of the crisis were in the gay communities of North America and later of Europe, which have been characterized as the very exemplars of sexual hedonism. And there can be no doubt that the easy sexual interactions of the gay culture of the West Coast or New York did help the rapid spread of the HIV virus within the gay community. But the most striking feature of the response to the epidemic from the gay community was the way in which it brought out a new culture of responsibility, for the self and for others (Weeks, 1995). The discourse of safer sex is precisely about balancing individual needs and responsibility to others in a community of identity whose organizing principle is the avoidance of infection and the provision of mutual support. The sexual ties of the new gay cultures of Western society proved to be strongly imagined community ties which produced a massive effort of collective self-activity in developing community-based responses to HIV and AIDS which showed the way forward for publicly funded services in Britain and elsewhere (Adam, 1992; Weeks, 1995). But in turn AIDS has raised complex issues about citizenship, and especially about the degree to which the execrated and threatening person with a life-threatening syndrome who nevertheless fails to engage in 'safer sex' can be fully included in the social (see for example Watney, 1994; Woodhead, 1998).

New forms of mutual responsibility and autonomy are also manifest in what I have described as families of choice, the varied patterns of domestic involvement, sexual intimacy and mutual responsibilities that are increasingly displacing traditional patterns of marriage and the family (Weston, 1991; Blasius, 1994; Weeks et al., 1999). All these, I would suggest, are examples of what Giddens (1992) calls 'experiments in living' which many of us in late modern societies are forced to engage in. There are, of course, constraints – economic, social cultural, personal – which severely limit free choice. It is easier for some people to adopt different lifestyles than others. Many are still trapped, as I have already acknowledged, in patterns of exclusion and poverty. Yet traditional ways of life are no longer viable or meaningful for very many people, who have no choice but to choose. They have to find ways of living together which are meaningful for them. For many that is a profoundly frightening threat; for others it is an opportunity for inventing themselves afresh.

New Subjectivities

Just as detraditionalization destabilizes traditional patterns of relationships, so traditional concepts of the self and individual and collective identities are fundamentally undermined. Increasingly today identity is not something you assume or are born into or that has to remain fixed all your life. It is something that you make for yourself, as part of what has been called the 'reflexive project of the self' (Giddens, 1992). We can no longer assume, either, a single identity from which all social action proceeds. We have multiple possible identities, as men or women, black or white, straight or gay, Welsh, British, European or whatever, each of which carries different, and often contradictory, loyalties, claims and commitments. Identities are varied and changing. We can no longer regard ourselves as one thing throughout all our lives. Identities are 'projects', 'narrative quests', 'performances' (MacIntyre, 1985; Butler, 1990; Giddens, 1992; Garber, 1992). We are no longer, perhaps, necessarily today what we were yesterday or will be tomorrow. We are hybrids (Bhabha, 1990; Sinfield, 1997). This does not mean a dissolution of the self, but a recognition that the task of finding an anchor for the self, a narrative which gives meaning to all our disparate potential belongings, is a task of invention and of self-invention (Plummer, 1995).

Poststructuralist and postmodernist questionings of the Enlightenment myth of the unitary self have opened up a whole series of questions. What is it, for instance, that gives unity to the self? For Michel Foucault it is in an important sense about being an artist of the self, creating an aesthetics of your own life (Foucault, 1988). Others, like Agnes Heller (1984), have raised critical questions about what constitutes a meaningful life, how we balance a strong sense of ourselves with the involvement with significant others which alone makes our lives have meaning. These are profoundly important issues concerning ethics and values, and in a very real sense the postmodernist challenge has led not to an abandonment of quest for meaning, but on the contrary a search for meaning, a meaning, however, that is constructed by us and not for us in some hidden heaven (Weeks, 1995).

The question of the nature of the self is not simply a product of wild surmise and theoretical speculation (Melucci, 1996). Globalization has dissolved many of the differences between cultures at the same time as it has reinforced new particularisms. New technologies have fundamentally questioned the fixity of our sense of self and of body. Reproductive technologies have made it possible to by-pass the traditional human processes in the creation of new individuals. A new obsession with health and fitness has led to a refashioning of the body along new lines. Cosmetic surgery can remake the body from the size of one's breasts to the shape of one's nose, from the colour of one's hair to the pigmentation of one's skin. Genetic engineering opens possibilities for choosing the sex of one's offspring, eliminating those with inherited diseases, eliminating the unfit, even, if we accept the wilder-eyed enthusiasts, eventually choosing sexual orientation. Information technologies have led to a new sense of the self – the cyborg, the body without limbs (Haraway, 1991) – communicating with other cyborgs through the virtual community of the Internet. The body itself has become a reflexive project, no longer the fixed point on which identity is built, but something to be made and remade through the maze of shifting potential identities.

But perhaps more relevant to our immediate analysis has been the impact of the new social movements of the past 30 years, growing out of these wider transformations, making use of them, building on them and transforming them, but making possible new ways of life, new ways of feeling which both stress individual fulfilment and collective involvement. The women's movement and the lesbian and gay movements of the past 30 years have done more than simply reflect pre-existing identities. They have helped to make new identities possible through their collective experiences. They have provided a focus of meaning. In turn, of course, they pose fundamental questions about politics, cultural belonging and personal needs (see, for example, Cooper, 1995).

These new subjectivities and identities are cultural creations. They are, I have argued elsewhere, fictions, individual and collective narratives which we invent to make sense of new circumstances and new possibilities. But that does not make them any the less significant. They may be fictions, but they are necessary fictions: they provide the means through which we negotiate the hazards of everyday life in a world in a process of constant change (Weeks, 1995). And they provide the stimulus and the necessity for the experiments in living which we have discussed. If traditional identities, located in a sense of place or hierarchy or class or status, are no longer viable, and if identities are narrative structures, they need anchor points. For many people today those anchor points are provided by new patterns of relationships, which offer the possibility of being an individual in a freely chosen set of commitments, and new narratives which sustain them.

New Stories

Plummer (1995) has talked about human beings as inveterate storytellers, and societies as webs of stories and narratives which through their interaction bind us together. We live in a culture of storytelling, but what is startling to the social scientist about the last 30 or 40 years is the ever proliferating catalogue of new stories, new narratives, that have emerged, both reflecting wider social changes and providing the language which makes change possible. New stories emerge when there are new people to listen to and understand them through interpretive communities. The new stories about gender, sexuality and the body that have been told since the 1960s have been possible because of the emergence of new movements and communities that both give rise to and circulate and rewrite these stories. The most common narratives are stories which tell of discrimination, prejudice and empowerment, stories which tell of coming out as lesbian and gay or as a strong, independent woman, stories of victimization and of survival, stories of difference and of similarity, stories of identity and stories of relationships. These new stories about the self, about sexuality and gender, are the context for the emergence of the sexual citizen because these stories telling of exclusion, through gender, sexuality, race, bodily appearance or function, have as their corollary the demand for inclusion: for equal rights under the law, in politics, in economics, in social matters and in sexual matters. They pose questions about who should control our bodies, the limits of the body, the burden of custom and of the state. They are stories which spring up from everyday life, but in turn place new demands on the wider community for the development of more responsive policies, in economics, welfare, the law, culture. In the case of AIDS, people living with devastating illness have taken the lead in defining both medical practice and caring relationships (Epstein, 1996). Non-heterosexuals have challenged the hegemony of patterns of marriage by demanding partnership rights or same-sex marriages (Sullivan, 1997). Counter-discourses, oppositional knowledges, grassroots politics and self-activity have undermined traditional political forms, and begun to define new agendas. There has been an accumulation of new social and cultural capital, where new voices, new collective subjectivities have put forward their claims through a variety of social and political practices (Blasius, 1994; Weeks, 1996).

I am not claiming that these new social forms have swept all opposition away. Where there is power, there is resistance, while resistance in turn gives rise to new forms of power. Yet what is remarkable about the changes is the way in which, despite the various forms of hostility they have engendered, the transformations are still going on, working their way through the undergrowth of everyday life. We live in a world of uncertainty, where old values are dying, majestic institutions are crumbling, but new forms, new values are still having to be struggled for. In this climate it is not surprising that we have seen the rise of new fundamentalism, whether embodied in the Christian right in the USA (see, for example, Herman, 1997), or in the various transnational political religious identities which have emerged over the last decade – Islamic fundamentalism, Hindu revivalism and so on (Bhatt, 1997). Concerns with the body, differentiation between men and women, and sexual identity are central to these movements. Nor is fundamentalism, which Giddens (1994) has described as a refusal of dialogue, a refusal to recognize diversity and difference, confined to religion. Various forms of fundamentalism have been manifest in the new social movements as much as in the old social forms, as the 'sex wars' in the USA dismally confirm (see Duggan and Hunter, 1995). The new pluralism can itself become a new form of fundamentalism if we believe that every distinct identity and community must be marked off by wars and barbed wire from another. The challenge of the late modern world is not to find a new unitary system of values, or to retreat into a hard-won new identity, but rather to balance diversity with common values. That is the task of what I have called radical humanism (Weeks, 1995), a project of shaping and constructing the human bond, not as a way of obliterating difference, but as a way of recognizing and respecting it. The challenge for a new politics of self and of sexuality is therefore huge.

The idea of sexual or intimate citizenship is simply an index of the political space that needs to be developed rather than a conclusive answer to it. But in this new world of infinite possibility, but also ever-present uncertainty, we need pioneers, voyagers, experimenters with the self and with relationships. The would-be sexual citizen, I suggest, represents that spirit of searching and of adventure.

Conclusion

To conclude, I want to spell out some of the implications of what I have argued for a politics of everyday life. The sexual liberation movements that emerged in the 1960s, like related movements around race, spoke within a discourse of emancipation. Structural inhibitions to the achievement of freedom, whether class, racism, patriarchy, heterosexism, were identified, and political strategies developed that argued for their overthrow, though usually in radically vague ways. By the 1980s, especially in countries that experienced a New Right hegemony, those millenarian enthusiasms were dampened and identity politics became concerned with the attainment of the particular: not the emancipation of humankind, but rights for this group rather than that. What are the prospects today?

I suggest that increasingly today we are necessarily concerned with the politics of everyday life. That does not mean that the old agenda is now totally irrelevant: in many parts of the world basic rights, of freedom from want and tyranny, freedom of expression and to be, freedom to live, are far from being attained. But today in most Western countries many of the rights that seemed unattainable even a generation ago are taken for granted. Social exclusions continue, but there are few societies in the developed industrial world that are not committed to broadening the definition of inclusion. Politics will continue to be concerned with macro issues about the economy, welfare provision, national identity, international involvement; but they can no longer ignore micro issues, because the transformations I have described are changing the possibilities of life for the vast majority of Western populations. New problems, new possibilities, are setting new agendas, concerned with the quality of life. Sexual politics, and the claim to sexual citizenship, are not marginal to, but at the heart of contemporary politics because they are centrally concerned with the quality of life. So let me list, summarily, some of the issues which are likely to be central to post-millennial politics:

- achieving a new settlement between men and women;
- elaborating new ways of fulfilling the needs for autonomy and mutual involvement that the family can no longer (if it ever could) fulfil;
- finding ways of dealing with the denaturalization of the sexual: the end of the heterosexual/homosexual binary divide, the new reproductive technologies, the queering of identities;
- balancing the claims of different communities with constructing new common purposes, recognizing the benefits of individual choice while affirming the importance of collective endeavours;
- learning to live with diversity at the same time as building our common humanity.

A list is not an agenda, nor does it provide a map; but it helps to identify the terrain. The claim to sexual citizenship is not an answer to these issues. The importance of the would-be sexual citizen is that by claiming a hearing s/he is beginning to pose new challenges to, and to require new responses from, the body politic.

Note

1. This section is based on research conducted for a project funded by the Economic and Social Research Council, entitled 'Families of Choice: The Structure and Meanings of Non-Heterosexual Relationships' (reference no. L315253030). The research took place between 1995 and 1996, as part of the ESRC's research programme on Population and Household Change, and was based in the School of Education, Politics and Social Science, South Bank University, London. The director of the project was Jeffrey Weeks, with Catherine Donovan and Brian Heaphy as the research fellows. The core of the research involved in-depth interviews with 48 men and 48 women who broadly identified as non-heterosexual. Female interviews are denoted by 'F', the male interviews by an 'M', each followed by a number.

References

Adam, Barry D. (1992) 'Sex and Caring among Men: Impacts of AIDS on Gay People', pp. 175–83 in Ken Plummer (ed.) *Modern Homosexualities: Fragments of Lesbian and Gay Experience*. London: Routledge.

Andrews, Geoff (ed.) (1991) *Citizenship*. London: Lawrence and Wishart.

Anthias, Floya and Nira Yuval-Davis (1992) *Racialized Boundaries: Race, Nation, Gender, Colour and Class, and the Anti-Racist Struggle*. London: Routledge.

Beck, Ulrich and Elisabeth Beck-Gernsheim (1995) *The Normal Chaos of Love*. Cambridge: Polity Press.

Bhabha, Homi (1990) 'The Third Space', in Jonathan Rutherford (ed.) *Identity: Community, Culture, Difference*. London: Lawrence and Wishart.

Bhatt, Chetan (1997) *Liberation and Purity: Race, New Religious Movements and the Ethics of Postmodernity*. London: UCL Press.

Blasius, Mark (1994) *Gay and Lesbian Politics: Sexuality and the Emergence of a New Ethic*. Philadelphia, PA: Temple University Press.

Butler, Judith (1990) *Gender Trouble: Feminism and the Subversion of Identity*. New York and London: Routledge.

Cooper, Davina (1995) *Power in Struggle: Feminism, Sexuality and the State*. Buckingham: Open University Press.

Donovan, Catherine, Brian Heaphy and Jeffrey Weeks (forthcoming) 'Politics, Power and Participation: Citizenship and Same Sex Relationships' (currently under review).

Duggan, Lisa and Nan D. Hunter (1995) *Sex Wars: Sexual Dissent and Political Culture*. New York and London: Routledge.

Dunne, Gillian (1997) *Lesbian Lifestyles: Women's Work and the Politics of Sexuality*. Basingstoke and London: Macmillan.

Epstein, Steven (1996) *Pure Science: AIDS, Activism, and the Politics of Knowledge*. Berkeley, Los Angeles and London: University of California Press.

Etzioni, Amitai (1995) *The Spirit of Community: Rights, Responsibilities and the Communitarian Agenda*. London: Fontana.

Evans, David (1993) *Sexual Citizenship: The Material Construction of Sexualities*. London: Routledge.

Evans, David (1995) '(Homo)sexual Citizenship: A Queer Kind of Justice', in Angelia R. Wilson (ed.) *A Simple Matter of Justice? Theorizing Lesbian and Gay Politics*. London: Cassell.

Feminist Review (1997) 'Citizenship: Pushing the Boundaries', *Feminist Review* 57 (Autumn).

Finch, Janet and Jennifer Mason (1993) *Negotiating Family Responsibilities*. London: Routledge.

Foucault, Michel (1979) *The History of Sexuality, Volume 1. An Introduction*. London: Allen Lane.

Foucault, Michel (1988) 'The Ethic of Care for the Self as a Practice of Freedom', in J. Bernauer and D. Rasmussen (eds) *The Final Foucault*. Cambridge, MA: MIT Press.

Fukuyama, Francis (1997) *The End of Order*. London: Social Market Foundation.

Garber, Marjorie (1992) *Vested Interests: Cross-Dressing and Cultural Anxiety*. New York and London: Routledge.

Giddens, Anthony (1992) *The Transformation of Intimacy: Sexuality, Love and Eroticism in Modern Societies*. Cambridge: Polity Press.

Giddens, Anthony (1994) *Beyond Left and Right: The Future of Radical Politics*. Cambridge: Polity Press.

Haraway, Donna (1991) *Simians, Cyborgs, and Women: The Reinvention of Nature*. London: Free Association Books.

Heller, Agnes (1984) *Everyday Life*. London: Routledge and Kegan Paul.

Herman, Didi (1994) *Rights of Passage: Struggles for Lesbian and Gay Equality*. Toronto: University of Toronto Press.

Herman, Didi (1997) *The Antigay Agenda: Orthodox Vision and the Christian Right*. Chicago, IL and London: Chicago University Press.

Holland, Janet, Caroline Ramazanoglu, Sue Sharpe and Rachel Thomson (1998) *The Male in the Head: Young People, Heterosexuality and Power*. London: The Tufnell Press.

Jamieson, Lynn (1998) *Intimacy: Personal Relationships in Modern Societies*. Cambridge: Polity Press.

Kaplan, Morris B. (1997) *Sexual Justice: Democratic Citizenship and the Politics of Desire*. New York and London: Routledge.

Lister, Ruth (1996) 'Citizenship Engendered', in Dave Taylor (ed.) *Critical Social Policy: A Reader*. London: Sage.

Lister, Ruth (1997) *Citizenship: Feminist Perspectives*. Basingstoke and London: Macmillan.

MacIntyre, Alistair (1985) *After Virtue: A Study in Moral Theory*. London: Duckworth.

Marshall, T. H. (1950) *Citizenship and Social Class*. Cambridge: Cambridge University Press.

Melucci, Alberto (1996) *The Playing Self: Person and Meaning in the Planetary Society*. Cambridge: Cambridge University Press.

Mulgan, Geoff (1997) *Connexity: How to Live in a Connected World*. London: Chatto and Windus.

Plummer, Ken (1995) *Telling Sexual Stories: Power, Change, and Social Worlds*. London: Routledge.

Plummer, Ken (1997) 'The Public Story and the Private Life: Dilemmas of Intimate Citizenship', unpublished paper, delivered at European Sociological Association Conference, University of Essex, August.

Rayside, David (1998) *On the Fringe: Gays and Lesbians in the Political Process*. Ithaca, NY and London: Cornell University Press.

Richardson, Diane (ed.) (1996) *Theorising Heterosexuality*. Buckingham: Open University Press.

Richardson, Diane (1998) 'Sexuality and Citizenship', *Sociology* 32(1): 83–100.

Rorty, Richard (1998) 'The American Road to Fascism', *New Statesman* 8 May: 28–9.

Sedgwick, Eve Kosofsky (1990) *Epistemology of the Closet*. Berkeley and Los Angeles: University of California Press.

Sinfield, Alan (1997) 'Queer Identities and the Ethnicity Model', pp. 196–204 in Lynne Segal (ed.) *New Sexual Agendas*. Basingstoke and London: Macmillan.

Stepan, Nancy Leys (1998) 'Race, Gender, Citizenship', *Gender and History* 10(1): 26–52.

Stevenson, N. (ed.) (1998) *Cultural Citizenship*. London: Sage.

Sullivan, Andrew (ed.) (1997) *Same-Sex Marriage: Pro and Con: A Reader*. New York: Vintage Books.

Turner, Bryan (ed.) (1993) *Citizenship and Social Theory*. London: Sage.

Waites, Matthew (1996) 'Lesbian and Gay Theory, Sexuality and Citizenship: Review Article' *Contemporary Politics* 2(3): 139–49.

Walby, Sylvia (1994) 'Is Citizenship Engendered?' *Sociology* 28( ): 379–95.

Watney, Simon (1994) *Practices of Freedom: Selected Writings on HIV/AIDS.* London: Rivers Oram Press.

Weeks, Jeffrey (1985) *Sexuality and its Discontents: Meanings, Myths and Modern Sexualities.* London: Routledge.

Weeks, Jeffrey (1995) *Invented Moralities: Sexual Values in an Age of Uncertainty.* Cambridge: Polity Press.

Weeks, Jeffrey (1996) 'The Idea of a Sexual Community', *Soundings: A Journal of Politics and Culture* 2: 71–84.

Weeks, Jeffrey and Janet Holland (eds) (1996) *Sexual Cultures: Communities, Values and Intimacy.* Basingstoke and London: Macmillan.

Weeks, Jeffrey, Catherine Donovan and Brian Heaphy (1998) 'Everyday Experiments: Narratives of Non-Heterosexual Relationships', in E. Silva and C. Smart (eds) *The New Family?* London: Sage.

Weeks, Jeffrey, Catherine Donovan and Brian Heaphy (1999) 'Families of Choice: Autonomy and Mutuality in Non-heterosexual Relationships', in Susan McRae (ed.) *Changing Britain: Population and Household Change.* Oxford: Oxford University Press.

Weston, K. (1991) *Families We Choose.* New York: Columbia University Press.

Wilson, Angelia R. (ed.) (1995) *A Simple Matter of Justice? Theorizing Lesbian and Gay Politics.* London: Cassell.

Woodhead, David (1998) 'Safer Sexual Citizenship: The Effects of Community Development Sexual Health Promotion on HIV Negative Gay Men in the AIDS Epidemic', unpublished PhD thesis, South Bank University, London.

Jeffrey Weeks is Professor of Sociology at South Bank University, London. His publications include *Against Nature* (1991) and *Invented Moralities* (1995).

On the Way to a Post-Familial Family
From a Community of Need to Elective Affinities

Elisabeth Beck-Gernsheim

Prologue: Stages in a Controversial Debate

I N WESTERN INDUSTRIAL societies of the 1950s and 1960s, paeans
were being sung to the family. In West Germany it was enshrined in the
Constitution and placed under special state protection; it was the
recognized model for everyday life, and the dominant sociological theory
regarded it as essential to a functioning state and society. But then came the
student and women's movements of the late 1960s and early 1970s, with
their show of resistance to the traditional structures. The family was exposed
as ideology and prison, as site of everyday violence and repression. But on
the opposite side, others appeared in the arena 'in defence of the bourgeois
family' (Berger and Berger, 1984) or rediscovered it as a 'haven in a
heartless world' (Lasch, 1977). A 'war over the family' broke out (Berger
and Berger, 1983). Suddenly it was no longer even clear who or what
constituted the family. Which types of relationship should be described as
a family and which should not? Which are normal, which deviant? Which
ought to be encouraged by the state? Which should receive financial
support?

Meanwhile, in the late 1990s, the discussion has become still more
confused. Many theorists perceive massive changes, perhaps even the end
of the traditional family; others criticize what they call the constant talk of
crisis and argue that the future belongs with the family; while a third group,

■ *Theory, Culture & Society* 1998 (SAGE, London, Thousand Oaks and New Delhi),
  Vol. 15(3–4): 53–70
  [0263-2764(199808/11)15:3–4;53–70;006059]

lying somewhere in between, prefer to speak of tendencies towards pluralism. What makes the debate particularly stimulating is the fact that all sides
appeal to empirical data, and especially to demographic statistics.

In this article I shall first look at two positions which emphasize
continuity and stability of the family. In considering these, I will show that
the black-and-white alternative 'end of the family' or 'family as the future' is
not appropriate. The focus should instead be on the many grey areas or,
better, the many different shades in the niches inside and outside the
traditional family network. The main argument here will be that these
forms signal more than just pluralism and contiguity, more than just a
colourful motley thrown together at random. For a basic historical trend can
be discerned in all this variety, a trend towards individualization that also
increasingly characterizes relations among members of the same family. A
shorthand way of saying this is that a community of need is becoming an
elective relationship. The family is not breaking up as a result; it is
acquiring a new historical form. Paradoxically, we could say that the
contours of a 'post-familial family' are taking shape (Rosenmayr, 1992).[1]

The Construction of Normalcy

On the Handling of Figures

Not long ago a respected daily paper carried a feature article under the
programmatic headline 'The Family Is Not a Discontinued Model' (Bauschmid, 1994). The first sentence already makes the point: 'Sometimes it is the
normal situation which amazes the observer: 85 per cent of children and
young people under eighteen in the Federal Republic grow up in complete
families with natural parents who are still in their first marriage.'

The statistic is indeed surprising, and it is therefore worthy of closer
examination. Where does it come from? What is the basis of calculation?
Three points immediately strike one. First, the cited figure takes children
and young people in 'complete' families as its reference. The picture is
therefore distorted in advance, because it excludes those who decide against
a family. Two groups that have clearly grown in recent years are missing –
men and women who do not marry in the first place, and those who remain
childless.[2] Second, the author writes that the figure comes from the year
1991, but in reality it covers a period stretching from 1970 to 1987.[3] And
already within that period – even more in the years since then – a clear shift
has taken place towards non-traditional forms of living. Since 1970, for
example, the proportion of children born out of wedlock has been constantly
rising;[4] and those born within it face an ever greater risk that their parents'
marriage will break up (Nauck, 1991: 427). Third, population figures that
give a picture of family life say nothing about whether people live willingly
or unwillingly in such relationships. Nor do they say anything about the
dynamic concealed behind these statistics. It is therefore necessary to look
beyond the objective data and to investigate their subjective meaning. Then
it becomes relevant to consider what sociological studies of the family

show:[5] namely, that in many relationships there are partly open, partly submerged conflicts over the domestic division of labour and gender life-projects, and that although traditional arrangements still largely prevail, there is increasing dissatisfaction on the part of women. In short, a considerable potential for conflict is visible beneath the surface normality.

What we find, then, is a screening-out of groups which do not fit the image of normality (single persons, the childless); a disregard for the declining trend in the traditionally normal family (more children born outside marriage, more divorces); and also a disregard for the conflict potential within so-called normal families. One thing is obviously common to these three elements: they all lead to a picture that emphasizes the aspect of continuity and systematically underestimates the aspect of change. It is not so much normality as constructions of normality that are involved.

Redefinitions and Immunization

In an essay entitled 'Family in Dissolution', the sociologist Laszlo Vascovics trenchantly criticizes those who point to radical changes in the family. He sees here just the long-familiar talk of crises: 'Over the last two centuries, crisis and breakdown of the family have again and again been "detected" or predicted' (Vascovics, 1991: 186). And he is quite clear about his own conclusions:

> The family as nuclear or conjugal family has kept its dominance up to the present day.... The 'normal chaos of love', as it has been called, continues to display quite clear and dominant patterns of the partnerships which ... in most cases lead to a quite normal family. (Vascovics, 1991: 197)

In order to assess this view of things, it is important to know how Vascovics defines the 'normal family'. In fact, practically everything goes into his definition. With or without a marriage certificate, temporarily or for life, once or a number of times – everything is indiscriminately included in the nuclear family or its precursors. Even people living alone become 'partnership-oriented' within this framework, because in Vascovics' view they do not in principle exclude a marital or non-marital partnership and even partly aspire towards one. Most non-marital partnerships are said to be 'at least geared to a medium-term perspective'. And if such couples separate, it can still be assumed 'that they will sooner or later enter into a non-marital long-term relationship with another partner'. It is true that there has been a decline in birth-rates, but this changes nothing with regard to the normal family. 'Parenthood has not ceased to be an important aim for young women and men.' Developments such as later parenthood show nothing new:

> Why should there be a difference in how late and early parenthood, shorter and longer-lasting families, are regarded? It is in the nature of things that a family will be founded at one point in the life cycle and dissolved at another. (Vascovics, 1991: 188–94)

Within this conceptual schema, Vascovics is undoubtedly right that the normal family is alive and flourishing. But the series of redefinitions that allows him to argue this mostly discards what a short time ago constituted the essence of marriage and family: legal certification, binding force, permanence and so on. If, amid massive change, all this is simply disregarded, then obviously no change will be left. It is as in the race between the hare and the tortoise: the normal family is there already. Proof to the contrary is impossible, because everything that looks or could look otherwise is simply built into the original concept. This is what theory of science knows as immunization – explanations which cannot be refuted and so are not really meaningful.

The result is that the central questions are systematically left out. For example, it is well known from the data available that most men and women do indeed say that having children is one of their aims in life. The interesting question here is why do young people *fail* to achieve this aim more often than previous ones. What are the barriers, the resistances? Or do other goals in life nowadays have greater attraction? Furthermore, it is hardly surprising that most single people do not dismiss all thought of a partnership. But far more intriguing is the question of why they *actually* live alone. What are the resistances or the rival goals? Finally, not much can be said against the statement that every family starts at some point and comes to an end at another. It is as correct as it is trivial. What is not at all trivial is when the family is founded and especially why it is ended – through death or through divorce. How many go on to found another family? How many let it all drop? How many set up several families in succession?

If such questions are not asked, if instead all forms of private life (with or without children, with or without a certificate, with or without permanence) are bunched together under the heading of the 'normal family', then all contours go by the board. Change? The perspective does not allow for it. And so it nowhere comes into view. The conclusion is fixed in advance: 'Nothing new under the sun.'

Family and Individualization: Stages in the Process of Historical Change

The emphasis on continuity of the family will now be contrasted to an approach that consciously places new elements at the centre of analysis. To draw out what is new, we shall take the discussion on individualization as our reference, focusing first on the historical changes that can be located in the lifespan of the individual. Individualization is understood as a historical process that increasingly questions and tends to break up people's traditional rhythm of life – what sociologists call the normal biography. As a result, more people than ever before are being forced to piece together their own biographies and fit in the components they need as best they can. They find themselves bereft of unquestionable assumptions, beliefs or values and are nevertheless faced with the tangle of institutional controls and constraints which make up the fibre of modern life (welfare state, labour market, educational system, etc.) (Beck and Beck-Gernsheim, 1993). To put it bluntly, the normal life-history is giving way to the do-it-yourself life-history. What does this imply about the family? How is the relationship between family and individualization to be conceived? Above all, what is new in all this?

The Obligation of Solidarity

It is advisable to start by glancing back at the preindustrial family. As many studies from social history have shown, this was essentially a relationship centred upon work and economics. Men and women, old and young people each had their own place and tasks within it. But at the same time, their activities were closely coordinated with one another and subordinated to the common goal of preserving the farm or workshop. Members of the family were thus exposed to similar experiences and pressures (seasonal rhythms, harvest, bad weather, etc.), and bound together by common efforts. It was a tightly knit community, in which little room was left for personal inclinations, feelings and motives. What counted was not the individual person but common goals and purposes. In this respect the preindustrial family may be defined as a 'community of need' held together by an 'obligation of solidarity' (Borscheid, 1988).

> Family, household and village community made productive assets out of the estate, ensured that the many efforts were not just a labour of Sisyphus, partly afforded the possibility of welfare and social prestige, and promised some security in the event of destitution, sickness and old age. Unless one was integrated into a family and a village community, one was virtually nothing, an impotent creature looked down upon by society.... In this network of dependence, it was not individual freedom but the material interests of one's own family, farm and village that were uppermost in people's minds. For better or for worse, everyone was tied to this community; it was at once their sheet anchor and their lead weight. (Borscheid, 1988: 271f)

As many historical documents testify, family members were not bound to one another only in love and affection; tension and mistrust, even hatred and violence, were not uncommon. Yet the basic experience remained one of mutual dependence, to which personal wishes and dislikes had to be subordinated in case of conflict. There was not much scope, then, for individuals to break out. To go one's own way was possible (if at all) only at a high personal cost.[6]

With individualization came the decisive historical break. The family lost its function as a working and economic unit, and started up a new relationship with the labour market. In a first phase, it was chiefly men who were involved in gainful employment outside the home. The imperatives of the performance-oriented society meant that what counted was now the individual person rather than the community. Women, however, were initially relegated to the realm of home and children, to the newly forming space of the private. (At least that was the model for the rising bourgeoisie, institutionally underpinned through the administration of justice, education, philosophy and so on.) Within this framework of relations between the sexes, which was geared in principle to a 'halved modernity' (see Beck, 1986: 179), a new form of dependence began to assert itself: the woman became dependent on the man's earnings, while he needed her everyday labour and care to be capable of functioning in the workplace. The obligation of solidarity that had characterized the preindustrial family went on existing in a modified form.

The Welfare State and the Logic of Individually Designed Lives

A new stage in the history of the family and individualization began with the gradual development of the welfare state, first around the end of the 19th century but above all in the second half of the 20th. A series of social security mechanisms (old age pension, sickness and accident cover, etc.) was introduced to give some protection against the rigours of the market, and various forms of material assistance to weaker groups (income support, education grants, housing benefit, help with buying a home, etc.) were meant to assure greater social justice. One result of such measures was that even if individuals could not function in the labour market, or could do so only to a limited extent, they still became less dependent on family, goodwill and personal favours. The beginnings of social security thus guaranteed a minimum existence beyond the family. Individual members of the family were no longer unconditionally required to fit in and to knuckle under; they could also get out in the event of conflict. The logic of individually designed lives was thus given a boost, and ties to the family were considerably loosened.

> Insofar as the state bestows its gifts upon individuals rather than the families to which they belong, it becomes more likely that young people on a grant will leave their family, that large households extending over several generations will split up, or that married couples in employment will be able to divorce. By reducing economic constraints, the state increases the scope for individual action and mobility. But it thereby also increases the probability that people's lives will move outside collective contexts. (Mayer and Müller, 1994: 291)

The Demand and Pressure for Women to Have a 'Life of their Own'

Another major break occurs with the change in women's normal life-history – something which also began towards the end of the last century but has greatly accelerated since the 1960s. Let us summarize this as concisely as possible (for a more detailed account see Beck-Gernsheim, 1983). As women move at least partly outside the family as a result of changes in education, occupation, family-cycle, legal system, etc., they can no longer rely on men as providers. Instead, in ways that are naturally often contradictory, a perspective of autonomy and self-sufficiency is held out to them.

The 'subjective correlate' of such changes is that women today increasingly develop, and must develop, expectations, wishes and life-projects which relate not only to the family but also to their own persons. At the level of economics first of all, they have to plan ahead for some security in life – if need be, without a man. They can no longer think of themselves just as an 'appendage' of the family, but must increasingly come forward as individuals with their own interests and rights, plans and choices.

The power of the family – above all, of the husband – has been correspondingly restricted. Unlike most of their forebears in previous generations, women are no longer referred to marriage as the route to economic security and social status. They can choose, perhaps not altogether freely but more than before, whether they really want to marry or to stay single, and whether to seek a divorce rather than put up with endless conflicts if the marriage does not turn out as they hoped. This means that, in women's biographies too, the logic of individual design is gradually asserting itself and the obligation of solidarity is further breaking down.

Meanwhile, feminists have analysed this development with new categories and concepts. Whereas traditional sociology always conceived the family as a unit with homogeneous interests and positions in life, there is now a contrasting focus on gender difference. Whereas 'the family' always used to occupy the whole field of vision, now men and women are becoming visible as separate individuals, each linked to the family through different expectations and interests, each experiencing different opportunities and burdens. In short, the contours of distinctively male and distinctively female lives are now becoming apparent within the family.

Individualization and the Staging of Everyday Life

As a result of historical developments, then, a trend towards individualization has made itself felt. This increasingly affects relations between family members too, setting up a special kind of dynamic. A number of examples will help us to understand what is meant by this 'staging of everyday life', as we shall call it. More and more coordination is needed to hold together biographies that tend to pull apart from one another. At a number of levels, the family thus becomes a daily 'balancing act' (Rerrich, 1988) or a permanent 'do-it-yourself' project (see Beck and Beck-Gernsheim, 1993; Hitzler and Honer, 1994). The character of everyday family life is gradually changing: people used to be able to rely upon well-functioning rules and models, but now an ever greater number of decisions are having to be taken. More and more things must be negotiated, planned, personally brought about. And not least in importance is the way in which questions of resource distribution, of fairness between members of the family, have come to the fore. Which burdens should be allocated to whom? Who should bear which costs? Which claims have priority? Whose wishes have to wait?

The Divergence of Tempos and Abodes

In preindustrial society, it was the demands of the family community centred on work and economics which directly set the course of everyday life. As the farm or workshop occupied the central place, each family member usually acted within a radius of which the others could easily keep track. And the distribution of tasks, having been practised for generations, followed a familiar rhythm that was tightly defined and coordinated.

Starkly contrasting with this is the everyday family life in highly industrialized societies. Most men are in employment outside the home, and so are an increasing number of women. The children go to school and spend more and more of their leisure in organized activities outside the home (sports club, painting class, music lessons, etc.), in the new forms of 'insulated childhood' spread right across the city (see Zeiher, 1994). Family life no longer happens in one place but is scattered between several different locations. Nor a fortiori is there a common temporal rhythm, for the family's life is structured by different social institutions: the timetable of kindergarten, school and youth organization, the working hours of the husband and wife, the opening hours of shops, the schedule of public transport and so on. Most important of all, the flexibilization of working hours directly intrudes upon family life, as it produces irregular and fluctuating tempos that do not correspond to such requirements of living together as continuity, stability and coordination.[7]

It is extremely difficult to tie together the threads of these different rhythms. The watchword is: 'Join together what is moving apart!' (see Rerrich, 1994) so that everyday family life becomes a kind of 'jigsaw' that is hard work rather than a game (Rerrich, 1991). The individual pieces have to be put together time and again, the temporal and spatial arrangements compared and collated. This is vividly shown by the results of a detailed empirical study (Jurczyk and Rerrich, 1993). The lives of individual family members, with their different rhythms, locations and demands, only rarely fit together naturally. Much more often, discrepancies appear and lead to repeated attempts to establish a balance. A harmonious everyday life is thus an 'achievement based on a great deal of preparation' (Rerrich, 1993: 311), which requires the family coordinator to be a skilful timetable-juggler. Usually it is women who perform this task which entails considerable practical and emotional effort, often with the help of a grandmother, au pair girl or child-minder. The need to plan, organize and delegate is thus growing all the time as the family becomes a kind of small business. 'Elements of rationalization and calculation are marching into private life' (Rerrich, 1993: 322). My, your, our time becomes the issue in a struggle between time of one's own and a quest for common time. And it is not uncommon for this to result in tension and competing demands – especially between men and women. Who will take responsibility for what? When and for how long? Whose need for time has priority? Who is free when?

Multicultural Families

In preindustrial society, when a man and a woman got married they nearly always shared a wide repertoire of local experiences, values and attitudes. For life-worlds were then far more closed than they are today, and marriage opportunities were greatly limited by factors ranging from class and property to ethnic origin and religion. In comparison, the everyday life-world is nowadays much more thoroughly mixed: people from different regions and social strata meet and often marry one another. The old barriers erected by the law or by the wider family have not completely disappeared, but they are much weaker than they used to be. The principle of a free choice of partner has become generally accepted, so that people who live together (with or without a marriage certificate) often come from quite different backgrounds. Or, as Berger and Kellner put it in a classic text, the modern choice of partner is characterized by the meeting of two strangers.

> Marriage in our society is a dramatic act in which two strangers come together and redefine themselves.... the term 'strangers' [does not] mean, of course, that the candidates for the marriage come from widely discrepant social backgrounds – indeed, the data indicate that the contrary is the case. The strangeness rather lies in the fact that, unlike marriage candidates in many previous societies, those in ours typically come from different face-to-face contexts. (Berger and Kellner, 1974: 160)

The marital relation thereby acquires new meaning, but also, of course, is subject to new strains. For the great opportunity of personally chosen togetherness – namely, the creation of a common world beyond the legacy of family and kin - requires that both participants make enormous contributions. Within the system of modern marriage, the partners are not only expected to construct their own form of togetherness; they *must* do so.

> Marriage and the family used to be firmly embedded in a matrix of wider community relationships.... There were few separating barriers between the world of the individual family and the wider community.... The same social life pulsated through the house, the street and the community.... In our contemporary society, by contrast, each family constitutes its own segregated sub-world.... This fact requires a much greater effort on the part of the marriage parties. Unlike in earlier situations in which the establishment of the new marriage simply added to the differentiation and complexity of an already existing social world, the marriage partners now are embarked on the often difficult task of constructing for themselves the little world in which they live. (Berger and Kellner, 1974: 162–3)

This is especially true of bi-national or bi-cultural couples, where each partner comes from a different country or culture. Such unions also existed in earlier epochs, of course, but their number has increased considerably in recent times, owing to migration of labour, political upheavals and political persecution, mass tourism and foreign travel for education or business. In Germany, every seventh couple marrying today is nationally mixed.[8] What Berger and Kellner saw as characteristic of modern marriage is here even more applicable. For in nationally mixed marriages, the strangers are 'even stranger and the differences in socialization are greater' (Hardach-Pinke, 1988: 116).

Today in every marriage, different lifestyles, values, ways of thinking and communicating, rituals and everyday routines have to be fitted together in one family world. In the case of bi-national/bi-cultural marriages, this means that both partners must achieve the 'construction of a new inter-cultural reality' (Hardach-Pinke, 1988: 217), build an 'intercultural life-world' (Hardach-Pinke, 1988) or a 'bi-national family culture' (Scheiber, 1992: 87ff). They act within a space that has been little structured before-hand, as two different worlds meet. In this situation, for which there is no preparation and no specific rules, the partners have to work out arrange-ments of their own (Scheiber, 1992: 45).

Much that used simply to happen, without any questions asked, must now be weighed up and decided upon. Where shall we live: in your country or mine, or perhaps in a third where neither has the advantage of its being home? Shall we stay here or later move to your home country? Who has which opportunities where? Who must bear which burdens where? Who will be without legal status, job protection or pension cover? Do we communi-cate in your language or mine, or in a third, or in whichever suits the occasion? Which festivals and holidays will we celebrate? What shall we do about family visits and all the many branches of the family? What about the division of labour at home? How are the children to be brought up: in your religion or mine, in your language or mine? What forenames will we choose, reflecting which of our origins?

To repeat: there are no models for any of these decisions. Each couple goes its own way, seeks its own forms. Whether they choose to follow one or the other cultural tradition in its entirety; whether they try to find forms combining elements from both; whether they test out several options and perhaps keep switching around (Scheiber, 1992: 44ff) – all this will depend on their previous history, actual place of residence and plans for the future, as well as on the cultural preferences and prejudices in their surroundings. Each bi-national couple lives out its own story, its own distinctive version of bi-national family culture.

The biography of each partner is far from unimportant in this process. The one who comes from a different country is 'the stranger' here. Perhaps their background was one of poverty and hunger, or perhaps of torture, persecution and escape; anyway they have gone through experiences and anxieties quite different from those of people in their new surroundings. Their life is, to a greater or lesser degree, cut off from their own cultural roots, their socialization, their language. If their mode of expression, behaviour and appearance becomes noticed, they live with the stigma of 'the other' (see Goffman, 1963). They have to face humiliating treatment and mistrust at the hands of courts and officials, landlords and employers. They live without protection, and if their legal status is insecure they can have their work permit withdrawn and perhaps even be deported. True, the native partner is not unaffected by all this, but he or she is in a comparatively secure position and can take steps in self-defence. It remains completely open what attacks from the outside will mean for the couple's relationship: in one case it may be tested to the point of breakdown, while in another it may be made all the stronger. But whatever the outcome, the structure of their relations is typically such that one partner is more exposed than the other. So, differences between their social positions establish themselves. There is an imbalance, more or less pronounced, between their respective opportunities and dangers.

Finally, a bi-national/bi-cultural marriage also makes both partners confront their own origins, with sometimes paradoxical results. Someone who looked for the attraction of 'the other' in a relationship with a foreigner suddenly discovers the 'native' element in his or her own self. 'One sees how deeply rooted is one's own value system – indeed, in many respects one sees it for the first time' (Elschenbroich, 1988: 368). Contemplating the children's future brings memories back with particular force, making it necessary to confront one's own socialization and history, values and desires – one's own identity. The question 'Who am I, what do I want?' is posed anew in the course of a bi-national marriage. And it leads on to further questions that call for a crucial decision: 'What do I want to keep?', 'What can I give up?', 'What is important to me?'

Divorce and its Consequences

The number of divorces has risen dramatically in the course of the 20th century. Every third marriage ends in divorce in the Federal Republic of Germany, every second one in the USA.[9] Children too are increasingly affected. A German study that compared children born in 1960 and in 1980 came to the following conclusion: 'During these twenty years, the risk of being affected in childhood by parental separation has risen more than threefold' (Nauck, 1991: 427).

When divorce occurs, the situations of men and women, adults and children, develop in different directions. This is true first of all in a directly geographical sense: one partner (nearly always the man) moves to another dwelling and perhaps another town (so as to make a fresh start). Women and children stay behind, but it is not uncommon for them to move too at a later date (to cheaper accommodation, closer to grandparents and so on) – which means a change in surroundings, school and neighbours. New economic situations are especially important: a drop in income usually takes place, depending on the laws of the country concerned. In the USA the standard of living sharply declines for women and children, while it not infrequently rises for men (because they often pay no maintenance) (Cherlin, 1992: 73f). In Germany money, or lack of it, is more evenly divided and most men have to contend with a reduced budget, but still the women and children generally are worse off (Lucke, 1990).

In addition, a new organization of everyday life becomes necessary after a divorce. It has to be negotiated, often fought over, between the two who used to be a couple. Who keeps the apartment, who gets which share of the household goods, which keepsakes? How much maintenance will be paid for whom? And above all, who gets the children and what are the custody rights? Man versus woman: claims and demands are raised, rights and duties redistributed. New agreements are sought, often with a great deal of argument. Instead of a common daily life and a common abode, there are now separate 'access' times for the father. When should he come, and for how long? How much is he entitled to have the child at weekends and holidays? In extreme cases, the man or woman may even try to settle things by force: the number of child kidnappings has also been increasing.

Family therapists, lawyers and judges see every day how wounding and bitterness, rage and hatred can escalate between ex-partners after a divorce. But even when the separation is calm and reasonable, it inevitably leads to a new relationship among husband, wife and children. Much more clearly than before, they confront one another as individuals eager to assert their own interests and pursuits, their own wishes and rights. The ex-partners differ in how they think not only about the future but also about their time together in the past – often too about who was to blame and how the whole thing should be seen (he always had other women, she always threw their money around).

In between are the children (on their situation see Cherlin, 1992; Furstenberg and Cherlin, 1991; Wallerstein and Berlin Kelly, 1980; Wallerstein and Blakeslee, 1989). Naturally they have wishes of their own. As various studies have shown, they usually hope that the parents will get together again. Yet the parents still go their own way regardless. The children then have to learn to live with divided loyalties. Where fights break out over who they should stay with, they are asked by the court whether they would prefer to live with the mother or the father. However carefully it is done, the child is being asked to make a statement against one or the other parent – and when little care is taken, the child directly experiences the parents' manoeuvres and attempts to gain influence. Where visiting rules are in force but the ex-partners cannot overcome their sense of hurt, the children become involved in a post-divorce battle in which they are sounded out about the lifestyle and new relationships of the former spouse, or used as carriers of information between the warring fronts. Nor is that always all. In some families, the children become split between the parents, as brothers and sisters too may divide against each other, Much more often, however, their relationship to the father rapidly tails off as he disappears from their immediate horizon. Relations with the paternal grandparents also grow weaker and more problematic, sometimes partly prevented by the mother as a way of wiping out all reference to the father (Cherlin and Furstenberg, 1986: 136ff).

What all this means for the growing child is a matter of dispute. Many studies indicate that children, being sensitive and vulnerable, often suffer lifelong disturbances when early relations are severed (see Wallerstein and Blakeslee, 1989). Others suggest that children are more flexible, robust, even thoroughly adaptable, and that although the period after a divorce is certainly a dramatic crisis, the children usually get over it and settle into the new conditions (see Cherlin, 1992; Furstenberg and Cherlin, 1991). It may be that both interpretations are not completely wrong, but also not completely right; perhaps they are both too narrow. In keeping with what has been said so far, I would therefore like to propose a third interpretation. The series of events connected with separation may, that is, involve a special kind of socialization, the essence of which is a message of, and a hard lesson in, individualism. If children manage to come to terms with changing family forms, this means that they have had to learn to sever close bonds, to cope with loss. They learn early what it means to be abandoned and to part. They see that love does not last for ever, that relationships come to an end, that separation is a normal occurrence in life.

Conjugal Succession and Elective Family Relationships

Many divorced people later remarry or cohabit with a new partner who was also married before and may also have children of their own. More and more children thus grow up with one non-biological parent. On closer examination, these step-families appear in a sense to be a variant of the bi-cultural family. According to recent findings, they are a 'curious example of an organizational merger; they join two family cultures into a single household' (Furstenberg and Cherlin, 1991: 83). Here too, values, rules and routines, different expectations and everyday practices – from table manners and pocket-money to television viewing and bedtime hours – have to be negotiated and agreed. In addition, many children move backwards and forwards between their different family worlds, between the 'everyday parent' who has custody and lives with a new partner, and the 'weekend parent' who does not have custody and may also have a new family. This may well lead to complex relationship structures that can be presented only in diagrams with many ramifications. 'Marriage and divorce chains',[10] 'conjugal succession' (Furstenberg, 1989), 'multiparent families' (Napp-Peters, 1993), 'patchwork families' – all these are concepts designed to make the new family forms easier to grasp. One key characteristic, of course, is that it is not clear who actually belongs to the family. There is no longer a single definition – that has been lost somewhere in the rhythm of separations and new relationships. Instead, each member has their own definition of who belongs to the family; everyone lives out their own version of the patchwork family.

> Let us consider the case in which a married couple with two children divorces and the wife retains custody of the children. . . . If we ask the divorced mother who is in her immediate family, she certainly would include her children, but she might well exclude her ex-husband, who now lives elsewhere. If we ask her children who is in their immediate family, however, we might get a different answer. If the children still see their father regularly, they would probably include both their father and their mother as part of their family. And if we ask the ex-husband who is in his immediate family, he might

LIVERPOOL
JOHN MOORES UNIVERSITY
AVRIL ROBARTS LRC
TEL. 0151 231 4022

include his children, whom he continues to see, but not his ex-wife. Thus, after divorce, mother, father and children each may have a different conception of who is in their immediate family. In fact, one can no longer define 'the family' or 'the immediate family' except in relation to a particular person. (Cherlin, 1992: 81)

In this constellation it is no longer the traditional rules of ascription (descent and marriage) which determine the family bond. The key factor now is whether the social relations stemming from it persist after the divorce. Where these relations are broken or gradually fade, there is also an end to the ties of kinship. What could be seen emerging in other family constellations of modernity is here fully displayed: maintenance of the family link is no longer a matter of course but a freely chosen act. In the situation following a divorce, kinship is worked out anew in accordance with the laws of choice and personal inclination – it takes the form of 'elective affinities'. As it is no longer given as a destiny, it requires a greater personal contribution, more active care. As one study of patchwork families puts it: 'From the huge universe of potential kin, people actively create kin by establishing a relationship – by working at becoming kin. And they have wide latitude in choosing which links to activate' (Furstenberg and Cherlin, 1991: 93). Many relatives by the first marriage continue to be 'part of the family'; many by the second marriage are added to them; and others remain outside or drop out.

The outcome no longer follows a predetermined model. For where there is a choice, personal preferences more and more become the yardstick; each individual draws his or her own boundaries. Even children growing up in the same household no longer necessarily have the same definition of who belongs to the family (Furstenberg and Cherlin, 1991: 93). What all this means is that 'conjugal succession implies greater fluidity and uncertainty in kinship relations. Cultivating family ties may become more important as less can be taken for granted about the obligation of particular kin to one another' (Furstenberg, 1989: 28f). This confronts everyone involved with new questions that need to be answered; new rules of solidarity and loyalty become necessary.

> It will be extraordinarily interesting to see the relative strength of consanguinal and affinal bonds within families whose members have been multiplied by successive marriages. How will grandparents divide their inheritance among biological grandchildren whom they barely know, stepgrandchildren acquired early in life, or stepgrandchildren acquired from their own second marriage who have helped to nurse them later in life? Do biological fathers have more obligation to send their biological children, who have been raised by a stepfather, to college or their own stepchildren whom they have raised? (Furstenberg, 1989: 29)

When such networks take shape, the net result of divorce for the children is an enlargement rather than a narrowing of their kinship boundaries. The character of the ties does, however, change in the process. No longer taken for granted, they become thinner and more fragile, more dependent upon personal cooperation and also upon external circumstances (such as a change of place). This kind of bonding contains special opportunities but also special risks. On the other hand, we should not underestimate the value of bonding which, precisely because of its weakness, encompasses a wide kinship network. But on the other hand, 'this thinner form of kinship may not be an adequate substitute for the loss of relatives who had a stronger stake in the child's success' (Furstenberg and Cherlin, 1991: 95). Today, through divorce and remarriage, people are indeed related to more people than they used to be, but the obligations involved in the bond have been decreasing.

Prospects for the Future

Whereas, in preindustrial society, the family was mainly a community of need held together by an obligation of solidarity, the logic of individually designed lives has come increasingly to the fore in the contemporary world. The family is becoming more of an elective relationship, an association of individual persons, who each bring to it their own interests, experiences and plans, and who are each subjected to different controls, risks and constraints.

As the various examples from contemporary family life have shown, it is necessary to devote much more effort than in the past to the holding together of these different biographies. Whereas people could once fall back upon rules and rituals, the prospect now is of a staging of everyday life, an acrobatics of balancing and coordinating. The family bond thereby grows more fragile, and there is a greater danger of collapse if attempts to reach agreement are not successful. Since individualization also fosters a longing for the opposite world of intimacy, security and closeness (Beck and Beck-Gernsheim, 1995), most people will continue – at least for the foreseeable future – to live within a partnership or family. But such ties are not the same as before, in their scope or in their degree of obligation and permanence. Out of many different strivings, longings, efforts and mistakes, out of successful and often unsuccessful experiments, a wider spectrum of the private is taking shape. As people make choices, negotiating and deciding the everyday details of do-it-yourself relationships, a 'normal chaos' of love, suffering and diversity is growing and developing.

This does not mean that the traditional family is simply disappearing. But it is losing the monopoly it had for so long. Its quantitative significance is declining as new forms of living appear and spread – forms which (at least generally) aim not at living alone but at relationships of a different kind: for example, without a formal marriage or without children; single parenting, conjugal succession, or same-sex partnerships; part-time relationships and companionships lasting for some period in life; living between more than one home or between different towns. These in all their intermediary and secondary and floating forms represent the future of families, or what I call: the contours of the 'post-familial family'.

Notes

1.   Leopold Rosenmayr (1992) speaks of a 'post-familial family'.

2.   These trends are more marked in West Germany, but they are also on the increase in East Germany. As to singles, the percentage of men and women who stay single over their lifetime has been increasing continuously, in West Germany since 1930, in East Germany since 1950 (Engstler, 1997: 85). As to cohabitation, in West Germany, the number of non-married couples living together rose tenfold between 1972 and 1996, from 137,000 to 1,408,000. In East Germany, this number rose from 327,000 in 1991 to 442,000 in 1996 (Engstler, 1997: 62). As to those without children, in West Germany, of women born in 1945, 13.3 percent remained childless; of those born in 1960, approximately 23.3 percent will remain so. In East Germany, until recently the number of women remaining childless was very low, but it is now also increasing (Engstler, 1997: 96, 103).

3.   The figures quoted by Elisabeth Bauschmid evidently come from Bernhard Nauck's article (1991), based on research work carried out in 1988. The forms of family in question refer to the period from 1970 to 1987.

4.   In West Germany, the number of children born outside marriage rose threefold between 1965 and 1997, from 4.7 percent to 14.3 percent (Statistisches Bundesamt 1990: 116; for 1997, data from the Federal Bureau of Statistics in Wiesbaden, not yet published). In East Germany, nearly half of the children (44.1 percent) were born outside marriage in 1997 (data from the Federal Bureau of Statistics in Wiesbaden, not yet published).

5.   See the survey contained in Elisabeth Beck-Gernsheim (1992).

6.   See the example of an 18th-century divorce, in Bock and Duden (1997: 126).

7.   For more data on the growth of flexitime working (weekend, shift, part-time work, etc.), see Gross et al., 1987, 1989.

8.   According to the latest available figures, for the year 1996, from the Federal Bureau of Statistics in Wiesbaden. This points to a rapid increase in such marriages, which still only accounted for a twelfth of the total in the second half of the 1980s. See also Engstler (1997: 83).

9.   For recent figures see Engstler (1997: 88, 90), and Cherlin (1992: 7, 24).

10.   The concept of 'divorce chains' originated with the anthropologist Paul Bohannan and was adopted by other authors such as Cherlin (1992: 83).

References

Bauschmid, Elisabeth (1994) 'Familie ist kein Auslaufmodell', *Süddeutsche Zeitung* 4 January: 4.

Beck, Ulrich (1986) *Risikogesellschaft. Auf dem Weg in eine andere Moderne.* Frankfurt am Main: Suhrkamp.

Beck, Ulrich and Elisabeth Beck-Gernsheim (1993) 'Nicht Autonomie, sondern Bastelbiographie', *Zeitschrift für Soziologie* 3: 178–87.

Beck, Ulrich and Elisabeth Beck-Gernsheim (1995) *The Normal Chaos of Love.* Cambridge: Polity Press. (Orig. 1990.)

Beck-Gernsheim, Elisabeth (1983) 'Vom "Dasein für andere" zum Anspruch auf ein Stück "eigenes Leben" – Individualisierungsprozesse im weiblichen Lebenszusammenhang', *Soziale Welt* 3: 307–41.

Beck-Gernsheim, Elisabeth (1992) 'Arbeitsteilung, Selbstbild und Lebensentwurf. Neue Konfliktlagen in der Familie', *Kölner Zeitschrift für Soziologie und Sozialpsychologie* 2: 273–91.

Berger, Birgitte and Peter L. Berger (1983) *The War over the Family*. Garden City and New York: Anchor Press/Doubleday.

Berger, Birgitte and Peter L. Berger (1984) *In Verteidigung der bürgerlichen Familie*. Reinbek: Rowohlt.

Berger, Peter L. and Hansfried Kellner (1974) 'Marriage and the Construction of Reality', in R. L. Coser (ed.) *The Family: Its Structures and Functions*. New York.

Bock, Gisela and Barbara Duden (1977) 'Arbeit aus Liebe – Liebe als Arbeit', pp. 118–99 in *Frauen und Wissenschaft. Beiträge zur Berliner Sommeruniversität für Frauen*. Berlin.

Borscheid, Peter (1988) 'Zwischen privaten Netzen und öffentlichen Institutionen – Familienumwelten in historischer Perspektive', pp. 271–80 in Deutsches Jugendinstitut (ed.) *Wie geht's der Familie?* Munich: Kösel.

Cherlin, Andrew J. (1992) *Marriage, Divorce, Remarriage*. Cambridge, MA: Harvard University Press.

Cherlin, Andrew J. and Frank F. Furstenberg (1986) 'Grandparents and Divorce', ch. 6 in *The New American Grandparent*. New York: Basic Books.

Elschenbroich, Donata (1988) 'Eine Familie – zwei Kulturen', in Deutsches Jugendinstitut (ed.) *Wie geht's der Familie?* Munich: Kösel.

Engstler, Heribert (1997) *Die Familie im Spiegel der amtlichen Statistik. Aktualisierte und erweiterte Neuauflage 1998*, ed. Federal Ministry for Family, Senior Citizens, Women and Youth. Berlin.

Furstenberg, Frank F. (1989) 'One Hundred Years of Change in the American Family', in Harold J. Bershady (ed.) *Social Class and Democratic Leadership: Essays in Honor of E. Digby Baltzell*. Philadelphia, PA.

Furstenberg, Frank F. and Andrew J. Cherlin (1991) *Divided Families: What Happens to Children when Parents Part*. Cambridge, MA: Harvard University Press.

Goffman, Erving (1963) *Stigma: Notes on the Management of Spoiled Identity*. Englewood Cliffs, NJ.

Gross, Hermann, Ulrich Pekuhl and Cornelia Thoben (1987) 'Arbeitszeitstrukturen im Wandel', in Der Minister für Arbeit, Gesundheit und Soziales des Landes Nordrhein-Westfalen (ed.) *Arbeitszeit '87*, Part 2. Dusseldorf.

Gross, Hermann, Cornelia Thoben and Frank Bauer (1989) *Arbeitszeit '89. Ein report zu Arbeitszeiten und Arbeitszeitwünschen in der Bundesrepublik*. Cologne.

Hardach-Pinke, Irene (1988) *Interkulturelle Lebenswelten. Deutsch–japanische Ehen in Japan*. Frankfurt am Main: Campus.

Hitzler, Ronald and Anne Honer (1994) 'Bastelexistenz. Über subjektive Konsequenzen der Individualisierung', pp. 307–15 in Ulrich Beck and Elisabeth Beck-Gernsheim (eds) *Riskante Freiheiten. Individualisierung in modernen Gesellschaften*. Frankfurt: Suhrkamp.

Jurczyk, Karin and Maria S. Rerrich (eds) (1993) *Die Arbeit des Alltags*. Freiburg.

Lasch, Christopher (1977) *Haven in a Heartless World: The Family Besieged*. New York.

Lucke, Doris (1990) 'Die Ehescheidung als Kristallisationskern geschlechtspezifischer Ungleichheit', pp. 363–85 in Peter A. Berger and Stefan Hradil (eds) *Lebenslagen, Lebensläufe, Lebensstile*. Göttingen: Schwartz Verlag.

Mayer, Karl Ulrich and Walter Müller (1994) 'Lebensverläufe im Wohlfahrtsstaat', in Ulrich Beck and Elisabeth Beck-Gernsheim (eds) *Riskante Freiheiten. Individualisierung in modernen Gesellschaften*. Frankfurt: Suhrkamp.

Napp-Peters, Anneke (1993) 'Mehrelternfamilien – Psychosoziale Folgen von Trennung und Scheidung für Kinder und Jugendliche', *Neue Schriftenreihe der Arbeitsgemeinschaft füre Erziehungshilfe* 49: 12–26.

Nauck, Bernhard (1991) 'Familien und Betreuungssituationen im Lebenslauf von Kindern', pp. 389–428 in Hans Bertram (ed.) *Die Familie in Westdeutschland*. Opladen: Laske und Budrich.

Rerrich, Maria S. (1988) *Balanceakt Familie. Zwischen alten Leitbildern und neuen Lebensformen*. Freiburg: Lambertus.

Rerrich, Maria S. (1991) 'Puzzle Familienalltag: Wie passen die einzelnen Teile zusammen?' *Jugend und Gesellschaft* 5–6.

Rerrich, Maria S. (1993) 'Gemeinsame Lebensführung: Wie Berufstätige einen Alltag mit ihren Familien herstellen', in Karin Jurczyk and Maria S. Rerrich (eds) *Die Arbeit des Alltags*. Freiburg: Lambertus.

Rosenmayr, Leopold (1992) 'Showdown zwischen Alt und Jun?', *Wiener Zweitung* 26 June: 1.

Scheibler, Petra M. (1992) *Binationale Ehen*. Weinheim: Deutscher Studienverlag.

Statistisches Bundesamt (ed.) (1990) *Familien heute. Strukturen, Verläufe, Einstellungen*. Stuttgart: Metzler-Poeschel.

Vascovics, Laszlo (1991) 'Familie im Auflösungsprozess?', pp. 186–98 in Deutsches Jugendinstitut (ed.) *Jahresbericht 1990*. Munich.

Wallerstein, Judith S. and Joan Berlin Kelly (1980) *Surviving the Breakup: How Children and Parents Cope with Divorce*. New York: Basic Books.

Wallerstein, Judith S. and Sandra Blakeslee (1989) *Second Chances*. New York: Ticknor & Fields.

Zeiher, Helga (1994) 'Kindheitsträume. Zwischen Eigenständigkeit und Abhängigkeit', in Ulrich Beck and Elisabeth Beck-Gernsheim (eds) *Riskante Freiheiten. Individualisierung in modernen Gesellschaften*. Frankfurt: Suhrkamp.

Elisabeth Beck-Gernsheim teaches Sociology at Erlangen University. Her publications include *Das halbierte Leben. Männerwelt Beruf, Frauenwelt Familie* (Frankfurt: Fischer, 1980), *Die Kinderfrage. Frauen zwischen Kinderwunsch und Unabhängigkeit* (München: Beck, 1988), *Technik, Markt und Moral. Über Reproduktionsmedizin und Gentechnologie* (Frankfurt: Fischer, 1991), translated as *The Social Implications of Bioengineering* (New Jersey: Humanities Press, 1995), *Welche Gesundheit wollen wir? Dilemmata des medizintechnischen Fortschritts* (Frankfurt: Suhrkamp, 1995) and *Was kommt nach der Familie? Einblicke in neue Lebensformen* (München: Beck, 1998), the translation of which will be published by Polity Press in 1999.

On the Elementary Forms of the Socioerotic Life

Sasha Weitman

For Elizabeth Beck-Gernsheim and Ulrich Beck

> ... le discours amoureux est aujourd'hui *d'une extrême solitude*. Ce discours peut être parlé par des milliers de sujets (qui le sait?), mais il n'est soutenu par personne; il est complètement abandonné des langages environnants – ou ignoré, ou déprecié, ou moqué par eux, coupé non seulement du pouvoir, mais aussi de ses mécanismes (savoirs, sciences, arts). Lorsqu'un discours est de la sorte entraîné par sa propre force dans la dérive de l'inactuel, il ne lui reste plus qu'à être le lieu, si exigu soit-il, d'une *affirmation*. (Roland Barthes, *Fragments d'un discours amoureux*)

IN HIS LAST and most important work, Durkheim (1960c) demonstrated that religious rituals serve to imbue worshippers with the realization that they are more than mere individuals, that they are 'members' of something vaster, more potent, more enduring, indeed, something far more real, than they themselves are. This greater something, the deity they worship, turns out on analysis to be none other than an idealized representation of the collectivity. Religion's work, then, is, literally, socialization – getting individuals to reidentify themselves as members of the collectivity. Durkheim's great merit lay not only in advancing this spectacular proposition, but in his detailed demonstration of how the rituals, symbols and experiences of religion perform this work of socialization. Thus, he showed how it is on holidays, when families converge from all parts of the territory of the clan to partake, together, in elaborate religious rites (of commemoration, expiation, etc.), that all these individuals feel inspired by super-human powers, come to associate these powers with the collectivity, and to re-experience and reaffirm themselves as clan members.

- *Theory, Culture & Society* 1998 (SAGE, London, Thousand Oaks and New Delhi), Vol. 15(3–4): 71–110
[0263-2764(199808/11)15:3–4;71–110;006060]

Religious rites are 'designed', as it were, to stir in them experiences so dramatic, so empowering, so real yet so unreal, that when the festivities are over and the holiday makers repair back to their respective hunting and gathering grounds to resume their everyday life routines, they continue to be under the spell of these extraordinary experiences and to feel and behave not as plain individuals, but as clan members.

What I will try to do in this article is begin an analysis of erotic sexuality in the spirit of Durkheim's social analysis of religion. Thus, based on an analysis of the peculiar things we do and feel when we make love, I propose, first, to uncover the implicit logic that generates and sustains these doings and feelings. Second, I proceed to suggest that the logic that governs love-making is the same as the logic of sociability, and of sociality in general, and that this homology calls for gathering erotic and social occasions under one and the same rubric, that of the 'socioerotic' (since the term 'social' has been denatured through overuse). Third, I conclude with a discussion of how socioerotic domains fit into a larger world structured and governed mainly by interest- and power-driven conflictual fields.

Before launching into an exposition of these claims, however, some preliminary clarifications are in order.

Preliminary Clarifications

First, what is 'erotic sexuality'? By it I mean here the kind of sexuality engaged in by lovers who love one another, at least in the course of their intercourse. It differs from sexuality *tout court* in that it entails more, much more than mere copulation. Erotic sexuality is, literally, love-making, a kind of sex which Alberoni (1987) has called *le grand érotisme* – and for which the phoneme 'sex' is grossly dissonant. Besides being able to last for hours, this kind of sex may also begin hours, even days, before the lovers engage in actual sexual intercourse, and may linger on well after the completion of the sex act. In this kind of love-making, lovers love not only the sexual parts of their mate but their whole body, especially its anatomic and kinesic peculiarities (the texture of the hair, the grain of the voice, the feel of the earlobes, the way s/he smiles, smokes, frowns, 'the wiggle in her walk/the giggle in her talk'). Even traits that, in others, may detract or irritate (wrinkles, scars, speech defects) are, in the mate, eroticized and feverishly desired. Moreover, in this kind of sexuality, not only is the mate's body fetishized, but so are details of his or her personal belongings (the coffee cup s/he drinks from, the gloves, the jacket, the scarf s/he wears, the cigarette lighter, the perfume, the handwriting, the beat-up old car s/he drives), as are the time, the place, the circumstances, even the ambient weather con-ditions, of their first or subsequent amorous encounters.

Second, what are social phenomena 'proper'? Following Weber – rather than, in this respect, Durkheim or Simmel – sociologists today use 'social' in an omnibus sense to designate virtually any and all matters involving two or more people, including purchases at the greengrocer's, committee meetings, transactions with a bank clerk, patient–physician consultations, staff–line relations in the factory, you name it. None of these, however, is 'social' in the ordinary language sense of the term: we don't refer to an appointment at the dentist's as a social rendezvous. In this article, as in plain English, 'social' will designate a *sub*set only of interpersonal occasions, those characterized by affability, fellowship, good-will, respect and deference and the like, as connoted by common expressions such as 'a very social fellow', 'social clubs', 'social calendar', 'social events', 'social work', even 'socialism'.

Third, why research erotic sex (of all things!) to theorize social occasions proper? Why not platonic love, or friendship, or filial–parental relations, fraternal and sororal ties, or neighborly relations, or any other less scabrous instances of sociality? True, any of these provides substantial grist for the same theory mill. If, nonetheless, I choose to study erotic sex, it is, first, 'because it is there', to use the climbers' standard reply to those who ask them why they want to scale the forbidding mountain. Second, because it seems self-evident, once you have thought of it, that erotic sex is a most privileged site in which to search for keys to the larger realm of sociability and of sociality in general. Third, erotic sex, perhaps more than any other single interpersonal ritual, presents today's researcher with a cornucopia of freely accessible visual records, many of them from the mass media, records that still await, indeed cry out, to be analyzed and decoded, so that we may, at long last, begin to make sense of this massively travelled yet, amazingly enough, still largely uncharted domain.[1]

Which brings me, fourth, to the materials on which this study relies. They are not field observations, nor laboratory data, nor responses to questionnaires or interviews, on the erotic doings and feelings of real-life people. Rather, they are pictures culled from popular magazines (of the GP-type, incidentally, not the X-rated type), many of them in familiar commercial product advertisements. (Unfortunately, space limitations prevent me from presenting them in this article.) The choice of these materials raises a number of issues, of which one only is taken up here. My reliance on these materials was not dictated only, or even mainly, by the inaccessibility of erotic sexuality to standard methods of social science research. It was dictated by the fact that this study is and wants to be a study of the *ideal* of erotic sexuality, not of the lived reality of it. Note that the ideal to be studied is a historically located, culturally quite specific ideal, not a universal ideal (there is no such universal ideal). Still, why this deliberate focus on an ideal, given the general preference of social scientists in general, and of sociologists in particular (as opposed to, say, moral philosophers), for studying the real? Three reasons stand out.

One is that, since the middle of this century, we have been living in the most ideal-driven, the most 'romantic' era ever. By this I mean that ours is a time characterized by the tendency of individuals (immortalized by Flaubert's *Madame Bovary*) to be guided in real life by habitus dispositions acquired in the course of prolonged immersion in the imaginary world of fiction, and less so by dispositions acquired in the course of coping with real life and with real people. Never before in human history have so many been so intensively and extensively exposed to the direct radiation of fictional materials as in this century. There is little doubt that this life-long immersion in 'the lustrous bath' of hyperrealistic and glamorized images (Barthes, 1964a: 50) has had deep formative effects on virtually all of us, and that older agencies of socialization (family, peer-group, church, school, workplace, profession, neighborhood) have had correspondingly lesser impacts.[2] This, then, is a first reason for wanting to study erotic sexuality in its ideal, imaginary, mass-cultural state.

A second reason is that real-life sex is, much of the time, a confusing amalgam, a resultant of the interplay of diverse, heteronomous logics. Thus, besides being driven by its own erotic logic, real-life sex may also be affected by a power-driven 'political' logic, by an interest-driven 'economic' logic, by a semiotic logic of impression-management, by a hygiene-driven logic of disease-avoidance and the like. By contrast, sexuality as represented in culturally idealized images of it, particularly in the kitschy kind of images this article draws upon,[3] is shown not only in 'hyperritualized' forms (Goffman, 1979), but also virtually unadulterated by all those other exogenous logics. Just as a chemist interested in the properties of a given substance prefers to work on a purified sample of it rather than on a raw chunk as it was found in nature, so, given that my interest is in the *generic* properties of erotic sexuality, I too prefer to begin the analysis of it based on idealized images of it than on records of real-life instances of it.

A third reason is that implicit ideals underpin all critical analyses of social realities, including critical analyses by sociologists. Thus, social critiques of institutions like schools, hospitals, geriatric homes, courts of law, penitentiaries, are made on the grounds that they violate or deviate from social ideals, largely left unspecified, of what such institutions could and should be. Likewise, critiques of extant, real-life sexuality draw on ideals, also usually left implicit or woefully under-articulated, of what erotic sexuality could and should be.[4]

In what follows, erotic and social ideals will be formulated as parts of a largely implicit, indeed secretive, 'constitutive logic' – or, if you will, a 'generative grammar'. The point of my analysis is to formulate this elementary logic or grammar in terms of a parsimonious few elementary principles ('laws'), each of which in turn is made up of somewhat more specific norms ('rules'). The logic of erotic sexuality will be presented in Part 1 below, and that of social occasions proper in Part 2.

1. Erotic Sexuality

Erotic Reality

Erotic sexuality is constituted as a separate, distinct reality (in the Schützian social phenomenological sense) which, following Murray Davis

(1983), I will call 'erotic reality'. It is a reality lovers shift into to engage in their erotic doings and experience their erotic feelings, then shift out of to slip back into their daily lives.

In erotic reality, individuals see, feel and relate to things (the physical surroundings, the weather, passing events, the passage of time itself), to others and to their own selves, very differently from the way they see, feel and relate to these in their everyday realities. Besides being different, erotic reality is also extraordinary, with those in it experiencing everything more keenly, vividly, deeply, sentimentally ('*la vie en rose*') than in everyday life. In short, it is a reality in which people not only 'experience' but, to use Dewey's (1958) expression, they 'have experiences', even 'peak experiences'. The broader significance of partaking in erotic reality is that participants can retain, as they return to their everyday lives, lingering memories of a different, extraordinary reality, where they felt more alive, more susceptible, to events in and around them, more stirred by them, than in their everyday realities.

Erotic reality is, largely, a social construction. It does not emerge naturally, as if by spontaneous generation.[5] It is deliberately set off in time (evenings, nights, weekends, vacations); it is segregated in space (home, bedroom, hotel, cat-house, secluded beach, back seat of a car); it is stage-set (drawn curtains, dimmed lights, burning logs in the fireplace, mood music, sexy clothes); it is aided by the intake of special foods, alluring scents (perfume, incense) and of mood-altering substances (liquor, certain drugs). But, most important, erotic reality subjects love-making, even if lovers are unaware of it, to an implicit logic of its own – better still, to a regime of constitutive laws and rules which, if violated, are liable to jolt lovers out of erotic reality and return them abruptly to their everyday realities.

It is to the formulation of these laws and rules that the following pages are devoted.

The Body

The first law governing erotic sexuality is the law of the body, of the centrality and paramountcy of the body – one's own and that of the other. The body, or, more precisely, the erotic body, is the site, the raison d'etre, the subject and the object, of erotic sexuality.

In everyday life, the self is made up of various component parts and dispositions (roles, statuses, etc.). As it shifts into erotic reality, however, it frees itself of most of these and becomes increasingly centered on the body, coextensive with it, in particular with its erotically charged parts. Undressing in erotic reality has a twofold significance. One, obvious, is to reveal the body, the centerpiece of erotic life, as at the unveiling of a statue. The other, less obvious, is to shed, along with the clothes, the roles and statuses of which the lovers' selves are composed in everyday life. As Murray Davis (1983) put it with his usual verve, to disrobe is to disrole.

Erotic 'embodiment' – Davis's term for what Catholic-bred Sartre (1943) called 'incarnation' – refers to the ethnomethods whereby the self is reduced to, or focused around, its bodily part, and induced into erotic reality. These methods serve to draw attention to the body, to arouse sexual desire and intensify it till it becomes well-nigh compelling. Self-embodiment – or self-seduction – refers to methods by which we reduce our own selves to our bodies and induce ourselves into erotic reality (e.g. by imagining ourselves making love with a particularly desirable other, by reading or by watching pornographic materials, etc.). Seduction, per contra, refers to the stratagems by which we embody others, reducing them to their erotic bodies, and making them desire ours (Garfinkel, 1967: ch. 5).[6]

Why is the body so central in erotic reality? After all, lovers do engage in long-distance interaction – phoning, writing, sending flowers or detachable parts of themselves (locks of hair, scented letters, lipstick-imprinted napkins) – and they manage by these and other telecommunications to stir considerable erotic emotion in one another. Yet they often feel and say that none of these even begins to compare with, let alone to substitute for, actually being together. Underlying this belief is the deep-seated and widely held notion that relations are somehow more real when the loved one is there 'in person'. Only when their bodies are close at hand do lovers feel, only then do they seem to know, that their liaison is 'for real', 'something no one can take away from us'. Conversely, so long as their bodies have not yet been directly involved, and regardless of what else they may have felt, said and done one to the other, lovers can still swear, to themselves no less than to others – and without even feeling that they are doing so in bad faith – that 'nothing, really nothing, happened between us'.

Why is this direct involvement of the body taken as a sign of the reality of the relation? Perhaps because it stems from an atavistic notion that, in the last analysis, the only things we can be sure of, really sure of, are those which we can sense with our own senses, especially with our 'proximity senses' (Schachtel, 1949) of touch, smell and taste. Perhaps, too, because of the widespread belief that 'the body does not lie': like it or not, cheeks blush, eyes shine, the skin perspires or gets goose pimples, nipples harden, the phallus stands erect and turgid, the vulva becomes tumescent. Thus it may be felt that our bodies willy-nilly 'give off' tell-tale signs that can hardly be feigned, and thus can serve as 'lie detectors' with respect to what is being claimed verbally.[7] But, whatever the bases for this belief, the important thing for the present analysis is in what bodily presence yields for our lovers. Much as cohabitation in a larger sense, what bodily involvement yields is the feeling, nay, the felt certainty, of the reality of the liaison. It is as if, by being physically together, lovers can pinch not only their own selves but their mate as well, to reassure themselves that what is happening to them is really real, that they are not dreaming or imagining things. It is as if, intuitively, the body serves as the ultimate token, the proof and the guarantor of the reality of their experience of being – or of having once been – together, really together.

Pleasure

The law of the body, then, determines the site, the object and the subject on which, with which and for which erotic sexuality is engaged. The second law, the law of pleasure, concerns what erotic sexuality 'is all about', the whole 'point' of it, which is to enjoy erotic pleasure, as much of it as possible, in as many kinds, variations and degrees as lovers can imagine. Lovers in erotic reality obey one central paramount 'obligation', one categorical imperative – to surrender to Eros, to Desire, to be hedonists, to submit to the rule of what Marcuse (1955) called 'Libidinous Reason'. Ideally, subjects shifting into erotic reality enter a world and a subjective state of mind in which, like customers in a *cordon bleu* restaurant, they feel entitled to expect everything – the mate, the setting, the doings to be engaged in, the feelings to be felt – to contribute to their erotic pleasure, and nothing to detract from it.

Actually, the law of pleasure is a *regime* of pleasure, made up of a cluster of more specific rules. These include (but the list below is neither comprehensive nor systematic) rules of painlessness, of naturalness, of playfulness, of largesse, of self-gratifying givings, of aesthetics and of escalation.

Painlessness   In erotic sex, a direct derivative of the law of pleasure is the 'Thou shalt not suffer' rule. Ideally, erotic sexuality is wholly pain-free, lovers feeling entitled not to endure any suffering whatsoever, physical or emotional, in the course of their love-making. Painful eroticism is an oxymoron. If it is painful, it is not erotic; and if it is erotic, it is not painful. Sexual masochism refers to taking erotic pleasure in treatments (spankings, whippings, lacerations, humiliations, bondage) which, *outside of erotic reality*, would be felt as painful, even unbearable, by the very persons who imperiously demand to endure them in erotic reality, let alone by those who can't imagine why or how anyone can get any pleasure from such treatments.

Naturalness   Likewise, the rule in erotic reality is for pleasure to come freely, spontaneously, 'naturally'. Lovers are 'overcome' by pleasure, much as we are overcome by laughter on hearing a good joke. Otherwise, if pleasure is feigned or otherwise forced, it is not pleasurable, hence, ideally, is out of place in erotic reality. In erotic reality, the consumption of alcohol and of certain drugs is explained by lovers as helping them feel more natural, more relaxed, less inhibited, less constrained, less self-conscious, than they might otherwise feel.

Playfulness   Erotic love-making is play-like in a triple sense. First, in that lovers make love for its own sake, for the pleasure of it, not as a means to achieve or promote some ulterior or extrinsic end. Second, in that, even when engaged in for its own sake, it is not taken 'seriously', so that nothing the lovers do or fail to do (whether they score 7+ on the Richter scale of orgasmic tremor, or, indeed, whether they score at all) is taken to be of any real consequence. The playfulness of love-making, then, by uncoupling it from all negative consequences, extrinsic or intrinsic (fear of failure, disappointment, frustration, shame, conception) serves as yet another enabling condition for the free, unhampered enjoyment of it. Erotic sexuality is play-like in yet a third sense, in that lovers engage in it, literally, 'for the fun of it' – for the thrills, the delights, the joys ('the joy of sex') it gives them, for the gay mood it puts them in and for the happiness with which it fills their hearts. Whence the ticklings, the horsing around and the other puerile things lovers indulge in before, during and after their love-making. Whence, too, their gigglings, their hysterical fits of laughter and their calf-like smiles of beatitude.

Largesse   Prospective   lovers come to erotic reality bearing gifts, i.e. free donations, the most important one being, by far and away, their own selves. Lovers 'give themselves' to one another, 'body and soul'. Following Mauss (1967) and Lévi-Strauss (1967), I refer to these as mutual *gifts*, not as 'exchanges of sexual services', for the ideal of erotic love is definitely *not* patterned on a you-scratch-my-back-and-I'll-scratch-yours model. Calling them gifts is meant to highlight the fact that the donations are given freely, with no strings attached, with no obligations on the part of the recipient to return in short order equivalent favors, because any such obligation is liable to make the gift onerous rather than purely pleasurable.[8] Lovers in erotic reality are not into book-keeping, and nothing could be farther from them than to tally tits received against tats paid out so as to ensure that they have not been short-changed. This is not to imply that there are no expectations of reciprocity in love-making. There are, as we shall see in the section on mutuality. But these expectations are so moot, so non-contingent, so unstringent, that they enable lovers to experience the giving of them not as 'costs' or 'investments', but as freely and gladly given gifts (Bourdieu, 1994: ch. 6).

Pleasurable Givings   One reason why lovers can easily afford such largesse toward one another is that, in erotic sex, gift-giving (kissing, caressing, squeezing, bringing the mate to orgasm) is itself pleasurable. Here, the giving of oneself is by no means sacrificial – it is not 'oblative', to use a favorite term of Bourdieu's. This is because, in erotic sex, giving is itself experienced as intrinsically pleasurable for the benefactor, no less than getting is for the beneficiary, and on occasion giving may even be more pleasurable. In fact, the very distinction between giving and getting, transplanted from everyday reality, is largely untenable in erotic reality. Thus, it is best *not* to conceive of love-making as an exchange, a give-and-take, of sexual services. More fitting metaphors would be of an erotic Kula Ring or a round-robin of erotic favors, in which lovers pleasure themselves directly and indirectly by pleasuring their mates, both in the active mode (via 'givings') and the passive mode (via 'gettings').[9]

Aesthetics   Given that bodily gifts are expected to produce as much erotic pleasure, and as little displeasure, as possible, erotic reality puts a high premium on aesthetics, though not in any disinterested Kantian sense of the term.[10] Thus, on entering erotic reality, lovers make themselves as beautiful or handsome as they can, displaying to advantage their erotic assets and keeping their liabilities under wraps. They brush their teeth, sweeten their breath, scrub their bodies, spray aromatic scents on their intimate parts, pluck unwanted hair, trying to eliminate all vestiges of 'dirt' (Douglas, 1966). To enhance their facial traits, they artfully style their hair and apply all manner of make-up. To enhance the sex appeal of their bodies, they wear their most body-flattering clothes. They dim the lights to show themselves off from their best angles and keep their imperfections out of sight – and also, and no less, to spare themselves having to face up to their mate's aesthetic liabilities. In brief, they try to make themselves as attractive as they can, and to see their mates in a similarly flattering light, all this not out of some high-minded commitment to beauty for its own sake but, rather, out of an unabashed desire to give and to get as much erotic pleasure as they can.

Escalation   Last, erotic activity has a built-in step-wise escalatory dynamic, whereby lovers gradually bring one another to ever-higher thresholds of pleasure, until, as with positive feedback loops in cybernetic systems (Bateson, 1972), the tension becomes too unbearable, and they fall apart, exhausted, after one last, great, violently pleasurable tremor, the orgasm.

To sum up: ideal-typically, erotic reality is a reality in which everything conspires to provide lovers with pleasure, nothing but pleasure and always more pleasure, literally until they can take it or give it no more. Having partaken of this reality, they can return to everyday life filled with alluring (though largely ineffable and quickly fading) memories of having had a taste not only of a world free from the frustrations, irritations, setbacks, humiliations, apprehensions, torments and other major and minor miseries of everyday life, but also of a cornucopia-like world overflowing with polymorphous joys and pleasures – i.e. a taste of paradise on earth if there ever was one.

Inclusions

Up to here we have seen that erotic love-making centers on the body and revolves around the enjoyment of sensual pleasures. Next I consider what these pleasures are, and how they are generated. Based on the materials of this study, I will propose below that the pleasures in question entail *experiences of erotic inclusion*, produced and sustained by *ritual practices of erotic inclusion*. I have classed these practices by the constitutive rules that give rise to them – alterity, exclusiveness, mutuality and unions. What all these practices have in common is that each, in its own way, contributes to the lovers feeling 'included' (or, if you will, loved), rather than feeling excluded, unwanted, unloved.

Alterity   As with the proverbial tango, it takes two (at least) to make love. Even auto-eroticism requires an imaginary playmate to fire the erotic imagination and produce half-way 'satisficing' results. I propose to call this requirement the rule of alterity.

For reasons as yet unclear to me, erotic love with someone yields considerably more pleasure than even the most sophisticated means of auto-erotic stimulation. Whatever the reasons, however, adherence to this rule ensures that the pleasures of love-making are not wholly self-administered, that aspiring lovers do not settle for masturbation. Insofar as it is adhered to, this rule does for individuals what the incest taboo does for families: it makes them turn outward in search of erotic gratifications, causing them to socialize, as it were, their autarchic, narcissistic tendencies.

What lovers can retain from this fact, as they return to their daily realities, is, to paraphrase Zborowski (1952), that 'love is with people', that we depend on others to obtain what love has to offer, and that dependence is not just a curse, that it can be a blessing as well. Sartre (1943) concluded his monumental treatise of human existence – which, incidentally, contains a most singular phenomenological account of the sex act – with the famous saying that *l'enfer, c'est les autres* (hell is others). The present analysis suggests that, in erotic reality, the opposite conclusion imposes itself: that, inasmuch as there is a paradise (on earth), that paradise, too, is others, or, at any rate, a particular other. Returning to our lovers, what they can take back from the alterity of their brief but magic sojourns in erotic reality is the old sociological (and socialist) adage that, together, they can do far more good for themselves than they possibly could on their own. From which it follows that dependence can be an emotionally desirable condition, just as desirable and on occasion even more desirable (in terms of the pleasures it can yield) than independence, and that it is therefore just as human (i.e. just as reasonable) to yearn for dependence – especially co-dependence – as it is to yearn for independence.[11]

Exclusiveness   True, erotic sexuality requires an other, but, equally true, it is also usually restricted to One Particular Other. This means in effect that lovers choose only one mate from among a large pool of potential others and, by the same token, that they themselves have been so chosen. In other words, a rule of exclusiveness is in force that enables each lover to feel simultaneously Chosen as well as Chooser. As a result of this rule, each lover may feel in a state of grace, as does the winner of a lottery, for being (of all people!) the Chosen One, elected to be the sole recipient of all this love and adoration. In time, this feeling may even turn to hubris, to the intoxicating illusion that only s/he has 'what it takes to really fulfill the other, that no one else can be or do for the other what s/he can'. It is as if each lover thought, 'I did not know, before I met him (her), that I was this attractive, this unique, this different, this special. But it is a fact that, of all the others, it's me s/he wants, me, me, only me, no one but me.'

What lovers can retain from this exclusiveness, then, and take back with them to the realities of their everyday lives, is the precious, if fast-fading, self-feeling that they are unique, special, irreplaceable, in a word, *charismatic* – regardless of what all others (in everyday life) may think and say. Another thing they may retain from the exclusiveness of erotic love, in particular after the loss of their lover, is, again, how dependent they are, but, this time, not on others-in-general (George Herbert Mead's 'Generalized Other'), but on one particular Other (Mead's 'Significant Other'), in order to enjoy this precious sense of their uniqueness, their specialness, their charisma.[12]

Mutuality   This rule combines what Goffman called the rule of 'demeanor', which, in a social situation, entitles us to *recognition*, i.e. to be accepted 'at face value' and to be treated accordingly, and the complementary rule of 'deference', which obliges us to recognize and treat all others in the social situation as they present themselves. Applied in erotic reality, mutuality entitles lovers to be recognized by their mate as they present themselves, thus to have their sexual aversions and proclivities respected and catered to, whatever they might be. In fact, it entitles them to even more than that. Not only to the mate's compliance with their every wish ('my wish is your command'), but also to the mate's taking visible pleasure in catering to these wishes ('my wish is your delight'). This, then, is why in erotic reality lovers are so very oriented to each other (rather than remaining wholly self-centred), and why they become so alive and solicitous to each other's every desire (rather than remaining attuned only to their own desires). This is also why they are so intent on discovering their mate's innermost secret desires, even, and especially, those not known even to the mate, and why they take such pleasure in ministering to these desires.

Note that the rule of mutuality is not to be confused with the rule of equality. Thus, where the latter stipulates that what is good for the goose is also good for the gander, mutuality stipulates that the goose's wishes are the gander's commands, and vice versa, regardless of whether there is any symmetry, equivalency or proportionality between their respective wishes.[13]

From the mutuality of erotic reality, then, lovers give and get full recognition. Here, as perhaps in no other reality, not even in the closest friendships, individuals can feel wholly and unconditionally accepted and loved just as they are – or, better still, just as they want to be. Not only are they themselves loved but so are their wishes, even their unconscious wishes, those that not even they knew they had until they were revealed to them by their mate. What lovers hope to find in erotic reality, then, and what they can retain from it for the realities of everyday life, are moments, however brief, when they could be wholly themselves, when they needed to be ashamed of nothing, when their every want and aversion were recognized, respected and catered to.

Unions Feelings of erotic sexual inclusion, we have seen, result from lovers implementing the rules of alterity (which make them feel co-dependent), of exclusiveness (which make them feel distinguished) and of mutuality (which make them feel recognized). But, cardinal though they be, these rules are essentially meta-erotic. They provide the frame (Goffman, 1974), the conditions of possibility, in which doings that, otherwise, might be construed and experienced as mere 'sexual intercourse' ('screwing', 'laying', 'scoring', 'fucking', 'working', 'copulating'), are experienced instead as 'love-making'. In and of themselves, however, these rules still do not explain, do not make sense of, the actual doings, active and passive, lovers commonly engage in – why they draw close, undress, kiss, embrace, squeeze, lick, nibble, open up, penetrate, take in and the like. Nor do they explain the emotions lovers commonly experience in the course of love-making – excitement, power, tenderness, faintness ('weak as a kitten'), languor, vertigo, liquidity, self-dissolution. It is to these, then, that I now turn, in an effort to make sense of them as well. Based on the materials I pored over, I propose the general rubric of 'erotic unions' for all these doings and feelings, because, objectively, they can be described as interpersonal unions of sorts, and because, subjectively, lovers engage in them out of a conscious desire to unite, to 'become one' with one another. Erotic unions, I found, are achieved by any of four broad classes of erotic ritual practices which I have designated as rapprochements, appropriations, participations and entrustments.

Rapprochements These refer to the lovers' attraction, to their 'magnetism', for each other, expressed in their feeling drawn to one another, and in their actually drawing physically ever closer, as if out of an urge to overcome and to obliterate all space and distance between them. Thus, they make ever bolder incursions into each other's private spaces – symbolically (by addressing each other with growing 'familiarity', making increasingly intimate verbal insinuations at one another); microecologically (by sliding up and moving ever closer to one another); and, above all, tangibly (by making physical contact, at first tentatively, then touching feverishly anywhere they can ['can't keep my hands off of you'], plastering and rubbing their bodies one against the other's, until, impatient with their clothes, since they too are now 'in the way', they tear these off, fling them aside, and proceed, naked as on the day they were born, to make bare-skinned, full body-to-body contact).

These progressive rapprochements, then, these increasingly intimate get-togethers, constitute a first mode, mostly proxemic and tactile, by which lovers embody their desire to become united. They congregate, seeking to, as it were, form an aggregate, by pressing their bodies so tightly together that, for a moment, they seem and feel conformed to one another, as in the Chinese yin–yang symbol, as if pressed into forming a single, solidary body. What they can retain from this, and bring back with them as they return to their daily realities, are memories of a different, of an alternative reality, in which they felt not as mere *separanda*, mere isolates, but, on the contrary, close, so unbelievably close to the other, that neither could tell any longer where one ended and the other began.

Appropriations   These are the practices whereby lovers embody their desire to appropriate and to be appropriated by one another, to take and be taken, to have and to belong, to make the other 'mine, all my own' and, simultaneously, to become 'all yours', 'yours only'. The erotic doings by which this desire for mutual appropriation is embodied come in the form of (friendly) takeovers and interlocks. Takeovers consist of a whole variety of ways to embrace (put in braces) and to enclose the other, using grips, grasps, clasps, hugs, clutches, holds, box-ins, pin-downs and the like. The desire to be held and fastened ('hold me tight, tighter') is indicated by how the lover who is held often assists in 'tightening the noose' the other has enlaced him (or her) with. These, then, constitute a first way whereby lovers embody their possessive want of the other, and, concomitantly, their desire to be possess-ively wanted by the other. The other way is by means of 'interlocks', by which I refer to the various kinds of mutual intrusions and incorporations, in which the penetrations and invasions by one automatically become the captures and engulfings by the other. The effect of these interlockings, as in the case of engaged gears, is that lovers become so enmeshed, so inter-twined, so imbricated one in the other that they come to feel inextricably bound up with and to each other, like the members of a chain-gang.

What these mutual appropriations may yield for our lovers is a short-lived feeling of permanent inseparability, a feeling that theirs is not just a liaison, a passing relation, but a relationship, a lasting tie. What they might retain from these doings and feelings, and take back with them to their everyday realities, are memories of brief moments when they felt united to someone 'for ever and ever', 'from here to eternity'.

Participations   These refer to the seemingly never-ending give-and-take of erotic favors lovers tirelessly lavish on one another. The emphasis here, however, is not on what these erotic favors consist of but, rather, on their dialogicality (Bakhtin, 1977), that is, on the fact that each long stare is met with an equally long stare in return, each squeeze by a reciprocal squeeze, each hug, each kiss, each sigh, each caress, each lick, by hugs, kisses, sighs, caresses, licks in return. These erotic con-versations (joint pourings) vary in content and in form, entailing turn-takings or simultaneity, symmetry or asymmetry, complementarity or reciprocity, synchrony or asynchrony. What they all have in common, however, and is of special interest to us here, is that they all entail lovers *doing things together* – taking part in (participation), and feeling part of (partnership), the joint enterprise, the cooperative venture known as the love-making of a couple. Inasmuch as each of the lovers' participation is – or, rather, is felt by them to be – of a very different nature – e.g. key and lock, yin and yang, lover and beloved, conqueror and vanquished – this differential partnership may give birth to the erotic variant of the kind of solidarity Durkheim (1960a) called 'organic'.

Through such participations, then, lovers give yet another embodied expression of their desire to unite with one another, this time by being and by feeling 'in' and 'part of' a going concern. In erotic sex, the expression is largely kinesic, accomplished by concerted movements, as in a wrestling bout. What lovers can retain from such participations, as they return to their daily lives, are memories of a reality in which they enjoyed, even if only briefly, the fulfilling experience of membership, of full partnership in a joint undertaking.

Self-entrustments Anyone who has ever given sustained thought to a couple's sexual exertions cannot but have wondered why it entails mutual squeezings, kissings, huggings, rubbings, lickings, nibblings, scratchings, caressings, kneadings, pressings, etc. The fact that these practices are so familiar does not make them any the less peculiar, and they make one wonder why it is through them in particular that we make love, that we embody our love. This question becomes all the more intriguing when we note that many of these doings have the same basic structure: one lover exposes – indeed, offers, tenders – highly vulnerable parts of the body to the mate (neck, nape, ears, lips, tongue, armpits, breasts, groin, cock, vagina, anus, etc.), to which the mate responds, not only by refraining from a sadistic aggression on these undefended vulnerabilities but, intriguingly enough, by ritual *pseudo*-aggressions that consist of attenuated mock-attacks on the exposed parts, performed in slow motion, gently, softly, suavely, soothingly. Thus, lovers engage in touching without impacting, taking without grabbing, caressing without abrading, holding without gripping, stroking without striking, kneading without bruising, nibbling without biting, kissing without producing hematomas, scratching without scraping, hugging without choking, entering without breaking, squeezing without bone-crushing, smacking without slamming and the like.

I do not know why the practices of love-making fall into these peculiar patterns, that is, why acts of love look like ritualized acts of violence,[14] nor why they produce in lovers such extremes of pleasure. Considered semiotically, however, these rituals seem like the equivalent, in the realm of interpersonal relations, of 'confidence-building measures' in the realm of international relations. Thus, the rites of love-making suggests that basic trust among lovers is generated through rites of mutual self- entrustment, whereby lovers entrust their security in the hands of the mate, as they wouldn't dream of doing with other parties. These self-entrustments have not only a disarming, appeasing, effect on the mate, but arouse in him (or her) deep feelings of tenderness which, intriguingly, find their expression in defanged, attenuated, play-forms of violence. It is as if war-making and love-making use many of the same ingredients (border violations, incursions, entrapments, hand-to-hand engagements, inducing weakness, confusion, loss of self-control, etc. in the other), but have their sources in opposite dispositions. Thus, where war-making is deadly serious and is engaged in out of sheer malevolence, love-making is in jest, lighthearted, playful, and is engaged in out of pure affection.

What lovers can take back from these rounds of pleasuring and pleasurable ritual pseudo-aggressions, as they return to their everyday realities, are memories of a world in which they need not be on the defensive, nor, therefore, on the offensive, a world in which they feel free from violence, real or symbolic, a world in which they can trust others, thus give themselves over, without fear of coming to harm, to the enjoyment of mutual ministrations of pleasure.

What do all these practices of erotic inclusion, especially those of erotic union, accomplish in the way of socially pertinent effects? Viewed together, what they seem to produce are experiental states in which lovers cease feeling like isolates in a largely indifferent, exploitative, domineering or hostile world and, instead, come to relate to each other as 'lovers'. That is, they put themselves in the rather extraordinary position of being able to make love to themselves by making love to the mate, activating the mate as they would their own limbs, to pleasure their own selves with the auto-motivated body of the other, in cyclical reiterations of positive feedback.

Why, one wonders, do lovers prefer to thus pleasure themselves 'by proxy', as it were? Why do they derive more pleasure from the ministrations of a mate than from those they can dispense to their own selves? In other words, why do they prefer socio-eroticism to auto-eroticism? The answer to this fundamental question is by no means obvious, all the more so if we think of how much better we know our own erotic predilections and our fluctuating moods than any mate possibly ever could. (The only discipline I am aware of that has given serious thought to this question is psychoanalysis.) Whatever the ontogenetic or the phylogenetic explanation of this phenomenon, however, its social function, if I may be pardoned the expression, is to keep alive the commonsense notion, in everyday reality, that the key to happiness, erotic or other, may lie not in our separate individual selves (as suggested by the autarkic myth of Robinson Crusoe) but, rather, in our coupling with an other, and in our becoming so 'with', so 'in', so 'of' that other, that the very distinction between us becomes as problematic as that between the different parts of our own self.

Erotic sexual bonds   Based on what precedes, I propose to define erotic bonds as the experiences lovers generate in one another by means of the rituals of love-making. These experiences are of a different reality from the one we know in our everyday lives. They are felt to be real, because they are centered on the body, our own and that of another. They are pleasurable, and they revolve around experiences of inclusion – of co-dependence, of distinction, of recognition, of various kinds of union with another – of closeness, of possession and of belonging, of membership and personal security. This, then, is what I propose erotic sexual bonds are: they are what they do for lovers, and what they do, ideally, is give them the kind of experiences I just listed.

Intermission: 'Il n'y a pas d'amour heureux' (Aragon)

Readers who have borne with me thus far must have been wondering about the extravagantly romantic, idyllic, indeed kitschy picture I have sketched of the realm of erotic love. I could, of course, answer that what I have drawn here is a picture of love-making only, not of a love relationship as a whole, and, moreover, of a specific cultural ideal of love-making, not of love-making as it actually is, or ever was, in real life. Still, the reader may insist, shouldn't even this ideal allow for the disappointments, hurts and angers that inevitably accompany love-making? As one reader (Illouz, 1995, pers. comm.) put it to me, 'If it is all so good, why is it so bad?'

The answer is that, yes, these miseries are closely linked to erotic reality, but no, they are not integral to it. They are linked to it in the sense that love-making is forever shadowed by everyday reality, and is liable at any moment to revert back to it. An anonymous phone call, an unexpectedly cool welcome, an inappropriate remark blurted out at the wrong moment – any of these can yank lovers abruptly out of erotic reality and catapult them straight back into everyday reality. That, however, is no reason for claiming that the two constitute one and the same reality, or that the one cannot be thought without the other. This is because erotic reality is experienced and constructed differently from everyday realities, regardless of how readily lovers may slip and fall back from one into the other. To fuse the two is like claiming that peace cannot be thought in abstraction from war, or leisure in abstraction from work. Each of these is constructed and experienced as a reality in its own right, is governed by its own logic, its own laws and rules ('*à la guerre comme à la guerre*'), and generates its own practices and feelings, all of which differ radically from those that make up the realities that are opposed to them. It may be that one is simply an upside-down version of the other but, then again, it may turn out that this is not the case. For example, Simmel (1955) argued that quarrels (conflicts) are *not* the obverse of 'good', harmonious relations, that they are forms of sociation in their own right, and that their real binary opposite are relations of indifference, i.e. non-relations.

2. Social Occasions Proper

I said at the outset that my interest in erotic sex is rooted in the hypothesis that erotic sexual rituals and experiences hold important keys for cracking the code of social occasions proper. The time has now come to make at least a prima facie case (though little more than that) for this hypothesis.

Under this rubric of social occasions proper, I am thinking here, among others, of interaction rituals (greetings, farewells, etiquette); rites of hospitality (invitations, visits to the ill, hosting guests); formal occasions (receptions, cocktail parties, balls, banquets, reunions, testimonials); dyadic bonding rites (flirtation, courtship); rites of passage (birthdays, weddings, confirmations, anniversaries, initiations, inaugurals, going-away parties, funerals, wakes); informal socializing (get-togethers in pubs and cafes, intimate dinners, outings, picnics); social games (parlor games, card games, ball games, chamber music, singalongs, dances and other pastimes). What I will do in the second part of this article, then, is to try and show, almost telegraphically, that the inner logic of social occasions proper corresponds, by and large, to that of erotic sexuality. Needless to say, not *all* laws and rules of the one will apply equally to the other, and there are probably some that apply to erotic sexuality but not to social occasions, as well as vice versa. Note also that here as before I will not be analyzing social occasions as they actually are in real life, but in their ideal state, that is, as it is felt in the ambient culture that they should be.

Social Reality

Like erotic encounters, social occasions, too, are constituted as fairly distinct and discernible life-worlds – hereafter, social realities – that people shift into so as to partake of social ritual practices and experiences, then shift out of in order to return to the realities of their everyday lives. Social realities, too, are more or less neatly bracketed, so that participants know that they are in them and conduct themselves accordingly. They are often scheduled to take place at special times – tea time, coffee break, banana time, after hours, weekends, holidays. They are often located in places or sites deliberately set aside and especially designed for them, such as (depending on the occasion) the salon, the den, the garden, the hotel lounge, by the side of the pool, at the social club, in cafes, neighborhood pubs and restaurants, at country inns and seaside resorts. They too are more or less consciously stage-set and directed, so as to create and impart their own ambiance of mild euphoria and genteel civility, distinct from the ambiance that characterizes everyday life.[15] In order to generate and to sustain the activities, experiences and ambiance characteristic on these occasions, social realities are also governed by an implicit logic of their own, made up of its own constitutive laws – of Presence, of Enjoyment and of inclusions – which, in turn, resolve each into more specific rules or norms, such as those of deference and demeanor, of civil inattention, of precedence, of mutual orientation, of politeness and the like. Note that the logic of social reality, though also implicit, is less subject than the logic of erotic sexuality to what Bourdieu (1994) has called 'the taboo on explicitation'. As a result, the analysis in the pages that follow will be more in line with intuitive common sense, hence will entail less in the way of ground-breaking analysis than the foregoing analysis of erotic sexuality.

Presence

We have seen how the body plays a key part in erotic reality. In social reality, there is a similar, though more attenuated requirement, that of bodily presence, of physical thereness, albeit, sometimes, only a partial, even a very minimal presence. Thus, in social relations proper, special significance is attached to the involvement of embodied elements such as the grain of the voice (Barthes, 1981), the scent of the body, the feel of the skin, the handwriting, the 'autographed' dedication, the 'original' work of art (Benjamin, 1971), even the photographic snapshot.[16] The more 'social' the relation between two or more persons, the more they expect to relate to each other 'in person', i.e. to bring their bodies to the encounter or, at the very least, to invest some embodied parts of themselves in it. Typically, the norm of *noblesse oblige* refers to the obligation to attend social events in person, to 'make an appearance', however minimal. Put otherwise, the more social the relation, the more immediate (non-mediated) the interaction. The theorist *par excellence* of what occurs the moment individuals come in physical co-presence ('face-to-face'), was Erving Goffman. Which is but another way of saying that Goffman was, first and foremost, a student of what I have called social occasions proper.[17]

Why is physical presence, even minimal, even if only 'symbolic', felt to be essential in and for social relations proper? Why does friendship require that we pay a visit in person to the sick friend at the hospital, and not be content with having our secretary send a get-well note or make a phone call on our behalf? Part of the answer may lie in the fact that it is when we are there in person, and only then, that we become, at least potentially, immediately and wholly available to the other, for it is only when we are physically there that we can be ready for any eventuality. This may be one reason why distant relations between close relatives (such as between elderly parents and their now adult 'children', or between spouses living in different cities) are problematic. For no matter how often we may call, write or even visit – we are not *there*, hence we are not really available, directly and immediately, when we might be needed to lend a hand. This, then, may be one underlying 'reason' why presence, physical thereness in real time, is viewed as a decisive signifier, as a tell-tale sign, of how 'real' a given social relationship is felt to be. It may even be an underlying factor in the break-up of certain 'strong' relationships (like marriages), because of the realization by one of the parties that, married or not, the other is not really there most of the time, in particular when s/he is needed.

Enjoyment

Like erotic reality, social reality too is ruled by a pleasure principle, though here again, a more modest, more moderate, more disembodied version of it. Social pleasures differ from erotic sexual pleasures not only in their being largely non-'carnal', but also in their often being substantially milder, less intense, less exciting, less profoundly stirring. Whereas in erotic reality lovers are rank hedonists, maximalists striving for peaks of pleasure – not content, as in the lyrics of Carol King's popular song, until they 'feel the earth/move/under my feet' – participants in sociable occasions often make do with mere ripples of pleasure, with experiencing feelings of enjoyment, of cheerfulness, of mild euphoria.[18]

As in the case of erotic reality, the law of enjoyment also resolves, under closer examination, into a set of more specific constitutive rules and norms, of which the following is a partial list.

Tact   In social reality, the *least* participants expect from one another is to be spared being made to feel embarrassed, shamed or otherwise upset. In fact, on many social occasions little more than that is expected, at least by guests. To ensure this, social occasions are governed by a rule of 'tact', of considerateness, that enjoins participants to refrain from doing unto others what the latter do not want done to them. Derivatives of this rule include, among others, *traffic rules* (Goffman, 1971: ch. 1) to prevent participants from bumping into each other; *conversational rules* to ensure that they do not just talk but also listen, that they patiently wait for their turn before taking the floor, that they give an acceptable excuse before breaking off to join another circle; *norms of civil inattention* (Goffman, 1971: 209n) to make them demurely look away when catching sight of someone in a compromising state; *norms of expressive moderation* to make them refrain, in public, from extreme manifestations of happiness, since there could be others around who may be pained (because of worries or sorrows they carry within them) by such uninhibited shows of pleasure.

Freedom   The norm, or at least the desideratum, at social affairs is for participants to feel free, loose, at ease and, accordingly, to act natural. Social conduct that is or appears gauche, belabored or otherwise constrained detracts from the enjoyment of the occasion for all concerned, and is therefore considered inappropriate. Needless to say, feeling free and acting natural does not mean or imply that one is moved by inborn organic impulses, as when one yawns, belches or scratches an itch. It means, rather, especially in the context of social occasions, that norm-driven conduct has been so thoroughly internalized and embodied as to have become integral to one's habitus, to one's innermost acquired need-dispositions. Just as the competent playing of ball games puts a premium on players' strokes and movements on the field or court being executed easily, smoothly, as if effortlessly – rather than jerkily, awkwardly, hesitatingly and self-consciously – so social occasions put a premium on interpersonal conduct that, likewise, is easy, relaxed, flowing, elegant, that is, free and natural.

Aesthetics   Social occasions, like erotic relations, have a distinct bias toward the aesthetic, where by the aesthetic I mean that which pleases, especially the mind and the distance senses. With this in view, organizers schedule social occasions at times (for example, at around nightfall) when the unseemly details of ordinary everyday life are more easily kept out of sight. Likewise, they locate these affairs in visually pleasing sites (a terrace with a grand view of the city, or overlooking the sea) to serve as decor for the occasion, and thus make them that much more enjoyable. They see to it that the place is swept clean, spruced up, brightly lit and cheerfully decorated and beribboned, as befits a properly social occasion. The finest tablecloths, crockery, glasses, silverware, serving dishes are brought out of the cupboards and laid out for the occasion. The finest foods and spirits are served by discreet, barely visible waiters and waitresses gliding among the guests.

The latter fit themselves out in their most festive clothes and wear their most precious jewelry. All this beautification work is done not out of commitment to some abstract aesthetic ideal of beauty for its own sake but, as mentioned above, so as to maximize the enjoyment of all present.

Play   This is the property which, for Simmel, was at the very heart of 'socialbility'. Like games, social occasions are playful in that they are ruled by a spirit of non-instrumentality, of inconsequentiality and of having some fun.

Non-instrumentality means that socializing is engaged in for its own sake, not as a means for attaining an ulterior goal. Thus, guests are expected to come to parties essentially in order to *socialize*. In the course of so doing, they may nibble on assorted appetizers (to please their palates, to keep from getting hungry) and sip alcoholic drinks (to cheer up, to relax). They do *not* socialize in order to stuff their bellies on the hosts' food or fill their gullets on their booze. They flirt for the sake of flirting, not with a view to 'scoring'. Likewise, they refrain from protracted 'shoptalk', from wheeling and dealing, from politicking, from gathering intelligence on behalf of interested parties, from seeking to 'make friends and influence people'....

As for the rule of inconsequentiality on social occasions, it insists on the importance of *not* being in earnest. Social talk is 'small talk', meant to perform what Jakobson (1960) called a 'phatic' function. Likewise, guests may, on social occasions, play gambling games, but the stakes are set low enough so that none risk losing their shirts. Women may dress sexy, even act a little raunchy, and men may respond accordingly. But it is all done in jest, with no intentions of 'serious involvement', and all but the socially inept and the incorrigibly jealous know that it is only 'flirtation', that is, light-hearted, good-humored, frivolous, inconsequential banter, with no intention by either party of 'going all the way'. For Simmel (1950, 1984), feminine coquetry, especially as expressed in sexual flirtation, represented the quintessence of sociability, precisely because, being 'pure sociability', it is neither instrumental nor consequential. No one, therefore – except, again, the socially underdeveloped, the hopelessly serious and hard-bitten mis-anthropes – can *lose* at socializing. The worst that can happen is that they fail to partake in the enjoyment such occasions have to offer.

Which brings me to the third of the play characteristics of social occasions, what they have to offer. Ideally, these affairs are deliberately constructed by those who organize them in such a way that all present – except the hired help, of course – 'have fun', 'have a good time'. For this to happen, all are expected to smile and laugh much of the time, these being outward signs of inner euphoria, as well as inducers of euphoria in others. Guests are expected to entertain one and all with funny jokes and amusing stories, or, if they can't do so, to serve as appreciative audiences for the stories and jokes that others tell them. On such occasions, a premium is placed on guests who are 'the life of the party', the kind who, the moment the music plays, pick a partner off the couch, dance up a storm and draw others onto the dance floor, as well as on the kind who, later, will pick up a guitar or an accordion and sing songs that cause everyone to join in and to feel together, as in 'the good old days' when they were young and poor but were having the time of their life.

Generosity On social occasions, guests are expected to come bearing gifts, a premium being laid on bringing 'just what the host wanted', or, better still, 'just what the party needed' (like great dance music, champagne, caviar, hilarious jokes, the latest, hottest and juiciest gossip, good ideas for games, a contagious good mood), so as to make the occasion into an even more smashing hit than it already is. Most importantly, participants are expected to give generously of themselves to contribute to the enjoyment of all present. They are expected to make special efforts to make themselves look as attractive as possible (dressing *up*, wearing make-*up*, etc.), to be on their Sunday best behavior (polite, pleasant, charming with one and all), to 'pay attention' to and show manifest interest in what others say to them, to laugh heartily at their jokes (no matter how insipid), to dole out flatteries, especially to the comely, to cheer up the morose, to flirt with members of the opposite sex (and not only the attractive ones among them), to invite others onto the dance floor (especially those too shy to join in on their own), to entertain and let themselves be entertained, to express keen interest in others, to congratulate them on their successes and commiserate in their problems, to wish them well, to toast to their future, to assist the hosts, if need be, with the serving of foods and beverages, and later with the clearing of dishes – all this, in an effort to contribute with largesse to everyone having a 'grand time' at the gathering.

Self-Gratifying Givings Social occasions are governed not only by the norm of giving gifts that please the recipient, but also and no less by the norm of deriving – or at least of giving the impression of deriving – genuine pleasure from the act of gift-giving. A verbal expression of this norm is provided by standard formulas like 'We are pleased/delighted to inform you that we have awarded you such-and-such award.'

Pleasurable Receivings   Just as it is *de rigueur* to enjoy the giving of a gift, it is equally obligatory, on social occasions, to enjoy receiving it, and to show one's delight with it, even when the gift in question it is not to our liking. (In *The Brothers Karamazov*, Dostoyevsky characterizes Alyosha as a 'real saint', not only because he knew how to give, but also, and more importantly, because he knew how to receive.)

Escalation As in erotic sexuality, social occasions, especially those which Goffman (1982) termed 'ceremonials', are often deliberately staged to induce mounting tension (suspense, rising expectations), this by scheduling a stepwise crescendo of gratifications. Thus, festive dinners and banquets offer an escalating series of courses culminating in a smashing *pièce-de-résistance* (fresh smoked brisket of beef flown in straight from Ontario) or a spectacular dessert (*bananes flambées* carried by a phalanx of waiters filing in to the sound of a rousing march). Toddlers' birthday parties culminate with the spectacular performance of a clown or magician. Banquets lead up to much awaited, after-dinner toasts and testimonials. Stag parties are staged to reach a peak with the surprise appearance of a stand-up comedian, a belly-dancer or a stripper.

Social Inclusions

In social reality, rites of inclusion are those whereby people generate and sustain, in themselves as well as in others, *feelings of inclusion*, that is, feelings associated with including others and with being included by them. Defining these feelings (or, for that matter, any feelings) is no easy task, and I will not attempt to do so here. Suffice it to say, for the purpose at hand, that they are verbally rendered by expressions such as feeling 'at home', 'in', 'part of', 'equality', 'acceptance', 'belonging', 'first-class', 'membership', 'affiliation', 'we-feeling', 'pride' (Scheff, 1990) and the like.

Feelings of social inclusion can be induced by any of a variety of ritual doings that I cannot begin to enumerate here, not only because the list would drag on and on but, mainly, because this variety has yet to be inventoried and codified.[19] All I will do here is continue making a prima facie case for the proposition that the laws and rules that generate the rituals and experiences of social inclusion are roughly the same as those which generate the doings and experiences of erotic inclusion.

Alterity   Just as erotic sex requires an other to do it with, so socializing requires others, usually several others, in order to take place. This, of course, is so virtually by definition. (I say 'virtually' because being alone physically does not necessarily mean that we are alone mentally or even emotionally: we *might* be communing 'mystically' with an absent other.) Still, in general, why do we require actual others in order to socialize? Perhaps it is out of a doxic belief that 'life is with people' (Zborowski, 1952), that living in isolation makes life meaningless, miserable, a calamity to be avoided at any cost. After all, prison wardens have long since known that a most effective punishment, indeed torture, is to let inmates languish in solitary confinement.

Exclusiveness   Social occasions are usually open to several participants, at times even to as many as care to join, or so it would seem. But a closer examination invariably reveals that participation in such affairs is always restricted to a chosen few, de facto when not de jure. America may invite all the world's downtrodden to its shores ('Give me your tired, your poor, your huddled masses'), but granting them entry visas is another matter. Reasons given to explain the exclusiveness of social affairs are legion (not enough seats around the dinner table, not enough food for everyone, the need to match guests with one another, etc.) but the bottom line, the Pareto residual, is that socializing is selective and exclusive by its very nature. Which is why inclusion in social affairs has the effect on the Included Few of making them feel privileged vis-a-vis the Excluded Many, of inducing or reinforcing in them a feeling that they are special, superior, chosen, charismatic, distinguished (Bourdieu, 1979).

Mutuality As I already mentioned, the rule of mutuality combines the rules of deference and demeanor. Thus, if on a social occasion a professor presents himself as an expert on a given topic, the rule of demeanor entitles him to his colleagues' ostensive recognition of him as such, while the rule of deference obliges them to treat him accordingly, even if they know him to be an ignoramus on that topic. What this rule yields for members of social occasions, at least for the duration of them, is the non-negligible satisfaction of feeling that they are viewed and treated by significant others as they themselves wish to be seen and treated – non-negligible because, to many, it happens so seldom in the realities of everyday life.

Unions These are all the social rituals whereby people make one another feel 'associated', 'united', 'solidary' with one another. Here, as in erotic sexuality, we have, first, *rapprochements*, by which individuals draw close to one another, closer, any rate, than they do to others, as in their differential clusterings around the dinner table, at cocktail parties, in the prison courtyard or, more permanently, in the neighborhoods where they buy their homes. But in social reality rapprochements are not limited to proxemic means. Here members can 'come close' to one another also, perhaps even more frequently so, by becoming visibly alike, e.g. by conforming to some common pattern, thus producing the impression in others and the feeling in themselves of bearing a 'family resemblance', of association by similarity. They achieve this effect, for example, by wearing 'uniform' clothes, by speaking the same dialect, by sporting the same insignia, by riding the same make of motorbike, by growing the same kind of beard or moustache, or having the same haircut and the like. All these conformisms have the effect of producing and sustaining in consociates the feeling Durkheim (1960a) chose to call 'mechanical solidarity', the unity we feel vis-a-vis others on the basis of our mutual perceptions of one another as similar.

A second way feelings of union and solidarity are induced and sustained is by means of *participations*. Thus, social affairs are invariable organized around common doings – eating together (commensality), conversations, joke- and story-telling, singing in unison, music-making ('jamming'), dancing, playing games, jointly picking on a scapegoat, gossiping about absentee third parties and the like. Participations, then, entail doing things together, regardless of what these joint doings may be. They constitute another way in which social occasions induce and sustain in members feelings of union, of solidarity. Since it is produced by taking part in joint doings, this dimension in the feeling of union may be termed a feeling of 'partnership'. Note that when the joint doings entail a clear division of responsibilities – as in team sports for example – participants may also feel united by what Durkheim called 'organic solidarity', i.e. the feeling of being incomplete without the other/s, and of being whole again with the other/s.

A third way feelings of union are induced on social occasions is by means of *appropriations*. Here again, appropriations come, first, in the form of symbolic friendly 'takeovers', by means of which we symbolically enclose others, encompass them, adjoin them to us, as if annexing them. Such takeovers take the form of shoulder-holds, hand-grips, bear-hugs, walking hand-in-hand or arm-in-arm, dancing in closed circular formations (*rondes, horas*, or by enlacing a single partner). Emblems of takeover-style appropriations include rings (finger bands, earrings, nose rings, armbands, wristbands), collars and chains (chokers, ties, necklaces, bracelets, anklets, chainlets, decorative handcuffs) and pins (going-steady pins, club membership pins). These annexations give participants the feeling of possessing, of owning and, just as importantly, of belonging, of having been annexed. The other form of social appropriation consists of 'interlocks', in which individuals enter one another's spaces and, in so doing, are taken in by one another, thereby becoming locked into one another, like engaged sets of gears. Social examples of such social interlocks include: invitations by and visits to consociates; mutual feedings, whereby we insert ourselves in the other via the Trojan horses of tasty morsels; reciprocal gift-givings; verbal addressings or references to one another using possessives (*my* darling, *my* wife, *our* family) and we-statements (*we* feel that...; it was *our* decision to...); familiarities (winks of complicity, wisecracks, intimate queries, etc.); mutual confidings and confessions. The cumulative effect of such symbolic appropriations may be to produce in participants a certain feeling of being 'involved', 'implicated', hence also of a certain inseparability, as that which ties the members of a chain-gang.

Finally, we saw earlier that erotic love-making entails *entrustments*, in which the exposure of vulnerabilities by one elicit pleasurable pseudo-aggressions by the other. The reader may also recall that, seen semiotically, it is as if much love-making consists of a drawn-out palaver, with lovers taking turns in, as it were, 'saying' to each other, 'Here is a particularly susceptible part of me – you could hurt me but I am sure you won't', and the mate 'responding' reassuringly 'I could indeed hurt you, but I won't.' A similar dialogue seems to take place on social realities, where much socializing consists of 'opening up' to other consociates, that is, of dropping our defenses and exposing our weaknesses, in the expectation that they in turn will respond by dropping their own defenses and letting us in on their weaknesses. What I want to propose here is that these mutual self-entrustments to the goodwill of consociates are peace-making rites – in fact, that peace-making *consists* of such mutual self-entrustments to the goodwill of others. On social occasions, then, consociates open their borders to one another, surrender their safety, exchange assurances that they come each to the other peaceably disposed. Consider, for example, what takes place in brief, perfunctory greeting rites between acquaintances. On meeting, they doff their caps (exposing their heads), utter peace formulas (shalom, salaam, salut), flash smiles (baring their teeth amicably, rather than snarling menacingly), offer their fighting hand to be gripped and held by the other, embrace one another (but without choking each other), stand at ease (rather than cocked like guns ready to fire), exchange jokes, flatteries and other niceties, until, ready to break off the encounter, again they smile, doff their caps, grip and shake hands, and bid each other peace.[20] Most social occasions entail such rites of appeasement, of reassurance, with parties repeatedly 'turning the other cheek' to one another, not out of masochism, but as gestures that elicit in return reciprocal shows of vulnerability, in a mounting and widening spiral of confidence-building gestures.

These rituals serve to reaffirm the peaceableness of relations among consociates in social life. Peaceable relations mean more than relations of non-belligerence, in which conflicting parties refrain from attacking one another but, armed to the teeth, are ready to do so at the drop of a hat. Peaceable relations are a key feature of civil society and civilized culture. 'Civil' society is, above all, non-military society and 'civilized' culture is demilitarized culture, where members can routinely go about their business without fearing, or even giving a thought to, the risk of being attacked by others. Thus, in civil society, members can and do walk about unarmed, freely and nonchalantly; they can look straight ahead, rather than let their eyes dart apprehensively in all directions, lest they be suddenly set upon from behind or from the flank; they can hold their heads high, leaving their throat exposed; they can stand about in easy, open-bodied stances; they can look directly at people coming their way, even strangers, and pass them by without even looking back, unafraid of being shot, mugged or stabbed in the back.

The Realm of the Socioerotic

I began this article with an analysis of erotic sex and showed how its peculiar doings and experiences are generated by a few laws and their respective subsidiary rules. Then I went on to show how the same type of laws and rules, though in attenuated versions, also serve to generate the broad class of interpersonal occasions that, in ordinary English, are designated as 'social'. Viewed in this way, erotic sex turns out to be so homologous with social occasions proper, and in many ways seems such a pure and intense version of such occasions, that a hard and fast distinction between the two becomes nearly impossible to maintain.[21] What seems to be called for, therefore, is to view erotic affairs and social affairs proper as instances of a broader class, which I propose to call the realm of the 'socioerotic'.[22]

Now the idea of a nexus between the sexual and the social is hardly new, Freud having advanced it boldly and forcefully a hundred years ago.[23] Others who also drew attention to this nexus include, to mention but a few who readily come to mind, Simmel (1984), Bataille (1957), Lacan (1966), Lorenz (1966) and Lévi-Strauss (1967). Curiously, sociology's two most prominent theorists of the domain of the social, Durkheim at the macro level, and Goffman at the micro level, never drew an explicit connection between the sexual and the social, let alone saw in the former the essence of the latter.[24]

The main conclusions of this analysis are: that there exists a distinct realm of interpersonal affairs, the realm of the socioerotic; that this realm entails a variety of rites, rituals, occasions and relations, ranging from perfunctory social contacts (greetings, openings and closings, etc.) at one end, to elaborate social ceremonies and erotic sexual rituals at the other end; that this realm is governed by its own distinct logic, which can be formulated in terms of a few general laws and their respective rules; that these laws and rules generate and sustain distinct practices (socioerotic rites) and experiences (socioerotic emotions), all of which involve the body to one degree or another, revolve around the production and experience of pleasurable experiences, and consist for the most part of various and sundry rites of inclusion; finally, that it is these practices and attendant experiences that forge the social bonds that tie people to one another and to larger social formations.

The broader importance of this socioerotic realm is that it provides people (though in dismally unequal proportions) with memories of and longings for what have been variously referred to as bonds, ties, relationships, attachments, affiliations, membership, belonging, fellowship, etc., and with concomitant experiences of happiness, gratification, fulfillment and the like. This realm, then, is one of the sources of *hope*, that important intangible which gives people something to look forward to, to work for, to wait for, even to suffer for – in brief, something to live for.

3. Socioerotic Realms and Conflictual Fields

Socioerotics in Social Theoretical Perspective

It may be instructive, in bringing this article to a close, to consider how the realm of what I have here called socioerotics has been theorized by sociologists past and present, and how it might be rethought in light of what has been said of it in this essay.

The professional credo of mainstream sociologists of an earlier generation was that, appearances to the contrary notwithstanding, the 'real' motive force in many domains of human endeavour is 'social', that is, socioerotic. Philosophers philosophize less out of a categorical imperative to pursue the truth than for the aura it brings them in the eyes of their students, their relatives, their neighbors and the general public. Politicians are drawn to politics less out of a commitment to improve society than in order to be featured in the media, to be recognized in the street, to bask in the admiration and gratitude of those for whom they do favors. In general, this sociological credo holds that in the case of many people, ostensibly utilitarian endeavours – like striving for an academic degree, for career advancement, for a higher income, for professional success, for a higher standard of living – stem, at bottom, from social considerations. Whether we like it or not, whether we admit it or not, we are moved more by social motives proper – the desire for acceptance, recognition, peer esteem, prestige and, as a corollary, the fear of being left out, left behind ('keeping up with the Joneses') or otherwise humiliated and ashamed – than by many of the other reasons we give or that are imputed to us (ambition, materialism, intellectual curiosity, moral commitment and the like).[25] Besides pointing to the latent socioerotic motives of individuals, sociologists of this earlier school also tended to underscore the 'social functions', also usually latent, of the patterns they studied, that is, their contributions to the overall solidarity and performance of the larger collectivity.[26]

Since the agitated decade of the 1960s, however, and to the end of the 1980s, different winds have been sweeping the field. Variously spearheaded, in the USA, by 'conflict theorists' like C. Wright Mills, Immanuel Wallerstein, Charles Tilly, Theda Skocpol and Randall Collins, and by exchange and rational choice theorists (George Homans, Peter Blau, James Coleman) and, in Europe, by Louis Althusser, Michel Foucault and Pierre Bourdieu, by New Left Marxist theory and by feminist theory, a new breed of sociologists have come aboard who think rather differently about socioerotic phenomena. Their stance on such matters as love, cohesion, morale, solidarity, identity, community and the like, has been one of skepticism (there are more pressing matters to concern ourselves with), of cynicism (active interest in these matters serves to divert attention from the struggles of the weak against the strong) or of indifference (there is not a single entry on socioerotic topics in Coleman's monumental *Foundations of Social Theory*). Collins (1975) did accommodate socioerotics in his 'conflict sociology', but essentially as resources mobilized in the service of collective conflicts. Even Bourdieu (1990, 1994), despite the finesse and sophistication of his writings on socioerotic matters, explains them, *in the last analysis*, as emergent properties ('perverse effects'?) of struggles over domination, as 'effects of power'. So the realm of the socioerotic, which earlier sociologists had theorized as rock-bottom infrastructure, has become, for critical conflict sociologists of the post-1960s, little more than epiphenomenon, ideological superstructure, objectivating practice, symbolic violence. For the New Sociologists, the really decisive forces in human affairs, down even to the intimate couple and the family, are internecine struggles over exploitation and accumulation, over domination and control. In what is, to my mind, the most compelling elaboration of this position, that of Bourdieu, socioerotics comes close to being theorized as 'symbolic violence', that is, as the pursuit of war – of interpersonal struggles – 'by other means', suaver, smoother, milder, more 'benevolent', more 'symbolic'.[27]

What we have here, I should like to submit now, are two kinds of theoretical radicalisms, two kinds of 'reductionism' if you prefer – one, sociologistic (*social*istic in the generic sense), the other utilitarian (*capital-i*stic in the broad Bourdieu–Collins sense). The former, founded by Durkheim, Freud,[28] and their respective schools, looks for (and usually finds) in most human institutions, including in some fairly repressive ones, a substratum of socioerotic motivations or a superstratum of social functions. The latter, epitomized by Marx and Pareto, and more recently by, each in his own way, Coleman, Tilly, Collins, Foucault and Bourdieu, looks for (and usually finds) behind seemingly innocuous socioerotic patterns and institutions (like romantic love), hidden mechanisms for the promotion of positional and capital interests of the haves at the expense of the have-nots.

There is no doubt that each of these two kinds of theoretical radicalism draws on an important truth, which is why each has chalked up some impressive scientific achievements to its credit. Despite their respective strengths, however, and notwithstanding their intellectual (and ideological) appeals, neither of them is, or can be, persuasive as general social science theories, for they both suffer from the same basic flaw, namely, that each aspires, implicitly or explicitly, to produce the social science version of what physicists designate as a 'unified field theory'. This, I propose, is an impossible mission, for it ignores one of the most fundamental discoveries of the social sciences, namely, that *the realities humans live in and live by are, largely, realities of their own making, constructed around whatever laws and rules they have concocted and succeeded in imposing and perpetuating.*[29] Whence it necessarily follows that *any* social theory that draws its basic model from *one* such socially constructed reality – be it *homo economicus* from the constructed reality of the free market, *homo politicus* from that of the agora or *homo sexualis* from that of the boudoir – and proceeds to extend it to other realities (using *homo economicus*, for example, to make sense of the 'dating and rating complex' [Waller, 1937]), is bound from the outset, at best, to partial success only (Gary Becker, 1981) and, in the hands of the less talented, to pathetic failure.[30]

Socioerotic Realms in a World of Conflictual Fields

An alternative approach, that strikes me as more productive and more pertinent to the domain of human affairs, is a modified version of Schütz's social phenomenological approach. In this purview, human social existence is constituted of distinct realms – Husserl's 'life-worlds', Berger and Luckmann's 'realities', Wittgenstein's 'language games', Goffman's 'frames', Geertz's 'cultural systems' – each of which is socially constructed, sustained and governed by a logic that is *irreducible* to the logic of any of the other realms. Thus, socioerotic logic cannot be reduced to the logic of conflictual fields, or vice versa. To quote Pascal's famous aphorism, 'The Heart follows reasons that Reason cannot follow'.

This is not to imply that, like oil and water, socioerotic realms and conflictual fields do not mix, that they are necessarily separate, segregated realities.[31] To be sure, actual love-making ('sexual intercourse') is performed in secluded niches, but other, less brazenly sexual conducts – sexy self-displays, sexual flirtation and bantering, even so-called 'sexual foreplay' (kissing, groping) – often do take place in locations not especially designed for them, like sidewalks, public benches, cafes, pubs, the office, even (here in Israel) between drivers of adjacent cars waiting for the traffic lights to turn green. The same holds, a fortiori, for the bulk of the more innocuous forms of socioerotic conduct. As Goffman never tired of showing, such conducts pop up virtually whenever and wherever people come together, variously mixed with conducts pertaining to other realms of reality (industrial, professional, administrative, pedagogic, commercial, political, therapeutic, etc.).[32] We all know how the logic of conflictual fields can invade, pervade, even dominate socioerotic realms, just as, conversely, socioerotics can suffuse conflictual fields, growing and spreading through them, even to the point of displacing field logic and taking its place.[33] At the macro level, this process been amply documented in, among others, studies of 'informal organization in formal organizations' (Selznick, 1943), as well as in ever recurring charges of 'nepotism', 'favoritism', 'corruption' and 'sexual hanky-panky' (nowadays 'sexual harassment') in public bureaucracies. And, at the micro level, suffice it to think of all the time and attention most of us devote each day, when we run into colleagues at work, to addressing them warm greetings, flashing grins, dispensing flatteries, making solicitous inquiries, laughing at dubious jokes, putting up with racist and sexist chatter, and performing gratuitous favors (like, in response to their queries, telling them what time it is or showing them the way to the toilets). Even the most business-like letters, however ruthless their substance, invariably open with an affectionate 'Dear Sir/Madam' and close with a sincerest 'Yours truly'. All these civilities, all these niceties, are unmistakably socioerotic in nature, so that everyday reality in the fields – even in some of the most dog-eat-dog fields – is perfused with socioerotics. The question on which I would like to conclude this article is *why*? What's a nice thing like socioerotics doing in a place like this?

One view attributes the omnipresence and irrepressibility of socioerotics to people's inborn or inbred socioerotic nature ('man is a social animal'). In this view, life is rife with socioerotics because, to paraphrase Goffman, humans 'cannot not socialize'.[34] Consider, again, the workplace: regardless of what severe measures are used to suppress socioerotics at work, employees always manage to find locations (in corridors, by the water cooler, at the john, in the snack bar, on the phone) and times (coffee time, lunchtime, commuting time) in order to socialize (to gossip, flirt, exchange niceties, make dates). Some theories (like those associated with the 'Human Relations' school) hold that, far from being dysfunctional, socioerotics in industrial organizations contributes to, indeed is indispensable for, their effective day-to-day operation, cutting down on friction, fostering morale and cohesion, and sustaining the climate of trust necessary for information to flow freely throughout the firm.[35] More recent theories have challenged this view, emphasizing that these socioerotic formations, whether or not they are 'functional for the organization', serve management's interests, often directly at the expense of the bulk of the employees (Hochschild, 1983;

Kunda, 1993; Shenhav, forthcoming). More generally, such critical theories denounced the extent to which the logic of fields (like the logic of commodification) has pervaded and corrupted socioerotic realms (Hochschild, 1994).

But what all these organizational theories and counter-theories have in common, besides agreeing on the ubiquity and inevitability of socioerotics at the workplace, is that they do not address, let alone answer, the key question of what employees themselves look for, and apparently find, in these socioerotic rituals and occasions. They do not begin to explain, for example, why so many of them willingly, indeed eagerly, take part in management-sponsored socioerotic events (picnics, excursions, office parties, testimonials), often contributing from their own personal resources to ensure the success of these occasions, even as they fully know or suspect the self-interestedness of management in backing these affairs.[36]

The explanation suggested here is the embarrassingly obvious, yet, in today's sociology, the even more embarrassingly neglected one, that people – that is, most of us – willingly and eagerly take part in socioerotic activities in order to indulge . . . our socioerotic desires. Not only in order to indulge such desires (we rarely do anything for one reason only), but often mainly, rather than out of crypto-political, crypto-economic, or some other crypto-utilitarian considerations.[37] What I have tried to do in this article, via an analysis of familiar socioerotic occasions, is to begin identifying and naming the specific kind of experiences people seek, and sometimes find, in these occasions (or else they would not return to them, or yearn for them, so obsessively). In particular, what people seem to look for in socioerotic realms is to *get away from everyday reality*, in order to, instead, *enter a wholly different realm of reality*, that I have called socioerotic. Socioerotic realms are characterized, first of all, in that they bring participants in touch with *real people* – not actors, agents, fiduciaries or role players, but real, live, physically present, readily accessible, warm-bodied, particular others. Second, these realms are designed and organized to provide participants with *socioerotic pleasures*, and to exempt them from the *social violences* they are used to (but never get used to) enduring in conflictual fields.[38] These socioerotic pleasures people seek are *experiences of inclusion*, whereas the *social violences* from which they seek a respite are *experiences of exclusion*. A closer examination of experiences of inclusion points to, among others, the following:

- The pleasure of *openness* (to others) generated by the rule of alterity and, as a corollary, the freedom from the meaninglessness and anomie of living only for oneself.
- The pleasure of *charisma* generated by the rule of exclusiveness and, as a corollary, the freedom from feeling common, ordinary, indistinct, passed over, left out, left behind.
- The pleasure of *acceptance* generated by the rule of mutuality and rituals of recognition and, as a corollary, freedom from the shame and anger produced by being misrecognized and mistreated.

- The pleasures of *solidarity*, generated by various rules of union, including the pleasure of *intimacy* – of feeling close, and of not being made to feel estranged; the pleasure of *membership* – of active partnership in a joint enterprise, and freedom from the humiliation of not being invited or welcome to partake in it; the pleasure of *possession* – of having and of belonging, of feeling that the desired others are 'ours' and that we in turn are 'theirs'; the pleasure of *ontological security* – of feeling completely safe among others whom we fully trust, and freedom from the insecurity we feel in the company of untrustworthy, potentially malevolent others.

One conclusion of this article, then, is that socioerotic realms grant us 'psychosocial moratoria' (Erikson, 1950b) from the social violences and miseries we inflict and endure in conflictual fields, that is, with time-outs for licking our narcissistic wounds and restoring our bruised egos, but also for enjoying, even revelling, in the interpersonal pleasures, large and small, such occasions have to offer. A second conclusion is that socioerotic occasions serve as matrices, as microfoundries, for the production and reproduction of the bonds that attach us to others, to larger groups, to our own selves, indeed to life itself. A third conclusion is that socioerotic realms serve to keep alive our hopes and dreams for a different and better world, ruled more by a social logic (a socio-logic) and less by the Hobbesian logic of conflictual fields. All of which is but another way of saying that socio-erotic realms are key sources – along with play, dreams, religion, music, song, poetry, dance, theater and the plastic arts – of what Marcuse (1964) called the *'other dimension'* of alienated society.

Notes

Many read and commented on an earlier draft of this essay, but I am particularly grateful for the detailed critiques and warm encouragements from Francesco Alberoni, Ulrich Beck, Elisabeth Beck-Gernsheim, Pierre Bourdieu, Donald Cohen, Lewis Coser, Murray Davis, Anthony Giddens, Mark Gottdiener, Arlie Hochschild, José-Enrique Rodríguez-Ibáñez, Allan Silver, Alfred Willener, Yves Winkin and Eviatar Zerubavel. Among my local friends and colleagues, I owe special thanks to Kalman Applbaum, Edith Astruc, Yosl Bergner, Judy Cooper-Weill, Avi Cordova, Shlomo Deshen, Zali Gurevitch, Shmuel Eisenstadt, Haim Hazan, Eva Illouz, Diana Luzatto, Guillermo Olmer, Motti Regev, Ditti Ronen, Ofer Sapir, Ronen Shamir, Chen Saraf, Moshe Shokeid and Natan Sznaider, all of whom, likewise, made extensive comments on an earlier draft of this paper.

1.   Sexologists have reported, *ad nauseam*, on the 'behavioral' aspects of sex (how, when, where, with whom, with what frequency, etc., people do it) and have cross-tabulated these 'variables' with the usual externalities (gender, age, race, occupation, income, religion, etc.). They have 'explained' (in the narrow statistical sense of 'explain') everything about sex, except the *Ding an sich*. Hard as it may be to believe, erotic sexual relations as such, considered as an elaborate interpersonal ritual, have yet to be *made sense of*.

2.   Mainstream sociology, even media sociology, has yet to really wake up to this development. To paraphrase Gitlin (1978), to ask whether the media have an impact on people is like asking whether water has an impact on fish. One of sociology's most urgent needs today is for a new George Herbert Mead (or a new Piaget, a new Freud, a new Lacan) to theorize our socialization by these media.

3.   Schudson (1984: ch. 8) has nicely dubbed the genre 'capitalist realism'.

4.   Sociologists usually profess to be more interested in 'reality' than in 'ideals', forgetting that ideals often constitute history-making realities in their own right, as Weber insisted on showing all along his career, e.g. via his notion of 'ideal interests'. Among contemporary sociologists who unabashedly profess an interest in researching ideals, three may be singled out here: Jürgen Habermas (1984), Luc Boltanski (1990) and Allan Silver (1995).

5.   But the generically 'sexual' elements of sexuality (tumescence, erection, orgasm) are rooted in our organic make-up and, as such, are irreducible to social construction. What socially constructed erotic reality does is awaken and sustain sexual excitement, it directs it to some objects (rather than others), it sets certain aims for it (rather than others) and, above all, it makes us experience all these physiological processes in specific culture-determined ways.

6.   For some, seduction relies mainly on flirting with promises of one's body (Weitman, 1992), while for others it relies on flirting with promises of a permanent relationship (Felman, 1980).

7.   If, as claimed by folk wisdom, the penis is 'the only organ in the male body that cannot lie', then this organ gives the lie to Eco's (1979) oft-quoted dramatic claim that 'a sign is anything we can lie with'.

8.   For two different analyses of gifts, see Schwartz (1967) and Bourdieu (1994: chs 5, 6)

9.   Actually, the distinction between active and passive is also fairly untenable in erotic reality, as are, indeed, many other classic distinctions drawn from and serviceable in everyday reality, such as between mind and body, freedom and necessity, subject and object, affect and cognition, rationality and irrationality, submission and power, egoism and altruism, individuality and self-dissolution, violence and gentleness, even between self and other.

10.   For a spectacular social critique of Kantian aesthetics, see Bourdieu (1979).

11.   Durkheim (1960a) also thought of the moral ideal of co-dependence as morally equal or superior to the allegedly superior ideal of independence. More-over, he thought (as had Comte before him) that the ideal of dependence was more in line with the highly differentiated society of the future.

12.   Note that the feeling of charisma does not *originate* in erotic reality but, in all likelihood, in infancy and very early childhood when, as a result of our parents' doting, many of us began life basking in the feeling that we are the most special, most fascinating, most desirable, most wonderful little thing in the world. When Freud and his followers (Bergmann, 1991) speak of the finding of love as a 'refinding', part of what they have in mind is that the loving subject has found again, at long last, the thrill of being, to someone, the 'apple of my eye'. Interest-ingly, some of the most influential psychoanalytical theorists of our time have in common the fact that they pointed to the narcissistic origins (rather than oedipal origins) of the capacity and the life-long desire to bond, like Kohut (1971), Selma Fraiberg (1967) and Lacan (1966).

13.   Alberoni (1983) calls mutuality the 'Communist Principle' of 'from each according to their capacities; to each according to their needs.'

14.   The most persuasive theory I have come across is the one advanced by Konrad Lorenz (1966), but it is an evolutionary theory that offers little insight into why, phenomenologically, the expression of love takes these ritual, pseudo-aggressive forms. Another theory that seeks to grapple seriously with this problem is existential psychology (see for example Maslow, 1960).

15.   Note that Goffman's (1959) early use of the notion of 'everyday life' lends itself to confusion, as it covers not only the public rituals performed in the 'front areas', but also all that goes on behind the scenes, in the 'back areas'. In my terms, what we have in the front areas is, or seeks to be, social reality proper, while what takes place backstage is everyday reality. See, on this, Cas Wouters's (1986) work on the trend to 'informalization', i.e. to norms encouraging us to conduct ourselves in front areas much as we do in back areas, a trend I see as partly responsible for the increasing intrusion of the culture and practices of everyday realities into those of social realities.

16.   Barthes (1964a, 1980) invoked this element of presence to explain the emotion a photographic snapshot (e.g. of a relative we hardly knew) occasionally stirs in us. Such snapshots have on us what he terms a 'reality effect', because we sense the 'was-thereness' (*l'avoir-été-là*) of the subject, of her having once been before the camera *in person*, so that the picture we are now contemplating results from light rays having bounced off *her* body onto the photosensitive emulsion. Which is but another way of saying that we relate to such pictures as we relate to *relics*, i.e. objects that were once in actual physical contact with the subject.

17.   In the presidential address he sent to the ASA shortly before his death, Goffman (1982: 2) wrote: 'Social interaction can be identified narrowly as that which uniquely transpires in social situations, that is, environments in which two or more individuals are physically in one another's response presence. My concern over the years has been to promote acceptance of this face-to-face domain as an analytically viable one, a domain which might be titled ... the *interaction order* – a domain whose preferred method is microanalysis.'

18.   Note, however, that social occasions are liable to stir up deeply hostile passions, like smouldering resentment and hate. For a general discussion of such passions, see Weitman (1973).

19.   In his last paper, Goffman (1982: 6–7) proposed that social interactions come in four kinds: (1) brief, perfunctory 'contacts', (2) 'conversational encounters', (3) 'platform presentations' and (4) 'celebrative social occasions'. (Note in passing that *sexual* encounters, whether erotic or other, do not fit into any of the above, reinforcing the impression that, for Goffman, such encounters are not part of the 'interaction order'.)

20.   I once witnessed Etienne Decroux, the legendary French master of acting and mime, explain how, in 17th-century royal court society, the elaborately stylized entries, greetings and exits of courtiers consisted largely of presentations, offered to all present in equal proportions, of the various vulnerable parts of the body: the bared head, the wide open eyes and face, the exposed throat, the flanks, the armpits, the pectorals, the abdomen, the groin, the knees, the Achilles' heel. By comparison with these courtiers, Decroux added (and demonstrated), nowadays our own bodily stance, gait, entry, greeting and exit rituals bring to mind how

Neanderthal man must have carried himself – hunched over, eyes darting to the left and to the right, hands over the groin, arms close to the flanks, legs held tightly together, as if he expected to be pounced upon at any moment by some wild beast or by another Neanderthal.

21.   Anyone who has doubts about this should read Albert Scheflen's (1965) paper on 'quasi-courtship' in psychotherapeutic sessions.

22.   Simmel's (1950) rubric for this realm, 'sociability' is too specific to subsume such phenomena as erotic sexuality, parent–child relations, friendship, etc. Parsons's (1951) notion of the 'socio-emotional' might have been suitable, were it not for my allergy to Parsonian terminology. In the 1970s, some (Wispé, 1967, 1978) suggested 'positive social behavior' or 'pro-social behavior', but these terms are too bi-polar (positive vs negative, pro- vs anti-), and strike me as too simplistic for designating this realm. Goffman's (1982) term 'the interaction order', is far too general. More recently, Maffesoli (1993) has been using the term 'sociality' ('socialité'), which I find suitable but presents problems of declination to adjectival, verbal and adverbial forms. I thought of using the 'social properly so-called', or the 'generically social', but these expressions struck me as too prim, or too academic, as well as too cumbersome. 'Socioerotic' strikes me as right, because it connotes what I think is distinctive to this realm and at the heart of it, namely, the elements of alterity, of desire and of pleasure. 'Sociolibidinal' might have done as well, except for the biologistic ('metapsychological') connotations of libido, especially in psychoanalytic theory. Some 30 years ago, Murray Davis (1973) suggested 'philemics' to designate his proposed science of intimate relations. I'd go along, if he agreed to extend the term's 'catchment area' to *all* socioerotic realms, not just to intimate couple relations.

23.   Long before Freud, the idea of a close linkage between sexuality and sociality had already been advanced, like much else, by Plato in *The Symposium*. Curiously enough, and despite its obvious relevance to sociology, this idea was not picked up by mainstream sociology – not even by Parsons (1951), despite his having borrowed freely from Freud for his own theory of child socialization. Inasmuch as this idea is alive at all in sociological circles nowadays, it is mainly in feminist theory, particularly among object-relations theorists like Nancy Chodorow (1978). An earlier generation of sociologists that did see in Freud a major theorist of social bonding included David Riesman (1949), Maurice Stein (1960) and especially Philip Slater (1963, 1966). For a dissenting view concerning the usefulness of Freudian theory to a theory of social relationships, see Robert Weiss (1968).

24.   Durkheim saw the essence of the social in *religion*, while the early Goffman saw it in the *theater*. Other important conceptualizations of the social have included *gift-giving* (Mauss, Lévi-Strauss), *play* (Simmel, Bateson), *ritualized aggression* (Lorenz), *transgression* (Bataille), *utilitarian exchange* (Blau, Homans, Coleman) and *power struggles* (Nancy Hensley, Jessica Benjamin, Bourdieu, Collins). For a recent comprehensive survey of the anthropological literature and a valiant, if not altogether persuasive attempt at producing 'a unified theory of social relations', see Alan Fiske (1991).

25.   See, for example, Rainwater (1974).

26.   I would not be surprised if the most frequent title in sociological and anthropological writings of this period was 'The Social Functions of . . .'.

27. Likewise, Foucault (1982) had written in a similar vein of the 'pastoral power' of the modern state, of the therapeutic power of the 'helping professions' and, toward the end of his life, of the power relations embodied in regimes of self-improvement.

28. Freud the clinical theorist, not the metapsychologist (Klein, 1976).

29. Bateson (1968: 217) formulated this principle as follows: 'The propositions ... about the world in which we [humans] live are not true or false in a simple objective sense; they are more true if we believe and act upon them, and more false if we disbelieve them. Their validity is a function of our belief.'

30. Witness the current spate of omnipotent theories (sociobiology, psychobiology, brain-science) ready to explain any and all social phenomena, especially those belonging to the socioerotic realm.

31. It is the recognition that these disparate realities are not necessarily separate and that, in fact, they usually are variably mixed and combined with each other, that makes me qualify my own approach as a *modified* version of social phenomenology.

32. For a superb microanalytic documentation of how 'quasi-courtship' (read: sexual) elements pervade all types of psychotherapeutic relations, see Scheflen (1965).

33. This fact was repeatedly bemoaned by Pareto, and led him to advance his theory of the circulation of elites, according to which elites fall when they become too 'soft' – i.e. too moved by emotional, humanitarian considerations of 'sociality' and the like – and, consequently, become increasingly incapable of acting out of cool, even cold-blooded, interest-driven considerations.

34. I think that Goffman himself subscribed to this view, given his oft-repeated claim that, willy-nilly, people lapse into their social song-and-dance routines the moment they come face-to-face with one another. Another indication of this are, from the 1970s on, his many admiring passing references to the work of ethologists (e.g. Morris, 1967). The view that humans have an ontologically social nature also seems implicit in the thinking of social scientists identified with 'the communitarian movement'.

35. What turned numerous sociologists in the 1960s against this functionalist turn of mind was the knee-jerk tendency of its practitioners – notably Merton, notwithstanding his insistence that functional analysis entails pointing up 'dysfunctions' as well as 'eufunctions' – to highlight the positive functions of almost anything they studied, including of notoriously repressive institutions like New York City's mob-controlled political machine (Merton, 1968: 125–36). I should add that the original impetus behind the rise of critical-conflictual theories in the 1960s was essentially a *social* impetus: to expose and denounce many of the repressive and exploitative institutions which mainstream sociologists had defended as 'functional'. Thus, power-driven and interest-driven theories like C. Wright Mills's (1963) in the USA and Bourdieu's (1979) in France arose to tear off the pseudo-benevolent masks of the elites and expose the interests (as opposed to the social 'functions') served by their institutions, notably the seemingly innocuous cultural institutions. Subsequently, however, since about the mid-1970s, a new wave of yuppie sociologists adopted these power-driven theories, no longer as weapons in the fight for a better society, but essentially as *prises de position*, as stances in the field. (Yuppies are those whose pose – rhetoric, appearance, style – conveys rebellion, leftism, anarchism, bohemianism, but whose actual conduct in the field

is guided by opportunistic careerist calculations. Of yuppyism it may be said that it is a case of Protest Ethic turned into Spirit of Careerism.) In a first moment, then, post-1970s sociology marginalized, in the name of social commitments, the study of socioerotic phenomena, along with the functionalists who had praised them. Then, in a second moment, even the social commitments were dropped, and the upshot is that we have been left today with a denatured sociology, largely emptied of both social substance and social commitment, and so riveted on power and on interests that it has become more akin to political science and to economics (both of them 'dismal sciences') than to what it had been from its inception in the 19th century till the end of the 1960s.

36.   For a political critique of such conduct among employees, see Mills (1951) or Whyte (1956).

37.   Durkheim (1960b) repeatedly enjoined sociologists to adhere strictly to the methodological principle of the 'homogeneity of cause and effect'. The mindless disregard of this principle by American sociologists since the 1970s – and, in their wake, by many sociologists elsewhere in the world – in favor of multivariate, multidimensional, 'interdisciplinary' theories and methods is, I think, one of the deepest of the many traps sociology has dug for itself, then proceeded to fall into.

38.   For a rich and frequently moving documentation and discussion of such miseries, see Bourdieu (1993).

References

Alberoni, Francesco (1983) *Falling in Love*. New York: Harper and Row.

Alberoni, Francesco (1987) *L'Érotisme*. Paris: Ramsey.

Ariès, Philippe and André Béjin (eds) (1985) *Western Sexuality: Practice and Precept*. Oxford: Blackwell.

Bakhtin, Mikhail (aka V.N. Volochinov) (1922/1977) *Le Marxisme et la philosophie du langage: essai d'application de la méthode sociologique et linguistique*. Paris: Minuit.

Barthes, Roland (1964a) 'Rhétorique de l'image', *Communications* 4: 40–51.

Barthes, Roland (1964b) 'Éléments de semiologie', *Communications* 4: 91–135.

Barthes, Roland (1967) *Système de la mode*. Paris: Seuil.

Barthes, Roland (1977) *Fragments d'un discours amoureux*. Paris: Seuil.

Barthes, Roland (1980) *La Chambre claire*. Paris: Seuil.

Barthes, Roland (1981) *Le Grain de la voix*. Paris: Seuil.

Bataille, Georges (1957) *L'Érotisme*. Paris: Minuit.

Bateson, Gregory (1968) 'Conventions of Communication: Where Validity Depends on Belief', in Jurgen Ruesch and Gregory Bateson *Communication: The Social Matrix of Psychiatry*. New York: Norton.

Bateson, Gregory (1972) *Steps to an Ecology of Mind*, Part II. New York: Ballantine Books.

Beck, Ulrich and Elisabeth Beck-Gernsheim (1995) *The Normal Chaos of Love*. London: Polity.

Becker, Gary (1981) *A Treatise on the Family*. Cambridge, MA: Harvard University Press.

Benjamin, Walter (1971) 'L'Oeuvre d'art à l'heure de sa reproductibilité technique', pp. 87–126 in *Essais 2*. Paris: Denoël. (Orig. 1936.)

Berger, Peter and Thomas Luckmann (1967) *The Social Construction of Reality*. Garden City, NJ: Doubleday.

Bergmann, Martin (1991) *The Anatomy of Love*. New York: Fawcett.

Bertilsson, Margareta (1986) 'Love's Labor Lost? A Sociological View', *Theory, Culture & Society* 3(2): 19–35.

Boltanski, Luc (1990) *De l'amour et la justice comme compétences*. Paris: Métailié.

Bourdieu, Pierre (1979) *La Distinction*. Paris: Minuit.

Bourdieu, Pierre (1980) *Le Sens pratique*. Paris: Minuit.

Bourdieu, Pierre (1990) 'La Domination masculine', *Actes de la Recherche en Sciences Sociales* 84: 2–31.

Bourdieu, Pierre (1993) *La Misère du monde*. Paris: Seuil.

Bourdieu, Pierre (1994) *Raisons pratiques*. Paris: Seuil.

Brown, Norman O. (1959) *Life against Death*. Middletown, CT: Wesleyan University Press.

Brown, Norman O. (1966) *Love's Body*. New York: Random House.

Chodorow, Nancy (1978) *The Reproduction of Motherhood*. Berkeley: University of California Press.

Collins, Randall (1975) *Conflict Sociology*. New York: Academic Press.

Davis, Murray (1973) *Intimate Relations*. Glencoe, IL: Free Press.

Davis, Murray (1983) *Smut: Erotic Reality/Obscene Ideology*. Chicago, IL: University of Chicago Press.

Dewey, John (1958) *Art as Experience*. New York: Putnam.

Douglas, Mary (1966) *Purity and Danger*. London: Routledge and Kegan Paul.

Durkheim, Emile (1960a) *De la division du travail social*. Paris: Presses Universitaires de France. (Orig. 1902.)

Durkheim, Emile (1960b) *Règles de la méthode sociologique*, 2nd edn. Paris: Presses Universitaires de France. (Orig. 1902.)

Durkheim, Emile (1960c) *Les Formes élémentaires de la vie religieuse*. Paris: Presses Universitaires de France. (Orig. 1912.)

Eco, Umberto (1979) *A Theory of Semiotics*. Bloomington: Indiana University Press.

Elias, Norbert (1973) *La Civilisation des moeurs*. Paris: Calmann-Lévy. (Orig. 1939.)

Erikson, Erik H. (1950a) *Childhood and Society*. New York: Norton.

Erikson, Erik H. (1950b) 'Identity and the Life-Cycle', *Psychological Issues* 1(1).

Felman, Shoshana (1980) *Le Scandale du corps parlant*. Paris: Seuil.

Fiske, Alan Page (1991) *Structures of Social Life: The Four Elementary Forms of Human Relations*. New York: Free Press.

Foucault, Michel (1976–84) *Histoire de la sexualité*, 3 vols. Paris: Gallimard.

Foucault, Michel (1982) 'Power and the Subject', *Critical Inquiry* 8: 777–95.

Fraiberg, Selma (1967) 'The Origins of Human Bonds', *Commentary* 46(6): 47–57.

Freud, Sigmund (1920/1952) *Three Essays on the Theory of Sexuality*, London: Imago.

Garfinkel, Harold (1967) *Studies in Ethnomethodology*. Englewood Cliffs, NJ: Prentice-Hall.

Giddens, Anthony (1992) *The Transformation of Intimacy: Sexuality, Love and Eroticism in Modern Society*. London: Polity.

Gitlin, Todd (1978) 'Media Sociology: the Dominant Paradigm', *Theory and Society* 6: 205–53.

Goffman, Erving (1959) *The Presentation of Self in Everyday Life*. Garden City, NJ: Doubleday.

Goffman, Erving (1971) *Relations in Public*. New York: Harper & Row.

Goffman, Erving (1974) *Frame Analysis*. New York: Harper & Row.

Goffman, Erving (1977) 'The Arrangement Between the Sexes', *Theory and Society* 4: 301–31.

Goffman, Erving (1979) *Gender Advertisements*. London: Macmillan.

Goffman, Erving (1982) 'The Order of Interaction', *American Sociological Review* 48(1): 1–17.

Gurevitch, Z.D. (1990) 'The Embrace: On the Element of Non-Distance in Human Relations', *Sociological Quarterly* 31(2): 187–201.

Habermas, Jürgen (1984) *The Theory of Communicative Action*. Boston, MA: Beacon.

Halton, Eugene (1992) 'The Reality of Dreaming', *Theory, Culture & Society* 9(4): 119–39.

Hochschild, Arlie (1983) *The Managed Heart*. Berkeley: University of California Press.

Hochschild, Arlie (1994) 'The Commercial Spirit of Intimate Life and the Abduction of Feminism: Signs from Women's Advice Books', *Theory, Culture & Society* 11(2): 1–24.

Illouz, Eva (1996) *Consuming the Romantic Utopia: Love and the Cultural Contradictions of Capitalism*. Berkeley: University of California Press.

Jakobson, Roman (1960) 'Linguistics and Poetics', pp. 350–77 in Thomas Sebeok (ed.) *Style in Language*. Cambridge, MA: MIT Press.

Klein, Melanie (1950) *Contributions to Psycho-Analysis*. London: Hogarth.

Klein, Robert (1976) 'Freud's Two Theories of Sexuality', *Psychological Issues* 9: 14–70.

Kohut, Heinz (1971) *The Analysis of the Self*. New York: International Universities Press.

Kunda, Gideon (1993) *Engineering Culture*. Philadelphia, PA: Temple University Press.

Lacan, Jacques (1966) *Écrits*. Paris: Seuil.

Lévi-Strauss, Claude (1967) *Les Structures élémentaires de la parenté*, 2nd edn. The Hague: Mouton.

Lorenz, Konrad (1966) *On Aggression*. New York: Harcourt Brace & World. (Orig. 1963.)

Luhmann, Niklas (1984/1986) *Love as Passion: The Codification of Intimacy*. Cambridge, MA: Harvard University Press.

Maffesoli, Michel (1982) *A l'Ombre de Dionysos*. Paris: Méridiens.

Maffesoli, Michel (1993) 'La Sociologie comme connaissance de la socialité', *Société* 35: 1–7.

Marcuse, Herbert (1955) *Eros and Civilization*. Boston, MA: Beacon.

Marcuse, Herbert (1964) *One-Dimensional Man*. Boston, MA: Beacon.

Maslow, Abraham (1960) 'Some Parallels Between Sexual and Dominance Behavior of Infrahuman Primates and the Fantasies of Patients in Psychotherapy', *Journal of Nervous & Mental Disease* 131: 202–12.

Mauss, Marcel (1967) *The Gift*. New York: Norton. (Orig. 1923.)

Merton, Robert (1968) 'Manifest and Latent Functions', in *Social Theory and Social Structure*, enlarged edn. Glencoe, IL: Free Press.

Mills, C. Wright (1951) *White Collar*. New York: Oxford University Press.

Mills, C. Wright (1963) 'The Cultural Apparatus', in *Power, Politics and People*. New York: Oxford University Press.

Morris, Desmond (1967) *The Naked Ape*. New York: McGraw-Hill.

Parsons, Talcott (1951) *The Social System*. Glencoe, IL: Free Press.

Phillips, Adam (1994) *On Flirtation*. London: Faber & Faber.

Rainwater, Lee (1974) *What Money Buys: Inequality and the Meanings of Income*. New York: Basic Books.

Riesman, David (1949) *The Lonely Crowd*. New Haven, CT: Yale University Press.

Sartre, Jean-Paul (1943) *L'Être et le néant*. Paris: Gallimard.

Schachtel, Ernest (1949) 'On Memory and Childhood Amnesia', pp. 3–49 in Patrick Mullahy (ed.) *A Study in Interpersonal Relations: New Contributions to Psychiatry*. New York: Grove Press.

Scheff, Thomas (1990) *Microsociology*. Chicago, IL: University of Chicago Press.

Scheflen, Albert (1965) 'Quasi-Courtship Behavior in Psychotherapy', *Psychiatry* 28(3): 245–57.

Schudson, Michael (1984) *Advertising, the Uneasy Persuasion*. New York: Basic Books.

Schwartz, Barry (1967) 'The Social Psychology of the Gift', *American Journal of Sociology* 73: 1–11.

Seidman, Steven (1991) *Romantic Longings: Love in America, 1830–1980*. New York: Routledge.

Selznick, Philip (1943) 'An Approach to a Theory of Bureaucracy', *American Sociological Review* 8: 47–54.

Shenhav, Yehuda (forthcoming) *Deus Ex Machina*. Cambridge: Cambridge University Press.

Silver, Allan (1995) ' "Two Different Sorts of Commerce": Friendship and Strangership in Civil Society', in Jeff Weintraub and Krishan Kumar (eds) *Private and Public in Thought and Practice*. Chicago, IL: University of Chicago Press.

Simmel, Georg (1950) 'Sociability', pp. 40–57 in Kurt Wolff (ed.) *The Sociology of Georg Simmel*. Glencoe, IL: Free Press. (Orig. 1950.)

Simmel, Georg (1956) *Conflict and the Web of Group Affiliations*. Glencoe, IL: Free Press. (Orig. 1908.)

Simmel, Georg (1984) *On Women, Sexuality and Love*. New Haven, CT: Yale University Press. (Orig. 1923.)

Slater, Philip (1963) 'On Social Regression', *American Sociological Review* 28(3): 339–64.

Slater, Philip (1966) *Microcosm: Structural, Psychological, and Religious Evolution in Groups*. New York: Wiley.

Slater, Philip (1967) 'The Social Bases of Personality', pp. 595-643 in Neil Smelser (ed.) *Sociology*. New York: Wiley.

Stein, Maurice (1960) *The Eclipse of Community*. Princeton, NJ: Princeton University Press.

Turner, Victor (1969) *The Ritual Process: Structure and Anti-Structure*. London: Routledge and Kegan Paul.

Waller, Willard (1937) 'The Rating and Dating Complex', *American Sociological Review* 2: 727–34.

Weiss, Robert (1968) 'Materials for a Theory of Social Relationships', pp. 154–63 in Warren Bennis et al. (eds) *Interpersonal Dynamics*, rev. edn. Homewood, IL: Dorsey.

Weitman, Sasha (1973) 'Intimacies: Notes Toward a Theory of Social Inclusion and Exclusion', pp. 217–38 in Arnold Birenbaum and Edgar Sagarin (eds) *People and Places: The Sociology of the Familiar*. New York: Praeger.

Weitman, Sasha (1992) 'On Flirtation', *Studio Art Magazine* 36: 24–9 (in Hebrew).

Wernick, Andrew (1991) *Promotional Culture: Advertising, Ideology & Expressive Symbolism*. London: Sage.

Whyte, William H. (1956) *The Organization Man*. New York: Simon and Schuster.

Winkin, Yves (ed.) (1981) *La Nouvelle Communication: Bateson, Birdwhistell, Goffman, Hall, Jackson, Scheflen, Sigman, Watzlawick*. Paris: Seuil.

Wispé, Lauren (1967) 'Positive Forms of Social Behavior: An Overview', *Journal of Social Issues* 28: 1–19.

Wispé, Lauren (ed.) (1978) *Altruism, Sympathy, and Helping*. New York: Academic Press.

Wolff, Kurt (ed. & trans.) (1950) *The Sociology of Georg Simmel*. Glencoe, IL: Free Press.

Wolff, Kurt (1962) 'Surrender and Religion', *Journal for the Scientific Study of Religion* 2(1): 41–7.

Wouters, Cas (1986) 'Formalization and Informalization: Changing Tension Balances in Civilizing Processes', *Theory, Culture & Society* 3(2): 1–18.

Zborowski, Mark (1952) *Life Is with People*. New York: International Universities Press.

Zerubavel, Eviatar (1997) *Social Mindscapes*. Cambridge, MA: Harvard University Press.

Sasha Weitman teaches at the Department of Sociology and Anthropology at Tel-Aviv University [sashaw@spirit.tau.ac.il]. His past research includes old regime France and the Revolution, statistics of given names (in Israel), and the semiology of (mass-mediated) femininity. He is currently writing a book, *Eros and Solidarity*, and is organizing a series of conference sessions (within a larger congress) on sociality and solidarity, to be held in July 1999 at Tel-Aviv University.

Bohemian Love

Elizabeth Wilson

THE TERMS 'Bohemia' and 'bohemian', which came into widespread usage in the 1840s and seem to have lost much of their meaning today, were always ambiguous and contested. The ambiguity alluded, in part, to the contradictory status of artists in Western capitalist society. One artistic reaction was to dramatize the role of artist as rebel and outcast: 'bohemian' became an identity.

The bohemian was always defined in terms of an opposite: sometimes s/he was the Artist as opposed to the 'philistine' or bourgeois; sometimes the phoney artist as opposed to the 'real' artist, so that the identity was always ambiguous. To trace the general evolution of this identity would go far beyond the scope of this article (but see Wilson, 1996). One of its central components, however, was a rejection of bourgeois marriage and conventional family norms and the espousal of a view of eroticism as a source of inspiration and as the raw material for works of art. It would be possible to argue, as some feminists have, that one result of this was the sexual objectification of women in the visual arts; on the other hand, the search for experience that could be translated into art took some artists into realms of excess and transgression, and ultimately involved a blurring of life and art that was characteristic of bohemian circles.

I propose to explore bohemian love at three discrete moments of its development: in the French literary culture of the 1830s, when the earliest groups of bohemians flourished (although they did not use the term bohemian at that time); in the German bohemian culture of the period before the First World War; and in Greenwich Village at a slightly later period. I trace the changing meaning of bohemian love, but willingly admit that this remains speculative, since it would be part of a much larger history of romanticism to demonstrate this evolution. Some might also argue that it should be of little interest to us today since bohemian cultures have waned in importance. In the final section of the article, however, I shall argue that,

■ *Theory, Culture & Society* 1998 (SAGE, London, Thousand Oaks and New Delhi),
   Vol. 15(3–4): 111–127
   [0263-2764(199808/11)15:3–4;111–127;006061]

LIVERPOOL
JOHN MOORES UNIVERSITY
AVRIL ROBARTS LRC
TEL. 0151 231 4022

on the contrary, bohemian 'ideologies' of love, if we may call them that, continue to influence us and indeed form a hidden undercurrent that remains unacknowleged in contemporary debates on morality between traditionalists and liberals.

In 1831, the first performance of Alexandre Dumas the Elder's play, *Antony*, caused a sensation, and its hero took his place alongside Byron and the tragic poet Thomas Chatterton as a model for rebel artists. In love with Adèle d'Hervey, a married woman who returned his love, Antony considerately killed her in order to preserve her virtue. Many years later Théophile Gautier, a member of a group known as the Little Circle or *Les Jeunes France* – one of the earliest groups of writers and artists that could be described as a bohemian subculture – attended a revival of the play, and recalling that famous first performance, when Alfred de Vigny's mistress, Marie Dorval, and the great actor Brocage had played the leading roles, wrote that this was 'modern love' in all its intensity, the fateful meeting of the fallen woman and the 'fatal man' (Gautier, 1874: 92).

'Modern love' was romantic love. The romantic movement privileged feeling over reason, and in reaction against 18th-century 'sense' romantic love expressed 'sensibility' and stood for authenticity and the truth of feeling. This is of course the great paradox and irony of modernity: that as scientific advance, representing reason and rational thought, transformed the material world, it unleashed unprecedented unreason and violence. Romanticism was one expression of this, as it moved in the direction of this underlying irrationalism. There was a tiger inside the iron cage of modernity, roaring and rattling its bars.

The 'modern love' explored in *Antony* signalled, moreover, the development of a crisis in relations between the sexes and a crisis in definitions of gender. George Sand explored one painful aspect of this crisis in her novel *Lélia*, published in 1833. The eponymous heroine of *Lélia* described the frigidity that had turned her into a sadistic predator, unable to abandon herself, although she longed to do so. She described the complete divorce between her body and her soul, caused by over-intellectualism, which made it impossible for her to be the equal of anyone: 'The coldness of my senses places me below the most abject of women, the exaltation of my thoughts lifts me above the most passionate of men' (Sand, 1833: 16).

George Sand was already a successful writer and a notoriously unconventional young woman, who had left her husband and was living with her lover, but the apparent freedom of her life was itself problematic. Sand was known to dress as a man on occasions (although she was not the only woman of the period to do so), and she herself later stated that this was so that she could explore Paris unaccompanied, an activity otherwise impossible for any woman – certainly any middle- or upper-class woman – no matter how emancipated. Her relationships, with Chopin and Alfred de Musset among others, in which she was often the older and more dominant partner of weak, rather feminine men, were fraught with difficulties, and her apparent masculinity gave rise to rumours of lesbianism, Alfred de Vigny, for example, becoming jealously convinced that her friendship with Marie Dorval was overtly sexual. Sand was so famous that, as a notoriously unwomanly woman, her persona contributed to the myth of the *femme fatale* in 19th-century European literature, a figure who became sadistic, lesbian, even vampiric (de Courtivron, 1980).

Certainly George Sand's discussion of erotic love in *Lélia* raised the troubling issue of the relationship of erotic pleasure to gendered identity. Théophile Gautier's novel, *Mademoiselle de Maupin*, published in 1835, made this its central preoccupation. The novel has been interpreted as a testament to the doctrine of 'art for art's sake', so that the ambiguous passion of the hero, d'Albert, for Mademoiselle de Maupin becomes a metaphor for the relationship of the artist to his art. Gautier's preface to the novel certainly constituted a defence of the transcendence of art, but the novel itself seems to attempt something more radical. It reads as a meditation on the impossible nature of 'modern love', and it anticipates Freud's questioning of the nature of sexual identity and the ambiguities of gender by 70 years.

Set in the 17th century, *Mademoiselle de Maupin* tells the story of a triangular love affair. At a country château d'Albert and his mistress Rosette meet a mysterious young man, Théodore, to whom both are strangely drawn. Matters come to a head during some amateur theatricals in which Théodore plays a female role, when d'Albert realizes to his horror that he is falling in love with the person he believes to be a man in drag. But of course Théodore is a woman – Mademoiselle de Maupin – in disguise, and the double error of the plot, whereby d'Albert falls in love heterosexually but believes his love is homosexual, while Rosette, also enamoured of Théodore, believes she has fallen in love with a man, 'acts to place homosexual love, both masculine and feminine, at the centre of a tale in which no-one actually admits to it' (Bénichou, 1992: 525). The novel ends ambiguously after Théodore/Mademoiselle de Maupin has slept with both Rosette and d'Albert during the course of a single night before leaving both of them forever.

Gautier used the well established conventions of theatrical drag to go beyond his investigation of romantic love, and although *Mademoiselle de Maupin* has been dismissed as narcissistic, this seems unfair, for the novel develops into an incoherent, but deeply felt exploration of sexual ambiguity, questioning the very nature of gender in a manner for which there was no adequate language at the time. The passage, for example, in which 'Théodore' reflects on her condition suggests a genuine disruption of gender boundaries (Gautier, 1966: 356):

> I was imperceptibly losing the idea of my sex, and I remembered only at long intervals, hardly at all, that I was a woman. . . . In truth, neither of the two sexes is mine. . . . I belong to a third sex apart, which has as yet no name.

While 'Théodore' feels she belongs to a third sex, d'Albert confesses to the normally repressed male wish to be a woman: 'I have never wished anything so much as to encounter in the mountains those serpents which cause one to change sex, as Tiresias the prophet did' (Gautier, 1966: 112).

In the context of these ambiguities of gender, it is hardly surprising if homoeroticism appears in the novel as the most romantic – because most transgressive – form of erotic love. For the romantics, brother–sister incest had been a fashionably forbidden form of heterosexual love. Byron, the template for all fatal men, had exploited this theme in his work and more than hinted at its existence in his life. Love of one's own sex, however, far surpassed this in crossing the boundary between the fashionably sinful and the satanically damned; d'Albert describes his passion for Théodore as utterly compelling (Gautier, 1966: 266):

> ... as compelling as the perfidious sphinx with the dubious smile and ambiguous voice, before whom I stood without daring to attempt an explanation of the enigma ... to love as I loved, with a monstrous, inadmissible love... to feel oneself devoured by longings that even the most hardened libertines would regard as insane and inexcusable; what are the ordinary passions beside this?

– and this was the logical conclusion of 'modern love' since it was always a *fatal* and a forbidden passion: erotic love as transgression, destiny and death.

In *Lost Illusions* and *Pleasures and Troubles of Courtesans*,[1] written in the same years as Gautier's novel, Honoré de Balzac dealt directly with homosexual love, linking it to another fatal figure, whose characteristics contributed to the idea of the bohemian. In these works he traced the adventures of Vautrin, criminal, priest, policeman and homosexual, a character based on the real-life Charles Vidocq, a notorious criminal who did change sides and become a police chief, and who in 1828 published his memoirs (which, needless to say, contain no hint of deviant sexuality).

Vautrin is a satanic figure, endowed with enormous strength and cunning, yet he is also heroic and, in his love for Lucien de Rubempré, poignant and even tragic. Lucien, the would-be poet, is, by contrast, a weak, effeminate and narcissistic dandy, who, although he is supposed to be in love with the devoted courtesan, Esther, is fatally seduced by and appears to succumb to Vautrin's power. Lucien's self-centred passivity opens up a disturbing vista of ambiguous masculinity by contrast with Vautrin's charisma.

Balzac does not present Vautrin as a bohemian character, yet the character reminds us that as well as displaying features of the doomed aristocrat, Byron, the emerging figure of the rebel artist or bohemian was simultaneously linked to the underworld. Indeed, the term 'bohemian' had originally been used in French exclusively to refer to the semi-criminal underworld, and Jerrold Siegel has described the way in which, by the 1840s, the figures of *flâneur*, investigative journalist, spy, criminal and revolutionary became blurred, contributing to the ambiguity of the bohemian identity (Siegel, 1986). Many of these marginal figures contributed to the ephemeral political newspapers and journals that sprang up and died, and Marx, who was inevitably embroiled in this world himself, however much he tried to distance himself from it, lumped '*literati*' in with 'the whole indefinite, disintegrated mass, thrown hither and thither, which the French term *la bohème*' (Marx, 1970: 137) – in other words, his *lumpenproletariat*.

The combination of aristocratic outlawry and underworld associations marked the emergent bohemian out as quintessentially anti-bourgeois. To flout the conventions and restrictions surrounding sexual behaviour in 19th-century society was one obvious form of rebellion. Nineteenth-century bohemian men consorted with prostitutes and lived openly with their mistresses, refusing the conformity of bourgeois marriage. Bohemian women – with considerably more difficulty – laid claim to the same rights to sexual freedom as men. The majority of rebel artists were, unsurprisingly, heterosexual and the bohemian legend has tended to emphasize the wine, women and song aspect of bohemian lifestyles. Behind this reassuring jolllity, however, lurked more disturbing possibilities: the homoeroticism and bisexuality that were central to bohemian life.

It was not surprising that sexual dissidents should have gravitated to circles in which the bourgeois conventions relating to sex were suspended or actively challenged, yet the incidence of homosexuality in bohemian circles was more than a matter of social convenience. A possible disturbing link between sexual deviancy and artistic creativity was simultaneously recognized and disavowed.[2] To explore deviant eroticism was more than simply rebellious, for it involved the exploration of forbidden areas of experience, it permitted the assumption of new identities, it heightened awareness. As Paul Schmidt has suggested, 'to be homosexual, even bisexual, is to be constantly aware of one's life in a way that heterosexuals are not forced to be ... to be aware of another possibility, another dimension'. Homo- eroticism, Schmidt argues, separates sex from the reproduction of the species, and thereby denies time, becoming, potentially at least, a perpetual present moment of the extraordinary, of magic and exaltation. Because Western culture has delegitimated it, reducing it to the status of a psychological aberration, it has been experienced as a state of alienation and negation, when it might more constructively be seen as a cultural potentiality. Yet the very marginality of the lesbian and the queer is a privileged viewpoint from which s/he gains a different perspective of critical vision (Schmidt, 1980: 235).

Even without the open espousal of homosexuality, it seemed uncertain what masculine identity was to be in the new urban society. Charles Baudelaire identified new, more virile types of womanhood in the labyrinth of city life: lesbians, female labourers and prostitutes. At the same time the society of the spectacle was feminizing men; both as obscure writer and as passive consumer the voyeuristic *flâneur* or bohemian became a kind of woman as he observed the urban world, a point brought out by Walter Benjamin (1985: 40; and see Buck-Morss, 1986), who understood the hesitancy of the *flâneur* and his wanderings in the urban labyrinth as a form of impotence – the perpetual deferral of the moment of consummation – rather than perceiving this figure as mastering the world with his gaze, as some feminist theorists have insisted (Wilson, 1999).

Théophile Gautier was a heterosexual bohemian, who rejected marriage, but lived for 20 years with Ernesta Grisi, mother of his two daughters, and had numerous other liaisons. Many bohemians, such as Gérard de Nerval, remained bachelors and little is known of their erotic lives (Bénichou, 1992). He and fellow bohemians, such as Baudelaire's friend, Alexandre Privat d'Anglemont, seem to have seen themselves much more as being *immersed* in urban life than in mastering it.

Gautier's friend, Charles Baudelaire, was yet more equivocal. Ten years or so younger than Gautier, he was the perennial rebel and poseur, the ultimate anti-bourgeois and bohemian. The adored son of a young woman and a much older man, who died when he was six, Baudelaire became enmeshed in a triangle of oedipal jealousies when his mother was united *en secondes noces* to a handsome army officer, to whom she seems to have been much more passionately attached than she had been to Baudelaire's father. The stepfather, General Aupick, opposed Baudelaire's literary ambitions, but more serious even than that was the way in which Baudelaire felt he had been displaced in his mother's affections.

Baudelaire became the black sheep, and remained so throughout his life, plagued for most of it by poverty (partly as a result of his own extravagance) and the syphilis that eventually killed him. His lifelong 'immaturity', his failure to settle down and lead a respectable life, his endless difficulties and disappointments in the literary world, his Creole mistress and frequent flights from one sordid lodging to another in attempts to ward off his creditors, all these questioned the assumed natural order, the bourgeois conventions and the complacency of the philistine. But where Gautier flirted with transgression, Baudelaire flung himself into the role of outcast and *homme damné* (Pichois and Ziegler, 1991).

In later reminiscences his friends insisted obsessively on Baudelaire's beauty when, as a young man, he was a meticulous dandy, his black ensembles enlivened only by the whiteness of his shirt and an oxblood cravat. Théodore de Banville wrote ecstatically that 'if ever the word seduction might be applied to a human being, it was to him', and described his beauty as 'at once virile and childlike ... seeing him, I saw what I had never yet seen, a man who was as I thought a man should be' (de Banville, 1842: 73–74). Gautier was franker about Baudelaire's 'perhaps rather too insistent stare' and his lips 'as ironic and voluptuous as the lips of the faces painted by Leonardo da Vinci'. He described how 'the nose, fine and delicate, a little rounded, with flared nostrils, seemed to smell vague, far off scents', while 'a vigorous cleft accentuated the chin, like the finishing touch to a statue; rice powder gave the carefully shaved cheeks a bluish, velvety bloom; the neck, as white and elegant as a woman's, appeared casually, rising from a shirt collar which was turned back' (Bandy and Pichois, 1957: 22). The youthful dandy, another friend remembered, took great care of his appearance, 'to which he brought a feminine coquetry'. He was proud of his small, soft, beautifully manicured hands (a trait shared with Byron) and took pride in 'an exaggerated cleanliness, with just a hint of scent and rice powder' (Croset, 1867: 15).

The communard and republican Jules Vallès, who belonged to a younger generation of bohemians, knew Baudelaire only in middle age and dissented from the admiration of those who had known him as a young man: 'He had the head of an actor; shaven cheeks, rosy and bloated, a greasy nose, bulbous at the tip, his lips simpered nervously, his expression was tense ... he had something of the priest, something of an old woman and something of the ham about him. Above all he was a ham' (Bandy and Pichois, 1957: 168). At this period he often reminded his friends of a priest – a defrocked one, presumably[3] – except that in Vallès' cruel description he more closely resembled a raddled old queen.

There *was* something of the homosexual manqué about Baudelaire. His thwarted but persistent attachment to his mother could have been a homosexual scenario, and homoerotic meanings have been read into some of his poems. The nature of his relationships with his mistresses is uncertain and his friend Nadar suggested that Baudelaire was a virgin (notwithstanding his syphilis). His misogyny may have been in part a defence against an inner femininity, while his fascination with dandyism (Baudelaire, 1971: 171–6) is also consistent, since the self-sufficiency of the dandy was part of a deviant and ambiguously gendered identity; on the one hand the dandy was a strangely asexual being, on the other homosexuality was reputed to be widespread among the Parisian dandies of the 1830s and 1840s (Citron, 1961: 183).

Puccini's opera, *La Bohème*, based on Murger's writings, was first performed in 1896, the year in which George du Maurier's novel *Trilby*, which also owed much to Murger, was published. These works purveyed a popular, commercialized image of bohemian life in the late 19th and early 20th century, and, reassuringly for their public, entirely obscured the dimension of doomed romantic passion central to Gautier's 'modern love'. Yet in the same period a Bohemia more radical than any yet seen developed in Wilhelmine Germany, and in the Expressionist Bohemias of Munich and Berlin Gautier's 'modern love' underwent a very different and even more significant transformation. The belief in romantic passion as a fatal destiny was ceding to the idea of eroticism as sexual liberation: a move from the tragic to the ecstatic, from the doomed to the utopian, from emotion to sensation.

Anarchism was a potent force in the German bohemian rebellion, whose headquarters were situated in the Munich suburb of Schwabing and in Berlin, against the authoritarian, patriarchal world of Wilhelmine Germany, but of even more enduring importance was psychoanalysis, a catalyst for the 'erotic revolution'. 'The bohemian way of life', wrote one Munich bohemian, 'was being drawn into the maelstrom of the twentieth century, and the most important role in the social critical destruction of the "good old days" was played by Sigmund Freud's concept of psychoanalysis' (Jung, 1961: 89).

In 1908 Ernest Jones, who was to become Freud's most important British disciple, spent some months in Munich, and it was in a Munich cafe that he witnessed his first demonstration of a psychoanalytic session. It was given by Otto Gross, and was in many ways, Jones said, an unorthodox one. 'The analytic treatments were all carried out at a table in the Café Passage, where Gross spent most of the twenty-four hours – the cafe had no closing time. But such penetrative power of divining the inner thoughts of others I was never to see again' (Jones, 1959: 173).

Otto Gross, 'erotic Dionysus', drug addict and psychoanalyst, was the electrifying figure at the centre of the 'erotic revolution'. Jones described him as

> ... the nearest approach to the romantic ideal of a genius I have ever met, and he also illustrated the supposed resemblance of genius to madness, for he was suffering from an unmistakable form of insanity that before my very eyes culminated in murder, asylum and suicide. (Jones, 1959: 174)

Gross (Green, 1986; Mitzman, 1977: 77–104) was the adored, and to begin with dutiful son of an ultra-Prussian patriarch, Hans Gross, jurist, magistrate and expert on detection. (His classic work on the subject is quoted in detective stories by Georges Simenon and Keating.) Otto studied medicine and then worked as an assistant at Kraepelin's psychiatric clinic in Munich, but after he had graduated in 1899 he sailed for Latin America, where his lifelong addiction to narcotics seems to have begun.

In 1903 he married Frieda Schlosser (a Wagner enthusiast who had also considered doing social work at Toynbee Hall in London). Two years later the relationship between father and son had become intensely antagonistic, as Otto developed theories of sexual repression and free love that he did not hesitate to put into practice. His involvements with women rapidly became scandalous and even sinister. Among his love affairs was one with a young woman, Regina Ullman, which he ended when she became pregnant. Not only did he not help her in this difficult situation, but she claimed he left poison in her reach, hoping she would commit suicide (Michaels, 1983).

Gross became involved in a series of scandals at the Munich outpost of Ascona, a settlement on the shores of Lake Como in the Italian-speaking part of Switzerland. In 1900 a group of seven Germans from Munich had arrived, with the intention of setting up a commune. Among them were Ida Hofmann and Lotte Hattemer, emancipated women who wore reform clothing, left their hair loose (then extremely shocking) and travelled around by themselves.

In 1906 the leading Schwabing anarchist, Erich Mühsam, and his companion, Johannes Nohl, were staying with the two women at the same time as Gross, who had been involved with Lotte Hattemer. She was suicidally depressed and her lover, as with Regina Ullmann, provided her with poison. Unlike her predecessor, she did commit suicide.

A year later Gross became involved with the sisters Else and Frieda von Richthofen, also radical, emancipated women. Else had been a school-friend of Frieda Gross and had married Edgar Jaffé, a wealthy industrialist turned academic who was associated with Max Weber's circle; her sister Frieda was unhappily married to an English professor, Ernest Weekley.

As a result of their relationships with Gross, both Else Jaffé and Frieda Gross gave birth to sons, both of whom were named Peter (much scope for psychoanalytic interpretation there). Otto's most intense love, however, seems to have been reserved for Frieda Weekley. She felt equally passionately about him, for it was her first erotically fulfilling relationship. What thrilled her, she afterwards wrote, 'was his vision, his new approach to human problems'. She was, she said, passionately grateful to him for giving her a new faith, that 'the human world could be happier and better than it was and more charitable'. Yet she resisted her lover's urgent demands that she leave her husband, recognizing his lack of balance: 'The everyday life he ignored. On visions alone you can't live. He hardly knew whether it was night or day ... somehow ... something was wrong in him; he did not have his feet on the ground of reality' (Lawrence, 1961: 90–1).

The two Friedas afterwards shared another lover, Ernst Frick, later accused of having detonated a bomb in Zurich, but by the time of his arrest Frieda Weekley had eloped with D. H. Lawrence, with whom she spent the rest of her life. Frieda Gross was left miserable and impoverished while her husband continued on the path that was to lead to his destruction.

Like so many men as well as women, Leonhard Frank had been overwhelmed by the force of Gross's personality when he first arrived in Munich. He became part of Gross's circle, and fell in love with another member of the group, Sophie Benz. After a time Gross objected to the monogamous nature of this relationship, and in 1911, by which time he had introduced her to cocaine, he travelled with her to Ascona. Leonhard Frank saw her for the last time at Munich railway station (Frank, 1954: 45):

> Her hair and dress were dirty as though she had slept for weeks out of doors. Her shrunken, waxen face was that of a dead girl still unaccountably breathing. The doctor [Otto Gross] sniffed cocaine in full view of the travellers standing around him, and repeated the dose a few minutes later. He had lost all self control. There were spots of blood on his crumpled collar. Blood and pus ran from his nostrils.

In Ascona the Lotte Hattemer episode was replayed with the suicidal Sophie. Gross refused to allow her to be hospitalized and, as with Lotte, provided poison with which she, like her predecessor, killed herself.

Gross was arrested soon afterwards (although for reasons unconnected with her death), partly at the behest of his father, and shut up in an asylum, but such was the uproar in the youth movement and the intellectual community that a protest campaign succeeded in gaining his release a year later, although on condition that he underwent an analysis with Wilhelm Stekel. His last years were spent in Prague and in Berlin, where he died in 1920, completely destitute (Jung, 1961).

Gross acted out the whole youth crisis of the period. As an answer to that crisis he had tried to adapt psychoanalysis to a radical world-view. His work had begun to diverge from Freud's by 1908 or 1909, when, anticipating Wilhelm Reich, he redefined the sexual drive as a benign force which is distorted by social institutions. The logical conclusion of this position was that to act on all one's sexual desires was to diminish repression and was in itself liberating. This was similar to the gratifying idea that the sexual act was inherently revolutionary and that sexual intercourse therefore automatically advances the revolution, a view propagated by Erich Mühsam, for example, when, in 1913, he listed in the first issue of the expressionist journal *Revolution* a 'few forms of revolution'; these included tyrannicide, creation of a work of art and the sexual act.

Mühsam – who devoted his life to direct action, played a leading role in the Munich *Räterrepublik* of 1919 and was murdered in Oranienberg concentration camp by the Nazis in 1934 – believed as passionately in the erotic as in the workers' revolution. While still a schoolboy in Lübeck he and a friend, Curt Siegfried, began to write for the newspapers and move in journalistic circles. Even at this early age Mühsam was interested in the workers' movement and revolutionary struggle; Siegfried by contrast was an aesthete who took Wilde's Dorian Gray as a model: 'he dressed in the height of elegance, wore a large chrysanthemum in his buttonhole and claimed to be tired and blasé.' In 1903 he put a revolver to his head and shot himself (Mühsam, 1958: 25).

It would be possible to read a homoerotic subtext into Mühsam's account of this friendship, and Mühsam chose homosexuality as the subject of his first book, published in 1903. Given his hatred of German patriarchal society in general and of his own father in particular, it is hardly surprising that Mühsam argued for the validity of erotic love between men, since it attacked the authoritarian family at its core, questioning the rigid Prussian definition of manliness. Indeed, this revolt was at the heart of the erotic revolution and German bohemian circles of the period, and Mühsam remembered an evening in a Berlin cafe when a friend asked which of the group had had a harmonious relationship with his family: 'without exception, we were all apostates from our background, all were black sheep' (Mühsam, 1958: 17).

Not only did Mühsam defend homosexuality in print, for many years he was content to let it be believed that he was homosexual, although he does not discuss this in his memoirs, and also had a reputation for womanizing. Whatever its nature, his most important relationship between 1904 and 1909, his 'wandering years', was with Johannes Nohl, with whom he travelled between Berlin and Munich, to Paris, central Europe and

Ascona. Nohl, another defector from a cultured bourgeois family, was openly homosexual, usually recalled in memoirs from the period with a string of young boys in tow, and he was, like Curt Siegfried, a Wildean character. Mühsam and he were thought to be lovers during their visit to Ascona in 1907 (at the time of Lotte Hattemer's suicide) and Mühsam dedicated his collected love poems to Nohl when they were published in 1913, although by this time the two men had moved apart, and both later settled down in relatively conventional marriages.

With the exception of Frieda Lawrence, it might seem that the bohemian women of Schwabing suffered more than they benefited from the 'free love' of the period. However, this was not true of the 'Queen of Schwabing', the 'Schleswig Holstein Venus' and 'Pagan Madonna', Gräfin Franziska zu Reventlov, Mühsam's friend and the lover of Ludwig Klages and many others. Like Frieda Lawrence she came from an upper-class family, which may have given her the confidence to rebel against her family and strike out on her own.

She was beautiful, 'a Danish type', wrote one admirer,

> ... small, petite, supple, un-made up, far more Parisian than the real Parisians with all their rouge, a little brash, offhand, very witty, a little sentimental. On her dainty feet she stalked through the sodden Munich suburb of Schwabing and seemed always untouched, washed and shining, even when she almost sank. (Fritz, 1980: 28)

Mühsam recalled especially her huge blue eyes, hearty laughter and tragi-comic aura, while Frieda Lawrence described her at the age of 40 as having 'the face of a young madonna', in spite of the wild life she had led.

Her attempts to achieve success as a painter and later as an actress met with no success. She had better luck with journalism and wrote two autobiographical novels, but poverty was a perennial source of bitter torment and hilarity. This being the case, she had no qualms about accepting money from men in payment for sex. She sometimes worked as a masseuse, seriously considered becoming a courtesan, and in her diaries recorded numerous occasions on which her erotic encounters proved remunerative. In 1898, for example, she met three students with whom she had supper and an 'orgy', for which they paid her 150 marks (Reventlov, 1971: 85):

> Afterwards I told them something about my life and my plans for acting ... and we killed ourselves laughing. Then between lust and tragedy and I know not what. 'We will live together so that you can become a star'.... Marie had stayed with Bubi [her baby boy] and I returned home at four o'clock in the morning through the beautiful dawn. I did not let them accompany me, since I wished to retain my incognito.... Oh, dear God, if they only knew that I was a countess, had been married, etc.

So her casual erotic liaisons involved performance, disguise and a kind of make believe. Even when she engaged in what others might have perceived as prostitution, she was the princess in disguise, was to some extent simply slumming.

Her belief in women's freedom was not feminist in the usual sense, although she had feminist friends, for she believed that the path to women's liberation lay through the freeing of their sexuality. In her novels she wrote of herself as a 'martyr for freedom' and a 'gladiator of the new time', but she also wrote in her diary that 'working women are always rather horrible' and believed that writing and gainful employment generally made women old and ugly (Fritz, 1980: 88).

She evaded the pleas of Otto Gross that she should undergo psycho-analysis, remaining sceptical as to its merits. This scepticism – from a radical bohemian point of view – might be shared by any observer of the transformation undergone by Freudian theory after it was exported to Greenwich Village.

The influence of psychoanalysis after it had crossed the Atlantic inaugu-rated – or at least was part of – a further transformation in bohemian love, and indeed of Bohemia generally. The American Bohemia that flourished in this picturesque corner of Manhattan was a more open, less extreme Bohemia than the German. From the early years of the century until 1917, when the USA entered the war, Greenwich Village was a utopian alternative community, its radicals attempting 'a cultural revolution in which no aspect of life was to be exempt from revolutionary change' (Fishbein, 1982: 4).

The Village was a Mecca for independent women, not only artists, but socialists, feminists and all kinds of radical campaigners – and also eccentrics. The journalist Hutchins Hapgood went so far as to assert that 'the restlessness of women was the main cause of the development called Greenwich Village' (Hapgood, 1972: 152).

Mabel Dodge was the great salon hostess of the Village. She was supported by a wealthy husband, although they no longer lived together, and in her magnificent double apartment just north of Washington Square she organized 'Evenings' throughout 1913 and most of 1914. The usual format was to invite a speaker, whose talk would be followed by discussion. Early in 1914 Dr A. A. Brill, who was responsible for bringing Freud to the USA for his first lecture tour, spoke on psychoanalysis. This was probably the first formal discussion of Freudian theory in Greenwich Village (Watson, 1994: 137).

Mabel Dodge was at this time engaged in a turbulent affair with John Reed, who later chronicled the Russian Revolution in his book, *Ten Days that Shook the World*. After the end of this relationship and an equally unsatisfactory relationship with a sculptor, she eventually moved perma-nently to Taos, New Mexico, where she married Antonio Luhan, an Ameri-can Indian.

Mabel Dodge was one of the first Villagers to undergo a course of treatment with Dr Brill, but in her memoirs she recalled that 'he had not much use for my radical friends, and he considered that their beliefs were generally only rationalized prejudices, and that their prejudices were due to their conditioned early years and that when they got together they bolstered up each other's complexes' (Dodge Luhan, 1936: 572). Psychoanalysis, she decided, was little more than 'a kind of tattletaling'.

Harnessed to the erotic revolution in pre-war Munich, Freudian theory was de-radicalized by its passage across the Atlantic, possibly partly because of Brill's own personality and prejudices. Its role in the Village was to de-politicize, to emphasize the personal and individual side of New York's 'cultural revolution' rather than the political. At this time Max Eastman and Floyd Dell were editing the radical socialist magazine, *The Masses*, together. Both were immediately attracted to the new doctrines of psychoanalysis, and were soon writing articles publicizing Freud's views in the popular press. In the December 1915 issue of *Vanity Fair*, for example, Dell wrote that 'psychoanalysis is the greatest discovery made by intellectual conversationalists since Bergson and the IWW [the anarcho-syndicalist movement, International Workers of the World]' (Watson, 1994: 145). The mocking tone was typical of his style, but he took Freud very seriously, and in 1917 he underwent analysis with Dr Samuel Tannenbaum.

Dell was one of the most influential chroniclers of the Village at this period, yet although he lived a bohemian life there and had a number of love affairs with independent women, including Edna St Vincent Millay, his attitude towards its radicalism of lifestyle and belief in 'free love' was always rather cynical and mocking, and his course of analysis seems to have crystallized his judgement that Greenwich Village and bohemian ways of life generally were immature and 'adolescent'. The Village, he decided, 'was a place where people came to solve some of their life problems ... a moral health resort, that is what it was'. The women of this community claimed to believe in free love, but secretly longed to get married, and some of them 'saw in the Village only a better place than the home town to find husbands' (Dell, 1933: 287). By the late 1920s his hostility to independent women was explicit:

> I did want to find marriage ... I did not care if my new sweetheart were not an intellectual. Her beautiful breasts were perfect for the suckling of babies. ... I felt quite sure now that I did not want to be married to a girl artist; I wanted to be married to a girl who would not put her career before children – or even before me. One artist in the family was enough. (Dell, 1933: 283)

His second wife, Marie Gage, whom he married in 1919 and with whom he departed to the suburbs, *had* been an intellectual, a socialist and feminist at the University of Wisconsin, who was later prosecuted in California for her activities in organizing, as a pacifist, against the war effort. After her marriage to Dell at the age of 23, however, she devoted herself to the roles of wife and mother. This masculine insistence on a traditional role for women, even in Bohemia, was not unusual, and Ellen Trimberger has explored the way in which a whole generation of male radicals in Greenwich Village, including Max Eastman and Hutchins

Hapgood, had difficulty in aligning their supposedly radical ideals and belief in feminism with their desire for love relationships in which women remained subordinate (Trimberger, 1984: 184). Psychoanalysis could all too easily be wheeled in to justify such views.

Yet the influence of psychoanalysis was double edged. On the one hand, as it developed in the USA, and to a lesser extent in Britain, into an adjustive therapy, it became increasingly intolerant of bohemian eccentricity. Social movements and radical ideals were dismissed as a collective neurosis that merely represented each individual radical's rebellion against his or her father, politics reduced to a neurotic and misguided side-effect of family conflict. On the other hand, however, Freudian theory as popularized did promote a belief in the importance of sexual fulfilment, even if this was supposed to be restricted to marriage relationships.

Such views gradually infiltrated the puritanical Anglo-Saxon societies on both sides of the Atlantic as part of the consumerism which assisted the commercialization of many aspects of bohemian life. The commercialization of Bohemia was quite apparent in Greenwich Village by the end of the First World War, according to Malcolm Cowley, who chronicled its development from – as he saw it – radical haven to tourist attraction. He believed that the changes he perceived were partly due to the split between the political radicals and the aesthetes. The politicos had no place in President Wilson's conservative and virulently anti-Bolshevik America, but the aesthetic bohemians, or those whose rebellion was largely personal, 'could continue to exist safely'.

Indeed, Cowley maintained that this second group was essential to the marketization of more and more aspects of life. The anti-puritanism pioneered in Bohemia had now triumphed all over the USA, he felt. It had been spread by business, forced to create new markets once the pioneering phase of American expansion ceased. It was not, Cowley argued, that Greenwich Village had *caused* the consumer ethic or the moral revolution, but its ideas had shaped the form these took, and he was being only partly ironical when he suggested that the bohemian ideals of self-expression and paganism (Cowley, 1964: 62):

> encouraged a demand for ... modern furniture, beach pyjamas, cosmetics [and] coloured bathrooms with toilet paper to match. *Living for the moment* meant buying an automobile, radio or house, using it now and paying for it later. *Female equality* was capable of doubling the consumption of products – cigarettes, for example – that had formerly been used by men alone.

Across the whole continent, he insisted, women who had never set foot in Greenwich Village were bobbing their hair, smoking in the street, meeting to gossip in black and orange tea rooms and giving parties at which they and their guests drank cocktails.

The bohemian ways of life which were commercialized for mass consumption, included, or perhaps it would be more accurate to say, implied a pre-existing environment that was accustomed to diluted forms of Freudian theory, as this had been filtered through Bohemia and its lifestyles and was now influencing many more strata of society.

Conclusion

Finally, then, two themes merge: bohemian love; and the infiltration of mass culture by bohemian morality. This second theme goes far beyond the scope of this article, but central to it was a fundamental change in the way the whole of Western society viewed erotic love. By 1900 few would have shared Lord Chesterfield's 18th-century view of sexual love, that 'the pleasure is momentary, the posture ridiculous and the expense damnable'.[4] In the 19th century the bourgeoisie had been seduced by the romantic movement, which had seemed to express a refinement of feeling far removed from the coarse and cynical worldliness of the 18th-century aristocracy (and perhaps Byron's fascination for a mass public had arisen because he was both aristocratic and romantic). The middle classes adopted romantic love as their own, although in squeezing it to fit a new form of marriage and familialism, they suppressed its tragic elements in favour of happy endings. The figures of fallen woman and fatal man have continued to haunt Western culture, incarnated in new forms – Marilyn Monroe, Ann Rice vampire heroes and, most recently, Princess Diana and Dodi Al Fayed – but conventional marriage is based on similar ideals.

We no longer believe in self control and sublimation, nor do we believe that familial duty must always triumph over wayward desire. The 19th-century bourgeoisie attempted to domesticate Gautier's 'modern love', but today liberal Western society has gone much further in adopting what is essentially a bohemian belief in the transcendent value of erotic passion as the touchstone for the authenticity of relations between the sexes. There is a widespread belief that these relationships must be spontaneous, and marriage itself has become a celebration of that unique spontaneity between two individuals rather than a religious and contractual obligation with wide-ranging responsibilities in terms of family and property. To the bohemians we partly owe the liaison between romanticism and consumer culture in which transgression, excess and the triumph of feeling and sensation triumph over more traditionally Enlightenment values, with Sigmund Freud as the Enlightenment midwife to an offspring that no longer salutes Enlightenment values. In this sense, we can say that even if – as many claim – Bohemia is in decline or has disappeared altogether, today we are all bohemians.

Notes

1.   Inappropriately entitled *A Harlot High and Low* in the Penguin translation.

2.   Evidence that this disavowal continues to operate may be found in the Penguin editions both of *Pleasures and Troubles of Courtesans* and of Arthur Rimbaud's *Collected Poems*. Balzac's translator, Rayner Heppenstall, suggests that to interpret Vautrin's love for Lucien as homosexual is to put a 20th-century spin on what was

more likely to have been a 'normal' degree of affection between an older and a young man. Yet it does not require a particularly close reading of the novel to grasp the absurdity of this assertion. In a semi-comic interlude, for example, Vautrin, in prison, discovers a former lover there. Balzac refers to this (male) lover as Vautrin's paramour and mistress, and tells us that he is being held in a section of the prison especially reserved for 'queens' and for the 'third sex'. Oliver Bernard, in his introduction to Rimbaud, also rather ludicrously states: 'I do not think his homosexuality matters nearly so much as what sort of person he was', as though the poet's sexuality could possibly be divorced from 'the sort of person he was', and even the most dedicated Foucauldian would surely dissent from the view that even if one rejects the idea of sexual 'master identities' an individual's sexual behaviour is still relevant in the context of his life and work as a whole. Both these introductions were written in the 1960s, but it is rather significant that Penguin has seen no reason to update them.

3.   Jean-Paul Sartre (1963: 194) describes Baudelaire in similar terms.

4.   This remark is attributed to Lord Chesterfield, but it has not been possible to locate it in his letters.

References

Bandy, W.T. and Claude Pichois (eds) (1957) *Baudelaire devant ses contemporains*. Monaco: Éditions du Rocher.

Baudelaire, Charles (1971) 'Le Dandy', pp. 171–6 in *Écrits sur l'art*, 2. Paris: Le Livre de Poche.

Bénichou, Paul (1992) *L'École du désenchantement: Sainte-Beuve, Nodier, Musset, Nerval, Gautier*. Paris: Gallimard.

Benjamin, Walter (1985) 'Central Park', trans. Lloyd Spencer with help from Mark Harrington, *New German Critique* 34: 1–27.

Buck-Morss, Susan (1986) 'The Flâneur, the Sandwichman and the Whore: The Politics of Loitering', *New German Critique* 39: 99–140.

Citron, Pierre (1961) *La Poésie de Paris dans la littérature française: de Rousseau à Baudelaire*. Paris: Éditions de Minuit.

Cowley, Malcolm (1964) *Exile's Return: A Literary Odyssey of the 1920s*. London: Bodley Head (revised edition). (Orig. 1934.)

Croset, Edmond (1867) 'Fantaisie Baudelaire', *La Vogue Parisienne*, 7 Septembre.

de Banville, Théodore (1842) *Petits études: mes souvenirs*. Paris.

de Courtivron, Isabelle (1980) 'Weak Men and Fatal Women: The Sand Image', in George Stamboulian and Elaine Marks (eds) (1980) *Homosexualities and French Literature: Cultural Context/Critical Texts*. Ithaca, NY: Cornell University Press.

Dell, Floyd (1933) *Homecoming*. New York: Farrar and Rinehart.

Dodge Luhan, Mabel (1936) *Intimate Memories: Volume Three: Movers and Shakers*. New York: Harcourt Brace and Co.

Fishbein, Leslie (1982) *Rebels in Bohemia: The Radicals of* The Masses *1911–1917*. Chapel Hill: University of Carolina Press.

Frank, Leonhard (1954) *Heart on the Left*, trans. Cyrus Brooks. London: Arthur Barker. (Orig. 1928.)

Fritz, Helmut (1980) *Die Erotische Rebellion: Das Leben der Franziska Gräfin zu Reventlov*. Frankfurt: Fischer Verlag.

Gautier, Théophile (1874) *Histoire du Romantisme*. Paris: Charpentier.

Gautier, Théophile (1966) *Mademoiselle de Maupin*. Paris: Garnier-Flammarion. (Orig. 1835.)

Green, Martin (1986) *Mountain of Truth: The Counter Culture Begins: Ascona 1900–1920*. Harvard, MA: University Press of New England.

Hapgood, Hutchins (1972) *A Victorian in the Modern World*. Seattle: University of Washington Press. (Orig. 1939.)

Jones, Ernest (1959) *Free Associations*. London: Hogarth Press.

Jung, Franz (1961) *Er Weg nach Unten: Aufzeichnungen Aus Einer Großen Zeit*. Berlin: Hermann Luchterhand Verlag.

Lawrence, Frieda (1961) *The Memoirs and Correspondence*, edited by E. W. Tedlock. London: Heinemann.

Marx, Karl (1970) 'The Eighteenth Brumaire of Louis Bonaparte', in Karl Marx and Friedrich Engels *Selected Works*. London: Lawrence and Wishart.

Michaels, Jennifer (1983) *Anarchy and Eros: Otto Gross's Impact on German Expressionism*. New York: Peter Lang.

Mitzman, Arthur (1977) 'Otto Gross: Anarchism, Expressionism and Psychoanalysis', *New German Critique* 10: 77–104.

Mühsam, Erich (1958) *Unpolitische Erinnerungen*. Berlin: Verlag Volk and Weit.

Pichois, Claude and Jean Ziegler (1991) *Baudelaire*, trans. Graham Robb. London: Vintage.

Reventlov, Franziska Gräfin zu (1971) *Tagebuch*. München: Langen Muller.

Sand, George (1833) *Lélia*. Paris: Henri Dupuy.

Sartre, Jean-Paul (1963) *Baudelaire*. Paris: Gallimard.

Schmidt, Paul (1980) 'Visions of Violence: Rimbaud and Verlaine', in George Stamboulian and Elaine Marks (eds) *Homosexualities and French Literature: Cultural Context/Critical Texts*. Ithaca, NY: Cornell University Press.

Siegel, Jerrold (1986) *Bohemian Paris: Culture, Politics and the Boundaries of Bourgeois Life, 1830–1890*. New York: Viking.

Trimberger, Ellen Kay (1984) 'Feminism, Men and Modern Love: Greenwich Village 1900–1925', in Ann Snitow et al. (eds) *Desire: The Politics of Sexuality*. London: Virago.

Watson, Steven (1994) *Strange Bedfellows: The First American Avant Garde*. New York: Abbeville Press.

Wilson, Elizabeth (1996) 'The Death of Bohemia?', pp. 46–60 in P. Büchler and N. Papastergiadis (eds) *Random Access 2: Ambient Fears*. London: Rivers Oram Press.

Wilson, Elizabeth (1999) 'The Invisible Flâneur', in Elizabeth Wilson *City Streets, City Dreams*. London: Verso.

Elizabeth Wilson is Professor of Cultural Studies at the University of North London. Her publications include *Women and the Welfare State* (Tavistock, 1977), *Adorned in Dreams: Fashion and Modernity* (University of California Press, 1985) and *The Sphinx in the City* (University of California Press, 1993). She was a founder member of the editorial board of *Feminist Review*.

Otto Gross and Else Jaffé and Max Weber

Sam Whimster with Gottfried Heuer

This article divides into three sections. The first is an introduction to the love letters of Otto Gross to Else Jaffé, and the next, a translation of the letters. The third section is a commentary on love and eroticism and contrasts the standpoints of Otto Gross and Max Weber. An Appendix provides the German text of the Otto Gross letters.

Introduction

The selection of letters below were written in 1907 by the libertarian psychoanalyst Otto Gross to Else Jaffé. They are immediately recognizable and understandable as love letters – the sort of letter that needs no introduction; perhaps even the sort of letter that should remain private to the addressee. Isn't it unscrupulous to read, transcribe, and publish some-one's love letters? The stimulus to this exercise was the *Theory, Culture & Society* Special Issue edition on 'Love and Eroticism'. In the many hours spent deciphering Otto Gross's manically driven handwriting and puzzling over the sequence of pages, questions of prying and prurience kept surfacing in my mind.

It is not too hard to justify publication. Both Otto Gross and Else Jaffé are dead and their affair happened a very long time ago. Otto died in 1920 and Else in 1973. (She was born in 1874, he was born in 1877.) The letters were handed over to Martin Green by Else Jaffé's daughter Dr Marianne von Eckardt with the approval of Else Jaffé. It was an affair she presumably wanted posterity to know about, even though she denied it in her lifetime (Green, 1988: 367). The relationship did result in a child – Peter, who was born Christmas Eve 1907 and died in 1915. This would seem to settle any ethical issues of privacy, and the lingering doubts that remain may, perhaps,

■ *Theory, Culture & Society* 1998 (SAGE, London, Thousand Oaks and New Delhi),
   Vol. 15(3–4): 129–160
   [0263-2764(199808/11)15:3–4;129–160;006062]

be put down to the sense of strangeness of encountering someone else's emotional world.

Besides, the narrative framework of these letters belongs to intellectual history. It is the subject of the justly celebrated book, *The von Richthofen Sisters* by Martin Green (1988), which should be consulted for the complete story. Here I will confine myself to providing the essentials required for understanding the letters and attempt to unravel a complex and highly dramatic narrative.

Else was the eldest of three daughters of Freiherr Friedrich von Richthofen and his wife Anna Marquier (Byrne, 1995: 14–38). Despite the title and the name, her family had limited wealth and sometimes were forced into debt. A 'good' marriage was not only a convention but a pressing necessity for the three daughters. Each daughter did 'well' in the marriage market but none enjoyed a stable marriage. Joanna, who was the youngest, married a regimental commander twice her age and had her first child at the age of 18. She was a society queen and had a number of lovers. Frieda married Ernest Weekley, who was professor of English at Nottingham University. Frieda found English middle-class life stuffy and boring, and she increasingly found her husband to be conventional and timid. She left him finally in 1912, when she eloped with the English novelist D.H. Lawrence.

Else was taken under the wing of Marianne and Max Weber, who met her as a young woman in Freiburg in the mid-1890s. Among the Richthofen sisters Else was seen as the clever and studious one. The Webers encouraged her to become a teacher, then to enter university – one of the first women to do so. An adolescent Frieda remembered being taken to a lecture by Else at the University of Heidelberg and pushing their way through a crowd of male students. Else completed her doctorate with Weber and Otto Wagner as supervisors and became a factory inspector in Mannheim. At this time – 1902 – she married Edgar Jaffé (born 1866) who had recently given up working in the family firm of merchants. He was a wealthy man who then turned to academia, becoming an economist at the University of Heidelberg. Edgar built a large splendid villa overlooking the Neckar for Else and himself and the four children who were born in 1903, 1905, 1907 and 1909. Else reverting more to type, resigned her post as factory inspector after a year and a half and became a leading light in the academic and social life of Heidelberg.

The marriage was not happy – an uneasy match of beauty and money. Else and Edgar visited Munich, where Frieda and Otto Gross had moved in late 1906. Frieda Gross was a close friend of Else's. She was an idealistic, gentle and refined presence. Born in Graz, Austria in 1876 she had been sent to live with her aunt in Freiburg when her mother died. There she had attended the Institut Blas and it was at this boarding school for girls that Frieda and Else became firm friends. Frieda Richthofen, who was also sent to the school, recalled the girl from Graz, 'Friedel is terribly attractive, I fell under her spell as a child, we clambered over fences then, and we still do the same now' (Gross and Weekley, 1990: 197). The school in Freiburg was the starting point of the immensely influential sorority of Frieda Schloffer, and Else and Frieda von Richthofen. In 1906 in Munich the Grosses and the Jaffés had much to discuss. Otto and Frieda had become part of the bohemian scene of Schwabing, Munich's artists' quarter where cafes and clubs celebrated a new frivolity and experimental lifestyle that embraced free love and drugs and satirized the oppressive atmosphere of mannered 'society'.

Neither Edgar nor Else were obvious candidates for this, first, counter-cultural movement. Edgar would be counted as no longer young and was not physically what the Schwabingers called an 'erotomorph'. He was something of a 'control freak' – terribly contained and patient and an intelligent academic (he wrote the standard treatise on English banking) but prone to excitable states when he couldn't stop himself talking. Frieda Gross liked Edgar and her quiet and powerful charm would have relaxed him. Else, with her doctorate and job, looked as if she was going the way of the Fabian Beatrice Webb – renouncing physical pleasure for higher, better causes – 'Social Asceticism' as Otto Gross ironized it (Gross and Weekley, 1990: 175).

Otto was a psychologist who was working within a clinical tradition of psychopathology at Emil Kraepelin's recently opened clinic in Munich. At this point of his career Gross was attempting to incorporate Freud's writing into his own research and was becoming increasingly frustrated with academic psychiatry that explicitly rejected Freud's insights into the causes of neurosis. He himself suffered from neurotic disturbances. In early 1907 Frieda Gross reported to Else that Otto would only work at night, which was when he visited patients, and he would not wash or take off his clothes. In addition he indulged in bouts of morphine and cocaine use and had already undergone two or three cures for addiction. When Else met him in 1906 he was a luminous, penetrating intelligence. His central insight was that it was not fathers alone as individuals who formed the repressive structure of personality in their children but that instead it was the structure and culture of a patriarchal society that had institutiona-lized repression in the family. His solution was to call for an expressive and unrestrained sexuality, which the unique conditions of Schwabing had shown to be possible (see Michaels, 1983, and Hurwitz, 1979). Otto had a calling and a message of fulfilment and happiness for a generation of adults who felt acutely uncomfortable with their upbringing, seemingly ingrained but now susceptible to analysis and treatment. Both the Jaffés fell under his spell. Early in 1907 Else and Otto started an affair. Edgar also had affairs but ones of no length of time – for example with Franziska zu Reventlow, one of Schwabing's more amazing spirits (Reventlow, 1971: 441).

The history of Else's affair with Otto is famous, but partly through the reflection of her sister Frieda's more famous affair with Otto Gross. The chronology of 1907 is complex and it requires careful unravelling. Frieda von Richthofen – then Mrs Ernest Weekley – also started an affair with Otto in the spring of that year. One of the main arteries of sexual modernism is seen to flow into the 20th century through Otto Gross, Frieda von Richthofen/Weekley to D.H. Lawrence. For Otto, Frieda Weekley became the embodiment of the erotic woman – 'the Woman of the Future', as indeed she became for D.H. Lawrence who married her in 1914 (see Worthen, 1992: 393–425 and Kinkead-Weekes, 1996: 5–42). This has tended to distract from Else's place, or rather, as we shall see, Else's place within the sorority of Frieda von Richthofen and Frieda Gross. Martin Green has cast Frieda von Richthofen as the goddess of love, Aphrodite, and Else as the goddess of wisdom, Athene. This distracts a little from Else's erotic strengths and needs. She remained more or less unhappily married, she required and found lovers, and a number of descriptions of her show her as much girlishly flirtatious as regal beauty (Weber, 1994: 369, 372). Else's strength of character and her own specific motives are a determining part of what happened in 1907 and its repercussions afterwards.

The translation and transcription here of the Otto Gross to Else Jaffé letters facilitate a better grasp of the events, and with that, the psychological interactions of 1907. The Otto Gross to Frieda Weekley letters have already been published in 1990 by John Turner (Gross and Weekley, 1990). In addition to the Otto Gross to Else Jaffé letters, there are the Frieda Gross to Else Jaffé letters, and the correspondence of Marianne and Max Weber.[1] The chronological sequence of most of Otto's letters is very hard to establish, since he never dated his letters. Although the Otto Gross to Else Jaffé letters overlap with the Otto Gross to Frieda Weekley letters, in the absence of any dates cross-referencing between the letters is frustrating. It is, however, possible to discern some of the narrative threads within and between both sets of the letters, which allows a reasoned ordering. In addition, the Frieda Gross letters often give a partial date and they become an important source of reference. Hence my numbering of the letters should be taken as putative.

One of the only dates that Otto gives is on a postcard on his return to Munich, 2 February 1907. This is a possible indication about when the relationship started. Because Else had Otto's baby on 24 December 1907, it is reasonable to suppose that by April she knew she had become pregnant. Letter 3 reveals a frustrated Otto trying to get in contact with Else with Edgar writing to say she had to rest. The reference to Schiemann could be the same Frank (Schiemann) who is asking Frieda Gross for money. (It could also refer to Leonhard Frank.) Frieda Gross in a letter of 23 March warns Else about this. 'Frank pumpt mich täglich an – nein manchmal ist ein freier Tag dazwischen' (Frieda Gross, Tufts Archives). Frieda's letter also tells Else that she and Otto have agreed a 'pact' whereby each shall have 'absolute freedom'. This, says Frieda, is a relief because she will no longer have to feel responsible for Otto. But at the same time she does not feel she is thereby free of Otto – 'there is a compartment of my soul that has to be unreservedly kept for Otto'. Frieda's letter is very depressed. She has a

3-month-old baby, Peter Gross and, as she repeats, Otto is always in her mind. She reports that Otto has put off going to Heidelberg. Otto did, however, get to Heidelberg – certainly by 17 April when Frieda Gross writes again to Else. The contents of this letter make clear that Else has confessed her relationship with Otto to Frieda, for Frieda condones their affair and she affirms her trust and love for Else. 'Bethel, ich weiss nicht, mir kommt vor, ich hab' Dich eigentlich lieber als die Männer.' Besides with the 'lad' (Bub) away, i.e. Otto, she can recuperate her shattered nerves.

There were a number of reasons why Frieda was so on edge, even allowing for the fact that her own psychological state was one of her constant preoccupations. Otto was meant to be correcting the proofs of *Das Freud'sche Ideogenitätsmoment und seine Bedeutung im manisch-depressiven Irresein Kraepelins* which was published later that year. He was also meant to be writing a paper on 'Die cerebrale Sekundärfunktion' for the International Congress of Psychiatry at Amsterdam in September 1907. In a letter of 28 April 1907 from Munich, Frieda instructs Else that Otto must be made to finish this work. Otto obsessively held on to proofs. It is also most likely that he was taking too many drugs in this period. Frieda believed in her husband's career and, in retrospect, we can see that this was a crucial juncture in Otto's intellectual development as well as his stability. Baby Peter Gross we have mentioned.

Then, in addition, Frieda Weekley had appeared in Munich that spring, probably at the beginning of April, visiting Frieda Gross.[2] Later that summer Otto wrote to Frieda Weekley, 'Do you still remember how you chose me in your wonderful aristocratic way?' (Gross and Weekley, 1990: 188). Under the freedom pact it is entirely plausible that Frieda Gross would have known about both affairs. Otto's philosophy was to keep everything in the open. Secret affairs belonged to a repressive culture. This might explain her reluctance to journey to Heidelberg with Otto (although Marianne Weber does report in a letter to Sophie Rickert that she and Max had met Otto and Frieda Gross at the Jaffés on the 23 April) (Weber, 1990: 394, n. 2.).

When eventually Frieda Weekley met up with her sister in Heidelberg (we don't know exactly when – probably in May), Frieda discovered her sister was pregnant and Else went ballistic about Frieda's affair. As Frieda Weekley recorded it in a letter to Otto later that summer:

> ... if I wasn't so pleased for her about the baby, I'd envy her for it, I'd like to see her again my last memory of her is dramatic and not a happy one, our meeting in Heidelberg was quite in the manner of 'Brunnhild und Krimhild' I can laugh now but at the time it cut us both to the quick. (Gross and Weekley, 1990: 196)

Undoubtedly this was the principal factor that led Else to start an affair with a doctor named Völcker and to tell Otto about it. In Letter 5, later, Otto realizes he knows this person and he vents his rage. He also complained extensively of Else's 'jealous revenge' to Frieda Weekley (Gross and Weekley, 1990: 174–9). This is the background to Letters 6 and 7 in which he tries to recover his position after insulting Völcker as belonging to the 'levelling of society' and the 'lower caste' and after accusing Else of 'crime' and 'perversion'. Otto's own rhetoric is Nietzschean 'yea-saying' and the affirmation of a higher sort of person who belongs to the peaks under the sun and not in the valleys. In Letter 8 he recovers Else's affection after a telephone conversation and asserts his own erotic creed with considerable force, to the effect that the Erotic transcends mere lust, which is merely the animal pleasure of two people as opposed to the Erotic as the creation of a union greater than the two.

Letter 9 records his struggle with withdrawal from drugs, which Else must have insisted upon probably during his stay in April in Heidelberg. In Letter 9, around July/August, he confirms he has the love of all three women. This was Otto's high point, personally and theoretically, his Zarathustra moment. It was also his moment of greatest danger, since it was the love of three women who had so intellectually elevated him. As Frieda Weekley noted, 'such a love mustn't go downhill, the others must be considered and you won't find 3 people like the 3 of us on every street-corner'. Otto recognized the danger himself in a letter to Frieda Weekley, 'I have felt in myself *too much* creative power, too many high intentions – there is a sentence in Heraclitus that is dreadfully true: the sun dare not exceed the bounds of its course – otherwise the spirits of revenge would seize it. – Now I feel it is *me* they are about to grab' (Gross and Weekley, 1990: 174) At the time he feared Völcker would poison his relationship with Else, but what most likely turned Else against him was his return to drugs. On 17 August Frieda Gross reported her worries about Otto to Else, and it may have been the forthcoming conference at Amsterdam that might have caused Otto to relapse.

Once Else had withdrawn her love for Otto, Frieda Gross would have been reduced to helplessness in the face of her husband. If the strong Else could not keep Otto on track, and Else's letter of 15 December (below) was a devastating documentation of his failings, what hope was there for Frieda? In fact she retreated to Else's at Heidelberg for the winter of 1907/8, so marking the start of the separation within their marriage. Otto kept corresponding with Frieda Weekley into the year of 1908. She was desperate to liberate herself from her marriage with Weekley, but fearful of the risk of endangering her children. Else eventually warned her sister of just how dangerous a prospect Otto was.

> You have to remember the tremendous shadows around the light – can't you see how he almost destroyed Frieda's life? That he's not able to constrain himself for even a quarter of an hour, whether it be for a person or an objective value? As a 'lover' he's incomparable, but a person doesn't consist of that alone. God it's useless to say anything. You are under that tremendous shadow of suggestion which emanates from him and which I myself have felt. (quoted in Green, 1988: 53)

Otto's fall – from the Three Graces – plunged him out of orbit. He didn't fall to ground but entered a series of spectacular and eccentric orbits, some of which drew him into contact with the Jaffés and the Webers in later years, in 1913 and 1914 (see Whimster, 1998). His reply to Else's letter, which is printed by Martin Green, is surprisingly robust and intelligent (Green, 1988: 58–9).

Such is the chronology insofar as it can be pieced together. It does shed a contextual light on the letters and their significance. But much of their impact must remain unknown. How, for instance, did they affect Else? What effect did the arrival of the small bulging envelopes with their coarse handwriting – like a felt tip – have on the Jaffé household when they arrived? Did Else gather the letter up and take it to her room? How did she hold the letter – grasped in her lap quickly turning the pages, or at arm's length held by finger tips? The imagination fills the space of what cannot be known. All we have are the letters; not the affair but the writing of love; not the passion but the violence of words.

The Letters of Otto Gross to Else Jaffé

The Translations

Postcard
Sender: Dr Otto Gross, München, Zieblandstr. 12/III
To: Frau Dr Else Jaffé, Heidelberg
Date stamped at Heidelberg, 2.2.07

Dear Else,
The first person I saw was M[ühsam]!, whose business is seemingly at an end and with whom I now sit in Café Stephanie.[3] I can use that. Otto.

Letter 1
My Else,
I must write yet again <u>such</u> a letter as previously – there is just a good hour in which there is uncertainty and the flickering of hope and also a last belief in happiness that will not yet die – there are still a couple of rays of sunshine in which I can still greet the day.

I can still speak to you once more of love – that I can do so arrived suddenly like a wonderful gift. It came through a couple of new and dizzying perspectives which threw everything into confusion – it was as if everything would rise up and cancel each other out with nothing left but a stillness – and high and great before me stands nothing other than this immense and wonderful love – and now within myself there is a quite specific, warm lustre of youth, which tomorrow will be gone, and a hope and a belief in myself – and the many, many colours and lights of the ascending life which give a splendour to everything. Today for the first time I have become conscious of their magnificence and tomorrow they will be no more, tomorrow they will be gone forever, and in life the first signs of fading and disappearance. And this night, it is still there and this strong, hot, magnificent love, this night carries within it something like joy. I can speak to you of love and greet you with my love as before. Oh Else, I have never otherwise understood what this love, this happiness has been – how it all was so very much more than I understood, how far more beautiful and richer still in wonderful happiness. You unspeakably beloved, it was so wonderfully beautiful!

And something tremendous will be missing – that will never reach completion. Else, I no longer understand this – can something like this really be lost? I still want to tell you something tremendous – even today to put into words the tremendous love – I have to love you with an unspeakable love, so hot and strong. And now having grasped your beauty as never before – 'invincible love' as you recently said – I believe that is my destiny henceforwards. Else, I will never let you go!

Letter 2 [page 6 of a missing letter]

. . . all that makes her admirable – I would very much like to help her and I think that she must have more influence on Edgar than anyone else.[4] Else, if in the end Edgar was at last free from this ill-fated love for you – Else do you see the prospects that open up with this possibility? Else, it is a fraud and a shiver of wild hope – but for Edgar it is after all only a misfortune to be with you – and both of us, for whom the hours and years full of unheard possibilities trickle away – we whose love is strangled by the narrow bounds of time – Else – Your Otto.

Letter 3

My Else,

I will telegraph you early tomorrow – you must not be angry with me for that, I am no longer able to stand the worry. You know of course that Edgar said in his letter that you urgently needed to recuperate and that therefore you do not write yourself because you are not well. And since then no more news and no answer. Or perhaps you no longer like me? Please tell me outright whatever it is – only not this silence which takes away all my strength. Else, have I then displeased you? – Yes, if only it was something – if only you are well – and then if you could love me just a little bit.

Else, are you perhaps angry that I approved of Schiemann's requests? Further: obviously totally without my agreement, he has written wholly on his own account a formal begging letter to Edgar, for which I have no responsibility!! Understand me correctly: I am whole-heartedly happy if he gets something from you, only for God's sake I hope you [Ihr] do not get annoyed with me – that is much more important to me than how Frank fares. I don't know whether this goes against comradeship – if your [Deine] feelings are put at risk, then for me all friends will become completely insignificant.

Please, please write to me soon, I know not whether I may still say: my Else. I love you so.

Your Otto.

Letter 4

My Else,

I love you with an insatiable yearning, with a pressing desire to have you by my side now – and to feel myself great and free in your love – Else – I long for the immeasurable fullness of your love – that your love in its engulfing and glowing unfathomableness carries me again to the heights – as before – Else, I don't know what would become of me, if it were no longer so. Else what have you given to me – how did you raise me up and make me great with the yea-saying of your love? – with the yea-saying of an unfathomable soul, in which I knew myself to be justified – knew myself blessed. How have you redeemed all the sources of my best possibilities – given me the fructifying belief in myself in whom you have believed. Only now do I see what you gave to me at that time, how my life has ascended, deepened and developed. I knew I was confirmed by you at that time, if only I went forwards on my own resources and when I moved away from everyone else, you remained for me, who you were. Beloved – I could at this time look forwards to life with such a perfect confidence – it was as though nothing could subjugate me.

I send you the first part of that work which is for you – in this work I have begun to move out of the great shadows and on my way, to work beyond Nietzsche and Freud.[5] And that I was capable of this confidence – have become capable after long, long resignation! – this was the new life energy which I obtained from you. Else, we never have enough time to speak. Were we to meet sometime, then I could speak to you about my work and my plans and the development of my production, then you would know what I owe to you. And above everything stands for me the one thing, that you have made me better – that you have freed in me the great power of the will to give – all this you probably know already. I've often said it to you. You should only remember what your love has made of me – and give your love to me again as you loved me at the time: trusting....

Else, give this to me again, the trusting love – the belief in myself – and even a little joy about myself. My life had become so rich and sunny through the consciousness of existing for your joy, of being simply so for your joy – to know this joy which has made me free and strong! – and I shall always long for it.

I must still say to you that just now I am totally overcome by a terrible yearning, which in part is also because Friedl [Frieda Weekley] has just given me the most joyful hopes. Out of this joy it is essential for me, Else, to have you again – to be allowed to exist for your joy again . I feel that I will lose the capacity for joy altogether, if the relationship between you and me is not again what it was then.
Answer soon, beloved, soon –
Your Otto.

Letter 5
My Else,
You know that with the deepest, I would say, knowing sadness I have never looked into the future together with you. I have the ill-fated eye to see all the last secrets of a soul and this is destined to cause me pain. This is exactly the case now, as in your letter there stands a gesture of your soul before my gaze when you promised me happiness sometime in the future – when at no time have I been able to believe in this – when we have talked of our next meeting and I could feel that this future happiness was no more than a dream. Do you still remember everything, Else – how you have often consoled me, how often you have laughed so when we have talked about this very next meeting and

then when every time I had to add: 'If you actually <u>still love</u> me then....' Do you still know that, Else? You – can you now also understand, what for weeks has really tortured me – <u>why</u> I was so <u>unsettled</u> about you? Your silence and your last letters – over the whole recent period it's been like a great nightmare for me – You will also know it Else: I have felt every single hour of happiness with you with all the splendour and the melancholy of a farewell feast –

Else, I have a great favour to ask you – don't do this one thing <u>ever again</u> – don't overcome me by making me <u>small</u>! I feel this coming again – it cannot be a pure belief that I did not separate the concepts clearly in the problem of 'absolute values'. It was already there at an earlier time, Else. That hurt me at the time more than anything <u>else</u>, Else, and if <u>this time you were objectively right – subjectively</u> the same secret will was there as was there before. Else, don't do it. Else, for God's sake be great and honourable towards what's been and for your own memory – your own recollections in later times. Else <u>don't do that one thing</u>!

Else, now I must remind you of something particular about me – simply so that you really understand me. I sense that your earlier reaction to the surgeon has revived again.[6] This much I see primarily <u>as an effect</u> of the start in the change of your feelings for me – and only <u>secondarily</u> as a strengthening factor with a retroactive effect. Else, this gives me a bitter feeling – I believe you will imagine this entirely correctly from the outset! – the feeling of having to compete, of the <u>juxtaposition</u> to a man whose type is defined for all time by my manner to you – whose social <u>equality with me</u> remains the expression of a stupid and bad <u>coincidence</u> – the expression of a social order which <u>I</u> find, for as long as I could think, unnatural and grotesque – which itself again only signifies the expression of the levelling, that is, <u>the destructive</u> historical forces. Here, a <u>real instinct</u> is alive in me – a <u>law</u> becoming flesh of the <u>unique</u>, age-old and immortal sexual morality demanded by life itself – the higher breeding instinct of the <u>separation of the castes</u>. To jump over the gulf between the castes – that in every really natural form of society was <u>the sexual crime</u> – I say 'perversion' instead of 'crime'. Else, for God's sake please do not misunderstand me – I feel the necessity to tell you <u>everything</u> that is going on inside me. I want to be completely understood by you. Believe me, life would be easier not having a knowledge of the caste hierarchy.

Else, I must now ask you for an answer to a question. I feel the complete <u>necessity to speak with you</u>, to be together with you, when we are not constrained and hindered by any <u>external</u> demands whatever they may be – that we must now for <u>truth's</u> sake create for ourselves the <u>same</u> situation, which for the sake of happiness we had thought so right. And indeed now <u>as soon as possible</u>. But now consider: that should only then be, if we are allowed to expect that our <u>truth</u> will be, that everything will be again as once before. Else, if that is <u>gone</u>, then it should be ended <u>with the celebration of joy</u> which we celebrated in our last meeting – and for the sake of our <u>memories</u> we will <u>renounce that</u>, ending the incomparable beauty with the greatest imaginable sadness. Else, until now our last shared memory is the incomparable day of joy at Wolfrathshausen[7] – until now what was <u>consummated</u> is also the <u>last</u> shared experience. That remains for us in the future as something of incomparably high value, whose eternal memory should really only be endangered by the blossoming of life itself. Else, you must now ask yourself with all your strictness the deepest truth, whether your feeling for me has started to decline – and if you recognize this in the depths of your soul – that your experience with me has now run its course – then destiny has been kind to us for the sake of our shared memory and the radiant purity of this memory. And if you find another answer in your soul, if you believe in the possibility that our lives are to be determined by a common happiness, then call me to you – Else, then call me soon? I will come immediately you call me. Then, Else, make the agony of waiting as short as possible, since during this wait, during this uncertainty every hour is torture. – Your Otto.

Letter 6

My Else,

my dear, dear – I wait anxiously for any news from you – I worry about you – particularly after the fear in the night of travelling, fear until the telegram came – and then even more anxiety, and always the questioning – Else, beloved, I know nothing about you, nothing about how you are – I know nothing about our great hope and whether it still exists. Else, I notice how many anxious thoughts about you I have to repress – while writing now the worry rises up. Send me news soon, Else – best of all by telephone! Tomorrow morning Sunday I will be in Café Stephanie from 11–1 and then again in the evening from 7 o'clock – please, please call me there!

Think of it, I must endure such worry: how you are getting on, Else, and whether you are not sad and how you were later on in the night just gone – you dearly beloved, you!

Else, about here I will tell you, as soon as I am clearer and in a quiet mood. Frieda [Gross] is again beautiful as in the final period before the birth, and is clear and quiet and freed from all disturbing nervousness – so quiet – beautiful, as I had not yet known her. She is much more seriously fond of M. [Erich Mühsam],[8] as I had expected, and M. is touchingly happy and in every respect faultlessly noble – To me Frieda is loving as never before, and I would now be completely happy with her, if I had the courage to believe fully in happiness – until now it is still so incredible and mysteriously beautiful – her nature is now like the expression of a profoundly serious and joyous love – in which I do not yet dare to believe.

Else – I have to think of you endlessly – with a burning, tremendous love – with anxiety and hope and tenderness and yearning – farewell beloved!
Otto
Little Peter is incredibly dear, but I can scarcely look at him, I must always worry about the other one ...[9]
Greetings to Edgar, I look forward to seeing him!

[Letter continues]
Friday
Forgive me that I dare once more to write to you – this does not need an answer, nor any positive action – but I must make good the blame in order to correct false pictures, which I have caused. Both the last letters are true, what I have written about my love and about my view of the world is true. The express letter after the first telephone call is terribly false, the product of my

withdrawal [from drugs]. This symbolization of social hatred against the man and his race through sinful and impossible slanders against you is dreadful and always alien to me, a sick form of expression of a physical aversion against something in you. That you are continually new every new day turns this symbolization into madness. Your body is holy to me for all time – and do absolve me from the blame that I could think of this depiction. It was for you the superhuman effort, not to fall back into morphine, the aversion against him, the horror, of seeing you going away from me to the enemy in my fearful imaginings – the suggestion of language and its meanness, simply because I myself had once contributed this and therefore stood in connection with it – for me this is incomprehensible like a terrible dream! Forgive me this sin of madness! Because of this iniquity I have become a stranger to you – don't let this iniquity stick to me! – It is true that it dejects me terribly that my directly opposite type is affirmed by you – that there must be two souls which alternate in you, the one with him and his world, the other which was kindred to me. . . . That his part of your soul must perceive me at least as a stranger, while my part promised itself to me as your best – here in this form must be represented the incompatibility, which in my view of the world expressed itself as caste division. That he and I as friends of one person exclude one another – that is a truth – which has crushed me, when I guessed his identity – and what drove me right out of my mind was that you had not seen the same thing, that you – after everything that you knew about me and my opinion of this man and also his characteristic hate against me – that you held relationships to him and to me as compatible. Here the shock before the incomprehensible really took hold of me – and what now remains as truth of that iniquitous letter is again this: one must now awaken a complete soul and a life sunken into the depths so that you once again become the person I knew and love so unutterably. Well before the change there was a telephone conversation between us in the evening. There you were completely with me and you were quite finished with him – then my letter arrived, which estranged and separated you from me. Now I wonder, if in that same moment had we met after all, whether you would not have found entire and total grace in me. Then the experience simply would have been one of going beyond this man and everything he has represented to you. Then you would have been right after all, that was my principle in my sense – then you would have been right to tell me 'in my arms', that it was he and that you were now free from him – just as I really have often advised you, and how I would have thanked you with the greatest joy – and you would have been right that 'something wonderful was awaiting us'. You would then have been safe and remained in my world.

And had you wished simply not to deny and reject the memory, that would not have been a tendency towards what is common nor a lack of distance and differentiation but rather it would have been a recollection of your own development – of all your longing and wrestling and striving and hoping and erring of all your own, which would have been behind you and overcome – 'abreacted'[10] in one last return of 'converted' sensuality to its origins, to an open and pure sensuality – then it was a purification, then it was great and pure! – and it must have remained valued and undamaged for you as the symbol of your own striving soul. And then you would have arrived, have come to me so pure and beautiful, purified to the core as never before.

If I have hit on the truth in this sense then I, and only I, have pushed you away from me and into the opposite. Then mine is the guilt for which I do not dare to ask for forgiveness – I must bear it, if such a guilt can be borne. What is required for the return of this love which redeems the lowest and the highest is not only a continuous transformation of the soul but actually the recovery of a long lost other soul.

Now today I believe that in this terrible destruction and despair I have completely overlooked one possibility which all of a sudden becomes clear to me and perhaps is the truth. What I say from now on is an assumption – I believe though that I should place this at your disposal just in case.

Letter 7

My Else,

Now you will have got my second letter and will know what's what – You must have taken me for terribly stupid when my first letter appeared to be the answer to your letter! – Isn't that so, now you know everything, how I mean it – you unspeakably beloved! You, on the telephone yesterday, that was a terrible torture of Tantalus – I was so despairingly in love with your voice – I saw and felt you – the magic of your fine nuances and this new clarity, and the wonderful sureness that now comes to it – your voice yesterday was so pure and faithful and it had the resonance of newly discovered depths.

Do you know, I have longed so much for your friendship, for the dependability that rates higher than anything unpredictable – do you know why now and only now I can reckon on this sort of friendship? Why I have this unconquerable suspicion of all the unpredictble 'dark and great passions'? And then, why I know I can now depend on you? You see – this is my leading ideal – the great elemental force of the soul, the erotic must be like water – blessing, fructifying, loved, mastered – and that is my guiding knowledge: He who rapes the erotic, the erotic will rape him. Only he who recognizes the erotic and affirms it, as it actually is – only he masters it, even to the extent that he can promise to be always himself.[11] Else you know now approximately what that means: I can count on always dealing with you yourself – do you understand this feeling of unendingly pure air in which I now breathe – breathing bliss in every thought of you?

Farewell, adored and beloved, farewell!

Letter 8

My Else,

Please write to me as many lovely things as possible in the time to come – and without reciprocity, for I am strengthening my abstinence [from morphine] and under these circumstances I can only manage stiff and meagre sentences while actually longing especially for love and light – and moreover one draws stupid conclusions from each nothing and one believes oneself abandoned or in other ways sees ghosts. Anyway relatively soon I hope to have redeemed my looks accordingly.

Else, could perhaps Munich be considered instead of Stuttgart? Because I think I will probably recover my looks sufficiently before I can travel. I crave feverishly to be with you. Else, in the future would it please you to be together with me? You would <u>also</u> have <u>Frieda</u> – luckily I have <u>more</u> to offer than myself alone.

Come! Else, come!

P.S. But not right now, I am still not <u>handsome</u> enough for you!!

Letter 9

My Else,

<u>now I do have</u> a document, that you love me – as in the dreams of my highest longings.... Else, your letter has given me unending jubilation and a great and pure <u>stillness</u> – the sheer harmonious beauty in which love becomes a blessing to everything maturing – what a precious maturity and what sweetness you had saved up! The green chrysanthemum[12] – Else, a gesture of a fresh and youthful innocence lives again in your letter – just as when you once nudged me with your lovely head in our little country house. I'm always transported <u>there</u> again, whenever I re-read your letter – I want to try and hold your head again in my hands, so near to me do you often feel then – <u>if</u> only I could hold you and kiss you! And rejoice that you want to tell me the story '<u>in</u> <u>my arms</u>' – *dans l'intimité* – do you remember? Rejoice, above all, that we now <u>understand</u> one another, understanding each other in the utmost yea-saying to a happy, flourishing life – Else, with the settling of our last dangerous difference have you drawn the poisoned thorn from your soul and our happiness? Else, do you really know that <u>this</u> moment is <u>not</u> such a one as has often been experienced? That <u>this</u> kind of love and trust that we now give to each other, has <u>not often</u> been lived by anyone. It is the <u>first</u> blossoming of a new <u>world</u>-spring that flowers for the beauty of <u>our</u> love! You, this new spring of a re-awakening human innocence – is this not like the kiss that awakens Sleeping Beauty?

Else, I thank you that you thought of extinguishing the last shadows of that sombre memory in a flood of light and blessing love.

Else, with <u>this</u>, completely undreamed of, a wonderful strength of loving has been set free – out of the depths – a new happy force of a rejoicing love wants to carry you to the sun. Else, the love for you which only now realizes itself in its limitlessness – <u>only now since the last confining pressure</u> <u>is wiped away</u> – only now, since I now know that my love is allowed to <u>enjoy</u> <u>itself</u> in its expansive strength. Else at this moment of understanding that <u>you</u> now <u>freely permit</u> my love for your sister – from your own fullness of strength and love and joy you <u>freely permit</u> the will to every pleasure – in <u>this</u> moment of blessed understanding <u>I have felt you and me so namelessly merging</u> <u>together and mysteriously being united.</u> I cannot describe it to you, Else – I just want to be able to say to you somehow what an inexpressible happiness it is for me, <u>to be now united with you.</u> I can probably say this only in your arms, only in the ecstasy of soul to soul – woe to me at the moment of fatal happiness and in the symbol of the utmost union.

Else, farewell – and may you <u>enjoy</u> happiness – farewell, tell me – do you understand me entirely? Do you understand, <u>why</u> I am so happy?

One Letter: Else Jaffé to Otto Gross
15 December

Dear Otto,

I will at least not give you grounds for any justified reproach that 'we' never answered your letters. Of course you won't hear anything from me which will put an end to your state of not knowing everything inside-out, since I can only write to you as a spectator of the situation – I cannot say anything about Frieda [Gross], she must do that for herself. You know yourself how difficult it is for another person to work you out! So you should take nothing of what I write as coming from her indirectly – it was the fear that you might do so that has stopped me up to now from writing to you.

You are quite wrong if you believe that I very much want to see you as inconsistent. I simply believe that life does not allow to us to live without compromises. I willingly admit that I first thought you were somehow forced to give up the relationship with Rega U[llmann].[13] Now I see the conflict quite differently – this relationship and your (as it must seem to those of us outside it) inconsiderateness to Frieda [Gross] are only symptoms of a development deeply rooted in your nature.

Friedele was quite right when she said to me in the summer, 'Don't you see that Otto is the prophet of whom it can only be said: He who is not for me is against me.'

Now to a certain extent the prophet has consumed in his fire the last remnants of the human being, Otto, and has taken from him the capacity to love persons individually in their individuality and according to their essence. That is an old, old story – and that other prophet said of his brothers: I have no brothers – you (the disciples) are my brothers! For you there are now only followers of your teaching (something of this was always there), no longer a particular wife loved for her essential self. It can scarcely be any other way. Now naturally one can imagine that a wife renounces her personal needs in love and, totally consumed in the holy fire, makes every sacrifice to remain next to him in whose goals she completely believes. But what if she cannot completely believe, Otto?

If she cannot completely believe, could she not still remain with the human being for the sake of her own love – but would the prophet tolerate this without continually wrestling with her soul, without himself disintegrating in this struggle?

This is how I see the situation. I won't say definitively that you love Frieda less than before, although – measured by the usual standards – that could hardly be doubted. At any rate the quality of feeling has changed. (And you certainly don't think of little Peter any more!)

I must say one thing, however. It seems quite pointless to make any sacrifice for you or your causes, because you are destroying your capacity to achieve anything by your senseless attacks on your own health. We really don't know how much of what makes your ideas so troublesome for us – the lack of discrimination, the need for nuances and the capacity to distinguish individual human beings – is caused in the end by morphine. You already know how this makes living with others so difficult.

I am sad, Otto, when I think of you – it seems to me you are going further and further away, and even the hope of being with you now and then as with a friend becomes so small when I think of everything that you would demand assent to. And life settles over everything that has happened and kills it quite dead – isn't that awful?

Your Else.

Love and Eroticism: The Cases of Otto Gross and Max Weber

To draw the contrasts between Max Weber and Otto Gross is to summon extremes. Weber was an elite member of the progressive cultural Protestant leadership in Germany. He was a reformer and a modernizer. As an academic he pioneered new standards of objectivity and science. As a person he was disciplined, ascetic, virginal and of a sometimes passionate disposition. One cannot go quite so far as saying each man stood for entirely different things. Weber was not the typical chauvinist and authoritarian Wilhelmine patriarch, and he campaigned for equality of rights for women. He did not belong to the *Gründerzeit* generation as did the hated figure of Otto's father Hans, and he belonged to the academic avant-garde as opposed to the conservative establishment of Berlin University.

It is Else Jaffé who makes the contrast possible and inevitable. She wanted to bring the two men together. Otto's prophetic mode and radical intellect *might* have been taken in hand by Weber's expansive mind and his interest in strong value positions. Weber might have been expected to think through the consequences of the programme of affirmative eroticism. For Otto, Weber presented a psychoanalytic challenge of some complexity. Weber was repressed but he appeared to practise this as a deliberate form of conduct. He was not anti-erotic, rather he sublimated sexuality into eroticism and into cultural forms that would now be described as decadent. He was an ascetic who knew well enough Nietzsche's critique of puritanism in the *Genealogy of Morals*. Weber had made these choices as a young man, certainly by the time that Else met him at Freiburg University in the mid-1890s. By the mid-1900s Else also knew that Weber was being increasingly restricted, not to say throttled by these choices. In Otto's terms he had cut himself off from the vital forces of eroticism. Weber would have regarded this as vitalist nonsense, but Else, as a confidante of Marianne and prized by Max, would have known he was plagued by depression, incapable of maintaining balanced emotional relationships with people, and was unable to find any way out of his psychological maze.

In submitting Otto Gross's paper to the *Archiv für Sozialwissenschaft und Sozialpolitik* through Weber, Else was trying to bring about a dialogue between the two men. In reality the gulf between the two was too wide to be bridged and Weber's reply to her in September 1907 is a tirade of no-saying (Runciman, 1978: 383–8; Helle, 1994: 214–23). Weber's central objection to Otto Gross's article was its contravention of scientific value freedom, which was canonical to Weber's conception of the *Archiv*. Weber thought Freudianism had yet to establish its scientific credentials, although he did acknowledge the value of Freud's insights for cultural and religious studies.

Otto Gross's programme advocated affirmative eroticism as a way of break-ing through the repressive structures of patriarchalism. Weber said, quite nastily, this was to dress base sexual instincts in the language of theory. He repeated his complaint in a subsequent letter to Marianne, saying that Otto believes it dirty not to express the erotic. Anybody, opines Weber, with any psychological knowledge can recognize the level from which Otto Gross is operating. Gross needs a formalism to save him from a descent into goatish instincts. Gross shows a complete lack of discrimination which any psy-chiatrist would say is a form of degeneration (Weber, 1990: 463).

Weber's crude psychological reductionism prompts a closer look at the linkages Gross did pioneer between love and eroticism and its praxis. In this field Gross established the 20th-century tradition of a libertarian psychology – the precursor of Wilhelm Reich, R.D. Laing and the post-structural anarchism of Deleuze and Guattari. Weber, as will be noted, took the field of the erotic into the already established tendency of decadence. Gross wanted to turn Freud in a Nietzschean direction, some might now say, 'back to Nietzsche'. Gross's Nietzscheanism was the strident naturalism of *Thus Spoke Zarathustra* and *The Twilight of the Idols*, especially the last which opens with an account of philosophical decadence and the love of argument and dialectic of the mind by the urbanite. Nietzsche demanded a return to 'natural instincts' and a naturalism in morality in place of Christianity's castration of passion and the elevation of the masses to equality with the strongest. Social Darwinism had led to the survival of the weak and the humbling of the strong. What was needed was not the degenerate anarchism of socialism but a noble anarchism of the individual. This is the point from which Gross develops his new sexual morality. Out of the 'Epoch of Decadence' as he called it in his letters to Frieda Weekley (Gross and Weekley, 1990: 188–9) and in drawing Else Jaffé toward erotic purity (Letters 6, 7 and 9), a new deep, social type will emerge. In living the erotic ideal a new inequality and strength will arise. This is Nietzsche's 'pathos of distance' (Nietzsche, 1968: 91), the necessary contempt for the masses, the degeneration of life and the levelling of democracy. The new ascending life will have its superiority marked through beauty. This is the Nietzschean theme which Otto Gross acts out repeatedly in his letters to both Frieda Weekley and Else Jaffé.

And, of course, as we know, Otto did act out his schema. Nietzsche, compared to Gross, was a mere fantasist. Gross inserted himself at the centre of his new erotic ideal. He launched his ideals into anarchist thought which in this period was one of the strongest currents outside official politics. The elevation of the erotic ideal was, as we also see, achieved through the love of three women, who for a period of time in the summer of 1907, overcame human nature in their unanimity for Otto Gross. Otto was incapable of holding and retaining this trust, yet his Nietzschean gospel of the erotic did penetrate and affect anarchist thought, permanently (Michaels, 1983: 21–3). Some of his elitism does not read too prettily to late 20th-century ears, but it has to be remembered that in this period there was a huge swell in anarchist, communitarian and pacifist thought that culminated in the meeting of student fraternities and other 'New Age' groups in the Hohen Meissner in 1913 (Nipperdey, 1993: 121-3.) It was the First World War that wiped out this youthful, civilizing force (see the recent essay by Carl Levy, 1998: 83–109.)

For Weber, as well as Carl Jung and Freud, one might note, Gross's engagement was a threat to their own scientific projects. Freud wrote to Karl Abraham in 1909, 'I believe that in publicly announcing certain things one would saw off the branch on which civilization rests; one undermines the impulse to sublimation. . . . The extreme attitude represented by Gross is wrong and dangerous to the movement' (quoted in Jones, 1955, II: 139). Gross preached 'abreaction', a cathartic purging of built-in repressions through free sexuality. Gross's anarchism meant that he saw little to save in civilization. On sublimation Weber's thought ran in the same direction as Freud's. For Weber, eroticism was a culture of sublimation and refinement, and ran directly against Gross's naturalism.

Aside from Weber's rejection letter of September 1907 there is a less well-known incident which is disclosed in the *Max Weber Gesamtausgabe, Briefe* (1994). At the end of 1909 Else started a long-lasting relationship with Weber's younger brother Alfred. This caused havoc in the Jaffé household and, to a lesser extent, in the extended Weber family. Marianne and Max Weber were called in to intervene and broker various compromise arrangements, arising not least from the violently antagonistic relationship that had blown up between Alfred Weber and Edgar Jaffé. The disclosure in the *Gesamtausgabe* is that Max Weber himself declared his love to Else at this time. His suit was turned down and their relationship subsequently deteriorated so that in 1914 they were refusing to meet one another (Whimster, 1998: 58).

During the crisis that marked the start of Else's relationship with Alfred Weber, Max had gone round to visit Else to speak with her alone. This was a declaration of love by Max himself, which Else described in a letter to Alfred the next day.

> He was like the embodiment of a godly love who says: Go forth my child, live, suffer, be happy – I let you go with difficulty but you belong to mother earth and to those who are your brothers. But do not forget, I am always there for you, I am close to you, no destiny can push us apart. I wait.

And to Alfred Else commented, 'he has a truer love for me than you! Yes. Because you love life more than anything and therefore me, since I love it with you. – And he has so little' (Weber, 1994: 367).

Actually Max had not declared his love for Else, this is Else's inference. He sublimated his love for her by reading a poem to her. In Otto's terms he repressed his emotions, failed to abreact, failed to say, 'Ich liebe dich.' (In Else's account she has Max address her as 'Du', but in his letters to her, Else was still 'Sie'.) In Freud's terms Weber sublimated his libido into, or through, an artistic form. But from reading his academic writings – the '*Zwischenbetrachtung*' – we may infer that Weber was sublimating his desire *into eroticism*. The erotic was not, as for Otto, a theoretical practice, nor was it, as for Freud, a displacement into something different – from libido to art, from id to civilization. Rather the erotic was a cultivated form of sexuality, an intensification of what would otherwise be brute natural instinct (Whimster, 1995: 447–62). In his personal life, as David Chalcraft has established, Weber enjoyed eroticism, in its cultural form, yet always withheld its physical enjoyment – a tantric practice of his own making. From the early 1890s he possessed a number of cycles of erotic etchings by Klinger whose theme was that sexual consummation was succeeded by decay and death. In the same way Weber celebrated Wagner's *Tristan und Isolde* as a story of forbidden love celebrated only at night and in death (see Gane, 1993: 156–72; Chalcraft, 1998: 197–214). Weber's eroticism was decadent; literally so because it terminated in death, and doubly so, for Otto, because it was a repression of life and hygiene. In the critical episode in January 1910 between Else and Max, the force of love must have severely tried the conventions of eroticism.

One can conclude in this way because Weber reprises Otto's themes, and Else wanted it so. But if one reads the poem that Weber read out to Else, it becomes apparent that Weber's world was a tone poem entirely different to that of Otto's. The poem is 'Requiem' by Rilke. Max Weber was likening Else to a water sprite dancing around the figurehead of a ship. The mariner wants to grasp hold of the sprite but the sprite cannot be secured. She has '*Leichtsein*', what now translates as 'lightness of being'. Rilke's poem condemns those who try to hold love and restrict its freedom. This was Otto's guilt. Max 'who has so little' mortifies himself with the lines: 'We need in love to practise only this:/ Letting each other go. For holding on/comes easily; we do not need to learn it.' (Wir haben, wo wir lieben, ja nur dies:/ einander lassen; denn daß wir uns halten, das fällt uns leicht und ist nicht erst zu lernen) (Bly, 1981: 157).

Appendix: Letters of Otto Gross to Else Jaffé –The German Texts[14]

Postcard
Sent from München, received in Heidelberg, stamped 2.2.07
An: Frau Dr Else Jaffé, Heidelberg
Absender: Dr Otto Gross, München, Zieblandstr. 12/III

Liebe Else,
Der Erste, den ich gesehen habe, ist M[ühsam]!, dessen Sache nun augenscheinlich zu Ende ist und mit dem ich jetzt im Stephanie zusammensitze. Ich kann das brauchen.
Otto.

Otto Gross to Else Jaffé, Letter 9

Source: Published by kind permission of Tufts University Archives.

Letter 1

Meine Else, ich muss Dir doch noch einmal einen <u>solchen</u> Brief wie früher schreiben – es ist gerade noch eine gute Stunde, in der noch Ungewissheit ist und kleine Flammen von Hoffnung und auch noch ein letztes Glauben an Glück, das noch nicht sterben will – es sind noch ein paar Sonnenstrahlen da – ich kann den Tag noch grüssen –

Ich kann Dir noch einmal von Liebe sprechen – dass ich's noch einmal thuen kann, das ist so plötzlich wie ein herrliches Geschenk gekommen – Es kam durch ein paar neue verwirrende Perspectiven, die Alles unklar durcheinander geworfen haben – es war auf einmal so, als ob sich Alles gegenseitig aufheben würde, als wäre nichts mehr übrig als eine Stille – und hoch und gross vor mir steht nichts als diese übergrosse und wunderbare Liebe – und in mir selber ist gerade jetzt noch ein ganz bestimmter warmer Glanz von Jugend, der morgen nicht mehr sein wird – und eine Hoffnung und ein Glauben an mich und viele, viele Farben und Lichter des aufwärtssteigenden Lebens, die alle heute noch wie immer glänzen und die ich heute zum erstenmal ganz bewusst in ihrer Köstlichkeit erkenne und die morgen nicht mehr sein werden – und morgen wird etwas weg sein für immer und im Leben ein erstes Welken und Schwinden – und diese Nacht noch ist es da und diese heisse starke herrliche Liebe trägt diese Nacht noch etwas wie <u>Freude</u> in sich. Oh Du, ich kann Dir da von Liebe reden und Dich mit meiner Liebe grüssen wie sonst – oh Else, ich habe ja niemals sonst begriffen, was diese Liebe, was dieses <u>Glück</u> gewesen ist – wie war doch alles so viel <u>mehr</u> als ich begriffen habe, um wie viel schöner und reicher noch an wunderbarem Glück. Du namenlos Geliebte, es war so wunderbar schön!

Und etwas Ungeheueres wird fehlen – das schliesst sich nicht mehr – Else, ich kann es nicht begreifen – <u>kann</u> etwas Solches denn wirklich verloren gehen? Ich möchte Dir noch Ungeheueres sagen – die ungeheuere Liebe noch heute in Worten sagen – ich muss Dich ja so namenlos lieben, so heiss und stark – gerade jetzt noch Deine Schönheit begreifend wie nie zuvor – 'Liebe unüberwindlich', das hast Du ja neulich erwähnt – ich glaube, das ist mein Schicksal fortan – Dich, Else, krieg' ich nimmer los!

Letter 2

... das Alles macht sie bewunderungswerth – ich möchte <u>ihr</u> gerne helfen und denke, <u>sie müsste auf Edgar besser einwirken als irgendeine</u> – Du, Else, wenn Edgar am Ende noch einmal <u>frei</u> würde von dieser unseligen Liebe zu <u>Dir</u> – Else verstehst Du, die Perspective, die hinter <u>dieser</u> Möglichkeit sich aufthut? Else, es ist ein Schwindel und Schauder von toller <u>Hoffnung</u> – es ist für Edgar doch nur ein <u>Unglück</u>, neben Dir zu sein – und <u>wir</u> beide, denen die Stunden und Jahre voll unerhörter Möglichkeiten verrinnen – wir, deren Liebe die engen Grenzen der beschränkten <u>Zeit</u> zum Ersticken schnüren – Else –
Dein Otto

Letter 3

Meine Else,
Ich werde Dir morgen früh <u>telegraphieren</u> – Du darfst mir darum nicht böse sein, ich halte die Sorge nicht mehr aus. Du weisst doch, dass Edgar in seinem Brief erwähnt hat, dass Du der Erhohlung dringend bedarfst und dass Du <u>deshalb</u> nicht selber schreibst, weil Du nicht wohl bist. Und seither keine Nachricht, keine Antwort mehr – Oder bist Du vielleicht nicht mehr gut auf mich? Bitte sag's doch

heraus, was immer es ist – nur dieses Schweigen nicht, das alle Kräfte zerrinnen macht – Else, hab' ich Dir denn missfallen? – Ja, wenn's nur noch so Etwas ist – wenn Du nur gesund bist – und dann erst wenn Du mich nur noch ein klein wenig lieb haben kannst –

Else, bist Du mir vielleicht böse, dass ich Schiemann's Anliegen befürwortet habe? Ferner: Natürlich ganz ohne mein Dazuthun, ganz auf eigene Faust hat formell einen Pumpbrief an Edgar geschrieben – da kann ich nichts dafür!! Versteh' mich recht: ich freue mich natürlich von ganzem Herzen, wenn er von Euch was kriegt – ich will nur um Gotteswillen nicht, dass Ihr Euch über mich ärgert – das ist mir eben wichtiger als wie es Frank ergeht. Ich weiss nicht, ob das gegen die Kameradschaft ist – wenn Deine Stimmung in Frage kommt, dann werden mir alle Freunde von Herzen nebensächlich –

Bitte, bitte, schreib' mir bald – ich weiss nicht, darf ich denn noch sagen: meine Else? – Ich hab' Dich so lieb –
Dein Otto.

Letter 4
Meine Else,
ich liebe Dich mit unstillbarer Sehnsucht – mit einem drückenden Verlangen, Dich jetzt bei mir zu haben – in Deiner Liebe mich gross und frei zu fühlen – Else – ich sehne mich nach der unmessbaren Fülle Deiner Liebe – dass Deine Liebe wieder in ihrer fluthenden und leuchtenden Unergründlichkeit mich in die Höhe trage – wie ehemals – Else, ich weiss nicht, was mit mir werden soll, wenn's nicht mehr so wird – Else, was hast Du mir doch damals geschenkt – wie hast Du mich erhöht und gross gemacht mit dem Ja-Sagen. Deiner Liebe – mit diesem Ja-Sagen einer unergründlichen Seele, in der ich mich gerechtfertigt wusste – gesegnet wusste – Wie hast Du doch alle Quellen meiner besten Möglichkeiten erlöst – mir den befruchtenden Glauben geschenkt an mich selber, an den Du geglaubt hast – Ich sehe ja doch erst jetzt, was Du mir damals gegeben hast, wie sich mein Leben damals gesteigert und vertieft und entwickelt hat.... Ich wusste mich damals von Dir bestätigt, wenn ich nur aus mir selbst heraus vorwärts gieng – und wenn ich mit Allen aus einander gerathe, Du bliebst mir, die Du warst – Geliebte – ich konnte in dieser Zeit so voller Zuversicht ins Leben schauen – es war, als könnte nichts mehr mich unterdrücken. Ich schicke Dir den ersten Theil jener Arbeit, die Dir zu eigen ist – in dieser Arbeit habe ich das begonnen, mich über die grossen Schatten auf meinem Weg, über Nietzsche und Freud hinüberzuarbeiten – Und dass ich fähig war zu dieser Zuversicht – fähig geworden nach langer, langer Resignation! – Das was doch diese neue Lebensenergie, die ich von Dir bekam –

Else, wir haben ja nie Zeit, genug zu sprechen – kämen wir einmal dazu, dass ich mit Dir an meinen Arbeiten und Entwürfen, die Entwicklung meiner Production besprechen könnte, dann würdest Du wissen, was ich Dir verdanke. Und über Allem steht mir das Eine, dass Du mich besser gemacht hast – dass Du die grosse Kraft des Geben-Wollens in mir befreit hast – Das weisst Du ja wohl schon. Alles – ich hab' Dir's ja schon oft gesagt – Du sollst Dich nur erinnern was Deine Liebe aus mir gemacht – und deine Liebe mir wiedergeben, sowie Du mich damals geliebt hast: vertrauend....

Else, das gieb mir wieder – die vertrauende Liebe – den Glauben an mich und wieder ein wenig Freude an mir – Mein Leben war so reich und sonnig geworden durch das Bewusstsein, zu Deiner Freude da zu sein – zu Deiner Freude gerade so zu sein – Um diese Freude zu wissen, das hat mich frei und stark gemacht! – und darnach sehne ich mich immer.

Ich muss Dir noch sagen dass mich gerade jetzt die Sehnsucht wieder so arg überfällt, das ist z. Th. auch deshalb, weil Friedl mir gerade jetzt die frohesten Hoffnungen schenkt – Aus dieser Freude heraus wird es mir unentbehrlich, Dich, Else, wiederzuhaben – Dir wieder zur Freude dasein zu dürfen – Ich fühle, dass ich die Freudefähigkeit überhaupt verliere, wenn es nicht zwischen Dir und mir wieder so wird wie damals –

Antworte mir bald, Geliebte bald –
Dein Otto.

Letter 5

Meine Else, Du weisst dass ich nie anders als mit einer tiefsten – ich möchte sagen-wissenden Traurigkeit mit Dir zusammen in die Zukunft gesehen habe. Ich habe den unseligen Blick für alle letzten Geheimnisse in einer Seele, aus denen mir Schmerz zu kommen bestimmt ist. So, gerade so wie jetzt aus Deinem Brief ist eine Geste Deiner Seele vor meinem Blick gestanden, wenn Du mir irgend einmal ein Glück in der Zukunft verheissen hast – wenn ich dann eben niemals daran zu glauben vermochte – wenn wir von unserem nächsten Zusammensein geredet haben und ich auch dieses nächstes Glück der Zukunft als nicht viel mehr als einen Traum empfinden konnte. Weisst Du noch Alles, Else – wie oft Du mich getröstet, wie oft Du so herzlich darüber gelacht hast, wenn wir von diesem allernächsten Zusammensein geredet haben und wenn ich auch da wieder jedesmal beifügen musste: '– Wenn Du mich nämlich dann noch lieb hat –' Weisst Du's noch Else? Du – kannst Du jetzt auch verstehen, was mich jetzt wieder schon seit Wochen im Grunde so gemartert hat – warum ich eigentlich um Dich so unruhig war ? Dein Schweigen und Deine letzten Briefe – es war die ganze letzte Zeit wie ein Alb auf mir – Du wirst es auch wissen, Else: ich habe doch jede einzelne Stunde des Glückes mit Dir mit aller Pracht und Schwermuth des Abschiedsfestes gefühlt —

Else, ich habe eine grosse Bitte an Dich. Else – das Eine thu' nicht mehr, dass Du mich damit überwinden willst, dass Du mich klein machst! Ich fühle das wieder kommen – es kann nicht reiner Glaube sein, dass ich im Problem der 'absoluten Werthe' die Begriffe nicht klar geschieden hätte – es war schon früher einmal, Else – das hat mir damals weher gethan als Alles sonst – Else, und wenn Du auch diesmal objectiv Recht hättest subjectiv spricht darum doch derselbe geheime Wille mit wie eben damals – Else, thu's nicht – Else, um Gottes willen sei gross und ehrlich gegen das Gewesene, gegen Deine eigene Erinnerung – Dein eigenes Rückerinnern in später Zukunft – Else, das Eine thu' nicht!

Else, nun muss ich Dich noch an ein bestimmtes Moment in mir erinnern – einfach damit Du mich gut verstehst. Ich fühle heraus, dass Deine frühere Reaction auf den Chirurgen sich wiederbelebt hat – soviel ich sehe im Wesentlichen als Folge der beginnenden Aenderung in Deinem Gefühl für mich höchstens in zweiter Linie als verstärkender Factor auch wieder zurückwirkend. Else, das giebt mir ein bitteres Gefühl – ich glaube, Du wirst es Dir übrigens schon vorneherein ganz richtig vorstellen! – das Gefühl des Concurrierenmüssens, des Nebeneinanderges-telltseins mit einem Menschen, dessen Art eben meiner Art zu Deinem bestimmt ist in aller Ewigkeit – dessen sociale Gleichberechtigung mit mir der Ausdruck eines dummen und bösen Zufalls bleibt – der Ausdruck einer Gesellschaftsordnung, die ich, seitdem ich denken kann, als widernatürlich und grotesk empfinde – die selbst wieder nur den Ausdruck der nivellierenden d.h. der zerstörenden historischen Kräfte bedeutet. Hier ist ein wirklicher Instinct in mir lebendig – das fleischgewordene Gesetz der einzigen vom Leben selbst geforderten uralten und unsterblichen Sexualmoral – der Hochzucht-Instinkt der Kastentrennung. Die Kluft der Kasten zu überspringen – das war in jeder noch wirklich natürlichen Societät das sexuelle Verbrechen – ich sage statt 'Verbrechen': 'Perversität' – Else, versteh' mich um Gottes willen nicht etwa falsch: ich fühle die Nothwendigkeit, Dir Alles zu sagen, was jetzt in meinem Innern vorgeht – ich will von Dir restlos verstanden sein – Glaub' nur, das Wissen um den Kastenrang ist ein Besitz, den nicht zu haben das Leben leichter macht. –

Else, nun muss ich Dich um eine Antwort auf eine Frage bitten – Ich fühle es für mich die vollkommene Nothwendigkeit mit Dir zu sprechen, mit Dir jetzt so zusammen zu sein, dass wir durch keine wie immer beschaffenen Anforderungen von aussen her behindert und eingeschränkt sind – dass wir jetzt um der Wahrheit willen die selbe Situation für uns schaffen müssen, die wir uns um des Glückes willen zurecht gedacht hatten. Und zwar nun mehr sobald als möglich. Nun aber überlege: das soll nur dann sein, wenn wir erwarten dürfen, das unsere Wahrheit sein wird, dass wieder Alles wird wie einst – Else, wenn dass vorbei ist, dann soll es mit dem Fest der Freude beendet sein, das wir bei unserem letzten Zusammensein gefeiert haben – dann wollen wir doch um unserer Erinnerung willen darauf verzichten, das unvergleichlich Schöne mit dem denkbar Traurigsten zu beschliessen – Else, bisher ist unsere letzte gemeinsame Erinnerung der unvergleichliche Freudentag von Wolfrathshausen – bisher ist das Vollendete zugleich das letzte gemeinsam Erlebte: das bleibt für alle Zukunft ein derartig unvergleichlich hoher Werth, das wirklich nur um das blühende Leben selber die unvergängliche Erinnerung gefährdet werden darf – Du, Else, musst Dich jetzt mit aller Strenge der tiefsten Wahrheit fragen, ob Dein Gefühl für mich den Niedergang begonnen hat – und wenn Du auf dem Grunde Deiner Seele erkennen wirst, dass Dein Erleben mit mir sich nun erfüllt hat – dann ist das Schicksal gütig gegen uns gewesen um unserer gemeinsamen Erinnerung willen und um der leuchtenden Reinheit dieser Erinnerung – Und wenn Du andere Antwort in Deiner Seele findest, wenn Du noch an die Möglichkeit glaubst, dass uns das Leben noch gemeinsames Glück bestimmt, dann ruf mich zu Dir – Else dann ruf mich bald? Ich komme augenblicklich sobald Du mich rufst –, dann Else, mach' mir die Qual der Wartezeit so kurz als möglich! Denn während dieser Wartezeit während dieser Ungewissheit ist jede Stunde Qual. –
Dein Otto.

Letter 6

(1907) [date not in Otto's hand]
Meine Else,
meine liebe, liebe – ich warte bang auf irgendeine Nachricht von Dir – mir ist ja bang um Dich – zumal nach der Angst in der Reisenacht, Angst bis das Telegramm kam – und dann noch weiter immer noch Bangigkeit, immer noch fragende Gedanken – Else, Geliebte, ich weiss ja gar nichts über Dich, nichts darüber, wie es Dir geht – weiss nichts um unsere grosse Hoffnung und ob sie noch besteht – Else, ich merke, ich muss so viel verdrängen an bangen Gedanken um Dich – jetzt unterm Schreiben steigt die Sorge herauf. Gieb mir bald Nachricht, Else – am besten telephonisch! Du, ich werde morgen, Sonntag, von 11–1 Uhr vormittag in

<u>Café Stephanie</u> sein und dann wieder abends <u>von 7 Uhr</u> ab – bitte, bitte, ruf' mich dort an !

Denk' Dir, ich <u>muss</u> ja doch Sorgen haben – wie es Dir geht, Else – und ob Du wohl nicht traurig bist und wie es Dir in der letzten Nacht dann noch gegangen ist – Du liebe Geliebte Du! . . .

Else <u>von hier</u> erzähl' ich Dir, sobald ich über Dich in klarer und dann in ruhiger Stimmung bin. Frieda ist wieder so schön wie in den letzten Zeiten vor der Geburt, dabei ruhig und klar, von aller störenden Nervosität befreit – so ruhig – prachtvoll, wie ich sie noch gar nicht gekannt hatte. – Sie hat den M. viel ernster lieb als ich erwartet hatte, und M. ist rührend glücklich, dabei in jeder Richtung einwandsfrei nobel. – Zu mir ist Frieda so liebevoll wie nie zuvor, ich würde mit ihr jetzt namenlos glücklich sein, wenn ich den Muth hätte, voll an's Glück zu <u>glauben</u> . . . es ist bisher noch unbegreiflich und so rätselhaft schön – ihr Wesen ist jetzt wie der Ausdruck einer tiefernsten und freudigen Liebe – an die ich eben noch nicht zu glauben wage –

Else – <u>an Dich</u> muss ich unendlich viel denken – mit einer heissen übergrossen Liebe – mit Bangigkeit und Hoffnung und Zärtlichkeit und Sehnsucht – Leb wohl, Geliebte.

Otto.

Das Peterl ist wahnsinnig lieb, aber ich kann's kaum ansehen, ich muss mich dann immer um's Andere sorgen. . . .

[along top of first page] Grüsse Edgar, ich freue mich auf ihn!

[letter continues]

Freitag

Verzeih, dass ich noch einmal wage Dir zu schreiben – das will nicht Antwort, nicht irgend etwas Positives – ich <u>muss</u> aber noch eine Schuld wieder gut machen und <u>falsche Bilder richtigstellen</u>, die ich verursacht habe. Wahr sind die <u>beiden letzten Briefe</u>, wahr ist, was ich von meiner Liebe und was ich von meiner Weltanschauung geschrieben habe – entsetzlich falsch und eine reine Abstinenzerscheinung ist dieser eine Expressbrief nach dem ersten Telephonieren – grauenhaft und mir selber ewig fremd ist diese Symbolisierung des socialen Hasses gegen den Mann und seine Rasse durch frevelhafte und unmögliche Beleidigungen gegen Dich – durch diese krankenhafte Ausdrucksform einer physischen Aversion gegen irgend etwas an Dir – Schon dass Du ewig neu bist an jedem neuen Tag, macht diese Symbolik zum Wahnsinn – Dein Körper ist mir heilig in alle Zeit – und nimm die Schuld von mir, dass <u>ich</u> auf <u>diese</u> Darstellung kommen konnte! Es war Dir übermenschliche Anstrengung, nicht in's Morphium zurückzufallen. Die Aversion gegen <u>ihn</u>, das Entsetzen, Dich von mir weg und zum Feind hinübergehend vor meiner angstvollen Phantasie zu sehen – die Suggestion der Sprache und ihrer Gemeinheit, gerade weil ich selber dies einst bearbeitet hatte und <u>daher</u> in Verbindung damit stand – und mir unbegreiflich wie ein schrecklicher Traum! Verzeih mir <u>diese</u> Wahnsinns Sünde! – Durch <u>diesen</u> Frevel bin ich Dir ein Fremder geworden – lass aber <u>diesen</u> Frevel nicht haften an mir! – <u>Wahr ist</u>, dass es mich furchtbar niederschlägt, dass mein directer Gegentypus von Dir bejaht wird – dass es <u>zwei</u> Seelen sein müssen, die sich in Dir ablösen, die <u>eine</u> mit <u>ihm</u> und <u>seiner</u> Welt, die andere die, die <u>mir verschwistert war</u> – Dass <u>sein</u> Theil Deiner Seele <u>mich</u> zuletzt als einen Fremden empfinden muss und <u>meiner</u> eben doch sich als Dein Bestes <u>mir</u> versprochen hat – Dass <u>hier</u> in <u>dieser</u> Form sich allerdings die <u>Unvereinbarkeit</u> darstellen muss, die sich in meiner Weltanschauung als <u>Kastentrennung</u> äussert. Dass <u>er</u> und <u>ich</u> als Freunde <u>eines</u> Menschen <u>einander</u>

ausschliessen – das ist eine Wahrheit – die eben hat mich niedergeschlagen, als ich gerade seine Person errieth – und was mich dann geradezu um den Verstand gebracht hat, das war, dass Du das Selbe nicht gesehen hättest, dass Du nach Allem, was Du über mich und meine Meinung über diesen Menschen und auch über seinen charakteristischen Hass gegen mich gewusst hast – dass Du Beziehungen zu dem und zu mir für vereinbar gehalten hättest – Hier hat mich eben wirklich der Schrecken vor dem Unbegreiflichen erfasst – was jetzt von jenem frevelhaften Brief an Wahrheit zurückbleibt, ist wieder dies: man muss jetzt eine ganze Seele, ein ganzes in die Tiefe gesunkenes Leben wieder erwecken, damit Du wieder die bist, die ich gekannt habe und so namenlos liebe – Ganz vor der Wendung war doch abends ein Telephongespräch zwischen uns – Da warst Du recht bei mir und eigentlich ziemlich zu Ende mit ihm – dann kam mein Brief, der Dich von mir entfremdet und getrennt hat – jetzt denke ich, ob nicht gerade in diesem selben Augenblick, wenn wir uns doch getroffen hätten, Du nicht gerade ganz und restlos die Anmuth bei mir gefunden hättest – Dann wäre das Erlebnis gerade das Hinauskommen über diesen Mann gewesen und über Alles, was er Dir repraesentiert hat – dann hättest Du eben doch recht gehabt, es war dann wirklich mein Princip in meinem Sinn – dann hättest Du recht gehabt 'in meinen Armen' mir zu sagen, dass er es war und dass Du jetzt frei bist von ihm – gerade wie ja auch wirklich ich es Dir oft gerathen habe und wie ich's Dir in höchster Freude gedankt hätte – und hättest recht gehabt, dass 'Wunderbares uns bevorgestanden hätte' – Du wärest dann sicher gewesen und geblieben in meiner Welt – Und dass Du die Erinnerung gerade nicht verneinen und abstossen wolltest, das wäre nicht ein Hang zum Gewöhnlichen gewesen und nicht ein Mangel an Distanz und Unterscheidung – das wäre die Erinnerung an Deine eigene Entwicklung gewesen – an all Dein Sehnen und Ringen und Streben und Hoffen und Irren – an all' Dein Eigenes, das hinter Dir gelegen hätte und überwunden gewesen wäre – 'abreagiert' in einer letzten Rückkehr der 'convertierten' Sinnlichkeit zu ihrem Ursprung, zu einer offenen und reinen Sinnlichkeit – dann war es eine Läuterung, dann war es gross und rein! – und musste Dir werth und unverletzbar bleiben als das Symbol deiner eigenen strebenden Seele. Und dann wärst Du gekommen, zu mir gekommen so rein und schön und in der Tiefe geklärt wie noch nie zuvor – wenn ich in dieser Deutung die Wahrheit getroffen habe, dann habe ich, nur ich, Dich von mir und in das Gegentheil gestossen – dann hab' ich eine Schuld, für die ich nicht um Verzeihung zu bitten wage – die muss ich tragen – wenn eine solche Schuld sich tragen lässt, dass es zur Wiederkehr dieser das Tiefste und Höchste erlösenden Liebe nicht einer nur continuierlichen seelischen Wandlung bedürfte, sondern geradezu der Wiedergewinnung einer verschollenen anderen Seele –

Nun glaube ich heute, dass ich in der entsetzlichen Zerrüttung und Verzweiflung gerade eine Möglichkeit ganz übersehen habe, die mir auf einmal klar wird und die vielleicht die Wahrheit treffen kann. Was ich von jetzt ab sage, ist Vermuthung – ich glaube aber, ich soll auch diese für alle Fälle Dir zur Verfügung stellen –

Letter 7
Meine Else,
Nun hast Du wohl auch schon meinen zweiten Brief und kennst Dich aus – Du musst mich für arg dumm gehalten haben, solang mein erster Brief als Antwort auf Deinen Brief erschien! – Nicht wahr, jetzt weisst Du Alles, wie ich's meine – Du namenlos Geliebte Du! Du, gestern am Telephon, das war eine furchtbare

Tantalusqual – ich habe mich so verzweifelt in Deine Stimme verliebt – ich sah und
fühlte Dich – der Zauber der feinen Nüancen und diese neue Klarheit, die schöne
Sicherheit die neu dazukommt – so rein und treu war Deine Stimme gestern, und in
ihr war ein Vibrieren aus neu erschlossenen Tiefen –

Weisst Du, ich habe mich doch so viel nach Deiner Freundschaft gesehnt –
nach der Verlässlichkeit, die über allem Unberechenbaren steht – verstehst Du,
warum ich jetzt und erst jetzt mit dieser Art von Freundschaft rechne? Warum ich
diesen unbezwinglichen Verdacht habe gegen alle die unberechenbaren 'dunklen
grossen Leidenschaften' – ? Und dann: warum ich mich jetzt auf Dich verlassen zu
können weiss? – Siehst Du: das ist mein leitendes Ideal: die grosse seelische
Elementarkraft, die Erotik muss wie das Wasser sein – segnend, befruchtend,
geliebt, beherrscht – und das ist mein leitendes Wissen: wer die Erotik vergewalti-
gen will, den vergewaltigt die Erotik. Erst wer die Erotik erkennt und bejaht, so wie
sie ist – erst der beherrscht sie auch soweit, dass er versprechen kann, immer er
selbst zu sein – Du, Else, weisst Du annähernd, was das jetzt heisst: ich kann
darauf rechnen, es immer mit Dir selber zu thun zu haben – verstehst Du dieses
Gefühl von so unendlich reiner Luft, in dem ich jetzt athme – Seligkeit athme in
jedem Gedanken an Dich – ?
Leb wohl, Geliebte, Angebetete – Leb wohl!

Letter 8
Meine Else,
Ich bitte Dich, schreib' mir jetzt in der nächsten Zeit möglichst viel Liebes – und
ohne Reciprocität: ich fange jetzt an die Abstinenz zu verstärken und da kommen
Zustände, in denen man nur steife magere Sätze herauspressen kann und dabei
gerade besonders nach Liebe und Helle verlangt – und überdies dumme Schlüsse
zieht aus jedem Nichts und sich Verlassen glaubt oder sonst Gespenster sieht – Ich
hoffe übrigens jetzt relativ bald mich wieder entsprechend verschönt zu haben – -

Du, Else, kommt es vielleicht in Betracht: München statt Stuttgart? Ich
denke nämlich, ich werde wahrscheinlich etwas früher schön genug sein als ich
reisen kann. Und ich fiebere nach einem Zusammensein mit Dir – Else, gefiele es
Dir, in Zukunft mit mir beisammen zu sein? Du hättest ja auch Frieda – ich habe
zum Glück ja mehr zu bieten als mich allein – Else, komm! komm!

P.S. Aber noch nicht gleich – ich bin noch nicht schön für Dich !!

Letter 9
Meine Else,
Nun hab' ich doch ein Document, dass Du mich lieb hast – wie in den Träumen
meiner höchsten Sehnsucht... Else, Dein Brief hat unendlichen Jubel in mich
gebracht und eine grosse reine Ruhe – die helle harmonische Schönheit, in der die
Liebe allem Reifenden segnend wird – was für ein kostbares Reifen und
Süsswerden hattest Du doch nur aufgespart! Die grüne Chrysantheme – Du Else,
in Deinem Brief lebt eine Geste – jugendfrische Unschuld wieder auf – dieselbe
wie damals, wie Du mich einst auf unserem kleinen Hof mit Deinem lieben Kopf
gestossen hast.... Da bin ich immer wieder hin versetzt, soft ich Deinen Brief
wieder lese – ich möchte oft mit den Händen nach Deinem Kopf zu fangen
versuchen, so nahe glaub' ich Dich dann oft bei mir – Wenn ich Dich fangen und
küssen könnte! Und jubeln, dass Du mir gerade 'in meinen Armen' von der
Geschichte erzählen wolltest – *dans l'intimité* – erinnerst Du Dich? Jubeln – vor
Allem, dass wir uns jetzt verstehn, verstehn im äussersten Ja-sagen zum frohen

blühenden Leben –Du Else, mit der Tilgung der letzten gefährlichen Differenz hast Du aus Deiner Seele und um unserer Beider Glück den vergiftenden Dorn herausgezogen – ? Else, weisst Du auch ganz, dass dieser Moment kein solcher ist, wie man ihn oft erlebt – -? Dass diese Art der Liebe und Treue in der wir uns jetzt einander schenken – nicht oft von Menschen gelebt worden ist – Dass es die ersten Blüthen in einem neuen Weltfrühling sind, die für die Schönheit unserer Liebe blühen! Du, dieser neue Frühling der wieder-erwachenden Menschheits-unschuld – ist das nicht wie der Kuss, der Dornröschen weckt?

Else, ich danke Dir, dass Du daran gedacht hast, die letzten Schatten jener düsteren Erinnerung mit einer Fluth von Licht und segnender Liebe auszutilgen.

Else in mir ist damit eine wunderbare Kraft des Liebens ganz ungeahnt frei geworden – so ganz aus der Tiefe heraus – eine neue freudige Kraft einer jubelnder Liebe die Dich zur Sonne hinauftragen möchte – Else, die Liebe zu Dir, die sich in ihrer Grenzenlosigkeit erst jetzt erkennt – erst jetzt seit auch der letzte beengende Druck gewichen ist – erst jetzt seit ich nun weiss, dass meine Liebe sich freuen darf an ihrer Expansionskraft selbst – Else, in diesem Augenblick des Begreifens, dass Du jetzt meine Liebe zu Deiner Schwester freigiebst – aus Deiner eigenen Fülle an Kraft und Liebe und Freude heraus den Willen zu jeder Freude freigiebst – in diesem Augenblick des seeligen Begreifens – da hab'ich Dich und mich so namenlos in Einander versinkend so unbegreiflich vereinigt gefühlt –

Ich kann's Dir ja nicht beschreiben, Else – ich möchte nur irgendwie Dir sagen können, welch' unsagbares Glück es mir ist, mit Dir jetzt einig zu sein – das kann ich Dir wohl auch nur in Deinen Armen sagen – ganz von Seele zu Seele wohl in Wollust sagen – weh mir gerade im Augenblick des tödtlichsten Glücklichseins und im Symbol der äussersten Vereinigung.

Else, leb' wohl – und mögest Du Dich freuen -freuen – Leb' wohl. Du, sag' mir: verstehst Du mich ganz? Verstehst Du, warum ich so glücklich bin? –

One Letter: Else Jaffé to Otto Gross
15. Dez.

Lieber Otto, ich will wenigstens Dir nicht Grund zu dem berechtigten Vorwurf geben, 'wir' antworten nicht einmal auf Deine Briefe. Freilich wirst Du von mir ja auch nichts, was diesem Zustand des Nicht-Ein- und Auswissens ein Ende macht, hören, denn ich kann Dir ja nur schreiben, wie mir als Zuschauer die Situation erscheint – über Frieda kann ich schon gar nichts sagen, das muss sie selbst tun, Du weisst ja selbst, wie schwer es für einen andern ist, sich in Dir auszukennen! Du darfst also nichts von dem was ich schreibe, als indirekt von ihr stammend, auffassen – dass Du's doch tun könntest, hat mich dazu gebracht, Dir nicht schon gleich zu schreiben.

Du wirst Dich doch wohl, wenn Du glaubst, ich wünsche so sehr, Dich inkonsequent zu sehen, ich glaube nur nicht, dass uns das Leben es gestattet, ganz ohne Kompromiss zu leben. Ich will Dir aber gern zugeben, dass ich zuerst fand, man müsse Dich irgend wie dazu bringen, die Beziehung mit Rega U[llmann] aufzugeben jetzt sehe ich den Konflikt doch anders – diese Beziehung, Deine – wie wir von uns aus es sehen müssen – Rücksichtslosigkeiten gegen Frieda sind nur Symptome einer tief in Deiner Natur begründeten Entwicklung:

Das Friedele hatte ganz recht, als es mir im Sommer sagte, 'Siehst Du nicht, dass Otto der Prophet ist, für den es nur heissen kann: wer nicht für mich ist, ist wider mich' –

Jetzt hat der Prophet gewissermassen den letzten Rest vom Menschen Otto ganz in seinem Feuer verbrannt und hat ihm auch die Fähigkeit einen Menschen, ein Individuum individuell, dessen Eigenart angepasst, zu lieben genommen. Eine alte, alte Geschichte ist das – auch jener andere Prophet hat von seinen Brüdern gesagt: Ich habe keine Brüder – Ihr (die Jünger) seid meine Brüder! – Es giebt für Dich jetzt nur noch – (etwas davon war ja immer da) Nachfolger Deiner Lehre, nicht mehr ein bestimmtes, um seiner Eigenart willen geliebtes Weib. Es kann kaum anders sein. – Nun lässt sich natürlich denken, dass ein Weib auf die persönliche Note in der Liebe verzichtet und ganz mitergriffen von dem heiligen Feuer, jedes Opfer bringt, um neben dem zu bleiben, an dessen Ziele sie ganz glaubt. – Wenn sie aber nicht ganz glauben kann – Otto?

Wenn sie nicht ganz glauben kann, könnte sie vielleicht noch um ihrer eigenen Liebe willen bei dem Menschen bleiben – aber würde der Prophet das ertragen, ohne ständig mit ihrer Seele zu ringen, ohne sich selbst zu zerfasern in diesem Kampf? –

So sehe ich die Situation – ich will nicht einmal mit Bestimmtheit behaupten, dass der Frieda weniger lieb hast als früher, obgleich – mit den üblichen Maassstäben gemessen – das gar nicht zu bezweifeln wäre. Die Qualität des Gefühles hat sich jedenfalls geändert. (An Dein Peterle denkst du schon gar nicht mehr!)

Eines muss ich aber noch sagen. Es scheint doch auch deshalb so nutzlos, Dir oder Deiner Sache Opfer zu bringen, weil Du selbst durch das sinnlose Wüten auf Deine Gesundheit Deine Leistungsfähigkeit zerstörst. Wir wissen ja gar nicht, wie viel von dem, was uns Deine Ideen unannehmbar macht, die Kritiklosigkeit, der gänzliche Mangel an Nuancierung und Unterscheidungsfähigkeit den einzelnen Menschen gegenüber, am Ende vom Morphium kommt. Wie dadurch auch die äusseren Seiten des Zusammenlebens erschwert werden, weisst du ja.

Ich bin traurig, Otto, wenn ich an Dich denke – du gehst immer weiter fort, scheint mir, und selbst die Hoffnung hie und da mit Dir als mit einem Freund zusammen sein zu können, wird so klein, wenn ich denke, wofür alles Du eine begehende Stellung fordern würdest. Und über alle gewesenen Dinge legt sich das Leben und macht sie ganz tot – ist das nicht furchtbar? Deine Else.

Notes

My thanks to Martin Green should be recorded for supplying me copies of the Otto Gross to Else Jaffé letters and for the spirit of openness in which he has encouraged this research. The original letters are to be found in the Tufts University Archives. Gottfried Heuer gave me indispensable help in the transcription and translation of these letters. Martin Green and Gerda Bender contributed further valuable suggestions.

1. The Frieda Gross to Else Jaffé letters are in the Tufts University Archives. Marianne Weber's letters are in the Bavarian State Library.

2. In her *Memoirs* Frieda Lawrence says this was in spring when the flowers were appearing and Otto Gross appeared in Café Stephanie in Schwabing pushing a pram with a 3-month-old Peter Gross (Frieda Lawrence, 1961: 93). Peter Wolfgang Gross was born 31 January 1907 (documents, Münich City Archive).

3. Erich Mühsam was a literary anarchist and central character in Schwabing (see Linse, 1998: 129–42).

4. This most likely refers to Frieda Gross.

5. See Introduction above, concerning Otto's paper for Amsterdam. It is quite probable that Else submitted this paper to Max Weber for publication in the *Archiv für Socialwissenschaft und Sozialpolitik*. Marianne wrote at the bottom of her copy of Weber's rejection letter of 7 September 1907: 'Über psychologistische Herrschaftsordnung. 1. Der Psychologismus seit Nietzsche und Freud' (Weber, 1990: 393).

6. This refers to Völcker.

7. A village 30 miles south of Munich.

8. Erich Mühsam had a relationship with Frieda Gross. He was also analysed by Otto and wrote to Freud congratulating him on the discovery of psychoanalysis. Subsequently he regretted his analysis, because he felt Otto had used personal confidences against him (see Linse, 1998).

9. Little Peter is Frieda and Otto's baby; 'the other one' is presumably a reference to Else's pregnancy.

10. A cathartic purging of repression through a free and unihibited sexuality. The term derives from Fliess and Freud. Gross's radical use of the idea departs sharply from Freud's understanding of psychoanalytic practice and the process of transference.

11. A crucial passage for understanding Otto Gross's doctrine. The erotic is an ideal that the 'dark passions' , i.e. hidden lusts, will defile.

12. Else's humorous comment on Otto's jealousy. Otto had previously sent Else white lilies, a symbolization of the purity of the erotic (see Gross and Weekley, 1990: 175).

13. Otto Gross was the father of one of her children. Otto refused to have anything more to do with Regina Ullmann. Else subsequently took Otto's daughter, Camilla Ullmann into her own family for lengthy periods of time (see Green, 1988: 57; Heuer, 1998: 21–31).

14. The original orthography has been retained.

References

Bly, R. (1981) *Selected Poems of Rainer Maria Rilke: A Translation from the German and Commentary by Robert Bly*. New York: Harper and Row.

Byrne, J. (1995) *A Genius for Living. A Biography of Frieda Lawrence*. London: Bloomsbury.

Chalcraft, D. (1998) 'Love and Death: Weber, Wagner and Max Klinger', in S. Whimster (ed.) *Max Weber and the Culture of Anarchy*. London: Macmillan.

Gane, M. (1993) *Harmless Lovers? Gender, Theory and Personal Relationships*. London: Routledge.

Green, M. (1986) *Mountain of Truth: The Counterculture Begins – Ascona, 1900–1920*. Hanover and London: University Press of New England.

Green, M. (1988) *The von Richthofen Sisters: The Triumphant and the Tragic Modes of Love*. Albuquerque: University of New Mexico Press. (Orig. 1974.)

Gross, O. (1907) *Das Freudsche Ideogenitätsmoment und seine Bedeutung im manisch-depressiven Irresein Kraepelins*. Leipzig: Vogel.

Gross, O. and F. Weekley (1990) 'The Otto Gross–Frieda Weekley Correspondence', trans. John Turner with Cornelia Rumpf-Worthen and Ruth Jenkins, *The D.H. Lawrence Review* 22(2): 137–225.

Helle, H. (1994) 'Max Weber über Otto Gross. Ein Brief an Else Jaffé vom September 1907', *Zeitschrift für Politik* 41(2): 214–23.

Heuer, G. (1998) 'Jung's Twin Brother. Otto Gross and Carl Gustav Jung. Gross' Children and Grandchildren', Occasional Paper, Association of Jungian Analysts.

Hurwitz, E. (1979) *Otto Gross. Paradies-Sucher zwischen Freud und Jung.* Zurich: Suhrkamp.

Jones, E. (1955) *The Life and Work of Sigmund Freud*, 3 vols. New York: Basic Books.

Kinkead-Weekes, M. (1996) *D.H. Lawrence, 1885–1930.* Cambridge: Cambridge University Press.

Lawrence, F. (1961) *The Memoirs and Correspondence*, edited by E.W. Tedlock. London: Heinemann.

Levy, C. (1998) 'Max Weber, Anarchism and Libertarian Culture: Personality and Power Politics', in S. Whimster (ed.) *Max Weber and Culture of Anarchy.* London: Macmillan.

Linse, U. (1998) 'Sexual Revolution and Anarchism: Erich Mühsam', in S. Whimster (ed.) *Max Weber and the Culture of Anarchy.* London: Macmillan.

Michaels, J. (1983) *Anarchy and Eros: Otto Gross's Impact on German Expressionist Writers.* New York: Peter Lang.

Nietzsche, F. (1968) *Twilight of the Idols* and *The Anti-Christ.* London: Penguin.

Nipperdey, T. (1993) *Deutsche Geschichte, 1866–1918. Arbeitswelt und Bürgergeist.* Munich: Beck.

Reventlow, F. (1971) *Tagebücher, 1895–1910.* Munich: Langen Müller.

Runciman, W.G. (ed.) (1978) *Weber: Selections in Translation*, trans. Eric Matthews. Cambridge: Cambridge University Press.

Weber, M. (1990) *Max Weber Gesamtausgabe: Briefe 1906–1908*, edited by M. Rainer Lepsius and Wolfgang J. Mommsen with Birgit Rudhard and Manfred Schön. Tübingen: Mohr.

Weber, M. (1994) *Max Weber Gesamtausgabe: Briefe 1909–1910*, edited by M. Rainer Lepsius and Wolfgang J. Mommsen with Birgit Rudhard and Manfred Schön. Tübingen: Mohr.

Whimster, S. (1995) 'Max Weber on the Erotic and Some Comparisons with the Work of Foucault', *International Sociology* 10(4): 447–62.

Whimster, S. (ed.) (1998) *Max Weber and the Culture of Anarchy.* London: Macmillan.

Worthen, J. (1992) *D.H. Lawrence: The Early Years, 1885–1912.* Cambridge: Cambridge University Press.

Sam Whimster teaches Sociology at London Guildhall University. His publications include *Max Weber and the Culture of Anarchy*. He is completing an ESRC-funded project to produce a catalogue of the Weber letters which are in open archives.

Gottfried Heuer is a professional member of the Association of Jungian Analysts and is in private practice in London. He will be publishing the Collected Works of Otto Gross in German on the Internet [http://www.ottogross.org/].

The Lost Innocence of Love
Romance as a Postmodern Condition

Eva Illouz

For if theater is a double of life, life is a double of true theater. (Artaud, *The Theater and its Doubles*)

Life does not imitate art; it only imitates bad television. (from Woody Allen's *Husbands and Wives*)

1. Introduction

ROMANTIC LOVE, a contemporary social commentator suggests, 'has been taken prisoner by discourse' and 'has become a dead artifact of an overwritten, overinterpreted culture' (Ignatieff, 1988). The idea that media shape our private dreams and acts of love has become a cliche, eagerly commented on by therapists and movies. In endless loops of ironic reflexivity, contemporary popular culture offers the spectacle of people who love each other while rehearsing the romantic icons of cinema (see for example movies such as Woody Allen's *Husbands and Wives* or *Sleepless in Seattle*). To what extent the cliche that love is a cliche is true, and if true to what extent it is new are the two questions I explore in this article.

The question of the relationship between romantic fiction and reality precedes, by far, the modern and postmodern era. *Don Quixote*, if one is to choose an 'inaugural' date, marks the first attempt in our cultural history to question the problematic relationship between reading, (chivalric) romance and reality. But if *Don Quixote*'s reader is rapidly placed into a skeptical (and comic) doubt about the reality the knight errant 'sees', she is never asked to doubt the authenticity of Don Quixote's *love* for Dulcinea. Don Quixote's *sentiments* remain outside the scope of the critical and comical distinction between reality and fiction. Only in the 17th century did a more

■ *Theory, Culture & Society* 1998 (SAGE, London, Thousand Oaks and New Delhi),
Vol. 15(3–4): 161–186
[0263-2764(199808/11)15:3–4;161–186;006063]

definite and clearly articulated interrogation of the relationship between reality, fiction and sentiment appear. The 17th-century French moralist La Rochefoucauld expressed this in his well-known maxim that 'many people would not have fallen in love had they not heard of it'. To use an anachronistic terminology, for La Rochefoucauld if culture induces love, it also falsifies it. Such a view was grounded on a deep-seated moral and religious suspicion of emotional intensity, deemed to incite false knowledge. The *passions* could be a reliable source neither of knowledge nor of moral conduct, and erotic (or romantic) love, more than the other passions, symbolized the vanity of human emotions and the frailty of reason.

During the following two centuries, this theme became insistent. As the theme of love took over popular and literary fiction and as fiction material, thanks to the print media, was distributed on a wider social and geographical scale, the cultural *malaise* about the presumed power of fiction to induce a (false) sentiment of love deepened. The historian Lawrence Stone goes as far as to write that:

> [Romantic love] is a product, that is, of learned cultural expectations, which became fashionable in the late eighteenth century thanks largely to the spread of novel-reading ... the romantic novel of the late eighteenth century and early nineteenth centuries has much to answer for in the way of disastrous love affairs and of imprudent and unhappy marriages. (Stone, 1977: 191)

In a somewhat similar vein, the system-theorist Niklas Luhmann affirms that romantic love is less a sentiment than a 'symbolic code'. Reminiscent of La Rochefoucauld's famous maxim about love is Luhmann's observation that 'English women who try to emulate characters in pre-Victorian novels have to wait for visible signs of nuptial love before allowing themselves to discover consciously what love is' (Luhmann, 1986: 8–9). Historically, it was as if the more love became a prominent theme of mass printed fiction, the more it was perceived to be an illusion, alien to what was presumed to be the experience of 'true' love and actively threatening the marriage institution. Or to put it differently, the growing representation of love in the print, and subsequently electronic, media has been increasingly accompanied by a form of cultural 'alienation': the more love was represented in print, and later electronic, fiction, the less it was recognized as a reality *sui generis* of romantic relationships. Flaubert's *Madame Bovary* epitomized this malaise and went a step further: Flaubert's heroine irreversibly crossed the boundary between 'life' and the 'novel', between the sign and its referent and paid with her own life for the confusion between fiction and reality, thus radicalizing the cultural *malaise* about mass printed romantic fiction. But Madame Bovary's tragic confusion did not refer to a moral discourse privileging marriage and 'true' love over the illusions produced by pernicious fiction. In Flaubert's narrative the power of romantic fiction pointed to the contradictions of the 19th-century petit-bourgeois family, and to the increasing centrality of love in the 'disenchanted' fabric of everyday life.

Thus, long before the so-called postmodern age, the relationship between romantic fiction and romantic sentiment was actively scrutinized in a way that resonated with a deep-seated moral suspicion of the passions and with newer cultural questions concerning the relationship between marriage and love. Did romantic fiction threaten the venerable institution of marriage by instilling 'dangerous' longings in men and women? If this question resolutely points to the relation between public discussions about fiction and social control, it also provides us with an opportunity to 'differentiate between what is specific to the postmodern and what may be an accumulation and intensification of tendencies long present within the modern, and even pre-modern' (Featherstone, 1992). How, in the context of postmodern culture, are we to understand the long-discussed link between romantic fiction and romantic autobiography? If, as so many commentators have argued, in postmodern culture 'models take precedence over things' (Kellner, 1989: 244), then what 'form' (in the Simmelian sense of this word) does the postmodern romantic autobiography take and what relationship does it bear to the highly stylized forms of mass media love stories? In an attempt to submit postmodern categories to systematic empirical examination, I examine these questions on the basis of in-depth interviews with 50 men and women interviewed in the USA.[1]

2. Love at First Sight: The Dwindling of a Myth?

The topic of love has been brought to the fore of sociological theory with Giddens's (1991, 1992) and Beck and Beck-Gernsheim's recent work (1995). Despite their differing perspectives, a number of striking commonalities emerge: all these authors view romantic love in the context of the transformations that modernity has brought to self-identity and characterize modern identity as a *biographical* category, to be managed and monitored by a reflexive self.[2] But while the Becks view love as the place where the contradictions between the nuclear family and the market are most blatant, Giddens views the romantic 'biography' as the framework par excellence within which the self shapes itself in the face of the 'disembedding mechanisms' of modernity. In a brilliant departure from the long-standing moral discourse on fiction and reality, Giddens argues that historically, romantic love has had an affinity with the novel and that it offers an overarching symbolic structure in which the self can orient itself, shape and 'author' its autobiography reflexively. That the contemporary experience of love is narrative is beyond doubt and is the departure point of this article. However, as I show in the following, the narrative biographical construction of the romantic self is far more contradictory than Giddens and the Becks suggest, because postmodern regimes of representation alter the symbolic categories within which 'reflexivity' takes place. Reflexivity may be the mechanism through which the self articulates a coherent biography, but it is also, as I show further, what *strains* the romantic biography by making it the site of contradictory *narratives of love*.

My discussion is based on in-depth interviews with 50 men and women who were asked open-ended questions about their romantic life. In addition, respondents were asked to interpret three love stories presented to them during the interview. My overall aim has been to understand how one's autobiographical narratives intersect with the symbolic structures within which these three fiction stories are interpreted.

The Stories

Story One presents the traditional ideal of romantic love which has pervaded our cultural representations of love: love at first sight, overwhelming force of love, the supremacy of love over reason and family considerations. Stories Two and Three present two different versions of the realist tradition of love: respectively, a 'residual' version in which the story is an attenuated version of the marriage of 'reason' organized by families; and an 'emergent' one presenting a professional couple whose relationship combines emotion with financial and professional concerns. The television serial *Thirty Something* provides many good examples of this last type of love story.[3]

Story One

On a Monday of June 19, – Floyd Johnson and Ellen Skinner, total strangers, boarded a train at San Francisco and sat down across the aisle from each other. Floyd crossed the aisle on Wednesday and sat in front of Ellen. Ellen looked at him and thought: 'I would say yes if he asked me to marry him.' As Floyd would say later 'they did all the talking with their eyes'. Thursday, the couple got off the train in Nebraska with plans to be married. Because they would need to have the consent of the bride's parents to get married in this state, they crossed the river to Council Bluffs, Iowa, where they were married on Friday.[4]

Story Two

When Robert turned 30, he felt he was ready to start a family. He told this to his parents, who were happy to hear that their son was ready to settle down. Robert's parents knew their friends' daughter, Theresa, who, they thought, was a promising match because of the many good qualities she and her family had. They decided to talk to Robert and Theresa to make the match. Both agreed and met late one afternoon. The first meeting was a bit awkward but they liked each other and decided to meet again. With time, the awkwardness disappeared as they came to know, understand and appreciate each other. Both families were happy. After a few months, Robert and Theresa started thinking about marriage. Robert told Theresa: 'I want you for my wife.' Theresa and Robert discussed the issue for a while and both came to the conclusion that their relationship was good and healthy enough to make a good marriage. They got married the first day of spring. It was a joyous and solemn celebration.

Story Three
Amy was successful in her professional life and had many good and reliable friends. But she was starting to feel she wanted a greater sense of security and stability in her life. One of her friends introduced her to Tom, whom she found lively and intelligent. Tom also liked her calm strength and warmth. They dated each other for a few months, and, except for occasional fights, they seemed to get along well. One night, Tom held Amy in his arms and told her how good he felt with her. Amy agreed with a kiss. Two years passed. Amy and Tom had known each other well enough to decide that marriage was the right decision. They waited eight more months to get married in order to get the professional promotion that would grant them a secure future. They married the following October and knew they were ready now to have the family they had wanted.

Story One – the 'typical' romantic story – overwhelmingly evoked similar responses: all respondents interpreted the man and woman's rapid decision to get married as an immediate, irrational and intense attraction. On the other hand, Story Two – a modern version of 'arranged marriage' – elicited a greater variety of interpretations: a 'fix-up', an 'arranged marriage', a 'relationship that begins without love but which might end up with love', or as 'a mature marriage of love'. Similarly, Story Three – a story about two people who plan marriage along with their career moves – was viewed as a 'Yuppie story of people who do not love each other', or as 'a nice combination of passion and reason' or as a 'modern love story'. Thus, while Story One was almost invariably interpreted as a marriage undertaken on the basis of impulsive passion, the interpretations of Stories Two and Three varied between 'a mature love' and 'a cold-hearted and calculated enterprise', which in turn indicates quite simply that slow-paced love stories have a less clearly codified meaning than fast-paced stories.

Confirming that the romantic model of Story One has thoroughly pervaded popular culture, respondents viewed the story as 'the most stereotypical', and 'closest to novels or movies', the 'typical story-book' or a 'Hollywood fantasy'. A small minority interpreted it as 'love at first sight', whereas almost all others viewed it as an infatuation, or, as many respondents enjoyed twisting the consecrated expression, 'lust at first sight'. The first interpretation is explicitly opposed to the second because 'often people think that it's love at the beginning of a relation when that's just infatuation, or a sexual need, but not necessarily love, they can be easily mixed up' (female, working-class, no profession). This careful separation boils down to a central feature of respondents' interpretation of the 'typical love story': namely the systematic attempt to demystify the 'love at first sight myth'. In answering an explicit question on the issue, most respondents, regardless of gender, class and education, said they do not believe in the idea of love at first sight.[5] Instead of interpreting Story One as the beginning of a possible life-long love story, as could have been the case in the Romantic tradition, respondents viewed it as '[sexual] chemistry at first sight', as merely the beginning ('infatuation') of a story which as such would not be viable. This interpretation shifts the life-long projected narrative of 'love at first sight' to a beginning *sequence* of a story with a rather different emotional tonality, that of 'sexual desire' or 'infatuation'.

It was not until the end of the 18th century that 'infatuation' began to acquire its modern sense of 'being foolishly in love'. Prior to that, it meant 'being fatuous and foolish' in an unspecified way (*Oxford Dictionary*). The concept of 'infatuation' dismisses the sentiment of 'love at first sight' by viewing it as the fleeting feeling of 'sexual arousal'. And this carries a double ideological message: that intense and immediate emotions are illusions that should not be relied upon, and that sexual attraction is an insufficient and even dangerous reason to choose a mate for life.[6] Respondents seem to activate two distinct narratives, one of sex (infatuation) and one of love. Indeed, as Seidman argues, at the same time that sexuality was integrated with love, political and medical discourses *disentangled* it from the emotions it was supposed to express and reinforce, thus legitimating sexuality for its own sake, with the further consequence, I would argue, of demystifying the cultural narrative of 'love at first sight' on the ground that it is 'just' sexual attraction. Whereas in the Romantic tradition sexual arousal was sublimated – and therefore made legitimate – into the scenario of 'love at first sight', today the claim of love at first sight is suspected of being a pretense for what one can now openly and legitimately acknowledge: sexual desire. *Because sex is now an acceptable and a necessary component of intimacy, and a form of self-expression, its sublimated expression in the cultural ideal of love at first sight is paradoxically jeopardized by the reign of sexuality for its own sake.* This in turn implies that narratives of love and narratives of sex are legitimately *constructed as separate and parallel life narratives which may or may not converge.* This has an important cultural implication; the Romantic narrative of love, which exalted without acknowledging sexual passion, has lost its cultural motivation, that of sublimating (authorizing by transfiguration) sexual passion. Love at first sight, like so much else in our culture, is submitted to a 'disenchanted' discourse of demystification. It is viewed as a cultural fabrication, a man- and woman-made invention caused by, as respondents dispassionately put it, 'hormones' and sexual drives.

To the intense narrative of Story One, respondents explicitly prefer a slower one where two people 'should know each other', spend time together and 'become friends' before they become lovers. These respondents therefore viewed Story One as 'foolish', 'risky', 'adventuresome', 'a sort of a fairy tale', 'cute as a story, but silly in real life', 'a silly story', 'teenage infatuation', 'unrealistic', 'unreal' or 'surreal'. Almost everyone considered the marriage of the protagonists as too hasty and 'most likely to have problems'. The view that to be *successful*, a relationship should rest on the secure ground of mutual knowledge and familiarity was almost unanimous. I examine more precisely the cultural content of this alternative narrative.

3. Real or Realist? Love and Everyday Life

On the surface, respondents substitute realist views of love for the model of intense and irrational love. Using metaphors such as: 'partnership', 'hard work', 'foundations', 'building', 'grow', 'working at love', respondents expressed the idea that if a romantic relationship is to be 'successful', true love has to evolve from time and mutual knowledge. Despite their differences in content and structure, Stories Two and Three were often lumped together into the same narrative frame when contrasted to Story One on the basis that both of them were slow, 'plausible', comfortable', 'more about friendship than passion and sex', 'nice and healthy', 'practical', 'wonderful' and 'realistic', a 'nice combination of love and practicality' or of 'comfort and passion'. The positive responses to these stories revolve around the idea that '[the characters] didn't jump', they 'feel very real', '[the relationship] provides a secure future', 'stability'.[7] The fact that both stories unfold and develop over a longer time span (a few months and a few years, respectively) and that the protagonists seem to ground their choice of partner on personality traits cues the reader into a 'realist' narrative model of love. Realist models of love are systematically opposed to 'fantasy-based' ('Hollywood', 'story-like') models, because they have the semantic and phenomenological properties of everyday life (Schutz, 1967).

(1) *Common sense* is a type of knowledge invoked in the course of everyday life.[8] Indeed the realist model is viewed by respondents themselves as the most commonsensical one. For example, one respondent justified her rejection of Story One as follows:

> *What do you think of this story* [Story One]?
> . . . it's sort of a fairy tale, I guess. It's something that I would never do; and it's like, *common sense* tells me that you don't do something like that. You hear those things and you think well that's stupid, that's dumb. (female, editor)

The perception that the first model is a fairy tale, while the second appeals to common sense is also articulated by other respondents:

> *Do you think that romance is important to keep love going between two people?*
> No, I really don't. I think it can even get in the way.
>
> *How so?*
>
> Because, especially if you're seeing a person *every day* or *frequently*, you have to accept at some point that you are dealing with a *real* person which has concerns which are very *down-to-earth*. And I think you can escape into an *unreal* world and it basically means that you are neglecting these concerns. (male, 25, PhD student)

The first model is perceived as unreal because it occurs outside the experience of everyday life. In contrast, the second exemplifies the attributes of 'realism' in being described as 'practical', 'down-to-earth', 'real', 'commonsensical'.

(2) *Time* – a realistic story is one that unfolds within the phenomeno-logical experience of the time of everyday life. The condensed, 'packed' time of the narrative model of love at first sight is perceived as 'unrealistic' because it does not fit the 'looser', longer and less dramatic plots of everyday life.

(3) *Sociality* – the different temporality of everyday narratives of love points to a different category of bond. Instead of love as the result of an immediate, intense and organic bond, respondents preferred to view love as evolving from 'friendship' and being 'comfortable', i.e. as a relationship that has the informal, casual and unceremonious character of everyday inter-actions and that unfolds progressively in linear time.

> [I]f I ever get married – I am 25 years old now – it's not going to be a [inaudible] encounter on the train. It is going to be with somebody who I have *grown with* as a friend and a confidant and a lover and *grown to* love as someone I want to *spend the rest* of my life with. This [Story One] is strictly the story book. (male, 25, 2 years of college, doorman)

(4) *Taken-for-grantedness of everyday life* – the realistic approach to love also demands that two people be 'compatible', i.e. that they should see their lives in a similar way. Explaining why Story One is not likely to have a successful outcome in the long run, one respondent said:

> I think they [protagonists of Story One] were wrong in getting married so spontaneously. I think they were dealing with infatuation and not real love, and I don't agree. I think they were not spontaneous but, uh, when you do something on a whim without thinking ... love is not enough [of a reason] to get married.
>
> *What more is required?*
>
> You need to be able to *get along with each other*. You need to be *compatible*. You need to, there is a lot more than just loving someone. That's why I didn't marry Paula after the first week or so. I was feeling madly in love, but with time I found out the problems of personality we had. We would have been irresponsible to get married after the first week. I do believe in love, perhaps infatuation at first sight, but not in terms of planning on the basis of that I think. (male, doctor, 30 years old)

Clearly for this respondent, and many others, the initial emotional intensity cannot be the ground for a long-term planning because everyday life takes on an autonomy of its own. The notion of 'compatibility' – central to the realist conception of love – hinges on the expectation that romantic love should be organized in the realm of everyday life which is then expected to 'flow' in a continuum of taken-for-granted actions. In order to function in the everyday world, there must be no doubt about the ordinary arrangement of objects and actions (see Schutz, 1967). The notion of 'compatibility' in turn expresses that romantic relationships, organized in the domain of everyday life, are expected to flow with, rather than interrupt the 'taken-for-grantedness' of everyday life.

(5) *Everyday life as work* – for the idea that love results from an immediate, effortless and organic bond, respondents substituted the notion that 'love is work'. For example:

> [I]f you're in a good love relationship, it means that it is alive, that it is changing. You put energy into it, you put effort into it, you give something to the other person, and they give something to you. It is always work. I don't think that relationships ever sit idle. Well, if you are people for whom romantic things occur, it's gonna occur. I don't think you can seek it out. I don't think it makes sense. (female, artist)

The idea of 'love as work' stems from the experience that everyday life is managed through delayed gratification rather than through play and instant pleasure. The relationship is here envisaged as a voluntary project requiring effort and skillful management. Furthermore, the metaphor of love as work reflects the pragmatic orientation of everyday life, which is geared toward 'making things work' rather than toward contemplation, aesthetic experiences or intense experiences.

All five characteristics of everyday life form the basic semantic categories of realist models of love. Thus almost all respondents viewed the narrative model of Story One as unrealistic and as a 'media construction', while they perceived Stories Two and Three as 'realistic' and grounded in everyday life. The two, clearly distinct, narrative models of love reflect a perceived opposition between 'Hollywood' (or 'story-like' or 'fantasy-like') and 'real life' love. This marked distinction in turn suggests that in sharp contrast to chivalric or Romantic or even Victorian love, which affirmed a heroic or 'authentic' self above and beyond the tribulations of everyday life, contemporary definitions of love are organized in the phenomenological and semantic categories of everyday life. This is easily explained by recent transformations in the history of love: in the course of the 19th century love became the legitimate motivation of marriage, especially in Protestant cultures, and was thus progressively disentangled from aristocratic and heroic forms of self-affirmation to be incorporated in the domain of everyday life via the bourgeois sanctification of family and the everyday (Taylor, 1989). If economic survival was the main vocation of pre-modern marriage, 'emotional survival' has become the main vocation of modern families who must maintain the dense emotional fabric of intimacy in everyday life. As Giddens suggests, love and intimacy become a *project*, only that I would add that this emotional project is located in everyday life.

This in turn qualifies the Becks' emphatic claim that '[love is] a kind of rebellion, a way of getting in touch with forces to counteract the intangible and unintelligible existence we find ourselves in' (Beck and Beck-Gern-sheim, 1995: 178). For contemporary definitions of love are deeply split: one way of experiencing love is indeed on the mode of 'rebellion'; but another – on which self-help literature endlessly capitalizes – is an attempt – unprecedented in the cultural history of love – to incorporate love in the discourse and phenomenological properties of daily life.

4. 'The Heart has Reasons which Reason Does not Know of'

The plot thickens for, when I turned from questions such as 'What do you think of this story?' to the question, 'Which story do you like best, and why?', the same respondents who had initially rejected Story One, when they were asked to compare it with the other stories, viewed it as the most 'interesting', 'original' and 'fascinating' of the three stories presented. Even though they earlier viewed it as a 'typical story-book romance', respondents paradoxically also said that it stimulated their imagination more than the other two. In other words, the fact that this story, by the respondents' own acknowledgement, is the most stereotypical, does not erode its cultural (and fantasmatic) power. The same respondents who evaluated it as 'stereotypical' and 'unreal' also viewed Story One as the 'true romantic [story]', 'the most passionate' and 'fun', 'the most interesting' and 'unconventional', 'it has spice and adventure', 'a wonderful romance', and 'spontaneous'. The characters are viewed as 'enchanted', 'enthralled' and 'totally spontaneous'. In the words of one respondent, the story is 'magical' and 'pure fantasy'. All these evaluations underscore the same idea: that the story embodies intense, impulsive and exceptional feelings, all of which are deemed typical of the genuine expression of the romantic sentiment. Because this story does not specify the nature and quality of the protagonists' feelings for each other, respondents must infer romance only from the suddenness or intensity or seeming irrationality of the protagonists' feelings, or from a combination of all these. Thus, even though almost all respondents disapprove of the haste with which this marriage occurs, they still consider it as an example par excellence of romanticism due to its affirmation of intensity and spontaneity, and thereby of pure passion.

These evaluations were expressed by the *same respondents* who had earlier dismissed Story One. And this in turn implies that respondents *alternatively rejected and praised the same story* depending on the question and the context in which it was asked and framed. Story Two – which was often interpreted positively at the beginning of the interview – later in the interview was rejected because it represented 'an arranged marriage', a 'business-like deal', or because it is 'cold, dry and clinical', 'conformist', a 'calculated decision' and 'unromantic'. That is, when evaluated in the semantic context of romance, Story Two was viewed as unappealing and old-fashioned. Similarly, later in the interview Story Three was deemed to be too 'rational', 'cold' and 'calculating', 'the dullest possible relationship', 'structured', 'mapped out', 'mechanical', 'typically yuppie', 'carefully planned', with 'no warmth' and 'unromantic' and 'too slow-moving'. And the protagonists of Story Three were viewed as looking for stability and security at the price – as one respondent put it – of 'sacrificing something important: Enchantment'. Thus, while these two stories satisfy criteria of realism and compatibility, they lack the romantic qualities found in Story One. That respondents affirm the two models simultaneously is exemplified by the following man. Earlier in the interview, this man had dismissed Story One as a simple infatuation and had claimed the other two stories more 'real' than the first. Later in the interview:

Which one of the three stories is the closest to your ideal of love?

I don't know. If you talk love, I guess the first one, because they never really thought about something else, they didn't have time to think about anything else, it's just ... I guess they just fell in love and they got married.

Which story is the furthest from your ideal?

[silence] I don't want to contradict myself now.

You can say whatever you want.

But I think I want to contradict myself.

That means you want to say 'Story One'?

You see, it's hard I don't really know whether this was love or not. To me this strikes me as if it was just ... they were just attracted to each other, right away. I don't know, I guess Story Two would be probably the furthest. That's my opinion. (male, janitor, 55, no high school education)

When asked to choose the story closest to his ideal, the respondent was faced with the contradiction inherent in simultaneously professing two incompatible narratives of love. This man's hesitations and self-conscious remarks point to his awareness of and discomfort with his inconsistency.

In their evaluation of the three stories, many respondents alternately instantiated both narrative frames – the idealist and the realist ones – at different points of the interview. *The narrative frame elicited by Story One served as the normative ground against which the other two stories were compared and contrasted, and vice versa.* The romantic and realist narrative frames were both held as ideal by the same people, who invoke them for different reasons at different points of the interview to evaluate either the stories' romanticism or the couples' chance of marital success.

5. Reality as Fiction

How do these narrative frames and their interpretations translate into respondents' autobiographical accounts of their own love stories? [9] According-ing to which narrative frame do people 'author' their own love stories? How do these interpretive frames come to bear in the construction of their own autobiographies? Despite respondents' insistence that the realist model is the most likely to be successful, *their most 'memorable' love stories almost*

always correspond to the basic structure and meaning of love at first sight.
Consider the following example of a man who declared earlier in the
interview that he found Story One the least appealing. When he related his
encounter with the woman he was involved with at the time of the interview,
he responded as follows:

> The most romantic moment that I can remember quite well was the first time
> that I met my former to present girlfriend, January 31st of last year, and I
> had been invited to a Super-Bowl party and she had been invited to the
> same party by mutual friends. And it was the kind of thing *that we looked at*
> *each other and we first saw each other it's like in the movies, you know where*
> *the whole rest of the world, everybody else, fades into oblivion and it's just you*
> *and her.* That's how it was like. We just knew right away that we were struck
> by this whirlwind of emotion, and we went to the fire escape away from the
> party. We talked and hugged, we left the party early. We went out to a place
> to eat, and we found ourselves hugging each other in the restaurant, because
> of this new found attraction, chemistry, love. And she asked me to drop her
> off, and it wasn't even a question of 'Am I going to take your number?',
> because we knew that there was this tremendous love that we had for each
> other. And that to me is the most romantic experience I can remember. It
> wasn't planned or anything, there was this tremendous tremendous love at
> first sight which subsequently was problematic. (male, doctor, 30, emphasis
> added)

Despite this respondent's earlier vehement dismissal of Story One, his
most memorable love story contains the main elements and visual imagery
of the narrative model of love at first sight as codified in popular cinema.
The stereotypical character of this narrative account is so marked that the
respondent himself self-consciously referred to such cinematic cliches of
love at first sight as the world 'fades into oblivion'. Moreover, although the
relationship subsequently turned 'sour', the story recounted is cut off from
the present and is narratively self-contained. That is, it does not offer a
diachronic continuity between the first meeting and its disillusioning
development but only rehearses the synchronic vividness and intensity of
the initial encounter.

Another response, from a married woman, further illustrates how the
model of love at first sight suffuses respondents' memories. She first tells
how, on a plane, she fell in love with a man who was sitting near her. She
then proceeds to tell another story, which is her other most memorable love
story.

> At the concert [in S. where she had just arrived] I sat near a man who – I just
> liked his energy and every time I looked at him, he kind of made me feel
> excited and he would look at me and smile and I would smile back and, I
> remember, I was having a particularly good time. I got up and danced with my
> friend Nancy and I kept thinking, should I go over and talk to him? I didn't.
> As we were leaving, he gave me his card and said – you know, I can't even

remember if he said anything. And I called him up a few days later and we talked. I went over to his apartment and I was tremendously attracted to him.

Did you have a relationship?

Yeah, all summer long.... It was a wonderful romance ... it was very exciting. It was in a place that I never lived in before. I didn't know anyone, that kind of thing. So it was a real adventure and I was kind of thrilled by the whole thing, and I was very excited. (female, 30, artist)

Although this woman is married, she did not choose her encounter with her husband as her most memorable love story but rather an adventure she lived, away from her routine environment. Like the previous respondent's, this story bears the characteristics of the adventurous model of love at first sight. It began intensely ('excitement' etc.), took place through silent communication (the eyes and the smiles). The attraction was felt before the actual sexual encounter, and it occurred in an unfamiliar environment under 'extraordinary circumstances', a long summer vacation. Conversely, when she described her relationship with her husband – which she did not cite even as her second most memorable story – she described a slow and progressive relationship that was neither intense nor engrossing.

The very structure of these 'most memorable' autobiographical accounts bears a certain resemblance to the structure of romantic-fiction narratives. Contrary to many narratives of everyday life, they have a clear beginning and a tight dramatic structure; events happen quickly and have a strong emotional effect on the protagonists; all stories have obstacles which prevent the protagonists from carrying on the love story into marriage or a long-lasting bond. Finally, they differ from the more continuous, open-ended, fuzzier plots of everyday life in that they all come to a sharply marked end: almost all memorable love stories have a strong narrative closure. [10] Only three out of the 50 interviewees cited a relationship that was *under way at the time of the interview* as their most memorable relationship; all the others had been brought to a clear closure.

The romantic self 'authors' its most memorable romantic memories by mimicking the intensely ritualized temporal structure of mass-media love stories. To use the terminology of German sociologist Georg Simmel, we might characterize the self-contained and tightly knit structure of these adventures as more *aesthetic* than the shapeless, unstylized and open-ended flow of everyday life stories. In fact it would be quite tempting to say that these autobiographical accounts bear the narrative mark of cinematic or written fiction. And yet, this conclusion cannot be drawn. These autobiographical accounts cannot be offhandedly reduced – as postmodern conventional wisdom would have it – to a copy or simulacrum of their fictional 'code' for, as Jerome Bruner aptly put it, 'Narrative imitates life, life imitates narrative' (1987: 13); and it is this always blurred and fuzzy boundary between life and texts that must be addressed and recast by a theory of love in the so-called postmodern culture.

6. Fiction as Reality

Lyman and Scott (1975) distinguish two categories of experiences: the 'ordinary' and the 'extraordinary'. In their classic study of social perform-ance, Lyman and Scott identify 'adventure' as a particular type of experi-ence that is isolated from the flow of daily events precisely because of its highly dramatic and tightly knit narrative structure. 'Adventures start and end with staccato notes. In contrast, routine life ... falls into a context of continuities; adventures are cut off from the entanglements of and connec-tions to everyday life' (Lyman and Scott, 1975: 149).

Interestingly enough, these authors use 'romantic affairs' as the para-mount example of the social experience of 'adventure'. As they explain, 'sex is always potentially adventurous because it uniquely combines physio-logical stimulation with social risks and psychological thrills' (Lyman and Scott, 1975: 151). Being attracted to someone and having a love affair are phenomenologically characterized by the fact they are physiologically, emotionally and cognitively more salient than other types of romantic experiences, which in turn might explain why they lend themselves to the dramatic and climactic structure of fiction stories. By contrast, long-term relationships are less salient because, as Lyman puts it in a later piece, the 'dramas [of everyday life] reside precisely in their dullness. They do not stimulate the imagination' (Lyman and Scott, 1975: 217).

Drawing from a quite different theoretical tradition, political econom-ist Tibor Scitovsky (1976) understands the experiences of the 'extraordi-nary' and 'ordinary' as being embodied into the drive to excitation and drive to comfort. The former is elicited when one experiences something new; while comfort is attained when an initial level of arousal is reduced, that is, when the excitation is stretched out over a *'longue'* or *'moyenne durée'* (Scitovsky, 1976). The two narrative categories of 'everyday life' and romantic 'adventure' or 'affair' tap into this distinction. While the narrative models of stories Two and Three reflect the drive to comfort, Story One centers on the drive toward excitation. In fact, 'comfort' is the word used most frequently in positive evaluations of Stories Two and Three, and 'exciting', 'spice', 'enchantment' and 'adventure' are cited in descriptions of Story One. The drive to excitation – here sexual excitation – is embedded in the first narrative frame and the second narrative frame codifies the 'comfort' to be found in sharing daily life with another person.

Thus the dichotomy between the romantic-fictional and realist-every-day narrative frames of love cannot be adequately reduced to a simple opposition between 'texts and reality' or 'representation vs simulacrum'. Both types of stories, the romantic and the realist, tap into *different categories of physical, psychological and phenomenological experiences*, one enacting the highly aestheticized, theatrical and stylized properties of 'adventure', and the other exhibiting the continuous and shapeless flow of everyday life; one motivated by the drive toward excitation, the other by the drive toward comfort. These two forms of experiences are embedded in the distinction between the uneventful routine character of everyday life and the outbursts of emotions that periodically erupt in the realm of everyday life and mark dramaturgic interactions.

The fact that these highly aestheticized autobiographical accounts are anchored within bodily experiences of excitation and comfort and in the universal distinction between routine and drama, gives a new twist to our inquiry about the postmodern condition of romance, one that includes the paramount reality of bodily experiences. As Featherstone (1992) suggests, certain forms of experience embedded in the body are codified and 'progressively submitted to the codification of cultural producers'. *These codes are in turn incorporated into life and provide stylized narratives within which one constructs and makes sense of one's experience.* The two narrative codes of love are anchored in distinct bodily and phenomenological experiences and undergo a process of stylization and aestheticization in the realm of mass media, with the results subsequently feeding back into everyday life.

Now, if the romantic experience is organized around these two phenomenological – and narrative – poles, what difference does it make that one type – and not another – is endlessly represented and codified in the highly visual and realistic narrative codes of media culture and (re-) enters the realm of everyday life via the consumption of mass media forms? Following Simmel, Featherstone (1992) contends that highly stylized and aesthetic narratives (such as my respondents' autobiographical accounts) can provide a way to overcome the heterogeneity of everyday life by supplying it with an art-like unity and coherence.

However, I would argue that these aestheticized narratives of love do not unify the romantic self with a 'heroic' telos but rather split it into incompatible narratives by making it *the site of contradictions.* Far from being viewed as a desirable or 'heroic' life narrative, the romantic ideal was treated by my respondents with suspicion, derision and ironic distance.

7. A Postmodern Romantic Condition

Most traditional societies privilege comfort and carefully attempt to control (or suppress) the expression of the drive to excitation exemplified in sexual attraction (Goode, 1968). The cultural ideal of romantic love has given a greater legitimacy to the intensity of passion and sexual attraction as it emphasizes the uniqueness of the loved one and restricts the possible number of partners by subsuming the romantic biography under a single life-long narrative of love ('*le grand amour*'). But this narrative of love almost never becomes a narrative of comfort. Since it must affirm the supremacy of passion, it is usually doomed to end with the parting or death of the lovers.[11] Postmodern romance has seen the collapse of overarching, life-long romantic narratives, which it has compressed into the briefer and repeatable form of the *affair.*

The 'affair' is related to the transformations undergone by sexuality after the Second World War (Seidman, 1991). During this period, sex for its own sake was progressively legitimized and promoted by the political discourses of feminist and gay liberation, a process that was aided by the powerful cultural idioms of the sphere of consumption. In its intrinsic transience and affirmation of pleasure, novelty and excitement, the affair may be dubbed a postmodern experience and contains a structure of feeling with affinities to the emotions and cultural values fostered by the sphere of consumption.

As Scitovsky argues, consumption rests on the drive toward excitation because the purchase and experience of new commodities are a source of pleasure:

> Novelty is a major source of satisfaction, to judge by the large quantity we avidly consume every day and the high value we place on it. First love, first taste of some special food, or a naked body, together with many firsts, are among our most cherished memories. (Scitovsky, 1976: 58)

In contradistinction to the teleological, absolute and single-minded Romantic narrative of 'grand amour', the affair is a cultural form that attempts to immobilize and repeat, compulsively, the primordial experience of 'novelty'. Moreover, the affair is undergirded by a consumerist approach to the choice of a mate. During the Victorian era, people chose from a very narrow pool of available partners and often felt compelled to marry their first suitor.[12] The contemporary affair, by contrast, presupposes variety and freedom to choose. This 'shop-and-choose' outlook is due to a much wider pool of available partners and to the fact that a marketplace viewpoint – the belief that one should commit oneself after a long process of information gathering – has pervaded romantic practices.[13] The double consumer motive of 'freedom of choice' – based on the perceived freedom to choose between various partners according to one's preferences – and of transient but renewable pleasures radically alters the pre-modern romantic and sexual sensibility.

The traditional Romantic narrative of 'le grand amour' was a double narrative of revelation – a sudden, unforeseen conviction of the unique desirability of another person, and of a kind of secular salvation: from love at first sight, the lover projected herself or himself whole into a future that could redeem their entire existence, even though they might die of it. Thus Emma Bovary clings to the idea that her relationship with Rodolphe is no mere 'affair' but rather the prelude to the great narrative she strives and waits for. In this respect, Emma stands on the threshold between the (modern) Romantic sensibility in which lives are spent waiting for or consuming themselves in a life-long 'master' narrative of love and the postmodern one in which several affairs – self-contained and 'local' narratives of love – occur serially in the course of a life.

The affair can be viewed as a postmodern expression of *intensities* or experiences of pure sensations, desire, pleasures, non-mediated by reason, language or a master narrative of self. In contrast to the pre-modern era, romantic intensities have eliminated the experience of 'waiting' – which was so central in Victorian women's lives – and are characterized by a total absence of the tragic. Tragedy is the inscription within a narrative structure of cosmic, ineluctable forces that rule over the individuals' lives. By their involvement, however, these forces raise those lives beyond the level of the merely individual, the subjective, the haphazard, giving human lives the weight of 'destiny'. In the equanimity with which they recount falling in and out of love, the respondents' autobiographical accounts bear a decisively untragic 'lightness'. Nowhere could I find the poignancy and existential gravity of the Romantic idea of the 'great love', because respondents – both men and women – did not project themselves into an all-encompassing narrative of love initiated by the revelation of a unique and eternal love. Their stories start in a mode of excitation rather than revelation. They have a sharply marked beginning and end – which is why they deserve the name of 'story' – but little intermediate narrative development, the frequent presence of an obstacle that might have driven such development (e.g. being already married, living in different places). Affairs then, are self-contained narrative episodes disconnected from one another in the flow of experience, resulting in a fragmenting of the experience of love into separate emotional units (the transitory settings of so many of these stories exhibit a corresponding spatial fragmentation). Romantic intensities similarly fragment time into what Jameson calls 'charges of affect' and thus contribute to the 'flat' present deemed characteristic of the postmodern contraction of time: temporality loses the unifying continuity of a life characterized by either a stable, enduring relationship or a grand (or grandiose) passion.

While human beings have doubtless always had sex before or outside marriage, the 'affairs' we have been looking at are peculiarly postmodern in a number of respects. First, like so much else in postmodern culture (Lash, 1990), they institutionalize liminality. Almost all the affairs recounted above took place on geographic, institutional and temporal margins, away from the routine space of home and work, outside the framework of family, marriage, job, in the exceptional time marked by romantic intensities and the merging of selves. This form of liminality provides postmodernity a defining rhetorical figure – the inversion of normative hierarchies and symbolic form – the reversal of identities and blurring of boundaries, social, aesthetic and cultural.

Second, the sexual flavor of 'liberation' since the 1960s makes the postmodern affair significantly different from the indiscriminate and power-ridden search for sexual pleasure embodied by the archetypical characters of Don Juan or Casanova. Contemporary affairs are more likely to be lived as sexual pleasure by *both* sexes, and in that respect reflect the diffuse androgyny of postmodern culture. Third, they do not contain elements of transgression and do not oppose any normative or moral imperative. Contrary to de Rougemont's account in *Love in the Western World* (1966), postmodern love is not set to fight any moral or social obstacle. Instead, the affair affirms the diffuse egalitarian eroticism and primal liberation of the instincts that, according to Daniel Bell (1980), has marked the postmodern onslaught on middle-class values. Finally, underlying the postmodern affair is a definition of identity based on lifestyle choices and consumer rationality. Although as yet there is little empirical data on this matter, I submit that the affair characterizes the romantic experience of those professionals and new cultural intermediaries, located in large urban centers, who are most proficient at switching between sexual pleasure and forms of economic rationality. One might even venture to suggest that the 'commitment phobia' so abundantly commented on in this population is a by-product of an identity largely based in the affirmation of autonomy through lifestyle choices, resulting in a reluctance to give up the freedom to choose and the prospect of 'finding a better mate'.

This discussion has not yet addressed the important question: why is the narrative of intensity more salient in people's memories, why does it have a stronger capacity to name the experience of loving than the narrative of everyday life?

The first obvious answer is that the phenomenological experience of the 'adventure' or the 'affair' is *cognitively* more salient than that of sharing everyday life with another. 'Extraordinary' experiences, by their nature, stand out from the stream of everyday life. They embody a form of bond in which emotions are dramatized, intense and ritualized. These dramatistic meanings of romance are sustained by a culture which privileges the consumption of leisure as a withdrawal from everyday life with the purpose of regenerating one's connection to society through the liberation of energy, the reversal of the constraints of everyday life (Illouz, 1997). Precisely because they lack the capacity to be ritualized, the meanings of everyday life are less susceptible to being codified in the highly stylized vignettes of mass culture. The meanings of everyday life are less formalized, fuzzier and therefore emotionally less intense than the meanings contained in leisure, 'adventures' and 'affairs'. Furthermore, one could make the claim that in contradistinction to religious teleology, contemporary culture hardly offers cultural frameworks in which the self can understand itself in a *diachronic* narrative. Contemporary (romantic) selfhood is better equipped to attend to and make sense of fragmented intensities than to overarching continuous time narratives. The experiential categories of love in the realm of everyday life thus conflict with the hedonism, intensity and aestheticism that are the basis of the experience of being a postmodern consumer and viewer.

This implies the following: the narrative within which the self *remembers its most significant* stories and the one within which the romantic self projects its chances for happiness do not match each other and may even contradict each other, thus thwarting the possibility of a continuous temporal structure containing a homogeneous self. The contemporary romantic self is marked by its persistent, Sisyphus-style attempt to conjure up the local and fleeting intensity of the love affair within long-term global narratives of love (such as marriage), to reconcile an overarching narrative of enduring love with the fragmentary intensity of affairs. This splitting of the romantic self into incompatible narrative structures, the patching of self-contained, discontinuous affairs into narratives of life-long love, breaks the coherent, heroic self of modernity into a 'collage' of conflicting narrative selves. And this collage, I want now to claim, is accompanied with a crisis of representation which we may qualify as postmodern.

Approached as fiction, Stories Two and Three are readily interpreted as expressions of 'realistic' love story. In respondents' own autobiographies, however, similar stories are interpreted according to a standard set by the affair and are consequently suspected of not referring to the actual feeling of love. In other words, when experienced, the realist narrative frame seems to empty itself of its signified, or at least to struggle to find one. By contrast, when the first narrative frame is presented as a fictional story, it is viewed as 'fabricated' and 'unreal', but when experienced, it is no longer viewed as an empty signifier but rather as the 'real referent' lived to its fullest meaning. For example, when asked to choose the most romantic story, one man chose (the realist) Story Two. But when the same man recalled and explained what had gone wrong in his most recent relationship, he said:

> [T]he last [relationship], we understood each other and we got along so well, but there was almost a spark missing.
>
> *What do you mean?*
>
> We were very compatible. We loved being together on a day-to-day basis. We got along very well. But the more romantic ideal side really never, uh, so I missed that.
>
> *What do you mean when you say that the romantic side was missing?*
>
> I felt almost as if I was going to bed with my best friend instead of with a lover. (male, music conductor, 30)

Clearly, this story has the 'fuzzy' character of the plots of everyday life and refers to the notion that compatibility is necessary if a relationship is to succeed. However, although this narrative model is normatively viewed as an ideal one, it is experienced as problematic in its lack of intensity and passion. This in turn prevents it from being incorporated into the romantic self as readily as the first model of love. Not only does the model of love that people normatively hold as the most likely to succeed diverge from what they experience as the most 'striking', 'interesting' or 'memorable' real-life love story, but the realist model of success is evaluated *against the backdrop of the love-at-first-sight model*, which renders it even more lacking in intensity and romance.

While the first narrative frame of intensity signifies romance without including the signified 'love', the second narrative frame, by contrast, offers this signified without the romantic signifier. This disjunction between the signifier of romance and the signified of love is one of the characteristic features of the 'postmodern' condition. In this disjunction appears a split autobiographical narrative structure: while the narrative signifier that best organizes respondents' most memorable stories embodies Jameson's intensities, this signifier is disconnected from the less memorable but longer-lasting narrative, that, respondents presume, captures the signified love.

Even more interesting is the way in which respondents accounted for this discrepancy. Far from being viewed as an existential dilemma or a tragedy of human existence, these 'semiotic quandaries' were analyzed and explained as *the by-product of mass-media culture*. For example:

Where do you think your ideas about love come from?

I think a lot of them come from the movies and they are I think, I think the movies have fucked us up a great deal in terms of our images about love.

Fucked us up?

Yeah, I think that like the first story would be more like in the movies. They meet in the train and fall in love instantly, and they run off and they get married, and we are supposed to believe that that's possible. And I don't think that it happens that way very often. So in that sense I think a lot of us spend our lives on trains hoping to fall in love. Sitting across the subway maybe I will meet my wife. It doesn't work that way. But there is still this expectation from the movies. (male, 33, actor)

Or:

Where do you think your ideas about love come from?

A large part I guess from media and from myths about love.

Which myths?

Oh, the myth about happily ever after and the myth of being swept off your feet, the myth you know, I think the most dangerous myth for women finding a man or being attached to a man somehow is, is so terribly important in order to make your life all right or something. I think those are very powerful for most people whether they think about it or even know it. I think those are probably the most powerful things, and I'm sure for me too even though I have thought about it a lot. Some of my ideas are from not wanting what my parents had and I guess mostly just from those images that you see in the media and that you see your friends all trying to live up to, probably the most influential things. (female, editor)

Respondents self-consciously used stereotypical expressions ('love conquers all', 'the princess being rescued', 'a man for every woman') to describe early expectations that they suspect were formed by media stories and images. Like postmodern artists and sociologists the respondents maintain the ironic stance that their representations and experiences are 'simulacra', imitations of manufactured signs devoid of referents. The romantic self perceives itself ironically, like a pre-scripted actor who repeats the words and gestures of other pre-scripted actors, simply repeating others' repetitions.

We have now come full circle: the same narrative structure that respondents view as 'Hollywood', 'unreal' and 'fabricated' is also the same one that respondents unproblematically use to name and recall their romantic love stories. On the other hand, the narrative viewed as authentically reflecting the real feelings of love is also the one respondents had more difficulties with as unproblematically referring to love.

8. Conclusion

The romantic experience of one respondent aptly recaps the above discussion and provides a conclusion to this part of my analysis:

What do you think of this story [Story Two]?

It's also romantic.

Romantic.

I suppose it's not romantic in the classical sense. It's nice. It feels good. I mean it's nice. What we discussed earlier vis-a-vis whether it's better to start off quickly or, the first one is obviously love at first sight kind of, whereas the second is more developing, two people who are comfortable and share certain qualities or interests or desires and love develops.

Do you think that Robert and Theresa marry for love?

I think the long-term possibility, prospect of having a long-term loving strong relationship, if they are not in love yet [*sic*].

Would you have liked to have met the partner of your life in the same way?

[long silence] I guess it wouldn't be my first choice but it would certainly be a reasonable.

Why not your first choice?

Well, it lacks the excitement or the strong attraction that is most desirable thing to have, the sort of excited attraction and the strong feelings and it does give, the story does give a sense that everyone is just kind of as if you choose a car.

So is it nice or not nice? You started by saying the story was nice.

Well if it had more of a sense – the story is a little vague in terms of whether in fact they do develop any kind ...

What is your impression? The story is vague on purpose so that I can see how you interpret it.

It wouldn't be my first choice ... maybe it's what I think I *should want* and maybe it would be more practical. . . . The truth of the matter is that one of the

reasons I didn't get married some years ago when I was engaged was it was
more of Story Two kind of situation and without real passion and excitement
attached to it and I ultimately decided to break it. And in some way I did
wrong.

In what way was it wrong?

Because I think in the long term it would have been a healthy and viable and
loving relationship. *Maybe there was a little less excitement than one is
promised by reading novels and watching what happens between Cary Grant
and Gina Lollobrigida and that's something I should have also. But even Cary
Grant and Gina Lollobrigida, sometimes have to sit in the living room and, ten
years later just read a book.* It's part of life. (male, doctor, 38, emphasis
added)

This respondent was aware that he held conflicting representations.
He also illustrates how the same narrative frame is interpreted differently
when used as a memory structure and as a projective structure. When it
structures his memory, Story Two is clearly not very exciting; but when
projected into the future, it is a desirable goal ('in the long run it would have
been a healthy story'). Moreover, this man also held media (cinematic)
representations responsible for instilling in him what he perceived to be
'unrealistic', 'fabricated' and incompatible models. The romantic self is the
site of deep contradictions that are not easily overcome even after one has
committed to living one narrative.

The difficulty in choosing one narrative is accentuated by the perception that the romantic self is the result of textual determinations, 'fabricated'.[14] The romantic self perceives itself in the halo of an ironic semiotic
suspicion. Like Baudrillardian sociologists, my respondents suggest that
their own lives are 'simulations', repetitions, of authorless signs empty of
any real referent.

If as Koselleck (see Habermas, 1990) argues, modernity is characterized by the increasing distance between reality and aspiration,[15] postmodernity is best typified by the self-conscious creed that this distance results
from imaginations over-exposed to the overcodified culture of the mass
media. It is not pure chance that Umberto Eco chose love to define the
postmodern:

I think of the post-modern attitude as that of a man who loves a very
cultivated woman and knows he cannot say to her, 'I love you madly',
because he knows that she knows (and she knows that he knows) that these
words have already been written by Barbara Cartland. [H]e loves her in an
age of a lost innocence. (Eco, 1985: 17)[16]

We may now offer an evaluation of the concept of 'postmodernism' for
social and cultural analysis. To the extent that a cultural interrogation about
the relation between romantic sentiment and romantic codes has been
present in the moral and epistemological discourse of 'modernity', the

postmodern claim that we have moved to 'hyperreality' seems to me to be at best unhelpful, and at worst gibberish. It may be the case that a media-saturated culture deepens and complicates the relation between the ways in which we sustain our experience and the codes that are available to us to construct such experience. But this cultural configuration does not represent a decisively new qualitative turn or radical departure from modern regimes of representation of love and remains, in any case, to be systematically and empirically investigated. What seems to be new, however, is a certain exhaustion of the Romantic paradigm of love, a systematic attitude of irony and unbelief, the demise of Love as a grandiose and threatening experience of the 'limits'. Love seems to have 'flattened' out in a culture where all forms of 'intensities' are actively encouraged and simultaneously demystified.

Thus, when one manages to disentangle the new from the old, it would seem that the postmodern romantic condition brings a crucial twist to La Rochefoucauld's saying that 'few people would fall in love had they not heard about it'; in the postmodern condition, many people doubt they are in love precisely because they have exceedingly heard about it.[17]

Notes

This article is a modified version of Chapter 5 in my book *Consuming the Romantic Utopia: Love and the Cultural Contradictions of Capitalism* (University of California Press).

I wish to thank Elchanan Ben-Porath, Nurit Bird-David, Jose Brunner, Avraham Cordova, Shlomo Deshen, Sigal Goldin, Haim Hazan, Guillermo Olmer, Moshe Shokeid and Sasha Weitman for many useful comments on previous drafts of this paper. Two anonymous reviewers for *Theory, Culture & Society* and Mike Featherstone have provided enlightening suggestions for which I thank them.

1.   I interviewed 50 men and women in three large urban areas of the East Coast of the USA. The interviewees were all white, natives, and had had romantic attachments prior to the interview. Some were married, some divorced, and others had never been married. In the broader study from which this article is drawn, respondents' romantic practices are compared along the dimension of class, defined by income, education and occupation. The sample comprised people working in working-class occupations, others in upper middle-class professions (cultural specialists and professionals). Each interview lasted approximately two hours and combined interpretation of cultural artifacts (photos of romantic couples, advertising pictures, stories, greeting cards) with questions pertaining to the respondents' romantic autobiography.

2.   'Reflexivity' has different meanings in Giddens's and Beck's work, but both have in common the view that the modern self chooses and plans according to some 'master concept' as a life-plan, a career, etc.

3.   None of the stories used mentions if or how much people love each other. However, they do indicate the channels through which the protagonists meet each other and how long it takes them to marry each other. Stories Two and Three associate the relationships with attributes of 'feeling good', 'healthiness' and

'solidity'. Each story contains an obstacle which delays the final decision to get married. It is respectively, parents' consent, the protagonists' shyness and awkwardness, and the professional promotion. All three stories end with a marriage so that the issue of the narrative would not affect the evaluation of the beginning and development of love. I turn now to analyze which narrative models inform the respondents' interpretations of the stories. Toward this end, I have analyzed respondents' reactions to the protagonists of the three stories, their interpretations of their motivations, and the evaluations of the level of 'romance', 'realism' and the 'likelihood of success' of each story. I also asked these respondents to tell me their 'most memorable' love stories, ones either taking place at the time of the interview or already ended. My overall goal was to determine whether there was a relationship between the respondents' life narratives of love and their interpretations of the fictional love stories I provided them with during the interview, and, if such a relationship was found, to understand the intersections between the cultural models used to interpret the three short stories and the respondents' own life stories.

4.   The story is adapted from an actual story first published in the *San Francisco Chronicle* and quoted by Ernest W. Burgess and Paul Wallin (1953: 151).

5.   The respondents most likely to believe in love at first sight are men, across all social groups, and occasionally working-class women. Middle-class women were rarely prepared to believe in this story.

6.   For example, although it is legitimate to marry someone because he or she is 'very smart' or 'very interesting', it is, to say the least, more problematic to claim to marry someone on the sole basis of sexual performance.

7.   This last claim does not always hold true, as some respondents said that precisely because the protagonists of Story Three are too concerned with financial security, and because they are a two-career couple, they will be likely to divorce.

8.   Common sense can be defined as 'a body of knowledge common to a group, pertaining to nature, human nature, and social situations and thought to be rooted in a uniformity of human experience' (Lindenberg, in van Holthoon and Olson, 1987).

9.   Luckman defines 'experience' as 'those events in the stream of consciousness which stand out as topics to which the self attends, which are memorable rather than belonging to the flow of "petites perceptions"' (in van Holthoon and Olson, 1987: 183). By asking for the respondents' own most memorable stories, one gains access to those events that are most significant for the romantic self.

10.   As Hernstein-Smith (1968) acutely notices, a 'closure' implies structure and differs from the mere ceasing of an activity.

11.   Famous examples include Rousseau's *Julie, ou la Nouvelle Héloïse*, Goethe's *Werther*, Hugo's *Les Misérables*, Puccini's *La Bohème*, Verdi's *La Traviata*, etc.

12.   This does not mean that the affair has the anarchic and 'disorganized' character often postulated by postmodern theorists. Quite the contrary, as the recent study on sexual behavior undertaken by Laumann and his associates suggests (1994), most people's sexual partners belong to a pool of people who are quite similar to them, and this despite the fact that barriers of locality, race, religion have been broken. This also suggests that the postmodern 'affair' is quite different from the indiscriminate and unbridled search for pleasure and the motive of male domination that characterize Don Juan's or Casanova's sexual quests.

13.   The falsity of this belief has been demonstrated by Whyte (1990) who, in his study of dating and marriage, shows that cohabitation or long periods of dating previous to marriage do *not* increase its chances for success.

14.   This is congruent with Baudrillard's (1983) assertion that in the postmodern era, the 'masses' (as he mysteriously calls them) know their own lives are simulations, repetitions of authorless signs devoid of any real referent.

15.   As Koselleck puts it: 'My thesis is that in modern times the difference between experience and expectation has increasingly expanded; more precisely, that modernity is first understood as a new age from the time that expectations have distanced themselves evermore from all previous experience' (in Habermas, 1990: 12).

16.   I thank Jose Brunner for having brought this article to my attention.

17.   I owe this last observation to Elchanan Ben-Porath.

References

Baudrillard, J. (1983) *In the Shadow of the Silent Majorities*, trans. Paul Foss, Paul Patton and John Johnston. New York: Semiotext(e).

Beck, U. and E. Beck-Gernsheim (1995) *The Normal Chaos of Love*, trans. Mark Ritter and Jane Wiebel. London: Polity Press.

Bell, D. (1980) *The Winding Passage, Essays in Sociological Journeys, 1960–1980.* New York: Basic Books.

Bruner, J. (1987) 'Life as Narrative', *Social Research* 54(1): 11–32.

Burgess, E.W. and P. Wallin (1953) *Engagement and Marriage*. Philadelphia, PA: Lippincott.

de Rougemont, D. (1966) *Love in the Western World*, trans. M. Beljooh. Greenwich, CT: Fawcet.

Eco, U. (1985) 'Reflections on "The Name of the Rose"', *Encounter* 64(4): 7–19.

Featherstone, M. (1992) 'The Heroic Life and Everyday Life', *Theory, Culture & Society* 9(1): 159–82.

Giddens, A. (1991) *Modernity and Self-Identity: Self and Society in the Late Modern Age.* Cambridge: Polity Press.

Giddens, A. (1992) *The Transformation of Intimacy.* Stanford, CA: Stanford University Press.

Goode, J.W. (1968) 'The Theoretical Importance of Love', *American Sociological Review* 33: 750–60.

Habermas, J. (1990) *The Philosophical Discourse of Modernity.* Boston, MA: MIT Press.

Hernstein-Smith, B. (1968) *Poetic Closure: A Study of How Poems End.* Chicago, IL: Chicago University Press.

Ignatieff, M. (1988) 'Love's Progress', *Time Literary Supplement* April: 15–21.

Illouz, Eva (1997) *Consuming the Romantic Utopia: Love and the Cultural Contradictions of Capitalism.* Berkeley: University of California Press.

Kellner, D. (1989) *Critical Theory, Marxism, and Modernity.* Baltimore, MD: Johns Hopkins University Press.

Lash, S. (1990) *Sociology of Postmodernism.* London: Routledge.

Laumann, E. et al. (1994) *The Social Organization of Sexuality: Sexual Practices in the United States*. Chicago, IL: University of Chicago Press.

Luhmann, N. (1986) *Love as Passion: The Codification of Intimacy*, trans. J. Gaines and D.L. Jones. Cambridge, MA: Harvard University Press.

Lyman, S. and M. Scott (1975) *Drama of Social Reality*. New York: Oxford University Press.

Schutz, A. (1967) *The Phenomenology of the Social World*, trans. G. Walsh and F. Lehnert. Evanston: Northwestern University Press. (Orig. 1932.)

Scitovsky, T. (1976) *The Joyless Economy*. New York: Oxford University Press.

Seidman, S. (1991) *Romantic Longings*. New York: Routledge.

Stone, L. (1977) *The Family, Sex and Marriage in England, 1500–1800*. New York: Harper and Row.

Taylor, C. (1989) *Sources of the Self*. Cambridge, MA: Harvard University Press.

van Holthoon, F. and D. Olson (1987) *Common Sense*. Lanham, MD: University Press of America.

Whyte, M.K. (1990) *Dating, Mating, and Marriage*. New York: De Gruyter.

Eva Illouz is Assistant Professor in the Department of Sociology at Tel-Aviv University. She is the author of *Consuming the Romantic Utopia: Love and the Cultural Contradictions of Capitalism* and is currently working on two other books.

Balancing Sex and Love since the 1960s Sexual Revolution

Cas Wouters

Introduction

PEOPLE LONG FOR sexual gratification and for an intimate relationship. These longings are interconnected, but not unproblematically. Today, some people (mostly men) even view them as contradictory. Traditions providing examples of how to integrate these longings have disappeared; the old 'marriage manuals' have become suspect or hopelessly obsolete, mainly because they hardly acknowledged, if at all, the sensual love and carnal desires of women. Statements such as 'the more spiritual love of a woman will refine and temper the more sensual love of a man' (van Calcar, 1886: 47) typify a Victorian ideal of love that is as passionate as it is exalted and desexualized (Stearns, 1994), with a rather depersonalized sexuality as a drawback and outlet for the man's 'wild' sensuality behind the scenes of social life. This ideal of love mirrors the Victorian attempt 'to control the place of sex in marriage ... by urging the desexualization of love and the desensualization of sex' (Seidman, 1991: 7). In the 20th century, particularly from the 1920s onward, this process was reversed in a 'sexualization of love' and an 'erotization of sex'. However, until the second half of the 20th century the dominant social code regarding the sexuality of women and men clearly continued to represent a lust-dominated sexuality for men and a complementary (romantic) love or relationship-dominated sexuality for women. In this 'traditional lust balance', female sexuality remained highly subordinated to male sexuality:

> A woman does not *take*, but *tempts* in order to be taken.... Copulation is performed *by* a man and *to* a woman. (Wattjes, 1930: 34)

■ *Theory, Culture & Society* 1998 (SAGE, London, Thousand Oaks and New Delhi),
Vol. 15(3–4): 187–214
[0263-2764(199808/11)15:3–4;187–214;006064]

> The newly married woman *is as a rule*, more or less completely 'cold' or indifferent to and in sexual intercourse. She must be *taught to love*, in the complete sense in which we here use the term. The husband may perhaps not succeed in imparting this erotic education; generally that is because he takes no trouble about it. She then *remains* permanently *frigid* ... (van de Velde, 1933: 271)

(It is no surprise, therefore, that the title page of the original Dutch edition of this international bestseller said: 'written for the physician and the husband', that is, not for women.)

Outside this literature, discussions of female sexuality usually had a negative tone centring on the 'prostitution issue' and the issue of 'immorality among the lower classes'. A new branch of this discussion expressed moral concern for what (from the 1920s to the 1950s) was called the 'amatrice' (female amateur):

> The appearance on the scene of the amatrice as a dramatis persona ... is connected to the appearance of a premarital female sexuality that could no longer as a matter of course be localised only within the lower classes nor be lumped automatically under the heading of prostitution. (Mooij, 1993: 136)

Up to the sexual revolution, a woman's sexuality and her reputation remained interconnected within social codes in such a strong way that, in retrospect, it gives the impression that 'as far as her reputation was concerned, a girl who admitted to having sexual needs might as well take a seat behind a window in the red light district' (van Dantzig, 1994: 1276). In the course of the century, more and more women have deviated from this code behind the scenes, but whenever caught in the glare of public attention, they gave rise to scandal and were treated like 'fallen women'.[1]

The 'traditional lust balance' was attacked in the 1950s, when the topic of female sexual pleasure and gratification gained considerable importance in sexual advice literature – *The Adequate Male*, translated into Dutch as *My Husband, My Lover*, is predominantly a good lover (Caprio, 1960). Especially from the 1960s on, the sexual longings of all women, including the 'respectable' and the unmarried, could openly be acknowledged and discussed. Then, for the first time, women themselves actively took part in public discussions about their carnal desires and a more satisfactory relationship between the longing for sexual gratification and the longing for enduring intimacy (love, friendship) – a more satisfying lust balance. Thus, emancipation of women ran in tandem with changes in public morality as well as in individuals' codes and ideals regarding love and sex. These changes coincided with rising tensions between the two types of longing. From the 1960s on, topics and practices such as premarital sex, sexual variations, unmarried cohabitation, fornication, extramarital affairs, jealousy, homosexuality, pornography, teenage sex, abortion, exchange of partners, paedophilia, incest and so on, all part of a wider process of informalization (Wouters, 1986), implied repeated confrontations with the traditional lust balance. People were confronted again and again with what might be called the lust balance question: *when and within what kind of relationship(s) are (what kind of) eroticism and sexuality allowed* and *desired?* This question is first raised in puberty or adolescence when bodily and erotic impulses and emotions that were banned from interaction from early childhood onwards (except in cases of incest) are again explored and experimented with:

> Sexual education predominantly consists of 'beware and watch out'. The original need for bodily contact or touching, which has a very spontaneous frankness in children, also becomes prey to this restriction in the course of growing up. Sexuality *and* corporality are thus separated from other forms of contact. Whenever two people enter an affair, the taboo on touching and bodily contact has to be gradually dismantled. For most people, this is a process of trial and error. (Zeegers, 1994: 139)

In this century, especially since the 1960s, it seems that a similar process of trial and error has been going on collectively, bringing about a collective emancipation of sexuality, that is, a collective diminution in fear of sexuality and its expression within increasingly less rigidly curtailed relationships. Sexual impulses and emotions were allowed (once again) into the centre of the personality – consciousness – and thus taken into account, whether acted upon or not. As the social and psychic distance between the sexes and the classes diminished (Wouters, 1995a, 1995b), both women and men became involved in a collective learning process – experimenting in mainstreams and undercurrents – in which they have tried to find new ideals and ways of gratifying their longing for both sex and love. The questions and answers with which they were confronted shifted and varied along with changes in the spectrum of prevailing interpretations of what constitutes a satisfying lust balance. This article aims at a description and interpretation of this collective learning process.

As studies of the connection and the tension between love and sex are rare, and historical studies of this area are even harder to find,[2] what follows is an 'essay'. It is an attempt to sketch a coherent picture of these social and psychic changes within and between the sexes, and to unfold a perspective that is inherent in the concept of the lust balance. This concept is taken from Norbert Elias, who used it in a wider sense, indicating the whole 'lust economy' (Elias, 1994: 456, 519).[3] Here, the concept is used to focus on the relationship between sex and love, a 'balance' that is perceived to be polymorphous and multidimensional (just as in Elias's concepts of a power balance and a tension balance): the attempt to find a satisfying balance between the longing for sex and the longing for love may be complicated by many other longings; for instance by the longing for children or by the longing to raise one's social power and rank.

Empirical evidence is drawn from a study of changes in the popular Dutch feminist monthly magazine *Opzij*[4] (Aside/Out of the Way), established in 1973, and from sexual advice books. In addition, reference is made to data resulting from sociological and sexological research, as well as from the experience of these decades. Some of these data refer to changes in actual behaviour but most of them refer to changes in codes and ideals of behaviour and feeling. This selection of empirical evidence also implies a stronger focus on women, the women's movement and the emancipation of women, and, by implication, on female sexuality. The reaction of men, their accommodation and the restraining of their sexuality will receive less attention, partly because for men there is no source of evidence comparable with *Opzij* that could be studied as diachronically and systematically: accommodation processes are rather 'quiet' on the whole.

This introduction will be followed by two longer sections. The first aims at describing significant changes in the lust balance since the sexual revolution. It is subdivided according to the four phases that are distinguished. The first phase is the sexual revolution itself. The second one, a phase of transition from the end of the 1970s to the mid-1980s, is characterized by the shift from 'sexual liberation' to 'sexual oppression'. In the third phase, there is a lust revival, and in the fourth, from the early 1990s onwards, a lust *and* love revival continues. The second section of this article consists of an attempt at interpreting and explaining these changes by presenting them as regularities in processes of integration and civilization.

Changes in the Lust Balance

The Sexual Revolution

The sexual revolution was a breakthrough in the emancipation of female sexuality even though many women throughout these years continued to think of sex in terms of duty (Frenken, 1976), sometimes worsened by the new 'duty' to achieve orgasm. Due to the 'pill' and an increase in mutually expected self-restraint (mutual consent) in interactions, the dangers and fears connected with sex diminished to such a degree that there was an acceleration in the emancipation of sexual emotions and impulses. Women's sexual desires were taken more seriously: men became 'more strongly directed at clitoral stimulation' and their aversion to oral sex diminished considerably – from more than 50 percent reported in the early 1970s to about 20 percent 10 years later (Vennix and Bullinga, 1991: 57). This means that increasing numbers of men learned to enjoy the woman's enjoyment and that many women have opened up to sexual fantasies and titillations. The dominant image of single females, if not already 'old spinsters', changed accordingly from 'failed-as-a-woman' and 'sexually deficient' into the opposite: sexy and independent. In a relatively short period of time, the relatively autonomous strength of carnal desire became acknowledged and respected. Erica Jong had her large audience dream about a pure form of instant sex, the 'zipless fuck':

> ... the incident has all the swift compression of a dream and is seemingly free of all remorse and guilt; because there is no talk of her late husband or of his fiancée; because there is no rationalizing; because there is no talk at *all*. The zipless fuck is absolutely pure. It is free of ulterior motives. There is no power game.... No one is trying to prove anything or get anything out of anyone. The zipless fuck is the purest thing there is. And it is rarer than the unicorn. And I have never had one. (Jong, 1973: 14)

For both genders, sex for the sake of sex changed from a degrading spectre into a tolerable and thus acceptable alternative, allowing more women and men to experiment with sex cheerfully and outside the boundaries of love and law. Until around 1970, the slogan of the advice literature that accompanied this process was that 'men should restrain themselves somewhat more and women should be a bit more daring' (Röling, 1990: 90), a slogan that was obviously attuned to men who came too quickly and women who did not come at all. From then on, interest and attention shifted from joint pleasures towards discovering one's own sexual desires and delights. In close connection with this, the ideal of love shifted further away from the Victorian ideal of a highly elevated marital happiness towards individual happiness and greater scope for each partner to develop themselves (Blom, 1993; Mahlmann, 1991; Swidler, 1980). In the early 1970s, the growing emphasis on individual development also came to be expressed collectively in the deliberately created 'apartheid' of discussion groups, refuge homes, pubs, bookshops, etc. 'for women only', expressing an outlook of 'emancipation-via-segregation' (van Stolk, 1991).

Sex-for-the-sake-of-sex was first and to a greater extent accepted among homosexual men, who almost seemed to realize the dream of the 'zipless fuck'. The far-reaching liberation of sexuality among them was a topic that was also frequently discussed outside their circles, with both an envious and a frightened tone. The comparison with homosexuals also had another function, put into words by Joke Kool-Smit (commonly credited with having triggered the second feminist wave in the Netherlands): 'feminists and homosexuals are each other's natural allies', she explains, not only because both groups are discriminated against, but from a

> ... much deeper similarity between the liberation of women and of homosexuals. Both demand the right not to behave like a woman or a man ought to, they do not accommodate to their sex role of strong man and soft woman. (*Opzij*, 1973[11]: 26)

However, as Kool-Smit continues, 'some male homosexuals ... are even more strongly adapted to male mysticism than the average hetero-man. And this group and feminists stand directly opposed to each other'. The

LIVERPOOL
JOHN MOORES UNIVERSITY
AVRIL ROBARTS LRC
TEL. 0151 231 4022

struggle for liberation from the straitjacket of sex roles obviously had priority, but as far as sexual liberation was concerned, Kool-Smit referred to lesbian women as a model:

> ... lesbian feminists could be an example for other women with regard to their relationships and in finding a distinct identity. For in these relationships where men are absent, emotional warmth need not come from one side only, and erotics can at last be separated from dominance. (*Opzij*, 1973[11]: 26)[5]

In their quest for a more satisfying lust balance, the two sexes tended to go in opposite directions. Led by their gender-specific definitions of lust, men tended to go towards a lust-dominated sexuality, towards sex for the sake of sex as (imagined) in the world of homosexual men, and women towards a love- and relationship-dominated sexuality in which physical love and psychical love are integrated and set apart from domination as (imagined) in the world of homosexual women. An undercurrent of women emphasizing lust by sharing the dream of the 'zipless fuck', also shared the mainstream women's longing for a sex that is pure, that is, uncontaminated by power and dominance.

In these years, increasing numbers of women and men will have experienced with greater intensity that the relationship between carnal desires and the longing for enduring intimacy is an uneasy one, and that the continuation and maintenance of a (love) relationship had on the whole become more demanding. The feelings of insecurity, shame, guilt, fear and jealousy, as well as the conflicts, divorces and other problems related to their drifting lust balance, were all perceived and discussed, for instance in the encounter and sensitivity movement, but hardly, if at all, by the women's movement. At the time, the spirit of liberation from the straitjacket of older generations and their morality, and the fervour of the movement did not allow much attention to be given to the *demands* of the liberation.

From 'Sexual Liberation' to 'Sexual Oppression'

In several respects the sexual revolution ended towards the end of the 1970s, as the voices raised against sexual violence became louder and louder. At that time, as the study of *Opzij* shows, in addition to sexual assault and rape, sex with children – incest in particular – and pornography also came to be included in the category of sexual violence. In the early 1980s, sexual harassment was added. As the women's movement turned against sexual violence, attention shifted from differences between the generations to differences between the sexes. Opposition to the sexual practices and morality of older generations diminished, while opposition to those of the dominant sex gained momentum (van Daalen and van Stolk, 1991). 'Greater sexual openness and more acceptance of sexuality had brought sexual abuse into sight' (Schnabel, 1990: 16), and this was another reason for the shift of emphasis from sexual liberation to sexual oppression. In the media, the

misery surrounding sex came under the floodlights. In the women's movement, heterosexuality was sometimes branded as 'having sex with your
oppressor', a sentiment also expressed in the lesbian slogan 'more sun,
fewer men'. In 1976, one of two lesbian women was reported to have said:
'We are interviewed because of being lesbians, because we make love to
women ... whereas this is the perfectly normal result of seeing yourself as
important and of refusing to live in oppressive conditions any longer' (*Opzij*,
1976[10]: 4–6). Hardly anything but 'soft sex' – sex that is not aimed at
intercourse – still attracted positive attention, and the phrase '*potteus
bewustzijn*' (lesbian consciousness) became popular as a kind of yardstick
for feminism.[6] Retrospectives on the 'years of sexual liberation' were also
increasingly set in a negative tone:

> It is appalling to notice how many people's thinking became stuck in the
> ideas of the sixties, at least with respect to sexuality. 'Anything goes' and 'the
> sky is the limit' are still their slogans and these stimulate a tolerance
> regarding any daughter–sister assault, which is a slap in the face of the
> victims. (*Opzij*, 1983[2]: 14)

The change of perspective and feeling from liberation to oppression,
occurring from the end of the 1970s into the first half of the 1980s, did not
imply an increase in attention to the demands of liberation, that is,
increased demands on self-regulation, such as the capacity to negotiate a
more ideal lust balance. Whereas before the fervour of the struggle against
the old morality had prevented this, now moral indignation about oppression
functioned as such a barrier. This indignation also produced a blinkered
view of the (gender-specific) difficulties connected with the emancipation of
sexual impulses and emotions. Directing public attention to the difficulties
of women in particular was met with moral indignation by feminists; it was
branded as 'individualizing', that is, as reducing structured male oppression
to individual problems of women. While the perspective did shift collectively from the other (older) generation to the other sex (men), it remained
almost exclusively directed *outwards*: the origin as well as the solution of all
difficulties was to be found in oppression by men.

Banning the psychical demands of emancipation from public discussions and from sight did not, of course, facilitate the quest for a new
lust balance, as may be concluded from two extreme ways in which it was
sought. One extreme consisted of a romanticization of old we-and-I feelings
– of traditional female solidarity and identity – and an attack on pornography as a form of sexual violence. Here, the implicit lust balance strongly
emphasises love and soft sex, coupled to tenderness and affection. This view
was the dominant one, and was also advocated by the intellectual avant-
garde of the women's movement. Only one author deviated strongly from the
general trend by expressing regret that a monthly like *Playgirl*, in comparison with magazines for homosexuals, contained so few pictures evoking a
visual pleasure that presupposed 'a pleasure in sex without the ballast of

love' (Ang, 1983: 433; Wouters, 1984). Other contrasting voices did not go nearly as far and, taken together, in the early 1980s their force seems to have shrunk to a marginal whisper. In that margin, the other extreme was to be found. It consisted of a tipping of the lust balance to its opposite side. According to tradition, a woman should have sexual desires and fantasies only *within* a romantic relationship, which was meant to last a lifetime. In a lust balance that is tipped the other way, a woman's sexuality could be aroused only *outside* such a relationship, in almost anonymous, instant sex. All public discussion focused on the first of these two extremes, while the second remained virtually in the shadows. Ironically, in emphasizing male oppression so strongly, the difficulties connected with the emancipation of sexuality were indeed reduced to the psychic and/or relational problems of individuals, thus leading precisely to the 'individualizing' that was so fiercely opposed at that time. A closer inspection of both extremes follows in the next two sections.

The Anti-Pornography Movement.   During the first half of the 1980s, protests against pornography were numerous and sizeable, sometimes even violent. In 1980, a massive anti-pornography demonstration was held. Slogans such as 'pornography is hatred of women' and 'pornography is sexual violence' became well known. In 1984, shortly before AIDS, a Dutch ministerial report on sexual violence was strongly against pornography and against 'the process of pornographization in the media, in the advertising industry and in mass-produced literature' (*Nota*, 1984: 47). To the extent that this stance was explained, reference was made to a romantic relational ideal of love, thus preventing any public recognition of the appreciation of sex, and certainly not of sex for the sake of sex.

  Although pornography certainly contains many examples of images that are degrading to women, the rejection of the whole genre was nevertheless remarkable. For one thing, the numerous protests against pornography usually suggested that only men were susceptible to this kind of titillation of the senses, and that therefore only men were responsible for the process of 'erotization', referred to as 'pornographization' in the ministerial report. At that time, there was already plenty of evidence – data derived from experimental research – to suggest that this is quite unlikely: images and fantasies of fortuitious sexual conquests by sexually active and dominant women could certainly titillate the female senses. This kind of research suggests that it is plausible to assume that both women and men are more strongly sexually aroused by fantasies and images of sexual chance meetings than by those of marital or bought sexual intercourse (Fisher and Byrne, 1978), that fantasies about 'casual' and 'committed' sex make no difference in women's sexual arousal (Mosher and White, 1980) and that women, just like men, are more strongly sexually excited by fantasies and images of sex that is initiated and dominated by someone of their own gender (Garcia et al., 1984; Heiman, 1977; at a later date also: Dekker, 1987: 37; Laan, 1994). Furthermore, research data also suggested that the difference between the sexes in experiencing pornography was relatively small, provoking more arousal and fewer conflicts and guilt feelings if women had been able to explore their sexuality more freely, just like men, and had developed a more liberal, 'modern' sexual morality (Sigusch and Schmidt, 1970; Straver, 1980: 55). An interesting (later) finding in this context is that on the whole, genital arousal – vascocongestion – occurs 'even when the erotic stimulus is evaluated negatively or gives rise to negative emotions and when little or no sexual arousal is reported' and that 'the gap between genital and subjective sexual arousal is smaller for women who masturbate frequently (10 to 20 times per month) than for women who masturbate less often or not at all' (Laan, 1994: 78, 164, 169). This finding suggests the interpretation that women who masturbate often are better informed about their carnal desires and/or indulge more (easily) in them. In addition to frequency of masturbation, frequency of coitus also yielded higher correlations between genital and subjective sexual arousal (Dekker, 1987).[7]

Women's public opinion on pornography was also remarkable in comparison with that towards prostitution and 'pornoviolence' – imagined violence as the simple, ultimate solution to the problem of status competition.[8] There have been hardly any protests by women against the spread of 'pornoviolence' in the media. In the second half of the 1970s, next to pornography, prostitution also became a significant issue. At first the women's movement was ambivalent about prostitution, but in the 1980s, the voices defending prostitutes increasingly drowned out the sounds of protest against them. Prostitutes even succeeded in winning the support of the mainstream women's movement. Yet in fact, on even more adequate grounds than those which apply to pornography, prostitution can be seen as a perverted expression of a sexual morality directed only towards male pleasure and to keeping women in the position of subordinates and servants. As far as 'consumption' is concerned they relate to each other as imagination (pornography) to action (prostitution), while the conditions and relationships of 'production' seem also to be in favour of pornography: the dangers for women are most probably larger in prostitution than on 'the set' or in a studio, and they are absent in the representation of sexual fantasies in books or paintings. In sum, the difference in moral indignation aroused by pornography and prostitution is not likely to be explained by a difference in the dangers of production or consumption. Nor can this difference be explained by a reference to the prostitutes' organization *De Rode Draad* (The Red Thread), which was established only in 1985.

Except as a symptom of women's solidarity,[9] the comparatively small extent of moral indignation at prostitution may be largely understood from women's sensitivity to the argument that there is little difference between the selling of sex in prostitution and in marriage – 'for the sake of peace, or as an expression of gratitude for a night out or a new dress' (*Opzij*, 1979[7/8]: 41). In this 'sex-is-work' view, prostitutes may seem to have the upper hand by staying more independent and obtaining higher financial rewards. In this view, lust has no place and sex brings more displeasure than pleasure:

women appear predominantly as sexual objects, not as sexual subjects. As such, it mirrors another view that was still widely held in the 1970s, the belief that men are entitled to have sex with their wives. In 1975, a detective of the Amsterdam vice squad was still shameless enough to say: 'I'm almost 60 years old now and I've raped my wife quite often. Yes, if she didn't want to [do it with me]' (*Opzij*, 1975[3/4]: 38). In addition to this sex-is-work view, the image of the 'prankster' emerged: 'naughty' women who (more often than not) enjoy the sex they are paid for – an example of women turning traditional double morality upside down.

The protests against pornography also evoke surprise because they go against the flow of the 20th-century process of informalization (increasing behavioural and feeling alternatives) and its inherent 'erotization of every-day life' (Wouters, 1990, 1992). Together, all these arguments seem to permit the conclusion that the anti-pornography movement, to a large extent, was an 'emancipation cramp'. It was predominantly an expression of the problems connected with the emancipation of sexuality: the attack on male pornography was a sort of 'best defence', concealing as well as expressing a 'fear of freedom' (in Erich Fromm's famous phrase), a fear of experiencing and presenting oneself as a sexual subject.

What is the Price of Sex?   In the margin of the public debate, some of the difficulties attached to the emancipation of sexual feelings sometimes surfaced more or less casually, one of them being the risk of tipping over to the other extreme of the lust balance. At this other extreme, sex was isolated by excluding sexual intimacy from other forms of intimacy, as these had come to be experienced as obstacles to sexual pleasure. Sexual desires tended towards the 'zipless fuck', to a 'sex without the ballast of love', while the forces which formerly forbade this - the social code and individual conscience – still had to be avoided with such energy and determination that their absence, so to speak, loomed large. This was expressed by a woman who said:

> For years and years I did not want any emotional commitment with men.... What I did do regularly at the time, though, was pick up a one-night stand. In fact, that suited me well.... Because I was not emotionally committed to those men, I was able to take care of my sexual needs very well.... It also gave me a feeling of power. I did just as I pleased, took the initiative myself and was very active. (Groenendijk, 1983: 368)[10]

A statement like this shows more than a shift of accent in the traditional mixture of love ('emotional commitment') and carnal desire. Here, the price of sex, to put it dramatically, is nothing less than love. The formulation – particularly the word 'because' – indicates that the lusts of the flesh can be given a free rein only if the longing for love is curbed radically, as radically as lust was curbed before. For this reason this was called 'the new withdrawal method': 'Don't go for happiness, just go for orgasm' (Rubinstein, 1983: 79). The coexistence of an abhorrence of subordination to men with a longing for a loving relationship will have made many women suspicious of their relational longing. They feared that if they gave in to this craving for love, they would lose 'the feeling of power' since they would (as usual) almost automatically flow into the devouring dependence of a self-sacrificing love (see Dowling, 1981). Therefore, what at first sight appears to be a fear of intimacy is in fact another expression of the 'fear of freedom'.

As an undercurrent, this lust balance formed the negative of that propagated by mainstream feminism, that is, the anti-porno movement. It is an open question as to how many women who in public turned against pornography and, by implication, against male sexual fantasies, to some extent combined this attitude in private with an escape from emotional commitment into volatile sexual affairs. What may be concluded, however, if only from the coexistence of these two extremes, is that in this period there must have been a tug-of-war between and within women; *between* women who ventured into giving free rein to sex for the sake of sex, and women who rejected this; and *within* women to the extent that women encountered both sides in themselves, and met them with ambivalence. The question of how many and how intensely women experienced this tug-of-war or ambivalence cannot be answered. From a longer-term perspective, it is obvious, however, that throughout the 20th century and especially since the sexual revolution, many women have been involved in the quest for a more satisfying lust balance, somewhere in between the extremes of 'love without the ballast or duty of sex' and 'sex without the ballast of love'. No woman will have been able completely to withdraw from this development and its inherent tug-of-war and ambivalence, if only because before the sexual revolution the social code allowed women to express only one side of the lust balance.

Lust Revival

In the latter part of the 1980s, the outlook of leaders in the women's movement was less exclusively outward, that is, focused on oppression by men. They developed a more relational view of oppression, a view that saw oppression as incorporated in the social code as well as within personality structures – the latter via the mechanism of an 'identification with the established'. Thus the difficulties and pressures connected with the emancipation of women and of emotions came to attract more attention. This was aptly expressed in the title of the inaugural lecture of a professor of women's studies: 'The Burden of Liberation' (Brinkgreve, 1988). Its point of departure was the insight that 'greater freedom of choice once again turned out to be a pressure to perform', as the historian Röling summarized it (1994: 230). Consequently, emancipation (and assertive use of the greater freedom of choice) was also seen as a learning process in which problems are expected to occur as a matter of course:

It is the complicated task of a 'controlled letting go', making heavy demands on affect control, and it is not to be expected that without a learning process this will proceed spontaneously and 'smoothly'. (Brinkgreve, 1988: 14)

In the latter part of the 1980s, this more reflexive outlook coincided with further emancipation of sexual impulses and emotions. In magazines like *Opzij*, more attention was given to themes like 'men as sexual objects', women buying sex, women's adultery, SM, positively evaluated passes and eroticism in the workplace, and also for 'safe sex' (owing to AIDS). These topics were discussed soberly. When an early attempt at commercializing this interest was made through the establishment of a Dutch version of *Playgirl*, the magazine had the cautious and typical policy of not publishing 'frontal nudes'. It was defended with the argument that:

> ... women have only in the last five years begun to discuss their fantasies. Male nudity does not eroticize.... It is power which makes men erotically appealing. Hence the popularity of romance novels in which the male star is a doctor, a successful businessman or an elderly father figure. (*NRC Handelsblad*, 21 October 1987)

Yet the wave of moral indignation at pornography faded away and in retrospect the anti-pornography movement was characterized as a 'kind of puritanism' (*Opzij*, 1988[9]: 43). From the mid-1980s onwards, a number of women-made, female-centred pornographic films showing women actively initiating and enjoying sexual activity appeared on the market (Laan, 1994: 163).

In this period, a sexologist relativized the importance of 'intimacy'. She wrote: 'in many ways, the need for intimacy can be a trap for women', and after having presented some examples of women who like making love to strangers, finding sexual pleasure, she concludes:

> Indeed, at times there is this double feeling: you *do* want that pleasurable experience of togetherness, you *do* want to have sex, but you don't bargain for a rather too intimate steady relationship. (*Opzij*, 1986[7/8]: 69)

In 1988, in a special issue of *Opzij* on 'Women and Lust', this argument was supplemented with a strong attack on the traditional lust balance:

> Tradition teaches a woman to experience her sexuality as predominantly relational and intimate. But it is an amputation through traditional female socialization to represent a sexuality so weakly directed at pleasure and lust.

The article, directed especially at 'career women who live alone', continues first with a plea to have 'sex for the sake of sex, to be erotic and horny but not emotionally committed' and then warns:

If a woman nevertheless (secretly) needs intimacy in order to enjoy sex, she will always be left with a hangover. After too many hangovers she will stop having this kind of affair. Then, she may help herself, that is, masturbate. That can be gratifying too. (*Opzij*, 1988[1]: 86–7)

In later years, this appreciation for masturbation is supported, although sometimes only half-heartedly, as in a review of the first issue of *BEV*, a 'lust magazine' for women:

I think we are on the brink of an individualization of sexuality, a development that very well befits the growing self-sufficiency of women and also accedes nicely to this age of video, telephone sex and special sex-shops for women. However, this image does not please me. What I sketch here, in fact, is an exact copy of what men are used to doing: they hurry to see a peep show during lunch hour, or use the company toilet to take the matter into their own hands. (*Opzij*, 1989[2]: 17)

A few months later, this author attacked a sexologist (Vennix), who had found that half of his female respondents repeatedly made love without the lust to do so, for creating the impression that women actually *are* like that. After having pointed out that these sombre data on '*the* female orgasm' were derived from questioning 'only married people', she concludes:

I think data like these should be connected above all to circumstances. Personally, I would resent it in any case, if from Vennix's research even *one* man might jump to the conclusion that the importance of *my* orgasm could possibly ever be overestimated. (*Opzij*, 1989[6]: 25)

A 'large study of sex and relationships', published in *Opzij* in 1989, comparing female readers of this magazine to a general sample of Dutch women, shows that the emancipation of women and of sexuality run in tandem. It concludes that *Opzij* readers in certain respects had become more like men – a 'masculinization'. They are, for instance, more playfully thinking about keeping up more than one relationship, and they rate having sex (masturbation as well as coitus) higher on a scale. On the other hand, a 'feminization' is concluded from their pursuit of 'a sex between equals, allowing, even stimulating dedication':

Traditional 'femininity', including tenderness, foreplay and passion, is not weakened in this process of renewal. On the contrary, men are expected to behave like this too. The renewal can be characterized as eroticizing feminization. (*Opzij*, 1988[1]: 70)

In this period, the Chippendales and similar groups of male strippers (who keep their G-strings on) appeared on the scene, and their success shows that the public titillation of female lust has become a socially accepted fact. Although the Chippendales do indeed make caressing movements in the direction of their crotches, their coquetry in military uniforms, however, is a continuing variation upon the tradition of the Mills & Boon romance novels in which women need to look up to a man before they are willing to nestle in his arms (van Stolk and Wouters, 1987a: 136–72). This pleasure in looking up shows how deeply rooted in the personality the longing for (male) protection is, while all the same it is based on the woman's subordination. It also shows the significance of 'identification with the established' as a defence mechanism.

Since all the changes described above represent movements in the same direction, it is plausible that from the mid-1980s onward, the difference between men and women regarding their lust balance – both ideally and in practice – has diminished. There was a certain lust revival, an acceleration in the emancipation of sexuality. The revival was limited, however, as can be demonstrated from the lack of commercial success of magazines aiming at female sexual fantasies, magazines like *Playgirl* and *BEV*: both disappeared after a few issues.

Lust and Love Revival

A research finding regarding the difference in appreciation of qualities of one's own partner and those of a fantasy partner possibly expresses a characteristic tension of the female lust balance, prevailing in the 1990s: women reported to particularly appreciate their own partner for qualities that are traditionally female – not macho, but sweet, tender, sensitive, emotional, honest, faithful, caring, devoted, companionable, all together 62 percent – whereas dreams about a (sex) partner mainly refer to corporeal characteristics like robust, big, handsome, dark type, sexy; all together 65 percent (Brinkgreve, 1995).

In the 1990s, further revival of female lust has been expressed in the successful sales figures of mailing businesses and chain stores marketing erotic articles for women, in particular from the sale of vibrators: both in 1993 and 1994 there has been an increase of 25 percent (*NRC Handelsblad*, 6 April 1995). In Germany, the network of female sex shops has become so dense in the 1990s that *Die Tageszeitung* has proclaimed the decade as that of the 'lusty lady' (6 March 1997). Owners of video shops have reported women's growing interest in porno videos. A 'sexuality weakly directed at pleasure and lust' has become more of a humiliating spectre, while at the same time the sex that prospers in anonymity, sex-for-the-sake-of-sex, evokes far fewer elated reactions, and not only in the context of AIDS. A Dutch trend-watcher claims: 'Sex for the sake of sex is out. . . . Sex is once again being perceived as part of a relationship (as it seems to have been before the sexual revolution)' (Kuitenbrouwer, 1990: 48–9). And an assertive heading in a book on 'erotic manners' reads: 'Sex for the sake of sex is old-fashioned' (van Eijk, 1994). These statements are backed up by research data on young people; they confirm: 'Free sex certainly has not become a new sin, but it is losing popularity.' As an ideal, 'most young people think of love and sexual pleasure as two sides of the same coin, and this goes for both boys and girls' (van der Vliet, 1990: 65; see also Vogels and van der Vliet, 1990). In 1995, 'having strong feelings for each other' sufficed for three-quarters of the Dutch school population (aged 12 years and older) as a precondition for having sex (Brugman et al., 1995). This attitude is reinforced by their parents: 'Many report the presence of a "relationship" to be decisive for their consent to a teenage child wanting to have sex. Some indicate that depth and stability of a relationship, more than age or anything else, makes having sex acceptable' (Townsend Schalet, 1994: 117; see also Ravesloot, 1997). Teenagers themselves in no way exclude the possibility of having sex for its own sake,[11] but in the longer run the ideal of lovers being matched to each other, including in bed, seems to have gained strength. This interpretation is supported by an increase in the number of young people between 17 and 24 years old who would consider an act of sexual infidelity to be the end of a relationship; in a 1979 survey, 41 percent held that opinion and in 1989/1993 this had risen to 63 percent. This very trend is most spectacular for cohabiting youngsters (by now a 'normal' way of life) from 30 to 65 percent (CBS, 1994: 15).

In the 1990s, the women's movement joined this trend under the new name of 'power-feminism'. Women's solidarity was no longer axiomatic, women could and did cooperate with men, and this attitude coincided with increasing attacks on those who still emphasized oppression. This was branded 'victim feminism' and denounced as 'victimism'. The attack was also aimed at romanticizing old harmonious (as well as unequal) relationships and the traditional lust balance of predominantly 'sweet and soft'; by calling that 'vanilla-sex' a larger variety of tastes is indicated as acceptable.

In the homosexual world as well, pioneers in the cultivation of sex for its own sake have lately expressed an ambivalent if not critical attitude towards this (tilted) lust balance. Opposing the lust profit of 'the streamlined way in which sex was organized, disposed of clumsy introductions and annoying questions', Stephan Sanders (1994: 47, 46, 13, 18) mentions the loss of lust in having sex without passion: 'the continuous coupling .. of more or less perfunctory fucks – the waiting, the posing desirably, the taking down of the trousers, the panting, the hoisting up of the trousers'. Here 'the suspicion that, despite all his efforts, his grip on his desire had not gained strength, but had rather weakened' is gnawing. This outlook implies the view that in the longer run, the absence of passion or emotional involvement limits the possibility of having a lustful orgasm. This is captured in the (1970s?) expression 'Fuck Romance!' that primarily relativizes romance to the point of sex, but in fact also sex to the point of romance.

On the whole, the changes of the 1990s can be interpreted as a lust *and* love or relationship revival. On the basis of continued reinforcement of the principle of proceeding only by mutual consent, mutual trust has been embedded in the prevalent relational or figurational ideal (van Stolk and Wouters, 1987b), to the extent that social interaction between the sexes has become more careful as well as more subtle. Because of the sensitivity and caution needed to proceed in such a way, erotic and sexual consciousness and tensions have expanded and intensified. Therefore, as 'no' became more unswerving,[12] latitude in sexual activity has enlarged and attempts at integrating sexual and relational desires have intensified. Together, these changes represent a shift in the ideal lust balance towards 'diminishing contrasts and increasing varieties' (Elias, 1994: 460ff), and they also represent a process of integration and civilization of the sexes. This diagnosis is confirmed by other data showing that 'on the whole, women feel like having sex more often, allow more sexual incentives more easily and have learned to discuss these matters more freely', whereas 'on the whole, men have learned to connect relational satisfaction and sexual gratification' (Straver et al., 1994: 154–64).

The emancipation of female sexuality and its counterpart, the bonding of male sexuality, will have certainly been channelled by literature (like feminist publications), by protest activities (like those against sexual violence and harassment) and by changes in the law (like making rape in marriage liable to penalty). But even more significant for explaining this process is the pincer movement that has affected men: they have found themselves between their longing for an enduring intimacy, on the one hand, which became subjected earlier and more strongly to more or less rigorous limitations such as desertion and divorce or the threat of them; and their increasing dependence upon their talent to arouse and stimulate a woman's desires, on the other hand, for satisfying their own sexuality.

Regularities in Processes of Integration and Civilization

In these changes in the relationships between the sexes and in their dominant lust balance, a few patterns can be discerned. These are regularities in all integrating and civilizing processes, to be presented in the following sections.

Lust Anxiety: Social and Sexual Fear of 'Heights' and 'Depths'

The first regularity is related to the mechanism of 'identification with the established': identifying with the uneven balance of power between the sexes functions as a psychical impediment in developing a higher-level and more integrated lust balance with more sex. It produces a lust anxiety that can be illustrated from a passage in a 1950s Dutch advice booklet on 'becoming engaged':

> Look at this engaged couple sitting in the car of a roller coaster. The car is pulled up slowly and then descends with flying speed down the steep slope. Other couples in other cars laugh and scream while falling into each other's arms, the fair sex seeking protection, as it were, from the sterner sex. But both of the engaged couple, who have turned-into-themselves, do not have the courage to do likewise. They braced themselves in the corner of their seat. They clench their teeth and lips and do not want to admit that they too were terror-struck when screeching down the slope. When at the end the cars are

stopped and the other couples go in search of the next amusement, arms dearly linked, the turned-into-themselves couple tell each other: 'There was actually nothing to it, it's a shame and a waste of money!' Well, a waste it certainly was, for they wasted an opportunity for people in love to let themselves go a little more on such an occasion than is possible when in serious company.

This lust anxiety is interpreted as follows: 'Quite often it is the result of a wrong kind of upbringing by dictatorial parents.... These dictatorially raised young people constantly ask themselves: "Is this permitted?" or "Is it allowed?" . . . They never really loosen up' (Mounier, n.d.: 13–15). Here, the explanation is found in the dictatorial relationship between the generations, but the same explanation can be applied to most expressions of lust anxiety in the relationship between the sexes: its inequality at least partly explains the greater difficulties of women in enjoying a lust balance with more sex. They remain afraid of the 'shame' of becoming more of a sexual subject, of the consequences of repudiating, if only in fantasy, the attitude of subordination. It is a 'fear of freedom'. From the fear of running wild through loosening up, they clam up. Their source of power and identity, the whole of their personality, is still strongly interwoven with the old balance of power between the sexes and also with the old lust balance, the old ratio of relational and sexual desires.

In this respect, homosexual women seem more like heterosexual women than homosexual (and heterosexual) men:

> Emotional involvement is the context within which most lesbian sexuality takes place. Lesbian couples indicate that closeness is more often a reason to have sex than arousal or orgasm. Monogamy is preferred by the majority of lesbians and most respondents act accordingly. (Schreurs, 1993a: 61)

And many lesbian women report having difficulties in taking sexual initiatives or in seducing their partners:

> In this context, their need to avoid even the slightest ring of dominance, power or male sexual behaviour, and to repudiate any behaviour that could possibly be experienced as an imitation of heterosexuality, is often mentioned as an impediment. (Schreurs, 1993b: 333)

From this outlook, the psychic repercussion of the uneven balance of power between the sexes is still a substantial barrier for continued emancipation of sexual impulses and emotions. This barrier might be conceptualized as a fear of social and psychic (including sexual) heights (Wouters, 1990: 74–5, 98). With regard to the men's accommodation process, the counterpart of this barrier might be conceptualized as social and psychic (including sexual) fear of depths, a fear of losing traditional sources of power and identity and of the jealousy and desertion anxieties that are involved, which prevent men from imagining and enjoying the pleasures of a more restrained kind of intercourse with a woman – the more 'civilized' satisfaction which this may bring. An example of someone struggling with this fear of depth comes from an interview with a man who sometimes watches pornographic videos with his wife and who reported being struck by a terrific stab of jealousy when his wife once said: 'It's odd, I'm 31 years old now and yet I only know your dick.' And he continued with an example of what he called the enormous gap between his emotions and his mind:

> For instance, the other day she asked me to lie at her side of the bed, so it would be pleasantly warm by the time she got in. That's what I did, and I don't see any reason why not, but I did feel like an idiot. I thought: 'Luckily my friends can't see me because they would laugh their heads off, Charlie impersonating a hot-water bottle.' (van Stolk and Wouters, 1987a: 133, 249)

Lacking data, it must remain an open question how many and to what extent men have suffered from impotence or other forms of loss of lust as an 'accommodation cramp'.[13] However, simply raising the question may suffice to suggest that the distinction between safe sex and emotionally safe sex (Orbach, 1994: 165) is significant for both sexes.

Three Types: Radicals, Moderates and Trend-Followers

Another important regularity follows from the fact that emancipation and accommodation are learning processes in which there are differences in tempo and emphasis, on which basis three different groups can be discerned: there are always radicals, moderates and trend-followers (see van Stolk, 1991: 59–60). With regard to the lust balance, these three types correspond to the three possibilities or scenarios that are open after the first few preliminary moves on the road of love and sex have been made:

> At that point, the outlines of different possibilities become apparent: one resigns oneself to one's partner's limits and satisfies oneself with what has been accomplished [followers]. The second possibility consist of a continued transgression of boundaries, the path of lust [radicals]. The third solution consists of preserving or reviving sexual tension and challenge in contact with the present partner [moderates]. (Zeegers, 1994: 140)

The lust balance of the radicals is strongly sex-oriented. They have become involved in the dynamics of lust as they continued to search for and to build up erotic and sexual tensions in situations or scenarios. In these dynamics, their sexual desire becomes specialized, while formerly lustful situations lose attraction:

> One thing I do occasionally regret. . . . If I compare myself to colleagues who, when looking at these girls in mini skirts, exclaim: 'Wow! What a delicious piece!', I can't help thinking: 'if you only knew what I've seen and done'. Do you understand? They still have that fantasy, that delightful 'Good God! What

would she look like under her knickers?' In fact, I don't have that fantasy any more. Because I've experienced so much. (Zeegers, 1994: 119)

The lust balance of trend-followers is mainly characterized by the longing for a lasting and taken-for-granted intimacy. Their sexual activity is directed at perpetuating their relationship: 'In the midst of social jostling and the ups and downs of personal positions and social identities, the family and, within that, sex, offer an *oasis of stability and predictability*, an area where one knows the dos and don'ts and who's who' (Zeegers, 1994: 131). Confronted with a widening range of socially acceptable behavioural and emotional alternatives, they clam up to some extent and stick to their routine, from fear of jealousy, desertion, loneliness, anxious about losing themselves and their relationship. The dangers traditionally connected with sex may have diminished since the sexual revolution, but for them the anxieties connected with those dangers carried on – an example of a cultural lag. Thus, they held on and stayed conservative where radicals and moderates continued the emancipation of sexuality.

The lust balance of the moderates is relationship *and* sex-oriented. They combine attention for both person and body in intimate activity: 'In letting oneself go, in knowing that the partner does that too, in showing a certain "childlike" lack of inhibition and in getting rid of feelings of shame, the feeling of mutual contact and appreciation is actualized' (Zeegers, 1994: 138–9). In this way, moderates have 'learned' to combine their longing for an enduring intimacy with their carnal desires.

One would expect an unequal division of the sexes among the three types, if only because the dangers and anxieties surrounding sex (rape, unwanted pregnancy, etc.) have always been (and are) greater for women than for men. In addition, for many women sex functioned as an important source of power (as a means of temptation, reward and punishment) and identity. On this basis it is also to be expected that the fear of giving up that traditional female pattern has been (and is) stronger. However, research into these three types revealed that moderates consist of just as many men as women. Moderates are reported to have developed the kind of sex in which 'lust and proximity are intrinsically connected, and even indulging in lust has the denotation of frankness'. This kind of sex 'is not a personal feature but a characteristic of the interaction with the partner' – that is, of the relationship (Zeegers, 1994: 138–40). This means that, as the principle of mutual consent became anchored and expanded both within a relationship and in having sex, the development of such a lust balance of greater uninhibitedness and candour in (sexual) behaviour and feeling has become more strongly a relational process as well as an individual one.

Phases in Processes of Emancipation, Accommodation and Integration

Just as the accomplishments of one generation become habitually taken for granted in the next, so the feeling of liberation, inherent in a successful emancipatory struggle, can topple over into its opposite when what was first an achievement becomes a taken-for-granted fact of life: when this happens, a feeling of oppression and of being burdened can become prevalent.

In the 20th century, the feeling of liberation prevailed in the 'roaring twenties' and again in the 1960s and 1970s. In those decades, entire groups were socially rising; there was a collective emancipation or, to put it differently, the most striking social pressure came from *below*. In such phases of emancipation and resistance, the *gains* in terms of we-feelings and I-feelings are usually emphasized and what prevails is the feeling of liberation from the straitjacket of old authoritarian relationships. In this phase, much of what was once considered to be bad luck is then experienced as injustice.

When collective emancipation chances diminish and disappear, another phase of accommodation and resignation has begun (for these phases, see Wouters, 1986 and 1990). In this phase, the most striking social pressure comes (again) much more unequivocally from *above*. When this occurs, the gains of the emancipation phase have largely come to be taken for granted, and thus the pressures of having to comply with authority relations are emphasized more strongly. The same goes for increased demands such as enlarged knowledge, ability, reflexivity and flexibility in dealing with others and oneself. Complying with these demands had been a precondition for reaping the gains of emancipation, but only when the pressure from above clearly prevails once again do they also come to be experienced as demands. This opens a perspective in which the *loss* and the oppression of old we-feelings and I-feelings are emphasized. In this phase, in deliberations as to whether one is confronted with bad luck or injustice and whether it is befitting to react with resignation or resistance, bad luck and resignation will usually get the benefit of the doubt. The following examples from the 1930s may illustrate this emphasis on the burden of liberation and on loss:

> By their equalization the sexes certainly have gained mutual understanding and conscious peacefulness in relating to each other, but they have lost happiness. (Haluschka, 1937: 178)

> If one only looks at photographs of life at the beach! Perfectly innocent if considered in themselves, but fatal in their effect, because, through lack of distance and deference, they continue to rob love of its poetry, its fine inner blossoming and spiritual contents. Love is in danger of becoming nothing but instinct or ambiguous friendship. (Haluschka, n.d.: 26)

The lust anxiety that speaks through these words, as well as the romanticization of the relationships and the lust balance of those 'happy days' of 'paradise lost', is expressed only in the margins of public debate in a phase of emancipation and resistance, when the feeling of liberation prevails.

In both phases, marriage was one of the institutions involved: while the old Victorian ideal of an elevated spiritual love lost vigour, the demand of always preserving one's marriage also lost precedence. Particularly in phases of emancipation, desires and interests of individuals gained importance – a shift in the we–I balance in the direction of the I (Elias, 1991). Moreover, by the 1970s, the social security provided by welfare arrangements had been transformed into an 'equanimity of the welfare state', on the basis of which many women have liberated themselves from the shackles of their marriage (van Stolk and Wouters, 1987a). In the 1980s and 1990s, as pressures from above gained precedence and collective emancipation chances disappeared, the longing for enduring intimacy has strengthened and intensified – a shift in the we–I balance in the direction of the we. In this most recent phase of accommodation and resignation, this longing will also have gained importance by the trimming down of social security and welfare arrangements, corroding the 'equanimity of the welfare state'.

Seen from a longer-term perspective, these alternating phases appear to change in a particular direction: in a spiral movement, both sides of the we–I balance, liberation as well as the burden of demands, are raised. This is the third pattern or regularity in the connection between changes in prevailing power and dependency relationships and in the dominant lust balance. On the one hand, the spectrum of accepted emotional and be-havioural alternatives expanded, but on the other hand an acceptable and respectable usage of these alternatives implied a continued increase of demands on self-regulation. Although sometimes one side is emphasized and sometimes the other, taken together they are best understood as phases in integration processes of sexes and classes within states (Wouters, 1995a, 1995b)

Intensified Tugs-of-War and Ambivalence

Coinciding with the spread of less uneven balances of power and depen-dency and of stronger ideals of equality, intimate relationships have become more strongly dependent on the style of emotion management of the partners involved: how to negotiate the terms of the relationship as two captains on the same ship without losing love and respect? At the same time, all kinds of conflict or conflicting needs and interests, formerly a tabooed non-topic, came out into the open and were subject to negotiation. According to traditional ideals, conflicts did not happen – female resig-nation would prevent them – and if they occurred, then they were seen only as natural phenomena, refreshing, like a thunderstorm. Since the 1960s, the art of 'conflict management' has developed, and marriage or living intimately together has become a conflict-prone balancing act (Mahlmann, 1991: 327).

As more egalitarian rules take time to 'sink in', both women and men have increasingly become subjected to a tug-of-war between old and new ideals (and power resources) and to related feelings of ambivalence. Most men and women seem to be egalitarian 'on the surface' and traditional 'underneath'. Most men react in accordance with the dynamics of established–outsider relationships: they do not want to accommodate and do not easily perceive the 'civilized' pleasures of a more egalitarian relationship. Therefore, they will use the 'gender strategy' of appealing to a woman's *old* identity underneath, trying to restore it, whereas most women will appeal to a man's *new* identity, trying to reinforce it and make it sink in. Therefore, 'sex and love are no longer given facts but talents to be exploited' (Schnabel, 1990: 16), and the art of obliging and being obliged as well as the art of escaping or sublimating these pressures has developed to increasingly higher degrees. As these demands increased, to lose oneself in making love was increasingly acknowledged as one of the ultimate forms of uncomplicated and unreflected existence. In the same process, the pursuit of a more stable and moderate lust balance also intensified. Recent discussions of issues like sexual harassment, pornography, rape in marriage and date-rape, can be understood as a common search for ways of becoming intimate and of keeping at a distance that are acceptable to both women and men. Precisely because of the sensitivity and caution needed to proceed in such a way, erotic and sexual consciousness and tensions have expanded and intensified, stimulating a further sexualization of love and an erotization of sex. This quest for an exciting and satisfying lust balance, avoiding the extremes of emotional wildness and emotional numbness, has also stimulated the emotional tug-of-war and ambivalence to a higher tension-level. That is so, if only because the increased demands on emotion management will have intensified both the phantasies and the longing for (romantic) relationships characterized by greater intimacy, as well as the longing for easier (sexual) relationships in which the pressure of these demands is absent or negligible, as in one-night stands. This ambivalence, together with an increasingly more conscious (reflexive) and calculating (flexible) emotion management as a source of power, respect and self-respect, is characteristic of processes of the decreasing segregation and increasing integration of classes and of sexes. This forms another, fourth pattern or regularity in the connection between changes in figurations and in lust balances: as long as those integration processes continue, these ambivalent emotions may be expected to accumulate and intensify, including both longings that make up the lust balance. This is why the body, nudity and sex are becoming increasingly prominent in the media (for Germany, see König, 1990), and why this trend is likely to persist; they contain the promise of natural physicality and of a harmoniously combined attention for both person and body in intimate activity. It may be expected that as the integration of the sexes continues to proceed, heightened sensitivity to this promise will accumulate as well, together with erotic consciousness and erotic tensions. However, because in the same process the ideal and longing to be known and loved body and soul will increase as well, both longings will remain connected to each other in heightened ambivalence.[14] Overall, this boils down to intensified longings, more contradictory desires, and thus, on the whole, less satisfaction or gratification ... unless people (once again) manage to deal with these contradictions in playful ways.

Notes

Thanks to Jonathan Fletcher and Stephen Mennell for improving my English and for their stimulating suggestions. Thanks also to Tom Inglis, Richard Kilminster, Peter Stearns and Bram van Stolk, whose comments helped me to improve the text.

1.   For this reason many scholars claim that the sexual revolution mainly consisted of the decline of the enormous distance that had grown between the public front kept up and actual behaviour (see, for instance, Bailey, 1994).

2.   See Blom (1993); Hatfield and Rapson (1994); Kooy (1968, 1983); van Zessen and Sandfort (1991); and Zwaan (1993). Besides the problem of distinguishing between changes in the lust balance as a dominant ideal and as a practice, there is an additional complication: studies of sexuality usually do not pay much attention, if any, to the kind of relationship in which it occurs; and vice versa, studies of loving relationships usually do not take a systematic interest in sex. Both kinds of research are even reported as attracting different kinds of respondents (Schreurs, 1993b: 332).

3.   The German words for 'lust balance' and 'lust economy' were translated into English as 'pleasure balance' and 'pleasure economy': 'The degree of anxiety, like the whole pleasure economy, is different in every society, in every class and historical phase' (Elias, 1994: 519).

4.   My thanks to Bram van Stolk who initiated this study of *Opzij* and presented me with his notes and photocopies. I would also like to thank Jon Fletcher; without his stimulating advice, this article would have remained behind the one-way mirror surrounding Dutch society.

5.   In 1974 Anja Meulenbelt, probably the foremost Dutch feminist, also contributed to this development by announcing her love affair with a woman under the title 'Homosex en feminisme' in *Opzij* (3: 7–9).

6.   In 1980, in a report entitled *Women and Sexuality: Ten Years After the Sexual Revolution*, the author excuses herself for being 'obliged' to discuss male sexuality: 'Because most women still [sic!] prefer to make love with men, we cannot talk about "her" sexual gratification without referring to "his" modeling of sexuality.' This author also advocates 'soft sex': 'Women can contribute a lot to the recognition of this "soft" pole. And this would not only liberate our own sexuality, but also that of men' (de Bruijn, 1980: 4, 23).

7.   The question of what determines whether genital arousal is interpreted as, and leads to, subjective sexual arousal, could not be answered by Dekker. He hinted at 'external information' such as 'appraisal of the erotic stimulus'. In her study, Ellen Laan could be more precise. She compared women's responses to the 'regular' man-made pornographic film and to a number of women-made, female-centred pornographic films: 'Contrary to expectation, genital arousal did not differ between films, although genital response to both films was substantial. Subjective experience of sexual arousal was significantly higher during the woman-made film. The man-made film evoked more feelings of shame, guilt, and aversion.... The largest contribution to female excitement might result from the processing of stimulus-content and stimulus-meaning ...' (Laan, 1994: 49).

8.   Tom Wolfe introduced the concept *pornoviolence*: 'Violence is the simple, ultimate solution for problems of status competition, just as gambling is the simple, ultimate solution for economic competition. The old pornography was the fantasy of easy sexual delights in a world where sex was kept unavailable. The new pornography is the fantasy of easy triumph in a world where status competition has become so complicated and frustrating' (Wolfe, 1976: 162).

9.   The difference in image-formation – the concept of prostitution draws attention more strongly to prostitutes than to their customers, pimps or managers, whereas the concept of pornography predominantly evokes the image of wallowing male consumers – seems to be the result rather than a cause of the anti-pornography movement. In prostitution women are 'real', whereas in pornography they are visually only a recording and tangibly absent. This may help to explain why women's solidarity is more easily and strongly directed at prostitutes than at female porno-stars.

10.   In his famous *The Culture of Narcissism*, Christopher Lasch presented a similar example: 'more and more people long for emotional detachment or "enjoy sex," as Hendin writes, "only in situations where they can define and limit the intensity of the relationship." A lesbian confesses: "The only men I've ever been able to enjoy sex with were men I didn't give a shit about. Then I could let go, because I didn't feel vulnerable"' (Lasch, 1979: 338).

11.   Suffering from a fatal disease, a few weeks before she died, the 15-year-old Floortje Peneder still frankly expressed the independent power of sexual desire, as is characteristic for her age. Under the heading *Wishes*, five of them, all numbered, are mentioned on separate lines, followed much lower, near the bottom of the page, by: 'A GOOD FUCK!!! (but that is out of the question).' A little later, her spirit rises above the fact that she is in hospital suffering from a fatal illness and adds: 'But look, these two sides in me are very strong. On the one hand . . . very well-behaved and respectable. But on the other hand (and that side is now much more important to me), I am a swinger. The pleasure of going to a pub, having a drink with friends, musing about sex (not just love, but real sex too) smoking and drinking together. To go out for a night with somebody, being able to say "Wow, I'll grab that sweet thing!"' (Peneder, 1994: 92, 111).

12.   Sado-masochism seems to be an exception, because here, lust seems to be derived from trampling on both 'yes' and 'no'. But this impression is largely deceptive, for the trampling happens within firmly defined borders. A German study, for instance, concludes that SM consists of carefully staged rituals, of which the high level of (mutually expected) self-restraint is the most striking character-istic (Wetzstein et al., 1993).

13.   When this issue was raised in *Opzij*, the tone was jeering: in a spoof interview with 'the last potent man', he finally became violent (1983[5]: 16). Four years later, the question was taken up somewhat more seriously, but the answer ('no need for that') overlooks the possibility of impotence as a transistory problem of accommo-dation: 'An equal relationship is pre-eminently an important support for sexual gratification, for only then can sexuality be liberated from ulterior motives like a display of power. Then you do what you do simply because you like it. And what can then fail?' (*Opzij*, 1987[1]: 46–8).

14.   The tension between these longings is likely to be heightened as well by a relentless curiosity for what was placed behind social and psychic scenes in former centuries, for both sex and death. In this 'emancipation of emotions' process,

awareness of bodily attraction and erotic longings will increase together with awareness of transitoriness, of death as the denial of endurance in any relationship.

References

Ang, Ien (1983) 'Mannen op zicht', *Tijdschrift voor Vrouwenstudies* 4(3): 418–34.

Bailey, Beth (1994) 'Sexual Revolution(s)', pp. 235–62 in David Farber (ed.) *The Sixties: From Memory to History*. Chapel Hill, NC and London: University of North Carolina Press.

Blom, J.C.H. (1993) 'Een harmonieus gezin en individuele ontplooiing', *BMGN* 108(1): 28–50.

Brinkgreve, Christien (1988) *De belasting van de bevrijding*. Nijmegen: SUN.

Brinkgreve, Christien (1995) *Droom en drift. Een onderzoek naar verborgen wensen van Nederlandse vrouwen*. Baarn: Anthos/Marie Claire.

Brugman, Emily, Hans Goedhart, Ton Vogels and Gertjan van Zessen (1995) *Jeugd en seks 95. Resultaten van het nationale scholierenonderzoek*. Utrecht: SWP.

Caprio, Frank S. (1960) *Mijn man, mijn minnaar*. Amsterdam: Strengholt.

CBS (1994) *Sociaal-culturele berichten 19. Trends in de leefsituatie van Nederlandse jongeren 1979–1989/1993*. Voorburg/Heerlen: Centraal Bureau voor de Statistiek.

de Bruijn, Gerda (1980) *Vrouw en seksualiteit. Tien jaar na een seksuele revolutie*, literatuurrapport 13. Zeist: Nisso.

Dekker, Joost (1987) 'Voluntary Control of Sexual Arousal. Experimental Studies on Sexual Imagery and Sexual History as Determinants of the Sexual Response', PhD dissertation, Utrecht University.

Dowling, Colette (1981) *The Cinderella Complex: Women's Hidden Fear of Independence*. New York: Pocket Books.

Elias, Norbert (1991) *The Society of Individuals*, ed. Michael Schröter, Oxford: Blackwell.

Elias, Norbert (1994) *The Civilizing Process*, trans. Edmund Jephcott. Oxford: Blackwell.

Fisher, W.A. and Byrne, D. (1978) 'Sex Differences in Response to Erotica. Love versus Lust', *Journal of Personality and Social Psychology* 36: 117–25.

Frenken, Jos (1976) *Afkeer van seksualiteit*. Deventer: Van Loghum Slaterus.

Fromm, Erich (1942) *The Fear of Freedom*. London: Routledge & Kegan Paul.

Garcia, L.T., K. Brennan, M. DeCarlo, R. McGlennon and S. Tait (1984) 'Sex Differences in Sexual Arousal to Different Erotic Stories', *Journal of Sex Research* 20: 391–402.

Groenendijk, H. (1983) 'Vrouwelijke seksualiteit uit het kader van pornografie', *Tijdschrift voor Vrouwenstudies* 4(3): 352–71.

Haluschka, Helene (1937) *Adam en Eva onder vier oogen*. Heemstede: De Toorts.

Haluschka, Helene (n.d.) *Hoe vindt U het moderne jonge meisje?* Heemstede: De Toorts.

Hatfield, Elaine and Richard L. Rapson (1994) 'Historical and Cross-Cultural Perspectives on Passionate Love and Sexual Desire', *Annual Review of Sex Research* 4: 67–97.

Heiman, J.R. (1977) 'A Psychophysiological Exploration of Sexual Arousal Patterns in Females and Males', *Psychophysiology* 14: 266–74.

Jong, Erica (1973) *Fear of Flying*. New York: Signet Books.

König, Oliver (1990) *Nacktheit: Soziale Normierung und Moral*. Opladen: West-deutscher Verlag.

Kooy, G.A. (ed.) (1968) *Sex in Nederland*. Utrecht: Het Spectrum.

Kooy, G.A. (ed.) (1983) *Sex in Nederland*. Utrecht: Het Spectrum.

Kuitenbrouwer, Jan (1990) *Lijfstijl. De manieren van nu*. Amsterdam: Prometheus.

Laan, Ellen (1994) *Determinants of Sexual Arousal in Women: Genital and Subjective Components of Sexual Response*. Amsterdam: University of Amsterdam, Faculty of Psychology.

Lasch, Christopher (1979) *The Culture of Narcissism*. New York: Warner Books.

Mahlmann, Regina (1991) *Psychologisierung des Alltagbewußtseins. Die Verwis-senschaftlichung des Diskurses über Ehe*. Opladen: Westdeutscher Verlag.

Mooij, Annet (1993) *Geslachtsziekten en besmettingsangst. Een historisch-socio-logische studie 1850–1990*. Amsterdam: Boom.

Mosher, D.L. and B. B. White (1980) 'Effects of Committed or Casual Erotic Imagery on Females' Subjective Sexual Arousal and Emotional Response', *Journal of Sex Research* 16: 273–99.

Mounier, P.J.J. (n.d.) *Gestroomlijnd leven voor de verloving*, Kanarie-boekje No. 212. Den Haag/Antwerpen: Succes.

Nota met betrekking tot het beleid ter bestrijding van sexueel geweld tegen vrouwen en meisjes (1984) 's-Gravenhage: Ministerie van Sociale Zaken en Werkgelegenheid.

Orbach, Susie (1994) *What's Really Going on Here?* London: Virago Press.

Peneder, Floortje (1994) *Het dagboek van Floortje Peneder*. Amsterdam: Nijgh & Van Ditmar.

Ravesloot, Janita (1997) *Seksualiteit in de jeugdfase vroeger en nu*. Amsterdam: Spinhuis.

Röling, H.Q. (1990) 'Samen of alleen. Initiatief en overgave in "Wij willen weten" (1938–1985)', *Amsterdams Sociologisch Tijdschrift* 17(2): 85–102.

Röling, H.Q. (1994) *Gevreesde vragen. Geschiedenis van de seksuele opvoeding in Nederland*. Amsterdam: Amsterdam University Press.

Rubinstein, Renate (1983) *Liefst Verliefd*. Amsterdam: Meulenhoff.

Sanders, Stephan (1994) *De grote woede van M*. Amsterdam: Bezige Bij.

Schalet, Amy Townsend (1994) 'Dramatiseren of normaliseren? De culturele constructie van tienerseksualiteit in de Verenigde Staten en Nederland', *Amster-dams Sociologisch Tijdschrift* 21(2): 113–47.

Schnabel, Paul (1990) 'Het verlies van de seksuele onschuld', *Amsterdams Socio-logisch Tijdschrift* 17(2): 11–50.

Schreurs, Karlein M.G. (1993a) 'Sexuality in Lesbian Couples: The Importance of Gender', *Annual Review of Sex Research* 4: 49–66.

Schreurs, Karlein (1993b) 'Sexualität und Bedeutung der Geschlechtszugehörig-keit bei lesbischen und heterosexuellen Paaren. Ergebnisse einer empirischen Studie in den Niederlanden', *Zeitschrift für Sexualforschung* 6(4): 321–34.

Seidman, Stephen (1991) *Romantic Longings. Love in America, 1830–1980*. New York and London: Routledge.

Sigusch, V. and G. Schmidt (1970) 'Psychosexuelle Stimulation durch Bilder und Filme: geschlechtsspezifische Unterschiede', pp. 39–53 in G. Schmidt, V. Sigusch and E. Schorsch (eds), *Tendenzen der Sexualforschung*. Stuttgart: Enke.

Stearns, Peter N. (1994) *American Cool*. New York: New York University Press.

Straver, Cees (1980) *Kijken naar seks*. Deventer: Van Loghum Slaterus.

Straver, Cees, Ab van der Heiden and Ron van der Vliet (1994) *De huwelijkse logica. Huwelijksmodel en inrichting van het samenleven bij arbeiders en anderen*. Leiden: NISSO/DSWO Press.

Swidler, Ann (1980) 'Love and Adulthood in American Culture', pp. 120–47 in Neil J. Smelser and Eric H. Erikson (eds) *Themes of Work and Love in Adulthood*. London: Grant McIntyre.

van Calcar, E. (1886) *Gelukkig – ofschoon getrouwd. Een boek voor gehuwden en ongehuwden*, trans. from the English. Haarlem: Bohn.

van Daalen, Rineke and Bram van Stolk (1991) 'Over revolutie en onwetendheid. Seksuele ervaringen en klachten van jongeren', pp. 34–54 in Peter van Lieshout and Denise de Ridder (eds) *Symptomen van de tijd. De dossiers van het Amsterdamse Instituut voor Medische Psychotherapie (IMP), 1968–1977*. Nijmegen: SUN.

van Dantzig, A. (1994) '06', *Maandblad Geestelijke Volksgezondheid* 11: 1276–8.

van de Velde, Th. H. (1933) *Ideal Marriage: Its Physiognomy and Technique*. London: Heinemann.

van der Vliet, Ron (1990) 'De opkomst van het seksuele moratorium', *Amsterdams Sociologisch Tijdschrift* 17(2): 51–68.

van Eijk, Inez (1994) *Bij jou of bij mij? Erotische etiquette*. Amsterdam: Contact.

van Stolk, Bram (1991) *Eigenwaarde als groepsbelang. Sociologische studies naar de dynamiek van zelfwaardering*. Houten: Bohn Stafleu Van Loghum.

van Stolk, Bram and Cas Wouters (1987a) *Frauen im Zwiespalt. Beziehungsprobleme im Wohlfahrtsstaat. Eine Modellstudie. Mit einem Vorwort von Norbert Elias*. Frankfurt am Main: Suhrkamp.

van Stolk, Bram and Cas Wouters (1987b) 'Power Changes and Self-Respect: A Comparison of Two Cases of Established–Outsider Relations', *Theory, Culture & Society* 4: 477–88.

van Zessen, Gertjan and Theo Sandfort (eds) (1991) *Seksualiteit in Nederland: seksueel gedrag, risico en preventie van aids*. Amsterdam: Swets & Zeitlinger.

Vennix, Paul and Marcel Bullinga (1991) *Sekserollen en emancipatie*. Houten/Antwerpen: Bohn Stafleu Van Loghum.

Wattjes, Prof. J.G. (1930) *Wijsgerige gedachten over Het Huwelijk*. Delft.

Wetzstein, Thomas A., Linda Steinmetz, Christa Reis and Roland Eckert (1993) *Sadomasochismus. Szenen und Rituale*. Reinbek: Rowolt Taschenbuch Verlag.

Wolfe, Tom (1976) *Mauve Gloves & Madmen, Clutter & Vine*. New York: Farrar, Straus & Giroux.

Wouters, Cas (1984) 'Vrouwen, porno en seksualiteit', *Tijdschrift voor Vrouwenstudies* 5(2): 246–50.

Wouters, Cas (1986) 'Formalization and Informalization: Changing Tension Balances in Civilizing Processes', *Theory, Culture & Society* 3(2): 1–18.

Wouters, Cas (1990) *Van minnen en sterven. Informalisering van de omgangsvormen rond seks en dood*. Amsterdam: Bakker.

Wouters, Cas (1992) 'On Status Competition and Emotion Management: The Study of Emotions as a New Field', *Theory, Culture & Society* 9: 229–52.

Wouters, Cas (1995a) 'Etiquette Books and Emotion Management in the 20th Century; Part One – The Integration of Social Classes', *Journal of Social History* 29(1): 107–24.

Wouters, Cas (1995b) 'Etiquette Books and Emotion Management in the 20th Century; Part Two – The Integration of the Sexes', *Journal of Social History* 29(2): 325–40.

Zeegers, Wil (1994) *De zonnige zijde van seks. De nawerking van positief beleefde seksualiteit*, FSW, Rijksuniversiteit Leiden: DSWO Press.

Zwaan, Ton (ed.) (1993) *Familie, huwelijk en gezin in West-Europa*. Amsterdam/ Heerlen: Boom/Open Universiteit.

Cas Wouters is a researcher in the Faculty of Social Sciences at Utrecht University.

Citysex
Representing Lust In Public

Henning Bech

I N MOST STUDIES of urbanization and the city, *'sexuality'* seems a dirty word, not to be found in indexes and almost equally rare in the text itself. This is hardly surprising, perhaps; in many parts of the academic world, the word can still be uttered only with the purpose of curing an illness – or as an indication that the speaker is suffering from one. In most studies of sexuality, however, *'city'* seems an equally dirty word, as absent from texts as are, indeed, other four-letter words.

Nevertheless, I want to put forward the thesis that the city is invariably and ubiquitously, inherently and inevitably, fundamentally and thoroughly sexualized; and that modern sexuality is essentially urban.

In pursuing this thesis, I shall pass through four battlefields. First, I shall specify what is to be understood by the term 'city'. Second, I shall present a description of some characteristic features of what I suggest is 'urban sexuality'. Third, there is the task of demonstrating in what way and how far there is a necessary relation between city and sexuality. A fourth problem – perhaps the theoretically most challenging one – concerns the nature of this alleged 'sexuality' of the city. If we were to stick to what are usually considered commonsense notions of sexuality, the problem would not be so great. In that case, we would possess a fixed point of departure in the shape of an inner *essence*, basically of the character of a *drive*; and the only task would be to investigate how the expression of this essence was moulded by the fabric of the city. Taking constructionist, or deconstructionist, criticisms of such 'essentialist' notions into account, however, raises the problem of the sense in which and the justification with which this alleged sexuality of the city can indeed be termed a 'sexuality'.[1] Finally, I shall add some remarks on the implications of my discussion, in relation to the study of sexuality as well as to wider issues of modern society and social change.

■ *Theory, Culture & Society* 1998 (SAGE, London, Thousand Oaks and New Delhi),
  Vol. 15(3–4): 215–241
  [0263-2764(199808/11)15:3–4;215–241;006065]

I

First, then, I shall deal with the question of *what is a city*, as a locus of modern sexuality. What is relevant in this context, I believe, is a concept which is capable of capturing the characteristics of the city as a *life space*, and as a particularly *modern* life space.[2]

Material for a basic conceptualization of the city as a life space can be found in a combination of two – analytically distinguishable – strands of sociological research and intellectual orientation. One is the rather formal and abstract reasonings of the tradition from Simmel (1957) and Wirth (1964) and their more recent followers such as Lofland (1973, 1989) and Hannerz (1980). Goffman (1959, 1963, 1971) may be added here; although he never specified his terrain as 'urban', he has been of great inspiration in the development of this line of research. The other strand is the social-historical and/or material phenomenological tradition from Kracauer (1964, 1976) and Benjamin (1974b, 1982), and their more recent followers such as Sennett (1977) and Berman (1982).

From these traditions a double-sided concept of the city as a life space can be distilled. From an objectifying point of view it can be defined as a *large, dense and permanent cluster of heterogeneous human beings in circulation*. From a phenomenological point of view it can be seen as an *ever-changing large crowd of varied strangers moving among one another*. This concept is a relative one, in the sense that the more an entity conforms to these criteria, the more of a 'city' it is. (For an extended discussion, see Bech, 1992b and Bech, forthcoming.)

Concepts like this have, as is well known, been highly disputed over the years. For instance, what was known in the 1970s and 1980s as 'urban sociology' (that is, a macro-oriented, Marxist or Weberian discipline, represented by Castells, Harvey, Lojkine, Pahl, etc.) rejected them fiercely or ignored them totally; at most, they were considered suitable in relation to a sphere of life regarded as 'real, but relatively unimportant' (Castells, 1975: 101–49; Saunders, 1981: 80–109; both making reference to the title of the article by Dewey, 1960). I am far from denying the relevance of macro-analysis of economic or political struggles over the structuring of urban physical spaces and the organization of collective consumption or the like. My point, however, is that when entering the spheres of 'circulation', 'reproduction' and 'consumption', economic and political (etc.) actors also inevitably enter particular *life spaces* where specific rules and possibilities exist; and this is what I am discussing here.[3]

As an abbreviation for the concept of the city as a life space I have found the expression used by Lyn Lofland very adequate: the city is *a world of strangers*. It should be noted that the concept of the stranger in this context does not imply that the other is 'peculiar' or that one is oneself 'estranged' or 'alienated' from her or him. Nor is the stranger an outsider intruding upon a community. Too often such pre-modern notions have been confused with concepts more adequate to the realities of modern life (see

Lofland, 1973: 183 n. 14). To use another expression of Lyn Lofland's: the modern city is a *routine* world of strangers (1973: 176–80).[4]

To make the concept of the city relevant for the study of modern societies, a further socio-historical specification is needed. Considerable parts of what is to qualify as a city must be *open* or *public* space, in the sense that it is accessible to all (or almost all) with regard to legal and social regulation and financial means, and that it is in fact frequented by various specimens of the varieties of human beings.

By adding the component of openness to the concept of the city, I have, indirectly, commented upon a particular form of criticism in terms of gender, class or race. Some critics have argued that the subject of the city is *male* (or, more radically, that the city as such is male). A standard point of reference of these arguments has been the question of the gender of the 'flâneur', as the prototypical urban subject (see, for example, Wolff, 1983; Pollock, 1988; Massey, 1991). Others, however, have pointed to the continual presence of women as well as the particular female spaces (such as the *grands magasins*) within the Western city; and also to the fact that the developmental trend has been in the direction of an equalization of the position of man and woman in urban public space.[5] Thus, I believe, we may maintain that the city and its prototypical subject are not to be conceptualized as male (in contrast to 'female') at the basic level. Analogous reasoning may be put forward regarding the argument that the subject circulating in the urban world of strangers is basically bourgeois, petit-bourgeois or new middle class (Häussermann and Siebel, 1987: 11–21, 239f; Featherstone, 1991: 75f, 104–11).

Since this is contested terrain and can fuel heated controversy, I shall enter into some more detail. I do not, of course, deny that there are differences in the ways various groups have made or make, or have been made to make, use of the city.[6] The main point, however, is this: the 'heterogeneity' or 'variety' of human beings circulating in the city must not be conceived of as generically restricted, for in that case the concept would not capture what is particular and essential to the modern city. To make my point by using gender as a case once again: a concept of the city which does not make reference to spaces populated by women as well as men is simply incompatible with an essential reality of modern cities. The *routine world of strangers* that I spoke of before is largely a routine world of men *and* women, as well as of different races and classes. In this world, men do not point or gape when and because they see a woman in the street.[7]

Objecting that this 'routine' world of gender-, race- and class-mixed strangers occupies a fairly limited space in most cities is, I believe, missing the point. What is particular and essential to the modern city, and therefore important to take into account in an adequate conceptualization, is the fact that these spaces do exist and cannot reasonably be 'thought away'; their extension is, in this respect, secondary.[8] On the other hand, the concept of the modern city as a world of strangers should not be restricted to making reference merely to space which is 'generally' public, that is, open to and frequented by all sorts of human beings. Many of the particular and essential qualities of the modern city are related to the simultaneous existence and dialectics of such generally public spaces *and* only partially open worlds of strangers. One may, of course, very well deplore the fact that generally public space is limited by social powers and cultural norms, and that it is perhaps becoming even more restricted by the interventions of commercial or political agents; but it is difficult to imagine the modern city as a space in which certain parts may not be shut off to the general public while still being worlds of strangers, open to particular groups of the public (women, for instance).[9]

Another objection might point to the fact that the existence of public space is dependent upon a number of factors outside the city itself. But so indeed is the very existence of the city as a world of strangers: historically, this depends, for instance, upon political conditions allowing the concentration and circulation of great numbers of people. However, once established, the city obtains a logic of its own, and exerts an influence of its own, not reducible to the factors that constituted it historically or continually help to reconstitute it.

During the last 50 years or so, the city as a basic life space has been increasingly supplemented and supplanted by another: what I call *the telecity* (Bech, 1992b, 1996). This is characterized by co-presences that are not 'physical' (in the sense associated with the city: that is, cannot be perceived, in principle, by all five senses) but are telemediated. On the other hand, it is still a world of strangers, and to this extent urban (for which reason I am somewhat reluctant to talk of it in terms of the 'post-urban' and the like). It is, moreover, still a world of co-presences, constituted between somebody who is present *at* (in front of) a telemedium and somebody who is present *on* (by way of) it.

The roots of the telemediated social world can, of course, be traced back very far in the history of humanity. The most developed form empirically realized at a more universal level is multichannelled television combined with video recorders (and perhaps with interactive 'telematic' systems – videotex, videophone – though for technological and financial reasons more advanced forms of these are available only for a minority).[10]

The conceptualization of the social world of watching television as an *urban* one – carrying the characteristics of a world of strangers – is, I believe, an important addition to the prevailing approaches in the study of modern telemedia (as well as of the city). Thus, the social life space I am talking about as the telecity is not identical to the one constituted between 'sender' and 'receiver' in the sense of 'communication analysis' or 'media analysis'. 'Senders' are only relevant to the telecity insofar as they are sensibly present among the strangers, for instance on a screen. Nor has the concept of the telecity and its implications been worked out in 'cultural studies' approaches to television, since these mostly stress the contents of the process of watching various programmes, and not the formal properties pertaining to it as a social world of strangers. And the recently intensified orientation of research known as qualitative reception studies has paid much attention to interactions among those watching television, but little to the simultaneous involvement of the viewers in television's world of strangers.[11] Modern sexuality is very much related to the telecity in this sense. In what follows, however, I shall concentrate primarily on urban, not on tele-urban sexuality.

II

After this outline of the basic characteristics of the city as a world of strangers, I shall proceed with the discussion of the main thesis of this article: that the city is fundamentally sexualized, and that modern sexuality is essentially an urban one.

First, a brief description of some of the characteristic features of what I suggest is indeed the sexuality of the city. I shall start by summarizing a short story from a fairly new 'erotic' magazine that has become quite popular in Denmark. It is about a woman who rides in a bus during the rush hour. Perhaps by mere chance she acquires a taste for it – because, to the rhythm of the movements of the overcrowded bus, she can be pressed against young men and 'inhale the mild and inciting fragrance of the male. Male *stranger*' – as it says in the text.

One day she squeezes in between *two* young men; the firm buttocks of the one in front of her contract against her belly, and the 'big piston' – I quote, of course – of the one behind her grows and squeezes in between her buttocks, which have adhered to his crotch. And while strap-hanging with one hand, she lets the other slide into the trousers of the man in front of her and rhythmically milks his 'stony, short and thick log'. The man behind her lifts up her dress and drapes the folds of it 'down like secretive portières that shelter from curious side-long gazes' while he 'fucks her, first in her front hole and then in her rear one'. There *are* in fact certain rules of conduct in urban public space which one must observe if others, for their part, are to be able to observe the rules of 'civil inattention' and 'non-involvement'. Soon the man in front of her lets go, and immediately after the one behind her follows suit, while she, too, 'comes and comes and comes'.

That is it; and she returns to 'reality', lying in her bed with one hand in her vagina and the vibrator up her behind. Her husband comes home from work and asks if they should go out on the town and eat Chinese and if they should have a little cuddle first, to which she coos: 'Mmmh, I've actually been lying in bed waiting for you.'[12]

This little story, I believe, represents many of the features characteristic of urban sexuality. There is the excitement of the amount of *supply and abundance, opportunity and freedom*. This is not merely related to the external wealth of mass and sensory flutter, but also to the inner, potential freedom from 'being oneself' connected with the anonymity and non-committedness of urban relations.

Further, there is the *consumerism* of picking and choosing and discarding again, and of the more and more, the trade in numbers and amounts, *mass* consumption in more than one sense of the word. There is the focus on *surfaces* and on *bits and pieces* – not the other person as a whole human being but his or her surface or only a part of it. These *are* indeed the pleasures of what throughout modernity has been so eloquently denounced by the invectives of alienation and objectification, instrumentalization and fetishization (Bech, 1989).

There is also the *relation to those around* – the play on their possible non-involvement or involvement by watching, joining in, interrupting, condemning or prohibiting. Sexuality *in* the mass is also always potentially sexuality *of* the mass; and it is inherently related to *public authority*, which may monitor and punish it – be it in the shape of the man or woman in the street, or of some lower rank guard, or the police themselves. (And you never *really* know whether the policeman himself is joining in in his own way, do you? Or whether she is turned on by all the gear and leather she is wearing?)

A further element, close to this, relates to the unspoken but very effectual *norms* or 'rules' of urban behaviour. Thus, for instance, there are norms of positioning oneself in public space, of looking and touching (or non-touching). Urban sexuality trades on the existence of these norms, as well as on the provocation inherent in them towards transgression and restoration.

Another important element in urban sexuality is the art of *positioning* oneself, or making use of the positions that one has somehow ended up in. This, I believe, is also vividly demonstrated in the little story I have related.

The story, however, is partially misleading on one important point. In it, considerable emphasis is put on relations of an immediately *tactile* character (if I may phrase it that way). Although such things no doubt do happen once in a while, and particularly in some spaces of the city, I believe that they should be seen in relation to a more basic and universal form of urban tactile sexuality. This is characterized by the simultaneous presence of closeness and distance; and the visual and other sensual stimulations inherent in this are intensified by the awareness of the rules of urban conduct I spoke of earlier.

Missing from the story of the woman in the bus is also another aspect: the importance of the *visual* in the sexuality of the city. This importance is connected with the fact that in the social world of strangers people are only surfaces to one another, and that the surface therefore becomes an object to be evaluated and styled according to aesthetic criteria (Bech, 1997: ch. V.3). Now, the gaze which sees the surfaces of others and which is active in the design of one's own, sees and evaluates on sexual criteria as well. Thus, surfaces are styled with a view to their potential signification of sexuality; and gazes are attracted to them for that very reason, *or* because they are actively scanning the surfaces in search of sexual attractions.

There is also the interplay of gazes and glances known as *cruising* – an art form involving a wealth of rules to be observed and transgressed. Sometimes cruising is stationary, merely a game of the eyes, but often it is also set in motion, when gazes and glances are given legs to walk on. One of the things which may be frustrating in very crowded spaces is that they leave no room for such *qualified cruising*. On the whole, *motion and movement* are important in urban sexuality: hiding and hunting, taking the position of the active or the passive; and notably, the latter position is not merely one you are put into, but also one you *take*.

Further, I should like to stress the *relentlessness* of the sexuality of the city. On the one hand, you are *exposed* to the gaze and the physical closeness of others, and their movements are at least partially beyond your control. On the other hand, you yourself are anonymous and bear no personal obligations towards others and are indeed free to consume them in relentless ways. *Danger* and *power* are inherent in all this, as well as the possibilities of *success* and *failure*, getting turned on or turned down. The pleasurable side of this might be termed the sadomasochism of urban sexuality; the less pleasurable side is, of course, tiresome, intolerable or frustrating. Notably, however, relentlessness is crossed by and combined with the deference and demeanour associated with the rules of urban sexual behaviour. As I mentioned earlier, these are not merely external limits to the game, but constituents of it in their own right. The pleasure of urban sexuality is very much related to the skilled knowledge and application of these rules, the mastery of the art.

Finally, one should not forget that urban sexuality is, at least sometimes, a *being-with*, a togetherness – be it in the communion of a sexualized diffuse mass, or in the bounded encounter of two (or more) people (Bech, 1991a: 60f, 1997: ch. IV. 11). There is an erotic intensity that tends to dissolve borders or at least cause them to oscillate; and the joinedness and sharedness makes of it something to care for.[13]

III

Now, we know that such conduct and experience do take place in the city: *sometimes* and *for somebody*. It has been observed and documented in casual or more systematic ethnographic reports from for instance trains, discotheques, prostitution, taxis and, not least, the parts of the city used by gay men (or more broadly, the city as used by gay men).[14] But is such rather sporadic empirical evidence really sufficient to prove my thesis of the ever- and omnipresent sexualization inherent in the life space of the city? Isn't this merely the business of a few sexual perverts or maniacs, *male* at that?

First, there is nothing wrong per se in studying a larger subject from some particularly characteristic part of it. Such procedure by way of the exemplary or prototypical is a widely used and well established methodological and rhetorical tool in the social sciences (see, for example, Plummer, 1983; Atkinson, 1990). Recently, for instance, the transformation of intimacy has been studied by Anthony Giddens (1992) from the ways and experiences of gays and lesbians; and Zygmunt Bauman (1991) has used the figure of the wandering Jew as a prototype for the study of wider features of modernity. And these are merely two of the recent examples from an almost infinitely expandable list.

As for the study of the modern *city*, a number of different characters have, more or less explicitly and extensively, been used as prototypical figures: the poet, the flâneur, the street whore, the photographer, the sandwichman, the detective, the ragpicker, the shopping woman, the journalist and the – urban – sociologist.[15] Thus, the competition might seem severe as to who should be considered *the* prototypical figure in the study of the city; however, urban reality is rich, and some figures are no doubt appropriate for the investigation of some aspects of city life, whereas others are to be preferred in relation to other aspects. In my own research, I have proceeded primarily by way of analysis of the 'modern' male homosexual; and there is a sense in which he can reasonably be considered the prototypical figure *par excellence* in relation to urban life. Most people primarily enter the city at two moments in their lives. In the course of their life history there is the moment of youth, the period of passage from one family to another. And in the repetitive course of everyday life there is the moment of transport, the time of passage to and from work-place and family.[16] As for the prototypical figures mentioned above – the journalist, the flâneur, etc. – the city as a life space occupies a larger place in their lives; nevertheless, most of them usually return to family after working or walking; and, in any case, their existence is not permeated by the urban. The male homosexual, however, is 'thrown upon' the city as his basic life space; and upon analysis each of his 'peculiarities' can be phenomenologically reduced to being (co-)constituted by this situation (or: situatedness).[17]

Thus, there is good reason to approach the study of city life from the prototypical figure of the modern male homosexual; and the exposition above of the characteristics of urban sexuality has relied to no small extent on my research and analyses of this special creation.[18] However, it must be determined to what extent this sexuality is indeed related to the *city*, and consequently to all subjects circulating there, and not merely to some extra-urban particularity of the male homosexual.

An obvious and often outspoken objection relates to gender: for *women*, we are assured, sometimes very emphatically, the city is primarily a place of danger, violence and male power; and insofar as it is sexualized, this is a sexuality of men harassing or assaulting women.

There can be *no doubt whatsoever* that the sexual positions of men and women in urban space are in fact not equal, and that very many more women are sexually assaulted by men than the other way round.[19] On a less violent level, reference is sometimes made to the case of the flight seat (an urban universe, it seems, fairly familiar to the sort of academics discussing these matters – myself included). A man is seated there, legs wide apart and elbows firmly planted on both armrests – or rather, well beyond. This leaves a woman who happens to get seated next to him an unhappy alternative. Either she can squeeze in, make herself as tiny as possible, keep her legs crossed or pressed together and clasp her arms tightly to her body. Or she can claim her right of equal space, either by words – in which case she runs the risk of appearing rude and creating an unpleasant atmosphere; or by using her arms and legs – and having interpreted as a sexual invitation.

One should not, however, take the point concerning the city's calamities for women too far. First, there are considerable differences between the cities of, for instance, the USA, Scandinavia, Japan and Italy.[20] Male assaults are not always and everywhere equally grave and common; and, indeed, the vast majority of women in public space are *not* incessantly assaulted by men. This holds true for the micro-logic of the flight seat as well: it is fairly likely that the man will remove his elbow or leg if the woman makes a physical claim to her share of space, simply because he respects common rules of behaviour in public. It may also be that he is just not sexually attracted to her. And is it not possible that *she* is attracted to him and might enjoy the game of the heat of legs? And indeed, why should it be considered appalling and offensive to talk of such tiny and harmless little pleasures in public? Some feminists have also warned against the political consequences, as well as the factual indistinctiveness, of the trend within feminism of 'reliance on the iconography of female victimization' in relation to sexuality and the city: this can 'cast women in the roles of victims requiring male protection and control' and 'turn feminist protest into a politics of repression'.[21]

The main point, however, is that male violence and gendered power have no necessary relationship to the city as a world of strangers. To be sure, in modern societies there is a particular potentiality of male violence and power, since these societies are not merely urbanized, but also *gender problematized* (see later, section IV). This potentiality, however, is not in itself a consequence of urbanization, nor is it restricted to the city; indeed, it has often been stated that, statistically, women are more safe in the street than in the home. It may be objected that the city has specific forms of male violence and power. But, again, this does not make them a necessary consequence of the city; further, we must ask *what specifies* the specifically urban forms of power and violence. The answer to this will, I believe, return us to the particular characteristics of the city as a life space: that it is a world of strangers.

These considerations give occasion to explicate the level of abstraction of the reasonings presented here on urban sexuality: they attempt to identify phenomena related by necessity to the life space of the modern city. There is nothing strange or illegitimate in this sort of abstraction: if we did not make it, we would mix up what is particular to the city and (for instance) what derives from non-urban power relations or economic relations.[22]

In short: there is nothing inherent in the city which must make of it a place of male sexual power and violence; although these may happen *in* the city, they are not *of* the city (to use the distinction of Hannerz, 1980: 3, 248). This conclusion is in line with those reached by other scholars, such as Elizabeth Wilson (1992: 103).

However, we are still lacking a more positive demonstration of the thesis that the sexualization described above is universal among city users,

JOHN MOORES LIVERPOOL UNIVERSITY
AVRIL ROBARTS LRC
TEL. 0151 231 4022

and that it is a necessary concomitant of the city. In fact, I do not think that my thesis can be verified in any very orthodox empirical manner. Given the delicate nature of the subject matter, interviewing about people's sensations and sentiments would probably have to be conducted in the qualitative way; and the task of carrying out such qualitative interviews with representative samples of the population of the city seems overwhelming.[23] I proceed in other ways, by reasoning of a more theoretical, phenomenological nature and by appealing to what seems difficult to doubt.

First, we may be fairly certain that the fact that *somebody sometimes* sexualizes is well known to every grown-up user of the city. They will have heard of it, or read of it, if they have not experienced it themselves – but they almost certainly have, since rather explicit sexualization in gazes, surfaces and positionings is not unusual – that much we know from the ethnographic and other reports.

This common awareness – that sexualization is at large and roaming around the city – compels everyone to realize that he and she may become the object of somebody's sexualization – and indeed that they may themselves sexualize. From this follows an essential *choice* connected to urban life: how does one want to relate to sexualization? On a basic level, this is a sort of constant or chronic choice that one must, so to speak, always carry about and make over and over again. But of course, this is often not done deliberately and reflectedly in the course of everyday life in the city. I do think, however, that it is, phenomenologically speaking, present and can be caught at certain moments: those related to decisions concerning positioning and the uses of the gaze in urban space, as well as the moment of dressing. The latter used to be particularly accentuated for women; as we all know, it is in the process of becoming equally significant for men. It is indeed a very crucial moment in everyone's life in modern societies: it is the point where you decide to confirm to which sex you belong as a gendered being, and it is also the point where you decide whether and how far your surface is to be sexualized.[24] An important factor in the individual's making of such choices of sexualization is her or his reaction to the pleasures perceived to be connected to it.

In this 'deduction' of the universality of sexualization in the city, I have proceeded from the assumption that the majority of people were, so to speak, originally innocent inhabitants of the urban world, and that they would have to be *taught* sexualization from the explicitly sexualized behaviour of individuals or minority groups, or from the general discourse and narratives on such matters. This may be the case to some extent.[25] However, it is also partially a theoretical device that I have used for the purposes of argument, indeed a rhetorical one.

I do not believe that such primary innocence is very common among city users. The potentialities of sexualization are so firmly embedded and flagrantly apparent in the fabric of the urban as a life space that it seems impossible to be in the city without *sensing* these potentialities. One indication of this, I believe, is the fact that readers are able to perceive and capture what goes on in the little story of the woman on the bus. Although this is not, I suppose, something very many people have experienced themselves, but merely erotic or pornographic fantasy, it is definitely not a tale from the world of schizophrenia or the Kalahari. It is, in a way, a *familiar* fantasy, because it is not far from the sensations, the awareness and the fantasies that people themselves have experienced in the spaces of the city.

In this way, modern mass pornography has its truth value. It mirrors the rise of the particular modern life spaces of the city and telecity and the sentiments, experiences and fantasies connected to living there. Pornography often mirrors this directly in its content: very much of it is about people meeting strangers and having sex in public places, or about posing and peeping in relation to visual media. And visual pornography mirrors the modern life spaces and their experiences by its very *form*: it does itself constitute a space within the telecity where telemediated surfaces of strangers are sexualized. Pornography is perceivable, recognizable and stimulating to the mass of people precisely because of this: because they already know of its universe from the mass life spaces they move in.[26]

So much for the problem of the universality of sexualization in the modern city. In discussing this, I have simultaneously answered the question of how it is to be explained. Only in the mode of an omnipresent potentiality can sexualization be demonstrated as an inevitable consequence of the particular characteristics of the urban as a life space. The actualization of this potentiality – in affirmed and accentuated forms of experience and conduct – cannot be deduced as necessarily determined by the characteristics of the city. On the other hand, the potentiality is so firmly located and deep-rooted in the urban as a life space, and so invitingly and incitingly present, that it seems very unlikely that it should not be realized, as what might be termed a 'guided response' to the fabric of the city. And, once actualized, sexualization is, as I have demonstrated above, reproduced by the very consequences which it sparks off, as well as by the pleasures inherent in it, that is, by its very qualities of being *sexual*.

IV

But indeed: why should such modes of experience and conduct be termed *sexual*? What is the sense and the justification of this word, given the insight of constructionism that there is no eternally fixed and secure point of reference in these matters, no *essential* sexuality?

In order to elucidate this, I shall return to a particular instance of the alleged sexualization in the city. Here, as I said earlier, everything can be turned into a turn-on for someone's sexualized gaze. However, some surfaces and surface designs seem to be of a more universally recognized 'sexual' character within the modern city. The Marlon Brando type of leather jacket seems to be one of them, the protruding female leg in a black stocking another. This poses the question why certain surface shapes and materials are capable of functioning as such more universally recognized signs of sexuality.

We are entering here the realm of what is often known as fetishism (in a more narrow sense of the word), a domain theoretically occupied by psychoanalysis. In the 'primary scene' (*one* of them), or in his fantasies of the primary scene, the boy is shocked by the discovery of the female's lack of a penis, of her being castrated. Fetishism is the outcome of the denial of this awful recognition: the movement of the eye or the hand is, so to speak, wound back to some point of the women's body or attire which it passed before reaching the wound, in particular to such parts as may be taken to bear some resemblance to the phallus so horrifyingly missing (see Freud, 1927).

This may seem to provide a smooth and complete explanation of various fetishisms such as that of the protruding female leg. It may, however, be reasonable to utter some cautionary remarks. First, instead of discovering the hidden infantile psychological roots of fetishism, psycho-analysis may merely be mirroring a broader social process going on in modern societies. One of the characteristic features of such societies is the particular *problematization of gender*, as the social functions and spaces once reserved for males as what seemed to be their natural domains were now becoming invaded by women. This problematization of gender at the social level was accompanied by an accentuation of what seemed indubi-tably certain in relation to gender difference: that is, biological differences. Gender was reduced to sex organs, the proof of gender difference was the carrying out of the sex act (with a member of the 'opposite' sex, that is). From that centre, however, this particular sexualization spread to the rest of the body as well as to all the traditional differences in the cultural wardrobes of masculinity and femininity: all of this came to be experienced in the light of or seen as symbolic expressions of sex organs and sex acts.

Here, no doubt, is to be found part of the answer to the question of the sense in which the urban phenomena described above can be termed 'sexuality'. And from this point of view, psychoanalytic explanations of fetishism appear as an ideological reflection of a particular transformation of social experience – a distorted reflection, turning social processes into psychological essences. Further, psychoanalysis may not merely be mirror-ing, but also co-productive in the more detailed formation and elaboration of this experience of gender and sexuality, as its theories and concepts produce the links that help connect the accessories of gender wardrobes to the sex organs of the body. In other words, the concepts and theories of psychoanalysis help *sexualize* the rest of the bodily as well as traditional cultural differences.[27]

So far, the sense and the justification of the term 'sexual' have been sought by making reference to certain processes and phenomena not particularly related to the urban; and indeed, modern sexualization has a number of different sources. However, many of the aspects of the various fetishisms on display in the city seem to have a closer relationship to the characteristic features of this life space. Thus, there is an accentuation of the *visible* and the *visual*, of the quality of *surface*, of *distance* and the *alien*, of the *potential tactility* of materials and shapes. To this extent, fetishism resembles quite a lot of the other 'sexual perversions' enumerated in the elaborate catalogues of medicine and psychiatry towards the end of the 19th century: they actually presuppose the *city* as a social life space. Thus, for instance, some psychiatrists had found what they catalogued as *frotteurs* – that is people (men) who obtained sexual pleasure by rubbing against strangers (women) in the throng; another group listed were those (men) who found satisfaction by, unnoticed, managing to steal the handkerchiefs of female strangers in the crowds of the streets (Krafft-Ebing, 1907: 194–7, 382–4; see also Foucault, 1976: 58–60). All in all, *very* much of what goes on in the 'sexuality' of the urban – whether officially classified as perversion or not – is *only possible* within the city.

This brings us once again to the question of the sense and the justification of the term 'sexual' in relation to such urban phenomena. This, I believe, is to be found in the reference of the word to a certain *mood* or *'tuning'* pertaining to being-in-the-city, more specifically a certain *excitement*. And again, the particular quality of this excitement is identifiable and communicable to people because and insofar as they have experienced it themselves. This was one more reason for recounting the story of the woman in the bus; since by that means I might, literally, *re-present* an experience, make it present again.

To say that the sense of the phrase urban *sexuality*, and the legitimation for its use, lie in the experience of a certain excitement may seem banal. Considering the theoretical point of departure – constructionism's radical relativization of all 'sexuality' – it is not so banal. What I have ended up with is this. On the one hand, there is nothing essential about urban sexuality. It is indeed a historical and social construction, dependent upon the life space of the city and thus particular to or particularly prominent in modern societies. On the other hand, there is, *within* this modern construction of urban sexuality, a sort of fixed point or essence: a special excitement. It can, of course, be explained in relation to its background, as I have tried to do, and the symbolic aspects of it can be analysed in relation to their inner hidden meanings. But it cannot be *reduced* to causes and meanings; it has a particular quality which cannot be apprehended by way of explanation and interpretation. Metatheoretically, I would relate this to Heidegger's concept of the fundamental *'Gestimmtheit'* – that is, 'being tuned' – of being-in-the-world (Heidegger, 1967: §§29, 30, 40).[28] In any case, social science has to accept and respect that it is simply there, and can merely try to re-present it adequately.

V

In concluding, I shall briefly point to some implications of the intimate relation between city and sexuality (though not all of these implications can be corroborated by the discussion I have presented in this short article). For an extended discussion see Bech (1992b and forthcoming).

The urban world of strangers is a particular and important life space of modern societies. Quantitatively, it is not the most extensive setting of most people's lives, but it does occupy some time space, as a field for transport, for shopping, for entertainment, for seeking new relations.[29] Qualitatively, however, it is in important ways *the* primary life space: *all* forms of social life in modernity are constituted on the background and under the influence of it; and the urban world of strangers is the one that can be fallen back on when couples, families and networks break – it is *always* there.

In view of this importance of the city as a life space in modern societies, it is astonishing that reflections upon it are so often absent from social theory. Thus, for instance, the urban is not to be found in the theories of Schutz, Heller and Habermas, situating the 'everyday life' and 'life world' of these theories rather airily.[30] Moreover, given that urbanization implies sexualization, the lack of reflections upon such sexuality is an equally unfortunate (and even more widespread) omission in social theory. In fact, urban sexuality is one of the bonds of integration in modern societies; it is also co-constitutive of many of the particular features to be found in the modern modes of life that are established on the background of the city (such as therapy and 'communities of taste' – see Bech, 1992b). Further, it is co-constitutive of the basic de-traditionalized character of all ways of life in modern societies; and it is one of the major channels through which people from 'traditional' societies become acquainted with and integrated into global modernization (through immigration and tourism, respectively, as modern urban phenomena; see Necef, 1997). This, by the way, poses a problem for the ideas of *difference, multiculturalism* and the like, which have become dominant values in cultural critique during the 1980s and 1990s. *Urban sexualization* constitutes a modern *universal*, running counter to the accentuation of the local and the particular, a *homogenizing* complication for the celebration of difference.

In relation to the study of sexuality, more specifically, one implication of what I have said is, of course, that modern sexuality should not be studied without considering its relation to the city and the particular characteristics connected with this. Moreover, attention should be given to the constitutive importance of the city as a life space, that is to the spatial construction of the social and the symbolic, and not merely to the social and symbolic construction of space.[31]

A further implication is that the invectives of *alienation, objectification, instrumentalization* and *fetishization* – so common, explicitly or implicitly, in the study of sexuality – are fairly lame and inadequate as tools of analysis and cultural critique. Given the importance of the city in people's lives and the fact that the urban world cannot easily be 'brought away', nor even 'thought away', one will have to live with such 'alienated' and 'objectified' forms of sexuality and, I suggest, make the best of them (without, however, making a lifestyle out of them, which is hardly a viable solution either, see Bech, 1989).[32]

Another implication of my discussion, connected with the importance of the urban in modern sexuality, though not reducible to it, is that the study of sexuality should not ignore the *emotional* or *sensual* character of its subject-matter.[33] In constructionist approaches to the study of sexuality, heavy emphasis has been put on narratives, tales, texts, discourses, meanings, categories, perceptions, attitudes, labels, roles, scripts, language, signs, symbols, significations, codings, representations, ideas, ideologies and identities. The emphasis on such 'matters of consciousness' is no doubt related to constructionism's background in or heritage from, on the one hand, symbolic interactionism and culturalist phenomenology in the social sciences, and, on the other hand, the textual disciplines of the humanities (literature and semiotics, history and herstory); and the trend has been further accentuated by the recent currents of deconstructionism and postmodernism. Correspondingly, a *discursified* and *textualized* sexuality has been constructed as the primary object in the study of sexuality. This is not without its own '*Gestimmtheit*': its own 'tuning' and sensuality, but one that has little relation to any reality outside the social spaces constituted between text, reader and writer, or speaker and listener.[34] However, to state the fact very plainly: modern sexuality is not merely a discursive or textual phenomenon – although its particular qualities may be re-presented by some textual devices rather than by others. This is not to say that there may not be quite a lot of ways in which one can talk and write in a scholarly and adequate fashion about the sensuality of sexuality; nor will I myself feel obliged to do this every time by way of a pornographic tale, although this may, once in a while, be appropriate and stimulating.

Afterword

In a recent paper, Carrol Smith-Rosenberg has recalled the importance of 'Exploring the Feminine Erotic' (Smith-Rosenberg, 1993, see also 1975). At first glance, her article may seem the absolute antithesis of mine: whereas she is trying to identify an erotic beyond the realm of modern 'sexuality', I have been talking of sex, sex and sex again.

I do not, however, think that there is necessarily a conflict between the two articles, or that they are mutually exclusive. Thus, Carrol Smith-Rosenberg observes that by insisting upon the discursive, many contemporary analysts have failed to study the aura of feelings – a point, I think, not far from one of mine. Further, she stresses the importance of examining the construction and deployment of sexuality and erotic sensations within each culture we study; and what I have been trying to do is in fact to identify a *particularly* *modern* form of sexuality.[35] Moreover, the question might indeed be asked if it would not be better designated by the term 'erotic'. At least it has not so very much to do with medical or other common notions of sexuality; it refers to a particular excitement which is, generally, not one related to copulation or orgasm. And even if it might be found to be, most appropriately, termed 'sexuality', it does not exclude the existence of other, 'erotic' forms of feeling and excitement. And, just as I stress the importance of studying sexuality, I acknowledge the value of turning attention to the erotic – feminine and masculine – outside the realm of sexuality. Only I would, from my point of view, stress the forms of erotic feeling and excitement related to the urban world of strangers. Thus, I believe, many of Billie Holiday's or Frank Sinatra's songs speak of aspects of the particular erotic of the city, for instance of the *sentimentality* adhering to the brief encounters among strangers. To illustrate this, I should like to refer you to the words of one of Frank Sinatra's songs – 'Beautiful Strangers', the words and music by Rod McKuen.[36]

Notes

Earlier versions of this article were presented at a departmental seminar at the Sociology Department, University of Essex, 28 January 1993; at a seminar on 'Sexual Cultures and Gender' at the Centre for Women's Research, University of Copenhagen, 7 June 1993; at the International Conference on 'Geographies of Desire', SISWO, University of Amsterdam, 18–19 June 1993; and at the Second Congress of the European Federation of Sexology, University of Copenhagen, 2–5 June 1994. A German version is published in *Soziale Welt* 46(1), 1995: 5–26. I would like to thank Zygmunt Bauman and Rob Shields for their comments.

1.   'Constructionism' in the study of sexuality derives from a variety of intellectual sources: symbolic interactionism, Freudian left, anthropological relativism, new social history, feminism, lesbian and gay studies. Among the seminal works are Simon and Gagnon (1967a, 1967b, 1967c), McIntosh (1968), Gagnon and Simon (1973), Plummer (1975, 1981), Smith-Rosenberg (1975), Foucault (1976), Weeks (1977, 1981, 1985).

2.   I conceive of modernity as a particular conglomeration of phenomena and factors, coming together and tangling in (North) Western societies during the latter half of the 19th century. All of these factors have differential histories; some of them were fairly new by the end of the 19th century (e.g. psychiatry and psychology as theoretico-practical apparatus); others are much older (although they might have gained new forms) and may thus be found at other points of world history (e.g. the city).

3.   Accordingly, the concept of the city that I am presenting here does not exclude other concepts of relevance when studying other dimensions of the complex phenomenon of the city. I am merely claiming that the world of strangers is *one* dimension (among many other dimensions) of the urban world; moreover, that it is an *essential* dimension, in the sense specified in the rest of this section (section I); finally, that it is, in some particular regards, the *primary* life space of modernity (see section V below). In recent years, some (though not all) of the 'urban sociologists' of the 1970s and early 1980s have in fact taken a more positive stance on the dimensions of urban life that I am referring to here. Compare, e.g., Harvey's more recent work (1989) with his writings from the 1970s.

4.   As appears from the conceptualizations given above, I do not, in this article, make any distinction between the city and the urban world. Thus, wherever a routine world of strangers exists, there is city; and, conversely, wherever this is not

the case, there is no city. This criterion is also quite helpful in discussions on whether, when and in what way X-town or Y-polis is city or not.

5.   For example Williams (1982), Chaney (1983), Davidoff and Hall (1983: 340ff), Wilson (1985, 1991, 1992), Bowlby (1985), Benson (1988), Wehinger (1988), Young (1990), Nava (1992: 97–122); cf. also references in note 21. There is by now quite a body of literature on 'women and space' or 'women and the city'; however, very little of it deals with the city as a world of strangers. Thus, the blank spots noted years ago by Lyn Lofland (1975) and Gerda Wekerle (1980: 195, 200) still remain largely uncharted. A number of interesting studies have appeared in the *Journal of Contemporary Ethnography* (and the predecessors of this 'thrice-named' journal).

6.   There is an extensive literature documenting various aspects of this. A few examples, particularly relating to women, are Boys (1984), Pickup (1988), Tivers (1988), Valentine (1989, 1993).

7.   These qualifications to the concept of the 'modern' city – not just a world of strangers, but a routine world of gender-, race- and class-mixed strangers – bring to the forefront the question of whether the term 'postmodern' or 'late modern' might not be more adequate here. I would not object to such terminology, as there has been, of course, a pronounced development concerning the 'routine' of this sort of urban world since the 18th, 19th or early 20th century. Obviously, an open, routine world of gender-, race- and class-mixed strangers may be found also before modernity, at least to some extent. In many cases, however, openness has been restricted in terms of gender, class or caste; and the world of strangers has not been so routine for such huge proportions of people as it is in modern, and, specifically, in contemporary modern societies.

8.   Of course, it *is* possible to 'think away' these public parts, but then one would end up with a concept which was not relevant to the study of modern cities and societies. A 'radical feminist' claim that the modern city – qua world of strangers – is male and that the actual presence of women is accidental or due to male grace or cunning, would have to explain the necessity of such an alleged relation between worlds of strangers and masculinity, as well as the necessity of its exclusion of women. Besides, I think such a position would end up in a political cul de sac intolerable to those advocating it: if the city is inherently and exclusively male, there is no point in fighting for women's rights to enter and frequent it; instead, the world of strangers should be abolished – but this is hardly possible either. In other words: hoping and fighting for better opportunities for women seems incompatible with such 'radical feminist' conceptions of the city.

9.   It has been argued that many spaces are neither strictly public nor strictly private, but mix characteristics of both (e.g. Dixey, 1988; Lofland, 1989; Bailey, 1990; Chaney, 1990; Wilson, 1992). I do not disagree; my main criterion – world of *strangers* or not – is analytical (but, I believe, of much usefulness also in more concrete analysis). I must emphasize that the concept of 'public' employed in this article is strictly related to the 'world of strangers'. Thus, it does not refer to the politics of what is often called the 'public sphere' (see note 30). Nor does it refer to economic distinctions of public and private. Nor does it refer to common anthropological distinctions, to the extent that these do not consider worlds of strangers.

10.   Obviously, this is in the process of changing, with the developments in picture transmission technology connected with the Internet. However, this new

version of the telecity has produced new restrictions concerning 'openness', related to generation and education.

11.   See e.g. Morley (1986, 1995), Gunter and Svennevig (1987), Lull (1990). Among the works sharing some interest in the formal qualities of the sociality of 'the telecity' – in, from my point of view, more or less reasonable ways – are McLuhan (1964), Benjamin (1974a), Sontag (1977), Baudrillard (1983), Duyves (1987). There is, however, also an affinity to some 'cultural studies' approaches (like e.g. Fiske, 1989). Zygmunt Bauman has commented on and elaborated my concept of the telecity (in Bauman, 1993: 173ff, 1995: 93, 138). For a more extended discussion see Bech (1992b and forthcoming).

12.   Høst (1990). According to a statement by the publisher from this period, the magazine had a Danish circulation of 37,000 copies (Bøggild, 1990) (in a population of 5 million). It may be added that the writer of the short story is a woman (according to the name given: Eva Høst); that the magazine was expressly catering to the erotic interests of women; and that the editorial board was quite influenced by women. Recently, another – hardly less explicit – 'erotic' magazine has become more popular: *Tidens kvinder*, edited by and catering to women.

13.   The particular being-with or 'communionality' of (some) urban sexuality is related to the 'underdetermination of tactility', the 'ambivalence of caress', as analysed by Bauman (1993: 92ff). This, as well as other of its formal characteristics, may place such sexuality in a somewhat transverse relation to some of the distinctions elaborated by Bauman (and not simply as their in-between, as intermediate stations or mixtures of these social forms): neither meeting nor mismeeting, neither proximity nor distance, neither rational rule-following of heteronomously regulated society nor emotional meltdown of crowd sociality. There is also an affinity to Maffesoli's (e.g. 1985, 1991) ideas on the intimate relation between sociality and sexuality.

14.   The scholarly literature dealing thematically with such issues is far from immense. When presenting earlier versions of this article, I have sometimes encountered the objection that there is an extensive, indeed a 'vast' empirical literature in sociology and geography concerning sexuality and the city. A careful examination of the references produced on such occasions has invariably led me to the conclusion that *this is not so* (and I emphasize this). For instance, the growing body of literature on various sexual and gender groups' creation of community or neighbourhood space – notwithstanding the importance of these studies – is not of relevance to the present investigation of sex in the world of strangers. However, there is an accumulating body of work on homosexual sites, experiences and practices (for some references, see Bech, 1997: Part IV and Bech, 1991a). Other strands of contributions can be found in some versions of feminism and/or in studies inspired by Walter Benjamin (see notes 21 and 15 for some references). Further, the debate initiated by the new journal on *Gender, Place and Culture* (see Bell et al., 1994) is very promising. And there is, of course, an extensive literature on prostitution – but one may wonder how much of this does in fact deal with the particular qualities of sexuality? Here are a couple of my favourites from the literature on sex and the city: Henslin (1971), Delph (1978), Bailey (1990), Wilson (1992).

15.   Much of the discussion on such urban prototypes is inspired by Walter Benjamin (1974b, 1982) and Siegfried Kracauer (1964, 1971, 1976). See e.g. Madsen (1977), Sontag (1977: 55f, 75ff), Frisby (1985), Buck-Morss (1986, 1989:

185ff, 304ff, et passim); Kleinheinrich (1986), Wilson (1992), Andersen (1993: 28–66). There is also an influence from the Chicago School (see e.g. Lindner, 1990: 17–150). As for the shopping women: see Williams (1982), Bowlby (1985), Benson (1988), Walkowitz (1992: 41–80).

16. Although most people primarily enter the city during these two 'moments' of their lives, the city as a world of strangers does, nevertheless, exert an enormous influence on everybody's lives, in various modes of *potentiality*. See Bech (1992b, forthcoming).

17. See Bech (1997: Part IV and 1991b, 1992a). It is not possible in this brief article to reproduce the detailed argument I have presented in hundreds of pages during my research over the last decade; on this point, then, as well as on others, I have to refer the critical reader to other of my works.

18. Obviously, this is not identical to claiming that all 'homosexuals' are hunting for sex all over the city all around the clock. Again, I refer to the detailed discussion of the homosexual, the urban, sexuality, the heterosexual and modernity in Bech (1997, esp. Parts IV & VI; see also 1991a, 1996).

19. There is an excellent exposition of the many facets of this in Deegan (1987).

20. Much contemporary writing on urban life tends to generalize from the rather peculiar realities of US cities. Much other writing proceeds from the rather peculiar British *fantasies* of the city. (See the excellent 'archaeology' of contemporary British notions of urban life and sexuality: Walkowitz, 1992.) Neither case is necessarily the most adequate for the elaboration of theories and concepts on urban life.

21. Walkowitz (1992: 245; cf. also Walkowitz, 1982). Along similar lines a number of feminist historians have, while in no way ignoring socially constructed gender dissymmetries, pointed to the active part played by women in the sexuality of the city (see Gordon and Dubois, 1983; Peiss, 1983; Stansell, 1986: 83–101, 125–9, 171–92; Meyerowitz, 1990; Ryan, 1990: 68–129). Cf. also Smith (1992), Golding (1993), Rubin (1993), Califia (1994: 71–82), Munt (1995).

22. To be sure, I do not think that gender problematization and the city do not in actual fact interact – indeed, they may tend to interlock; but this is a topic outside the scope of the present article, which is concerned with aspects of urban sexuality *not reducible to* gendered power relations that originate outside the urban. Undifferentiated claims like 'the history of sexuality is the history of male power' have all too often functioned as blinkers if not taboos against the study of these other aspects of sexuality.

23. Since some readers tend to get rather heated by the porn tale related at the beginning of this article, I would like to spell out the methodological problematics pertaining to an investigation of the issue in question. Obviously, I do not believe that the porn narrative constitutes any proof in itself. However, I do not think there is any empirical material available, or any method to make it available, which would produce proofs in this sensitive matter. Ethnographies and other qualitative methods may always be accused of dealing with non-representative material. Citing from the huge non-academic literature and other cultural products celebrating urban sexuality does not prove its general existence, as little as the widespread anti-urban literature bewailing the omnipresence of urban sexuality proves its infrequency. This state of empirical affairs can*not* be remedied by a cumulative examination of existing social science investigations of the subject matter – since, as stated earlier, there are very few of these. Finally, I should like to remind the

critical reader that my elaboration of the characteristics of urban sexuality does in fact build on empirical work, others' as well as my own, as presented in Bech (1997; see also 1991a, 1996).

24.   You may, of course, dress decently, or resignedly count yourself out from being sexually attractive. Either way, however, presupposes the awareness of sexualization: how else would it be possible to dress decently? The notion of 'choice' employed here does, of course, relate to Sartre's considerations (1943). An objection to this sort of reasoning is exemplified by Coleman (1990). Most of the time there is, he argues (in relation to masculinity), simply no problematic of 'impression management' like the one postulated by social constructionists: people simply *do what they do*, without considering whether or not they are making a satisfactory presentation of themselves. This objection is, I think, partially begging the question, since no one would really deny that such 'spontaneity' and 'natural-ness' are predominant in many instances. The question is whether there is, nevertheless, insecurity at a more fundamental level; and my argument is that this must be the case *precisely in modern societies* because these are urbanized and gender problematized (and homosexualized and sociologized), thereby making such problematic choice more than just an occasional (or 'occasioned') exception.

25.   Indeed to no small extent, given the pervasiveness of various kinds of discourse on such matters (see note 31).

26.   Obviously, people can *imagine* some of the qualities of urban sexualization without ever having been part of a world of strangers. Yet the difference between imagining on the one hand, and experiencing and recognizing on the other, has to do with the particulars and specifics of the 'object' of these mental activities.

27.   The above critique of psychoanalysis is elaborated in greater detail in Bech (1997: chs III.4, III.8, IV.19; see also 1990).

28.   More specifically, the particular excitement of sexualization is a fundamental '*Stimmung*' of *modern* being-in-the-world, i.e. of being-in-the-city. Obviously, analogous phenomena can be found wherever there are worlds of strangers through-out history, as is richly demonstrated in the literature from many periods. What is particular to *modern* urban sexualization is its routineness, ubiquity and general-ness. Thus, modern being-in-the-world is *essentially* sexualized.

29.   However, for most people the world of strangers of the city *and* the telecity conjunctively does play a major quantitative role as a life space (see Bech, forthcoming).

30.   Thus, Habermas' *grand theory* of modern society has no room for the urban: it is not 'system', but nor is it 'life world', or '*Gesellschaft*' as a structural component of life world, in Habermas' sense of these words. Although these concepts of his belong to a very abstract level of reasoning, the component (related to '*Gesellschaft*') of '*Zugehörigkeit zu sozialen Gruppen*' and the corresponding one of '*Gruppenidenti-tät*' do not point in a direction relevant for the study of the city as a life space (see Habermas, 1981 vol. II: 182–228). This conclusion is not modified by the rhetorical use, in Habermas (1982), of the concept of life world in relation to the city. Nor is his concept of 'public sphere' relevant (1981 vol. II: 471–88; cf. also his earlier work on this, 1962). This is also the reason why discussions of Habermasian or similar concepts of the 'public sphere' are not considered in this article, e.g. the feminist critiques by Carole Pateman (1987), Nancy Fraser (1987), Joan B. Landes

(1988), Gillian Rose (1990), Seyla Benhabib (1992) and others. They simply deal with another topic than the one treated here (although, of course, an important one).

31. Although the latter is certainly important: popular, commercial and high culture products do not merely celebrate or lament citysex and sexy city (or simply presuppose it as a 'natural' setting) but also advertise it and seduce people to delight in sexualized city life. See e.g. the chapter on Brighton in Shields (1991) and the sections on sex tourism in Urry (1990).

32. The invectives of alienation, etc. have often been connected to critiques of economics, consumerism and power, as well as to utopian ideas of the disappearance of alienation, etc. with the overthrow of capitalism or patriarchy, or with the instalment of non-'materialist' values. The argument of this article points to other and inert connections related to the city – which is one more reason for treating the relationship of city and sexuality in abstraction from systems of economics and power that do not originate in the urban.

33. In the words of Anthony Giddens, one may speak of the 'innocence of sexuality itself' (in the sense of a historicized, socialized sexuality), or 'the pleasure and fulfilment that episodic sexuality can provide' (1992: 144, 147). Or, with a different wording and, perhaps, a bit of a different accent: one should not forget the *lust, lewdness and lechery* of 'episodic sexuality', or of more diffuse voyeurism, cruising and stimulated participation in the motions of the crowd. Nor should one forget the joys of sexualized posing, styling and ritualizing in the urban world.

34. This emphasis on the discursive in (the study of) modern sexuality is sometimes related to the influence from Foucault. Apart from the fact that it could be found in the literature before he started writing thematically on the topic, I do not think that Foucault, in his later years, did in fact insist that vehemently upon the discursive. In the first volume of *The History of Sexuality* he emphasizes the interconnectedness of discourses *and* practices *and* institutions in the modern '*dispositif*' of sexuality; and in the introduction to the second volume he characterizes this '*dispositif*' – from another, I would say phenomenological, point of view – as an '*expérience*' (Foucault, 1984: 9ff).

35. 'Particularly modern' in the sense specified in note 28.

36. 'Beautiful Strangers', words and music by Rod McKuen, Warner Bros. Records (1969). For copyright reasons I am unable to quote the lyrics.

References

Andersen, S. (1993) 'Udfordringer til blikket: En diskussion af by- og billedoplevelser herunder oplevelsen af dokumentariske fotografier', MA thesis, Institute of Cultural Sociology, University of Copenhagen.

Atkinson, P. (1990) *The Ethnographic Imagination: Textual Constructions of Reality*. London: Routledge.

Bailey, P. (1990) 'Parasexuality and Glamour: The Victorian Barmaid as Cultural Prototype', *Gender & History* 2(2): 148–72.

Baudrillard, J. (1983) *Les Stratégies fatales*. Paris: Éditions Grasset et Fasquelle.

Bauman, Z. (1991) *Modernity and Ambivalence*. Cambridge: Polity Press.

Bauman, Z. (1993) *Postmodern Ethics*. Oxford, UK and Cambridge, MA: Blackwell.

Bauman, Z. (1995) *Life in Fragments: Essays in Postmodern Morality*. Oxford, UK and Cambridge, MA: Blackwell.

Bech, H. (1989) 'The Aestheticization of Sexuality: The Pleasures of Alienation and Reification', paper presented at the International Conference on Sexuality and (Post)Modernity, University of Copenhagen, 11–13 December.

Bech, H. (1990) 'Mandslængsel: Hankøn i moderne samfund', *Varia* 1: 83–97.

Bech, H. (1991a) 'Schwule Existenz und ihr Verschwinden: Die Postmodernisierung der Homosexualität?', pp. 59–69 in *HIV/AIDS – Homosexualität/Bisexualität: Dokumentation des Internationalen Symposiums 6.–9. Oktober 1991 in Hamburg.*

Bech, H. (1991b) 'Recht fertigen. Über die Einführung "homosexueller Ehen" in Dänemark', *Zeitschrift für Sexualforschung* 4(3): 213–24.

Bech, H. (1992a) 'Report From a Rotten State: "Marriage" and "Homosexuality" in "Denmark"', pp. 134–47 in K. Plummer (ed.) *Modern Homosexualities: Fragments of Lesbian and Gay Experiences.* London and New York: Routledge.

Bech, H. (1992b) 'Living Together in the (Post)Modern World', paper presented at the European Sociology Conference, 26–9 August, University of Vienna.

Bech, H. (1996) '(Tele)Urban Eroticisms', *Parallax* 2: 89–100.

Bech, H. (1997) *When Men Meet: Homosexuality and Modernity.* Cambridge: Polity Press and Chicago, IL: University of Chicago Press. (Revised English edition of *Når mænd mødes.* Copenhagen: Gyldendal, 1987.)

Bech, H. (forthcoming) *Modern Life Spaces* (working title). London and New York: Routledge.

Bell, D., J. Binnie, J. Cream and G. Valentine (1994) 'All Hyped Up and No Place to Go', *Gender, Place and Culture* 1(1): 31–47.

Benhabib, S. (1992) *Situating the Self: Gender, Community and Postmodernism in Contemporary Ethics.* Cambridge: Polity.

Benjamin, W. (1974a) 'Das Kunstwerk im Zeitalter seiner technischen Reproduzierbarkeit', pp. 471–508 in W. Benjamin *Gesammelte Schriften. Band I.2.* Frankfurt am Main: Suhrkamp. (Orig. 1935.)

Benjamin, W. (1974b) *Charles Baudelaire: Ein Lyriker in Zeitalter des Hochkapitalismus* (contains: 'Das Paris des Second Empire bei Baudelaire' [orig. written 1938]; 'Über einige Motive bei Baudelaire' [orig. published 1940]; 'Zentralpark' [orig. written 1937–8]), pp. 509–690 in W. Benjamin *Gesammelte Schriften. Band I.2.* Frankfurt am Main: Suhrkamp.

Benjamin, W. (1982) *Das Passagen-Werk. Bd. I und II.* Frankfurt am Main: Suhrkamp. (Orig. c. 1927–40.)

Benson, S. (1988) *Counter Cultures, Saleswomen, Managers, and Costumers in American Department Stores, 1890–1940.* Urbana and Chicago: University of Illinois Press.

Berman, M. (1982) *All That Is Solid Melts Into Air: The Experience of Modernity.* New York: Simon & Schuster.

Bøggild, P. (1990) 'Der er penge i dansk kiosk-erotik', *Information* (daily newspaper, Copenhagen) 4 November.

Bowlby, R. (1985) *Just Looking: Consumer Culture in Dreiser, Gissing and Zola.* New York and London: Methuen.

Boys, J. (1984) 'Women and Public Space', pp. 37–54 in Matrix (ed.) *Making Space: Women and the Man-Made Environment.* London and Sydney: Pluto Press.

Buck-Morss, S. (1986) 'Der Flaneur, der Sandwichman und die Hure. Dialektische Bilder und die Politik des Müssiggangs', pp. 96–113 in N. Bolz and B. Witte (eds) *Passagen. Walter Benjamins Urgeschichte des neunzehnten Jahrhunderts.* München: Fink.

Buck-Morss, S. (1989) *The Dialectics of Seeing: Walter Benjamin and the Arcades Project.* Cambridge, MA: MIT Press.

Califia, P. (1994) *Public Sex: The Culture of Radical Sex.* Pittsburgh, PA: Cleis Press.

Castells, M. (1975) *La Question urbaine.* Paris: Maspéro.

Chaney, D. (1983) 'The Department Store as a Cultural Form', *Theory, Culture & Society* 1(3): 22–31.

Chaney, D. (1990) 'Subtopia in Gateshead: The MetroCentre as a Cultural Form', *Theory, Culture & Society* 7(4): 49–68.

Coleman, W. (1990) 'Doing Masculinity / Doing Theory', pp. 186–99 in J. Hearn and D. Morgan (eds) *Men, Masculinities & Social Theory.* London: Unwin Hyman.

Davidoff, L. and C. Hall (1983) 'The Architecture of Public and Private Life: English Middle-Class Society in a Provincial Town 1780–1850', pp. 327–45 in D. Fraser and A. Suttcliffe (eds) *The Pursuit of Urban History.* London: Edward Arnold.

Deegan, M. (1987) 'The Female Pedestrian: The Dramaturgy of Structural and Experiental Barriers in the Street', *Man–Environment Systems* 17(3–4): 79–86.

Delph, E. (1978) *The Silent Community: Public Homosexual Encounters.* Beverly Hills, CA: Sage.

Dewey, R. (1960) 'The Rural–Urban Continuum: Real but Relatively Unimportant', *American Journal of Sociology* 66: 60–6.

Dixey, R. (1988) 'Means to Get Out of the House: Working-Class Women, Leisure and Bingo', pp. 117–32 in J. Little et al. (eds) *Women in Cities: Gender and the Urban Environment.* London: Macmillan.

Duyves, M. (1987) 'The Minitel: The Glittering Future of a New Invention', pp. 70–9 in *Homosexuality, Which Homosexuality?: Papers from the Conference, Social Science*, supplement, Free University, Amsterdam.

Featherstone, M. (1991) *Consumer Culture and Postmodernism.* London: Sage.

Fiske, J. (1989) *Television Culture.* London: Routledge.

Foucault, M. (1976) *Histoire de la sexualité I: la volonté de savoir.* Paris: Gallimard.

Foucault, M. (1984) *Histoire de la sexualité II: l'usage des plaisirs.* Paris: Gallimard.

Fraser, N. (1987) 'What's Critical about Critical Theory? The Case of Habermas and Gender', pp. 281–303 in S.I. Benn and G.F. Gaus (eds) *Public and Private in Social Life.* London and Canberra: St Martin's Press.

Freud, S. (1927) 'Fetichismus', pp. 311–17 in S. Freud *Gesammelte Werke Bd. XIV.* Frankfurt am Main: S. Fischer Verlag.

Frisby, D. (1985) *Fragments of Modernity: Theories of Modernity in the Work of Simmel, Kracauer and Benjamin.* Cambridge: Polity Press.

Gagnon, J. and W. Simon (1973) *Sexual Conduct: The Social Sources of Human Sexuality.* Chicago, IL: Aldine.

Giddens, A. (1992) *The Transformation of Intimacy: Sexuality, Love and Eroticism in Modern Societies.* Cambridge: Polity Press.

Goffman, E. (1959) *The Presentation of Self in Everyday Life*. New York: Double-day/Anchor.

Goffman, E. (1963) *Behavior in Public Places*. New York: Free Press.

Goffman, E. (1971) *Relations in Public: Microstudies of the Public Order*. New York: Basic Books.

Golding, S. (1993) 'Sexual Manners', in V. Harwood et al. (eds) *Pleasure Principles: Politics, Sexuality and Ethics*. London: Lawrence & Wishart.

Gordon, L. and E. Dubois (1983) 'Seeking Ecstasy in the Battlefield: Danger and Pleasure in Nineteenth-Century Feminist Sexual Thought', *Feminist Review* 13: 42–54.

Gunter, B and M. Svennevig (1987) *Behind and In Front of the Screen: Television's Involvement with Family Life*. London: John Libbey.

Habermas, J. (1962) *Strukturwandel der Öffentlichkeit. Untersuchungen zu einer Kategorie der bürgerlichen Gesellschaft*. Darmstadt: Luchterhand.

Habermas, J. (1981) *Theorie des kommunikativen Handelns. Band I und II*. Frankfurt am Main: Suhrkamp.

Habermas, J. (1982) 'Moderne und postmoderne Architektur', *Arch+* 61.

Hannerz, U. (1980) *Exploring the City: Inquiries Toward an Urban Anthropology*. New York: Columbia University Press.

Harvey, D. (1989) *The Condition of Postmodernity*. Oxford: Basil Blackwell.

Häussermann, H. and W. Siebel (1987) *Neue Urbanität*. Frankfurt am Main: Suhrkamp.

Heidegger, M. (1967) *Sein und Zeit*. 11. Unveränderte Auflage. Tübingen: Max Niemeyer. (Orig. 1927.)

Henslin, J. (1971) 'Sex and Cabbies', pp. 193–223 in J. Henslin (ed.) *Studies in the Sociology of Sex*. New York: Appleton-Century-Crofts.

Høst, E. (1990) 'Omstigning til Paradis', *Cupido* (Copenhagen) 7: 2–5.

Kleinheinrich, J. (1986) *Kopenhagener Panoramen um 1900. Varianten der Grossstadtapperzeption und der poetischen Transformation von Grossstadterlebnissen im journalistischen Oeuvre Herman Bangs*. Münster: Haus Hölker.

Kracauer, S. (1964) *Strassen in Berlin und anderswo*. Frankfurt am Main: Suhrkamp. (Orig. 1925–33.)

Kracauer, S. (1971) *Der Detektiv-Roman. Ein philosophisches Traktat*, pp. 103–204 in S. Kracauer *Schriften Band I*. Frankfurt am Main: Suhrkamp. (Orig. written 1922–5.)

Kracauer, S. (1976) *Jacques Offenbach und das Paris seiner Zeit*. (= S. Kracauer, *Schriften Band 8*). Frankfurt am Main: Suhrkamp. (Orig. 1937.)

Krafft-Ebing, R. (1907) *Psychopathia Sexualis*. (Dreizehnte, vermehrte Auflage, herausgegeben von Dr Alfred Fuchs). Stuttgart: Enke.

Landes, J.B. (1988) *Women and the Public Sphere in the Age of the French Revolution*. Ithaca, NY and London: Cornell University Press.

Lindner, R. (1990) *Die Entdeckung der Stadtkultur: Soziologie aus der Erfahrung der Reportage*. Frankfurt am Main: Suhrkamp.

Lofland, L. (1973) *A World of Strangers: Order and Action in Urban Public Space*. New York: Basic Books.

Lofland, L. (1975) 'The "Thereness" of Women: A Selective Review of Urban Sociology', pp. 144–70 in M. Millman and R.M. Kanter (eds) *Another Voice: Feminist Perspectives on Social Life and Social Science*. New York: Anchor Press.

Lofland, L. (1989) 'Social Life in the Public Realm: A Review', *Journal of Contemporary Ethnography* 17(4): 453–82.

Lull, J. (1990) *Inside Family Viewing: Ethnographic Research on Television's Audiences*. London: Comedia.

Madsen, P. (1977) 'Tidens smerte og storbyens atmosfære', in O. Harsløf (ed.) *Omkring Stuk*. Copenhagen: Reitzel.

Maffesoli, M. (1985) *L'Ombre de Dionysos: contribution à une sociologie de l'orgie*. Paris: Méridiens Klincksieck.

Maffesoli, M. (1991) 'The Ethic of Aesthetics', *Theory, Culture & Society* 8(1): 7–20.

Massey, D. (1991) 'Flexible Sexism', *Environment and Planning D: Society and Space* 9: 31–57.

McIntosh, M. (1968) 'The Homosexual Role', *Social Problems* 16: 182–92.

McLuhan, M. (1964) *Understanding Media: The Extensions of Man*. London: Routledge & Kegan Paul.

Meyerowitz, J. (1990) 'Sexual Geography and Gender Economy: The Furnished Room Districts of Chicago', *Gender & History* 2(3): 274–96.

Morley, D. (1986) *Family Television: Cultural Power and Domestic Leisure*. London: Comedia.

Morley, D. (1995) 'Television: Not So Much a Visual Medium, More a Visual Object', pp. 170–89 in C. Jencks (ed.) *Visual Culture*. London and New York: Routledge.

Munt, S. (1995) 'The Lesbian Flâneur', pp. 114–25 in D. Bell and G. Valentine (eds) *Mapping Desire: Geographies of Sexualities*. London and New York: Routledge.

Nava, M. (1992) *Changing Cultures: Feminism, Youth and Consumerism*. London: Sage.

Necef, M. (1997) 'Ethnic Sex in the Multi-Ethnic City: The Role of Sexuality in the Integration of Immigrants', Paper presented at the conference on 'Transformations in the Plural City', 28–31 May, Bergen University, Norway.

Pateman, C. (1987) 'Feminist Critiques of the Public/Private Dichotomy', pp. 103–26 in A. Phillips (ed.) *Feminism and Equality*. Oxford: Blackwell.

Peiss, C. (1983) ' "Charity Girls" and City Pleasures: Historical Notes on Working-Class Sexuality, 1880–1920', pp. 74–87 in A. Snitow et al. (eds) *Powers of Desire: The Politics of Sexuality*. New York: Monthly Review Press.

Pickup, L. (1988) 'Hard to Get Around: A Study of Women's Travel Mobility', pp. 98–116 in J. Little et al. (eds) *Women in Cities: Gender and the Urban Environment*. London: Macmillan.

Plummer, K. (1975) *Sexual Stigma: An Interactionist Account*. London: Routledge & Kegan Paul.

Plummer, K. (ed.) (1981) *The Making of the Modern Homosexual*. London: Hutchinson.

Plummer, K. (1983) *Documents of Life: An Introduction to the Problems and Literature of a Humanistic Method.* London: Allen & Unwin.

Pollock, G. (1988) 'Modernity and the Spaces of Femininity', in G. Pollock *Vision and Difference: Femininity, Feminism and the Histories of Art.* London: Routledge & Kegan Paul.

Rose, G. (1990) 'The Struggle for Political Democracy: Emancipation, Gender, and Geography', *Environment and Planning D: Society and Space* 8: 395–408.

Rubin, G.S. (1993) 'Thinking Sex: Notes for a Radical Theory of the Politics of Sexuality', pp. 3–44 in H. Abelove, M. Barale and D. Halperin (eds) *The Lesbian and Gay Studies Reader.* New York and London: Routledge.

Ryan, M. (1990) *Women in Public: Between Banners and Ballots, 1825–1880.* Baltimore, MD: Johns Hopkins University Press.

Sartre, J.-P. (1943) *L'Etre et le néant: essai d'ontologie phénoménologique.* Paris: Gallimard.

Saunders, P. (1981) *Social Theory and the Urban Question.* London: Hutchinson.

Sennett, R. (1977) *The Fall of Public Man.* New York: Knopf.

Shields, R. (1991) *Places on the Margin: Alternative Geographies of Modernity.* London and New York: Routledge.

Simmel, G. (1957) 'Die Grossstädte und das Geistesleben', pp. 227–42 in G. Simmel *Brücke und Tür.* Stuttgart: K.F. Koehler Verlag. (Orig. 1903.)

Simon, W. and J. Gagnon (1967a) 'Homosexuality: The Formulation of a Sociological Perspective', *Journal of Health and Social Behavior* 8(3): 177–85.

Simon, W. and J. Gagnon (1967b) 'The Lesbians: A Preliminary Overview', pp. 247–82 in J. Gagnon and W. Simon (eds) *Sexual Deviance.* New York: Harper & Row.

Simon, W. and J. Gagnon (1967c) 'Femininity in the Lesbian Community', *Social Problems* 15(2): 212–21.

Smith, A.M. (1992) 'Resisting the Erasure of Lesbian Sexualities: A Challenge for Queer Activism', pp. 200–13 in K. Plummer (ed.) *Modern Homosexualities: Fragments of Lesbian and Gay Experience.* London and New York: Routledge.

Smith-Rosenberg, C. (1975) 'The Female World of Love and Ritual: Relations Between Women in Nineteenth-Century America', *Signs* 1(1): 1–29.

Smith-Rosenberg, C. (1993) 'Exploring the Feminine Erotic: Some Reflections on the Social Purity Movement in Nineteenth-Century America', paper from the seminar on Sexual Cultures and Gender, 7 June, Center for Women's Research, University of Copenhagen.

Sontag, S. (1977) *On Photography.* New York: Farrar, Straus & Giroux.

Stansell, C. (1986) *City of Women: Sex and Class in New York 1789–1860.* New York: Alfred C. Knopf.

Tivers, J. (1988) 'Women with Young Children: Constraints on Activities in the Urban Environment', pp. 84–97 in J. Little et al. (eds) *Women in Cities: Gender and the Urban Environment.* London: Macmillan.

Urry, J. (1990) *The Tourist Gaze: Leisure and Travel in Contemporary Societies.* London: Sage.

Valentine, G. (1989) 'The Geography of Women's Fear', *Area* 21(4): 385–90.

Valentine, G. (1993) '(Hetero)sexing Space: Lesbian Perceptions and Experiences of Everyday Spaces', *Environment and Planning D: Society and Space* 11: 395–413.

Walkowitz, J. (1982) 'Male Vice and Feminist Virtue: Feminism and the Politics of Prostitution in Nineteenth-Century Britain', *History Workshop Journal* 13: 79–93.

Walkowitz, J. (1992) *City of Dreadful Delight: Narratives of Sexual Danger in Late-Victorian London*. London: Virago.

Weeks, J. (1977) *Coming Out: Homosexual Politics in Britain, from the Nineteenth Century to the Present*. London: Quartet.

Weeks, J. (1981) *Sex, Politics and Society: The Regulation of Sexuality since 1800*. London: Longman.

Weeks, J. (1985) *Sexuality and its Discontents: Meanings, Myths and Modern Sexualities*. London: Routledge & Kegan Paul.

Wehinger, B. (1988) *Paris-Crinoline: Zur Faszination des Boulevardtheaters und der Mode im Kontext der Urbanität und der Modernität des Jahres 1857*. München: Fink Verlag.

Wekerle, G. (1980) 'Review Essay: Women in the Urban Environment', *Signs* (Supplement) 5(3): 188–214.

Williams, R.H. (1982) *Dream Worlds: Mass Consumption in Late Nineteenth-Century France*. Berkeley: California University Press.

Wilson, E. (1985) *Adorned in Dreams: Fashion and Modernity*. London: Virago.

Wilson, E. (1991) *The Sphinx in the City: Urban Life, the Control of Disorder, and Women*. London: Virago.

Wilson, E. (1992) 'The Invisible Flâneur', *New Left Review* 191: 90–110.

Wirth, L. (1964) 'Urbanism as a Way of Life', pp. 60–83 in L. Wirth *On Cities and Social Life*. Chicago, IL: Chicago University Press. (Orig. 1938.)

Wolff, J. (1983) 'The Invisible Flâneuse: Woman and the Literature of Modernity', *Theory, Culture & Society* 2(3): 37–46.

Young, I. (1990) 'The Ideal of Community and the Politics of Difference', pp. 300–23 in L. Nicholson (ed.) *Feminism/Postmodernism*. New York: Routledge.

Henning Bech is senior lecturer in sociology at the University of Copenhagen. His latest book is *When Men Meet: Homosexuality and Modernity* (Polity Press and University of Chicago Press).

Love and Structure

Charles Lindholm

Theory and Love

I N THIS ARTICLE I intend to consider a question that has been little discussed by sociologists; that is, how culturally and historically specific is the experience of romantic love? As Bertilsson (1986) has shown, social theorists writing about love have generally considered romantic involvement as a variable connected to the modernization process. Weber and Habermas on the one side, and Parsons, Simmel and Luhmann on the other, have presented romantic love either as an instrumental aid to the maintenance of an ever more rationalized society or as a functional resource for increasing social integration and communication in a social universe that is fragmented and atomistic. An exception is Sartre, for whom love has an absolute existential reality as a powerful expression of the unrealizable desire to absorb the freedom of the Other.

Whatever the moral perspective taken (and apart from Sartre), romantic love has usually been perceived by social theorists to be a relatively modern and particularly Western phenomenon; a direct consequence of the evolution of an uncertain 'risk society' which has liberated individuals from the moorings of kinship, social status and religion without offering any alternative points of attachment or security (Beck, 1995). As Robert Solomon writes, 'We should expect to find romantic love arise in precisely those epochs and cultures where self-identity is in question, when traditional roles and relationships fail to tell a person "Who I am"' (1981: 57). The appearance of romantic love is also thought to coincide with the advent of a leisure culture, where self-cultivation is possible; it has been linked with the modern 'invention of motherhood', smaller family size, and a greater emphasis on the emotional tie between husband and wife that occurred in response to the industrial revolution.

In this context, the romantic dream of an erotic bonding to an idealized and unique beloved is understood to serve as a substitute for outmoded loci

- *Theory, Culture & Society* 1998 (SAGE, London, Thousand Oaks and New Delhi),
  Vol. 15(3–4): 243–263
  [0263-2764(199808/11)15:3–4;243–263;006066]

for identity, offering an experience of self-transformation, personal choice, a meaningful future and sensual expansion. It also simultaneously buttresses some of the central premises of modern culture, including individualism, autonomy, and the hope of personal salvation through the 'meeting of souls'. As the basis of marriage and the family, romantic love, the most intimate of relationships, is at the heart of the mechanism by which contemporary society reproduces itself.

According to Giddens, this new ideal reached its pinnacle in 19th-century Europe, as 'notions of romantic love, first of all having their main hold over bourgeois groups, were diffused through much of the social order' – a diffusion indicated and promoted by the hugely popular literature that provided a new 'narrative form' for love relationships (1992: 26, 40). A number of historians, the most famous being Stone (1977, 1988, 1992), Flandrin (1979) and Shorter (1975), have validated this depiction of the history of romantic love through their influential portraits of the origin of the modern family in the social and spatial mobility and the disruption of kin networks that marked the beginnings of the industrial age.[1]

For these writers, romantic love is essentially a kind of culturally constructed eroticism remarkable for its idealization and etherealization of the desired other. As Giddens writes: 'Romantic love made of amour passion a specific cluster of beliefs and ideals geared to transcendence' (1992: 45); while Stone, in blunt fashion, defines falling in love quite simply as 'an urgent desire for sexual intercourse with a particular individual' (1988: 16)

Most theorists agree that it is precisely the erotic aspect of romantic love that gradually takes center stage in modern intimate relations, over-whelming elements of idealization, which are taken to be sublimations of the sexual drive behind the romantic impulse. This is because eroticism is, in Weber's words, 'the most irrational and thereby real kernel of life, as compared with the mechanisms of rationalization' (1946: 345). As Bertilsson documents, this purported shift toward heightened sensuality in modern personal relationships was greeted with trepidation by functional-ists, who feared unleashing the erotic would undermine fragile social bonds; Weber, too, worried about the brutality of purely sexual relations. Others have been more positive about the demise of sexual inhibition, following Marcuse (1966), who hoped the liberation of eroticism would energize social emancipation. For example, Giddens has recently applauded the replace-ment of romantic fantasy by freely and frankly negotiated 'pure relation-ships' based on the utilitarian exchange of 'reciprocal sexual pleasure' and terminated at will when the relationship ceases to offer sufficient erotic satisfaction to either partner (1992: 62)

The assumed sexual nature of romance has provided the basis for the most radical challenge to modern social theory about romantic love, which has been offered not by sociologists but by sociobiologists. Taking their cue from contemporary evolutionary theory on inclusive fitness, they have argued that romantic attraction to an idealized other is a mechanism genetically encoded in human beings as a consequence of the inexorable efforts of nature to optimize reproduction and the nurturing of offspring.[2]

From this point of view, romantic attraction is an adaptation serving to negate the human male's innate predisposition to maximize his genetic potential by engaging in sexual promiscuity. Instead, romantic idealization keeps him tied to his beloved, where his labor and protection are required for the necessary task of childraising. Unlike social scientists, sociobiologists understand romantic attraction as a universal phenomenon, though most would admit that cultural and historical factors may intensify or lessen the idealizing impulse.

In general, neither sociologists nor sociobiologists make significant recourse to ethnographic case studies or cross-cultural material that could help to validate or refute their basic assumptions. Instead, Western history is invoked to verify the uniqueness and modernity of romantic love, or else reference is made to the sex lives of simians. Unfortunately, the absence of cross-cultural material is not simply due to the researcher's unwillingness to make use of ethnography (though that may indeed be the case). It is also a result of the widespread lack of interest of anthropologists in the topic. Indeed, most ethnographers have tended to agree with the famous anthropologist Ralph Linton, who wrote the following lines in his influential early textbook:

> The hero of the modern American movie is always a romantic lover, just as the hero of an old Arab epic is always an epileptic. A cynic may suspect that in any ordinary population the percentage of individuals with capacity for romantic love of the Hollywood type was about as large as that of persons able to throw genuine epileptic fits. However, given a little social encouragement, either one can be adequately imitated without the performer admitting even to himself that the performance is not genuine. (1936: 175)

In Linton's version, romantic love is nothing but a self-delusion, derived from the arts, that allows lovers to persuade themselves that their sexual desires are actually ethereal and transcendent.[3] It has no cross-cultural analogues and, in fact, does not actually exist even in the West except in fantasy emulation of novels and movies.

The anthropological acceptance of Linton's debunking perspective meant that fieldworkers, who have no hesitation about investigating such distasteful subjects as cannibalism and incest, have had, to this point, very little to say about the seemingly more appealing topic of romance. Exceptions to the ensuing silence have tended to be efforts to demonstrate that romantic love is an exclusively Western phenomenon (see Hsu, 1983; Endelman, 1989),[4] or else have fallen into either the instrumentalist or functionalist camp. For instance, Yehudi Cohen followed the instrumentalist line when he attempted to show that incorporative state systems favor romantic love as a means of undermining the solidarity of local lineages unified by arranged marriages (1969);[5] meanwhile, a series of articles and

counter-articles inconclusively discussed the possible functional relationship between 'love marriage' and various residence patterns (Rosenblatt,
1966, 1967; Coppinger and Rosenblatt, 1968; Mukhopadhyay, 1979).[6]
Some authors, such as Berndt (1976) and Abu-Lughod (1990) have been
content to translate the love poetry recited in their respective field sites, and
others, such as Jankowiak and Fischer (1992), have surveyed ethnographic
material to make a sociobiological case for the universality of passionate
experiences of 'falling in love'.

But, for the most part, Linton's self-assured dismissal of the possibility
of romantic love in other cultures has had large repercussions for our
understanding of the history and cultural specificity of romance and idealization. For example, Hunt, in his popular study of romantic culture in the
past, cites anthropological research to back his claim that:

> ... by and large the clanship structure and social life of most primitive
> societies provide a wholesale intimacy and broad distribution of affection;
> Western love, with its especially close and valued ties between two isolated
> individuals is neither possible nor needed. (1959: 10)

The Nature of Romance

Is this really the case, or does anything analogous to romantic love exist in
societies that are non-Western, and even 'primitive'? Is romantic love, in
fact, universal, as the sociobiologists claim? In the following pages, I want to
argue for the first proposition, against the second. But to begin to make this
case we first need to distinguish sexual attraction, which is more or less
omnipresent (though sexual desire, too, is more culturally constructed than
is generally admitted), from romantic love, which is, as Giddens writes,
'much more culturally specific' (1992: 38).

A basic error of sociobiologists has been to assume that romantic love
is simply a mechanism for directing sexuality in order to maximize the
production and nurturing of children. However, in cross-cultural examples,
the beloved is very rarely the person one marries, and reproduction and
romantic attraction usually do not coincide. For example, in my own
fieldwork site in northern Pakistan, the patrilineal Pukhtun organized
marriages to cement alliances between clans, while individual men
pursued romances clandestinely. Prostitutes and adolescent boys were the
objects of their romantic idealization, and neither of these ever produced
children.[7] It is also difficult for sociobiologists to account for the fact that in
Europe, where romantic love has prevailed in marriage, birth rates are much
lower than in societies where marriages are arranged.

Social theorists and historians similarly understand romantic idealization as a veneer over eroticism, though they believe this veneer to be a
particularly modern social phenomenon coinciding with the breakdown of
traditional society. However, this link is also challenged when we consider
material from other cultures where romantic idealization is elaborated yet
chastity is enjoined between the lovers. For example, consider the southern

European expressions of courtly love in the medieval period. Here, in a transformation of the cult of the Virgin Mary, the courtier explicitly denied any carnal feelings for his beloved, who was worshipped as an angel above the realm of earthly lust, not to be sullied in thought or deed. These courtiers singing of *fin amor* were often married men with active sex lives and children, and the lady herself was always a married woman, with husband and children of her own. However, romantic love was not to be found in these legitimized sexual relations, but only in adulation of the lady. To assume this chaste and idealizing ideology was simply a mask disguising sexual desire is taking for granted what one wishes to prove; rather, we should take at face value the truth of the courtier's song: that is, that the lady was, *for the poet*, beloved as a creature of sanctified innocence and virtue.[8]

If this example seems too exotic, we need look no further than our own Victorian forebears. The familiar split between whore and virgin was a reality for the Victorians, and sexual desire was, as much as possible, divorced from middle-class marriage, since women of culture were assumed not to have demeaning sexual impulses. Men demanded virginal purity in the women they married, while, from their own accounts, wives often actually managed to live up to the ideal. Sexual contact between a husband and his beloved wife was regarded as an unfortunate necessity of marriage, engaged in as a duty; men overcome by sexual passion were expected to spend themselves in the company of prostitutes, whom they certainly did not love. This characteristic Victorian division between love and sexuality is a mode of feeling that must be taken on its own terms.

If romantic love is not to be understood as a kind of gloss over sexual desire, what is it? As Alberoni has remarked, talking about romantic love has been hampered by the absence of an adequate ordinary language to discuss the topic. The dominant epistemes for romantic love which are generally recognized as conventionally appropriate are those of poetry or obscenity, both of which remove the experience from rational discourse (Alberoni, 1983). Poetry renders love ineffable, obscenity reduces it to the comic, so that any study of romantic love appears either to be missing the point altogether, or else to be engaging in voyeurism under the guise of research.

But sticking to the utilitarian and causal language of science is no solution. As we have seen, this language tends strongly to reduce romantic attraction to something else, that is sexual desire, the exchange of pleasure, maximization of the gene pool and so on. These utilitarian images do not do justice to the subjective idealization of the other that is reported by lovers to be at the core of romantic involvement. The striking problem of achieving an adequate discourse once again directs our attention to the crucial and ambiguous place that romantic love occupies in our thought; in fact, it is precisely the elaboration of a special language of love that can be taken to indicate the existence of what Goode (1959) has called a 'romantic love complex' within any culture. To define romantic love, then, we ought to begin by listening to the words and examining the actions of people who believe and experience romantic relationships to be of ultimate importance to their lives. By this means, we may be capable of escaping the restrictions of technical language and achieve a picture of romance that has the ring of truth in it, yet is not novelistic or poetic, nor one that assumes love equals lust.

And, in fact, within our own culture, what the words and deeds of lovers tell us is that romantic love is not necessarily sexual, though it is thought to lead to sexual involvement. Rather, it is more akin to a religious experience – a vision of the beloved other as a unique, transcendent and transformative being who can 'complete' one's own life. From this alternative perspective, love is not motivated by the desire to reproduce, or by sexual desire, or by an ideal of beauty; rather, the beloved other is adulated *in themselves* as the fountainhead of all that is beautiful, good and desirable. As Francesco Alberoni puts it, when we fall in love 'the possible opens before us and the pure object of eros appears, the unambivalent object, in which duty and pleasure coincide, in which all alienation is extinguished' (1983: 23).

It is crucial to note that this adulation is offered in spite of the beloved's *actual* characteristics; in other words, falling in love is an act of imagination in which the other is invested with absolute value; the beloved can even be loved for their very faults. Singer calls this idealistic form of love the 'bestowal tradition' to stress the lover's creativity in manufacturing the perfection of the beloved.[9]

From within this framework, any overt or covert calculated appraisal of the other as a good provider, a useful ally, a potential mate, a vehicle for sexual enjoyment, or even as an avenue to God, is felt to be a sin against the very nature of romantic love, which is defined and experienced as spontaneous, total and boundless in its devotion to the actual person of the other – to love 'for a reason' is not to love at all.[10] We love because we love, and not because of anything that the beloved other has to offer us beyond themselves.[11]

In Singer's account, this alternative notion of unqualified love has deep intellectual and spiritual roots in the West: its heritage includes the Jewish concepts of *nomos*, transformed into Christian notions of God's unconditional, unreserved and undeserved love for humanity (*agape*) as expressed in the sacrifice of Jesus.[12] The notion of God's boundless love of humanity made love itself a value in Western culture, while simultaneously devaluing sexuality. Love was further humanized in the cult of Mary and, as we have seen, afterwards was secularized in the courtly love that bound the courtier to his lady. As Singer writes: 'Henceforth the Christian could hold not only that God is Love but also that Love is God' (1984: 340).

In this context, and over time, 'the idea that love is the unmerited sanctification of the sinner degenerated into the notion that sinners become sanctified through *any* love whatsoever. God disappeared, but there remained the holiness of indiscriminate love binding one worthless person to another' (1984: 341). Love became reciprocal and individualized, as it was secularized and institutionalized into the romantic experience that is the expected prelude to marriage in contemporary culture in the West and, increasingly, everywhere in the world.

It is this secularized form of romantic love that has been portrayed in songs, poems, novels and films as an ultimate value in itself: compelling, overwhelming, ecstatic, uniquely blissful – indeed, the most powerful emotional event of one's life. This is the love in which, as the young Hegel writes, 'consciousness of a separate self disappears, and all distinction between the lovers is annulled' (1948: 307); it is the love apostrophized by the philosopher Roberto Unger as 'the most influential mode of moral vision in our culture' (1984: 29). And, as Hervé Varenne argues (1977), it provides the core symbol by which community is understood and legitimated in modern egalitarian society. It is also the experience which Giddens (1992) sees vanishing under the influence of a reflexive social world of plastic sexuality, replaced by the 'confluent love' of utilitarian individualists engaged in pragmatic 'pure relationships'.[13]

Romance and Structure

Having established the idealizing nature of love, we are now in a position to consider whether some of the assumptions made about it are accurate. For instance, although most social theorists believe romance to be a modern Western phenomenon, this is clearly not the case. Ample literary evidence indicates that an ideal of romantic love was well developed, at least among the literate elite, in several large-scale non-Western state systems of the past. For example, the love suicide plays of Japan's Tokugawa period give powerful dramatic evidence of a pervasive and irresolvable conflict between the desire for an idealized other and social obligations. And in an earlier era, Lady Murasaki's *Tale of Genji* portrays the transforming power of love in the Japanese court of the 10th century. In India, the myths of Krishna as a lover, the ancient legend of Pururavas and Urvasi, the stories of the Mahabharata (especially of Ruru and Pramadvara), and the poetry of Bhartrihari and Bilhana, all show aspects of the compulsive, idealizing and transcendent power of love.[14]

But romance does not require a cultivated leisure class, nor, as we have already noted, was it necessarily associated with erotic relationships – as we discover in the literary tradition that inspired the troubadours, that is, the poetry of the Middle East, which always stresses the sexual purity of the lovers. According to Ibn al-Jawzi (d. 1200), who was the most prolific medieval writer on romantic love, the convention of chastity derived from the early Bedouin, who 'loved passionately but spurned physical union, believing that it destroys love. As for the pleasure resulting from union, it is the affair of animals, not of man' (quoted in Bell, 1979: 33–4). His portrait is validated by the philologist al-Asmai (d. 828) who did research among the remote tribes. He writes:

I said to a Bedouin woman: 'What do you consider love to be among you?' 'Hugging, embracing, winks, and conversation,' she replied. Then she asked: 'How is it among you, city-dweller?' 'He sits amidst her four limbs and presses her to the limit,' I answered. 'Nephew,' she cried, 'this is no lover, but a man after a child!' (quoted in Bell, 1979: 134)

Massignon tells us that the high evaluation of chaste love (*hubb udhri*) may be traced to the 7th-century Bedouin Yemeni tribe of the Banu Udhra, who believed that 'to die of love is a sweet and noble death'. According to Massignon, Udhritic love was linked to a deep notion of the 'election to a religious and sacrificial life by the unexpected appearance of a "kindred soul"' (1982: 348, 349). The transcendent other who inspired this elevated state was believed above all to be a spirit embodied in a human being, and the relationship was not to be soiled by physical contact. Instead, the beloved was regarded as pure and was internalized through avid contemplation, so that eventually the two became one.[15]

What sort of society is likely to favor this kind of idealizing and chaste relationship? We know very little about the ancient Bedouin, but we do have an ethnography of a group who live in an analogous environment and who have a similar stated belief in chaste love: these are the nomadic Marri Baluch of the rugged southeastern deserts of Iran, as described in a classic work by Robert Pehrson (1966).

The Marri inhabit a harsh, isolated and unforgiving world. They are highly individualistic, self-interested and competitive, and expect opportunism and manipulation from all social transactions. Their personal lives are dominated by fear, mistrust and hostility; secrecy and social masking are at a premium, while collective action and cooperation are minimal. Yet among these people, as Pehrson writes, romantic relationships are idealized, and a love affair 'is a thing of surpassing beauty and value' (1966: 65), implying absolute trust, mutuality and loyalty; such a love is to be pursued at all costs. Romance is both the stuff of dreams, and of life. Frustrated lovers among the Marri may commit suicide, and become celebrated in the romantic poems and songs which are the mainstay of Marri art. As one Marri woman tells Pehrson 'it is very great, very hard, to be a lover for us Marri' (1966: 62).

Unlike Western love relationships, romance among the Marri stands absolutely opposed to marriage, which is never for love. It is, in fact, shameful even to show affection for one's spouse. True romance has to be secret, and with a married woman of a distant camp. This is a dangerous matter, since other camps are hostile, and adultery is punishable by death. The striking contrast to the West is a consequence of the social organization of the Marri, who live in small patrilineal, patrilocal campsites ruled lightly by a religiously sanctioned central authority, called the Sardar.

Although political domination does occur, the local units, permeable and shifting as they are, nonetheless have considerable solidity and autonomy, judging their own disputes and controlling their own means of production within a framework of traditional knowledge and local consent. The patrilineal patrilocal ideology means that members of the camp site have absolute rights and duties to one another that are legitimated by close blood ties and co-residence. Participation in blood feuds, payment of fines, rights to pasturage and the punishment of adultery all are incumbent on the minimal lineage group.

However, this minimal group is not one of cooperation and friendship. The camp members, despite their ties, work separately, have their own tents and property, cooperate as little as possible, and are mutually suspicious and rivalrous. If they could, they would separate, but the need for defence and a varied labor pool keeps the camps together; a need validated by the rights and duties of kinship. Within this inimical but constraining structure, Marri men continually manipulate to get a share of the power and status that derive from the center. By gaining a loyal following among his cohorts, the poor herdsman can make a claim for becoming the local factotum of the Sardar, thereby gaining points over one's nearest, and most disliked, lineage mates and rivals.[16] Marriage in this context is not a matter of personal choice and attraction. Instead, Marri men use marriage in an instrumental fashion to establish relationships which will help them to pursue their political interests, while women are treated as chattels, to be controlled and dominated for the honor and benefit of the patriarch. As one woman says: 'You know what rights a woman has among us Marris. She has the right to eat crap – that's all' (Pehrson, 1966: 59).

In this context, romantic involvement, with all its risk, is the only human relationship in the whole of Marri culture felt to be of value in and for itself, and not simply as a means to the instrumental ends of personal power and prestige. It is understood by the Marri Baluch to be opposed to marriage in every way. Marriage is a public and sanctioned relationship between superior men and inferior women, often within the camp and the lineage, and always among allies; it is pre-eminently politically motivated, and it is expected to be cold and hostile at best. Romance on the contrary is secretive, private, and conducted with strangers who are actually potential enemies. Its only possible political consequences are disastrous enmity and feud. Romantic love has the potential for dividing groups while it unites the lovers, while marriage aims to solidify groups, while permitting no attraction within the asymmetrical couple. In marriage, the woman is inferior and despised, while in romance she is honored and revered.

Like the ancient Bedouin, the Marri also claim that a true romantic relationship, in contrast to marriage, is not sexual. Theoretically, at least, the male lover worships his beloved as a pure being and is worshipped in return; forgoing the connotations of female inferiority and degradation that the Marri (like many patrilineal peoples) believe to be implicit in the sexual act, the romantic couple immerse themselves in mutual gazing, spontaneous recitations of poetry and the reciprocal exchange of confidences and love tokens.[17] For the Marri, then, romance is with a distant other, and it is consciously perceived as negating the rivalries of power, the inferiority of women and the constraints of the marriage tie. It is chaste and highly idealistic. This romantic complex occurs within a relatively rigidly structured, but characteristically competitive, social formation. Far from providing the basis for reproducing the dominant social configuration, romance in this instance opposes it in every way

Though on a different scale, the Marri pattern resembles that found in many centralized, highly stratified traditional state systems, where love also opposes the web of manipulation predominating in daily life. In these systems, group membership is determined by lineage, and certain traditional obligations and standards of behavior provide identity markers and a degree of solidity. But, as among the Marri, these systems also involve intense internal rivalry and a ubiquitous pursuit of status validation. Marriage relationships function solely for the public end of achieving social mobility and prestige. Far from being a haven, marriage is a political act in a politicized world.

The court society of Louis XIV is a case in point. In his brilliant work, Elias (1983) shows how the nobility, struggling within itself for favor from the king, burdened by traditional obligations and standards, and pressed from below by the ambitions of the newly rich, elaborated a fantasy of romance and a cult of gallantry and service to women that belied the courtier's public posture of complete emotional control and the calculating character of all interactions.[18] The cult emphasized romantic love as a relationship outside of ordinary life. As among the Baluch, sexuality was devalued in the romantic myth, which poetically stressed the feelings of ecstasy and longing experienced by pure lovers.

In this context, we find the image of the courtesan as friend and confidant, with whom a nobleman could interact freely and without constraint, who was treated with the utmost respect in society, and to whom the highly controlled nobleman sometimes lost his heart in a most uncontrolled way. The pattern is, of course, a familiar one in many traditional state systems, where inequalities of power, the traditions and obligations of noble identity, a continual jockeying for prestige and a politicization of marriage combine to make the appeal of the courtesan's love very great.

In another example, Grimal (1986) and Elias (1987) document the evolution of male–female relationships in imperial Rome. Traditionally, conjugal love between husband and wife was considered ridiculous and impossible; as Seneca writes, 'to love one's wife with an ardent passion is to commit adultery' (quoted in Grimal, 1986: 252). Rather, lineages were tied together through sacred marriage bonds based on Roman virtues of austerity and piety. But the expansion of the imperial society, the increase in state domination and its capacity to codify and enforce civil law, the vast multiplication of wealth and the growth of slavery all coincided with a greater independence for women and gradual loosening of the ties of duty binding husband and wife. Divorce, formerly not thought of, became common, while fines, child marriage and tax incentives were required to induce matrimony among patricians. Noble women, often wealthy property owners because of inheritances passed down from their elderly husbands and their own fathers and brothers, could become players in imperial power games and rivals with men, and marriage became, at least among the elite, a contractual tie between equals.

At the same time, slave women (or boys) without honor filled the brothels of imperial Rome. Patrician men, escaping from their political responsibilities and struggles with their wives, frequented these houses and sometimes found themselves falling deeply and hopelessly in love with the concubines installed there. This love was a release from relations of obligation and rivalry found in arranged marriages and in the intrigues of the court. However, love with a slave led noblemen inexorably into relationships where uncertainty about the sincerity of one's mistress became obsessive. The noble lover often enough found himself the dupe of a manipulative courtesan. Tibullus, an embittered lover, accordingly names his beloved 'Nemesis' – the sister of tenderness and deceit (quoted in Grimal, 1986: 164).

This characteristic configuration favoring romantic idealization apparently exists within objective conditions of extreme pressure, ecological or social, so that human life is experienced as involving struggle, mistrust and pervasive and intense interpersonal rivalry of competing individuals. But the world in which the individuals act is not fluid and formless as is the case in modern society. There is a legitimate social identity above that of the isolated free agent – be it the minimal lineage of the Marri, or the noble's position in the court. Romantic engagement does not make the world go around in such a system. Instead, it stands opposed to the more formal structures that provide a high degree of social integration.

Furthermore, rigidity and closure of the social structure are marked in these systems, as is the continual manipulation for power within the constraining moral order. Where the European or American lover is seeking a secure identity in an untrustworthy world, the Marri nomad, French courtier or Roman aristocrat, though also living in a world that is untrustworthy, knows quite well what he or she is looking for, and knows exactly how to get it. The ceaseless quest for power and prestige within a closed social world intrudes into the marriage contract, meaning that romantic love is found only secretly, outside of marriage.

Such societies also have elaborate notions of the complementarity of lover relations, which often reverse the actual sexual asymmetry of the public world. This complementarity can coincide with an exaggerated idealization of the female, leading to the idolatry of women in medieval romance or of courtesans in the French court. Similarly, Roman poets idealized their beloved slave prostitutes as *domina* – literally reversing the role of master and slave. This is, conjecturally, related to the increased inequality of the sexes and classes in centralized social systems, and to the degree of fantasizing that these stratified systems promote.[19]

From these cases, it is evident that under the conditions of strong social constraint, well-formed primordial identities and intense rivalry for power that are found both in centralized stratified societies, and in certain kinds of highly structured and internally competitive simpler social formations, the idealization offered by romantic love may offer a way of imagining a different and more fulfilling life. But because of the objective reality of the social world, romance can never form the base for actually constructing the family, as it has in Western society. It must instead stand against and outside of the central social formation, and will in consequence be more fantastic and unrealistic in its imagery, more dangerous in its enactment, than in the flexible, egalitarian and atomistic cultures of the modern world.

Romance in Fluid Societies

However, all instances of romantic love in the non-Western context are not so markedly different from the Western model. In fact, it is precisely in some of the most 'primitive' of social formations, where people do not have complex kinship structures or central authority, and live by means of hunting and gathering, that we find romantic idealization taking a form remarkably similar to that characteristic of the West. This is because the fluid, competitive, insecure and risky social formation of the modern world resembles, in essential ways, the lifestyles of hunting and gathering societies operating under especially harsh ecological conditions.

Although a comparison between the emotional life characteristic of our modern and extremely complex society and a society of great simplicity may seem far-fetched, important structural and emotional correspondences can be found at the level of ordinary social interaction. For instance, the exigencies of the environment in both cases make individual self-reliance and isolation a necessity, so that all persons may believe themselves to be standing alone, acting out of self-interest in order to survive. And even though in small-scale traditional societies identity markers may be clear enough, difficult ecologies and internally hostile social structures make life itself dreadfully insecure and other people unreliable. These are truly societies in which risk and danger are pervasive, and where the nuclear family and the reciprocal affection of husband and wife are the only source of solace and refuge.

Perhaps the clearest example of a romantic love complex resembling that of the modern West to be found in the ethnographic record is among the hunting and gathering Ojibway Indians of the Northern Great Lakes region.[20] As the ethnographer Ruth Landes writes, for the Ojibway:

> ... lovers have a completely romantic attitude that counts the world well lost for love. (1969: 56)

> Sentimental and romantic love are valued tremendously and marriage is supposed to be the fulfillment of this attraction. (1937: 104)

> What is essential is to have a loved person who can be idealized; and often this is realized in unions that are externally drab. (1969: 120)

Love is described by the Ojibway themselves as an experience of great intensity, valued in itself, focused on one idealized and beloved other, and worth the ultimate self-sacrifice. Nor is this simply an ideal. The life histories recorded in Landes's *Ojibwa Woman* show that romantic love was a central event in people's lives; one which often went against their rational best interests and exposed them to great suffering and peril, and even led to suicide should their lover be unapproachable. The similarity of their concept of love to that of the West was recognized by the Ojibway themselves, who quickly adapted American love stories and songs into their own language

Along with their belief in love, the Ojibway are like modern Western society in other crucial ways. Their society was characterized by extremes of competitive individualism, coupled with a highly developed concept of personal property, which was held even within the nuclear family. According to Landes, 'individuals may grumble, especially close relatives, and there is a weak notion of fair play; but these are as nothing compared with the valuation placed on ruthless individualism' (1937: 87). There were also few, if any, primordial groups or ties among the Ojibway providing a sense of solidarity and identity. There were no ascribed positions of authority, no stable structures of hierarchy. Even the social roles of men and women were not highly articulated, and each could do the work of the other. Clans, though perhaps cohesive in the past, had long since ceased to have any importance, and the only significant kinship structure was a vague division between parallel cousins and marriageable cross-cousins. Easy divorce made the family itself insecure.

Nor did residence provide coherence, since families lived in isolation during the harsh winters, and shifted residence regularly in the summer. Constant mobility was partly an effort to find better hunting grounds, but also partly a result of a pervasive distrust of those nearby, combined with a readiness to take insult at minor slights, and a deep fear of treachery from neighbors. This fear was not unrealistic. As Hallowell notes, quoting an Ojibway: 'When I meet [my enemy] face to face I will give no evidence of my hostility by gesture, word or deed' (1940: 400). Aggressive sorcery was also commonly practiced in secret, destroying the health of an unsuspecting enemy. In Ojibway society, then, a smiling face could not be trusted, as it might easily be masking rankling hatred

The Ojibway social world was evidently quite like the modern 'risk society' of possessive individualists, with its blurring of differentiating ascribed boundaries, its mobility, its competitiveness, and its pervasive sense of mistrust and insecurity. The Ojibway also lived in an extremely harsh physical environment; one in which starvation was a very real possibility, leading to an intensification of pressure on individuals in a way analogous to the pressure caused by adaption to the constant technological change in the modern world.[21]

For comparative purposes, it would be valuable to discover what the Ojibway share with other societies that also have a similar ideology and experience of romance. Unfortunately, as I have noted, the ethnographic record concerning romantic love is weak, since love was not considered a topic worth discussing by serious anthropologists. It is significant, then, that in the few cases where we find indications of romantic idealization coincident with marriage,[22] they indeed tend to occur in simple dispersed hunting and gathering societies under conditions of considerable ecological stress. These cultures include the Murngin, the Ainu, the Ona, the Yahgan, the Ife, the !Kung, the Western Apache and the Hottentot. From these admittedly fragmentary findings we can postulate that it is likely that societies with extremely fluid social relations marked by mobility and competition, operating according to individualistic worldviews within harsh or otherwise insecure environments, may find meaning and emotional warmth in the mutuality of romantic relationships. Romance in these societies is associated with marriage, since the couple is idealized as the ultimate refuge against the hostile world, and functions as the necessary nucleus of the atomized social organization.

Sexual Freedom and Romance

There is, finally, another very different type of social formation I can mention only in passing which seems to favor romantic love. These societies are neither centralized and rigid, nor are they atomistic, or under any extreme social or ecological pressure. Rather, they are group-oriented, non-individualistic cultures that strictly control marriage, but that offer compensation to their youth by means of an institutionalized premarital sexual freedom; a freedom that often leads to powerful romantic attachments and idealizations.

Examples of this type are found in tribal India, Southeast Asia and in the Oceanic cultures where romantic love seems to occur. In these cultures, the young people live together in clubhouses, which offer a private and separate enclave away from the responsible world of adulthood. Here they can pursue sexual encounters, but only with those partners whom they can never actually marry. Within the clubhouse there is a free and easy atmosphere of equality and reciprocity between the sexes. But eventually couples form and are faithful to each other. Sometimes this relationship develops into one of deep involvement that is felt to be the most powerful emotional tie in a person's life. This doomed romance is also regarded as the highest possible cultural and aesthetic value, and is celebrated in song and story.

The clubhouse, with its equality and dyadic love, is considered to be a kind of paradise that everyone experiences in adolescence, and which the rest of life cannot match, for in adulthood men and women are unequal and unloving, and life is a series of responsibilities and obligations, revolving around duties to one's extended lineage. Romantic attachment stands in radical contrast to adult husband and wife relations, and in each of these societies stories are common of lovers committing suicide out of despair at the inevitable separation that is entailed by marriage.

Most of these societies appear to have an elementary marriage pattern of generalized exchange (mother's brother's daughter marriage) which Lévi-Strauss long ago realized entails considerable stress and risk (1969). Furthermore, they are unusual in that they are disharmonic in their residence and kinship reckoning (i.e. matrilineal and patrilocal, or vice versa), so that the resident core are not lineage mates. It seems plausible that this marriage form, which obliges insecure long-distance exchanges of women, often in an internally contradictory social organization of disharmonic residence and kinship, may be one relevant variable in the elaboration of romantic love in such cultures. Romance, confined to unmarried members of the group through the establishment of the clubhouse, is a powerful binding mechanism, affirming the intimacy, reciprocity and transcendent quality of life and love in the group prior to the necessary relationships with outsiders. In providing an emotional glue, binding people to the memory of the paradise of their youth, romantic love helps to integrate a social formation that has serious centrifugal qualities. As in the modern world, romance, while centered on the dyad, makes the group possible, but only as a nostalgic memory, not as the foundation of the family.

We then have three sorts of social configuration in which an elaboration and idealization of romantic love occurs; the West appears to be a subtype of fluid social organization, having evolved from a more hierarchical and rigid system in the past.[23] Because of the paucity of data, it is impossible to 'fill in the boxes' as to what kinds of societies will *not* have an elaborated belief in romantic love, although, from the ethnographic record, it appears that such beliefs are rare indeed (we discovered only 21 possibilities out of 248 cases); but this may well be a fault of the record-keepers. It does seem likely that relatively stable societies with solidified extended families, age-sets and other encompassing social networks that offer alternative forms of belonging and experiences of personal transcendence through participation in group rituals are not prone to valuing romantic involvement. Hunt's formulation, that the intimacy of clan life precludes the development of romantic dyads, seems to be more or less correct – but his formula simply does not account for some crucial variations where the social order is fragmented and perilous, or where internal rivalry eats away at solidarity, or where intense adolescent sexual dyads are broken apart by long-distance marriage exchange.

Conclusion

Western expectations and beliefs about romantic love clearly develop out of our unique historical trajectory and cultural background. But this obvious truth should not blind us to deeper correspondences between our emotional lives and the emotional lives of people in cultures different from our own, who report the same sort of intense idealization of a beloved other, the same feelings of exaltation in their presence and suicidal despair in their absence. Though sparse, ethnographic material demonstrates that romantic love is not necessarily the prerogative of a leisured class; it does not require a complex society; it is not solely heterosexual, nor does it always lead to marriage; it is not intrinsically linked to capitalism, small families, sexual oppression, a cult of motherhood or a quest for identity; it is neither a disguise for lust nor evidence of evolution at work. Rather, romantic attraction is an attempt to escape from certain types of social contradictions and structural tensions through the transcendental love of another person. As such, it is experientially akin to the experience of religious ecstasy.

Notes

I would like to thank Owen Lynch, William Jankowiak, Laurie Hart-McGrath, Cherry Lindholm, Mike Featherstone and the anonymous reviewers of *Theory, Culture & Society* for their suggestions, which have improved this article immeasurably. I especially want to express my deep gratitude to Andrew Buckser and Susan Buckser (née Rofman) for their invaluable help in the original research and analysis.

1.   This claim is much disputed by other researchers studying the early family, as summarized in MacFarlane (1986, 1987), but strong (and, to my mind, convincing) opposition has not had much success in dislodging the dominant paradigm.

2.   For good accounts of modern sociobiological theories on love, see Jankowiak (1995) and Fisher (1992). The sociobiological argument was first proposed by Schopenhauer, who believed romantic love to be the means by which the Will created the future. As he writes, 'if Petrarch's passion had been satisfied, his song would have been silenced from that moment, just as is that of the bird, as soon as the eggs are laid' (1966: 557). Simmel makes the same case, with greater subtlety, arguing that the tragic dimension of romance derives precisely from the contrast between the subjective sense of the uniqueness of the beloved and the objective reality of the impersonal force of nature (1984).

3.   In philosophy, Jean-Paul Sartre has taken a similar view of love in a famous section in *Being and Nothingness* (1956), where he scathingly imagines the bad faith of a young girl absently permitting her hand to be stroked by a suitor while she simultaneously imagines herself admired solely as a creature of purity and abstract intellect.

4.   This argument has been countered by Jankowiak (1992).

5.   Cohen's pioneering comparative work was partially vitiated by the fact that in the cases cited romantic love was not correlated with marriage at all, but (as is usual cross-culturally) with extramarital affairs, and therefore did not necessarily interfere with lineage solidarity.

6.   Much of this debate was rendered meaningless by a confused definition of love and the assumption that marriage by choice was marriage for love.

7.   See Lindholm (1981, 1982) for more on romantic love in this society.

8.   See Boase (1977) for a comprehensive review of this literature. Of course, romantic relations between the courtier and the lady were sometimes erotic, but the ideal was that they should not be so, and the ideal is what is crucial for analysis, since it is the ideal that is the measure of action. Other instances of chaste love will be documented below.

9.   Singer (1987) also rightly notes that in fact both appraisal and bestowal are necessarily intermingled in modern romantic love – we idealize others partly for what their characteristics are. But what is important from my perspective is that it is analytically possible and necessary to distinguish the idealizing aspect of love from purely erotic aspects.

10.   In this sense, Giddens's 'confluent love' based on the exchange of pleasures is the antithesis of romantic love.

11.   As Singer puts it: 'Love supplements the human search for value with a capacity for bestowing it gratuitously' (1984: 14). Giddens (1992) argues that this form of love is necessarily asymmetrical and gender specific but this is not inherently the case, as further examples will show.

12.   As Anders Nygren writes: 'Eros *recognizes value* in its object, and loves it – Agape loves, and *creates value* in its object' (1958: 210). Bertilsson laments that 'in the social theories of love, its passionate (solitary and extraordinary) side needs the countervailing force of reciprocal love' which she links to agape (1986: 33). I agree with her as to the narcissistic narrowness of social theories of love, but when we look at personal accounts, we often find expressions of selfless devotion.

13.   Whether romance is vanishing or not, and what will replace it if it does, is a question that I cannot consider here, but refer the interested reader to Lindholm (1988a, 1990, 1995, forthcoming) for my point of view.

14.   Cohen (1969) makes a strong case for the ubiquity of some form of romantic idealization in centralized state systems – see note 6.

15.   This ideal of sexless merging later degenerated into an esoteric practice among some Sufis who sought mystical communion by gazing at beautiful boys. The notion that romantic love must be heterosexual is not a part of the Middle Eastern view of love, and some of the great classics of medieval romantic literature concern love between men – the most famous being the love of King Mahmud of Ghazna for his Turkish slave Ayaz.

16.   The potential for minimal social movement is of crucial importance, not the degree of movement possible. An absolutely rigid structure would not evolve the love complex noted here because social pressure would be absent.

17.   As in the case of the troubadours, whether all (or any) love affairs are chaste is irrelevant; what is important is that this is the cultural ideal of romantic love the Marri respect, and attempt to enact in their own lives.

18.   See Lindholm (1988b) for more on the cultural correlates of emotional masking.

19.   In this context, it is worth noting Scheff and Mahlendorf's argument that the idealized love of young Werther for Lotte in Goethe's classic is associated with Werther's inferior position in a rigid status hierarchy. As they write: 'infatuation and hero-worship are both manifestations of unacknowledged shame' (1988: 78).

20.   Andrew Buckser's undergraduate thesis on love among the Ojibway (1986) deserves recognition here as the inspiration for this section.

21.   It is significant that the Ojibways' greatest terror is of possession by a cannibal spirit, the windigo, which will drive them to devour their fellows.

22.   This research was done by two students (Andrew Buckser and Susan Rofman) who read through the Human Relations Area Files (HRAF), focusing especially on

small-scale societies and on the categories 'basis of marriage' (581), 'suicide' (762) and 'ideas about sex' (831).

The 'basis of marriage' category was chosen because cultures with romantic love often link love and marriage. However, I tried to correct for the assumption that love and marriage go together and also get at the intensity of the romantic love ideology in the culture by using the category of 'suicide'. Since romantic love, by definition, means that life without the beloved is not worth living, my reasoning was that suicide, stemming from rejection, grief at a lover's death or frustrated marriage plans, would be a good indicator of romantic idealization. Excluded here were suicides from hurt pride or as revenge. The final category, 'ideas about sex', turned out to be the file that yielded love stories and myths, which I assumed to reveal underlying beliefs about idealized relationships. The relationship between image and act is, of course, neither simple nor direct; but for my purposes even the discovery of pervasive romantic imagery was regarded as significant.

In doing their ratings, the researchers worked independently, selecting cases that they believed might warrant further study based on frequency and directness of the data, and scoring them on the degree to which romantic love appeared to exist in the society, both as ideal and as action. These cases were then compared by the researchers, who found that they were in general agreement in their ratings. A final list of societies where romantic love might be found was then made up, along with references and representative quotes. In 248 cultures researched in the HRAF, 21 societies were rated highly likely to have such a complex. Five were in Oceania (Murngin, !Kung, Tikopia, Tonga, Trobriands), three in Africa (Ashanti, Hottentot, Ife), five in Asia (Marri, Ainu, Gond, Miao, Semang), five in North America (Blackfoot, Commanche, Crow, Ojibway, Western Apache) and three in South America (Mataco, Ona, Yahgan).

23.   Though see MacFarlane (1986) on the fluidity of early English and northern European society, which he sees as conducive to a romantic love complex among the poor quite different from that later elaborated among the elite.

References

Abu-Lughod, L. (1990) 'Shifting Politics in Bedouin Love Poetry', in C. Lutz and L. Abu-Lughod (eds) *Language and the Politics of Emotion*. Cambridge: Cambridge University Press.

Alberoni, F. (1983) *Falling in Love*. New York: Random House.

Beck, U. (1995) *Ecological Enlightenment: Essays on the Politics of the Risk Society*. Atlantic Highlands, NJ: Humanities Press.

Bell, J. (1979) *Love Theory in Later Hanbalite Islam*. Albany: State University of New York Press.

Berndt, R. (1976) *Love Songs of Arnhem Land*. Chicago, IL: University of Chicago Press.

Bertilsson, M. (1986) 'Love's Labour Lost? A Sociological View', *Theory, Culture & Society* 3(2): 19–35.

Boase, R. (1977) *The Origin and Meaning of Courtly Love*. Manchester: Manchester University Press.

Buckser, A. (1986) 'Love in a Cold Climate: Romantic Love and Social Structure Among the Canadian Ojibway', undergraduate honours thesis, Department of Anthropology, Harvard University, Cambridge, MA.

Cohen, Y. (1969) 'Ends and Means in Political Control', *American Anthropologist* 71: 658–87.

Coppinger, R. and P. Rosenblatt (1968) 'Romantic Love and Subsistence Dependence of Spouses', *Southwestern Journal of Anthropology* 24: 310–18.

Elias, N. (1983) *Court Society*. New York: Pantheon.

Elias, N. (1987) 'The Changing Balance of Power between the Sexes – A Process-Sociological Study: The Example of the Ancient Roman State', *Theory, Culture & Society* 4(2–3): 287–316.

Endelman, R. (1989) *Love and Sex in Twelve Cultures*. New York: Psyche Press.

Fisher, H. (1992) *Anatomy of Love: The Natural History of Monogamy, Adultery and Divorce*. New York: Norton.

Flandrin, J.L. (1979) *Families in Former Times: Kinship, Household and Sexuality*. Cambridge: Cambridge University Press.

Giddens, A. (1992) *The Transformation of Intimacy: Sexuality, Love and Intimacy in Modern Societies*. Stanford: University of California Press.

Goode, W. (1959) 'The Theoretical Importance of Love', *American Sociological Review* 24: 38–47.

Grimal, P. (1986) *Love in Ancient Rome*. Norman: University of Oklahoma Press.

Hallowell, A.I. (1940) 'Aggression in the Salteau Society', *Psychiatry* 3: 395–407.

Hegel, G. (1948) *Early Theological Writings*. Chicago, IL: University of Chicago Press.

Hsu, F. (1983) 'Eros, Affect and Pao', in F. Hsu (ed.) *Rugged Individualism Reconsidered*. Knoxville: University of Tennessee Press.

Hunt, M. (1959) *The Natural History of Love*. New York: Alfred Knopf.

Jankowiak, W. (1992) *Sex, Death and Hierarchy in a Chinese City: An Anthropological Account*. New York: Columbia University Press.

Jankowiak, W. (ed.) (1995) *Romantic Love: A Universal Experience?* New York: Columbia University Press.

Jankowiak, W. and E. Fischer (1992) 'A Cross-Cultural Perspective on Romantic Love', *Ethnology* 31: 149–55.

Landes, R. (1937) *Ojibwa Sociology*. New York: AMS.

Landes, R. (1969) *The Ojibwa Woman*. New York: AMS.

Lévi-Strauss, C. (1969) *The Elementary Structures of Kinship*. Boston, MA: Beacon Press.

Lindholm, C. (1981) 'Leatherworkers and Love Potions', *American Ethnologist* 9: 512–25.

Lindholm, C. (1982) *Generosity and Jealousy: The Swat Pukhtun of Northern Pakistan*. New York: Columbia University Press.

Lindholm, C. (1988a) 'Lovers and Leaders: A Comparison of Social and Psychological Models of Romance and Charisma', *Social Science Information* 27: 3–24.

Lindholm, C. (1988b) 'The Social Structure of Emotional Constraint: The Court of Louis XIV and the Pukhtun of Northern Pakistan', *Ethos* 6: 227–46.

Lindholm, C. (1990) *Charisma*. Oxford: Blackwell.

Lindholm, C. (1995) 'Love as an Experience of Transcendence', in W. Jankowiak (ed.) *Romantic Love: A Universal Experience?* New York: Columbia University Press.

Lindholm, C. (forthcoming) 'The Future of Love', in V. De Munck (ed.) *Love and Culture*. New York: Columbia University Press.

Linton, R. (1936) *The Study of Man*. New York: Appleton-Century.

MacFarlane, A. (1986) *Marriage and Love in England: 1300–1840*. Oxford: Blackwell.

MacFarlane, A. (1987) *The Culture of Capitalism*. Oxford: Blackwell.

Marcuse, H. (1966) *Eros and Civilization: A Philosophical Inquiry into Freud*. Boston, MA: Beacon Press.

Massignon, L. (1982) *The Passion of al-Hallaj: Mystic and Martyr of Islam: Vol I The Life of al-Hallaj*. Princeton, NJ: Princeton University Press.

Mukhopadhyay, C. (1979) 'The Function of Romantic Love: A Re-appraisal of the Coppinger and Rosenblatt Study', *Behavior Science Research* 14: 57–63.

Nygren, A. (1958) *Agape and Eros*. Philadelphia, PA: Westminster Press.

Pehrson, R. (1966) *The Social Organization of the Marri Baluch*. Chicago, IL: Aldine.

Rosenblatt, P. (1966) 'A Cross-Cultural Study of Child Rearing and Romantic Love', *Journal of Personality and Social Psychology* 4: 336–8.

Rosenblatt, P. (1967) 'Marital Residence and the Function of Romantic Love', *Ethnology* 6: 471–80.

Sartre, J.-P. (1956) *Being and Nothingness*. New York: Philosophical Library.

Scheff, T. and U. Mahlendorf (1988) 'Emotion and False Consciousness: The Analysis of an Incident from *Werther*', *Theory, Culture & Society* 5(1): 57–80.

Schopenhauer, A. (1966) *The World as Will and Representation*, Vol. 2. New York: Dover.

Shorter, E. (1975) *The Making of the Modern Family*. New York: Basic Books.

Simmel, G. (1984) *On Women, Sexuality and Love*. New Haven, CT: Yale University Press.

Singer, I. (1984) *The Nature of Love, Vol. 1: Plato to Luther*. Chicago, IL: University of Chicago Press.

Singer, I. (1987) *The Nature of Love, Vol. 3: The Modern World*. Chicago, IL: University of Chicago Press.

Solomon, R. (1981) *Love, Emotion, Myth and Metaphor*. Garden City, NJ: Anchor Books.

Stone, L. (1977) *The Family, Sex and Marriage in England, 1500–1800*. New York: Harper and Row.

Stone, L. (1988) 'Passionate Attachments in the West in Historical Perspective', in W. Gaylin and E. Person (eds) *Passionate Attachments*. New York: Free Press.

Stone, L. (1992) *Uncertain Unions: Marriage in England, 1660–1753*. Oxford: Oxford University Press.

Unger, R. (1984) *Passion: An Essay on Personality*. New York: Free Press.

Varénne, H. (1977) *Americans Together: Structured Diversity in a Midwestern Town*. New York: Teacher's College Press.

Weber, M. (1946) 'Religious Rejections of the World and their Directions', in H. Gerth and C.W. Mills (eds) *From Max Weber*. New York: Oxford University Press.

Charles Lindholm is Professor of Anthropology at Boston University. His latest books are *The Islamic Middle East: An Historical Anthropology* and the forthcoming *Is America Falling Apart?* co-authored with John A. Hall. He is also the author of *Charisma*.

'Falling in Love with Love is Falling for Make Believe'
Ideologies of Romance in Post-Enlightenment Culture

Mary Evans

> ... being inclined to marry, he soon fancied himself in love. ...
> (Jane Austen, *Mansfield Park*)

T
O 'FANCY' OURSELVES in love is one of the dominating themes of post-Enlightenment narrative fiction. From Austen to Tolstoy to E.M. Forster, novelists of 19th- and 20th- century Europe have discussed the possibilities, the evasions, the betrayals and the tragedies of the emotion which their characters have described as love and which they have pursued against the better interests and claims of family and rationality. Indeed, narrative fiction has taken a sceptical view of love and a great many words have been employed to demonstrate that romantic love is one of the most futile of human relationships. In this, of course, narrative fiction has positioned itself against the tide of romance and romantic fiction which developed in Europe from the 19th century onwards. The rise of romance, always organized around heterosexuality, ran counter to the thesis of much of fiction, which is that characters who believed themselves 'in love' were deceiving themselves.

Thus I shall argue in this article that 'love', as we have constructed it in the West, has always had a bad press, and that the account of it to be found in fiction is not an account which endorses it. On the contrary, novelists – whether female or male – offer endless accounts of the impossibility of love when constructed as romance and its inevitably negative

■ *Theory, Culture & Society* 1998 (SAGE, London, Thousand Oaks and New Delhi),
Vol. 15(3–4): 265–275
[0263-2764(199808/11)15:3–4;265–275;006067]

impact on human actions. Furthermore, what has existed as a consistent tension about love, and its meaning, is the way in which women and men (whether heterosexual or not) have positioned themselves in relation to love. But these positions do not follow straightforward gender divisions of the kind which would suggest that men are against love while women are for it. Thus a tradition can be established in which women are as much critics of romantic love as men, and as concerned as male authors to demonstrate the problems of an emotion which is constructed only in terms of the private world of the home and the bedroom. Romantic fiction is always associated (in terms of authorship and readership) with women, and yet what is suggested here is that although this association is empirically correct, it does not account for all that women have to say about love, or – on occasions – the depth and range of women's distaste for romantic love.

In terms of English post-Enlightenment fiction the most profound, and the most articulate, critic of romantic love is Jane Austen. In all of her novels she consistently mocks, satirizes and writes with deep contempt of those characters seduced into marriage by the physical appearance or apparent good nature of a partner. Clever, thinking, apparently rational men such as Mr Bennet in *Pride and Prejudice* find themselves – because of the fancies of love – married to women they cannot love and barely respect. Sexual attraction, the erotic tensions produced by a social code of strict boundaries, create situations where what appears to be love can easily develop. Unhappy marriages and ill-matched partners then result from those courtships in which the appearance and the expectation of love was allowed to take precedence over rational understanding. Austen is, as Alasdair MacIntyre (1994) has argued, the definitive moralist of the Enlightenment and her morality – and her moral sense – is at its most sure in setting out the conditions on which heterosexual marriage should be established. Those conditions are three-fold: the characters should learn to speak with honesty to each other, the characters should respect the differences between themselves and the characters should locate their relationship within a social as much as a personal world. In those relationships which Austen dooms to disappointment (Maria Bertram and Mr Rushworth in *Mansfield Park* or Charles and Mary in *Persuasion*) the characters have seen, prior to marriage, only fantasies in the other party. Women see in men rescue from home or the unmarried state, men see in women a hope of personal intimacy and both parties see in the other a means of solving and resolving individual difficulties.

In contrast to those unions in Austen where we can imagine, if not see or read about, the dark looks and the deep disappointments of marriage, we are offered pictures of marriages which can succeed – precisely because the characters are not, in any romantic sense, 'in love'. They may well have acquired, through trial and tribulation, a considerable respect and affection for the other party but that affection has been based on a key component of workable relationships: Socratic conversation and discourse. In these exchanges, in which ideas about topics as diverse as Cowper, landscape gardening and human fidelity have been discussed, the characters have established that the spoken word has meaning and is the basis for both action and principle. Words, in Austen's fiction and epistemology, have a direct relationship to expectations about human behaviour. It is not quite the ethos of mercantile capitalism ('My word is my bond') which is being articulated here, but the shared assumption between characters of moral worth is that words are used precisely and with care and not as a form of unfettered and unlocated exchange. Moreover, the conversations between parties who will marry well suggest that what is recognized is precisely that distinction between the senses and rational behaviour which Austen wants us to recognize and acknowledge. For example, in his first declaration to Elizabeth Bennet Darcy expresses the tensions produced in him by his feelings: 'In vain have I struggled. My feelings will not be repressed' (Austen, 1975: 221).

In Austen's world, what we are presented with is a refusal of both love and romance. Romance is foolish and illusory, while the idea of romantic love is as suspect. Yet at the same time as Austen systematically attacks romantic love as the organizing foundation for marriage she also makes plain her commitment to the idea of freely chosen relationships. She does not, for example, endorse – in *Mansfield Park* – Sir Thomas Bertram's determination that Fanny Price should marry Henry Crawford. Austen presents Sir Thomas as a firm believer in marriages contracted through sense rather than sensibility – a position not remote from her own – but at the same time she recognizes that the essentially forced marriage which Sir Thomas is advocating violates Fanny's own feelings and inclinations. Thus Sir Thomas speaks of the 'young, heated fancy' which people assume is necessary for marriage: a view of romantic love which is both close to Austen in its implicit critique of romance but also distant from her in that Sir Thomas prefaces his remarks by highly critical comments about 'modern' young women. Thus he berates Fanny:

> I had thought you peculiarly free from wilfulness of temper, self-conceit, and every tendency to that independence of spirit, which prevails so much in modern days, even in young women, and which in young women is offensive and disgusting beyond all common offence. (Austen, 1976: 372)

The 'modern' young people of whom Sir Thomas speaks are, of course, those generations who are going to grow up within what is generally described as modernity and for whom love and romance are taken for granted as part of the culture. What Sir Thomas recognizes – as much from his own less than satisfactory marriage as from sustained thought – is that love is by no means a simple straightforward idea and that its meaning, and boundaries, have to be set by social as much as personal negotiation. But the boundaries which Sir Thomas – and Jane Austen – wish to set (namely that 'love' should be constructed within a discourse of rational thought and discussion) were increasingly eroded throughout the 19th and the 20th centuries. Modernity opted for love and romance; a combination most usually expressed in Western culture as romantic love. Within this expectation, it became part of the normative structure of society to assume that people would 'fall in love' (and equally out of love), and that being 'in love' would provide the necessary and absolute legitimation for the construction (or destruction) of relationships. 'Love at first sight', 'true love', 'endless love': all these descriptions of the nature of love became part of everyday speech and everyday assumption. Within a culture in which 'all you need is love' defined the aspirations of many individuals, the voice of Jane Austen – and other Enlightenment sceptics about romantic love – became muted and obscured.

In the literature (both fictional and otherwise) on the past 200 years of romantic love, there is a widespread assumption that the acceptance of romantic love as part of the normative discourse of the West is a victory for both women and for individual self-determination. The assumption thus takes for granted the idea that it is in women's interest for 'love' to be the crucial factor in defining relationships and that it is through expectations of romantic love that women escape arranged marriages and patriarchal control. For women, the words 'I don't love him' (and a heterosexual model is the general expectation of romantic love) are seen as the defining point in which women state their inclinations in a way that cannot be questioned. Equally, both women and men are assumed to be able to invoke love, or lack of it, as the organizing principle of long-term relationships. To fall out of love carries with it the expectation that a relationship will end, just as surely as falling in love generates expectations of the establishment of public relationships and households.

But exactly what love is, and what its part should be in the construction of social and personal relationships remains as little discussed as it is generally assumed. At the interview following his engagement to Lady Diana Spencer, Prince Charles was asked by an interviewer if he was 'in love'. The interviewer clearly expected – and indeed it was entirely to be expected – that the reply would be unequivocal and even enthusiastic agreement. What the interviewer received was an extraordinarily ambiguous and evasive reply, in which Prince Charles openly voiced an uncertainty about what love is. To listen to the conversation with the hindsight of the knowledge of the unhappiness of that marriage is to listen to the competing traditions and ideas about love which doomed the marriage. Diana Spencer, standing by Prince Charles as he equivocates about love, quite obviously expects a clear and unambiguous reply. As her glance away from Prince Charles suggested at the time, she was disturbed by the apparent absence in her future husband of wholesale participation in romance. The public knows, of course, that Prince Charles's very obvious ambiguity was the result of other affections and other pressures. It was quite impossible – given the way in which the marriage had been constructed – for Prince Charles to say that the forthcoming marriage was a result (like the choice of bride) of dynastic pressures and that at the very best he hoped that he and his future wife would be able to live together reasonably amicably.

To say this – to speak of the complexities of marriage – would, of course, have shocked and appalled many of the viewers of that interview. To admit openly that it is possible to enter a marriage and not to be 'in love' is tantamount to a refusal of Western culture and a distancing from one of the crucial tenets of popular culture. Prince Charles (or anyone else in that situation) could not have refused the whole idea of love, since to have done so would have amounted to a refusal of what is assumed as the basis of marriage. Yet from what has been written and revealed about the subsequent marriage it is clear that what contributed to its failure was a chasm of difference about the ideology of love, with one party demanding endorsements of love and romance which were simply not available. Until the end of her life, Diana Spencer was popularly constructed within a discourse of love and romance; the last relationship before her death was portrayed as 'finding love'. Within these descriptions there was little place for cynical comments about holiday romances or the victory of hope over experience.

The example of Diana and Charles, the doomed couple of the Windsor Horror Show, demonstrates all too clearly that for women love – and quite literally in this case – kills. Far from liberating women from patriarchal control or the pressures of arranged marriages romantic love actually traps women in false expectations and psychologically crippling demands. The feminist badges which were widely worn at the time of the Diana–Charles marriage ('Don't Do It, Di') were proved, tragically for all concerned, to offer good advice – even if the advice focused on the institution of marriage rather than on the ideology of romance. But in this emphasis what we can see is that romantic love, as an expectation, permeates not just the institution of heterosexual marriage but also the aspirations underlying all relationships, whether heterosexual or not. None of the feminist advice to Diana at the time of her marriage excluded or refused to endorse the possibility of romantic love. Nobody said, please don't do this because you are endorsing a deeply suspect idea about the formation of relationships. So Diana was not wrong to endorse the idea of love per se, only love situated in the frozen embrace of Prince Charles and his family.

The particular example of Diana Spencer and her unlucky and ill-fated pursuit of what Nancy Mitford once described as 'love in a cold climate' serves to illustrate the still endless enthusiasm for love and the expectation of love which Western culture has. When Nancy Mitford wrote her two bestselling novels about upper-class romance in the 1940s (*The Pursuit of Love* and *Love in a Cold Climate*) she did so from the vantage point of a cynical, and cosmopolitan, point of view which mocked and subverted the romantic expectations and aspirations of her heroines. Indeed, what Mitford did was to pour scorn on the idea of romantic love and point out that it was the product of adolescent imagination, limited experience and highly susceptible and ignorant ideas about the nature of social life. Her hapless heroines, who fall in and out of love, are portrayed as immature and fanciful, victims of a set of ideas which can only lead to misery and disappointment. Against these disappointments are set the arrangements and the relationships rooted in shared social position, commitments to children and households and internalized emotional hierarchies in which romantic love is given little account.

A reading of the history of love in the Western culture which begins with *Mansfield Park* and then discusses Nancy Mitford and Princess Diana is, necessarily, incomplete. Of the many complexities of the history of love which the account overlooks are the ways in which class, gender and ethnicity affect (as everyone knows) this phenomenon as much as any other part of social life. Indeed, the mantra of 'class, gender, ethnicity' is now intoned over all social events. What the three elements can tell us about the social construction of love is that it differs from class to class, gender to gender and exists – or does not exist – differently within different cultures. One of the most striking features of the history of love is that its history in post-Enlightenment Europe has been so contested: what we often accept as a fixed point in our culture is, in fact, one which has had diverse meanings. In particular, what we can observe from this history is that love, and romantic love most specifically, has often been regarded as lower-class, irrational and deeply suspect. Indeed, there is a great deal of evidence to suggest that love has been not just a personal, but also an ideological battleground. Put in bold terms: men and the socially powerful have regarded love as feminine and feminizing, while for women, and the less powerful, the achievement of the recognition of love has been a major social project which has gone hand in hand with the projects of the domestication of men and the achievement of female autonomy and citizenship. Love, therefore, has been in a sense a pawn in a social game which has been primarily about the control of the personal and the domestic space. Yet while love has been a weapon of the powerless, it has become a vehicle for their oppression: the paradox of the achievement of what might be described as a 'love culture' is therefore a poisoned chalice as far as the less socially powerful are concerned.

Every history of love (where boundaries often overrun into the history of sex and/or the erotic) begins with an account of homoerotic love in classical Greece. It is assumed that the starting point of Western civilization was a society in which males loved males and had sexual relations with women for the purposes of procreation. Little is generally said about the history of love in Europe between the disappearance of Greek civilization and the emergence of chivalry in the 12th century. At this point, we begin to enter a discourse which is identifiably modern, if only because courtly love is heterosexual and is generally accompanied by a great deal of heartache if not tragedy. At the same time, a rich literature of energetic sexuality (whether heterosexual or not) emerges. Lofty thoughts of endless fidelity and commitment were accompanied by accounts of lust and desire in which it was widely recognized that love and lust were two sides of the same coin. But in general, what was being established, albeit gradually and with many exceptions, was an expectation that the very nature of civilization, and the civilized person, was in some way associated with the capacity for at least a degree of romantic love. As the 16th and 17th centuries wore on, there is increasing evidence of the emergence of the bringing together of romantic love and heterosexual marriage and that this association was in itself associated with the process of civilization. 'Domestic felicity and harmony' became a goal of early modern Europe, and with it the acknowledgement that this could not be achieved without the participation of women in the domestic contract.

Thus *forming* that contract became one of the great issues confronting modern Europe: how to establish those desirably harmonious households which appeared to be based on freely chosen partners. The aristocracy and the Court still had to accept partners who would be acceptable for dynastic reasons, but for those not bound by constraints of inheritance and strategy there was considerable freedom to negotiate the choice of partners. Parents still exercised control around issues of suitability for many middle-class women, but these women now had a new weapon through which to establish their choice of marriage partner: that of romantic attraction. Whatever the threats and anger of Henry Fielding's Squire Weston, he could do nothing against his daughter's insistence on love as a basis for marriage. Romantic love had arrived, and had arrived as a legitimate basis through which marriage partners could be chosen.

In this – as suggested earlier – there seems to be a strong case for supposing that romantic love was a formative part of the gradual ideological emancipation of women and the public definition of a specifically feminine set of interests. Women – through the discourse of romantic love – could exercise choice in who they would marry and construct male behaviour in ways likely to produce love in women. Gallant forms of address, tests of devotion, commitments to fidelity, care and attention were part of the normal, and expected, behaviour of the man in love. Not to demonstrate at least some version of this behaviour suggested a degree of callous indifference to the other party and was, of course, unlikely to produce the hoped for result of love. Throughout the 18th century English novelists, both male and female, presented the man in love as a person temporarily divorced from silent and inexpressive masculinity, and constrained instead by the single desire to show himself in love. Heroes as diverse as Fitzwilliam Darcy in Austen's *Pride and Prejudice*, Tom Jones in the novel of the same name and (in the 19th century) Tolstoy's Count Vronsky in *Anna Karenina* all became apparently destabilized by their love for women.

But what these men (and others like them) became destabilized by was not so much love for women per se, but the adoption – in the process of becoming lovers of women – of what was seen to be unacceptable behaviour for men. Love for women became the way in which masculine emotional stability – a form of stability which gave a priority to the lack of expressiveness in men – was undermined. Tolstoy's *Anna Karenina* presents a definitive picture of the man undermined by love: at the height of his passion for Anna, Vronsky neglects his profession, his friends and social life. His falling out of love for Anna is accompanied by a return to the preoccupations of his previous existence. Vronsky's friends and colleagues accept the idea of 'being in love' and passionate preoccupation with a woman, but what they expect is that Vronsky will at some point return to 'normal' and his behaviour return to a more conventionally appropriate pattern.

The paradox of Vronsky's situation, and indeed the social role of the male heterosexual lover in the past 200 years, is that men are expected to adopt atypical masculine behaviour in the situation in which they are attempting to normalize sexual relations through marriage and courtship. Once marriage is arranged and organized, it is then possible for masculinity to return to the expected pattern of authority over women and an absence of sensibility. Thus across cultures and the social spectrum voices have endlessly spoken of the 'loss of romance in marriage' and bemoan the apparent disappearance of what had appeared to be a disclosure of highly individualized romance. The expression 'the honeymoon is over' suggests precisely that return to normality which marks off the period of courtship and romance as both different from ordinary life, and in some senses an essentially insincere aspect of experience. Romance as charade and disguise has always been recognized in literature and the arts: Mozart's opera *Cosi fan Tutte* is an entirely modern parody of the limits of romance and the limitations of the sentiments expressed by those in love. Dorabella's protestations that 'if I lost Ferrando, I think I'd bury myself alive', is met by the robust Despina with the comment that 'other men have everything these men have. Now you love one man; you will love another.'

Despina's prediction becomes, of course, entirely true. The final reconciliation of the two pairs of lovers ends, however, not in morbid tragedy of betrayed love and tearful infidelity but in a hymn to reason: the lovers join in a paean of praise to those 'who allow themselves to be led by reason'. Men *and* women have been shown to be equally ridiculous when they profess themselves 'in love' and the deceit engineered by Despina has had the effect of demonstrating the unreliable nature of romance. Yet at the same time new, and more serious, ties have emerged which allow that human beings need to form lasting attachments. To attempt to form these ties through romance and exaggerated sentiment, is, however, suggested as pointless and degrading for both sexes.

Cosi fan Tutte was completed in 1790 and with the novels of Jane Austen forms part of a radical Enlightenment critique of romantic love, while at the same time endorsing sexual equality and in particular the equal capacity of women and men for radical action. In both Mozart and Jane Austen women and men are equally duped by romance, and equally capable of behaving absurdly when influenced by the dictates of romance. Austen's Enlightenment hero, Mr Bennet in *Pride and Prejudice*, lives out a life of conjugal irritation because, he like many men, was flattered and affected by the smiles and charms of the young Mrs Bennet. Indeed, throughout her work, Austen maintains a radical and critical eye for the idiocies of both men and women in love and never falters from her determination that only rational choice, and rational discourse, can provide an adequate basis for human relationships.

To set out Austen's position in the late 20th century still carries with it the possibility that it will be rejected as a cold and calculating way of forming partnerships. Yet the accumulated evidence of the last centuries suggests that people in the West have suffered more in their personal lives from 'love' than from any other single ideology. From the middle of the 19th century romance emerged as both an industry and an ideology in Western societies, and consumerism rapidly endorsed and developed the possibilities of romance. Historians of shopping and consumption can point to advertising from the end of the 19th century which is precisely geared to expectations and situations of romance. The 'romantic', a term previously associated with the wild and the untamed, came to possess an entirely opposite meaning: the form through which sexual desire and attraction could be appropriately organized and sanitized for domestic consumption.

Against this culture of romantic love, women and gay men have fought ongoing battles of resistance and dissent. Women have criticized, mocked and lampooned romance as the form through which the domestic oppression of women has been organized. This entirely valid resistance has, nevertheless, had the effect of implicitly encouraging us to assume that romance is a plot by men to sugar the evil pill of patriarchal domesticity. It is entirely possible that some such calculations do exist, but the evidence of both literature and social reality suggests that romance is a discourse within which many men, as well as many women, feel uncomfortable. Moreover, the expectation of romance allows little space for individual differences in behaviour: to be romantic involves becoming an ardent suitor just as much as it involves the role of the sought after and the pursued. These roles – involving as they do behaviour which suggests diffidence and coyness – have now been identified as crucial to the misunderstandings which fuel aggression and violence between the sexes. The literature on rape and violence against women testifies to the ways in which cultures which condone romance are also beset with the misreadings of romance. Far from giving individuals a guide to the expression and articulation of emotional feelings, romance distorts and limits the possibilities of human relationships.

In their recent account of love in Western societies Ulrich Beck and Elisabeth Beck-Gernsheim (1995) have argued that the category of 'love' is becoming less coherent and more likely to be constructed by individual choice rather than external circumstance. To the Becks, in an account which includes discussions of divorce, birth rates and the lived world of marriage, the idea of 'love' is never deconstructed or regarded as anything other than a once powerful – and fixed – category. Yet in many ways, the idea of 'love' in heterosexual relations has always been extremely unstable, and as likely to change as any other social ideology. What has changed a great deal (and certainly within the course of the last century) are ideas about what makes other people loveable. The meaning of love, as numerous historians, biographers and ordinary individuals have pointed out, has changed enormously in the course of the 20th century. For example, when Sylvia Plath wrote *The Bell Jar* (1963) – her searing critique of the cult of domesticity of the Eisenhower years – she attacks one conventional notion of 'love' (that provided by her mother and her mother's friends) only to endorse, at the novel's conclusion, the more explicitly sexualized version of love which was to become the benchmark for the latter part of the 20th century. What this construction of love did for women – in that it encouraged recreational heterosexuality and norms of sexual satisfaction – has been the focus of work by Barbara Ehrenreich (1983) and others. These critics – unlike the Becks – recognized that 'love' (in the sense of the reasons that people give for individual attractions) has changed but the cult of romance and romantic expectations has not. People of both sexes, and diverse sexualities, expect to 'fall in love' and with this expectation goes the unchanging view that it is possible to establish a life-long relationship with one other person who will make good the intimacies known in childhood and lost in adult life.

Every account of romance – be it in the cards sold in their millions on Valentine's Day or the high culture of romantic poetry – speaks for individual desire to recover the intimacy known (generally) between mother and infant. The wish to find 'the other' who will make good the agony of separation and the costs of autonomy provides an endless, and a historical, basis for romance. In a real sense, the sense of the biography which almost every human being experiences, we cannot but be romantic and search for the missing companion of our adult years. Romance, then, has a real foundation in human experience, however distorted and absurd it may become through commercial exploitation. The social tragedy of romance (unlike its many personal tragedies) is that just as it seemed possible to recognize the loneliness of the human condition (and Franken-stein's monster in Mary Shelley's novel spoke for everyone when he cried out for human companionship) and to attempt to build an ethic of love which would diminish that loneliness, social and material factors usurped romance and love and forced them into the endlessly infantilizing constructions that we know as 19th- and 20th-century love and romance. For a brief period in European history writers recognized and articulated the paradoxical reality of romance, but no sooner was this recognised than a version of love was constructed in which the sexes were separated by distinct moralities and expectations of sexual behaviour. Love became not the resolution of human need and desire, but the form through which it has transparently distorted the possibilities of human relationships.

References

Austen, Jane (1965) *Persuasion*. Harmondsworth: Penguin.

Austen, Jane (1975) *Pride and Prejudice*. Harmondsworth: Penguin.

Austen, Jane (1976) *Mansfield Park*. Harmondsworth: Penguin.

Beck, Ulrich and Elisabeth Beck-Gernsheim (1995) *The Normal Chaos of Love*. Cambridge: Polity.

Ehrenreich, Barbara (1983) *The Hearts of Men: American Dreams and the Flight from Commitment*. London: Pluto.

MacIntyre, Alasdair (1994) *After Virtue: A Study in Moral Theory*. London: Duckworth.

Mitford, Nancy (1949) *Love in a Cold Climate*. Harmondsworth: Penguin.

Mitford, Nancy (1954) *The Pursuit of Love*. Harmondsworth: Penguin.

Plath, Sylvia (1963) *The Bell Jar*. London: Faber.

Mary Evans is Professor of Women's Studies at the University of Kent at Canterbury. She is also co-editor of *The European Journal of Women's Studies*.

Introduction to Georg Simmel's 'On the Sociology of the Family'

David Frisby

S IMMEL'S ARTICLE 'On the Sociology of the Family' originally appeared in the Sunday Supplements (numbers 26 and 27) of the *Vossische Zeitung* in Berlin in two parts on 30 June 1895 and 7 July 1895 (Simmel, 1895a). Simmel was a relatively frequent contributor to this prominent Berlin newspaper in the 1890s. Indeed, the issue containing the second part of the article on the family also contained a review by Simmel of Georg Jellinek's *Die Erklärung der Menschen und Bürgerrechte* (Simmel, 1895b). A year earlier, Simmel had published an article in the *Vossische Zeitung* on 'Die Verwandtenehe' ('Consanguineous Marriage') in the Sunday supplements numbers 23 and 24 for 3 and 10 June 1894 (Simmel, 1894a), and on 'Der Militarismus und die Stellung der Frau' ('Militarism and the Position of Woman') in the editions for 21 and 28 October 1894 (Simmel, 1894b). The quality of the articles in the Sunday supplements was usually high and compares very favourably with their contemporary equivalents.

There are a number of contexts in which Simmel's contribution to the sociology of the family can be viewed. A year prior to the publication of 'On the Sociology of the Family', Simmel had published his influential programmatic essay 'Das Problem der Soziologie' (Simmel, 1894c), which appeared in English translation as 'The Problem of Sociology' with a supplementary note in 1895 (Simmel, 1895b; Frisby, 1994: 28–35), almost certainly translated by Albion Small. In this essay – which, as he wrote to Emile Durkheim's student Celéstin Bouglé, is one 'upon which I myself lay the greatest value and which contains my work programme (and the essential part of my teaching programme)' (Frisby, 1992: 179, n. 27) – Simmel

■ *Theory, Culture & Society* 1998 (SAGE, London, Thousand Oaks and New Delhi),
 Vol. 15(3–4): 277–281
 [0263-2764(199808/11)15:3–4;277–281;006068]

outlined the nature of his paradigm for sociology and a possible future sociological research programme. Sociology was to be the study of the forms of social interaction (*Wechselwirkung*) or sociation (*Vergesellschaftung*) as a specifically demarcated discipline. Clearly one of the most important forms of socialization (*Socialisierungsformen*) in human societies has been the family. In the context of Simmel's sociology, the variations in this form should be the object of investigation, as should its comparative study.

Like several of his essays from this period, the article commences with a brief justification for Simmel's sociological paradigm, before turning to a substantial discussion of the family. He distinguishes conceptions of sociology which view the discipline as a special branch of psychology, as an examination of the presuppositions common to all societies, and (which is Simmel's paradigm) as the study of forms of sociation. The significance of the study of the family from these perspectives lies in its capacity to serve as exemplar for the repetition of a social form, for the diversity of this form in a variety of social settings and the influence of manifold interests upon this form.

The article on the family may also be read in the context of Simmel's contributions to the sociology of gender. The study of social interaction between the sexes (including prostitution), a psychology of women, dimensions of the emergent Women's Movement in Germany, forms of intimate interaction such as flirtation and love, and the cultural and power constraints upon the development of a distinctive female culture are all themes which Simmel takes up in articles and essays at various times from around 1890 until his death in 1918. Some of these contributions to a sociology of gender (see Coser, 1977; Oakes, 1984; Dahme and Köhnke, 1985) are related to central themes in Simmel's social theory, such as social differentiation, the separation of subjective and objective culture, and the impact of the money economy and social relations. Others relate to the development of a psychology and philosophy of human relations, while yet others may be viewed as conjunctural interventions in the politics of the Women's Movement in Germany. Some of them are available in translation (see Oakes, 1984; Frisby and Featherstone, 1997).

If we turn to the text of the essay on the family, then – as with almost all of Simmel's essays and monographs – the essay provides no explicit references to the secondary literature upon which its author is drawing. However, it is clear that Simmel is drawing upon 19th-century ethnography, anthropology and sociology for his comparative evidence on the history and development of the family. Possible sources upon which he had already drawn are Herbert Spencer's *Sociology* (1885) and his *First Principles* (1862) and other writings.

The extent to which Simmel is taking up Spencer's themes, lines of argument and sometimes anthropological evidence in several of his early essays is apparent, for instance, from a reading of his 1894 essay on 'Militarism and the Position of Woman' and the essay on the family. Spencer's thesis that the transition from 'prevalent polygyny to exclusive monogamy' in family structures strongly correlates with the 'decline of militancy and rise of industrialism' (Spencer, 1885: 680) is a theme examined by Simmel in his essay on militarism (1894b). Also explored in the essay on the family is the relationship between family structure, the status of women and the role, if not the status, of children, all covered by Spencer in his evolutionary perspective on the emergence of the modern family structure.

In particular, some of the examples upon which Simmel draws are derived from Edward Westermarck's influential *The History of Human Marriage* (Westermarck, 1891), already in English and German translations. Westermarck's substantive comparative-historical study of marriage contains several themes that are dealt with by Simmel in his article, including the origins of marriage and marriage by purchase – a theme which he takes up in detail later in relation to money payment (Simmel, 1898) and which is developed most fully in his *Philosophy of Money*, first published in 1900 (Simmel, 1990). Several specific affinities could be drawn between Westermarck's and Simmel's treatment of marriage and the family. To give but one instance, Simmel's concluding remarks could be compared with those of Westermarck. Referring to the evolution of marriage, Westermarck (1891: 549–50) concludes that:

> The dominant tendency of this process [of evolution] at its later stages has been the extension of the wife's rights. A wife is no longer the husband's property; and, according to modern ideas, marriage is, or should be, a contract on the footing of perfect equality between the sexes. The history of human marriage is the history of a relationship in which women have been gradually triumphing over the passions, the prejudices, and the selfish interests of men.

The assumption of the improvement in the position of women in marriage is shared by Simmel, but without reference to their legal position. Simmel's focus upon the economic mediation of money and the shift from an historically indeterminate anthropological (and psychological) perspective to the contemporary situation renders his conclusion questionable. However, a full historical analysis of this article would have to return to the theoretical and practical parameters within which Simmel was working in the early 1890s, access to which has only recently been systematically provided (see Köhnke, 1996).

It is noteworthy that this essay on the family, like several others from the early 1890s and later that draw heavily on 19th-century ethnography, is not taken up in Simmel's major sociological text, his *Soziologie* (Simmel, 1908, 1993), even though the family is acknowledged to be a crucial form of sociation. One can only speculate on the reasons for this since Simmel did not justify extensively the grounds for choosing the essays for inclusion in this volume. What can be asserted is that the early confrontation with Spencer's sociology and social science programme and the reliance upon ethnological sources is much less in evidence in the *Soziologie* of 1908. There, Simmel is intent upon developing his own programme for sociology and extensive instances of its application to a great variety of areas, rather than confronting earlier sociological paradigms.

There is, however, one theme which Simmel takes up briefly in his essay on the family that is treated in later writings, namely the phenomenon of love. In the essay on the family, love is associated with a transition to individual choice of partners. In his later writings, Simmel examines different dimensions of the relationship between the self and the world, between the I and You, as flirtation, adventure, eroticism and love. These often more fragmentary reflections reveal contributions to a sociology of the emotions and a philosophy of life relations, elevating love to 'more-than-life', to something both within everyday experience and totally beyond it (as in the case of the adventure). Although located in the I–You relation, love creates a phenomenon beyond it, a third entity. As Dahme and Köhnke put it (Dahme and Köhnke, 1985: 20), 'In his late philosophy, sexual love is ultimately viewed' as an emotion that cannot be explained by other facts, as an 'inner act that cannot be analysed' or 'rendered intelligible through the co-operation of other elements'. Love is motivated neither egoistically nor altruistically, but rather is 'a "third" entity'. In this respect, the association of love with a third entity has affinities too with Simmel's conception of society as emerging out of the interaction of three or more elements.

Simmel's reflections on love remain incomplete. Some of their most illuminating strands are contained in notes and aphorisms. Thus, on eroticism, Simmel announces in his aphorisms:

> The erotic nature is perhaps the one for whom taking and giving are identical, those who give insofar as they take, and take insofar as they give. . . .

> What, at all events, the erotic person is *not*: a thrifty housekeeper, a differentiated professional person, a hypochondriac. (Dahme and Köhnke, 1985: 266)

Had they been developed, these and other reflections would have matched Simmel's more complete and even dialectical observations on flirtation, adventure and other phenomena. In his essay 'On Love', he explores the relationship between love and life, in which love is generated out of life but seeks to create its own autonomy from life – to be 'more-than-life'. As Oakes (1984: 6) aptly formulates its heterosexual theme:

> Although love is an instrument that serves the procreative needs of life, it now becomes an end in itself. Life is employed as an instrument to realize the existentially autonomous purposes of love. As a result, the erotic existence becomes detached from life and irreconcilable with its interests, an antagonism which is perhaps most clearly expressed in the conflict between the passions of eroticism and the forms of marriage.

In 1895, in his essay on the family, Simmel was still exploring differentiations in family structures, of which modern marriage was a distinctive form whose emergence remained to be explained.

References

Coser, Lewis A. (1977) 'Georg Simmel's Neglected Contribution to the Sociology of Women', *Signs* 2: 869–76.

Dahme, Heinz-Jürgen and Klaus Christian Köhnke (eds) (1985) *Georg Simmel. Schriften zur Philosophie und Soziologie der Geschlechter*. Frankfurt: Suhrkamp.

Frisby, David (1992) *Simmel and Since*. London: Routledge.

Frisby, David (ed.) (1994) *Georg Simmel: Critical Assessments*. London: Routledge.

Frisby, David and Mike Featherstone (eds) (1997) *Simmel on Culture*. London: Sage.

Köhnke, Klaus Christian (1996) *Der junge Simmel in Theoriebeziehungen und sozialen Bewegungen*. Frankfurt: Suhrkamp.

Oakes, Guy (ed.) (1984) *Georg Simmel: On Women, Sexuality and Love*. New Haven, CT: Yale University Press.

Simmel, Georg (1894a) 'Die Verwandtenehe', *Vossische Zeitung* (23 and 24) 3 and 10 June.

Simmel, Georg (1894b) 'Der Militarismus und die Stellung der Frau', *Vossische Zeitung* 21 and 28 October.

Simmel, Georg (1894c) 'Das Problem der Soziologie', *Jahrbuch für Gesetzgebung, Verwaltung und Volkswirtschaft* (18): 271–7.

Simmel, Georg (1895a) 'Zur Soziologie der Familie', *Vossische Zeitung* (26 and 27) 30 June and 7 July.

Simmel, Georg (1895b) 'The Problem of Sociology', *Annals of the American Academy of Political and Social Science* 6: 52-63.

Simmel, Georg (1898) 'Die Rolle des Geldes in den Beziehungen der Geschlechter', *Die Zeit* (14) 15, 22, 29 January.

Simmel, Georg (1908) *Soziologie*. Berlin/Leipzig: Duncker and Humblot.

Simmel, Georg (1990) *The Philosophy of Money*, 2nd enlarged edn. London: Routledge.

Simmel, Georg (1993) *Soziologie*. Frankfurt: Suhrkamp.

Spencer, Herbert (1862) *First Principles*. London: Williams and Norgate.

Spencer, Herbert (1885) *Principles of Sociology*. London:Williams and Norgate.

Westermarck, Edward (1891) *The History of Human Marriage*. London: Macmillan.

David Frisby is Professor of Sociology at Glasgow University.

On the Sociology of the Family

Georg Simmel

I

NEWLY EMERGENT SCIENCES enjoy the questionable advantage of having to offer a temporary home for all the current problems that cannot otherwise be adequately accommodated. The fact that their borders are inevitably indeterminate and undefended attracts all the homeless, until their growth gradually once again rejects the inappropriate elements, as it directs the sciences into preventive limits that are certainly disappointing, but for that very reason avoid future disappointment. Thus the confusing mass of problems which press upon the new science of sociology is beginning to thin out. It is beginning to distribute less indiscriminately the right to call it home, and although it is still far from settled what more precise form the peripheral lines of its field will have, serious scientific efforts can be seen everywhere that seek to determine such boundaries.

For a while, sociology seemed to be the magical word that would offer a solution to all the riddles of history and practical life, moral theory and aesthetics, as well as religion and politics, and in France, for instance, people still tend generally to adhere to this view. In contrast, in Germany and North America, those more modest theories have arisen which abstain from summarizing knowledge about everything that occurs within a society into a single science. They conceive of the new science either as a branch of psychology, specifically of the kind which deals with the socially caused and socially expressed mental states of the individual; or they view it as the science of the common presuppositions of all types of knowledge concerning society; or as the philosophy of social events; or, finally, as the investigation of the forms in which human beings are sociated and which display the same nature and development through all the variety of goals and contents around which societies crystallize.

For all these more circumscribed goals of sociology, the history of the

■ *Theory, Culture & Society* 1998 (SAGE, London, Thousand Oaks and New Delhi),
  Vol. 15(3–4): 283–293
  [0263-2764(199808/11)15:3–4;283–293;006079]

family is a matter of special importance. For in it we have a socialization of a few persons which is repeated countless times within every larger group in exactly the same form, and which proceeds from simple interests with which everyone can empathize and is, for these reasons, relatively easily recognizable. In addition, we have an extraordinary diversity of familial forms in the various cultural stages, and since the family in general is an enduring grouping through all the change of other life forms, we can often test the nature and strength of conjugal and kinship relationships by means of the family's influence upon them. Finally, despite their very simple structure, a great number of very different interests – erotic and economic, religious and social, interests of power as well as individual growth – unite marriage and the family. In this way, on the basis of a clear example, it can be demonstrated how all these factors, in their combination and with the changing predominance of the individual elements, affect the collective life of human beings. By commencing from these viewpoints, I should like to present here some facts and reflections that arise out of the most recent studies and socio-psychological analyses of the history of the family.

The most obvious historical supposition is that marriage has developed out of a state of animalistically unregulated and arbitrarily changing relationships between man and woman. Fixed orderings and limiting norms everywhere appear to be later stages of developments that began with meaningless chaos, and thus the specific, permanent relationships that we identify as marriage and the family seemed able to be only the result of social training and tested expediency. What one must call the minimum conjugal form is that relationship between man and woman which extends beyond the birth of offspring and in which there exists a commonality in provision for life.

This idea of an original absence of marriage found its main support in so-called matriarchy. As is well known, several decades ago it was discovered that it was not the father, but the mother who constituted the centre of the family among many primitive peoples and probably even in earlier stages of present-day civilized peoples. Even where marriage already exists, the child is frequently considered to belong to the mother's clan rather than that of the father, the child is not considered kin of the father and the child also does not inherit from him, but rather from the mother's brother. The most obvious thing was to explain this remarkable relationship as being a result and remnant of earlier conditions in which the father was not known at all, because there was no set institution of marriage and because promiscuity prevailed.

However, it has been very recently discovered that in several ethnic groups even the earliest subgroups have patriarchy, patriarchal descent and inheritance along the paternal line, while the more highly developed ones feature matriarchy, which was supposed to follow from, and characterize, the lowest stage. Among the most highly developed American Indians, who were already raising grain when the first Europeans arrived, and possessed a secure social organization, matrilineality is the rule; among the least developed ones, who lack both of the latter, patrilineality prevails. The very same relationship is found among the Australian Aborigines; indeed it seems certain that patriarchy was the earliest existent familial form. For reasons still unknown and not until later did matrilineality – that is, the child's membership of the mother's clan – develop from it, although here too, there can be no question of communal wives and uncertainty of paternity.

This main argument for an original lack of any individual and lasting relationship between man and woman therefore proves to be untenable. Indeed, this provides an interesting insight into the significance of all such reconstructions of the earliest conditions from the later ones. A researcher concludes from the consequence of jealousy the necessity of an original completely free, promiscuous condition. If, from the very beginning, there had been private property with respect to women, then any type of tribal formation and organization would have been impossible, because the jealous feeling of the men would have nipped any kind of close social life – any cooperative union – in the bud. In order for such a thing to have come into existence, in order to have formed large and lasting groups, then, one would definitely have to presume mutual toleration of the adult males, freedom from jealousy, i.e. the lack of any constraints on the relationships between every man and woman.

Another scholar draws exactly the opposite conclusion, namely that continuing jealousy would emerge from the latter circumstances. As long as regulated relationships between the sexes do not exist and the man cannot consider his wife his exclusive property, which is simply unavailable for the others, the struggle for women, since not all of them are equally desirable, would be a source of continual discord between the males. Only when men's relationships to women are separated and protected, when the possession of women was limited but in turn protected from the others, could the inner peace in a group and, subsequently, the larger and more lasting organizations emerge. Thus, the fact that we see such organizations before us and that the sense of jealousy keeps men apart leads some commentators to the conclusion that there were only anarchic circumstances at the beginning of human development and other commentators to the opposite conclusion, namely, that only regulated circumstances could have predominated.

An additional proof for the original lack of definite conjugal relationships was based on the fact that, among some peoples, the terms for nephew and niece are the same as for son or daughter, and those for male and female cousins the same as for brother and sister. Such terms could only have originated in the case where every woman stood in a conjugal relationship with all males of her group, and therefore even with her own brothers; in these circumstances, the father and the mother's brother, and consequently the son and the nephew, were often identical or at least could not be distinguished. Even though this situation is nowhere found to exist, nonetheless this terminology is claimed as proof that it must have previously existed, on the grounds that such naming systems always arose as an expression of real existing circumstances, but continue to live on long after they have been rendered meaningless by further development.

This argument for an original conjugal communism has also proved itself to be inadequate, especially since we now know the social constitution of the Australian Aborigines much better and have seen from it that the designation 'father' or 'son' among primitive peoples need not give any indication at all of some kind of kinship relation, but only of a difference in age, just as in some figures of speech still current among ourselves. The Aborigine divides the life course of every individual into three sections: child, young man or woman, old man or woman. Originally it was solely this generational stratification that decided which kinship expression was to be valid for individual persons. That is, the members of the older stratum were referred to indiscriminately as 'mothers' and 'fathers' of the younger stratum, and those of the oldest stratum as grandparents of the youngest. The expressions 'father' or 'mother', 'son' or 'daughter' thus in no way imply the physiological, blood-kin relationship that we connect with the same words, but rather only differentiations between old and young. Despite this, the Australian Aborigine knows quite precisely his own real father and mother, but he simply does not have a specific word that would be able to distinguish them conceptually from the other members of the same stratum. The extent to which merely a lack in conceptual and linguistic formation is present here, but not a lack of actual ability to make distinctions, is shown by the fact that many tribes do not even have a separate word for father and another one for mother. If they wish to characterize the gender differences within the older stratum, then they must add the word 'man' or 'woman' to the common expression. Just as it would be a mistake to assert here that this lack of a distinguishing expression indicates an impossibility or omission of distinction, then so too it would be equally erroneous to deduce from the undistinguished characterization of all older men as fathers that there existed here a real or previous ignorance of the father, that is, a form of conjugal communism.

Thus we are not compelled by any ascertainable fact to derive monogamous or any other definite conjugal form regulated by custom and law from an earlier condition of complete licence. Rather, it would be possible that humankind is by nature monogamous, like some animals – and especially most birds – and only falls into uncommitted relationships, into polyandry or polygamy, as a result of special circumstances of the type that modify and confuse natural tendencies in all areas of life. Some considerations support this view. First of all, complete, unregulated arbitrariness in the relation between men and women is not found among any known peoples in the world, and where it exists in part, peculiar contradictions within it show that it should not be viewed as a generally valid phase of human development. For instance, there are some primitive peoples among whom young girls enjoy complete freedom, and may indeed even be encouraged to have a large number of lovers, because this proves the power of their attractiveness – whereas they are absolutely faithful to their husbands from the moment of their marriage. Among other peoples, the complete opposite is reported: the strictest chastity on the part of the girls and the unlimited desire for amorous adventures on the part of the women. The reason why polygamy cannot be a typical conjugal form results from the simple fact that there are always only about as many women as men. Polygamy must therefore always be a privilege of the few, but must be denied to the great majority. Polyandry too occurs only under very special circumstances, in the highlands of Tibet, for instance, where the difficulty of making a living is so great that marriage appears to be a burdensome and difficult commitment, which is why several men share it. It has also transpired that most cases of polyandry proved to be a form of monogamy with a number of lovers rather than a conjugal form as such.

Alongside these forms, several types of mixed forms are also to be found, such as the so-called three-quarters marriages that have been observed in an Arabian tribe. Here, upon entering into marriage, the girl promises to be faithful to her husband for a certain number of days per week. A traveller very amusingly describes how the marriage gifts of the suitor are checked by the parents-in-law and at first found so insignificant that no more than two days of faithfulness per week can be promised, until finally, after passionate bargaining back and forth, the mother-in-law utters the saving words, 'My daughter will be faithful to you Mondays, Tuesdays, Thursdays and Fridays!' The temporary marriages of the White Muslims constitute another mixed form. These are legal marriages, that are dependent upon prescribed conditions and are usually conducted by priests, but only last for a previously agreed time – from one hour to 99 years. The children of such a legally fully recognized marriage are just as legitimate as are those of a permanent marriage. Finally, there is an odd conjugal form among the extremely primitive Australian Aborigines, who currently represent the lowest level of our species. Their tribes are largely divided into conjugal classes; among the Kamilaroi, for instance, there are two classes, in one of which the men are called 'Ippai' and the women 'Ippata', while in the other the men are called 'Cubbi' and the women 'Cubbota'. Now an Ippai may only marry a Cubbota, a Cubbi only an Ippata, and any marriage of an Ippai to an Ippata is absolutely forbidden, even if she is in no way a blood relative. On the other hand, an Ippai is considered potentially married to all Cubbotas, so to speak, and if he encounters a Cubbota in some remote village, then it is quite natural for them to enter a marital relationship, fleeting as it may be.

All these diverse forms of the relationship between man and woman are characterized as the results of special historical circumstances, and none of them reveals to us any 'primeval state', towards which some natural, universally uniform and presupposed drive was leading. If nevertheless such a drive does exist, then monogamy is no less well documented than is lack of regulation. Indeed, the development of marriage tends everywhere to move away from polygamic and polyandric forms towards monogamy. It is usually reported of the former that a *single* wife assumes a legal or customary leading position among the various wives of a husband; she may be the first-wed, or the most noble in birth, or the favourite wife. For this reason, even Zulu women, for example, strive to purchase a second wife for their husbands with their savings, because this second wife has the position of a maid with respect to the first. The position of *primus inter pares* occupied by the main wife in polygamy, as is inherent to such a position, tends to develop towards a position of *primus per se*; it sometimes happens that even the children of the secondary wives consider the chief wife their real mother.

The more important, both inwardly and outwardly, the position of this *one* wife becomes, the more deeply that of the others is depressed, until the point where this sociological separation process ends with only one wife existing and all auxiliary relationships with women becoming illegitimate or prohibited. It would be quite possible then to conceive of those other types of relationships as intermediary forms, while the monogamous instinct dominated both the preceding and the following conditions. This would be only one of the frequent cases in which the highest stage of development repeats the form of the lowest, but in a purified, protected and perfected manner. Yet this indubitable possibility is not yet a probability. Rather, what appears to me to be probable is that the infinite variety of conjugal forms has also corresponded to a variety of the original tendencies and instincts. Just as individuals within the same social group, despite all the similarity of external circumstances, can act in this respect in extremely different ways, with decidedly monogamous natures alongside those with decidedly polygamous tendencies so, equally, entire groups may have displayed quite contrary instincts and hence conditions, even at the earliest stages of their development. Here, as in many other issues, it is a mistaken indulgence with respect to the impulse for uniformity in our thinking to wish to lay a foundation at any price for the diversity of historical phenomena with an equality of the pre-historical starting point.

II

One may think of the primitive conjugal or non-conjugal relations what one wishes, but it still seems to me indubitable that the solid core around which the family grew up is not the relationship between man and woman, but that between mother and child. This is the stable point in the whole range of phenomena of conjugal life, a relationship which is essentially the same everywhere, whereas that between spouses is capable of infinite modifications. This is why, among primitive peoples, the relationship of the family father to the children is by no means the direct and naturally based one which we have. The child belongs to the mother, but it belongs to the father only to the extent that the mother belongs to him – just as the fruits of a tree belong to the person who owns the tree. As a cause or an effect of this, we frequently encounter an indifference, almost incomprehensible to us, with regard to who is the actual physical father of the child; as soon as the mother belongs to a particular man, the child is his, even if he knows that none of his blood is flowing in its veins. That is the root of the frequent lending and exchanging of women among primitive peoples.

What characterizes early familial forms therefore is not, as was once thought, the anonymity of the father, but rather the indifference with respect to who the father is in the physiological sense. I shall give a few striking examples of the extent to which the concept of the father can be a merely legal one, quite alien to the issue of blood relationship. Among some peoples, immature boys are engaged to mature girls, who have relations with other men, often with the fathers-in-law, until the boys mature. The children of these unions are considered unquestionably to be children of the boy, who is the legal owner of the girl. Among the Kaffirs, the son inherits his father's wives. He himself refrains from relations with them, but lends them to others, and children produced in this way are his own. That is to say – and this strengthens the idea in question here – they are considered to be children of the deceased, as is the case with the levirate marriage, and since all possessions of the latter pass over to his son, so too these children also belong to him, directly in fact, and not by means of a prior act of adoption or special recognition.

The most striking case, however, is the frequent phenomenon in primitive tribes that men specifically strive to get their wives to have intercourse with the chief, the priest or other such notables, because they believe that the children, which are still theirs despite this, will inherit the outstanding characteristics of the progenitor and that this will be to their benefit and that of their family. Here we see clear and consequently conscious progenitorship in such a sharp distinction to fathership that, taking the unity of the two for granted as we do, we can barely comprehend this distinction. The concept of the father had to undergo a long development before its original meaning, which only included the possession of the child by means of the possession of the mother, could develop into that of a direct and individual relationship between the progenitor and the child.

In all probability, this development is tied to that of private property. When the man had acquired and defended personal, more extensive property by means of struggle and labour, then he wished to leave it to an heir of his own blood. In my opinion, this dimension of the concept of blood inheritance considered here has grown and been strengthened by the concept of the inheritance of goods. The issue of paternity was not so significant, as it were, as long as no serious consequences with respect to property were associated with it. As soon as this interest appears, however, it brings about the demand for absolute marital fidelity on the part of the wife, although the same demand for men, as is obvious, does not spring from the same root and in fact developed the same degree of strictness much more slowly. This demand on the man probably only occurs to the extent that the equality of women grows, as a result of which those limitations to which women are subjected also appear to men as commandments of simple justice – even though the real cause which brought them into existence for women does not apply to men.

Yet this very reason for the emergence of conjugal fidelity – although it is naturally only one among many working together – brings us closer to the certainly evident fact that individual love, which – according to general opinion at least – is now the foundation of marriage and the defining basis for its qualities and direction, originally had nothing at all to do with marriage. Rather, on the contrary, the individual qualities and elements of marriage arose from separate and often very superficial causes and, in turn, it was they which brought about love as an individual relationship of the heart.

First, strict monogamy in marriage has probably only emerged out of the victory of the democratic principle. I already mentioned that the mass of men everywhere have always actually had to make do with *one* wife, simply because there has been no more than one woman available for each man. Wherever polygamy is legally permitted, there we consistently find that it is the privilege of princes, the wealthy or otherwise exceptional people. But to the extent that the broad masses gain rights vis-a-vis the rulers – and acquire not merely political but also moral rights – they shape their own norms of living into morally social laws, by which even those previously excepted from them are now bound. Monogamy, which appears to us in so many ethnological facts as a forced external limitation upon those who cannot be any better off anyway, becomes an inner moral law for everyone as social levelling grows.

This is the same explanatory principle that has been used to derive fasting as a sign of mourning, a custom which is common among many primitive peoples. The fear of the haunting spirit of the deceased moved the bereaved to placate it with generous offerings of food. But since there was very often barely enough food available, such offerings to the dead would lead to scarcities, to enforced fasting, which ultimately came to appear as a morally and religiously necessary consequence of every death.

Once monogamy had become the prevailing conjugal form, those subjective feelings attached themselves to it which are the result of long-prevailing conditions everywhere and which attest to the complete adaptation of individuals to such conditions. What is sometimes said today in justification of marriages of convenience, that love will come with the marriage, is without any doubt true of the historical development of our species. A reversal has taken place here that sociology can detect at many important points: what was a cause for the species is an effect for the individual and vice versa. It was only the validity of monogamy, that had arisen from economic and social circumstances, which brought about the specific feelings of love and lifelong fidelity in the first place; and now conversely, the emergence of this feeling is the impetus for the individual to marry.

The relationship of parents to their offspring has developed through a similar reversal. If all public and lasting institutions lead back to some kind of purpose and use for the social group, then one must also ask what is actually the original purpose of marriage, i.e. the cohabitation of the parents beyond the birth of their offspring? What moved human beings to go to a lasting, duty-laden and often restricting union, rather than merely the momentary satisfaction of the passions?

The social utility that impelled people in this direction was at first perhaps the greater cohesion, the inner support, that society drew from lasting unions. If we consider a group whose elements are in firm reciprocal commitments to one another, living in reliable circumstances, where one person has lasting support from another, which extends a chain of duties through the entire social circle, then such a group will prove more lasting and resistant in the struggle for existence than will another, whose elements know no reciprocal duties, but instead only momentary, arbitrary and therefore constantly fragmenting commitments.

The major social purpose of a secure marriage was obviously the better care for the offspring which it could guarantee, and which already led to marriage-like unions in the animal world. Marriage brings about a division of labour between man and woman which primarily benefits the children. The wife feeds the children and the husband furnishes the wife food; or the husband provides the food and the wife prepares it for him and the children. The combined or competing interest of the parents in the welfare of the children must tend to make the succeeding generation physically and mentally stronger than would have been possible in a group lacking in shared parental care, that is, without marriage. Over time, therefore, marriage creates a direct superiority of the group with respect to a group without marriage, in which the younger generation is abandoned either to the isolated powers of the mother or to communistic care that is devoid of personal interest.

The social functionality [*Zweckmässigkeit*] of marriage enables us to understand a remarkable trait in its development. Among the most diverse peoples around the world, a marriage is not considered to have been entered into in a legally binding manner until the moment when a child is born or expected. Among some tribes – in Asia, Africa and America – the wife remains in her parents' house until this point; in the Philippines and in a district of southern India there is no binding betrothal prior to this point; while in a Senegalese tribe the marriage is not celebrated until that point. In short, the origin of marriage as lying in the social purpose that it is there for the sake of the children makes it into a result of the creation of offspring in the history of the development of our species – whose respective stages are still revealed by these primitive peoples.

Just as love was a consequence of marriage until marriage became a consequence of love, so marriage itself is a consequence of the projection of the next generation until the current reverse relationship arose. It can be clearly seen in both reversals how social development leads more and more from the social interest and the social norm to the interest of the individual as the decisive element. Marriage is the social interest vis-a-vis the individual interest of love; within a different category, the existence and provision for the next generation is the social interest vis-a-vis the personal concern of marriage. This is why, in the earlier stages of development, the first-mentioned factors are the cause of the succeeding ones, whereas the causal connection is reversed in the later stages.

A different development which similarly terminates in the reversal of its starting point leads similarly to the emergence of love from marriage. One of the most frequent forms in which we encounter marriage ceremonies in earlier cultural stages is marriage by purchase or bride-price. The wife is considered first and foremost as a beast of burden, no better than a slave. Indeed, on the lowest level of culture, which does not yet have slavery, she is the only such beast of burden who can be relied upon. The desire to provide oneself with labour power is almost the only real individual interest out of which primitive man moves on to marriage. It is accompanied only by the desire for children, which, by the way, is by no means universal. That the two are connected is seen by the quite frequently encountered custom that credit is extended for the bride-price, but the children belong to the in-laws until it is paid in full. The woman is an object of economic value and therefore her relatives, who have so far been able to utilize her labour power for themselves, do not give her up for nothing, demanding instead an approximate capitalization of her labour value.

The purchase of a woman first of all indicates her low position within the marriage. In most cases, the mere fact of being sold implies that she has no will of her own, but is instead handled by her relatives like an object, and under this aspect she enters into marriage. In this context, the man's objective is to work her as much as possible in order to recover the purchase price. But that is only the superficial side of marriage arranged by purchase. I own what I have acquired with money absolutely and unconditionally, more completely than a possession that comes to me as a result of free will; in all respects, there is less obligation and less consideration attached to such an object. This will appear less harshly where the price consists in personal labour service to the bride's parents. Here at least there is an individual achievement, an employment of one's own personality, which leaves the object acquired in that way with a modicum of its own value, which does not utterly degrade it to the category of a 'thing'. This does occur, however, where women are purchased with money or objects of direct monetary value – cattle, wood or objects of clothing.

Of all the values that practical life has developed, money is the most impersonal. Because it serves as an equivalent for the most contrary things, it is itself completely colourless. All personal values, all individualizations of life end with money, which is why people say that geniality ceases where monetary transactions commence. Money possesses no qualities other than its quantity, and its incomparable significance for all the external things in life therefore corresponds to its complete lack of any relation to all inner, personal values of life. Now this nature of money influences the evaluation of all those things that can be acquired with it. We call something very special and noble that cannot be acquired by just anyone 'priceless'. If a woman sells herself, be it in marriage to a man to whom she is indifferent or in more transient forms, then it seems particularly repulsive to us because the most personal thing a person has to give is being exchanged for such an impersonal value as money. Something analogous is now seen on lower levels. It is generally true that women are treated particularly badly where they are purchased in marriage; their position improves when this conjugal form disappears.

The same thing, however, must now also develop the opposite psychological effect. Precisely because women are a usable object of ownership, the fact that sacrifices are made for their sake ultimately causes them to appear valuable. Everywhere, it has been said, ownership produces love for the possession. It is not merely that we make sacrifices for what we would like to possess, but also, conversely, we love that for which we have made sacrifices. If maternal love is the basis for countless sacrifices for the children, then the trials and tribulations the mother takes upon herself for the child's sake are indeed also a bond that connects her tighter and tighter to it. From this, one can understand why sick or otherwise handicapped children, who demand the sacrificial devotion of the mother, are often the ones she loves the most passionately.

The Church was never ashamed to demand the hardest sacrifices for the love of God, because it was very well aware that the greater the sacrifices we have made for a principle, the more capital we have invested in it, so to speak, the more firmly and intimately committed we are to it. It is therefore probable, psychologically, that the purchase of wives, just as, on the one hand, it degraded women at first must, on the other hand, have elevated them in the estimation of the husband.

This psychological feature is perhaps not completely removed from the modern family. The relatively good position of the woman in the latter corresponds to a material sacrifice of the husband due to his duty to support her, a sacrifice that is relatively much more significant than the bride-price for women in primitive peoples. Yet, because of the fact that this material sacrifice is distributed over the entire lifespan, and, in particular, that it directly benefits the wife herself and not her family, as was earlier the case – the transitional stage of which in later times was the provision of the bride-price to the bride by her parents as a dowry – so precisely those aspects of the sacrifice are preserved which tend to elevate the value of what is gained with it. The sacrifice for the acquisition of a wife, which originally expressed and increased her oppression, her exploitation and her character as an object, in this way contained the psychological feature whose formation led to a direct revaluation of her position.

Translated by Mark Ritter and David Frisby

Sex and Sociality

Comparative Ethnographies of Sexual Objectification

Laura Rival, Don Slater and Daniel Miller

THEORIZING HUMAN SEXUALITY has become a central task for social theorists engaged in the elaboration of new theories of personhood, identity and embodiment. New thinking about human sexuality has grown in a wide and diverse range of contemporary political and intellectual fields: radical feminism, gay, lesbian or queer theorizing, social history and anthropology. It is almost always social constructionist. Social constructionists follow Michel Foucault's historical approach to human sexuality. Their goal is to establish that human sexuality, far from being a natural phenomenon to be explained through fixed and inherent drives – and other biological givens – is (1) fundamentally constructed and contingent; (2) shaped by the hierarchical ordering of dominant social norms, as well as by the ideological and oppressive discourses of modern science; but also (3) reinvented by fully individuated subjects constituted through their sexual desires, who can resist the power of such discursive constructions, build new sexual communities, forge liberating subcultures, and define value systems that respect diversity and choice.

The radical social constructionist denial that there is anything given or natural in sexual organs and human sexuality corresponds to the goal of radical sexual politics: the full realization of all human potentialities, complete autonomy, and total liberation from norms and restrictions.[1] Such thinking puts sexual identities at the centre of social theory because it claims that sexual identities form the core of all social identities and partly determine social positioning. The claim here is that desire (which is by definition sexual, fluid and uncertain) constitutes the foundational core of self-identity, that self-identity requires continuity, and that the continuity of

■ *Theory, Culture & Society* 1998 (SAGE, London, Thousand Oaks and New Delhi),
Vol. 15(3–4): 295–321
[0263-2764(199808/11)15:3–4;295–321;006069]

the person and of her or his inner self is not the inevitable unfolding of some biological truth, but self-made history. We are free, according to this hyper-existentialist manifesto, to choose who to be and how to realize our sexual desires. The individual becomes the artist of his or her life, who 'constructs the self as a creative self' (Weeks, 1995: 45).

Radical social constructionism also challenges the long-established feminist distinction between 'sex', a natural, biological sexual identity, and 'gender', a socially constructed one. It makes sexual embodiment the privileged terrain to test the discursive construction of the real and the material (Butler, 1993). Whereas the earlier generation of feminist scholars challenged patriarchal ideologies that reduced women's prime contribution to society to their 'biological capacity' for nurturing and reproducing, the new gender theorists are fundamentally concerned with the historical subjectivity of sexed individuals and the embodiment of sexual identity, seen as indeterminate, ambiguous and multiple (Morris, 1995). For Judith Butler (1990, 1993), who argues that sexual identity is lived as a highly regulated performance, one is not female; one can only 'do' female. 'Female', a regulatory fiction, is never limited or constrained by an anatomical body, for whereas an individual's identity is fundamentally dependent on her or his sexual identity, this identity cannot easily be found in the body, because bodies are not naturally given. As Henrietta Moore (1994: 6) puts it, 'there are different ways of being gendered because there are different ways of living one's sexuality'. The individual subject as an effect of her or his sexual desire (a desire understood to be shaped by erotic activity rather than determined by genitality) is what social constructionists interested in human sexuality are trying to conceptualize.

Our purpose in this article is not to challenge the social constructionist approach to human sexuality but, rather, to cast a critical eye on the concept of sexual pleasure and on the primacy so many authors give to the construction of erotic roles. While this radical deconstruction of performative sexual identities has much to commend it, the notion of sexuality that underpins it is not ethnographically grounded in any particular social world. It therefore appears abstract, overgeneralized and possibly reflective of a peculiarly Western objectification of sexuality as a thing apart from mundane sociality. As a result, rather than problematizing (historicizing, contextualizing) the category 'sexuality', radical deconstructionists take it for granted and identify it with 'sexual desire' as a seemingly separated domain of erotic experience, love, sex, sexual representation, desire and so forth. Authors such as Butler go so far as to contend that biological reproduction is not a salient question for thinking about gender in our Western, end-of-the-millennium context. When remarking, for example, that 'most women will spend almost all their lives not pregnant, not giving birth and not suckling their young' (in Segal, 1994: 227–8), she implies that for a majority of women in industrialized societies, pregnancy and child-bearing are not the reality of female bodies, but the effects of biomedical and other ideological and prescriptive scientific discourses that produce sexual difference by eliminating all trace of categorical ambivalence on the body. Anthropologists, however, have shown over and over again that people experience sex as embedded in mundane 'reproduction' (including familialism, material and emotional care of the self, routine work for wherewithal, home-keeping and, indeed, life-giving as the potential source of parenthood), and that cultures everywhere relate discourses on sex to issues of procreation and fertility (see Gay-y-Blasco, 1997 and Busby, 1997 for two recent examples). What needs theorizing, therefore, is the relation between the pleasures of the body (sexual pleasure as one among others) and physical reproduction.

Our aim is to problematize sexuality as a domain readily identifiable and clearly objectified by showing that the utopian and transgressive use of sexuality in Western thought largely depends on constituting it as a sphere separate from the domain of mundanity, love and sociality. In order to examine the conditions under which sexuality is objectified as a domain for social practice and cultural production, we propose to start with an examination of Bataille's ideas on eroticism. We then explore sexuality as lived and represented by 'sexpics traders' on the Internet, the Huaorani and Trinidadians, before drawing from this cross-cultural comparative exercise general conclusions which should open the debate on how to re-orient the social analysis of human sexuality.

Bataille's Sacred Sex: Transgression, Sacrifice and Origin

Bataille[2] exemplifies one modernist strategy by which sexuality is constituted as transcendent and transgressive by virtue of its complete separation from nature, biology, function and mundane life, a strategy which also seems to infuse poststructuralist positions that seek to decentre identity as an entirely discursive or performative (cultural) accomplishment.[3] At the same time, Bataille's insistence on a dialectic of taboo and transgression allows us to explore the ways in which even transgressive sexualities are involved with a normative sociality. Bataille's philosophy is Manichaean. Society exists through the positive productivity of labour, order, taboos and morality, political involvement, and social solidarity. But these profane values and moral ideals are not sufficient to make us human; without the sacred (a form of negativity without cause) and eroticism (transgressive excess), we would not be able to make sense of the absurdity and meaninglessness of death, this (too real) impossible. Culture must recognize that social life has two faces, one rational and ordinary, the other destructive and sacred, and that true materialism is not located in the positive force of matter and reproduction, but, instead, in the creativity of the pure spirit encountered in the abject horror of loss, expenditure and death. To experience the sacred through the convulsions induced by orgasm or by the sight of a dead body constitutes the essence of humanity. Bataille's sexual economy is scatological: work and reason must be disrupted by eroticism, a form of violence that wastes energy and hastens the dissolution of the boundaries of the self. Eroticism, or the death of the subject in orgasm, is a necessary condition for achieving transcendence (the inner experience of self-loss); it is also the only form of true communication. At once immanent and transcendental, erotic sexuality lies beyond biological death, the absurd and monstrous condition of finitude which plagues humanity. In other words, we defy death and reach transcendence not by continuing ourselves through others (that is, by being productive, having children, giving ourselves to society and contributing to the general social good), but by engaging in transgressive, mystical and ecstatic experiences, such as erotic activity and watching corpses or moribunds. Bataille insists that the purpose of debauch is to lose oneself in order to become God-like,[4] not to feel sensual pleasure, emotional gratification, or physico-psychic release. The channel through which such experience is consummated is the woman's vagina, particularly that of the mother, the most forbidden woman, or that of a prostitute. A woman's vagina is the most obscene, the most taboo, and the most sacred object.[5] In Bataille's brand of materialism, the body, particularly the sexual organs when used for non-reproductive, wasteful activities, is sacred. The body is sacred because corruptible and mortal. Orgasm as an ecstatic, initiatory experience gains in mysticism if it is attained near a dead body, for both death and fornication are about non-differentiation and loss of individuation.

There are two aspects of Bataille's notion of eroticism we would like to highlight for the purposes of this article. The first one relates to the ways in which his reading of Marcel Mauss departs from that of Claude Lévi-Strauss. Lévi-Strauss and Bataille both interpret the archaic form of exchange represented by gift-giving as a total social fact which cannot be reduced to the rational and utilitarian workings of bourgeois economics. Lévi-Strauss's discussion of Mauss focuses on the Maori *hau* as obligation to reciprocate gifts, from which he abstracts exchange, central to his definition of culture as communication and symbolic order. But the significance of the gift for Bataille lies primarily in the American Pacific Northwest *potlatch* or ceremonial 'wars of wealth'. Archaic exchange, as he sees it, is not about the moral imperative of gift reciprocation; it is, rather, about excess and violence, that is, a totally gratuitous form of expenditure. Both Lévi-Strauss and Bataille interpret sexuality within a general economy which marks the passage from nature to culture. But whereas Lévi-Strauss analyses incest taboo (the rule which obliges men to renounce their sisters and daughters and exchange women in marriage) in terms of reciprocal exchange, Bataille sees the institution of incest taboo as a necessary prerequisite for its violation. For Bataille, who considers reproductive sex natural and animal, and, when performed within the domestic and profane domain of conjugality, a mere positive social expedient, the circulation of women between social groups is not as cultural a mark of our humanity as erotic desire and taboo transgression.[6]

The second aspect of Bataille's thinking on eroticism, we would like to stress, is that he does not see sexual arousal as being primarily about physical satisfaction. A tortured body and a fornicating one, to his mind, attain exactly the same degree of ecstasy. In Bataille's eroticism, sexuality is placed outside of and in opposition to society. It can thus be seen as a new form of moral absolutism based on forbidden longing and transgression which has very little to do with what passes for pornography today – such as it exists in the sex industry for instance. Pornography, rather, is a kind of service by which the needs for pleasure of individual consumers are fulfilled. 'Soft' or 'mainstream' pornography, in particular, is ultimately a form of sublimated energy based on the complementarity of the work of sex workers and the leisure of clients. It might be that porn sex, then, with its exploitation of the hedonic values promoted by the sexual liberation movement and its anti-taboo demands, is closer to a Reichian, rather than a Bataillian, view of sexuality.[7]

Reich's introduction to non-Western sexuality as cultural critique was via Malinowski. His book *The Function of Orgasm* (1993) was inspired by Malinowski's descriptions of the Trobrianders' natural approach to sexuality. Far from opposing culture to nature, Reich took the Rousseauian position that Western culture and its distorted morality foreclosed the true expression of sexual pleasure. Morality, Reich thought, should not be a matter of rules imposed from the outside (by the state or the church), but the natural response of a healthy individual to the situations of life. The natural state of the human body is to be healthy, satisfied and radiant with positive energy. In a way, we could say that for him the Westerner's body is more moral than his repressed mind. His critique of Western culture was therefore diametrically opposed to that of Bataille. Reich set for himself the task of making sexuality rational and positive in a society which he saw as utterly irrational and oppressive. For this, he focused his attention on the material and gender-neutral expression of sexual pleasure: orgasm, or libido. Libido, in his view, was less a state of mind than an objective substance equated to the life force (the *élan vital*), a wave of energy he hoped to measure quantitatively. He saw orgasm as an essentially involuntary release, the virtual loss of consciousness, and the loss of control over bodily movements. Unrepressed, healthy sex was ecstatic surrender, an essential component of the good life, which in no way depended on changing partners; on the contrary, Reich expected it to be especially achievable between balanced individuals forming long-lasting relationships based on true communication (for if language is deceptive, the body does not lie). Finally, as sexual relationships are inseparable from the social order in which they are embedded, Reich was actively promoting social reforms (including, among others, better housing, the abolition of anti-abortion and anti-homosexual laws, new marriage and divorce laws, free birth control advice and contraceptives, nurseries in the workplace, and sex education) aimed at liberating the sexual energy of all individuals – children, women and men alike. To conclude this point, if both Reich and Bataille were searching for a new moral order, while Reich based his model on the self-regulation of naturally good and measured desires freed from compulsion and external imposition, Bataille defended the idea that sexuality was not to be enjoyed, but experienced as a religious sacrifice, through shame, guilt and transgression. Bataille's conception of sexuality was religious in nature, and based on the heteronomic internalization of the sacred, which he located beyond morality, rationality and sociality.

However brief the summary of the ideas of these two thinkers, it makes it clear why they have had a major influence on contemporary views on human sexuality and why constructionists would discard Reich as a 'naturalizer' while praising Bataille as the enlightened authority on transgression and the experiences and discourses of transgressors. Our objection to such praise is no less clear: we are doubtful that transgressive behaviours illuminate normative discourses better than non-transgressive behaviours do. Whatever the categories to which they belong, in the Bataillian view transgressors represent marginal social identities whose social subjectivity is marked as being especially sexual. They create their singular individual identities by transgressing the dominant norms they refuse. It is not surprising, therefore, that their sense of identity, derived from their wish to adopt alternative norms, appears to be constituted in discourse even before it gets lived as embodied experience. As a contrary case, the next section argues that the ostensibly transgressive and extremely objectified or separated sexual domain constituted by the sexpics traders studied by Slater has actually to be understood in relation to normative, mundane, 'functional' and reproductive issues that structure both on-line and off-line contexts of their activities.

On-line Regulated Transgressions: Trading Sexpics on the Internet

Trading sexpics on IRC defines a very specific ethnographic setting: Internet Relay Chat is a system of communication in real time, via the Internet, through the exchange of typed lines of text. Individuals run software on their local computers that links them via ordinary Internet connection to networks with as many as 20,000 other people concurrently logged on. They can send lines of text to any of these people either individually or as participants in channels, public spaces in which a line of text typed by any one person can be seen by all the others. If one can send a typed line of text to anyone, one can send any digitized information, hence any kind of representation: still image, sound, video, text. This enables the activity of 'trading sexpics': the circulation, exchange, accumulation and consumption of sexually explicit representations. Moreover, the chat, the real-time communication via typed text, can itself become eroticized as representations, flirting, heated and pleasurable sex talk, cybersex, in which the actual encounter between participants becomes, as the typical comment goes, 'like being inside a piece of interactive pornography'. Trading and chatting intertwine, and often come to resemble each other, for sexuality seems to have been disembodied, hived off into strategies and skills of representation in a place apart.[8]

Sexpics trading on IRC would seem a likely candidate for representing a world-historical extreme in constituting sexuality as an objectified sphere that is both transgressive and separate from mundane life. Participants clearly see IRC sexpics trading and chatting as a place of sexual transgression and 'going beyond': this includes both looking at things forbidden and previously not experienced, as well as acting out desires in relation to the images or through conversation or fantasy with others. Women informants in particular have regularly told Slater that IRC allows them to explore desires which are too taboo, embarrassing or dangerous for off-line life: mainly bisexuality, exhibitionism, group sex and promiscuity. Informants often say that IRC's cardinal attraction is the licence simply to float pleasurably through a shamelessly eroticized space. These pleasures and transgressions evidently depend upon a clear separation of sexuality from 'real life': they are without commitment or consequence; the material resources on which they depend (finance, technology, symbolic capital, labour) are obscured from view and experienced as beyond any scarcity. IRC sexuality clearly mirrors the world constructed within mainstream pornography: there are no material cares or dangers (including disease); no enduring commitments; performance is unproblematic; desire is inexhaustible, as is desirability (everyone is desired and included). Bodies neither fail, nor make non-sexual demands. Nothing external challenges the integrity of 'the sexual'. It is not merely procreation that is excluded from both pornography and IRC: they edit out a mundanity that comprises everything which makes up the work of reproducing everyday life; there are no families, no paid or unpaid work, no necessary care of the body or self unless these are themselves eroticized. Indeed, both pornography and its circulation on IRC depend on eroticizing labour; they are worlds of pure consumption in which the moment of production (taking the picture) is seen as a sexual moment for both the models and the photographer.

The 'apartness' of IRC and its sexual domain depends on this ability to absorb everything within this undisturbed sexual moment. For example, references to bodily care on IRC ('I'm off to take a shower') tend to be eroticized ('she's wet and steamy now'). The pornographic on IRC has to be captured through transitive verbs: everything is, or can be, eroticized or 'pornographied'. 'To pornography' the other is to absorb her or him within this place of desire beyond the cares of the world. In this orientation, sexuality is neither an end in itself nor an acid which corrodes an oppressive social order. It is rather a colour that one might paint over the greyness of the mundane. This sense of 'pornographying' the other and the world is contained in one of the most common statements made in this setting: although the pictures and cybersex are obsessively, monotonously genital and orgasmic (in the end, everything is organized around people fucking and 'cuming' [word used by informants]), virtually everyone declares that cybersex is boring and that they don't look at the pics very much. What they do like is flirting, talking about sex, trading pics within a pleasurable chat, watching new pics scroll down their screen. In short, what holds people is a sensually coated ambience more than orgasmic stimuli. Interestingly, participants often talk about IRC itself and pornography in very similar terms: they are both places apart which allow the indulgence of amorphous pleasures, utopias without time or space which are also, because they are so pleasurable and because they seem to remove one from mundane space, time and needs, deemed 'addictive'. There is a constantly expressed fear, or guilt, about getting lost 'out there'.

These experiences of the separateness of sexuality objectified in a utopic place apart from the mundane are quite real to participants and constitutive of their world. However it would be quite wide of the mark to assimilate this to some of the contemporary theoretical agendas that have been projected on to 'cyberspace': it is not part of a project of deconstructing sex, gender or sexuality, but rather a way of experiencing pleasures within fairly stable constructions of these. Indeed, it could be argued that much of what I have been observing *aims at* finding a route back to mundane versions of sexuality and familiality.

This point can be elaborated on several levels. First, although participants on IRC are intensely aware of the performative nature of their on-line identities and encounters (you are what you type), they have a seemingly unchallengeable core belief in authenticity. Hence, performativity is not taken up as an opportunity to deconstruct notions of identity, but rather constitutes a pervasive series of issues about deception and credulity: it is a basis for disbelieving almost everything, treating most events and people as occasions for purely immediate pleasures, and for devising strategies for 'authenticating' the other (for deciding when and on what basis to accept their identity claims). There is a consistent assumption that all performances can be traced back to a real other to which they do or do not correspond (they can be true, deceptive, or 'true at some level', or 'just playing'). That which is performed, one's 'sexuality', is also deemed to be more or less true to a real self: hence IRC can be about exploring what had been 'hidden' within one, or repressed. More often, it is treated simply at the level of individual choice: 'this is what I feel like', 'this is what I like'. The exploration of desire is not deemed to produce a sexuality, but to gratify or develop an existing one. In this respect, the ideology of IRC on-line sexuality is not deconstructive but libertarian: anything goes, but nothing is particularly challenged. In other words, while privileging sexuality as a place of exploration and transgression, this ideology also uses sexuality as an idiom through which an authentic self finds its own normality, even by way of actions which outsiders might find to be extreme. IRC sexpics trading involves an almost consumerist normality in which individuals choose things in a manner that never gets near challenging the choosing self. This frequently takes an explicitly political form – even an organized form, as in resistance to the American Communications Decency Act – which clearly treats sexuality as the exemplary or foundational instance of modern freedom: uncompelled acts of choice by consenting adult egos. 'Extreme' sexuality then acts as an idiom through which to negotiate the most mundane and normative consumerist self.

Second, maintaining the sexualized ambience of IRC requires considerable mundane labour of social reproduction: organizing and policing channels, socializing newbies, overcoming endless technical problems, extending and adapting the software in order to make the right things happen smoothly (and usually automatically). For many, the technocratic concern with ordering this social world and its contents, maintaining its internal routines, is more important than the sexuality it contains. However, it is not only that sexpics trading venues are normative orders (neither lawless, nor amorphous, nor unstable), with complex mechanisms for sustaining themselves as such; it is also that their norms are extremely, almost bizarrely, conventional. Two examples may suffice. The first concerns the way conventional notions of sexuality are used to draw social and textual boundaries. There is heavy policing (by ops but also by ordinary participants) against a standard list of pariah sexualities (child porn, bestiality or rape). This does not involve either a deconstructive sense that our own 'normal' sexualities might arise in relation to the exclusions and inclusions we operate, nor a conservative rejection of particular sexualities as evil or wrong. Rather, there is, again, a libertarian sense of 'to each their own': 'people can do what they like as long as they don't do it here, and as long as it has nothing to do with me'. This is even clearer in the more major exclusion: male homosexuality is contained in completely separate networks and channels. The scene Slater has been investigating is entirely structured on the premise that men are heterosexual and women are bisexual. While most of the homophobia is implicit rather than open and aggressive, nonetheless, in these IRC venues core sexualities are not questioned or treated as performative. They are socially mapped on to normative boundaries between groups or camps that are not regarded as affecting each other. Moreover, the sexualities which are deemed permissible and are performed clearly mirror mainstream pornography: women's bisexuality encompasses their complete connectability, their position at the centre of all desires; men insatiably desire, but only women. Both the pornography traded and the sexualities that are enacted may include fairly extreme or 'hard' variations within these conventional structures, but these structures are rarely challenged.

A further example of the normativity of IRC transgression moves us beyond sexuality to economy. There is essentially an inexhaustible supply of 'free' sexpics on IRC: it is a post-scarcity and post-value world. And, yet, it is completely obsessed with rules of exchange and with exchange ratios. For example, much exchange is carried out by way of 'fserves', a program which allows one person to open their hard disk drive to another. One can look through the fserver's directories, choose and pick pics, and set an exchange rate ('send me 1:4'). Exchange values are then programmed into the software; they are also ethically enforced through constant, tedious castigation of 'leechers' and 'leeching', i.e. people who take without giving.

The fantasy space of on-line sexuality sits within ongoing everydayness, both on-line and off, defined as 'real' by participants. If we have questioned the trangressive character of this reality, we might now also question its apartness, as a sphere of sexual objectifications, from other and specifically 'off-line' realities. In fact, the ethnographic sense of the ways participants treat sexpics trading on IRC as a world apart from or connected to 'real life' is highly varied.[9] There are at least three different takes on this that emerge from people's talk. They may, first and most commonly, talk of sexpics activities as pure play: 'it is just fun'. It offers the freedom to explore kinds of fun and fantasy which are not accessible off-line (public sex, group sex, bisexuality) but which connect to 'real' (i.e. off-line) desires. But play is understood here in a classic way: it is clearly bounded, contained, 'real' only within a frame that clearly says 'play'. Participants seem quite clear that unless authentically grounded in real off-line bodies and identities then none of this should be taken too seriously. Indeed, taking this on-line world for real is the one consistently articulated notion of pathology. More dangerous than anything fantasized is the fallacy of taking fantasy for reality.

This danger, or temptation, of taking fantasy for reality arises not only from credulity but also from alienation: In this context, 'real life' means the world of immediate everydayness: home, family, paid and unpaid work milieus. Participants talk of everyday life as boring, a drudgery of maintaining self and family. And it is frequently characterized as a lonely place, a place where one is aware of one's separation from others, including one's partner or family. A large amount of chatting in sexpics venues is about everyday life. Many logged conversations move within minutes from tastes in porn to the problems of single-parenthood, money problems, dead-end jobs. IRC sexuality is explicitly understood as escapist in relation to the alienation and the loneliness. So too is IRC sociality: these are intense, yet uncommitted, encounters in which 'the other' seems to be (and in some respects is) 'in your head'. It is also understood, though, that this escapism can tend in two different directions towards 'realization', and these provide the alternative ways of relating sexpics trading on IRC to 'real life'. On the one hand, one can try to make cyber-relationships (sexual or not) ever more 'real', more embodied (by making them endure, by moving on to voice communication, or real-life meetings). This challenge to the everyday is often marked by the boundary-defining question: 'Is cyber-sex cheating on your RL partner?' Moreover, idealized ethics of the everyday are imported to govern cyber relationships (they can be cloyingly romantic, jealously monogamous, with clear rules about trust, honesty, spending time together, permissible sexual acts and so on which replicate on-line the structures of off-line domesticity). Rather than treating IRC as escapist, then, participants may want cyber-relationships and cyber-sexuality to *really* embody and actualize the ideals they have imported from their off-line life. On the other hand, sexpics trading and chat may be used to eroticize the everyday and the familial: as an aphrodisiac for real life, a way of getting both stimulation and ideas for the domestic. IRC space sometimes acts as a kind of erotic overlay on the domestic scene, giving it a charge; not to challenge relationships, but to make them a bit more exciting. Following this route, conventional domestic life is compatible with the sexualities enacted on-line, not challenged but rather revived by them. However, whether IRC sexpics trading is seen as escapist, ideal or therapeutic in relation to 'real life', each constitutes an intimate connection with the mundane which is clearly reflected on by participants.

The sexpics trading scene we have sketched above is difficult to assimilate to some of the contemporary poststructuralist and cyber agendas that have been projected on to 'cyberspace' (for key discussions see Bassett, 1997; Dery, 1994; Featherstone and Burrows, 1995; Haraway, 1990; Plant, 1995, 1996, 1997; Porter, 1997; Springer, 1996; Stone, 1996; Turkle, 1995). This scene does not simply lead us backwards from bodies and genders to the discursively constructed sexualities that structure them, but also forwards to the mundane versions of everyday life, domesticity and reproduction in which they are all embedded and on whose conventional normativity they draw. Whereas the 'apartness' of virtual realities and their potentially transformative impact on mundane or naturalized identities play a central part in the intelligentsia's reception of 'cybersex', ethnographic engagement in 'cyberspace' shows that, far from being the domain of 'lawlessness', transgression, danger and release from social bonds, taboos and the profane, on-line sexuality is experienced by IRC participants as a place that, in offering a total (because physically unbounded) freedom to transgress, allows them to raise all the promises of modernity (to constitute the self, in this instance through the privileged 'laboratory' of sexual desire), but then to contain them within tight normative constraints. These almost Durkheimian moral structures of sociality not only regulate their particular patch of cyberspace but do so according to norms that bring it very close to the mundane and domestic sphere which it, like the transgressive sexuality it contains, putatively escapes and challenges. It seems to us that this 'world apart' of inexhaustible and transgressive sexuality is circumscribed by mundane values of exchange ratios, technique, order and organization, and that a passion for cataloguing may play a far more significant role in its regulation than does sexual desire. We would like to argue that sexpics traders on IRC tend to use sexuality and sexual materials as another occasion to construct and reproduce a social order where moral interests and the care of reproduction take precedence over erotica. In our view, a proper understanding of such a highly objectified form of sexuality requires its comparison with forms of sexuality that do not appear so divorced from mundane and reproductive sociality. In the next section, we discuss the embeddedness of Huaorani sexuality, and the ways it is transparently constitutive of the social bonds into which it is integrated.

Sensual Reproductivity in the Amazon: Huaorani 'Two-Making' Sex

Ongoing common residence in the longhouse is the basis of sociality for the Huaorani of Amazonian Ecuador,[10] who practise sensuality, not as the realization of private fantasies, but as the bodily expression of sharing relations. The overall population is divided into dispersed networks of inter-marrying longhouses separated by vast stretches of unoccupied forest. Traditional longhouses are typically occupied by an older couple (often a man married to one, two, or three sisters), their daughters (with, when married, their husbands and children), and their unmarried sons; they may comprise between 10 and 35 members. Allied and inter-marrying longhouses form loose regional aggregates. Contact with groups belonging to other aggregates (considered potential enemies) is avoided. Relations between longhouse co-residents are more intimate, caring and close than those between blood kin living in different longhouses. Most marriages are uxorilocal and take place between cross-cousins. Men, who start their married careers in their wives' house-groups almost as strangers, are gradually incorporated as they father children. Gender and intergenerational differences are played down, and personal autonomy, egalitarianism and longhouse sharing highly valued (Rival, 1992, 1996, 1998, in press, forthcoming).

Persons and communities are conceptualized as processes that unfold in time through the cumulative experience of living side by side, day after day. By continuously feeding each other, eating the same food and sleeping together, people who live together develop a shared physicality of greater import than that resulting from genealogical bonds. Togetherness is expressed, and continuously reasserted, through sharing practices. The repeated and undifferentiated *action* of sharing that goes on within the longhouse turns co-residents into a single, indistinct substance, so that people living in the same longhouse gradually become of the same substance, literally 'of the same flesh' (*aroboqui baön anobain*). Longhouse members share illnesses, parasites, a common dwelling and a common territory. Sensual bonding, as diffuse as food sharing, unfolds as one aspect of the pleasure of living in each other's company. Everyone partakes in everyone else's care and well-being; the more people spend time together, the more they become alike.

Sensuality in this culture is not centred on genitalia, nor is it the exclusive domain of adult heterosexuality; it should not, therefore, be assimilated to 'sexual pleasure'. Children seek sensual pleasure as actively as adults do (or perhaps even more), for sensuality, which does not require sexual maturity, is an essential part of belonging to the collectivity. Huaorani culture does not eroticize sensuality, nor does it differentiate genital pleasure from other bodily pleasures. For example, no distinction is made between the pleasure and contentment felt during sexual intercourse, the pleasure and contentment of a 3-year-old caressing the breast of the woman from whom she or he is feeding, the merry feeling of someone stroking gently the body of a caressing companion,[11] the gratification caused by the action of delousing someone's head, or the pleasure of being deloused by someone's expert hands. It is, of course, extremely difficult for Westerners to accept that these intimate relations are not eroticized, and journalists of the British tabloid press would almost certainly report them as being sexual. To them, social relations are all potentially sexual and all based on power differential. Media coverage of 'deviant' sexual behaviour in our society reflects (or creates?) the fear that no relation is immune to the quicksilver effect of sexual desire, especially not the most intimate ones. Intimate relations between blood kin are represented as being no less sexually exploitative than those between strangers, and children as being, not innocent angels, but social agents capable of the same immoral actions as adults. By contrast, sexuality is never used in Huaorani society to create power differentials, or to transgress social norms. When Huaorani people talk about sensuality, they mean 'we live well' (*huaponi quehuemonipa*); to them, sensual pleasure, or promiscuous well-being, is simply one of the ways in which the longhouse sharing economy gets materialized (Rival, 1996). The need for comfort and physical contact is never construed as sexual, nor the desire for affection taken to be a desire for sex (see also Liedloff, 1986: 151, 152). It might be that anti-orgasmic sex is particularly valued on aesthetic grounds, or, perhaps more simply, that bodies are socialized to experience diffuse, unfocused pleasures. In any case, low-level sexual energy in this cultural context does not appear to be caused by the fear of losing life force or other vital substances through intercourse.

Whereas sensuality, like all forms of bodily pleasures, is amorphous and diffuse, reproductive sexuality, the conscious and focused action of making a child, is goal-oriented. As the Huaorani see it, sexuality is the reproductive activity by which heterosexual pairs (men and women who are not siblings, belong to the same generation, and are of approximately the same chronological age) are 'two-making' (*mina pa*), or 'sleep as one' (*arome mö*; *mö* means both 'to sleep' and 'to be married'), and, consequently, 'multiply through copulation' (*niñcopa*). *Niñe* is the action through which all sexed animals reproduce, from crocodiles, to birds, jaguars, monkeys or dogs. Making love involves two persons in one hammock, and only two, so if a man has several wives, he goes from one hammock to the next, in turn. Repeated intercourse is considered necessary for a woman to get pregnant, and for the foetus to grow. As it is believed that the foetus is made of equal quantities of male semen and womb blood, two or three genitors can contribute semen.[12] That the word *tapey*, which literally means 'let's make another child', is what women say to men when they want to copulate illustrates the fact that sexual intercourse is overtly geared towards repro-duction. Unless used between a woman and her (classificatory) husband(s), the word *tapey*, considered obscene, may be the cause of considerable embarrassment. Having babies is not seen as a by-product of sexual pleasure, but as a reward in itself, for adulthood is about pairing and giving birth to children.[13]

Finally, it must be noted that Huaorani culture does not represent men and women as classes of people constituted by and through sexual desire, except, perhaps, in myths on lethal sexual attraction between humans and animals. A great number of myths concern women who copulate with animals (anacondas, monkeys, tapirs and so forth). They invariably become pregnant, and, their insides devoured by the monstrous foetuses they carry, die. The myth of a young woman fatally attracted to a giant earth worm who resides underground beneath the longhouse and next to the hearth is particularly explicit about the awesome pleasure she derives from her repeated sexual encounters with the beast. The only myth about male bestiality relates the story of a man who finds the genitalia of the nutria (Amazon dolphin) identical to, and far more desirable than, those of a human female. He derives so much pleasure from copulating over and over again with the she-dolphin, that he ends up wasting all his blood and semen, drowns and dies in his animal lover's dwelling at the bottom of the river. On the basis of numerous conversations with informants as well as ethnographic observations, Rival understands these myths to express the asocial nature of excessive sexual desire and unreasonable attraction. They also, albeit more indirectly, suggest that sexuality is really about 'child making' (Rival, in press).

In ending this section, we would like to stress that our analysis of Huaorani sexuality and sensuality differs substantially from previous interpretations of sexuality in Amazonia, in particular from those offered by North American cultural anthropologists writing in the wake of the US women's liberation movement. These authors discuss sexuality in terms of sexual antagonism and 'war between the sexes' (Gregor, 1985; Kensinger, 1995; Murphy and Murphy, 1974; Siskind, 1973). They see Amazonia as the land of gang rape par excellence, and argue that masculine psychology, structured by anxiety, chronic sexual frustration and high levels of dissatis-faction, is fundamentally similar in both Euroamerican and Amazonian cultural settings. As they see it, Euroamerican and Amazonian men equally view women as alluring, emasculating and arousing primitive fears of dependence and loss of male identity. Gregor (1985: 201), for example, remarks that 'few Mehikanu relationships or institutions escape the tensions generated by sexual desire and frustration', and Kensinger (1995:78) that 'Cashinahua men and women agree that although it gives pleasure, sex is a source of danger.' Kensinger (1995: 75) adds that Cashinahua men think that women are 'stingy with their genitals' and offer sexual services in exchange for gifts, especially of meat (see also Siskind, 1973). Gregor finds this functional use of sex absolutely identical to what goes on in North America, where, he says, 'courtship and dating reflect the fact that sex is a service that women provide for men in exchange for financial and social commitment' (Gregor, 1985: 201). Following Murphy and Murphy's (1974) influential *Women of the Forest*, these authors propose a Freudian interpre-tation of masculine sexual frustrations, anxieties and defensive reactions as expressed in Amazonian myths, rituals and other cultural practices. This leads them to contrast, not personality types (these are structured by identical psychodynamics), but social arrangements, and to argue that lowland South American institutions make manifest the universal anxieties aroused by the separation from the mother, that similarly structure male individual personalities all around the world. Whereas the ongoing battle of the sexes and the pervasiveness of sexual ideas is blunted in Euroamerican societies (divided by class, education, religion, race, vocation and so forth), it is manifest in Amazonian men's houses, fertility and initiation rituals, gendered work activities and sexual ideologies. Lack of hierarchy and power asymmetry actually exacerbates sexual antagonism, which often becomes public, as villages form into two gender groups throwing insults at each other. Men may proclaim their superiority over women by virtue of possessing penises, but women normally ignore these proclamations and in no way see themselves as inferior to men (Kensinger, 1995: 75).

It is true that in some Amazonian societies cross-gender social inter-actions are conflictual, and that cosmologies are often male-biased. However, it would be wrong to interpret all complementary oppositions (self/other, kin/affine, victim/killer, virilocal/uxorilocal and so forth) in sexual terms, as if they were variations on the same universal theme. The fact that hostility between the sexes, confined to highly ritualized contexts, is largely absent from daily interactions should be analysed in the context of mundane activities, rather than in terms of symbolic structures. Moreover, the fact that cosmological systems are saturated with sexual and other bodily images (Reichel-Dolmatoff, 1971; Roe, 1982) should be understood as an expression of the importance of organic life, fertility and biological reproduction in Amazonian social philosophies.

As we have tried to show here, Huaorani sexuality is embedded in the care of reproduction. Sexuality as an objectified domain referring to the physical relations between the sexes does not exist as such. On the one hand, sensuality, the physical pleasure of harmonious living, is neither caused or expressed in sexual desire, nor restrictive: all longhouse residents, whatever their age, gender or kin affiliation, behave sensually towards each other. Entirely engulfed in the domestic and its organicity, sensuality is the *art de vivre* of individuals who have chosen to share a common residence. In a society that defines relationships with non-co-residents as dangerous and predatory, sensuality and intimacy form the two sides of the same everyday social reality. Reproductive sexuality, on the other hand, creates physical, spiritual and social bonds between a woman, a man (sometimes two) and a baby, the fruit of their copulation. This bond, considered neither more biological nor less social than the ties formed around eating the same food or sleeping side by side, is both the expression of individual growth and development (sexually mature youth are expected to pair with cross-sex, cross-cousin partners, and produce children), and the manifestation of intra- and inter-longhouse marriage politics. Social repro-duction depends on the formation of strong and long lasting heterosexual pairs. Married couples with adult offspring form the core of residence units, and solid alliances between longhouses invariably develop around strong brother–sister ties. Sociality, the good life and the creation of intimate communities through everyday sharing equally depend on gender comp-lementarity in reproduction, seen as the natural development of the human potential asserted against the inhumanity of predation and violent death. Killing and warfare, overtly aimed at breaking up house-groups, are in some ways considered the inevitable outcome of the tragic position of men in this society. Men do not exert violence against women,[14] but against their condition of incorporated husbands and fathers. Their aggression, caused by a form of homicidal fury (*pïï*), a typically male emotion, is not expressed sexually. Killing may start as a morally motivated act of legitimate vengeance, but it easily degenerates into the desire to kill for the sake of killing. Killers are driven to the solitary and asocial position of pure individuals who are not afraid of 'living alone with the trees' (Rival, forthcoming).

Sexed Bodies in Trinidad: Erotica and Health

If the Amazonian case demonstrates the possibility of a minimally objectified sexuality and the trade in sexpics appears, at first, to illustrate the maximal objectification of sexuality in the sense of being abstracted out as a thing in and of itself, then Trinidad presents an important third possibility for the comparative objectification of sexuality. Because of its continuous presence in dialogue, sexuality in Trinidad often appears as the maximally objectified perspective which seems to dominate most social relations. But in contrast to the case of sexpics, the ubiquity of sexuality in Trinidad is a sign of its importance as an idiom. So far from being abstracted as an autonomous medium of relationships, it becomes the linchpin which seems to hold together a huge field of practices and aspects of identity.

Research in recent years has continued to demolish the foundations of the crass stereotypes about race and sexuality that were once prevalent in the region, thus rendering the task of addressing sexuality directly easier. Even Fanon's (1986) most subtle and critical analysis of West Indian sexuality could be thought of as continuing the tradition of generalizing 'black' sexuality in terms which, in other discourses, have been used to characterize people as essentially animalistic or primitivist. In contemporary Trinidad, however, the discourse of sexuality plays a central role in a multitude of social and cultural dimensions, for all the island's diverse populations, including groups who identify themselves as South Asian, Chinese and Middle Eastern, and who would be more commonly stereotyped as having anything but such a relationship with sexuality.

The research we are concerned with is quite diverse in as much as it includes highly detailed ethnographic accounts of the interaction between factory floor workers (Yelvington, 1995, 1996), the study of the use of health care centres by teenage mothers (McCartney, 1997), the role of sexuality with respect to general issues of modernity (Miller, 1994) and the more specific arena of Carnival (Miller, 1991). What emerges from this work is first that sexuality is a highly overt and constantly foregrounded mode of social relations. This is true of the sexual act itself, where there is a constant discourse around sex as comparative performance with attention to amounts of sex, types of sex and sexual ability. A woman will stake her claim that few men could engage with her without risking a heart attack, and a man will be constantly concerned with the sexual encounters he may claim to have achieved. But the act of sex is also surrounded by a vast additional discourse that includes many 'sweet talk' rhetorics, as well as comparative insults making use of sexual innuendo. Claims are equally prevalent about who makes babies for whom as the evidence for sex, and there are activities such as dance that become a form of 'virtual sex' in that they provide public spectacles for encounters which are very close to simulated sexual perform-ance.

Earlier studies of sexuality in Trinidad (for example, Freilich, 1969) analysed sexuality in connection with the state of gender relations per se, and compared it to similar issues of gender and power elsewhere. The fact that male sociality is formed through boasting about and achieving sexual relations with women was particularly stressed. More recent studies, however, have tended to elucidate the more specific and nuanced use of sexuality in Trinidad both in itself and increasingly as a larger idiom which does not relate simply to sexuality and gender as separate aspects of identity or practice but which instead examines how sexuality unites diverse fields and sometimes seems foundational to them all.

These later ethnographic observers then argue for an anthropological encounter with this phenomenon which quickly goes beyond the super-ficiality of sex as an objectified arena directed only at itself as a topic. The importance of sex in Trinidad is clarified when it is seen as being about many other things that might not be related to this domain elsewhere. As Miller's (1991, 1994: 113–25) analysis of dance has shown, sex is above all an idiom. He researched a dance form called 'wining' which is character-istic of the many *fetes* (parties) that are most common in Carnival season but are also found at other times of the year. Wining is also the dominant dance movement within Carnival itself. The form of the dance clearly refers to sexual intercourse itself, and can be observed to operate as a discourse about the nature of sexual relations. Contemporary wining is dominated by women, especially during Carnival. Miller argued that as used in parties wining becomes an idiom through which the wider relationship between genders, which most commonly takes the form of acts of exchange, is developed as a commentary upon gender relations in general, as well as between any two particular individuals. Once established as marking the place occupied by sexual activity within gender relations, wining within contemporary Carnival is transformed by individual women into a largely autonomous dance, which then may be interpreted as the movement by which the larger history of Carnival as an objectification of freedom becomes a more specific experience of freedom experienced as the repudia-tion of normative sociality.

Yelvington's (1995, 1996) work on the factory floor extends these concerns with sexuality as idiom. He suggests that flirting and sexual innuendo have become the main forms in which power relations (both between the genders and between workers, and between managers and employers) have taken shape, and are exhibited and negotiated in daily practice. As in many other societies, skills developed in innuendo and allusion complement skills and reputations in the physical technologies of sexual practice, both with the same potential of becoming important components of power relations. These relations are as much about the tensions between competition and collaboration amongst peers as they are about living within hierarchized vertical relations evident in the organization of the work place.

McCartney's (1997) work starts with the issue of health and health care. She found that while the state often resorts to a rhetoric that sees teenage pregnancy as a problem and evidence of unhealthy practices with unhealthy consequences, teenage pregnancy is actually prompted by a counter-discourse in which sex and having babies are the single most important forms by which many people recognize the evidence for good health. It is the lack of active sexual relations and a lack of consequential conception that are viewed as a major cause and sign of ill health. So, far from the erotic nature of sexuality depending upon a separation from issues of reproduction, the phrase 'making babies' is crucial to any claim made by either males or females with respect to sexual prowess, access and above all sexual health.

From observations that start with issues of sexuality as an expression of health, McCartney then shows how these become the medium by which a person's maturation and development are understood. Sexuality thereby becomes fundamental to the sense of what it is to be a person. This then connects to Miller's observation (1994: 257–90) that the core contradictions of modernity in Trinidad, which in turn are projected upon a diverse range of distinctions such as ethnicity, age and class, are themselves increasingly reliant upon sexuality or its negation as their medium of objectification. As such the place of sexuality is best viewed within a comparative understanding of the potential of sexuality as a mode of human objectification. The degree of importance given to sexuality makes it more, rather than less, subject to clear limitations and moral discourses determining the definition of what is taboo or transgressive. In many respects, Trinidad appears a highly prurient society which clearly excludes forms of sexuality that are regarded as deviant. And the level of censorship of what in other areas would be seen as relatively mild forms of sexual transgression is generally high.

Generalizations are obviously much more problematic when talking about Trinidadian society than either the small-scale setting of the Huaorani, or the self-selected group of people studied in Slater's ethnography of sexpic exchanges on the Internet. Miller (1994) provides a much more detailed argument about how such generalizations should be read with respect to the diversity of contemporary Trinidadian experience. There are important sections of the population for whom these statements simply would not hold. He suggests that, although there might be a tendency for this dominance of sexuality and sexual technique to be associated with males, it is no more than a tendency; the clearest examples of this use of sexuality as discourse are actually found among women. Although McCartney's, Miller's and Yelvington's research involved a wide range of people asserting a variety of ethnic identities, in all three cases the research was dominated by female rather than male informants.

The case of Trinidad extends our attempt to use anthropology to forge a third path between the essentialism of psychological and of some psycho-analytical perspectives, and the relativism of some of the recent approaches to sexuality as performance. To be a person in Trinidad returns one to the materiality of sexuality, i.e. to the sexual act itself, the discourses of sex, and the basic question as to what sex is good for as a medium. While in some social contexts the key to sexuality is the social relation between those involved, Trinidadians exploring the possibilities of freedom demonstrate the ability to separate sex out from any concomitant social relation between sexual partners. A degree of engagement in wining or sex itself does not necessarily betoken the emergence of a social relation between those engaged. And if babies become signs of the health of their biological progenitors, neither of them may act as actual parents. The kin connections can move directly to the father's female relatives, while virtually missing out the father himself (see also Smith, 1988, for a comparison with Jamaica).

The case of Trinidad demonstrates how difficult it is to generalize about the implications of sexuality as a highly objectified medium. Objectification does not here imply separation out from the wider context of sociality or discourses which comment upon sexuality. Rather, the relatively abstracted form of sex and sex discourses means that this contextualization may be very different from that which might be expected if we assume that we know what the consequences of having sex or making babies would be in some particular region.

Conclusion: Human Sexuality, Potentialities and Objectifications

Our reason for picking these three ethnographic cases is that if each of them written in isolation could be disregarded as exotic or aberrant, placed together, we wish to argue, they suggest that sexuality and gender relations more generally are too pliable an arena of social practice to be limited to issues such as sexual desire as a motif of liberation or the parameters of gender conceptualization. It is not the ethnography but the theoretical speculation on the utopian potentialities of sexuality that needs to be rescinded in favour of such encounters with the comparative normativity of sexuality within society. There also seems to be a wider sphere of sociality at stake here, and this is the case whether the objectification of sexuality is minimal, as among the Huaorani, or maximal, as in the trade of sexpics on the Internet. Sexpics traders on IRC still connect transgressive sexuality with mundane sociality, including the care of reproduction, even if the connection is not as direct and as immediate as it is amongst the Huaorani.

While the poststructuralist appropriation of Bataille celebrates the liberation represented by the transgressive, a study of sexuality in social formations returns to the Durkheimian roots of Bataille's work, emphasizing transgression as a mechanism for creating and maintaining moral orders. It also returns us to the influence of Mauss on the study of comparative objectification. Some of the ethnographic material is compatible with Bataille's understanding of the moral foundation of sexuality. For example, the interpretation of wining as a medium for a quasi-transcendental release from the world in Trinidad (Miller, 1991) or the use of sexpics to transcend the conventional limitations of the concept of the self. Both of these suggest that wider segments of society, and not just a social theorist, may follow the logics of abstracted eroticism as part of an exploration of the potentialities of modernity. On the other hand, these three case studies firmly refute that any construction of the erotic is fundamentally dependent upon its separation from what Bataille regarded as 'functionalist' sexuality represented in particular by the connection between sexuality and reproduction. This assumption, part of a more general anti-functionalism central to Bataille's thinking, not only constituted one of the basic tenets of his work, but it has also continued to have a considerable influence on contemporary theories of sexuality and gender.

Our starting point was a study of the Huaorani which comes to serve as an example of just how far the element of separation – which we might have assumed to be intrinsic – can in fact be denied within ordinary human practices. Among the Huaorani, sexuality as a domain is entirely sub-servient to the concerns over reproductive sociality. Both sex and sensuality are directed to the making of other people than oneself. In a society where personal autonomy is a paramount value, individuals do not become subjects through loss or through the narcissistic satisfaction of erotic desires. Any potential for abstracted objectification is denied in its diffusion within the larger social formation. It would be easy enough to bracket the Huaorani as outside of such debates – as an 'exotic' Amazonian example typical only of anthropological relativism. This is why it is juxtaposed here with two other case studies. For the relevant section of the Trinidadian population we find the opposite situation, where sexuality per se is objectified to an extraordinary degree. Yet, far from depending upon a separation from reproduction, 'making babies' is the most important sign of erotic achievement. The evidence that they have made babies is what gives people adult status, a status which is fundamentally based on erotic power. More, sex and pregnancy are seen to be as essential to bodily health as food and sleep. The exchange of sexpics on the Internet may at first appear a clear case of such separation, but the point of encountering this practice through the laborious methodology of ethnography is to explore the wider context of this practice. It thereby becomes evident that those involved formulate and reflect upon the nature of their on-line sexual activities within the context of fairly conventional notions of domestic relations: for example, assumed norms of nuclear families, sexual fidelity/monogamy and strict separation of adult sexuality from children. These norms often also structure or contain the range of fantasy and representation that is exchanged. Here too the body and its pleasures should be interpreted in the context of social relations of production and reproduction.

What is true for the specific case of reproduction is also more generally the case for the contextualization of sexuality within normative and moral orders which define the nature of sociality in each case. Among the Huaorani an unobjectified sexuality remains within the diffused culture of sociality. In Trinidad what the state condemns as unhealthy is understood by most of the population as a primary sign of good health. Visitors are shocked by public cross-sexual rubbing of genitals, but those who engage in such behaviour are equally shocked by visitors kissing in public. Even within the trade in sexpics on the Internet, an arena that would usually be designated as transgressive, those who trade do so within normative conventions partly established within this practice and considerably over-lapping with very conventional notions that underpin everyday moral orders.

In conclusion, too much of the discussion of sexuality and gender today continues to be merely an adjunct of academics attempting to work through the potential logical implications of modernity, where sexuality and increasingly gender are assumed to be a proving ground for liberationist potentialities. Within such debates it is only too easy to imagine how our examples might be employed, the Huaorani encased within primitivist discourses about Amazonian Indians, and the Internet trade celebrated as the vanguard of technicist definitions of virtual futures. What we have tried to do here is to return both to the comparative study of mundane sexuality as normative social practice, which in no way diminishes the insights to be gained from addressing the extraordinary ability of human social groups to explore the range of differential objectifications that we isolate as sexual practice. We have shown that both eroticism and reproduction form integral parts of human sexuality, defined in terms of moralities and socialities in which sexual behaviour is always found to be embedded. By doing so, we have looked at forms and mechanisms of sexual objectification, without separating relational aspects from the performative construction of gender.

This article began with a discussion of the dominance of social constructionist perspectives on gender. As will now be evident, we are not trying to demolish the foundational conceptualization of gender as socially constructed; what we have done is to challenge the consequences and implications of this observation. What we challenge is the degree to which a philosophical discussion of the logical implications of social construction-ism becomes conflated with our attempt to understand the practice of gender. Merely recognizing the 'what could be' distorts our understanding because it pushes us towards an emphasis upon the extreme potentiality of aspects of gender such as sexuality as performance. By returning to the comparative examination of gender and sexuality in specific cultural contexts we return to the central task of empathetic understanding of what most people do. What our case studies show is that it would be quite wrong to assume that the mundane is somehow less interesting or instructive. In many ways the three cases are all equally astonishing for teaching us the diversity of what can be experienced as mundane. This also encourages us to return to those elements of gender such as reproduction, ethics, health and non-eroticized sensuality which may have been neglected in philosophical speculation upon the modernist logics of gender and sexuality.

It seems to us that Huaorani, Trinidadian and cyber views on human sexuality cannot be subsumed under the postmodern representation of sexuality as founded in desire and constructed in discourse. The Amazonian case demonstrates the possibility of a sexuality which never becomes an abstracted thing in and of itself, and is entirely subservient to social reproduction. In Trinidad, by contrast, both men and women demonstrate their success at performing highly eroticized and self-gratifying sexuality by making babies, but in no way as a means to achieve long-lasting relationships conducive to co-parenthood. Both men and women believe that not having sex is extremely unhealthy (celibacy causes headaches, back troubles and, eventually, madness), and that having sex without producing babies is equally unhealthy. Given that all sex in Trinidad is highly eroticized, the effect is to make reproduction subservient to the erotic, which is why young girls will strive to have babies despite all the efforts of their mothers to dissuade and prevent them from becoming pregnant. As for the Internet traders and chatters, domestic life and pornographic activities, which are apparently constituted as two entirely separate forms of objectification, can only exist in relation to each other. Slater's ethnography shows that the objectification of sexuality on-line appears to be fuelled at least as often by the urge to order sexuality (and IRC relationships and practices themselves) along ethical lines as it is by the desire to gratify it transgressively. Cultural norms regulate both relational domains, as well as their articulation. As we see it, the potentiality for human sexuality must be understood from the viewpoint of a particular creative actor, culture, which, in the end, can be regarded as the normativity of a given population. All sexuality falls under a normative regime of some sort.

Notes

1. Following Laclau (1990: 30, quoted in Weeks, 1995: 40) who proposes that 'the constitution of a social identity is an act of power and identity as such is power', Weeks (1995: 36) argues that alternative and oppositional sexual identities 'breach boundaries, disrupt order, and call into question the fixity of inherited identities of all kinds, not just the sexual'.

2. Our reading of Bataille's writings on eroticism, death and sexuality has concentrated on *L'Expérience intérieure* (1971), *L'Erotisme* (1957), *Les Larmes d'Eros* (1980), *L'Histoire de l'érotisme* (*Oeuvres Complètes*, vol. 8, 1976), as well as *Les Ecrits de Laure* (1977) by his companion Colette Peignot, which he edited and published, and which reflects graphically and poignantly his philosophical ideas. It has been guided by the scholarly works of Michèle Richman (1982, 1990), Daniel Hawley (1978), Jean-Claude Renard (1987) and Elizabeth Roudinesco (1986, 1995).

3. See Morris (1995) for an excellent review of the current research literature.

4. Bataille, who considers eroticism to be first objectified in human history as a religious activity, proposes a religious system which represents a dialectical reversal of Catholicism. The prostitute occupies the place that Mary is not granted. Whereas Mary gives birth to the son of God, the prostitute initiates man into becoming God. For Catholics, the flesh is sinful, weak, abject. In Bataille's creed, the flesh is perishable, grotesque, but sacred, for what is low becomes high.

5. Lacan (who married Bataille's wife, and was considered by Bataille's daughter as her true, caring father) was profoundly influenced by Bataille's vision of the vagina as a sacred, repulsive object. Lacan once aquired a painting by Courbet representing a woman's open sex after love-making. The painting was so shocking that his wife asked him to hide it behind another painting by Bataille's closest friend, Masson. This surface/public painting represented Courbet's painting of the vagina in a surrealistic, disarticulated fashion. In Lacan's structural analysis of the human psyche (the symbolic, the imaginary and the real), what he calls the real corresponds exactly to this realistic vagina covered by an abstract representation of it. Lacan on the whole defends Freud's interpretation of psychic reality, but he adds a new, irreducible and unspeakable element to unconscious desires and sexual fantasies: the non-symbolic, unimaginable material and external reality of the 'accursed share'. His theory is thus directly inspired by Bataille's notion of erotic expenditure, which itself constitutes the very core of the Bataillian sociology of the sacred. As in Bataille's notion of heterology, the real contains a morbid, dejectory, wasteful part, which cannot be returned to the psyche's imaginary or symbolic dimensions. Whereas Freud envisaged a subjective reality rooted in fantasy, Lacan conceived a desiring reality entirely excluded from all symbolizing processes, and unreachable through subjective thought: a black shadow or ghost escaping all forms of reasoning. The real is what cannot be represented, it is the mystical presence of sex as origin (Roudinesco, 1995: 211).

6. The gender implications of the nature/culture dichotomy are the same in Lévi-Strauss and in Bataille. For both, women are the supreme gift. For Lévi-Strauss, women are objects of exchange, and men and culture agents doing the exchange. For Bataille, men transcend their nature and become truly human, not by exchanging, but by profaning the pure gift (women). Women are natural, 'positive' beings who abandon themselves. Because they give themselves in pure abnegation of their subjective identities, they do not suffer the 'little death' (i.e. orgasm) as men do, and do not, therefore, experience transcendence. In both economies and symbolic orders, therefore, women are the intermediaries through which men construct culture against nature, either through reciprocal exchange or through transgression and expenditure.

7. A thorough comparison of their symmetrically opposed views on human sexuality is overdue. We do not know whether Bataille and Reich, who were born in the same year (1897), and who both extensively wrote on fascism and human sexuality, were aware of each other's work.

8. Increasingly, IRC communication now extends beyond text to 'streamed' sound and video (Internet phone systems and 'Cuseeme' video conferencing) so that people are increasingly embodied on-line as well as increasingly themselves presenced as representations. It is unclear yet how this might affect the sexpics setting.

9. Although Slater has not been able to speak to people off-line yet, he can report on the kinds of connections they make in chat and interviews.

10. They live in multi-family dwellings (longhouses) on hilltops away from rivers. They are nomadic, autarkic and highly endogamous hunters-and-gatherers who, by tradition, cultivate manioc anbd plantain sporadically for the preparation of ceremonial drinks.

11. The evangelical missionaries who translated part of the Bible into Huaorani had great difficulty in finding the right term for adultery. They finally settled for *nano tohue nono* (literally, 'someone who's having fun', and resorted to the made-up expression 'someone who's repeatedly having fun' (*èè quète ante nè tohuenga*) to translate 'prostitute'.

12. They will be socially recognized as co-fathers, as long as they are classificatory husbands (i.e. husband's brothers and classificatory brothers) to the child's mother, and as long as they respect couvade restrictions before and after the birth of the child (Rival, in press).

13. The few unmarried men I know live with their married sisters, and act as second husbands in terms of division of labour. The single mothers I know live with their mothers and married sisters. Their children have *no father*, for no man has shared substance with them through repeated intercourse, and no man has performed the couvade for them. There is 'no good reason' (*ononqui*), it is said, for the birth of these children.

14. Rape and domestic violence are entirely absent from social relations. The only form of physical violence consists in spearing 'enemies' during a killing raid. It is most often exercised by men against men.

References

Bassett, C. (1997) 'Virtually Gendered: Life in an On-line World', in K. Gelder and S. Thornton (eds) *The Subcultures Reader*. London: Routledge.

Bataille, G. (1957) *L'Erotisme*. Paris: Minuit.

Bataille, G. (1971) *L'Expérience intérieure*, in H. Ronse and J.M. Rey (eds) *Oeuvres Complètes*, vol. 5. Paris: Gallimard. (Orig. 1941.)

Bataille, G. (1976) *L'Histoire de l'érotisme*, in T. Klossowski (ed.) *Oeuvres Complètes*, vol. 8. Paris: Gallimard.

Bataille, G. (1980) *Les Larmes d'Eros*. Paris: Pauvert.

Busby, C. (1997) 'Permeable and Partible Persons: A Comparative Analysis of Gender and Body in South India and Melanesia', *Journal of the Royal Anthropological Institute* 3(2): 261–78.

Butler, J. (1990) *Gender Trouble: Feminism and the Subversion of Identity*. London: Routledge.

Butler, J. (1993) *Bodies that Matter. On the Discursive Limits of 'Sex'*. New York: Routledge.

Dery, M. (ed.) (1994) *Flame Wars: The Discourse of Cyberculture*. London: Duke University Press.

Fanon, F. (1986) *Black Skin, White Masks*. London: Pluto. (Orig. 1967.)

Featherstone, M. and R. Burrows (eds) (1995) *Cyberspace, Cyberbodies, Cyberpunk: Cultures of Technological Embodiment*. London: Routledge.

Freilich, M. (1969) 'Sex, Secrets and Systems', in S. Gerber (ed.) *The Family in the Caribbean*. Rio Piedras, Puerto Rico: Institute of Caribbean Studies, University of Puerto Rico.

Gay-y-Blasco, P. (1997) 'A "Different" Body? Desire and Virginity among Gitanos', *Journal of the Royal Anthropological Institute* 3(3): 517–36.

Gregor, T. (1985) *Anxious Pleasures. The Sexual Lives of an Amazonian People*. Chicago, IL: University of Chicago Press.

Haraway, D. (1990) 'A Manifesto for Cyborgs: Science, Technology and Socialist Feminism in the 1980s', in L. Nicholson (ed.) *Feminism/Postmodernism*. London: Routledge.

Hawley, D. (1978) *L'Oeuvre insolite de Georges Bataille: une hiérophanie moderne*. Paris: Champion.

Kensinger, K. (1995) *How Real People Ought to Live. The Cashinahua of Eastern Peru*. Prospect Heights, IL: Waveland Press.

Laclau, E. (1990) *New Reflections on the Revolution of Our Time*. London: Verso.

Liedloff, J. (1986) *The Continuum Concept*. London: Penguin. (Orig. pub. 1975.)

McCartney, K. (1997) 'The Socio-cultural Construction of Teenage Motherhood in Santa Maria, Trinidad', unpublished PhD thesis, University of Belfast.

Miller, D. (1991) 'Absolute Freedom in Trinidad', *Man* 26(3): 323–41.

Miller, D. (1994) *Modernity: An Ethnographic Approach*. Oxford: Berg.

Moore, H. (1994) *A Passion for Difference*. Cambridge: Polity Press.

Morris, R. (1995) 'All Made Up: Performance Theory and the New Anthropology of Sex and Gender', *Annual Reviews in Anthropology* 24: 567–92.

Murphy, R. and Y. Murphy (1974) *Women of the Forest*. New York: Columbia University Press.

Peignot, J. (ed.) (1971) *Ecrits de Laure* (Colette Peignot), followed by *A Life of Laure* by G. Bataille. Paris: Pauvert.

Plant, S. (1995) 'The Future Looms: Weaving Women and Cybernetics', in M. Featherstone and R. Burrows (eds) *Cyberspace, Cyberbodies, Cyberpunk: Cultures of Technological Embodiment*. London: Routledge.

Plant, S. (1996) 'On the Matrix: Cyberfeminist Solutions', in R. Shields (ed.) *Cultures of Internet: Virtual Spaces, Real Histories, Living Bodies*. London: Sage.

Plant, S. (1997) *Zeros and Ones: Digital Women and the New Technoculture*. London: Fourth Estate.

Porter, D. (ed.) (1997) *Internet Culture*. London: Routledge.

Reich, W. (1993) *The Function of Orgasm: Sex-Economic Problems of Biological Energy*, trans. Vincent Carfagno. London: Souvenir. (Orig. 1942.)

Reichel-Dolmatoff, G. (1971) *Amazonian Cosmos: The Sexual and Religious Symbolism of the Tukano Indians*. Chicago, IL: University of Chicago Press.

Renard, J.-C. (1987) *L' "Expérience intérieure"' de Bataille, ou la négation du mystère*. Paris: Gallimard.

Richman, M. (1982) *Reading Georges Bataille: Beyond the Gift*. Baltimore, MD: The Johns Hopkins University Press.

LIVERPOOL
JOHN MOORES UNIVERSITY
AVRIL ROBARTS LRC
TEL. 0151 231 4022

Richman, M. (1990) 'Anthropology and Modernism in France: From Durkheim to the Collège de Sociologie', in M. Mangarano (ed.) *Modernist Anthropology. From Fieldwork to Text*. Princeton, NJ: Princeton University Press.

Rival, L. (1992) 'Social Transformations and the Impact of Formal Schooling on the Huaorani of Ecuador', PhD Thesis, University of London.

Rival, L. (1996) *Hijos del Sol, Padres del Jaguar: Los Huaorani de Ayer y Hoy* (Children of the Sun, Fathers of the Jaguar, the Huaorani Today), Quito: Abya-Yala.

Rival, L. (1998) 'Marginality with a Difference: How the Huaorani Remain Autonomous, Preserve their Sharing Relations and Naturalize Outside Economic Powers', in Mesan Biesele and Peter Schweitzer (eds) *Hunters and Gatherers in the Modern Context: Conflict, Resistance and Self-Determination*. Providence, RI: Berghan Books.

Rival, L. (in press) 'Androgynous Parents and Guest Children: The Huaorani Couvade', *Journal of the Royal Anthropological Institute* 5(4).

Rival, L. (forthcoming) *Trekking Through History. The Huaorani of Amazonian Ecuador*. New York: Columbia University Press.

Roe, P. (1982) *The Cosmic Zygote*. New Brunswick, NJ: Rutgers University Press.

Roudinesco, E. (1986) *La Bataille de cent ans: histoire de la psychanalyse en France (1925–1985)*, vol. 2. Paris: Seuil.

Roudinesco, E. (1995) 'Bataille entre Freud et Lacan: une explication cachée', in D. Hollier (ed.) *Georges Bataille après tout*. Paris: Belin.

Segal, L. (1994) *Straight Sex: The Politics of Pleasure*. London: Virago.

Siskind, J. (1973) 'Tropical Forest Hunters and the Economy of Sex', in D. Gross (ed.) *Peoples and Cultures of Native South America*. Garden City, NY: Natural History Press.

Smith, R.T. (1988) *Kinship and Class in the West Indies*. Cambridge: Cambridge University Press.

Springer, C. (1996) *Electronic Eros: Bodies and Desire in the Postindustrial Age*. Austin: University of Texas Press.

Stone, A.R. (1996) *The War of Desire and Technology at the Close of the Mechanical Age*. Cambridge, MA: MIT Press.

Turkle, S. (1995) *Life on the Screen: Identity in the Age of the Internet*. New York: Simon and Schuster.

Weeks, J. (1995) 'History, Desire and Identities', in R.G. Parker and J.H. Gagnon (eds) *Conceiving Sexuality: Approaches to Sex Research in a Postmodern World*. New York: Routledge.

Yelvington, K. (1995) *Producing Power: Ethnicity, Gender and Class in a Caribbean Workplace*. Philadelphia, PA: Temple University Press.

Yelvington, K. (1996) 'Flirting in the Factory', *Journal of the Royal Anthropological Institute* 2: 313–33.

Laura Rival is currently Lecturer in the Department of Anthropology at the University of Kent at Canterbury. Her doctoral research was among the Huaorani Indians of the Ecuadorian Amazon (1989–90, 1991, 1994, 1996), on whom she has written a number of ethnographic articles and papers. Her doctoral dissertation was translated into Spanish under the title *Hijos del Sol, Padres del Jaguar. Los Huaorani de Ayer y Hoy* and published by Abya Yala (Quito, Ecuador) in 1996. She has also edited a volume on tree symbolism, *The Social Life of Trees: Anthropological Approaches to Tree Symbolism* (Oxford: Berg, 1998). She is currently preparing a monograph titled *Trekking through History: The Huaorani of Amazonian Ecuador* to be published by Columbia University Press.

Don Slater is Senior Lecturer in Sociology at Goldsmiths College University of London. Recent publications include *Consumer Culture and Modernity* (Polity Press, 1997). He awaits publication of *Markets, Modernity and Social Theory* (co-authored with Fran Tonkiss, Polity Press, forthcoming) and ' "Trading Sexpics on IRC": Embodiment and Authenticity on the Internet' (*Body & Society*, forthcoming).

Daniel Miller teaches at the Department of Anthropology, University College London. Recent publications include *A Theory of Shopping* (Polity and Cornell University Press, 1998), *Material Cultures* (UCL Press and Chicago University Press, 1998), *Capitalism: An Ethnographic Approach* (Berg, 1997), as well as *Shopping Place and Identity* (with P. Jackson, N. Thrift, B. Holbrook and M. Rowlands, Routledge, 1998) and *Virtualism: Towards a New Political Economy* (with J. Carrier, Berg, 1998).

The Nazi Eye Code of Falling in Love

Bright Eyes, Black Heart, Crazed Gaze

Andrew Travers

> It was very beguiling, that female arrogance. There were women who would
> not refrain from intimating that it was they who were more at home in the
> world. Who could not forbear, all unprovoked, to run up their mythic
> pennants. Instrument of Birth, Shroud Weaver. Bent never Broken. It
> became very primitive, very quickly. Talking some commonplace like
> genocide or the weather they performed a hula, a series of mudras. Your
> eyes are hot and deluded, they signalled, ours are clear. We have suffered
> your rantings, your violence, your febrile illusions and endured. We can look
> on all things the same, we can imagine serenity. Grow up, they said. (Stone,
> 1981: 225)

Introduction

THIS ARTICLE, LIKE a jealous husband grimly intent on denouncing
his wife as a bitch, will say that (as an instance) if Romeo and Juliet
had not committed suicide the day would have dawned when Juliet
would have hated the sight of Romeo as well as hating every sign of human
life. I shall arrive at the conclusion accommodating this instance via eyes
and their Western cultural code. To illustrate. Romeo from below Juliet's
balcony gazes at Juliet who, unaware of him, stares at 'two of the fairest stars
in all heaven' (*Romeo and Juliet*, Act 2, Scene 2). Focusing on Juliet's eyes,
Romeo flies into a literary conceit. He wonders whether, if Juliet's eyes were
exchanged with the stars ('What if her eyes were there, they in her head?'),
they would 'through the airy region stream so bright that birds would sing,
and think it were not night'. That is the eye code, which has it that any
woman whose love is pure and intense is lit up from within, culturally

■ *Theory, Culture & Society* 1998 (SAGE, London, Thousand Oaks and New Delhi),
Vol. 15(3–4): 323–353
[0263-2764(199808/11)15:3–4;323–353;006070]

speaking. I go on to say that light pours out of such a woman's eyes eventually to a point, when the love is opposed, of hating human life, and I assert then that eyes like Juliet's radiate a Nazi ideology.

The single example that drives my thesis is Tolstoy's character Anna Karenin in the novel of the same name (Tolstoy, 1901).[1] Tolstoy serves me well because his is a deeply meditated use of the subcode of eyes (Synnott, 1993: 206–27) within Western culture's 'love code' (Luhmann, 1986). (I write in a broad cultural context that ought to be refined at length in a hierarchy of genre contexts along the lines of Dyer [1979]). By directing my black look at Tolstoy's novel I find in Juliet's and Anna Karenin's shining eyes the darkness of an Auschwitz gas chamber.

There is no difference in this article between the eye code as it is employed by 'real' people, by Shakespeare, by Tolstoy or by Mills and Boon (e.g. in Mills and Boon, 'Kate stared up at him with wild, brilliant eyes, and found she was laughing and crying at the same time' [Hilton, 1982: 181] and, in Tolstoy, 'She was conscious herself that her delight sparkled in her eyes and curved her lips into a smile, and she could not quench the expression of this delight' [1901: 143]). This is to take as true Goffman's (1974: 562–3) nihilistic conviction that life is interactive for interactants when it imitates mostly bad art.

My method, then, is to use excerpts from a novel as phenomenological explications of everyday experience, which the excerpts are if (1) words are the very forms of perception (Clough, 1993) and if (2) one possible future of ethnography is a 'haunted realism' (Clough, 1992) of rewriting patriarchy's disavowed oedipally coded *desire* for objectivity, truth and fact. It is not my method to reinforce conventional polarities such as analyst/subject, expert/reader, literary theory/everyday life, scientific data/novelistic knowledge. I commit 'symbolic realism' (Brown, 1977) in which meaning inheres in linguistic tropes that deepen and refine rather than truncate perception. Further, my reading of Tolstoy is not structuralist, in that I am not searching for acontextual intra-textual relationships, and it is not functionalist, in that I am not trying (hermeneutically) to relate the text to its context of production. My orientation to Tolstoy is not unlike that of a reception theorist, therefore. Iser, for example, says that reading 'is cybernetic in nature', 'helps to create the impression that we are involved in something real', and 'is experienced as something which is happening' (Iser, 1975: 20). Thus literature is particularly interesting for sociologists to read because it 'questions or recodes the signals of external reality in such a way that the reader himself [herself] is to find the motives underlying the questions, and in doing so ... participates in producing the meaning' (Iser, 1975: 25). The ultimate dimension of a literary text, according to reception theorists, is a diffuse, pre-semantic 'imaginary', which provokes interpretations of every stripe. Interpretations tend to extrapolate their own semantic intentionality as being that of the text, and thus fail to address the imaginary of fiction (Iser, 1979). The most real theories arising from literary texts are at best heuristic, limited 'prospectings' of the imaginary that is lodged in social systems which tend to neutralize the questions that literature addresses. In every case the receptionist reading of literature is a pragmatic application of cultural-anthropological frames of reference. The reality uncovered in such reading belongs to society and is best revealed in literature. It makes sense therefore to ethnographize our culture's eye code by finding it in an outstanding literary work. which in its turn, as Goffman (1974) and Luhmann (1986) note, will be a strong model of conduct to which interactants indirectly or directly refer when undergoing their own eye-coded romantic engagements. Both Goffman and Luhmann imply that, since human behaviour is modelled on potent cultural representations, ethnography should grasp those representations the better to represent cultural members.

The eye code of falling in love, however gifted its expression and however benign its inception, always carries a Nazi virus – I argue – because, as Tolstoy reveals, it involves the surrender of reason to a cruel mysticism.

Perhaps it is disingenuous of me to say here that I am not assigning a Nazi ideology to Tolstoy any more than a musicologist assigns that to Wagner (but see McClary, 1991). 'Presentism' is one criticism of such reversals of epoch, and switching of meaning domains (from literary to political narratives) may also be criticized for violating conventional rhetorical distinctions that obtain between discourses that have discrepant political and epistemological goals. However, I am writing about how Tolstoy and his characters are read now, and the scholarly, hermeneutic representation of how they appeared a century ago is no part of my inquiry. And, when I come to compare Anna Karenin with Hitler and to parallel the relation Anna Karenin/Vronsky with Hitler/Goebbels, I am semiotically exploring – in this article – the phenomenon of an eye code and am not attempting to use cross-*genre* resemblances as the beginnings of an argument concerning the relationship between art and politics (for which see Adorno, Lukács, Goldman, Jameson, Eagleton and Peter Burger). Here and there in what follows I identify Tolstoy the author with his characters, but not so much, in my view, as he must have done in order to have written them in the first place. It seems to me a fair assumption that the deeper the fictional character is written the deeper will it draw on the author's experience. The distance of character from author might be thought of as similar to that between actor and role. The role or the written character will be the more vital the more it is rooted in the actor or writer. This is an assumption that I make at times in the analyses that follow, and it squares both with Clough's feminist social criticism technique of rereading an author's objectivizing desire and with the reception theorist view that interpretation should work from the imaginary of the text and not from semantically intentional impositions upon it.

I further show that analysts both of face-to-face interaction and of gaze – notably Mead, Goffman, Foucault, Lacan, Sartre and Mulvey – are not sensitive to the ways in which, through the eye code, eyes are seen by interactants. Several other propositions are ravelled up in this. The two most important are (1) that women in love destroy their social selves, feed on admiration, and spit out their lovers when they (the lovers) stand up for society (this is not quite like Simmel, 1984: 170–3) and (2) that social analysts, by virtue of not loving their phenomenon (not *identifying with* it [see Travers, 1995]), not fully experiencing it, do not do it analytical justice.

The methodological thinking above depends on my understanding human experience to be a product and producer of the cultural language(s) by which it is structured.[2] Though I respect Craib's (1995) point that experience is insulted by trivially social constructionist codes and though I do not nearly so much respect Russell's (1961) point that experience is always physiological arousal plus cognition, I pass over the remote possibility that just because some emotions are very powerful they are culture-free. Powerful cultural language forms, I say, generate powerful emotions that circularly generate powerful cultural language forms, for example, the language form of the physiology-plus-cognition argument.

Finally, I am intent on reminding readers that, since dyadic love is a primary social bond, there might be a sociological future in studying the gaze element of that bond's eye-to-eye language. But I am only explicating the case of Anna Karenin (even if at times I generalize from her to all women and some men) and Anna Karenin could be atypical.

Blinded by the Light

Tolstoy uses the eye code to beatify Anna Karenin. In the process he releases one of the seeds of my later critique (Tolstoy-Vronsky's assertion that when Anna's light switches off she is 'strange and unaccountable' [Tolstoy, 1901: Pt 2, ch. 23, 213]). Though much more is said by Tolstoy about Anna than can be distilled to a few pages, I dwell exclusively on how Tolstoy and Vronsky register Anna through the eye code. My implicit claim here is that, no matter the detail of Anna's characterization, it is narratively subsumed in the light of her eyes, whose code in Tolstoy works Anna up into a dazzling/mysterious creature, period.

The first time Vronsky meets Anna Karenin he is excited by an inner light animating her eyes and smile (Appendix: A). Soon after, when Vronsky briefly encounters Anna on a train, Tolstoy writes that 'irrepressible delight and eagerness shone in her face' (1901: Pt 1, ch. 30, 115). And the inhibiting presence of Anna's husband (Alexey Alexandrovitch) does not prevent Vronsky catching in her glance towards him 'a flash of something' (1901: Pt 1, ch. 31, 118). The woman whom Vronsky loves is always full of light, since he does not know her when the light goes out: 'It was as though … the real Anna retreated somehow into herself, and another strange and unaccountable woman came out, whom he did not love, and whom he feared, and who was in opposition to him' (1901: Pt 2, ch. 23, 213). (As I have said, I shall return to this 'strange and unaccountable woman'.) But even at the end of the novel when Vronsky no longer respects Anna she continues to shine in other men's eyes. After '[s]he had unconsciously … done her utmost to arouse in Levin a feeling of love – as of late she had fallen into doing with all young men...' (1901: Pt 7, ch. 10, 792), she appears light-filled and extraordinarily compelling (Appendix: B).

Anna's eyes in Tolstoy's words create Anna as a vital interactional presence who is yet particularly *her*. Missing from Tolstoy's eye/light descriptions, however, is an analysis of the eye code. In his references to Anna's eyes (e.g. 1901: 68–9, 115, 118, 785) Tolstoy is brazenly imprecise. A group of near-synonyms ('brilliant', 'flashing', 'shining') do not denote particular eyes so much as bounce off an otherwise unseen physical organ. Tolstoy never expands his equation of shining eyes and delight. Further, the emphasis given to Anna's inability to control the light in her eyes (to control her delight) has no basis beyond its assertion. It comes entirely from non-referential motor phrases such as 'against her will' and 'brimming over'. So, where we might expect special pleading of Anna's unique character to explain Vronsky's captivation, Anna is written as little more than a container of 'irrepressible' life that cannot be fully 'suppressed'.

Nebulous in his evocation of Anna's eyes, Tolstoy without fail makes her eyes motivate Vronsky's passion. Tolstoy seems to be dazzled by his own creation, who is only dazzling because he very conventionally says she is, employing a ready-made eye code that obscures a fictional heroine whom he is celebrated for masterfully revealing. Thus the eye code speaks louder than Tolstoy. But what does it say?

It says that Anna Karenin has and is a self that (a) will be born of strong emotion, (b) is involuntarily responsive to a personable male, (c) is charismatically fascinating, (d) appears like light in the instant of a glance or a look, and (e) powerfully declares itself, when it appears, as the self it will be in future towards the personable male and, indeed, towards anyone else. Such a self as Anna's is one whose coded manifestation is the liveliness of eye that it has at the expense of any other identity. Whatever Anna is in a clearly defined sense is lost in Tolstoy, who has it, from the eye code, that she (1) is alive beyond the interactional death of being finally and exactly definable and (2) is alive because she is too bright to be adequately described except as her coded eyes. Entailed is a portrait of Anna as a narcissist. For, in her interactions with Vronsky, Anna does not really see him until he stops completely *identifying with* her and begins to *identify* her *as* an adulteress (the distinction between *identifying with* and *identifying as* in the *identification of* self is elaborated in Travers, 1995). Seeing Vronsky refusing to surrender to her, Anna hates him (we come to this shortly).

Recapitulation Tolstoy writes his heroine Anna Karenin (a creation ranked by commentators[3] with Madame Bovary,[4] Juliet and Goethe's Charlotte[5]) as an effulgent being, and mostly just that. The reality-effect of Anna in Tolstoy's words is achieved by a culturally ready-made eye code, which itself is not explored. Love is said to light Anna up as though she were simultaneously bathed in spotlights and illuminated from within by a source of light that was only waiting to be switched on by Tolstoy-Vronsky's excitement (feminists might feel about this that Anna is subject to the remote control of phallic power changing her channel from humdrum to tragically beautiful). *Anna is not observed but beatified.* The novel *Anna Karenin* therefore is a several-hundred-page aria on an eye code inherited by Tolstoy from a culture that he adopts without question. The code has it, à la *Romeo and Juliet*, that women are brilliant, sentient objects when they fall in love with the 'right' men. Yet, if the light switches off by its own hand, Anna Karenin is 'strange and unaccountable', a woman to be feared, opposing the lover (Tolstoy, 1901: Pt 2, ch. 23, 213). In short, Vronsky throws a switch, Anna Karenin bursts into light, and thenceforth she is that light or 'unaccountable'.

Shattered Identity and Heightened Perspicuity

Tolstoy is not content with writing Anna Karenin from without, as it were parading her on his catwalk, hot to trot. He will penetrate her mind.

Anna, in the grip of her feelings, is said to see herself as Vronsky sees her. Avoiding 'her serious-minded friends' and going out 'into the fashionable world' Anna:

> ... gave him [Vronsky] no encouragement, but every time she met him there surged up in her heart that same feeling of quickened life that had come upon her that day in the railway carriage when she saw him for the first time. She was conscious herself that her delight sparkled in her eyes and curved her lips into a smile, and she could not quench the expression of this delight. (Tolstoy, 1901: Pt 2, ch. 4, 143)

Inwardly conscious of herself as identical to how she must appear to Vronsky, Anna's self, born again, emerges in strong emotion. From the moment of first realizing that Vronsky has followed her on to her train she is 'seized by a feeling of joyful pride' (1901: Pt 1, ch. 30, 115) while in later meetings she experiences 'an agitating joy...' (1901: Pt 2, ch. 4, 143). The self-shattering mixture of joy and pride derives from the *defeat* of a shame still felt by her residual married image of herself with regard to the image of an adulteress and from the *victory* of amatory delight in the remembrance of Vronsky. The quote in Appendix C exhibits clearly how Anna's passion throws her identity into a delirious chaos. The consuming emotion of a nascent self – loved by and loving Vronsky – drowns Anna's fear of becoming a social outcast. Love routs shame as well as any other self but the one that springs to life when seen with love. Not only does Anna's principal social identity (loyal wife of a high-ranking civil servant) disintegrate on impact with Vronsky but so too does Anna's inner organization which now finds its sanity by focusing on Vronsky alone.

With the new self comes a perspicuity hitherto shrouded in dutifulness. Fundamentally doubting her past identity, Anna starts to perceive with a keen and critical eye (trained on everybody but Vronsky). Recognizing her husband in the distance, for example, Anna notices as if for the first time that he is frigid, obstinate and sarcastic. And she becomes acutely conscious that, inasmuch as she had known this in the past, her acting towards its denial had been unpleasantly hypocritical. It takes just one glance for Anna – having fallen in love – to understand how crushing her husband is and always has been to the passionate self who she feels must be her real self (Appendix: D). *Anna's clear vision is a consequence of unforced love.*

(Love, Tolstoy implies, is more clear-sighted than unemotional detachment, but only if gazing at those who are not loved. To those who openly love it, the new self is greedily alive to just the signs that it is loved. But, when those signs disappear, Anna sees in Vronsky a partner as oppressive as her husband.)

Recapitulation   Having switched on Anna Karenin, Tolstoy enters her to find a turmoil of joy in which her past loyalties are exploding. Nothing is left to Anna except her wholehearted response to Vronsky-Tolstoy, 'a great love' that, looking around itself, regards other forms of life as ugly things. Her husband's ugliness itself causes Anna to cleave to the image of Vronsky as though Vronsky has become the exclusive origin of her life that now has a new and ruthless gaze.

The Love that Hates Society

The 'in love' self emerges from Tolstoy's eye code as a two-edged phenomenon. Superlatively alive, attractive and desirable, if appreciated, it is pitiless if opposed, then experiencing its opponent as an impositional and offensive object, the tolerance of whom in the past it disavows as hypocrisy. Tolstoy sharpens the pitiless edge of the 'in love' self all the way to a sweeping misanthropy.

To start with, from Anna's subjectivity, Tolstoy charts an increasingly hostile social world in which at every advance of the plot her husband's unsympathetic characterization stems from Anna's revulsion. So Anna's 'in love' self is displayed to the reader not only in her animated relation to Vronsky but also in her hatred of her husband (in whom, after Anna has fallen in love with Vronsky, Tolstoy never permits her to see humanity). Anna tells Vronsky that Alexey Alexandrovitch is a 'spiteful machine' (Tolstoy, 1901: Pt 2, ch. 23, 214) and a 'doll' (1901: Pt 4, ch. 3, 408), and, informing her husband that she is Vronsky's mistress, she sees in his face 'the solemn rigidity of the dead' (1901: Pt 2, ch. 29, 241). Even at his angriest – when searching Anna's room for love letters that will incriminate her in a divorce case – Alexey Alexandrovitch, with his mouth 'tightly and contemptuously shut', has seemingly unseeing eyes that 'stared darkly before him' (1901: Pt 4, ch. 4, 412). At every twist and turn of Anna Karenin's battle for independence from her husband, Tolstoy confronts her living self with her husband's deathly, black gaze.

But Anna's vitality begins to be opposed by Vronsky too. This first happens when she is bewildered by Vronsky's objection to her attending a major social event. She does not understand why her new self, ready to flaunt itself in all its emotional glory, should not eclipse the identity of a common-or-garden adulteress. Anna will not yield to Vronsky's protest: 'In that dress, with a princess only too well known to everyone, to show yourself at the theatre is equivalent not merely to acknowledging your position as a fallen woman, but is flinging down a challenge to society, that is to say, cutting yourself off from it for ever' (Tolstoy, 1901: Pt 5, ch. 32, 615). In this and similar distressing scenes Vronsky tries to curb Anna so that she reluctantly comes to see, instead of non-stop love and total surrender, 'coldness' (1901: Pt 5, ch. 32, 614), a 'cold, severe expression ... the beginning of indifference' (1901: Pt 6, ch. 32, 751), 'not merely a cold look, but the vindictive look of a man persecuted and made cruel' (1901: Pt 6, ch. 32, 754), and an 'obstinacy' of unforgiveness ('in his tone, in his eyes, which became more and more cold' [1901: Pt 7, ch. 12, 794]). Finally, there is a violent clash between Anna and Vronsky:

> 'No, this is becoming unbearable!' cried Vronsky, getting up from his chair; and stopping short, facing her, he said, speaking deliberately: 'What do you try my patience for?' looking as though he might have said much more, but was restraining himself: 'It has limits.'
>
> 'What do you mean by that?' she cried, looking with terror at the undisguised hatred in his whole face, and especially in his cruel, menacing eyes. (1901: Pt 7, ch. 24, 836–7)

Suddenly Vronsky has the same deathly gaze that Anna saw in her husband's congealed mask of a face. Anna's glimpse of this deathly gaze and her emotion of terror are one and the same experience of her self, that is, of a loving self from whom love is being withdrawn. But Anna's terror only makes her more beautiful to Vronsky: 'He felt at the same time that his respect for her was diminished while his sense of her beauty was intensified' (Tolstoy, 1901: Pt 5, ch. 32, 615). (This last *aperçu* – Vronsky's admiration increasing with his disrespect – will be returned to: it is the second seed of my critique). Anna can find neither sympathy nor comprehension when she tries to explain herself to Vronsky (Appendix: E). Plainly (in Appendix: E) she is talking about her loving self, which is far from extinguished by Vronsky's obstinacy. With her love rejected, however, Anna relapses into the same delirious, identity-doubting clarity that she let herself be sucked into after first realizing that Vronsky might love her. But now her former callous doubt that 'Vronsky was for her only one of the hundreds of young men, for ever exactly the same, that are met everywhere, [upon whom] ... she would never allow herself to bestow a thought...' (1901: Pt 1, ch. 30, 114) takes hold as a certainty. On this occasion of rejection, brighter and more lucid than ever, Anna feels estranged from Vronsky (Appendix: F). Yet the doubt about who she is to Vronsky and the light of her selfhood will eventually coincide:

> 'If I go away from him [Vronsky], at the bottom of his heart he will be glad.'
>
> This was not mere supposition, she saw it distinctly in the piercing light, which revealed to her now the meaning of life and human relations. (1901: Pt 7, ch. 30, 858)

It is in this 'piercing light' – of a rejected love beyond its return to everyday reality (Simmel's [1984: 170] 'empirical world') – that Anna commits herself to suicide, falling under the wheels of a train (Appendix: G). The suicide makes sense because en route to her death Anna experiences herself as never having been truly loved by Vronsky. Anna Karenin now lights up the whole world to reveal how hatefully it denies her passion:

And there's nothing amusing, nothing mirthful, really. It's all hateful.... Why these churches and this singing and this humbug? Simply to conceal that we all hate each other... (p. 856)

Never have I hated any one as I have that man [Vronsky]! she thought.... The servants, the walls, the things in that house – all aroused repulsion and hatred in her... (p. 856)

... the struggle for existence and hatred is the one thing that holds men together. (p. 857)

If without loving me, from *duty* he'll be good and kind to me, without what I want, that's a thousand times worse than unkindness! That's – hell! And that's just how it is. For a long while now he hasn't loved me. And where love ends, hate begins. I don't know these streets at all. Hills it seems, and still houses, and houses... And in the houses always people and people ... How many of them, no end, and all hating each other! (p. 859)

Aren't we all flung into the world only to hate each other, and so to torture ourselves and each other?' (p. 859)

It's all falsehood, all lying, all humbug, all cruelty! (p. 862) (Tolstoy, 1901: Pt 7, chs 29–31)

Thus Anna's final blazing reaction to Vronsky's profound affront. In this passage, self equals hate, and, to escape that hate, Anna takes one final step under a train wheel. Only by dying in Tolstoy's novel can Anna release her self from the darkness of a society that in the light of her love is vicious.

Recapitulation   Anna discovers in Vronsky the very obstinacy of Alexey Alexandrovitch whom she has fled, but her eyes and her light do not switch off. She inflates her narcissistic rage to challenge the whole world. Seeing in Vronsky the hateful memory of Alexey Alexandrovitch she also sees every sign of human life as no less hateful. Her vision at the end is savage. She asks if the purpose of human life is the hate of everybody for everybody else. In other words, her bright perspicuity looks at the world and paints it black. It is by committing suicide that Anna returns, in Tolstoy's account, to 'bright' childhood (Appendix: G), to a time before passionate love, to a place where Rousseau-esque thinkers, prior to Freud, sought human innocence.

Tolstoy touches a bare wire of social reality when he links Vronsky's loss of respect for Anna to an 'intensified' sense of her beauty (Tolstoy, 1901: Pt 5, ch. 32, 615). With a jolt we learn that the beauty *he* has bestowed on his fictional creation becomes even more beautiful because it is damned (by Tolstoy-Vronsky). This thought I shall pick up very soon in my suggestion that the eye code of falling in love is a Nazi ideology. But first a reprise from Tolstoy's next novel.

Tolstoy's Reprise

After publishing *Anna Karenin*, Tolstoy devoted himself to issuing pro-nunciamentos on every social problem of his day. This was his notion of political activism, coupled to an evolving cult of 'mother Russia' and the Russian peasant, whose values Tolstoy sought to emulate in his own conduct, despite the fact that he was insulated from the peasant experience by his autocratic control of his agrarian social experiments. Meanwhile, Tolstoy's wife Sofia, whom he had used as a copyist of draft after draft of his novels, filled her diaries with reproaches for the damage her husband's projects were doing to her life. Then, after writing almost no fiction for 20 years, Tolstoy begat another huge novel, *Resurrection* (1970). The plot of *Resurrection* is simple. A young man of position seduces a servant girl whom at the time he loves. He leaves her. She drifts into prostitution. Years later she is wrongly convicted of murdering a client. By accident, the young man, mature now, crosses paths with the 'murderess'. He feels guilt. Finally he follows the servant girl/prostitute to Siberia, after doing everything he can to lessen her sentence. It is as though Vronsky from *Anna Karenin* is given a second chance to prove himself to Anna, this time putting his beloved before a society that, 20 years on, Tolstoy (not just Anna) has decided is corrupt to the core. *Resurrection* (1970) begins with a scene that picks up where Anna's dying thoughts leave off:

> Though men in their hundreds of thousands had tried their hardest to disfigure that little corner of the earth where they had crowded themselves together, paving the ground with stones so that nothing could grow, weeding out every blade of vegetation, filling the air with the fumes of coal and gas, cutting down the trees and driving away every beast and every bird – spring, however, was still spring, even in the town. The sun shone warm ... the jackdaws, the sparrows and the pigeons were cheerfully getting their nests ready for the spring, and the flies, warmed by the sunshine, buzzed gaily along the walls. All were happy – plants, birds, insects and children. But grown-up people – adult men and women – never left off cheating and tormenting themselves and one another. It was not this spring morning which they considered sacred and important, not the beauty of God's world, given to all creatures to enjoy – a beauty which inclines the heart to peace, to harmony and to love. No, what they considered sacred and important were their own devices for wielding power over each other. (Tolstoy, 1970: 20)

This is Tolstoy speaking. But he is not opening a novel that will celebrate a tragic heroine of high rank in society. He is about to explore society's lower depths. Even so, he yet again falls for the eyes of his heroine:

> Her face was pale with the pallor peculiar to people who have been shut in for a long time and which puts one in mind of the shoots which sprout from potatoes kept in a cellar. Her small broad hands and as much of the plump neck as could be seen beneath the big collar of her prison cloak were the same colour. Her sparkling jet-black eyes, though they were somewhat puffy and one of them had a slight cast, were very lively and offered a striking contrast to the dull pallor of her face. (1970: 20–1)

> She lifted her head, and her black squinting eyes rested on him and looked beyond him, and her whole face shone with happiness. But the words she spoke were not at all what her eyes were saying. (1970: 318)

The eyes have it, to the last. Words, Tolstoy says, fail the eye code, which he leaves intact, though dimmed now by being given to a proletarian woman with a squint (why does she have to have a squint?).

Tolstoy's Heart of Darkness

When Anna's light switches off, Vronsky is afraid that Anna becomes someone else, 'strange and unaccountable'. And, when Anna defies both Vronsky and the social world from which he thinks he is protecting her (and which she might feel he is protecting from her), Vronsky finds her more beautiful but less worthy. 'Beautiful', Anna is just that while, switched off, she is not Anna (and 'very beautiful' – because angry – she is latterly immoral). This dual enigma is resistant to Vronsky's understanding.

(It does not cross Vronsky's mind that his pursuit and persuasion of Anna are responsible for her becoming the adulteress he finally *identifies* her *as*. Similarly, Tolstoy slurs the beauty he has created when [Appendix: B] he claims out of the blue that Anna indiscriminately incites love without thought for her victims, as though she were a vamp or a bitch or a professional *femme fatale*, which she is not, since she only loves Vronsky.)

Anna is a composite indescribability. Strangely dark and strangely bright, she does not belong, either way, to the social world from which Vronsky will not uproot himself and which Anna thinks will forgive and even revel in her great love. Tolstoy never does cope with this dual enigma. He might as well say what Simmel (1984: 170–1) says about romantic love:

> The tragedy of Romeo and Juliet lies in the *dimensions* of their love, for which the empirical world has no place. Nevertheless, because their love has its source in the empirical world and because its real development must be implicated in the contingencies of this world, it is subject to a fatal contradiction from the outset.

Simmel adds that the tragedy is not a tragedy of love versus the world but an inbuilt 'tragic quality' (1984: 171) that has 'drawn the energy of its genesis and existence from precisely this world, in which it finds no place' (1984: 171). However, Anna, like the adulteress of Hawthorne's *Scarlet Letter* (1965) before her, is more courageous and more reckless than the man who made her so. She will return her love to a world that will have none of it, to the point where Vronsky, defending the world's right to scorn it, alienates her. Tolstoy's heart of darkness is here – Conrad in his novel *Heart of Darkness* (1994) sums it up as 'the horror, the horror' (later to be cinematically Vietnamized by Francis Ford Coppola in *Apocalypse Now*) – in that place beyond society and at the limits of language and analysis where passion demands its dues of respect in a bloodbath of moral chaos. Things have moved on a bit lately. Now we have Irigaray (1985) and La Belle (1988) and, in films like *Fatal Attraction* and *Black Widow*, according to Denzin (1995: 167), two heroines who 'deploying all of their sensibilities . . . move to the dark side of the feminine and masculine soul' exposing the need for an 'empowering, multisensual feminine subjectivity . . . that . . . when released into society threatens the status quo'. Denzin says:

> Beyond the tain of the male mirror, the feminine eye opens the way for a new epistemology that goes beyond the masculine, ocular-based systems of knowing. . . . This new 'Private I' will lead to the production of a new model ethnographic textuality . . . a form of factual fiction that draws on the postmodern detective and her search for a moral truth about self. The postmodern detective, unlike his or her modernist counterpart, is no longer an objective observer of the world. This figure stirs up the world and is changed as a result of that project. (Denzin, 1995: 185–6)

But is this new 'Private I' more than Tolstoy's Anna Karenin? Perhaps Tolstoy knew all about stirring up the world 118 years ago, before the cinema was invented? Perhaps his developing solution, his heart of darkness, is just darker today? Anna Karenin may be as potent a double enigma as she ever was because she loves absolutely within a language and a culture that still cannot read such love except when it entails the validating high risk of suicide.

Deficiencies of Theories of Interaction and Theories of Gaze in the Light of Tolstoy's Heart of Darkness

In this section I unpick strands of thought that, when woven into the eye code strand of Tolstoy-Anna, create a propositional climbing rope that may be useful in future escape attempts from the maximum security of our culture's belief that love has a happy ending.

Mead

Mead's model of face-to-face interaction (1962) consists of two unspecified people calculatively taking into consideration the other taking him or her into consideration. The two interactants consider the other with their 'I's' while their 'I's' have inner dialogues with their respective 'me's' (a 'me' is an identity conceived by Mead as proof against interactional traumata). As in Cooley (1983), self and other are on the same plane of knowing, but, though Mead thinks he is more empirical than Cooley, he lacks Cooley's (1983: 121–2) idea that an interactant understands his or her self according to how he or she imagines that the other sees him or her ('imagines' means much more than that a self uses another self as a flat mirror [see Travers, 1994: 133–7]). Regrettably, Cooley did not develop his theory that social life is nothing but people's imaginings of one another, and that may be why readers such as Mead feel he leaves them no exits from their selves back into 'empirical' interaction.

Though Mead's interaction model is language-centred (for a critique see Stone, 1975), it has no truck with poetry, which some (Brown, 1977; White, 1978) would say is the truth of language. Thus Mead applied to Tolstoy would flatten Vronsky and Anna into caricatures, without hearts, without the least trace of human communion. For that reason alone Mead is a poor guide to interaction if compared with Tolstoy who at least allows that an eye code can be fatally decisive for selves. But Goffman discerns further flaws in Mead's vision.

Goffman

In his dissertation, Goffman (1953: 103) says that Mead overstates mutual calculation. Analysts should go beyond 'taking into consideration' and probe the *giving* of consideration ('a case may be made for the view that the best model' of the interactant is not a person but a Durkheimian sacred object [Goffman, 1953: 104]). Three years later, Goffman (1972: 85) deems Mead's blueprint of attitude-taking 'very much an oversimplification' because the interactants of Goffman's analysis do not act as mirror images of what others think of them: '[T]he individual must rely on others [through deference] to complete the picture of him of which he himself is allowed to paint only certain parts [through demeanour]'. A single self in Goffman's view is not an I–me dyad but a running project of 'joint ceremonial labor' (1972: 85). Goffman also thinks (like Stone, 1975) that Mead's distinction between significant and insignificant gestures leaves out the class of 'body idiom' (a 'conventionalized discourse' [Goffman, 1963: 34]) adapted to the conveying of marginal impressions of 'uncalculating spontaneous involvement' that can be denied if challenged (Goffman, 1963: footnote 2, pp. 34–5). (Even Goffman's [1969: 137] analysis of 'strategic interaction', he claims, is an 'advance' on Mead because 'it seeks out basic moves and inquires into natural stopping points in the potentially infinite cycle of two players taking into consideration their consideration of each other's consideration, and so forth'.)

Goffman's 'self', then, partially arises in a body idiom outside the official or collectively ratified perception of interaction. But, if it does that, most of all through the eye code, the rest of interactional reality will begin to pale in comparison. The self of eyes and the self of light, if strong enough, cannot but overshadow the Goffmanian conduct that is aligned to 'the mesh of norms that regulate socially organized co-mingling' (Goffman, 1969: 139). Certainly such an interactional self may be no more than Goffman's 'dramatic effect' (1959: 245) or 'changeable formula for managing oneself during [events]' (Goffman, 1974: 573) but it punches a hole in mundane reality (a hole through which Clough [1992: 107–11] suggests Goffman ought to have seen the Lacanian desire behind his frame relativism). Thus an interactant may experience 'heightened interaction reality' and 'ambiguity of frame' and 'internal disorganization' (Travers, 1992: 629–31) if, for example, eyes very meaningfully meet:

> He reached the whip before she did, and turned to present it to her. She bowed and looked at him: he of course was looking at her, and their eyes met with that peculiar meeting which is never arrived at by effort, but seems like a sudden divine clearance of haze. I think Lydgate turned a little paler than usual, but Rosamond blushed deeply and felt a certain astonishment. After that, she was really anxious to go, and did not know what sort of stupidity her uncle was talking of when she went to shake hands with him. (Eliot, 1957: 115)

In an instance like this no analysis – such as Goffman's – that programmatically gives social organization priority over selves (Goffman, 1983, 1993) will grasp social reality as it is experienced. Selves in the above quote are neither derived from deference-plus-demeanour nor from role-taking but from a mutual gaze and the cultural meaning invested in this with respect to the persons of that gaze. *To be sure, those selves see each other through a common eye code but it is one that, unlike the conventions of Goffman's 'interaction sui generis' and unlike the Meadian mirrorings of role-taking, allows an exit from both of those into the eyes, as if eyes are infinitely deep ('in a sudden divine clearance of haze').*

Foucault

To visualize society Foucault (1979) invokes a hypothetical system of prison surveillance in which unseen prison guards monitor prisoners' bodies. But, writes Sass, Foucault's work 'is haunted by a strange absence' of 'those characteristics of modern subjectivity and selfhood' (1987: 101) that are 'actually the complement and consequence of institutions, practices, and discourse structures' (1987: 104).[6] Taking the case of the psychotic judge Daniel Paul Schreber,[7] Sass (1987) demonstrates Foucault's missing subjectivity within surveillance society.

Schreber is his own vigilant observer, and he is never alone because it is he who observes himself. However, Schreber – in the exact image of Foucault's surveillance victim – can neither identify with his inner observer without abandoning himself nor identify with his body without abandoning his observer's view of it. Perpetually torn between omniscient consciousness and the substance of which it is conscious, Schreber believes himself to be composed of 'nerves' (his substance) that to remain alive have to be interesting enough to attract 'rays' (his reason). If the rays depart, Schreber is lost, and, if the rays come too close, he is threatened. Yet there is a state of 'soul voluptuousness' (Schreber's concept) which offers temporary identity-suspending relief from his nightmarish self-consciousness. Schreber has devious ways of getting to this state so that he might perform his natural bodily functions:

> I must therefore put up temporarily with such evils as bellowing when I want to go to sleep, empty myself, etc., to be able to do in concrete what is indispensable for one's bodily well-being: emptying in particular which one tries to prevent by miracles, I now achieve best when I sit on a bucket in front of the piano and play until I can first piss and then – usually after some straining – empty my bowels. However incredible this may sound it is true; for by playing the piano I force the rays trying to withdraw from me to approach, and so overcome the opposition put up against my effort to empty my bowels. (Schreber, quoted in Sass, 1987: 146–7)

Schreber, a limit case of riven Foucauldian subjectivity, can feel but not see how he is seen. Shot through with power from altogether elsewhere he is unable to look power in the face. How then, in a Foucauldian society of interactants whose selfhoods Sass describes as 'inner panopticons',[8] is any self seeable as such, unto itself?

I suggest that the Foucauldian self – to be seen as a full self and to experience itself so – must plunge its witness into a soul voluptuousness whereby the witness is bathed in the invigorating beauty of eyes that seem to have their true origin in an absolute and unimaginable superiority of vision. The subject of the-other-as-an-eye-coded self has to be irradiated by power that shines 'through' the other's eyes from a mystic beyond. If this happens, the subject has someone else to play its piano for it, as it were, while rapturously emptying its worthless ego before the other's supernatural presence:

> I could no longer contain myself.
> I walked – no, I was driven – toward the platform.
> There I stood, looking long into the face of the One.
> This was no speaker, but a prophet!
> Sweat streamed from his forehead. His eyes, two glowing stars, lit up his pale gray face. His fists were clenched.
> Word after word, sentence after sentence thundered like the Last Judgment. I no longer knew what I was doing.
> I was almost out of my mind.
> I shouted 'Hurrah!' No one thought anything of it.
> The man above me looked at me for a brief moment. The blue stars of his eyes struck me like rays of flame. A command! In this instant I was reborn.

All the dross I carried fell away.
I now knew where my future lay; I had found the pathway to maturity.
(Goebbels, quoted in Theweleit, 1989: 122)

For the Hitler self – who *is* his eyes to Goebbels – there is no reciprocity. Hitler (eyes first, words second) commands Goebbels who finds that his destiny is the pathway of slavish adoration (Anna Karenin's experience of Vronsky too is of his slavish 'setter-dog' adoration). In Foucault's world, then, selfhood may belong to moments of social fusion when powerless structures of the panopticon self collapse and reconfigure as even more powerless subjects of power-in-person. The self – in the limit examples of Schreber, Hitler and Goebbels – is either unspeakably charismatic or utterly under the spell of charisma. (The experience of everyday life, we should note, still has to jump into the realm of charisma to stay interactive [Travers, 1992].)

Of course, in real-life love relationships, the power of selves flows from a language that connects the love partners to exemplars (such as Anna Karenin and Vronsky) that stand over and beyond them. The exemplars actively and passively, as Goffman (1974: 562–3) argues, are the design of social interaction in which real people owe the reality that they have for one another to a borrowed light. The light of eye codes must be seen as real, however, if society is not to become a dance of the dead. Thus, in the everyday life of Foucault's surveillance world, people encounter one another as people only if, in their encounters, power is seen in eyes because eyes are read as seeing supernaturally. (Hitler has an effect on Goebbels similar to Anna Karenin's effect on Vronsky, not because Hitler is like Anna and Goebbels like Vronsky but because all four characters are plugged into the same cultural eye code.)

Speaking for and of the eye code, Simmel (1921: 358) suggests that full selfhood will be experienced by both sides when eyes meet: 'What occurs in this direct mutual glance represents the most perfect reciprocity in the entire field of human relationships.' But, says Simmel, '[t]his highest psychic reaction ... in which the glances of eye to eye unite men, crystal-lizes into no objective structure ... [t]he interaction of eye and eye dies in the moment in which the directness of the function is lost'. Nevertheless: '[T]he totality of social relations of human beings ... would be changed in unpredictable ways if there occurred no glance of eye to eye.'

Here, in the case of mutual absorption (Anna Karenin, I have said, is only absorbed in Vronsky's signs of love, whereas he is absorbed in *her*), we have the eye code well stated as a dialectic. Thesis: without eyes enjoying union, society – in its 'totality' – would be different. Antithesis: but eyes meet outside structure. This dialectic is what the eye code, through Simmel, seems to say directly, in accord with Foucault. Foucault and Simmel converge in a synthesizing belief that only in the eye code is there an exit from societal structures that could not exist without it. The possibility of exit via charismatic eyes, it follows, is the condition of subjective assent to the external human authority without which objectivity and power become powerless and societies run out into empty dramas of capital, technology, science and language. Foucault, however, averts *his* gaze from eyes and their codes (see de Certeau [1986] for an expansion of this, and Baudrillard [1987] for the argument that Foucault's gaze only mirrors the gaze of power, far too panoptically). But Foucault's message, via Sass's (1987) analysis of Schreber, is the same as Tolstoy's. Eyes of selves meet outside society in its eye code which prevents individuation and which incites a heart of darkness (de Certeau's 'black sun': 'For Foucault, unreason is no longer the outer limit of reason: it is its truth. It is the black sun imprisoned in language, burning unbeknownst to it', where things and words approach the condition of death [de Certeau, 1986: 173–4]).

Lacan

Lacan argues that a child becomes a self when it sees itself as being like the mirror image of its mother (Grosz, 1990: 31–40).[9] The Lacanian self disavows a shattering recognition of maternal absence, however. Desire originates in maternal absence, and it is the desiring child that seeks images *with* which it can *identify* (Travers, 1995). But, because it is definitionally incomplete, the child *always fails to conclusively identify with* the images wherein it finds itself.[10] The Lacanian child, emptied by every attempt to complete itself, goes on to internalize the father's language (law) that further divorces its self from understanding its origins in absence, lack and loss of the mother: 'What circulates between subjects in symbolic communication is of course ultimately the lack, absence itself, and it is this absence that opens the space for "positive" meaning to constitute itself' (Zizek, 1991: 131–2). The condition for 'positive' meaning (i.e. empty plenitude) is the phallus (a signifier without a signified).

Lacan believes that objective reality, the reality of the ego and the reality of scientific facts are unreal because they deny a true state of desiring. But the reality of desire cannot be seen directly. It must be courted in Lacan's case through 'a deliberate obscurity' (Grosz, 1990: 13) of indirection, circularity, ellipsis, humour, ridicule and word-play in a manner that veers between the flirtatious, the mocking, the seductive and the insulting, all the while 'stretching terms to the limits of coherence, creating a text that is difficult to enter and ultimately impossible to master' (Grosz, 1990: 17). Lacan's rather surrealist and possibly Artaudian intention is to write in the style of the unconscious, articulating the desire that undoes mundane reason. His paradoxical position is 'that the essential function of the ego is very nearly that systematic refusal of reality which French analysts refer to in talking about the psychoses' (Lacan, 1953: 12). Therefore the analyst should enter the 'Real', the lack of lack, where biological, organic and instinctual processes have not yet been traduced by the deadening ego. At the edge of his or her ego, as it were, the Lacanian analyst is committed to understanding how fantasy rules reality, how phallic signifiers induce insatiable desires and how the gaze of an Other is 'constitutively asymmetrical' (Zizek, 1991: 125) with the eye that is in search of objectivity. In Lacan, writing tries to meet the gaze of an Other, to know the uncanny sense of real reality that desire 'sees', and so to describe the self of Western eye codes by any other name.[11]

In the light of Lacan the observable self of eyes and light is a function of that Lacanian desire without which – for any subject – there would be no persuasive (pre-oedipal) signs of living reality in other persons. So further Lacanian insight into the eye code self would consist in reading eyes 'awry' (Zizek, 1991) from the point of view of a desiring primal doubt. Meanwhile, Lacan's theory adds to the eye code self of this essay the possibility (1) that it is alive in proportion to the experiential vacuity of its perceiver qua fixed identity and (2) that it is beautiful just because it is a desired reality that desire has succeeded in linguistically affixing to an innocent 'object' phenomenon.

Sartre

For its subject Sartre's (1956: 255) 'look' of the Other 'corresponds ... to a fixed sliding of the whole universe, to a decentralization which undermines the centralization I am simultaneously effecting'. But the decentralized self (Anna Karenin) can and does look back:

> Woman is the Other in a pure sense, the Other of whom I will never be able to say that from a certain point of view she is the same as me (same body, same activities, same love-making role). Her body is mysterious and inspires horror at the same time that it attracts. (Sartre, 1983: 393)

> A woman always sees things and people better. She notices right away a certain manner, a certain gesture that characterizes someone, that reveals something about him; and she's capable of expressing it. You would never have that in a conversation with a man. ... I love their sensitivity, their way of being, I love the profoundness of their conversation. (Sartre, 1978: 239)

Here we have the Anna Karenin of this essay in two easy propositions. Scrutinized (by Vronsky, by an alien, male social world), she decentralizes (disorganizes) herself (in Tolstoy as in Sartre) and at the same time she becomes a site of horror and acute perspicuity (in Tolstoy as in Sartre). Tolstoy describes this better than Sartre, however, especially when read by social theorists as a case study writer who puts the phenomenology on hold.

Mulvey

Mulvey's (1975, 1989a, 1989b) Lacanian insight that women in their cinematic representations are passive fetish objects imprisoned in the voyeuristic gaze of males who have not the faintest idea that their looking is premised on fear of castration has won a wide readership. But other feminist film theorists (e.g. Silverman, 1980; Rodowick, 1982; Williams, 1989: 48–9) doubt the wisdom of ascribing the male gaze to males alone.[12]

Ignoring the contributions to interaction studies of James, Cooley, Mead, Blumer, Denzin and Goffman (possibly because her connection between cinematic representation and actual bodily conduct is only hinted at), Mulvey in effect directs a Lacanian (male, therefore) gaze at stereotyped males. This may be why she is popular. However, her revisions (1989a, 1989b) of 'Visual Pleasure and Narrative Cinema' (1975) rewrite the word 'male' as a metaphor (in alignment with Freud [Mulvey, 1989a: 30–1]), so as to distance it from the first version, as convincingly as the reader will allow. There are no signs in Mulvey's writing that she would be able to analyse the Kareninian case of life itself being hateful to a passionate woman rejected in her uncompromising love. Mulvey's fascinating polarization of the genders (within the gaze) has no place for the other side of Anna Karenin's hate, her love of Vronsky. In addition, Mulvey is not up to date with analyses such as Denzin's (1995) that find in Hollywood films a genuine female gaze that plays havoc with male specularity (but, as I have said, I feel that Denzin is anyway pre-empted by Anna Karenin).

Nazi Ideology and Eye-to-Eye Interaction

I have suggested that the self of the eye code plunges its witness into a Schreberian soul voluptuousness whereby the witness is bathed in eyes' invigorating beauty that seems to have its true origin in an absolute and unimaginable superiority of vision. The subject of the-other-as-an-eye-code-self, I said, is as it were irradiated by power that shines 'through' a leader's eyes from a mystic beyond.

> ... not a single German – not even those who had never seen him face to face – was permitted to claim never to have been looked in the eye by the *Führer* ... [Citizens of the Third Reich] may never have seen him [Hitler] face to face, but they have felt themselves bathed in the light of his two 'stars' [Goebbels' description of Hitler's eyes is 'two great blue stars'], which they know were blue (though his eyes were brown as they come). (Theweleit, 1989: 130)

Similarly, Tolstoy demands that Anna Karenin be read as a great tragedienne, though she has no better legitimacy than her coded eyes, into which society should look and either obey or be subject to her hate. She is both a pernicious role model to fill up the 'empty self' (Cushman, 1990) and, inasmuch as she is treated as 'self-revealing', an extreme example of the 'despotic banal' (Finkelstein, 1991: 192). We might also want to say that Anna Karenin is as seductively charismatic as Marlene Dietrich wearing a man's top hat. The Dietrich message 'Fuck me and I'll fuck you' lies in her come-on eyes that intimately repel any intimacy other than slavish Vronsky-like adoration. And, since I have argued that all eyes need a degree of eye code charisma in order that interaction not cease to be interactive, I am saying here that any self is a self to the degree that it is a Nazi (but not all Nazis are fanatics, and there are degrees of fanaticism).

Conclusions: Fade to Black

Tolstoy's Anna Karenin is one of the most brilliant women in the Western cultural canon. And her brilliance streams out of her eyes according to a representational eye code that Tolstoy adopts without criticism. I have analysed how the code operates within Tolstoy in three different but associated ways.

First, Tolstoy beatifies Anna Karenin. The very moment she falls in love with Count Vronsky she acquires supernatural brilliance. But we are only *told* that. We are not *shown* how Anna's brilliance is brilliant. Thus Tolstoy reneges on naturalistic responsibilities that in other parts of *Anna Karenin* and in most of his oeuvre are amply fulfilled. An equation is set forth. Anna's reality is her brilliance and her brilliance is brilliant because it is hers. This tautology is the power of Anna Karenin as Tolstoy writes her.

Second, the authorial gift to Anna Karenin of eye-coded brightness entails that she has the quality of ruthless perspicuity towards all those who do not regard her with love. But the entailment of perspicuity follows a delirious inner deconstruction of her identity. Anna Karenin has to fall apart to fall in love. Only when her married identity has disintegrated can she see with a dispassionate icy clarity the deathliness of those, including her husband, who cannot recognize how she loves Vronsky.

Third, Anna Karenin eventually encounters the same cold detachment in her lover Vronsky that she had first aroused in her husband Alexey Alexandrovitch. Whenever Vronsky stands up for the society that Anna Karenin wishes to dazzle with her radiant beauty, he becomes for her just as much an uncomprehending enemy as had been Alexey Alexandrovitch. At the end, the society with which Vronsky as well as Alexey Alexandrovitch aligns – in the face of Anna's intransigent beatification alternating with her unaccountable darkness – is hateful to Anna Karenin. She cannot live in it, and will not. She commits suicide.

I have also suggested that there is a darkness in Anna Karenin, and that it can be traced to Tolstoy. Tolstoy writes that when Anna Karenin is not brilliant she is not herself. A light goes out, and Anna Karenin becomes someone else whom neither Vronsky nor the author fully recognizes, much less understands. Tolstoy actually uses the word 'unaccountable' for the 'dark side' of Anna Karenin. A review of Tolstoy's writing career indicates that he never does produce a satisfactory account of a woman's unaccountable darkness. Thus, in his late novel *Resurrection*, Tolstoy is still looking to the eye code for explanations of the power of his principal female characters. But in an interim short story, 'The Kreutzer Sonata' (1993), the sympathetic hearing that is given by the narrator to a man encountered on a train indicates Tolstoy's developing and near-Strindbergian horror of love between men and women:

> Passion, no matter with what forms it may be hedged round, is an evil, a terrible evil, to be combated, not fostered, as it is in our society. The words of the Gospel that 'whosoever looketh on a woman to lust after her, hath

committed adultery with her already in his heart', apply not only to other men's wives, but also and mainly to one's own. In our world as at present constituted, the prevalent views are exactly contrary to this, and consequently to what they ought to be. (1993: 89)

Her beauty was of a provoking, perturbing kind, such as would naturally characterize a pretty woman of thirty, well-fed, irritable, and no longer fatigued by the cares and responsibilities of motherhood. Whenever she passed she was sure to attract the looks of men, to magnetize them, as it were. She resembled a well-fed, wanton, harnessed horse that has long stood inactive in the stables, and from whom the bridle has been suddenly removed. There was no curb of any kind, as there is no curb of any kind to hold in ninety-nine per cent of our women. I felt this, and I was seized with horror. (1993: 106–7)

What I mean to affirm is that all husbands who live as I live must sooner or later give themselves up to indulgence or separate from their wives, or else must kill themselves or their wives as I killed mine. If there are people to whom none of these alternatives has proved a necessity, they are very rare exceptions. (1993: 109)

Here we see Tolstoy swinging from his Anna Karenin ideal and towards an identification with Anna Karenin's husband Alexey Alexandrovitch. At the start of this article, I adopted this latter identification as the article's point of view on Anna Karenin. My purpose was to be blackly obtuse towards the eye code so as not to be uncritically captivated by it.

In coming to my own view of the eye code, I note how Mead's sociology of I–me omits eyes, gaze and what Crossley (1995) calls 'corporeal expressivity' (though one should not forget Mead's internalized 'gesture'). Mead's understanding of such manifestations of the eye code as Anna Karenin can hardly be deemed a look, let alone a black look. Goffman, however, does write a 'carnal' sociology (Crossley, 1995) but again he is much more interested in eyes as monitors of vehicular bodily traffic, for example, than as culturally freighted expressions of beauties and brilliancies that can confound 'traffic' rules of social coordination. Goffman would see that on the surface Anna Karenin was behaving herself but he would not see that in her own eyes she is outside and transcending any belief in the value of interactional propriety. Goffman is capable of perceiving the likes of Anna Karenin, then, but not of registering the social perturbations that may follow upon the infatuation with her eyes.

Foucault, however, in Sass's reading, does give us a term (via Schreber) for infatuation with coded eyes, 'soul voluptuousness', the state of surrendering to eye brilliance. But Foucault's theoretic derision for the idea of human subjective experience prevents him from getting to the heart of soul voluptuousness. Lacan, though also alive to the type of woman Anna Karenin stands for, is not helpful either. Lacan writes from desire of what desire sees, but his writing is in darkness, outside egos and beyond the direct gaze of actual eyes. Sartre, again, is sensitive to the special nature of female perspicuity and its link to internal disorganization. But he throws up his hands before female Otherness, as though there is no way for him to penetrate a woman's eyes. Even the film theorist Laura Mulvey, who analyses the effect of gaze in cinematic representations of human figures, tends to leave the reader in the character of Alexey Alexandrovitch, looking blacky at brilliant women as though their brilliance is not itself a gaze like Anna Karenin's, a gaze that shows up the darkness of those who cannot and will not see her for the woman who she insists she is and whom she insists on dying for.

If falling in love is culturally coded to involve a woman in seeing through society (as if society is a conspiracy against her love) and if falling in love is represented by descriptions of a woman's eyes as brilliant, sharp and loaded with destruction, there is a concomitant darkness not only in those who will not return the woman's love but also in that same woman up against indifference and hostility. I have suggested that Joseph Conrad in his novel *Heart of Darkness* taps into this darkness and draws from it experience that – though an indispensable social bonding agent – is as much outside society as a great love. Conrad's narrator Marlow says of Mr Kurtz: 'Everything belonged to him – but that was a trifle. The thing was to know what he belonged to, how many powers of darkness claimed him for their own' (Conrad, 1994: 70). What Marlow says of Kurtz – in the perspective of this article – could now be said of Tolstoy or Anna Karenin:

> The point was in his being a gifted creature, and that of all his gifts the one that stood out pre-eminently, that carried with it a sense of real presence, was his ability to talk, his words – the gift of expression, the bewildering, the illuminating, the most exalted, and the most contemptible, the pulsating stream of light, or the deceitful flow from the heart of an impenetrable darkness. (1994: 67–8)

Here we have 'real presence', 'the illuminating' and 'pulsating stream of light' flowing from 'the heart of an impenetrable darkness'. Conrad comes close to identifying Kurtz with the African river at whose source Kurtz has become the greatest ivory trader of history, the white man as thief and seer. It is apt that Conrad's story is narrated by Marlow in the estuary of the Thames, on a moored cruising yawl. From the trading mouth of the British Empire a tale is told of the other end of the world, where '[n]o eloquence could have been so withering to one's belief in mankind as his final burst of sincerity. He struggled with himself, too. I saw it, – I heard it. I saw the inconceivable mystery of a soul that knew no restraint, no faith, and no fear, yet struggling blindly with itself' (1994: 95–6). Like Tolstoy, Conrad seems mesmerized by a cultural black hole, 'struggling blindly with itself'. Tolstoy looks for it in Anna Karenin, but only (in the years following her creation) to be frozen by her to a death mask of his former self. Conrad looks for it in

Kurtz, who in Marlow's opinion is a 'remarkable man' for only one reason: 'He had something to say' (1994: 101). But what is this something?

> He [Kurtz] had summed up – he had judged. 'The horror!' He was a remarkable man. After all, this was the expression of some sort of belief; it had candour, it had conviction, it had a vibrating note of revolt in its whisper, it had the appalling face of a glimpsed truth – the strange commingling of desire and hate. And it is not my own extremity I remember best – a vision of greyness without form filled with physical pain, and a careless contempt for the evanescence of all things – even of this pain itself. No! It is his extremity that I seem to have lived through. True, he had made that last stride, he had stepped over the edge, while I had been permitted to draw back my hesitating foot. And perhaps in this is the whole difference; perhaps all the wisdom, and all truth, and all sincerity, are just compressed into that inappreciable moment of time in which we step over the threshold of the invisible. Perhaps! I like to think my summing-up would not have been a word of careless contempt. Better his cry – much better. It was an affirmation, a moral victory, paid for by innumerable defeats, by abominable terrors, by abominable satisfactions. But it was a victory! (1994: 101)

One is put in mind here of Creed's (1986, 1987) cinematic explorations of Kristeva's 'abjection' and of Jardine's 'gynesis' as well as Clough's (1992) analyses of Steven Spielberg's relocation of oedipal logic in male-mothering systems. The eye code as I have revealed it in Tolstoy seems to take its brilliance from an equal and opposite non-representable abyss (Lacan) of pre-verbal monstrosity, a monstrosity that is maternal, colonial, white racist, voracious, postmodern, and in its way the most primordial Jungian archetype of them all, the feminine matrix that devours its male offspring in the demise of a masculine speech that has any pacific authority. It follows that the eyes of women in love will seem brighter and brighter the darker our future gets, and that only one ruse is left to the 'great male author', that of becoming, in the fashion of Patrick White, a drag artist whose camp Flaubertian literariness has found in Australia of all places the promise of unbridled feminism in its menfolk (Tacey, 1988). If Tolstoy becomes Alexey Alexandrovitch and Anna Karenin a prototypical Kurtz-cum-Hitler, then interaction sociology can only be aware of the eye code at its centre when abandoning itself to literature, perhaps. This article, having rehearsed the posture of Alexey Alexandrovitch in Mead, Goffman, Foucault, Lacan, Sartre and Mulvey, is poised for just such a self-destruct. Meanwhile it says that Anna Karenin and her emulators are more dangerous than ever before, so long as human interactants are driven by themselves to interact to the limits and beyond the limits of their everyday humanity, on behalf of Simmel's sociality.

Appendix

The following quotations from Tolstoy's *Anna Karenin* (1901) are referred to in the text.

A

Her shining grey eyes, that looked dark from the thick lashes, rested with friendly attention on his face, as though she were recognising him, and then promptly turned away to the passing crowd, as though seeking some one. In that brief look Vronsky had time to notice the suppressed eagerness which played over her face, and flitted between the brilliant eyes and the faint smile that curved her red lips. It was as though her nature were so brimming over with something that against her will it showed itself now in the flash of her eyes, and now in her smile. Deliberately she shrouded the light in her eyes, but it shone against her will in the faintly perceptible smile. (Pt 1, ch. 18: 68–9)

B

A peculiar brilliance lighted up Anna's face when she felt his eyes on her. (p. 785)

Levin talked now not at all with that purely businesslike attitude to the subject with which he had been talking all the morning. Every word in his conversation with her had a special significance. And talking to her was pleasant; still pleasanter it was to listen to her. (p. 785)

Anna talked not merely naturally and cleverly, but cleverly and carelessly, attaching no value to her own ideas and giving great weight to the ideas of the person she was talking to. (p. 786)

'Yes, yes, this is a woman!' Levin thought, forgetting himself and staring persistently at her lovely, mobile face, which at that moment was all at once completely transformed. (p. 786)

And she glanced again at Levin. And her smile and her glance – all told him that it was to him only she was addressing her words, valuing his good opinion, and at the same time sure beforehand that they understood each other. (p. 787)

And Levin saw a new trait in this woman, who attracted him so extraordinarily. Besides wit, grace, and beauty, she had truth. She had no wish to hide from him all the bitterness of her position. (p. 788)

... Levin was all the time admiring her – her beauty, her intelligence, her culture, and at the same time her directness and genuine depth of feeling. (p. 789)

And though he had judged her so severely hitherto, now by some strange chain of reasoning he was justifying her. ... (p. 789) (Pt 7, ch. 10)

C

She remembered the ball, remembered Vronsky and his face of slavish adoration, remembered all her conduct with him: there was nothing shameful. And for all that, at the same point in her memories, the feeling of shame was intensified, as though some inner voice, just at the point when she thought of Vronsky, were saying to her, 'Warm, very warm, hot'.... Moments of doubt were continually coming upon her, when she was uncertain whether the train were going forwards or backwards, or were standing still altogether; whether it were Annushka at her side or a stranger. 'What's that on the arm of the chair, a fur cloak or some beast? And what am I myself? Myself or some other woman?' She was afraid of giving way to this delirium. But something drew her towards it, and she could yield to it or resist it at will.... That peasant with the long waist seemed to be gnawing something on the wall, the old lady began stretching her legs the whole length of the carriage, and filling it with a black cloud; then there was a fearful shrieking and banging, as though some one were being torn to pieces; then there was a blinding dazzle of red fire before her eyes and a wall seemed to rise up and hide everything. Anna felt as though she were sinking down. But it was not terrible, but delightful. (Pt 1, ch. 29: 112–13)

D

At Petersburg, so soon as the train stopped and she got out, the first person that attracted her attention was her husband. 'Oh, mercy! why do his ears look like that?' she thought, looking at his frigid and imposing figure, and especially the ears that struck her at the moment as propping up the brim of his round hat. Catching sight of her, he came to meet her, his lips falling into their habitual sarcastic smile, and his big, tired eyes looking straight at her. An unpleasant sensation gripped her heart when she met his obstinate and weary glance, as though she had expected to see him different. She was especially struck by the feeling of dissatisfaction with herself that she experienced on meeting him. That feeling was an intimate, familiar feeling, like a consciousness of hypocrisy, which she experienced in her relations with her husband. But hitherto she had not taken note of the feeling, now she was clearly and painfully aware of it. (Pt 1, ch. 30: 116)

E

'For you it's a matter of obstinacy,' she said, watching him intently and suddenly finding the right word for the expression that irritated her, 'simple obstinacy. For you it's a question of whether you keep the upper hand of me, while for me ...' Again she felt sorry for herself, and she almost burst into tears. 'If you knew what it is for me! When I feel as I do now that you are hostile, yes, hostile to me, if you knew what this means for me! If you knew how I feel on the brink of calamity at this instant, how afraid I am of myself!' And she turned away, hiding her sobs.

'But what are you talking about?' he said, horrified at her expression of despair.... (Pt 7, ch. 12: 794)

F

And now for the first time Anna turned that glaring light in which she was seeing everything on to her relations with him [Vronsky], which she had hitherto avoided thinking about. 'What was it he sought in me? Not love so much as the satisfaction of vanity.' She remembered his words, the expression of his face that recalled an abject setter-dog, in the early days of their connection. And everything now confirmed this. 'Yes, there was the triumph of success in him. Of course there was love too, but the chief element was the pride of success. He boasted of me. Now that's over. There's nothing to be proud of. Not to be proud of, but ashamed of. He has taken from me all he could, and now I am no use to him. He is weary of me and he is trying not to be dishonourable in his behaviour to me. He let that out yesterday – he wants divorce and marriage so as to burn his ships. He loves me, but how? The zest is gone, as the English say.' (Pt 7, ch. 30: 858)

G

A feeling such as she had known when about to take the first plunge in bathing came upon her, and she crossed herself. That familiar gesture brought back into her soul a whole series of girlish and childish memories, and suddenly the darkness that had covered everything for her was torn apart, and life rose up before her for an instant with all its bright past joys. But she did not take her eyes from the wheels of the second carriage. And exactly at the moment when the space between the wheels came opposite her, she dropped the red bag, and drawing her head back into her shoulders, fell on her hands under the carriage, and lightly, as though she would rise again at once, dropped on to her knees. (Pt 7, ch. 31: 864)

Notes

Thanks to Andrea Fontana and two anonymous referees of *Symbolic Interaction* for helpful comments on a more panoramic draft of this article (February 1992) and for their helpful comments on its revision (March 1993). Thanks to Mike Featherstone and three anonymous referees of *Theory, Culture & Society* for helpful comments on a truncated version (February 1994) of the article as it now stands. Thanks to the anonymous referees of *TCS* who in a second review alerted me to some methodological difficulties of ethnographizing the eye code. Thanks also to Greg Smith for helpful comments on the first three versions as well as on this version.

1. Readers might be more familiar with the title *Anna Karenina*. The translator (Constance Garnett) of my edition writes in a 'Translator's Note': 'I have not adopted the form "Anna Karenina", but "Anna Karenin", since such a preservation of the feminine form of the surname is unparalleled in English ... [I]t is not the Russian habit to retain these feminine terminations ['a', 'eva', 'aia'] when speaking English.'

2. Which is the Sapir–Whorf hypothesis (Langsdorf, 1991: 146), the view of feminist, psychoanalytically oriented semioticians (Clough, 1992, 1993, but see Smith, 1993), the conviction of some social constructionists (Harré, 1986) and the theory of autopoiesis (Luhmann, 1986; Maturana, 1988, 1991).

3. See Gifford (1971) which contains appreciations of Tolstoy by over 50 writers including Dostoevsky, Turgenev, Chekhov, William James, Rilke, Lenin, D.H. Lawrence, Mann, E.M. Forster, Lukács, Gide and Poggioli.

4. See Travers (1995) where I analyse Emma Bovary as the paradigm self of patriarchal capitalism, in that she is a sign-set in thrall to 'a flawless and fluid and sharply televisual hallucination', Paris, the same Paris that powerfully influences American academics through Derrida, Foucault, Sartre, Barthes, Bourdieu, Baudrillard, Althusser and so on.

5. See Travers (1994: 125–9) where I analyse Werther's unrequited love of Charlotte as a colossally magnified form of Goffmanian deference.

6. Parker (1989: 66) thinks that Mead's 'I' originates in the Other and that Mead can learn from Foucault that the Other is 'historically constituted' in the 'mode of surveillance'.

7. Schreber is most famous as a case study which Freud developed from Schreber's memoirs (Schreber, 1955). Sass (1987) argues that Schreber's state of 'soul voluptuousness' and 'union of all rays' is not a regression but a perfectly reasonable antidote to the madness of subjectivity in surveillance societies.

8. The symbolic interactionist Paul Rock (1979: 110) also uses this formulation vis-a-vis Meadian selfhood: '[E]ach man is his own panopticon, an external monitor of himself . . .'.

9. As a true developmental psychology this idea is subject to challenge (Fridlund, 1992), but as a literary idea it goes unchallenged in much feminist film theory (De Lauretis, 1984; Penley, 1989). It is sometimes said that a problem for women is the male gaze (Silverman, 1984; Benjamin, 1984). The example of Anna Karenin, however, shows a female gaze operating to 'unwrite' men. Clearly Anna Karenin's husband and also Vronsky when he is being obstinate embody the patriarchal eyes of the law, but, equally clearly, when Anna sees those patriarchs as dead and deadening creatures, they recoil. Consequently it is not possible to map feminist theories of aggressive male gazing and powerless female subjectivity (such as Kappeler, 1986) on to my phenomenon.

10. 'The child identifies with an image that is manifestly different from itself, though it also clearly resembles it in some respects. It takes as its own an image which is other, an image which remains out of the ego's control. The subject, in other words, recognizes itself at the moment it loses itself in/as the other. The other is the foundation and support of its identity, as well as what destabilizes or annihilates it. The subject's "identity" is based on a (false) recognition of an other as the same' (Grosz, 1990: 41).

11. '[I]f we look at a thing straight on, i.e., matter-of-factly, disinterestedly, objectively, we see nothing but a formless spot; the object assumes clear and distinctive features only if we look at it "at an angle," i.e., with an "interested" view, supported, permeated, and "distorted" by *desire*. This describes perfectly the *objet petit a*, the object-cause of desire: an object that is, in a way, posited by desire itself. The paradox of desire is that it posits retroactively its own cause, i.e., the object *a* is an object that can be perceived only by a gaze "distorted" by desire, an object that *does not exist* for an "objective" gaze. In other words, the object *a* is always, *by definition*, perceived in a distorted way, because outside this distortion, "in itself", *it does not exist*, since it is *nothing but* the embodiment, the materialization of this very distortion, of this surplus of confusion and perturbation introduced by desire into so-called "objective reality". The object *a* is "objectively" nothing, though, viewed from a certain perspective, it assumes the shape of "something". . . . Desire "takes off" when "something" (its object-cause) gives positive existence to its "nothing", to its void. This "something" is the anamorphotic object, a pure semblance that we can perceive clearly only by "looking awry"' (Zizek, 1991: 11–12).

12. '[T]he male/active/voyeuristic/objectifying side of cinematic spectatorship has been stressed at the expense of the female/passive/identifying/fetishized (instead of fetishizing) side. Even more problematic is the way activity and passivity have been rigorously assigned to separate gendered spectator positions, with little examination of either the active elements of the feminine position or the mutability of male and female spectators' adoption of one or the other subject position' (Williams, 1989: 49).

References

Baudrillard, Jean (1987) *Forget Foucault*. New York: Semiotext(e).

Benjamin, Jessica (1984) 'Master and Slave: The Fantasy of Erotic Domination', pp. 292–311 in Ann Snitow, Christine Stanselle and Sharon Thompson (eds) *Desire: The Politics of Sexuality*. London: Virago.

Brown, Richard Harvey (1977) *A Poetic for Sociology*. Cambridge: Cambridge University Press.

Clough, Patricia Ticineto (1992) *The End(s) of Ethnography: From Realism to Social Criticism*. London: Sage.

Clough, Patricia Ticineto (1993) 'On the Brink of Deconstructing Sociology: Critical Reading of Dorothy Smith's Standpoint Epistemology', *Sociological Quarterly* 34(1): 169–82.

Conrad, Joseph (1994) *Heart of Darkness*. Harmondsworth: Penguin. (Orig. 1902.)

Cooley, Charles Horton (1983) *Human Nature and the Social Order*. New Brunswick, NJ: Transaction Books. (Orig. 1902.)

Craib, Ian (1995) 'Some Comments on the Sociology of the Emotions', *Sociology* 29(1): 151–8.

Creed, Barbara (1986) 'Horror and the Monstrous-Feminine: An Imaginary Abjection', *Screen* 27(1): 44–70.

Creed, Barbara (1987) 'From Here to Modernity: Feminism and Postmodernism', *Screen* 28(2): 47–67.

Crossley, Nick (1995) 'Body Techniques, Agency and Intercorporeality: On Goffman's *Relations in Public*', *Sociology* 29(1): 133–49.

Cushman, Philip (1990) 'Why the Self is Empty: Toward a Historically Situated Psychology', *American Psychologist* 45(5): 599–611.

de Certeau, Michel (1986) 'The Black Sun of Language: Foucault', pp. 171–84 in Michel de Certeau, *Heterologies: Discourse on the Other*. Minneapolis: University of Minnesota Press.

De Lauretis, Teresa (1984) *Alice Doesn't: Feminism, Semiotics, Cinema*. Bloomington: Indiana University Press.

Denzin, Norman K. (1995) 'Women at the Keyhole: Fatal Female Visions', *Symbolic Interaction* 18(2): 165–90.

Dyer, Richard (1979) *Stars*. London: British Film Institute.

Eliot, George (1957) *Middlemarch*. London: Zodiac Press. (Orig. 1872.)

Finkelstein, Joanne (1991) *The Fashioned Self*. Cambridge: Polity.

Foucault, Michel (1979) *Discipline and Punish: The Birth of the Prison*. New York: Random House.

Fridlund, Alan J. (1992) 'The Behavioral Ecology and Sociality of Human Faces', pp. 90–121 in Margaret S. Clark (ed.) *Emotion: Review of Personality and Social Psychology* 13. Newbury Park, CA: Sage.

Gifford, Henry (ed.) (1971) *Leo Tolstoy*. Harmondsworth: Penguin.

Goffman, Erving (1953) 'Communication Conduct in an Island Community', PhD dissertation, University of Chicago.

Goffman, Erving (1959) *The Presentation of Self in Everyday Life*. New York: Doubleday.

Goffman, Erving (1963) *Behavior in Public Places*. New York: The Free Press.

Goffman, Erving (1969) *Strategic Interaction*. Oxford: Basil Blackwell.

Goffman, Erving (1972) 'The Nature of Deference and Demeanor', pp. 47–95 in Erving Goffman, *Interaction Ritual*. Harmondsworth: Penguin. (Orig. 1956.)

Goffman, Erving (1974) *Frame Analysis*. Cambridge, MA: Harvard University Press.

Goffman, Erving (1983) 'The Interaction Order', *American Sociological Review* 48(1): 1–17.

Goffman, Erving (1993) 'Interview with Jef C. Verhoeven', *Research on Language and Social Interaction* 26(3): 317–48. (Orig. 1980.)

Grosz, Elizabeth (1990) *Jacques Lacan: A Feminist Introduction*. London: Routledge.

Harré, Rom (1986) 'An Outline of the Social Constructionist Viewpoint', pp. 2–14 in Rom Harré (ed.) *The Social Construction of Emotions*. Oxford: Basil Blackwell.

Hawthorne, Nathaniel (1965) *The Scarlet Letter*. New York: Harper and Row. (Orig. 1850.)

Hilton, Margery (1982) *The Beach of Sweet Returns*. London: Mills and Boon Ltd.

Irigaray, Luce (1985) *Speculum of the Other Woman*. Ithaca, NY: Cornell University Press.

Iser, Wolfgang (1975) 'The Reality of Fiction: A Functional Approach to Literature', *New Literary History* 7(1): 7–38.

Iser, Wolfgang (1979) 'The Current Situation of Literary Theory: Key Concepts and the Imaginary', *New Literary History* 11(1): 9–20.

Kappeler, Susanne (1986) *The Pornography of Representation*. Cambridge: Polity.

La Belle, Jenjoy (1988) *Herself Beheld: The Literature of the Looking Glass*. Ithaca, NY: Cornell University Press.

Lacan, Jacques (1953) 'Some Reflections on the Ego', *International Journal of Psychoanalysis* 34: 11–17.

Langsdorf, Lenore (1991) 'The Worldly Self in Schutz: On Sighting, Citing, and Siting the Self', *Human Studies* 14(2–3): 141–57.

Luhmann, Niklas (1986) *Love as Passion*. Cambridge: Polity.

McClary, Susan (1991) *Feminine Endings: Music, Gender, and Sexuality*. Minneapolis: University of Minnesota Press.

Maturana, Humberto R. (1988) 'Reality: The Search for Objectivity or the Quest for a Compelling Argument', *Irish Journal of Psychology* 9(1): 25–82.

Maturana, Humberto R. (1991) 'Science and Daily Life: The Ontology of Scientific Explanations', pp. 30–52 in F. Steier (ed.) *Research and Reflexivity*. London: Sage.

Mead, George Herbert (1962) *Mind, Self and Society*. Chicago, IL: University of Chicago Press. (Orig. 1934.)

Mulvey, Laura (1975) 'Visual Pleasure and Narrative Cinema', *Screen* 16(3): 6–18.

Mulvey, Laura (1989a) 'Afterthoughts on "Visual Pleasure and Narrative Cinema" Inspired by King Vidor's *Duel in the Sun* (1946)', pp. 29–38 in Laura Mulvey *Visual and Other Pleasures*. London: Macmillan.

Mulvey, Laura (1989b) 'Changes: Thoughts on Myth, Narrative and Historical Experience', pp. 159–76 in Laura Mulvey *Visual and Other Pleasures*. London: Macmillan.

Parker, Ian (1989) 'Discourse and Power', pp. 56–70 in John Shotter and Kenneth J. Gergen (eds) *Texts of Identity*. London: Sage.

Penley, Constance (1989) *The Future of an Illusion: Film, Feminism, and Psycho-analysis.* Minneapolis: University of Minnesota Press.

Rock, Paul (1979) *The Making of Symbolic Interactionism.* London: Macmillan.

Rodowick, D.N. (1982) 'The Difficulty of Difference', *Wide Angle* 5(1): 7.

Russell, Bertrand (1961) *An Outline of Philosophy.* Cleveland, OH: World. (Orig. 1927.)

Sartre, Jean-Paul (1956) *Being and Nothingness: An Essay in Phenomenological Ontology.* New York: Philosophical Library.

Sartre, Jean-Paul (1978) 'A Conversation about Sex and Women with Jean-Paul Sartre', *Playboy* January: 103–4, 116–18, 124, 139.

Sartre, Jean-Paul (1983) *Cahiers pour une morale.* Paris: Gallimard.

Sass, Louis A. (1987) 'Schreber's Panopticism: Psychosis and the Modern Soul', *Social Research* 54(1): 101–47.

Schreber, Daniel Paul (1955) *Memoirs of My Nervous Illness.* London: William Dawson.

Silverman, Kaja (1980) 'Masochism and Subjectivity', *Framework* 12: 2–9.

Silverman, Kaja (1984) '*Histoire d'O*: The Construction of a Female Subject', in Carol S. Vance (ed.) *Pleasure and Danger: Exploring Female Subjectivity.* London: Routledge and Kegan Paul.

Simmel, Georg (1921) 'Visual Interaction', pp. 356–61 in Robert E. Park and Ernest W. Burgess (eds) *Introduction to the Science of Sociology.* Chicago, IL: University of Chicago Press.

Simmel, Georg (1984) 'On Love (a fragment)', pp. 153–92 in *Georg Simmel: On Women, Sexuality, and Love.* New Haven, CT and London: Yale University Press.

Smith, Dorothy (1993) 'High Noon in Textland: A Critique of Clough', *Sociological Quarterly* 34(1): 183–92.

Stone, Gregory P. (1975) 'Appearance and the Self', pp. 78–90 in Dennis Brisset and Charles Edgley (eds) *Life as Theatre: A Dramaturgical Sourcebook.* Chicago, IL: Aldine.

Stone, Robert (1981) *A Flag for Sunrise.* London: Secker and Warburg.

Synnott, Anthony (1993) *The Body Social: Symbolism, Self and Society.* London: Routledge.

Tacey, David J. (1988) *Patrick White: Fiction and the Unconscious.* Melbourne: Oxford University Press.

Theweleit, Klaus (1989) *Male Fantasies*, Vol. 2. Cambridge: Polity.

Tolstoy, Leo (1901) *Anna Karenin.* London: Heinemann. (Orig. 1877.)

Tolstoy, Leo (1970) *Resurrection.* Harmondsworth: Penguin. (Orig. 1899.)

Tolstoy, Leo (1993) *The Kreutzer Sonata and Other Short Stories.* New York: Dover Publications Inc. (Orig. 1891.)

Travers, Andrew (1992) 'Strangers to Themselves: How Interactants Are Other than They Are', *British Journal of Sociology* 43(4): 601–37.

Travers, Andrew (1994) 'The Unrequited Self', *History of the Human Sciences* 7(2): 121–40.

Travers, Andrew (1995) 'The Identification of Self', *Journal for the Theory of Social Behaviour* 25(3): 303–40.

White, Hayden (1978) *Tropics of Discourse*. Baltimore, MD: Johns Hopkins University Press.

Williams, Linda (1989) 'Power, Pleasure, and Perversion: Sadomasochistic Film Pornography', *Representations* 27: 37–65.

Zizek, Slavoj (1991) *Looking Awry: An Introduction to Jacques Lacan through Popular Culture*. Cambridge, MA: MIT Press.

Andrew Travers was a Research Fellow in the Department of Sociology, Exeter University.

'On Me, Not in Me'

Locating Affect in Nationalism after AIDS

Cindy Patton

LOVE

>   Gay men are socialized as men first; our gay socialization comes later. From the day we are born we are trained as men to compete with other men. The challenge facing gay men in America is to figure out how to love someone you've been trained to 'destroy'.
>
>   The goal of gay male liberation must be to find ways in which love becomes possible despite continuing and often overwhelming pressure to compete and adopt adversary relationships with other men.
>
>   Men *loving* men was the basis of gay male liberation, but we have now created 'cultural institutions' in which love or even affection can be totally avoided.
>
>   If you love the person you are fucking with – even for one night – you will not want to make them sick.
>
>   Maybe affection is our best protection. (Berkowitz and Callen, 1983: 38–9)

This is not a call for 'gay marriage'. The authors link affection and liberation to place duty *in* sex, regardless of the duration of a relationship. The booklet appears at the end of an era – of mimeographed publishing, of a gay politic that was anti-misanthropic, that was based in a critique and dispersion of love, not in a reconstruction of love in the face of hate. 'Protection' is grounded in liberation, in countercultural activism, not in the free market writ small as personal responsibility. This drive to solidarity has been grossly misunderstood, or forgotten, or rejected, in recent criticism of early AIDS activists' use of 'undifferentiated' calls to safe sex. (Undifferentiated by sero-status ... but then, testing was not widely available until late 1985, not broadly accepted by 'consumers' until a few years later.) The Berkowitz/

■ *Theory, Culture & Society* 1998 (SAGE, London, Thousand Oaks and New Delhi),
   Vol. 15(3–4): 355–373
   [0263-2764(199808/11)15:3–4;355–373;006071]

Callen approach seeks a unifying critical relationship to masculine social-ization *against* the deadly reversion to capitalism's *every man for himself.* Thus, their advice is collective, not individual. But the homophobia of the emergent rightist patriarchy dramatically and continuously pressurized the love between men, between women. Grappling with the right loosened bond of solidarity, casting doubt on the role of dissident sex and queer affection as the experiential touchstone for political action.

What has been most difficult to understand and assess in this loping, decade-long dance between gay left and Christian right is the way in which our bodies have been pressed to assume a different affect – not just in relation to each other (the New Monogamy, the New Abstinence, which may only rationalize our exhaustion from a long period of economic speed-up) but in relation to our Nation. I want to make partial sense of the shifts of the 1990s by reinvigorating the antipathy toward family and romantic love that characterized that Long Decade. Extending Benedict Anderson's illuminat-ing discussion of 'political love' in the context of Internet mediated post-nationalism, I want briefly to review the trajectory of rightist responses to sexuality in the context of AIDS. I will then turn to several conservative and crypto-conservative websites that reorganize sex and love. I hope to show that while superficially 'relying on an archaic book and a primitive belief' ('Marc' responding on 23 March 1998 to the Pure Love Alliance website) and reading like 'puritanical, dangerous and uninformed literature' ('Sara' responding on 23 March 1998 to the PLA website), the particular juxtaposi-tion of sex and love to family characteristic of non-government abstinence sites masks a particularly frightening kind of nationalist ideology in our post-Cold War, transnational communication world.

From Smash the Family to Family Values

Let us indulge some memories of the Long Decade of the 1970s, an epoch that, from the standpoint of queer America, runs from about 1968, with the emergence of gay activist groups (catalyzed, of course, by Stonewall) to about 1985, when gay politics – even gay identity – were fatefully recon-figured by the consolidation of HIV testing.[1] Slogans like 'smash the family, smash the state' tripped lightly off the tongues of second wave feminists, socialists and various groups militating for sexual freedom. Viewed as a long arm of the state, it was clear that the family had to go. Romantic love was the ideological bad faith that bound body to couple, couple to family and family to state. Sex had to be revolutionary, anti-family and anti-state.

Then The Crisis came. Gay liberation needed to sustain group soli-darity in the face of loss (friends, mass) and political threats (quarantine, 'protecting' good gays from their monstrously promiscuous brothers through state-sponsored contact tracing or rumors of 'unsafe sex'). Left antagonisms toward named modes of relation posed no problem: for the tight-knit political micro-culture sustained in practices of sexual liberation, 'love' was a state of durable and transportable respect, not a government- or church-sanctified union. But this powerful will to celebrate bonds of pleasure in the face of biological – and soon, it seemed – political *death* was short-lived. In response to the emergence of a new conservatism, civil rights became, well, more *civil*, and affection was superseded by *anger* as the source of radicals' power.

The radical political analyses of the New Left tended toward the structuralist and anti-psychologistic. Activist rhetorics increasingly posited identity as the source of politics, as the affective mechanism for producing coalition across difference. From an objective standpoint, oppressions were the result of structurally different, though generally systematic and integrated forms of *power over*. Subjectively, oppressions were seen as quantitatively variable, but essentially the same: pain was pain. Any difficulty in identifying with others came not from differences among kinds of oppression but in the inability to calibrate one's fractional status as oppressor to one's states of oppression. This awkward project of knitting objectivist analyses of power systems with subjectivist accounts of their effects was central to the Rainbow Coalition. Stand-up comics now make fun of this deeply felt politics of cross-identification. A joke on the 15 April 1998 episode of the US sitcom *The Drew Carey Show*, which featured a plot about anti-(heterosexual) cross-dresser employment discrimination went, 'give me a black, transexual lesbian with a speech impediment, and I'll make her CEO'.

Even those of us who were activists during the Long Decade may not have recognized the extent to which our politics were a labor of, or rather, *on* affect. Certainly, we worked 'consciousness raising' – effected explicitly in CR groups, but more broadly through a rhetoric of liberation through self-criticism – into a particularity: 'coming out'. But in changing our consciousness, we were only dimly aware that we were breaking an attachment. Our characteristically Anglo-American philosophical assumption that pain is intersubjectively recognizable, is universal, obscured the fact that as Enlightenment subjects, especially as *Americans*, our most profound object of affection is the nation.

The fateful moment was somewhere in the mid-1970s, when a haphazard coalition of pro-gun, anti-abortion, anti-busing, pro-Panama Canal, prayers-in-public groups decided that the family was, in fact, the foundation of 'American' if not 'Western' culture. They didn't quote Hegel's *Philosophy of Right*, though they might have. Instead, they based their politics on the Bible and, in more secular versions, the 'great books' that preached duty to family and the power of *agape*, harnessed to hearth and *polis*, to overcome the evils of mercantilism and monarchy. At first this simply seemed ludicrous: even after the most violent feelings of the civil rights, Black Power, anti-war and feminist movements cooled, it seemed impossible that anyone would actually want to *go back*. The initial far right activism seemed more like a last gasp than the harbinger of a new form of citizenship. A crucial, but almost undetected shift began to occur in affective relations: among people who lived face-to-face; more radically, among individuals in their mode as citizens; and in collectivities in their sense of what it meant to be 'represented' as a people.

During the 1960s and into the 1970s, the separatist Christian right struggled with its relation to secular society. In the late 1970s, they converged with single-issue groups that had no overarching political ideology to form a loose *movement* – paradoxically, through direct mail campaigns that allowed organizers to yoke together these issues under the rubric of 'Family Protection', but without ever getting the 'family' together. Committed to mass organizing and unfamiliar with mass marketing techniques used by the new direct-mail-based rightist organizations, the left, feminists and gays did not unite in a rejection of the emerging family rhetoric. Indeed, periodicals like *In These Times*, *Gay Community News* and *off our backs*, to invoke only three of the most trenchant new-New Left periodicals of the late 1970s and early 1980s, began to debate how to reclaim the idea of family. As a result, although not uncontested by activists, a counter-rhetoric of famil*ies* was adopted by feminists, leftists and gay activists who believed it was possible to combat the right by including 'families we choose'. To some extent, liberal politicians took up and coopted this strategy, speaking about 'family' to assuage conservatives, but equivocating on the term's definition in order to keep feminists from decamping.

Astonishingly, in just a decade, it became progressive to support alternative families alongside the traditional ones, and to speak openly about the desire for the kinds of emotional commitments such bonds might ensure. Although it nagged at many people's political consciousness, no one could quite articulate why the desire for these warm fuzzy feelings might be politically problematic: we largely thought of emotions as 'natural' and, at any rate, pertaining to our relations in their most local sense. Thus, we found it clever when during the 1992 campaign Bill Clinton took this slippage in family/love to new heights: he countered Bush's 'family values' rhetoric by saying he wanted to 'value families'.

But, as the subsequent 'don't ask, don't tell'[2] policy and the effort to forestall gay unions with 'marriage protection' laws revealed, the commitment to anything other than heteronormative families was nil: domestic violence and divorce were preferable to 'parents' of the same sex. After only two decades of wresting sex from love, the two were uneasily re-shackled: for both right and left, the fundamental issue was, once again, the proper relation between sex and love. But in the context of calls to saf/ve sex, there was no simple alignment between the two. Debates about sexuality uneasily forced culturally different genealogies of sex – sex and love never ceased signifying differently for and as class, race, gender – onto a more starkly divided contest over the significance of acts per se. Sex was divided against itself: at once unimportant – commitment was the test of love – and the sine qua non of procreative pleasure, that which should be reserved as the material-ideal core of family.

For Ben, with Love

Benedict Anderson (1991) offers the idea of political love to describe the quality that attachment to nation has in the modern project. His *Imagined Communities* has been extended and reworked to analyze the mediations of people and place that exist in the variegated entity we call Nation.[3] But, finally, it is the affective relation to nation and not Nation's diversity that most agitates Anderson. He ponders 'why, today, they command such profound emotional legitimacy' (1991: 4) and he returns to this problematic after detailing the multiple and historically contingent forms of nation. I want to draw out this aspect of Anderson's work, perhaps exceeding his original intent, but not, I hope, infelicitously.

Anderson suggests several reasons why nation became the dominant – and dominating – form of geopolitical organization. First, the development of a semi-independent print capitalism allowed people who were widely dispersed to see themselves as existing in a coextensive time that alters the citizen's sense of place. Placement of news articles from different regions on the same page, for example, promoted a consciousness that *what's happening over there* is not something you learn about *later* when the news has *traveled* but something that is happening *here and now*. Although Anderson does not concern himself with the details of this bodily disposition, I want to suggest that we can speak quite literally of the citizen's proprioception – her capacity to know where her body *is*, in space. This new sensibility enabled the development of cross-regional consensus about politics among the literate middle classes and enhanced the sense that a nation was a community, even if that national identity – Anderson's 'imagined community' – exists in a different order of space.

There was an important reciprocal effect of this production of national time as simultaneity: people who did not live in limned spaces of Nation were living in the primitive past, existing in mythological rather than secular or civil time. To fall out of the material space of Nation was, thus, to be denied a separate historicity: this space–time complex of Nation meant that a literal long arm of Nation could instantiate anywhere, at any time, through the sense of national location that adheres to the traveling citizen. At least to some degree, we carry our nation with us: wherever my body is, so is my nation. The diplomatic immunity (what a curious way to phrase the translocation of a nation's sovereignty inside the territorial boundaries of another nation!) of the embassy and ambassadorial staff is only an explicit codification of the body-quality of any citizen of a recognized nation.

For Anderson, the space of imagined community is hypothetical, but I think we need not interpret discontinuous space as idealist. Indeed, it is quite material, in the instance and in effect. As recent work in postmodern geography has suggested, it was an error of essentialist materialisms to demand that physical space repeat the scientific assumption of molecular contiguity. Such accounts needed a concept like ideology to account for the domination of the mind from afar, conceiving power as an asymmetrically bifurcated system of oppression (e.g. Althusser's Repressive State Apparatus and Ideological State Apparatus), resulting in subsequent attempts to blur the differences between them, or explain their interconnection.

In fact, the most important distinction in modernity is not at the level of the 'state', which may act with direct or mediated force, but in the embodiment of space/time as simultaneously immediate – habitation and super-real nation. From a practical standpoint, the modern citizen's task is finding a style of living in between, of negotiating the alter-nation of multiple dimensions of space/time. Cedric Robinson's (1996) neo-materialist *Black Political Movements* finds an important lived alternative to the assimilation/separation dichotomy that has dominated thinking about American politics. He provides an account of maroon colonies, unsecurable swamps, and unincorporated territories that were extended and material experiences of contesting nation per se, not from 'outside', as when one nation rubs up against another, but from within. These unincorporated locales were not, for their inhabitants, part of a simultaneous, contiguous Nation. These renegades were neither assimilated to nor separate from democratizing America: they contested the very compulsion to wholeness – what I think of as 'geophagia' – of Nation. While they were unsuccessful as strategic contenders for the space they attempted to secure, runaway slaves, Native Americans and indentured whites nonetheless provided the basis of a political sensibility that rejects attachment to nation. If space and its occupation are understood this way, then the idea of Ideologic State Apparatus is both improbable and superfluous. There is a somatic link through the space–time of nation, and this Anderson calls political love. This affect toward the new entities Nation and People was strong enough to make millions of 20th century soldiers lay down their lives not for economic gain, but for the idea of nations and freedom.

I want to suggest that the specific qualities, the affect, of the citizen shifts as the calculus of Nation requires. Elsewhere (1996, 1997), I have argued that we have seen two changes in political love since the end of the Second World War. I would like to review these briefly, as they provide the historical backdrop for the reconnection of sex and love we will observe in the websites. A caveat: the formulation here may seem too dense, too heavy, too threatening to the thin texts I propose to examine. Take it as a pharmakon to stave off, for the moment, the symptoms of thought that we moderns suffer and cannot be rid of. If, as Lyotard suggests, the 'post-modern' precedes the modern, is the condition that necessitates the modern project, then the thin texts I propose to read are both 'pre-modern' – in the tone of their politics – and post- – in their mode of circulation. They precisely lack the 'depth' and symbolism that a hermeneutic of suspicion requires. They are surfacial, rather than superficial; they circulate at face value rather than communicate something more profound. If the modern project is an expansion of the distance and temporal lag between body and nation, then these 'simple' texts show more clearly, more algebraically, the linkages that are being worked over in the current refiguration of political affect. It is quickly obvious that these texts trade in Christian rhetoric. But to see them only as a throwback to a theocratic era is to succumb to the greasy night sweats and hallucinations of our humanist malaria. And it is not only we academics in the rarefied atmospheres of our offices who are sick from this air, but participants in the chats. If the website authors extend a rightist politics they sometimes disavow ('this is not about religion') then their on-line critics may double our own reaction: their simplicity is not a fact but a warning not to treat too lightly the flimsy evidence of our web.

From 'Walking in the Other Guy's Shoes' to Tough Love

In the late 1940s, in the heat of anti-communist sentiment, but also when American social issues like anti-semitism and racism were constructed as the work of individuals, I found emerging in popular culture and in immigration statutes (which represent in relief concepts of citizenship) a newly 'empathic' citizen. The new citizen somewhat shed the masculine trappings that had been required of the citizen who could kill Our Foes. Indeed, books like *Gentleman's Agreement* (Hobson, 1947) represent hypermasculinity as bigoted, as incapable of 'walking in the other guy's shoes', rendering America more susceptible to communist invasion. He hates his fellow man in favor of loving – too much – his nation. But this new affect did not represent a feminization of citizenship, since women were explicitly constructed as unable to control and define their 'identification' with their fellows. Instead, this new affect absorbs, desexualizes and mutes the violent impulses of the homoerotic warrior bond. The immediately post-Second World War citizen was the man who could balance his love of man with his love of country, sacrificing neither, and, thereby, strengthening America's ability to be hard-nosed in ferreting out foreign (or communist) influence, while remaining empathic toward the plight of those Americans who suffered from racism and anti-semitism.

Later, in the late 1980s, another refiguration of affect occurred: this time in the context of AIDS. Like the shift in the late 1940s, this new citizenship demanded a combination of toughness and sympathy. Once it was clear that, at least in the USA, HIV would be more or less contained among the poor (especially communities of color) and the queer, it was imperative to quell the panic over 'casual contagion'. Let me be clear that this containment had nothing to do with qualities intrinsic to the bodies of the poor or the queer, but rather resulted from the long-existing and intransigent organization of sex precisely along lines of class and (biological) sex. Heteronormativity consisted not only in the demand for man to bond with woman, but in the requirement that these bonds remain within class and, especially, racial boundaries. As an idea about prevention, the very framing of 'safe sex' was intrinsically and immediately problematic. It required an uneasy separation between trust and duty toward others on one hand, and the politics of sexual and social empowerment of several minority groups on the other (especially gay men, sex workers of all genders, and African Americans, already subject to complex and racist ideas about sexuality). From the left/feminist/gay/minority community activist perspective, it was essential to quickly and loudly disassociate AIDS from *types* of people. This would decrease panic-driven discrimination and would make it more likely that potentially 'at risk' individuals would attend to prevention messages or seek medical care. They argued that education about AIDS in general, but especially education about the sexual and drug use practices that could result in infection, ought to be discussed in a way that did not invoke negative stereotypes of class, race or sexuality. In an already conservatizing atmosphere in which right-wing groups were calling AIDS the scourge of God, activists demanded of government a 'value-neutral' language for campaigns. But what was 'value neutral' to those who are not bothered by sexual differences was perceived as a nefarious and irresponsible lie by those who deeply believe that God's plan calls virgins to bond for life in monogamous and procreative relations.

It was in the context of value neutrality that a sinister new concept of love re-entered the discussion of sex, but it took some time for the Christian right to work out how to connect Jesus's love and political love. Most readers will be familiar with the blatantly homophobic writings of people like Jerry Falwell and his colleagues at *The Moral Majority Report* (later renamed *Liberty News*). But there was another, more scientifically and theologically moderate position among mainstream Protestants, whose denominational bodies were debating ordination of gays. Once the initial panic about AIDS diminished, these folks were not too concerned about contracting HIV through casual contact or even 'contracting' queerness from ministering to gays. Splitting identity and acts, they reconciled their commitment to parishioners with their dislike of homosexual practice (especially in their queer clergy!) through the logic of 'love the sinner, hate the sin'. But this turned nasty in more conservative groups:

> Prayer Focus: AIDS – That God would prevent the spread of this dreaded disease to the general public, use it to expose the depravity of homosexuality and cause those who are practicing homosexuals to repent and totally reject their detestable life style. May He have mercy and bring healing to those AIDS victims who repent and turn to Him. (Intercessors for America, 1983)

Other groups more explicitly cloaked themselves in our all-important language of non-discrimination in order to redirect the citizen's duty:

> This [AIDS] pamphlet has been written for the benefit of heterosexuals and homosexuals alike. We believe that homosexual sex practices seriously threaten the well-being of the individual homosexual along with the well-being of our nation. Our goal is to diminish that danger for both. (Alert Citizens of Texas, 1984)

Even gay commentators were not entirely free of this tendency to divide responsible and irresponsible citizens, based on their individual responsibility for *acts*. But this usually required recourse to a story of the Long Decade. Centrist gay groups insisted that AIDS had unfairly represented gay men as driven by lust rather than by relationships. Typically, as, for example, in the enormously influential *And the Band Played On* (Shilts, 1987), political and personal development were homologized to depict the gay community of the 1970s as 'adolescent', but now chastened, emerging in the 1980s and 1990s as a mature political force populated by reasonable and duty-conscious homosexual citizens. By the late 1980s, moderate and rightist tendencies had converged on a strategy that could sustain covert homophobia while insisting that such a position was not discriminatory. Straights could be compassionate citizens who could pity the 'victims' of AIDS, but not provide funding for sex-positive education. Gays finally got to be citizens, but only if they were responsible homosexuals who, while they might not be able to reorient their (mostly, his) filthy desires, could take active steps (abstinence or, failing that, condoms and the resistance of bisexuality) to avoid polluting the nation. Safe sex is the civic obligation of the gay citizen and the act that distinguishes him from the compassionate citizen, who must by definition be separate from the class toward which s/he expresses sympathetic affect. As an affect that pre-empts intersubjective recognition (i.e. empathy, or the sense that 'you and I are *the same*'), sympathy allows acts of pity to hide anti-gay (and racist) hatred within political love. This is why so many heterosexuals do not see using condoms as an act of social responsibility, of solidarity with gay men, but as degrading, perverse. This also explains the recent US government decision to publicly acknowledge that needle-exchange programs save lives but refuse to allocate federal monies to support them.

Hypercommunity, or Politics without Bodies

Nothing has challenged both political economy and textual analysis more than the Internet. However complexly developed, questions of the political economy of communications systems are thrown into crisis by this high-tech but widely accessible means of intercommunication. Concepts like face-to-face communication falter, especially when conceived as the natural or modal form for which people provide compensations in other forms of communication. We don't know how people 'experience' their bodies when they enter this 'space'. We don't really even know who is on the Net. In fact, there is no consensus on a genealogy of the Internet. Is there a single precursor form of communication – say phone calling – out of which the Internet primarily developed? Or, does the Internet incorporate a variety of kinds of communicative function, each with its own sensibility and community, and place them alongside one another in technically parallel but experientially divergent streams? My attempt to locate a group called the 'Pure Love Movement' illustrates some of the complexities of doing research 'in' the Internet, and of knowing what to do with what you find.

I first heard of the Pure Love Movement from friends in Taiwan, who emailed me in distress wondering who was behind this group that had been organizing a branch there. Although my friends have the same web access as I (indeed, as antipodal subjects, are probably better users!), it seemed fitting, somehow, for me to track down the American origin of this supposedly global movement. I had followed the direct mail new/Christian right since the early 1980s, so I was well aware of the difficulty in defining 'groups'. Though the left and identity politics are also much more complex and varied than we often admit, the New Right quite consciously emerged as a phantom movement. Early 1980s writings by emerging rightist leaders cautioned against holding mass meetings and marches of the kind that had characterized civil rights and left activism. To a very great extent, the New Right emerged discursively and only later as an embodied movement. The late 1970s and early 1980s saw the convergence of a carefully crafted rhetoric with the bodies of politicians who were either newly entering electoral politics, or who shifted their ultra-conservativism to match the new requirement to use rightist Christian language.

By the early 1990s, the world-wide web presented another domain for propagating broadly conservative ideas about sex, love and politics, even less controlled by a specific organization or specific right-wing figurehead. Like renegades of the neo-anarchist left, young people with conservative politics could now communicate directly with anyone who could surf their way to them. Unlike the direct mail days, when one's name was sold from list to list, and therefore one could passively receive material of interest, websites link among themselves, or are indexed through the several 'search engines'. The widespread implementation of public access systems through public libraries and cyber-cafes means that a vast public exists for website inaugurators. They can offer new information more quickly and inexpensively than direct mail enterprises, which had to consider cost ratios of mailings to replies.

I did initially find the group that I believe had been organizing in Taiwan, but when I tried to find it again a year or two later (in 1998), the site was gone or renamed. So, when I decided to analyze this kind of Internet grouping, I did a content-driven (rather than 'word match') search using Yahoo. I hit 'abstinence' and, based on the search engine's algorithm, got a list of some dozen regional public health groups, Pure Love Alliance, several church-related sites, a few personal home pages – the most 'pure' form of democratic participation, the personal home page (see later) – including one ('Abstinence Safer than Sex') with fire-and-brimstone graphics reminiscent of those little comic books people hand out on the street. Interestingly, this site would not 'print', so my research 'time' there was 'real'. In the case of the other sites, I printed systematically from 'top' to 'bottom', allowing me to read and re-read these web-detachable words. Only one site (PLA) had a compilation of recent notes from the guest-book, which created something like a dialog between the site's creators and readers. But this suggestion of interactivity must be viewed with caution; the entries were more like letters than strings of chat. 'James' (24 March 1998) questions the relative lack of negative comments: 'How interesting and revealing that the only negative comments in this site are from the last day or two. Could it be that they are erased?' Nevertheless, the guest-book leavings allowed readers to allude to each other when responding to the site manager: Svemir Brkic in Macedonia (27 March 1998) says, 'It is also good to see many negative comments, even though they are sometimes obviously by people who did not read your materials carefully. When you are close to the target, you will most certainly be shoot [sic] at! Nobody will attack you if you are missing it.'

Just Wait

The two explicitly Christian (True Love Waits sponsored by the Southern Baptist Convention and Wait Trainer, a home page on the offensiveness-screened Christian web domain, integrityol) use two principal strategies to combat what they see as disinformation campaigns by public health agencies. Unlike the Abstinence Safer than Sex site, which eventually moves you to a picture of a gaunt (gay?) man who appears to be covered with KS lesions, neither uses explicitly homophobic rhetoric. Wait Trainer emphasizes that 'Heterosexual transmission accounts for 45% of AIDS cases among teenage girls.' But if these sites' response to government's neutral or AIDS Service Organizations' sex-positive campaigns has left overt homophobia behind, their lack of concern with the possible homo-sexual behavior of their audience suggests that they do not believe that Christian teens are tempted by homosexual practices. Indeed, both sites argue that most teens are not even having sex, or rather, most middle-class white teens are not. Wait Trainer cautions the teen reader not to be 'fooled into thinking all teenagers are having sex', but goes on to cite various studies that suggest that unplanned pregnancy is the domain of the poor.

True Love Waits goes further than Wait Trainer in linking Christianity and sexual abstinence. The campaign uses rock-concert-style 'super rallies' complete with Christian musicians who give testimony about their own sexuality. Harking back to the right-wing direct mail days, when the receiver was typically asked to send money and sign a pledge card of some kind, young people who take the 'abstinence challenge' are asked to sign 'covenant cards' that read: 'Believing that true love waits, I make a commitment to God, myself, my family, my friends, my future mate, and my future children to be sexually abstinent from this day until the day I enter a biblical marriage relationship' ('210,000 covenant cards were displayed on the national Mall in Washington, D.C., on July 29, 1994' and '340,000 cards stacked from the floor to the roof of the Georgia Dome'). Where Wait Trainer stages itself against prevailing safe sex advice, True Love Waits emphasizes the value of joining in an entire movement that will support the 'choice' of an individual to wait. Linking the emotional trauma of out-of-wedlock sex to the possible physical health sequelae of sex (or rather, though they don't say it, unprotected sex), they argue that you 'can't put a condom on your heart', a phrase that appears in several of the personal home pages.

With God as My Penis

Trying to be ultra-hip and 'in-your-face', the Pure Love Alliance sees its roots in the radical activism of 'Berkeley' in the 1960s. Confusing anti-war, civil rights and 'free love' movements of the Long Decade, PLA criticizes 'Madison Avenue' and 'Hollywood' as ideological trendsetters but emphasizes that 'members of PLA have diverse interests – from international service projects to abstinence & pure education, from ethnic reconciliation to promotion of democracy – we are all working to promote the timeless values on which a strong society must stand.' One protest, reported by Gary Jones-Locke, of Los Angeles, evoked ACT UP demos of the late 1980s in which protesters carried signs with numbers of dead.

> ... clad in white T-shirts bearing the slogan, 'Pure and Proud[,]' ... students marched with cardboard replicas of the stars embedded in Hollywood sidewalks, brandishing them high above their heads. The stars bore the names of Hollywood idols who practice 'free' sex, divorced recently or who died of AIDS, and were symbolic of the corruption of the nation's entertainment industry.

But the most interesting aspect of PLA is the argument it makes linking the body to nation via God. In their on-line newsletter, columnist Richard Panzer defines pure love as 'a new sexual revolution, a national movement for purity'. Pure love is one that 'cares about the consequences of one's acts, including the possibility that you may be creating a new life, and not just a new life, but even an entire lineage that may last for decades or for hundreds, even thousands of years!' (columnist Richard Panzer). This temporal yoking of sex and love to a 'lineage' finds even sharper focus in the 'simple truths' espoused by PLA: 'A strong family is the center of an enduring and prosperous community and nation.' After spelling out a complicated theory of love (quite similar to that in one of the non-aligned sites below) as having 'marriage', 'child' and 'parent' modalities, one contributor turns to the nature of God. Arguing through a hack version of object relations theory, Ed Fleck notes that just as 'we need an object, someone who resembles us and reflects our own character, nature, and deepest heart ... so does God.' Other contributors connect the mass movement dimension of True Love Waits with the anti-condom sentiment of Wait Trainer to produce a 'frank' discussion of 'who owns my sexual organ'. According to their analysis, God – not ourselves or our partners – 'owns' our sex organs. A truly liberatory sexuality is one that uses God's sex organs in the ecstatic act of procreation.

'This is not about Religion ...'

The most interesting sites come not from predictable sources like the Southern Baptist Convention but from ordinary people empowered by their use of new technologies. Laura Kate Van Hollebeke of Born Again Virgins of America (BAVAM) recounts her decision to fax a 'testimonial' to talk radio host Dr Laura Schlessinger, who 'preaches morals and integrity'. The good doctor read Laura Kate's words on the air and suggested that Laura Kate start the club she jokes about – Born Again Virgins, or BAVs. Laura Kate enlisted the help of a friend and started a web-site ('filed' under 'Sexless in Seattle'). Like the explicitly religious-group-based sites, BAVAM is constructed in response to the Long Decade: 'Then jump on the bandwagon, baby, it's time to set free the remains of the last sexual revolution and observe the next – the germ-free, accident-proof and emotion-safe sexual revolution.' Uncomfortably combining an unacknowledged post-feminism with recent tropes of conservative protestantism – being 'born again' and 'BAVtized' – the author says: 'This is not about religion, this is about self-worth – valuing your body, mind and soul.' The letters BAVAM reprints on the site are an interesting and secular mix, focused on how BAVAM 'makes it so cool to wait' ('Jessica'). Of particular interest is the 'affirmation' from 'Virgin Dude' Chuck:

> I am a guy and I even agree with you. I am so completely thrilled that someone has finally figured out a way to be cool about this subject of chastity. I am a 31-year-old virgin, and proud of it! I am getting married in eight months. My virginity will be my gift to my wife as will hers be her gift to me. There's not much more valuable than that.

Whether or not there actually is a 'Chuck', the inclusion of this reassurance seals the site's principal audience as female. Subtly adopting a conservative Christian precept about masculine sexuality, the stories the authors tell suggest that men are sex-driven animals. Significantly, with one exception, the women whose voices are represented in this site have all 'succumbed' to the 'just do it' ethos they attribute to 'the over-exposure of sex in our culture – sex on TV, in movies, magazines, and our roommates' bedrooms … if we're not doing "it", we are unsophisticated and out of touch'. Only through persistently announcing their intention to be Born Again Virgins do these worldly-wise young women stand a chance of 'remembering that you are worth waiting for!'

Terri Lester also started a home page out of a desire to 'do a service project in my community of Kansas City'. This non-religious-group based site also invokes the 'local' extending out to the global via the Internet. Like Laura Kate, Terri has searched for 'materials that I felt comfortable using'. Finding none she could use, Terri enlists the help of her (cyberspace?) friend 'Starlene', who has her own site: '(Visit Starlene [hotlinked], but don't forget to come back!!!!).' Starlene is a 'stay at home mother of two sons' who offers her views on various topics, including parenting, food, pets and including a 'Bohemian Café' where you can read Starlene's poetry. Hot-links from her site take us to a wide variety of locales, including 'queendom', a site that offers psychological testing, counseling, and lots of 'stuff' for 'bored' women. (Note: if you are looking for a really good web-site designer, you might 'call' Starlene: this is about the most hot-linked and sophisticated home page I've seen!)

Though her analysis replays the logic of the Pure Love Alliance, she argues that her approach is designed to 'talk about what we ARE doing – learning to love in the most healthy way possible! Healthy Love! Yeah!' rather than 'talking about what we're *not* doing (not having sex)'. She believes that:

> Safe/r sex is promoted as something noble, almost saintly, and abstinence is openly criticized as unnatural and unrealistic, even by government representatives. In the rush to persuade youth to embrace the condom, its limitations are glossed over or even completely ignored as if they were nothing more than obstacles standing in the way of the onward march of perfect public health and universal enlightenment.

Terri's Healthy Love site provides '36 questions and answers on practicing abstinence'. It is here that we can most clearly see the logic that underwrites all of these sites, regardless of their religious or post-feminist orientation. Terri outlines a complex argument in which the specificity of 'romantic' love is debunked. In her view, there are different types of love – love of children, love of siblings, married love and parental love – and these vary in intensity, but share five traits: 'permanence, affection, generosity, intimacy, security'. Sex is only to be found in married love, and only after this pentagonal base is built. Learning all of these forms of love occurs within the family, where a healthy marriage produces healthy children.

Significantly, Terri explicitly grounds her argument in common sense, liberal pluralism rather than a particular religion. In response to the FAQ, 'Isn't abstinence just for religious fanatics?' she replies, 'You don't have to be religious to abstain from sex, you just have to be sensible. Abstinence is simply the healthiest way to go, and we want to give everyone the opportunity, regardless of their beliefs or cultural background.' But religions in general are not far behind, and here we see most profoundly the extent to which her abstinence project is tied to 'political love'. Foregoing the straight-line arguments about love, God and America that were used in the religious sites, Terri has to work harder to bring the body back in line with nationalism. She has to build from desire to nation without forfeiting her pluralist inclusiveness. Admitting that 'physical sexual urges can be very strong' Terri relegates desire to a Darwinian logic: 'They're meant to be: that's what ensures the survival of humankind.' Dismissing relativism as 'confusion of values' that results in 'anarchy' instead of 'freedom', she subtly retrieves 'freedom' from its association with the Long Decade – as in 'sexual freedom' – to instead place it in the conservative frame of collective freedom, freedom of the whole to be safe from deviations in its parts. 'All cultures', she argues, ' agree on basic values and standards for behavior; it's mostly in the details that we differ.' She echoes secular rightists who reject multiculturalism by locating 'cultural difference' in 'details' and suggest that gays and lesbians and feminists have derailed the quest for true (as opposed to *special*) rights by, for example, African Americans. Terri simultaneously invokes difference ('give everyone the opportunity') and dismisses it as inessential ('All cultures have rules and customs governing the ways that people relate to each other'). The most important task is to consolidate the 'kinds of love' into an economic unit – the family – so that society can be 'based upon it'. Ultimately, Terri provides a 'clear, rational concept of love', divorced from desire and representing the control of mind over body: the model for intimate relations is identical in nature and practice to the bonds in society. Terri does not explicitly argue the link between society and nation, but as a post-Cold War writer, she doesn't need to; communism is no longer a threat, but the outer edge of difference that proves the rule that 'it' s mostly in the details that we differ'.

> In fact, *all* major religions – Hinduism, Judaism, Buddhism, Confucianism, Christianity, Islam, Sikhism, Jainism, Taoism – have supported the ideal of abstinence prior to marriage. Even communist societies have actively discouraged premarital sex.

Though oblique, compared with the blatant linkage of sex, God and country in the early 1980s rightist responses to the Long Decade, Terri subtly links the rationalized body with a national (and not transnational – capitalism has never, for the right, counted as a 'world order') project of implanting the value of abstinence. Like the other sites, this is not imagined simply as a return to established or traditional values, but as reconstructing the affect of the citizen.

'Love in a Cold Climate'? The Politics of Sex Revisited

It might appear that the AIDS crisis has offered an opportunity to revisit the politics of love – loves at different levels, of different kinds, of varying intensities and objects. Indeed, isn't that what is at play in ideas like compassion – a love toward those with whom one shares a social bond? Or volunteerism? Or even safe sex campaigns, with their varying emphases on 'communication' and commitment? But what happened instead was the assertion of community over and against the sex bond that was now explicitly or reluctantly thought of as dots on an epidemiological scatter map. We opted for love as democracy over love as an anti-social place of resistance against the patriarchy. Compassion was generalized as the emotional bond of an unarticulated populace toward its marked analogues, not the political action of a hegemony against another complex of interests. In the quest for self-determination, for safety, gay men and lesbians produced anti-national communities, materialized networks of recognition and aid without ever having achieved citizenship rights. The affect at play here has been overwhelmed in the neo-conservative rhetorics of sexual deferral, has been lost to the sentimental representation of the dyad of buddy–victim, or lifetime companion and dying partner.

Perhaps I am simply nostalgic for that time when we actively contested social and political theories that lauded the 'marital' or family bond, both supposedly derived from a biological urge to live and procreate. Maybe I long for the days when using family as the basis of grander feelings – like patriotism – seemed laughable. We were profoundly radical when we disavowed the pleasure and comfort offered to us through these affective flows. Admittedly, cutting away the neat, homologously structural unity of lover–family–nation left a gaping wound. We were so incisive in our recognition that the family was no more natural than the state, but we left the broader category of feelings of attachment, of affect, uncriticized. Because we saw the *desire to belong* as natural, rather than constructed, the best we could do was replace earlier attachments to home, country and Mom with negative politics. Many have lamented the lack of emotional wholeness of the 1960s and 1970s, but this was a symptom of violent detachment, not proof that we needed monofocal love. It was profoundly anti-national to dissociate ourselves from *heimat*, from belonging, es-pecially at a time when anti-communist paranoia still demanded allegiance to America. If affects are variable dispositions and not at all natural, then effacement of radical sentiments like 'smash the family, smash the state' must have resulted from *work* on affect. The politics of the 1960s and 1970s did not founder on any lack of attachment to something 'bigger'. The New Right did not simply gain adherents because they offered something – a comforting feeling of traditional hearth and home – the left lacked. Neo-conservativism represents an active refiguration of the citizen's affect toward Nation, a new political love masquerading as the return to lost sentiment.

I can't quite bring myself to formulate or advocate a new politics of love. Once attached to nation, love – indistinguishable from political love – is too dangerous a basis of social politics, probably antithetical to a material politics of the body. Love reappears as the glue that can hold some of 'us' together across our differences, the underlying thing expressed through all kinds of 'love-making' or underwriting all forms of household. Turning the love that dared not speak its name into 'families we chose' or 'alternative families', 'love we frame' or 'alternative love' or even that most fraught move, the 'love that knows no borders', cannot extricate us from the tendency of love to return us to Nation, to a nation that would rather maintain itself as the central love object than give all its people the tools they need to survive an epidemic.

Notes

The title of this article alludes to one of the first 'safe sex' slogans. It is unclear who coined the phrase – men from the Gay Men's Health Crisis, or from Boston's AIDS Action Committee – but buttons quickly made their way through gay circles in the Northeast. Significantly, the slogan precedes the phrase 'safe sex', indeed, it was intended to pre-empt obscuring a logical *approach* to sexual practice with a name. Naming suggests that there is a specific object to which the name refers, but what act is meant by safe sex? This would become a central battle from the late 1980s through the present, as is reflected in the rightist pamphlets and websites discussed here. The dual insight of 'on me, not in me' – that getting an infectious agent inside the body is the problem, that sex is, most radically, practices and not 'interiorities' – was quickly lost once 'safe sex' (or even safer sex) shifted attention onto an aura of vulnerability/invulnerability, and away from the surfacial quality of sexual practice.

2. I underscore the significance of widespread HIV testing for gay politics and gay identity. The strong popular association of HIV with gay men and gay communities, coupled with persistent attempts – through to the present – to mandate testing created the ideological possibility (very little different than the outrageous proposals to tattoo or quarantine) of scientifically identifying 'queers'. Given that the homophile and later gay liberation movements had fought for decades to demedicalize homosexuality, the return of objectivizing science was not only a problem for political strategy (endless amount of time spent convincing myriad agencies not to test, not to ask, not to disclose, etc.) but also a problem for the concept of identity. It was a traumatic coincidence that HIV testing appeared at the moment that the internal logic of 'identity' movements began to break down. During the Long Decade, a quasi-Marxian concept of consciousness combined with a properly queer idea (of closet/non-closet) to produce a hermeneutic of self which was enormously productive for the personal liberation and political intervention of a generation of activists. But coincidence is the wrong word: *founding condition of queer politics* is better. Let us not forget, though, that we did not cede the strong, now somewhat conservative idea of identity entirely of our own free will. The entirety of the gay identity/queer nation debates were haunted by the spectre of an HIV-tested body. Both gay civil rights groups and queer nation sought to limit the claim of science on the body of the homosexual.

3. The new policy made it illegal for the military to ask about sexual orientation, but it also forbade military personnel from announcing – in act or word – that they are gay or lesbian. This complicated policy referred to a series of contradictory decisions by the Supreme Court and lower courts that attempted to distinguish identity, speaking about one's identity or acts, and engaging in acts – with or without gay identity, with or without speaking. In effect, cases that tried to establish the right to announce one's orientation under free speech laws (sexual identity here would be something like political speech) were disregarded. The disruptive outcomes that might result from such speech (or, obvious acts that amounted to an announcement, and, therefore, speech) were considered potentially more dangerous than the limitation on free speech. In principle, a gay man or lesbian who conducted a quiet relationship that never came to light would not be in violation of the policy. Although this removed the problem of being thrown out of the military for lying about 'having ever been' a homosexual, a question asked under the old policy, one could still be thrown out for announcing – or having others announce for you – that you are gay or lesbian. While this is a huge distinction in the law, in practical terms it meant that rumors of someone's sexuality could – and did – provoke the kind of public discussion of their sexuality that amounts to 'telling'. The phrase 'don't ask, don't tell' is now widely used in American popular speech not just to refer to this absurd situation, but to indicate, more broadly, the kinds of statuses in which one can only be what one is by not acknowledging 'it'. The policy was found unconstitutional in 1997, and the government is currently appealing this decision.

4. Much of the work influenced by this book came before Anderson issued the expanded second edition (1991). Here, Anderson modifies the English Marxism that underwrites the fleeting interest in affectivity. More closely aligning with French poststructural theory allowed him to treat the disciplining practices of national pedagogies more rigorously and take more seriously the role of maps and flags as material (rather than symbolic) aspects of nationalist projects, but at the cost of keeping sight of the 'structure of feeling' that Nation entails.

Perhaps the best examples of the recovery of a concept of affect *after* post-structuralism are Judith Frank's (1997) *Common Ground*, which links literary representation with the production of a new affect in bourgeois England of the 18th century, and Eve Kosofsky Sedgwick and Adam Frank's introduction to their Sylvan Tompkins anthology, *Shame and Her Sisters*, which considers how a non-positivist understanding of the biological body yields an idea of affect that does not require a 'deep' interior or unconscious. In addition, Brian Massumi's work on Ronald Reagan profitably uses Deleuze to argue for a sense of place – proprioception – that arises on the body's surface rather than through a refusal of cognitive processes of placement. Here, the idea of 'knowing where your body is' that is developed in kinesthesiology as a condition prior to a mind–body split (in essence, instructing athletes to 'just do it') is de-essentialized: through somatic play and memory the body becomes as/in a place.

References

Abstinence Safer Than Sex. www.monmouth.com. 3 April 1998.

Alert Citizens of Texas (1984) 'Homosexuality: The Shattered Image', undated pamphlet, probably early 1984.

Anderson, Benedict (1991) *Imagined Communities: Reflections on the Origin and Spread of Nationalism*. London/New York: Verso. (Orig. pub. 1983.)

BAVAM! www.sexless.com. 3 April 1998.

Berkowitz, R. and M. Callen (1983) *How to Have Sex in an Epidemic: One Approach*. New York: Frontline Publications.

Frank, Judith (1997) *Common Ground: Eighteenth Century English Satiric Fiction and the Poor*. Stanford, CA: Stanford University Press.

Healthy Love: A Positive Approach to Abstinence. people.delphi.com/tglit/index.html. 3 April 1998.

Hobson, Laura Z. (1947) *Gentlemen's Agreement*. New York: Dutton.

Intercessors for America (1983) 'Prayer Focus', PO Box 1289, Elyria, OH 44036.

Massumi, Brian (1995) 'The Autonomy of Affect', *Cultural Critique* 31: 83–109.

Patton, Cindy (1985) *Sex and Germs: The Politics of AIDS*. Boston, MA: South End Press.

Patton, Cindy (1996) *Fatal Advice*. Durham, NC: Duke University Press.

Patton, Cindy (1997) 'To Die For', in Eve Kosofsky Sedgwick (ed.) *Novel Gazing*. Durham, NC: Duke University Press.

Pure Love Alliance. www.purelove.org. Guest-book read 30 March 1998.

Robinson, Cedric (1996) *Black Political Movements*. London: Routledge.

Sedgwick, Eve Kosofsky and Adam Frank (1998) *Shame and Her Sisters*. Durham, NC: Duke University Press.

Shilts, Randy (1987) *And the Band Played On*. New York: St Martin's Press.

Starlene. www.geocities.com/Heartland/7783/. 4 May 1998.

True Love Waits. www.marietta.edu/daviso/HOEM/tlw. 3 April 1998.

Wait Trainer. www.integrityol.com/waittrain/index.html. 3 April 1998.

Cindy Patton teaches in the Graduate Institute of the Liberal Arts at Emory University in Atlanta, Georgia. Her books include *Inventing AIDS* (1990), *Fatal Advice* (1996) and two forthcoming volumes, *Who I Am: The Making of American Political Identities* (with Harry Denny) and *Global AIDS/Local Context*.

Seductions of the Impossible
Love, the Erotic and Sacrifice in Surrealist Discourse

Michael Richardson

Sacrifice as an Inner Experience

THERE IS A notorious legend that, in establishing the secret society *Acéphale* in 1937, Georges Bataille wanted the community to be consecrated through the performance of a ritual human sacrifice. All the evidence suggests that he was sincere in this desire, and it has been suggested that one of the members of the group even volunteered to be the victim.

This desire may strike us as risible, if not just another surrealist scandal. Yet there can be no doubting that it was, within Bataille, genuine. It bore witness to his will to go as far as it was possible to go and, more significantly perhaps, to experience the primitive, raw sense of life that he felt had been lost in contemporary, rational, society. Sacrifice was not, for Bataille, an archaic rite which had only historical significance. On the contrary, he believed it had considerable implications for contemporary society that bear upon the foundations of our inner life. Sacrifice bore witness to elemental needs that were being repressed. To enquire into the nature of sacrifice was therefore to address an important contemporary issue. According to him, the closest we come to an experience of sacrifice is in eroticism. I will therefore not be concerned so much here with the historical significance of sacrificial practices as with the extent to which sacrifice itself has a reality in contemporary society.

It can hardly be denied, notwithstanding the attempt by René Girard in *Violence and the Sacred* to rationalize it, that sacrifice is the human act par excellence that contravenes rationality. Even if we accept Girard's

■ *Theory, Culture & Society* 1998 (SAGE, London, Thousand Oaks and New Delhi),
Vol. 15(3–4): 375–392
[0263-2764(199808/11)15:3–4;375–392;006076]

dubiously supported argument, sacrifice still stands as testimony to human irrationality (why should the killing of a surrogate victim be able to protect a community from its own internalized violence?).[1] Equally, few would deny, I think, that the collective experience of sacrifice is alien to the concerns of a technologized, rationalized, contemporary society. If this experience has been lost to our sensibility today, does it matter? Bataille and Girard agree – this is perhaps the only point upon which they would agree – that it matters very much.

Sacrifice is too widespread a phenomenon – both in time and space – to be easily generalizable. Yet theorists from Robertson Smith onwards mostly agree that communal bonding in some form is a crucial element of it. We can also say with some certainty that at its basis it represents an attempt by the human community to regulate its relationship with the cosmos. It is concerned with how we relate to the fact of our mortality, both personally and in a collective sense.[2] There seems little reason to deny the fundamental fact that Bataille saw as being at the root of sacrifice, that is that it arises from our consciousness of the reality of death. It is at the same time connected with the generative principle. It ties together the fact of birth with that of death. According to Bruce Lincoln, sacrifice is 'a ritual which effectively repeats the cosmology, shifting matter from a victim's body to the allofomic parts of the universe in order to sustain the latter against decay and ultimate collapse' (Lincoln, 1991: 170). For Luc de Heusch, too:

> To perform a sacrifice is, primarily, to try to outwit death. Human sacrifice represents the outer limit which many rites – in which the sacrificer is seen to project himself into the animal victim, losing a part of his 'having' in order to preserve the essential – strive to reach. (Heusch, 1985: 215)

Death and communication lie at its heart. This is where Bataille saw its lack in contemporary society as being so crucial: having lost the experience of sacrifice we have also lost a sense of the real meaning of death and of communication. Instead of being a series of communicating vessels, human society is fast being transformed into a mechanical structure whose fundamental nature is ceasing to be an organic part of us. We try today to outwit death not by means of communication with it, but by conquering its effects. Through understanding the structure of life we gain the knowledge and the power to prevail against death. At least potentially. And yet we also know that the will to conquer nature has dangerous consequences. No one today can doubt that the concerns of the ecology movement are significant, and that the most immediate of these concerns is that of restoring a sense of harmony to our relationship with the natural world. Consideration of the nature of sacrifice is therefore of great importance in allowing us to gain greater understanding of our relation with the rest of nature. The will to conquer nature is the same as the will to conquer death. Scientists still often delude themselves that it is possible to do this. This will to conquer nature reflects a denial of the notion of sacrifice. For while all sacrifice is a disruption of nature, a sign of mankind's disequilibrium, it is also, at the same time, an attempt to restore equilibrium and heal the breach that reflects our separation from the source of what we are. Sacrifice responds to human guilt, founded in primal loss. It encapsulates a transgressive moment; it is contagious and violent, while serving the ends of social solidarity. Its loss in contemporary society is the denial of this breach: having conquered nature, we are masters, potentially, of all that exists. This is the key issue that concerned Bataille. To assert the continuing relevance of sacrifice is to deny the claims of human mastery of the world. For what is at issue within sacrifice is the character of our relationship both with the world of death and with the world of nature. If sacrifice may be seen as a gift offered to death and to nature, it is one that implies complex obligations. It involves a highly complicated relation that bears upon the very construction of our own identity and reality. In order to understand this significance, we need to examine our internal consciousness to consider the psychic reality to which the sacrificial impulse responds. The experience within us that corresponds with sacrifice, he believed, was erotic activity.

To gain insight into Bataille's view that eroticism held the key to an understanding of sacrifice, we need first to consider the background against which he developed his theory. Crucial to this is the surrealists' examination of the nature of love and sexuality.

Towards a Re-Invention of Love

Surrealism took shape in the wake of one of the greatest 'sacrifices' in human history. The carnage of the First World War is sometimes spoken of as having sacrificed a whole generation of young people. This may be an abuse of the term: in distinction from ancient rituals of sacrifice the victims of the war did not, in any real sense, offer themselves willingly, nor were they offered up by society as freely given. On all sides, the losses were mourned either as the regrettable consequence of a necessary war, or as bearing witness to a world gone mad. It was a sacrifice over which society held no ritual control, that served no ritual purpose. Yet it did confront people with the terrible reality of death. The generation that was to constitute the surrealists had therefore experienced sacrifice at first hand in an entirely negative way. It was a sacrifice made to nothing but an abstract and worthless principle and it served a social order from which they felt thoroughly alienated. It inspired not collective guilt, but collective revulsion. It may be said to have been a sacrifice devoid of all internal necessity. As such it was less a sacrifice than a massacre, if one accepts the terms of the distinction made by Tzvetan Todorov (1984: 144). The element of disillusion this involves is an important strand that conditioned Bataille's later thoughts on sacrifice. It alerts us to the very real moral conditions that gave rise to it.

For surrealism – beyond all the hubris that surrounds it as an avant-garde grouping – may be said fundamentally to be a moral movement directed against the crisis of human consciousness that had come to the fore in the 1920s. It is well known that the surrealists opposed the moral codes of the dominant society. But they were equally doubtful about the myth of the artist as the violator of those codes. They were concerned to question the whole issue of contemporary morality, especially in the sexual domain. This is conveyed well in André Thirion's memoirs. The surrealists abhorred, he writes:

> ... the licentiousness of the artistic Bohemia that surrounded them. Drugs and homosexuality were condemned.... Sleeping around was just not done, and dirty jokes were forbidden. The golden rule was passionate love, preferably faithful, between two individuals of the opposite sex. And once passionate love had been exalted as the supreme good, unique love imposed itself as the ideal. One could love only once. Any other possibility would open the door to libertinage, with the complacency that involved for oneself and for others. (Thirion, 1976: 92)

Thirion no doubt overstates his case, but it was undoubtedly a milieu that was consciously seeking a new morality that would undermine the old moral values that had led to the debacle of the war.

As Thirion makes clear, the determination of the surrealists to re-evaluate social and personal values caused them to give a special place to love and sexuality, as they strove to 'reinvent love' as Rimbaud had demanded. Looking back on the history of the Surrealist Movement, André Breton recalled how important the issue of love had been and asserted that the major disagreements within surrealism had even more to do with personal issues relating to sexuality than to political questions, as had generally been maintained in histories of the movement (Breton, 1994: 111).

There has been a great deal of misunderstanding about surrealist attitudes towards love. Unfashionable as they may seem today, they need to be placed in historical context. They are alien to today's attitudes partly, of course, because they inevitably reflected to an extent the sexual mores of their time, which have become transformed during the century, but also, perhaps more precisely, because they were concerned to oppose those mores. As Thirion suggests, drugs and homosexuality were not condemned as such, but because of the fashionable posture they implied.[3] Before we condemn their attitude, therefore, we need to understand the context in which it developed. This is especially important because the surrealist view is based upon an attitude as fundamentally at variance with modern morality, which finds its basis in the acceptance of individual penchants as a natural right, as it was with that of its own time. Nevertheless, there is an element of moral puritanism in surrealism, which has remained largely consistent. This is shown by Robert Benayoun who, writing in 1963, is highly critical of sexual attitudes which he says exalt a sexual athleticism that is uncontrolled, inhuman and mechanical. Sexual familiarity and routine induce a lassitude and cynicism into sexual relations that reduce love and destroy the erotic sensibility. Sexuality today, he says:

... is conditioned by a blend of material security and moral insecurity: the permanent presence of a notion of annihilation that is not – due to the atomic spectre – simply abstract, the irreversible haste of vital rhythms and the avowed cult of violence, have augmented the morbid energy of ordinary sexual behaviour. (Benayoun, 1965: 11)

What is above all characteristic of surrealist attitudes has been a questioning of dominant assumptions in all spheres of life. In considering surrealist writings on sexuality, it is apparent that they have tended to discern a progressive dehumanization at play in contemporary attitudes. Against this, they sought to recompose an experience of the sacred – of the marvellous possibilities of life – within the framework of the sexual encounter itself.

The fascinating series of 'discussions' about sexuality that took place between 1928 and 1932 show the degree to which the issue of sexuality was considered significant by the first generation of surrealists. These have been collected and recently published in English translation (see Pierre, 1992). Their documentary value is limited. They no doubt tell us more about personal relationships within the Surrealist Group at what was a very difficult period than they do about what the surrealists really felt about sexuality.[4] Nevertheless, they are revealing about the structure of the surrealists' concerns.

The opening question holds a key which will underlie all of the discussions: 'A man and a woman make love. To what extent is the man aware of the woman's orgasm?' This question is more complex than it may at first seem. At issue is the very nature of love and the motivation of the desire that brings two beings together while, at the same time, maintaining their separateness. It implies a vast questioning of the otherness of the partner in sexual relations and the extent to which it is possible for love to overcome such a primordial separation. What is at stake, that is, is how it is possible to love when our own personal conditions by definition constantly militate against an involvement in the consciousness of another. The act of love promises a passage across this otherwise apparently insurmountable barrier while at the same time tending to emphasize it. If there is a passage, it is one that is marked with rapids, dead-ends and treacherous straits. Nevertheless, the moment of orgasm offers a promise that brings the possibility of resolution into its greatest relief, since at that moment we feel ourselves momentarily plunging into a beyond where we may lose ourselves and our personal values. At the same time the fleeting quality of the sensation has an aspect of illusion. What is the experience that men and women share at that moment? Do they genuinely experience a unique moment in which they transcend themselves in one another, or do they remain irrevocably separated, their experience nothing but a personal projection of their own vanity? This is a question that lies at the heart of the surrealist interrogation and underlies the way they approached love. It is also at the basis of Bataille's interest in sacrifice and marks the connection that he drew between it and eroticism.

If love was central to the surrealist attitude, these discussions show us a wide divergence of views between different surrealists. At one extreme some of them seem to have seen the necessity for a complete rupture between sexual activity and love. Here this view is given vivid expression, in very different ways, by Antonin Artaud and Paul Éluard, both of whom protest against the incorporation of love into discussions devoted to sexuality. For Artaud, who probably never had a physical relation with anyone and yet had several intense emotional relationships with women, the physicality of sex was obscene and could only serve to separate people. Artaud believed that the only true communication took place in the mind, a landscape of purity that was beyond physical desire. Éluard is curiously in agreement, even though he certainly finds nothing obscene about the sex act (he claims indeed to have slept with between 'five hundred and a thousand' women). Nevertheless he remains convinced of a fundamental incompatibility between sex and love. He seems to have considered sex as a purely physical need that had to be satisfied, but which had nothing to do with desire itself and had no bearing at all on the love relation. First-hand evidence of this is given a vivid form in the letters – full of tenderness and longing for a love that can no longer be present in physical form – he wrote to his (ex) wife Gala (see Éluard, 1989).

For Breton such an attitude – in whatever form it was manifested – implied an intolerable resignation. No matter how difficult the relations between the sexes were, he felt it was essential to confront the affective component in the relation as it was given physical form through desire.

In reading these conversations today it is easy to dismiss them for elements that appear in retrospect suspect. However, we need to remember that the surrealists were creatures of their time and it is far too easy to take a condescending view of them. It is perhaps more worthwhile to consider the extent to which they cast light on today's attitudes. Our own age, which has merchandized sex to a degree that cheapens and degrades its every aspect, has nothing to be smug about in relation to the attitude of previous generations. What concerned the surrealists above all – something that has remained consistent throughout the history of surrealism – was the affective relation between the sexes. For them the physical and technical aspects of sex were always subsidiary to the working through of desire. Love was an irruption of desire into an ordered existence based upon elementary needs and it pointed to a transformation of our very being. In our current mechanical world this vital issue is almost as unmentionable as sexual desire was for the Victorians. If today the most intimate details of sexual activity are rendered commonplace and subject to television discussion, if we live in a world in which sex is just another product (to which the consumer has the easiest access through 'good sex guides'), we also live in a world in which the determinants of desire have become lost in a generalized obscurantism. If it is possible today to ask the question, 'A man and a woman make love. To what extent is the man aware of the woman's orgasm?' it is so only in a burlesque way. How can a man today *not* be aware of a woman's orgasm? But this awareness simply indulges his own vanity. It no longer disturbs him, as it did the surrealists, since sex has become a purely biological *need* to be satisfied. For us it is generally nothing more than that. It no longer challenges our personal boundaries, indeed it tends even to reinforce them. Love ceases to be anything more than another social encounter, which we need to negotiate as best we can. Sex becomes normalized as a biological process (even to the extent that we are able to indulge our most outlandish personal penchants) and the otherness of the encounter is in the process denied. This implies a complacency that the surrealists put into relief. For even when Éluard displays a similar attitude towards sexual activity as a biological need, it does not satisfy him: real sexual relations lie far beyond the pure physicality of the sex act. Perhaps, then, we need the surrealists to remind us that the reduction of sexuality to a *need* is reductionist of our humanity and our personalities. If we are to confront what it is we are in the depths of our being, perhaps we need to remind ourselves that sex also involves *desire*, a desire for what is other, a desire that is so deep that it can never be satisfied and yet alone has the power to transform us and lead us to the heights. To reduce sexuality to a need is to destroy what may be the heart of our being. It is one with what Bataille saw as the will to deny the consciousness of death and its intimate link with the erotic. This also means that it denies love, at least in the terms that the surrealists conceived it, well expressed by Octavio Paz: love, he says, is 'the passionate vision of the *other*: a human like ourselves, yet enigmatic ... before the mystery of the beloved, the lover perceives himself as at once similarity and irreducible otherness' (Paz, 1987: 94).[5]

Love as Transgression

As discussed earlier, for surrealism love was explored as a value definitively set against the dominant values of society. This conception has tended these days to be reified as mad love, after a book by Breton originally published in 1937, one of his most important works.

We need to remind ourselves about what was involved in the idea of mad love, since it has become vulgarized, reduced to the status of a – generally adolescent – passionate infatuation. Recent French films (most notably *Betty Blue*) have given a particularly mournful tone to a condition now often assigned as the effect of a sort of chemical imbalance. This view could hardly be further from the idea of Breton and the surrealists. To understand what Breton meant by the idea of mad love, we might translate it today more accurately as 'extravagant' or 'lavish' love, that is love that is experienced in profusion and intensity, love that is, to use the term used by another surrealist, Benjamin Péret, sublime. Octavio Paz defines it well:

> Love is a choice ... perhaps a free choosing of our destiny, a sudden discovery of the most secret and fateful part of our being. But the choosing of love is impossible in our society. To realise itself, love must violate the laws of the world. It is scandalous and disorderly, a transgression committed

by two stars that break out of their predestined orbits and rush together in the midst of space. . . . Whenever it succeeds in realising itself, it breaks up a marriage and transforms it into what society does not want it to be: a revelation of two solitary beings who create their own world, a world that rejects society's lies, abolishes time and work, and declares itself to be self-sufficient. (Paz, 1967: 198)

Love is transgressive and unconstrained. It brings social norms into question but it also symbolizes a greater social bonding. Experienced as a total prestation, as an unconditional giving of oneself, love is society reduced to its simplest form, a community of two who exist only for one another. There is thus a paradox involved here. At its heart love is revolt, but it is a love that redeems and reveals society – that is, human communication – in its purest form. Bataille expressed this in a powerful way:

Only the beloved, so it seems to the lover – because of affinities evading definition which match the union of bodies with that of souls – only the beloved can in this world bring about what our human limitations deny, a total blending of two beings, a continuity between two discontinuous creatures. Hence love spells suffering for us in so far as it is a quest for the impossible . . . (Bataille, 1986: 20)

This quest is central to the exploration Breton undertakes in his book *Mad Love* (1987). It follows the concerns of *Investigating Sex* (Pierre, 1992), in so far as its central concern is with the otherness of the sexual encounter, but the focus for him has changed. At the time it was written, Breton was married to his second wife and his only daughter was about to be born. Preoccupied with new birth and more generally with the coming into being of things, Breton is concerned to integrate love into the flow of the universe. This is refracted through his love for his wife Jacqueline, who is celebrated by the book. Despite this, though, the tone is by no means idyllic. Storm clouds cover the horizon (the Spanish Civil War is in its early stages and Breton tells his unborn daughter – in a moving letter that concludes the book – that, if it had not been for her impending birth, he would have gone to fight for the Republic). This far away storm is not the only disquiet, though. The mood throughout is troubled. Although the book celebrates Jacqueline, she never appears to us in a defined way, but remains distant and almost ethereal. One senses that Breton felt that their love, although it was genuine, was, as most love is, fragile and had shallow foundations. It was not really of the crazy, total and impassioned kind that Breton dreamed about. Perhaps there is something here that already obliquely tells us that the couple would separate in a few years. In one episode Breton tells of a trip to the seaside when he felt unaccountably estranged from her as they passed a building in which a man had murdered his wife and this episode seems in some way to be symptomatic of their relationship.

In all probability, Breton himself never experienced the overwhelming power of reciprocal love in the intensity he desired. His writing as a whole bears witness to a tremendous longing that could never be satisfied. Although he had many loving relationships, and remained friends with most of his girlfriends, the delirium of absolute passion that is mad love seems to have remained beyond his grasp, as perhaps he always knew it would. The harmony of nature, nature reconciled within itself, must necessarily remain illusory. The differentiation of life inevitably works against it. The love he celebrates, love with a lethal shadow, is already encapsulated by that question that opens *Investigating Sex*. To what extent can the man ever be fully aware of the woman's orgasm? Or vice versa? The answer is probably to the same extent as the flower can be aware of the bee's feelings as it sucks her nectar. Nevertheless, the vertigo of the encounter remains and encapsulates the central mystery of life, and encapsulates, if only momentarily, our continuity with the rest of existence. This is the central issue of *Mad Love* – and indeed of the whole surrealist understanding of love – and it raises difficult questions about our personal relation not merely with the beloved, but also with the world. To love, in any meaningful sense of the word, is to make a sacrifice of oneself to the other. As such, it also involves a fundamental communication with the world.

To Eroticize the World

At the basis of Bataille's understanding of eroticism lies the view that creation is fundamentally a rending experience. By being born, we are torn out of the continuity of existence and cast into a world that is discontinuous with us. In eroticism we gain a glimpse of the continuity we have lost, which impels us towards a movement of resolution, in which we dream of recovering our original oneness. This is part of what Bataille calls the 'impossible'. It is also transgressive, both of social form and of our own identity. This makes love itself, as the surrealists believed, fundamentally transgressive. Yet if love is transgressive, it also at the same time pointed towards a greater sense of harmony, a harmony that connected the human sensibility with the flow of the universe. In this, the legacy of German Romanticism in particular, with its identification of the beloved with the universe, was crucial. The idea of the couple as a microcosm of universal form, which revealed the secret of creation, was central to this attitude. Octavio Paz wrote: 'If we are a metaphor of the universe, the human couple is a metaphor par excellence, the point of intersection of all forces and the seed of all forms. The couple in time recaptured, the return of time before time' (Paz, 1974: 53). By linking the human couple with universal flow in this way, Paz discloses one of the connections between the erotic and sacrifice, if we accept the idea that sacrifice embodies a will to re-create the world. In surrealism generally, the image of the couple is central, and links creation and destruction, life and death, in much the same way as in alchemy the hermetic couple stands at the highest point of the great work. This is also at the heart of the striving for a pure, preferably monogamous, love, since only such an absolute can make perceptible the point of intersection of apparent contradictions. Malcolm de Chazal expressed this perfectly: 'Sensual union in love: we are unanimously and unitarily two; sensual union in vice: we are alone and three' (Chazal, 1948: 36). In this conception, love is integrally erotic. And eroticism, as opposed to pure sensuality, becomes possible only in the lucid recognition both of the identity of the other and the fact that this identity is being violated in the fact of love. Eroticism, indeed, holds these contrary movements of maintenance and destruction of identity in tension.

Eroticism was defined by the surrealists as 'a sumptuous ceremony in a tunnel' (Surrealist Group, 1938: 11). The ritual framework this suggests was made more explicit at one of the surrealist exhibitions. The Exposition inteRnatiOnale du Surréalisme (EROS), prepared by the surrealists in Paris in 1959, was devoted to the theme of eroticism. It was organized very much under the aegis of Bataille, and explicitly explored the issues raised in his *Eroticism*, which had been published two years earlier. Bataille was invoked by Breton in the introduction to the show with two key quotations from *Eroticism*:

> Man's erotism differs from animal sexuality in that it calls the inner life into question. *Erotism is that part of man's consciousness which calls his own being into question.*

> *The inner experience of erotism demands from the person involved an equal sensitivity towards the anguish which provides the basis for interdiction and the desire which tends to violate it.* (in Breton, 1972: 378)

These two quotations – central to Bataille's understanding of eroticism – defined the focus of the exhibition. And it can be said that if Bataille was unable to perform a human sacrifice to bind together the participants in *Acéphale*, he must have recognized that with this exhibition the surrealists came close to giving the sort of genuinely contemporary expression of the sentiment informing sacrifice he had dreamed of. Like all of the exhibitions organized by the surrealists, it was much more than an art show. It was organized as a total environment, structured as a labyrinth of desire. Robert Benayoun sets the scene:

> At the entrance, under a ceiling of quivering pink satin flesh (courtesy of Marcel Duchamp), a 'vaginal' door pearled with dew opened onto a labyrinth permeated with sighs and swoons towards a Chamber of Fetishes and a red hall in which a cannibal feast was taking place. (Benayoun, 1965: 230–1)

This feast, prepared by Meret Oppenheim, emphasized the ritual quality of the event. But even more extraordinary was a ceremony organized by Jean Benoît to enact the provisions of the will of the Marquis de Sade (which were ignored at the time of his death). This ceremony consisted in the undressing of a fabulous monster that had been meticulously constructed by Benoît over several years (for details about it see Le Brun, 1996). Benoît himself wore the costume for the ceremony, at the culmination of which he branded himself with the word SADE. Those who witnessed the event testify to the power it had. As one of them, Alain Jouffroy, expressed it:

> ... the act, consisting in branding oneself with the letters SADE in a society as garrulous and disinclined to make gestures as the one in which we live at present in Paris, is obviously a challenge. A challenge to conformists, a challenge to all forms of laziness, a challenge to sleep, a challenge to all forms of inertia, in life as in thought. In absolute contradiction to the vulgarity peculiar to our time, such a ceremony can only be the object of derision in the conversations of our self-styled intellectuals. Rather, though, it represents a call to essentials, to the mysterious axis about which human beings turn, [to] the energy liberated by the sexual act, allowing us to shatter for a moment the bolted door of our consciousness. (Jouffroy, 1964: 34)

Through a sacrificial ritual, Benoît may genuinely be said to have enacted Sade's will, not in a literal sense but as a symbolic action. From the evidence we have of it,[6] the ceremony acted upon those who witnessed it in a powerful way as a purification and an affirmation of a community of feeling based upon a sense of awe. It bore witness to the internal and contagious impact that appears to be central to the sacrificial attitude, something which helps to explain the seeming paradox of affirming life through an enactment of death.[7]

The will within surrealism towards communal harmony, based in a re-invention of myth in contemporary terms, is very strong. It leads us back to the experience of sacrifice and to the importance that Bataille saw in it for our erotic relations.

Eroticism and Sacrifice

Bataille shared the environment of surrealism and was equally keen to 're-invent love' in terms of a new moral myth. As he said, love:

> ... promises a way out of our suffering. We suffer from our isolation in our individual separateness. Love reiterates: 'If only you possessed the beloved one, your soul sick with loneliness would be one with the soul of the beloved.' Partially at least this promise is a fraud. But in love the idea of such a union takes shape with frantic intensity.... (Bataille, 1986: 20)

Yet this promise is also intimately tied in with violence and violation: 'Only in violation, through death if need be, of the individual's solitariness can there appear that image of the beloved object which in the lover's eyes invests all being with significance. For the lover, the beloved makes the world transparent' (Bataille, 1986: 21). This violence is not that which Girard identifies at the heart of human society – that is violence linked with conflict and revenge – but a violence that is perpetrated upon us by the fact of our being born. It is this that is inherent to our nature: creation itself is a fundamentally violent act and it is only through the further violence of death that the breach it institutes can be repaired. In this sense, any death affects us as representing a sacrificial moment, but it is only when death itself is directly confronted – rather than the death of a particular individual – that we gain a sense of what the psychic reality of sacrifice within us is.

The violence of creation is experienced within us overwhelmingly as anguish, which emerges from the birth trauma that Otto Rank analysed so powerfully. In his book, *Foyers d'incendie*, which prefigures some of the themes of Bataille's later exploration, the Greek surrealist Nicolas Calas perceived the dialectic that was established at a fundamental level between life and anguish. This is felt within life – and within us – as a double tendency. As we seek to transcend the trauma through consciousness, it is constantly being restored through the memory (Calas, 1938: 221–3). This dialectic lies at the heart of the impulse to sacrifice and gains its most heightened communication in eroticism. Bataille puts it thus:

> There is no way out and the *communication of anguish* – which takes place in sacrifice – is not the solution but the introduction and the maintenance of rupture in the very centre, in the heart of humanity. It is only in the midst of anguish that this being which you are maintains enough consistency and yet leaves gaping the wound through which, hastening from all points of the universe, deadly destruction enters. Without your anguish, you would not be this faithful mirror of excess movements, of the vertiginous flight of day and night, which you have become. This is why it would not be for you to refuse that wild amplification of this pain which you are suffering from, of the splendour which follows you, and of your ultimate reality – which sacrifice is. (Bataille, 1988a: 195)

Eroticism and sacrifice are both facets of ultimate reality, bringing us into contact with what we are in the most fundamental way. Bataille experienced this unbearable anguish in his own life, especially in his searing relationship with Colette Peignot, in which he came close to experiencing the sort of sublime love that the surrealists spoke about. This relationship lasted for only four years, from 1934 to her death in 1938, but its effects persisted in Bataille's life (he considered it as being analogous of the love of Catherine and Heathcliff in *Wuthering Heights*) and there is a very strong sense in which Colette's death was experienced as a sacrifice by Bataille.

Yet he had no illusions that it might be possible to achieve reconciliation through passion. Erotic passion acted within human life like the storm in nature, breaking the oppression of a sultry day but also throwing everything into turmoil. In exploring this, he formulated what may be the clearest possible response to the question that permeates *Investigating Sex*. Considering the love relationship, he sees that the gulf separating us is very deep and he can see no way to bridge it. 'None the less,' he says, 'we can experience its dizziness together' (Bataille, 1986: 13).

For Bataille the condition of life itself is paradoxical and is determined by a pursuit whose resolution is inevitably 'impossible': any such realization would destroy itself at the very moment of the resolution by reason of the conditions that gave rise to it. Bataille did not believe in any possibility of hope or salvation from the human condition. Nevertheless it is open to us to affirm the sovereignty of each moment of life and this affirmation receives its greatest intensity in eroticism. The erotic impulse tears us away from ourselves, dissolving our personality and propelling us into a realm of terror and dissociation. It is in this that it is transgressive of social form, and it is also why Bataille considered that it was related to sacrifice: 'the lover strips bare the beloved of her identity no less than the blood stained priest his human or animal victim' (Bataille, 1986: 90).

This conclusion perhaps disturbs us, but it affirms our existence, not as isolated beings whose reality begins and ends with ourselves, but as part of a greater whole that constitutes existence. It serves to deflate human arrogance and integrate our sense of identity into the flow of the natural world.

On one point, Bataille's linkage of sacrifice with eroticism may initially appear tendentious, for in eroticism there is no victim. Nothing is actually sacrificed. Equally, no substitute is chosen to stand in for any community. Yet, Bataille's perception asks us to consider not the outward forms that sacrifice takes, but rather the internal necessity to which it responds. He wants us to question what is involved in the urge for sacrifice. It is true that in eroticism nothing material is sacrificed, that no gift as such is offered up. Yet the sacrificial element is contained within the relationship between the lovers, who mutually offer themselves to one another. The gift is that of their own identities. It may be an illusory offering, since the loss of identity is only momentary. But it is no less real for all that. In sexual abandon, we are suspended on the brink, and collapse back into our own separate personalities. The same thing is true of sacrifice, which momentarily unites the community in a paroxysm of transgression that mimics destruction without succumbing to it. In eroticism, we are transfigured by this movement, and gain a glimpse of what surpasses us. This reveals to us a possibility of a unity that is outside the conception of our ordinarily limited and discontinuous existence. It brings us into direct contact with death in a way that corresponds with the apparent impulse of sacrifice. As Bataille says, 'if love exists at all it is, like death, a swift movement of loss within us, quickly slipping into tragedy and stopping only with death' (Bataille, 1986: 239).

Bataille's exploration of the link between eroticism and sacrifice is an extension of the themes the surrealists introduced in the 1920s. In confronting our own identity with that of another in eroticism, we are also confronting what both affirms and destroys us. As an affirmation of life, sexuality is thus in complicity with death. Equally, time effectively stands still in the moment of sexual union, for in that moment the separation of partners is overcome and their separate personalities are dissolved.

As is well known, the basis of the surrealist attitude lies in a quest for a supreme point at which contradictions are no longer perceived. Within our human existence, it is the mingling of otherness, especially in the sexual act, that offers anticipation of the perception of such a point. The impetus of sexual attraction may emphasize our fundamental internal disharmony, but it is also what contains the possibility of its remedy. The confrontation of the nature of otherness – the desire to be *other* is also the desire to know the other through oneself – is the desire, ultimately, to transcend what separates our individual beings. This is the quest that surrealism set for itself. Contemporary discourse on the other hand seems largely to foreclose on debates about otherness, reaching an impasse in today's world where the rigours of 'political correctness' and the imposition of 'rights' upon any minority with the will to claim them has served to obfuscate the complexities involved in the construction of our sense of identity as human beings. This may become a search for easy solutions which may serve social equilibrium, but does nothing to confront essential antagonisms born from our fundamental being and identity.

Thus, Bataille's linking of eroticism and sacrifice remains significant for contemporary discourse. There is a need to recognize that the impulse of sacrifice is not negative but fundamentally affirmative to our sense of being and identity:

> It is the common business of sacrifice to bring life and death into harmony, to give death the upsurge of life, life the momentousness and the vertigo of death opening on to the unknown. Here life is mingled with death, but simultaneously death is a sign of life, a way into the infinite. (Bataille, 1986: 91)

Sacrifice shares with eroticism the fact that it is experienced within us as a loss, a loss that is welcomed as such. It offers a glimpse of what surpasses us, releasing infinity (or the possibility of infinity) into our lives and promising profusion and generosity. As such it embodies a moral sensibility that strives towards the assertion of the continuity of life in the desired encounter with an other who is nothing less than the infinity which, tied within our own limited existence, we are unable to appreciate.

This links with the essential impulses of surrealism – which arose out of the break-up of the moral certainties of the Victorian era and although reacting against those certainties never lost sight of the essential value of the moral framework itself – that serve to reveal the extent to which increasing material security in present-day society hides a considerable moral insecurity. This moral insecurity is manifested by a range of symptoms that may contaminate both social relations and our relation with the greater world. In their various explorations of sexuality, Bataille and the surrealists confronted this insecurity in a way that still offers a powerful illumination into some of the darkest recesses of our inner lives.

Notes

1. Girard's study seems to be set up against Bataille's view of sacrifice, even if this is not explicitly stated and even though Bataille is mentioned only once in the book. It fails to convince as a theory or even a study of sacrifice because Girard has a pre-established theory to which he fits a plethora of disparate data. This theory is extrinsic to the fact of sacrifice and emerges from consideration of the effects of violence within the community. If Girard's study has any value, it is as a theory of scapegoating, which is seen as being a response to internally generated violence. Sacrifice may be significant as part of this process, but almost all of the data we have about sacrificial practices indicates that internal violence is merely one element within sacrifice that tells us nothing about its essential qualities. Girard's failure to address the determinants of sacrifice itself can be measured by the fact that he decontextualizes his data, treating ethnographic facts in a particularly cavalier way and ignoring an obvious detail: the intensity of sacrifice occurs not primarily in response to internal violence, but to the level of violence directed *against* the community from outside (in the form of famine, drought, threats from neighbouring societies and so on). It is also often marked by its periodicity, in many societies being performed at specific seasonal events, most notably for the spring festival. Furthermore, it is not clear that the sacrificial victim is precisely a scapegoat, since no fault is ascribed to the victim. It would perhaps be more accurate to say that the sacrificial victim is a surrogate, standing in for the whole community, which is symbolically offering itself up as a gift. It seems difficult to accept the theory that violence as such is at the heart of sacrifice. Bataille seems to be much closer to the truth in saying that the essence of sacrifice is communication, and equally in asserting that the manifestation of violence within human society (which Girard seems to take for granted as the essence of mankind) is itself problematic, being tied in with our uniquely human consciousness of death.

2. It is curious to be writing this article at the time of the death of the Princess of Wales, an event that has had a very real quality of a sacrifice about it. It was permeated with the sense of collective guilt, and with feelings of purification and renewal that seem to have been central to the sacrificial attitude. It also represented a massive release of pent-up emotion, which shows how difficult it is for people today to express collective emotion. The modern attitude towards death and the fragmented nature of human relationships make it hard for anyone to share the grief they feel in a genuinely collective way. The death of the Princess has been one of the very few occasions in which it has been possible for this to occur. Shared loss is reserved for rare public 'icons' with whom we may, in an alienated society, feel we have a closer relationship than we have with those with whom we share our daily lives. Despite, or perhaps because of, the very real emotion expressed, it is difficult not to feel that there is something perverse about this. That Diana should have died in a car crash also seems significant. It is not, I think, far-fetched to draw parallels between road accidents in our society and sacrifice in ancient societies: it is through road accidents that we pay homage to the god we worship (that is, the god of technology), even if it is an involuntary form of sacrifice. What is different is the context and the fact that a sacred element is absent. In general, each road accident is a tragedy only for the immediate friends and relatives of the victims and has no collective charge. The death of the Princess of Wales shows that to be an inadequate emotional response to the suddenness of such death. It reveals that the restraint of emotional responses to death in our culture responds to the problem of

the sacrificial sensibility that Bataille identified and suggests that he was right to believe that this is an authentic issue in contemporary society.

3.   The apparent surrealist prejudice against homosexuality has been much commented upon, especially in relation to Breton's refusal to discuss it during the surrealist discussions about sexuality. We can only conjecture why Breton was so opposed to pursuing its discussion, but it should be pointed out in fairness that Breton's attitude is in part to do with the fact that during the 1920s homosexuality was a fashion among the modish set that Breton despised – his rejection of it is not so much a rejection of a particular sexual activity but lies in an equation he made between it and attitudes of superficiality and affectedness which he loathed; his exclusion of Sade and Lorrain from his condemnation makes it plain that more is involved in this than may at first appear. A problem of translation also accentuates this difficulty. What is discussed is not *homosexualité* (that is homosexuality as a sexual penchant) but *pédérastie*, which has a wider range of associations than in English, meaning both pederasty and more specifically the culture of homosexuality which also identifies homosexual behaviour with superficiality and which was a prevalent attitude among French intellectuals of the time. In stating that 'everything is permitted' for Sade and Lorrain, it is clear that for Breton it is not a simple condemnation of homosexuality itself. To some extent – or at least in some contexts – it might be said that the word used might perhaps be more accurately translated as 'homosexualism'.

4.   As Artaud said in the course of them, 'In investigations like this one, for most people a degree of ostentation inevitably intrudes. There is thus also a problem of whether such an investigation can distinguish between people who are being sincere and those who are not' (Pierre, 1992: 85). It should also be pointed out that it was a question of a game, the Game of Truth, which equally inevitably involved a certainly element of one-upmanship that was doubtless irresistible, especially among participants who were not getting on very well together. It is very clear, for instance, that Raymond Queneau, in particular, was winding Breton up for much of the time.

5.   In this respect there are interesting parallels between surrealism and the thought of Levinas, the great contemporary philosopher of the encounter with Otherness. Levinas indeed drew a distinction between need and desire and when he states that 'desire "measures" the infinity of the infinite' (see Levinas, 1987: 56), he is, I believe, expressing a fundamental surrealist perception.

6.   Around 200 people participated at this ritual. I have spoken about it to half a dozen of them, as well as to Jean Benoît himself, who all affirm that it was one of the most extraordinary events of their lives. Although self-mutilation has become a common theme for artists in the past couple of decades, these manifestations are generally rather self-indulgent and display very different intentions to Benoît. For instance, the work of Marina Abramovic or that of the Vienna Actionists is presented as performance and the mutilation is an integral part of their art. If it has an emotional impact it seems to respond to tragedy rather than sacrifice and be cathartic (in the classic Aristotelian sense) rather than contagious. What marked Benoît's act was its uniqueness and its irrevocability: like a sacrifice, it could never be re-enacted.

7.   Again, comparison with the death of the Princess of Wales is instructive here. There can be little doubt about the contagious – even unwonted – character of what followed. Above all, people seem to have been amazed by their own emotional

responses, and what was also surprising was the lack of mawkishness that was displayed. One feels that this could only have occurred because the death was such a violent one, which brought people face to face – in a way that is rare in contemporary society – with the reality of death.

Bibliography

Alexandrian, Sarane (1977) *Les Libérateurs de l'amour*. Paris: Seuil.

Bataille, Georges (1957) (1986) *Eroticism*, trans. Mary Dalwood. San Francisco, CA: City Lights; London: Marion Boyars.

Bataille, Georges (1985) *Visions of Excess: Selected Writings, 1927–1939*, trans. Allan Stoekl. Manchester: Manchester University Press.

Bataille, Georges (1986) 'Writings on Laughter, Sacrifice, Nietzsche, Un-Knowing', trans. Annette Michelson, *October* 36(Spring).

Bataille, Georges (1988a) *Inner Experience*, trans. Leslie Anne Boldt. Albany: State University of New York Press. (Orig. 1942.)

Bataille, Georges (1988b) *Guilty*, trans. Bruce Boone. Venice, CA: Lapis Press. (Orig. 1944.)

Bataille, Georges (1988c) *The Accursed Share*, vol. 1, trans. Robert Hurley. New York: Zone Books. (Orig. 1949.)

Bataille, Georges (1988d) *Theory of Religion*, trans. Robert Hurley. New York: Zone Books.

Bataille, Georges (1989) *The Tears of Eros*, trans. John Connor. San Francisco, CA: City Lights. (Orig. 1961.)

Bataille, Georges (1991) *The Accursed Share*, vols 2 and 3, trans. Robert Hurley. New York: Zone Books.

Benayoun, Robert (1965) *Erotique du surréalisme*. Paris: Jean-Jacques Pauvert.

Breton, André (1972) *Surrealism and Painting*, trans. Simon Watson Taylor. New York: Harper and Row. (Orig. 1965.)

Breton, André (1987) *Mad Love*, trans. Mary Ann Caws. Lincoln: University of Nebraska Press. (Orig. 1937.)

Breton, André (1994) *Arcanum 17*, trans. Zack Rogow. Los Angeles, CA: Sun and Moon Press. (Orig. 1944.)

Brown, Norman O. (1991) 'Dionysus in 1990', in *Apocalypse And/Or Metamorphosis*. Berkeley: University of California Press.

Caillois, Roger (1950) *L'Homme et le sacré*. Paris: Gallimard.

Calas, Nicolas (1938) *Foyers d'incendie*. Paris: Denoël.

Chazal, Malcolm de (1948) *Sens plastique*. Paris: Gallimard.

Éluard, Paul (1989) *Letters to Gala*, trans. Jesse Browner. New York: Paragon House.

Girard, René (1977) *Violence and the Sacred*, trans. Patrick Gregory. Baltimore, MD: Johns Hopkins University Press. (Orig. 1972.)

Heesterman, J.C. (1993) *The Broken World of Sacrifice: An Essay in Ancient Indian Ritual*. Chicago, IL: University of Chicago Press.

Heusch, Luc de (1985) *Sacrifice in Africa*, trans. Linda O'Birnen and Alice Morton. Manchester: Manchester University Press.

LIVERPOOL
JOHN MOORES UNIVERSITY
AVRIL ROBARTS LRC
TEL. 0151 231 4022

Hubert, Henri and Marcel Mauss (1964) *Sacrifice: Its Nature and Function*, trans. W. D. Halls. Chicago, IL: University of Chicago Press.

Jouffroy, Alain (1964) *La Révolution du régard*. Paris: Gallimard.

Laure (1995) *The Collected Writings*, trans. Jeanine Herman. San Francisco, CA: City Lights.

Le Brun, Annie (1996) *Jean Benoît*. Paris: Galerie 1900 2000.

Levinas, Emmanuel (1987) *Collected Philosophical Papers*. Dordrecht: Martinus Nijhoff.

Lincoln, Bruce (1991) *Death. War, and Sacrifice: Studies in Ideology and Practice*. Chicago, IL: University of Chicago Press.

Paz, Octavio (1967) *The Labyrinth of Solitude*, trans. Lysander Kemp. New York: Grove Press. (Orig. 1961.)

Paz, Octavio (1974) *Alternating Current*, trans. Helen Lane. London: Wildwood House.

Paz, Octavio (1987) 'At Table and in Bed', in *Convergences: Essays on Art and Literature*, trans. Helen Lane. London: Bloomsbury. (Orig. 1973.)

Paz, Octavio (1996) *The Double Flame: Essays on Love and Eroticism*, trans. Helen Lane. London: The Harvell Press. (Orig. 1993.)

Péret, Benjamin (1956) 'Noyau de la comète', in *Anthologie de l'amour sublime*. Paris: Albin Michel.

Pierre, José (ed.) (1992) *Investigating Sex: Surrealist Discussions 1928–1932*, trans. Malcolm Imrie. London: Verso.

Surrealist Group (1938) *Dictionnaire abrégé du surréalisme*. Paris: José Corti.

Thirion, André (1976) *Revolutionaries without Revolution*, trans. Joachim Neugroschel. London: Cassell.

Todorov, Tzvetan (1984) *The Conquest of America*. New York: Harper and Row.

Viveiros de Castro, Eduardo (1992) *From the Enemy's Point of View: Humanity and Divinity in an Amazonian Society*, trans. Catherine V. Howard. Chicago, IL: University of Chicago Press.

Michael Richardson teaches at the School of Oriental and African Studies, University of London. His most recent bok is *Georges Bataille: Essential Writings* (Sage Publications, 1998).

The Lesson of Fire

Notes on Love and Eroticism in Octavio Paz's *The Double Flame*

Maria Esther Maciel

Desire is greater than love but the desire of love is the most powerful of desires. (Octavio Paz, 1991a)

1

MANY LATIN-AMERICAN poets of this century have set about transforming their work – through the practices of creation, critical reflection and translation – into a kind of *ars combinatoria* of cultural signs from various times and spaces. Under the sign of plurality, they have not only carried on a dialogue with other Eastern and Western traditions, but also subverted the dichotomies between universalism and Americanism, identity and alterity, by putting Latin America in the global circuit of cultural exchanges. This is specifically the case with the Mexican poet and thinker, Octavio Paz, the 1990 Nobel Prize winner, who, along with the Argentine writer, Jorge Luis Borges, is considered to be one of the most important writers of the 20th century.

Born in a town on the outskirts of Mexico City in 1914, Paz began his poetic and intellectual activities in the beginning of the 1930s. Always in tune with the social and political events of his country and attentive to the literary innovations of the aesthetic avant-garde of Europe and the Americas, from his early career he conjoined creative activity to an interdisciplinary critical investigation of the past and present. Up until his recent death, in April 1998, Paz was constantly involved in this many-sided work:

■ *Theory, Culture & Society* 1998 (SAGE, London, Thousand Oaks and New Delhi),
   Vol. 15(3–4): 393–403
   [0263-2764(199809/11)15:3–4;393–403;006077]

he wrote countless poems and essays; he created theories of poetry; he made inroads into the territories of history, anthropology, politics, philosophy and the arts; he founded journals, took part in revolutionary aesthetic and political movements, indulged in polemics, confronted the powers-that-be, reinvented his own Mexican roots and carried on a dialogue with poetic voices from a number of traditions.

If the most important political gesture of his intellectual life was resigning the position of Mexican Ambassador to India, in protest against the massacre of 350 students by the Mexican government in October 1968, one could say that the direct contact with French Surrealism, in the second half of the1940s, was his most significant literary experience. Even though he did not entirely agree with the movement's principles, such as the unlimited belief in the powers of inspiration and the defence of so-called *engagé* art, Paz incorporated many Surrealist procedures in his poetry and way of thinking, which, however, is not sufficient to mark him as an adherent of this artistic current, since he added other relevant poetic experiences to the Surrealist legacy, such as the discovery, in the USA, of modernist Anglo-American poetry (especially T.S. Eliot and Ezra Pound), the influences of Spanish baroque – mainly by way of the emblematic figure of the Mexican poet Sor Juana Inés de la Cruz), the encounter with synthetic and visual forms of oriental poetry, the enthusiastic reading of the English and German Romantics, the critical and creative dialogue with the textual subversions of Stéphane Mallarmé and the theoretical passion for the structuralist ideas of Claude Lévi-Strauss and Roman Jakobson. Out of this mixture of experiences arose the complex *oeuvre* of the poet, into which the reader can enter by different paths, depending on the thematic emphasis that he or she wishes to privilege, due to the centrifugal force that issues from his works in the form of multifaceted languages and themes.

This possibility of travelling in diverse places while not being confined to any one allowed Paz to intervene in a decisive way in the paths of Latin American modernity and at its intersections with the cultural diversity of other continents, that is, to show that to be Mexican or Latin American is also an exercise of cosmopolitanism and openness to alterity. The consequence was international public recognition, especially with the Nobel Prize in 1990, awarded to Paz for his 'impassioned writing with wide horizons, characterized by sensual intelligence and humanistic integrity'.

There is no doubt about the pertinence of this phrase of the Swedish Academy to justify the prize, since the words 'passion' and 'sensual' best define the thought and writings of the Mexican poet. For him, if thought was also an exercise of the senses, there was no way of separating the 'passion for language' from the 'language of passion'. 'Seeing the world is spelling it' (Paz, 1990b: 15[1]), he said – which can only be viable through the direct, bodily, contact with the things of the world and with the desire to transform them into words capable of seducing the desire of the reader as well.

It was because he was moved exactly by this passionate impulse for knowledge, for life and for language that Octavio Paz dedicated a great part of his poetry and essays to themes of love, passion and eroticism. From the first poems written in the 1930s, through the essay *The Labyrinth of Solitude* published in 1950, where the question of love is treated in a more detailed way, an entire theory of this field began to be formulated and disseminated in many poems and essays, such as the important *An Erotic Beyond: Sade* published in 1994 among others, which investigate the various representations of eroticism and love in the cultural traditions of East and West. All of these works maintain a dialogue among themselves and show the tension between poetic creation and critical clarity, which makes it possible for the reader not only to find in a poem such as 'Blanco' the verbal and visual representation of theoretical reflections on poetry and eroticism, developed in texts like *Conjunctions and Disjunctions* (orig. 1969) and *The Bow and the Lyre* (orig. 1967), but also to detect in these works thematic and formal resonances with a number of other poems.

One might say that Paz's interest in this theme culminated with the publication of *La llama doble: amory erotismo* (trans. *The Double Flame: Essays on Love and Eroticism*, 1996), in 1993, when Paz was 79. Able to be read as a substantial summary of the ideas developed in earlier works, this book confirms not only the vitality of the poet's old age but also his inexhaustible passion for everything that concerns this theme.

It is precisely with respect to the ideas contained in this book that I should like now to discuss the concepts of love and eroticism developed by Paz, attempting as far as possible to relate them to other thematic concerns of the author and to studies made by other writers.

2

In a little book entitled *La Flamme d'une chandelle*, Gaston Bachelard shows that the flame is one of the greatest 'operators of images', in that it incites desire, brightness and memory in the poetic exercise of the imagination. For this purpose, he collects and investigates in the writings of various Western poets metaphors originating in the semantic field of fire, as well as examining some specific treatises on this theme. Among the collected images, one especially stands out, described by Blaise de Vigenère in his *Traité du feu et du sel*, of 1628:

> There are two flames in the rising flame: one white, which shines and brightens, with a blue root at the tip; another red, which is connected to the wood and the fuse that burns. (Bachelard, 1961: 33)

This is the same image with which Octavio Paz opens his book *The Double Flame* (1996a), only now as a metaphor eroticized and raised to the category of 'operational concept'. It is in and through this image that the entire treatise is constructed. Associating the red flame with eroticism and the blue flame with love – human representations of sexuality symbolized by fire – Paz defines the limits of and the confluences between both, by means of an intertextualized and interdisciplinary perspective, a kind of non-linear story of Western eroticism. This tendency to use a metaphor as a conducting wire for reflections of a theoretical nature is in fact recurrent in the work of the Mexican poet. As he privileges the poetic method even in treating inter-disciplinary themes, that is to say, the creative faculty of 'putting contrary or dissimilar realities in analogical relation' (Paz, 1990a: 138), he allows himself the liberty of interweaving thought and imagination, by composing a textual universe where the limits between the poetic and the discursive dissolve. This practice gives his discourse a hybrid form and attests to his propensity for paradox and plurality – indications of his being in tune (even though sometimes dissonant) with certain de-hierarchized forms of contem-porary thought.

It is exactly out of this variegated texture that *The Double Flame* is composed. Besides being a solid, though small, compendium on love and how its cultural forms are realized in human life – which in a way places it in the line beginning with Plato's *Symposium* and subsequent works such as Georges Bataille's *L'Érotisme* (1957), Soren Kierkegaard's *The Seducer's Diary* (1997), Roland Barthes' *A Lover's Discourse* (1985), and Denis de Rougemont's *Love in the Western World* (1983) – Paz's essay also takes the form of a poetic manifesto in defence of the faculty of feeling.

Rebelling against both the commercialization of desire, promoted by contemporary consumer capitalism, and the resulting decline of the idea of love towards the end of the century, Paz makes a claim – in a gesture that I would call 'post-utopian utopianism' – for the individual right to the freedom of the senses and the imagination as a necessary guarantee for humanity's survival. In this sense, he speaks of the urgent need to reinvent the very notion of the individual, today obliterated by the homogenizing force of the market, and he proposes an erotic re-education of society, based on the rehabilitation of the idea of love. Nor does he omit turning his text as well into a kind of ethical and political examination of the symptoms of our time, even while he takes up again – not without nostalgia – certain links he has maintained with Surrealism. This is particularly true if we think of the utopian strand of this current, constituted, as Fredric Jameson (1995: 173) has pointed out, by the attempt 'to endow the object world of a damaged and broken industrial society with the mystery and the depth, the magical qualities'. But, at the same time, we cannot forget that the utopian gesture of Paz is formed not as a project but as a desire, since the idea of utopia, after the overturning of the values that have made up the modern tradition, is only possible if thought of as something emptied of its historical commitment to the future, as a desiring gesture which is sheltered more and more in the spatialized temporality of the now. It is counting in on what he designates as 'nowness' that Paz converts the praise of love into a libel against the contemporary erasure of the transgressive character of eroticism which he sees as 'into a publicity department and a branch of commerce' (Paz, 1993: 159).

3

If that were not enough, Octavio Paz goes even further in *The Double Flame*, in treating the intersections between love, eroticism and sexuality – themes found throughout his work, beginning in the early poems and essays written in the early 1930s. He offers us as well a revision of his own biography. As he admits in the introduction, the book can be read as a kind of profession of faith, since it is the reconfirmation of the poetic pact that he made earlier in his life.

In addition to his theoretical and poetic reflections on this theme, one might add data from his personal and intellectual life, such as trips to Japan and India, the aesthetic movements he encountered, the books he read, his poetic influences and his own discovery of love at 50 years of age. As he emphasizes: 'poetry and thought are a single system', since they arise from the same source, life (Paz, 1993: 6).

It is not by chance, therefore, that Paz has indicated the intimate relationship between *The Double Flame* and 'Carta de Creencia', the poem that closes the book *Arbol adentro* (1987). The poem, divided into three parts, also starts with the image of fire and develops a chain of metaphors that is converted obliquely into an unfolding conceit on love. An exercise in 'otherness', the poem has an implicit affinity with certain aspects of the theory of love developed by Ortega y Gasset (1957) and to images from earlier poems of Paz himself, as well as exhibiting on the very surface of its language the relation between the I and the other, body and soul, thought and feeling, by making clear the convergence that exists between the erotic and the poetic act.

This convergence involves a special *topos* in the first chapter of *The Double Flame*, since it functions as an indirect justification not only of the analogical thinking that, as I have mentioned earlier, traverses the entire book, but also of the poetic journey of the author. The association poetry/ eroticism is one of the keys to understanding the unfolding of Paz's concept of poetic creation over the decades. For Paz, if a poem is a verbal erotic, eroticism is a corporeal poetic; in the same way that the poem turns language away from its natural and immediate end, which is communication, eroticism turns the body away from its primary function, reproduction. From this notion comes that of eroticism as a 'transfigured sexuality: a metaphor'.

To the imagination is attributed, in this process of the transfiguration of both sexuality and language, 'a cardinal and subversive function'. The imagination would be the inflaming element of deviation and the condition for both the poetic and the erotic act to take place, as acts of reinvention of the body and the word. This is because, as Paz (1993: 195) remarks, 'the imagination makes the phantoms of desire palpable'.

Octavio Paz sought, in a number of poems, to show clearly this 'inverse symmetry' between eroticism and language. Perhaps the poem 'Blanco' (originally published in 1966) is the most exemplary case. Fragmented into several separate poems and placed on the page in a non-linear form, it presents through the play of the right and left columns – in the movements of approaching and distancing – a ritualized simulation of the erotic act. In the poem, what is said materializes in the saying: the themes of eroticism and poetic creation are arranged through the sonorous and visual elements of the verbal material. The poem is thus made in the shape of the erotic ritual, as a ceremony of transfiguration. It is a movement that is seen, in a different way, in *The Monkey Grammarian* (originally published in 1974), a long and discontinuous poem in prose where the liturgies of the body and of language are formed as a search for a meaning beyond the signs that both one and the other emit. From this comes the detailed description of scenes (sometimes orgiastic) of eroticism, as well as the theatricalization – through poetic resources like the fragmentation of phrases, pauses, the suspension of meanings and the creation of a chain of metaphors – of the conjunction/disjunction between the I and the other. It is a repeated impulse in the direction of the abolition of duality and the provisional (or illusory) regression to unity, since Paz believes, and here lies the mystical dimension of his thought, this 'beyond erotic' to be our 'ration of paradise on earth' (1993: 195).

4

One could say that this premise which is central to Paz's work and, more specifically, the book in question, consists of what the poet absorbed through personal experience. Specifically I am referring to the six years he spent in India during the 1960s, when, as Mexican Ambassador in New Delhi, Paz both met the person who would remain his wife till the end of his life ('after being born, it was the most important thing that happened to me', he said in an interview) and discovered the radical nature of a tradition that would appear viscerally in his conceptions of love, of eroticism, of spirituality: Tantrism, considered the last and most transgressive expression of Indian Buddhism.

   The Tantric tradition, as Paz himself teaches us in several texts dedicated to the subject, among them the essay *Conjunctions and Disjunctions* (originally published in 1969), postulates the insertion of the body into the mystical project of spiritual liberation, electing the rites of eroticism, the orgiastic ceremony of the banquet, and the exploration, also ritualistic, of the materiality of language as forms of initiation for achieving illumination, the overcoming of duality symbolized by the masculine and feminine principles. In this sense, the human body – understood as a magical double of language and the universe – acquires an importance never before realized the spiritual history of India. One of the most important premises consists of the retention of semen and the transformation of the erotic release into food for the spirit; that is, the body is transformed into a way of initiation, an experience of ecstasy and 'disincarnation'.

Seduced by the transgressive principles of this sacred erotic, Octavio Paz makes use of them to compose some of his important poetic texts, such as 'Maithuna', besides the poems 'Blanco' and *The Monkey Grammarian*, mentioned earlier, and he also derives support for his theoretic reflections on eroticism, such as that presented in *The Double Flame*. Yet, he adds to these texts and reflections an element absent in the Tantric tradition, one with a more Westernized provenance (although showing influences of Arab eroticism): love conceived as the attraction for a single person, for the union of a body and a soul.

It can be said that, in rehabilitating love as the most powerful force of lived erotic experience, Octavio Paz continues the lyrical current, into the late 20th century, which originated in the theory/practice of courtly love in Provençal poetry, traversed the Romantic movement (in its various off-shoots) and arose again in the 20th century, in new guise, with Surrealism. These moments, either through reading or direct experience, had a strong impact on the conception of love adopted by Paz.

'A mysterious passionate attraction for a single person, that is, the transformation of the "erotic object" into a free and unique individual' (Paz, 1993: 35): with this definition Paz outlines the basic difference between love and eroticism. If eroticism is desire in movement, a thirst for otherness, love transforms the object of desire into a free subject. Freedom is an indispensable element here, since it allows that the other, the beloved person, gains recognition through his or her possibilities of flight. Just like eroticism, without which it could not survive, love is a ceremony and a representation, but also 'an irrational wager' on another's freedom. It is in this sense that, according to the poet, 'the emergence of love is inseparable from the emergence of woman' (Paz, 1993: 72) as subject of her own freedom, her own desire.

Through this argument, Paz offers a proposition that challenges accepted readings: Plato's *Symposium* would be seen less as a philosophy of love than a philosophy of sublime eroticism: in the first place, because it craves a kind of intransitivity, that is, it does not depend on an exclusive relation with another person, but a form of solitary and contemplative asceticism, in which the corporeal beauty of the object (or objects) of desire would only work as one of the possible ways of achieving love. Or, in Paz's words, what is lacking in this form of eroticism is 'the other, the other and its complement, that which converts desire into agreement: the free will, freedom' (Paz, 1993: 47). In the second place, woman would have been excluded from the theory, even though the main argument reproduced in the dialogue came from Diotima. Paz even comments that Plato would have found scandalous what our civilization, since the advent of Provençal poetry, has called love. And by extension, he would also have repudiated the cult that this poetic tradition has bestowed on women.

Although letting slip a certain romantic idealism – which, for us, participants in this end of a century, can sound both like nostalgia for the past and subversion of the present – Octavio Paz makes his own mark on the brief notes he gives us in *The Double Flame*. The ideas of Paz do not shun being a risk or a challenge, since they also have as their aim that which Paul Valéry chose as the driving force of his own poetic-intellectual career: *to make the reader think, to provoke internal acts.*

5

Although contentious, since any concept of love is unstable given the displaced and unclassifiable nature of the feeling, Paz's reading, paradoxical as it is, retains an unquestionable coherence. This does not prevent us, however, from being able to observe significant absences (or exclusions) from the various textual voices that meet in the book: Kierkegaard, Bataille and Barthes.

It is certain that Paz chose a sophisticated *paideuma*, from which he could construct his own reading of the theme. But one might also ask if, for example, the exploration of Kierkegaard's works *In Vino Veritas* (1976, an ironic re-reading of Plato's *Symposium*) and *The Seducer's Diary* (1997), would not have offered more support for the mapping Paz made. This also would have given him the opportunity to insert the theme of seduction into the matrix of feelings and sensations he composed around the idea of love. Kierkegaard, besides broaching – in the masks of the countless pseudonymous characters he created – themes like love, marriage and woman, gives us an entire treatise on the art of seduction, founded on poetic reflection, which both points to a Romantic vision (of an ironic lineage, in tune with the aesthetic precepts of the Romanticism of Jena) which anticipates certain contemporary readings of themes like seduction and the feminine, such as *The Seminar of Jacques Lacan – Book 20* (Miler, 1998) and Jean Baudrillard's *Seduction* (1991).

In *The Seducer's Diary*, one finds, in paradoxical conjunction, both the eroticism of the Platonic type and the Romantic love of Provençal origin, to which is added an unusual element of perversion. Johannes, the Seducer, chooses one woman, Cordelia, who captures him with a look and with whom he falls in love, creating from this situation a strategy to seduce her at the same time that he transforms the practice of seduction into a narcissistic exercise of refining both sensitivity and spirit. Paz could say, rightly: there is no voluntary surrender on the part of Cordelia; she is manipulated by the desire of the Seducer and converted into a way of access to something else, which would lead the relation to the exclusive field of aesthetic eroticism. The complexity of the text, however, brings in other elements which would make this argument relative. Johannes at first admits his spontaneous passion for Cordelia ('I am almost unable to stand on my feet', he confesses), and admits that it is at the same time a physical and spiritual attraction. The young woman is seen as a body and a soul; she has a name and a voice that she makes heard in the letters she writes to her lover. Johannes even says, in the manner of Paz: 'it is necessary that she [Cordelia] does not owe me anything, for she ought to feel free, love is only found in freedom' (Kierkegaard, 1997: 46).

This quote could lead us to associate the feeling of the Seducer with what Paz has called love. Nevertheless, what occurs between Johannes and Cordelia is a kind of displacement of the amorous relation – strategically provoked by the Seducer – to another order, which we might call perverse (in both dictionary and psychoanalytical meanings). On transforming this relation into an aesthetic and intellectual game, the protagonist attempts, by way of verbal artifice and ironic reflection, to destroy the woman as free subject. How? By his incorporating the freedom and the seductive force that Cordelia possesses, passing them through the sieve of calculation and returning them, in artificial form, to the young woman herself. This is a prismatic, refractive, process: what reflects itself turns against the reflected. As Baudrillard observes, the artificial, in this chain, is also ritual and sacrificial (Baudrillard, 1989: 107), which would lead to the Johannes and Cordelia relation being confined exclusively to the plane of eroticism, in the way Paz understood it.

This can be seen as rich material for understanding the paradoxical relation between love and eroticism in their distinct representations in the West, as are, too, the contributions of Roland Barthes and Georges Bataille to the same field. Barthes, by interweaving details of the daily living of a love experience with textual citations from various sources, creates a kind of scriptural constellation of discursive fragments on love. Bataille works with eroticism in the perspective of evil, death, violence and transgression.

If, in the case of Kierkegaard and Barthes, we can argue that they were not a part of Paz's theoretical and literary horizon (even if we find points of contact between them), in the case of Bataille the absence is rather strange, since he is one of the important references of Paz's thought especially in texts such as *An Erotic Beyond: Sade*, and *Claude Lévi-Strauss: An Introduction*.

In any case, one can say that on shying away from certain morbid and shadowy aspects inherent in the dominions of eroticism – explored especially by Bataille – Paz prefers to explore the sunny parts of this universe, by way of lightness, erudition, memory and poetic lucidity, from which arises the delicacy of *The Double Flame*: it is less an anthropological treatise than a confession of love for life.

Here I take up again the initial image of the flame, but now as a privileged metaphor of what, in this love, is passion: passion for the office of writing, reading, listening, making polemics, seeing, denying, affirming and existing, without which Octavio Paz would not have left the vast *oeuvre* and the luminous wisdom that are now given us – in his physical absence – as the most living testimony of his presence on earth.

This multiplied passion justifies, as we have seen, the potentiality that he always had to travel in distinct territories of knowledge, to remain in a state of vigilance in the face of the political problems of his time, to have a creative relation with the past and with traditions, to understand the paradoxes of his double condition of being a Mexican and a citizen of the world. It justifies, above all, his visceral complicity with poetry.

The essay *The Double Flame* is also the result of the substantive power of this passion, not only because it constitutes a study of the dominions in which it sets itself up, but also because it proposes a new conception of life, founded on the time of the now, which is also the time of the body and of death. As Paz says, 'love is not love *for* this world, but *of* this world; it is tied to the earth by the force of the gravity of the body, which is pleasure and death'(Paz, 1993: 207). It should, for this reason, be recovered in its dimension of presence, of the present. Its flame is the guarantee of our provisional eternity.

Note

I would like to thank Thomas Burns, who helped with the translation into English.

1.   All the translations of quotations from original Spanish and French editions are mine.

Bibliography

Bachelard, G. (1961) *La Flamme d'une chandelle*. Paris: Universitaires de France.

Bachelard, G. (1990) *The Flame of a Candle*. Dallas, TX: Dallas Institute of Humanities and Culture Publication.

Barthes, R. (1985) *A Lover's Discourse: Fragments*. New York: Hill and Wang.

Bataille, G. (1957) *L'Érotisme*. Paris: Éditions de Minuit.

Baudrillard, J. (1989) *De la seducción*. Madrid: Cátedra.

Baudrillard, J. (1991) *Seduction*. New York: St Martin's Press.

de Rougemont, D. (1983) *Love in the Western World*. Princeton, NJ: Princeton University Press.

Gasset, J. Ortega y (1957) *Sobre el Amor*. Madrid: Plenitud.

Guibert, R. (1973) *Seven Voices* (Interview). New York: Alfred Knopf.

Jameson, F. (1995) *Postmodernism, or, the Cultural Logic of Late Capitalism*. Durham, NC: Duke University Press.

Kierkegaard, S. (1976) *In Vino Veritas. La repetición*. Madrid: Guadarama.

Kierkegaard, S. (1997) *The Seducer's Diary*. Princeton, NJ: Princeton University Press.

Miler, J. A. (ed.) (1988) *The Seminar of Jacques Lacan – Book 20*, trans. B. Fink. New York and London: Norton.

Paz, O. (1970) *Claude Lévi-Strauss: An Introduction*. Ithaca, NY: Cornell University Press.

Paz, O. (1973) *The Bow and the Lyre*. Austin: University of Texas Press.

Paz, O. (1974a) *Blanco*. New York: New York Press.

Paz, O. (1974b) *Conjunctions and Disjunctions*. New York: Viking Press.

Paz, O. (1981) *The Monkey Grammarian*. New York: Seaver Books.

Paz, O. (1985) *Selected Poems*. New York: New Directions.

Paz, O. (1987) *Arbol Adentro*. Barcelona: Seix Barral.

Paz, O. (1990a) *La otra voz*. Barcelona: Seix Barral.

Paz, O. (1990b) *Pasado en Claro*. México: fondo de Cultura Economica.

Paz, O. (1991a) *Cuadrivio*. México: Joaquin Mortiz.

Paz, O. (1991b) *Other Voice: Essays in Modern Poetry*. New York: Harcourt Brace.

Paz, O (1993) *La llama doble: amor y erotismo*. México: Seix Barral.

Paz, O. (1996a) *The Double Flame: Essays on Love and Eroticism*. London: Haverill.

Paz, O. (1996b) *The Labyrinth of Solitude*. London: Penguin.

Paz, O. (1998) *An Erotic Beyond: Sade*. New York: Harcourt Brace.

Plato (1989) *Symposium*. Berkeley: University of California Press.

Maria Esther Maciel teaches in the Department of Semiotics and Literary Theory at the Universidade Federal de Minas Gerais, Brazil. Her publications include *As vertigens da lucidez: poesia e crítica em Octavio Paz* (São Paulo: Experimento, 1995) and *Borges em dez textos* (co-editor) (Rio de Janeiro: Sette Letras, Belo Horizonte: POSLIT, 1998).

Love, Gender and Morality

Mike Hepworth

'Now look me in the face, Mr Slope, boldly and openly.'

Mr Slope did look at her with a languishing loving eye, and as he did so, he again put forth his hand to get hold of hers.

'I told you to look at me boldly, Mr Slope; but confine your boldness to your eyes.'

'Oh, Madeleine!' he sighed.

'Well, my name is Madeleine,' said she; 'but none except my own family usually call me so. Now look me in the face, Mr Slope. Am I to understand that you say you love me?'

Mr Slope never had said so. If he had come there with any formed plan at all, his intention was to make love to the lady without uttering any such declaration. It was, however, quite impossible that he should now deny his love. He had, therefore, nothing for it, but to go down on his knees distractedly against the sofa, and swear that he did love her with a love passing the love of man. (Trollope, 1962: 231–2)

Victorian Romantic Love

IN THIS INCIDENT from Trollope's famous novel of clerical life (first published in 1857) the potential for female empowerment within the conventional Victorian rhetoric of romantic love is exploited by Signora Madeleine Neroni to the full. Mr Slope, a devious schemer committed to self-advancement, is out-manoeuvred by the perceptive and worldly-wise Signora Neroni who coolly returns Mr Slope's warm professions of attachment with the pertinent question: 'when are you to be married to my dear friend Eleanor Bold?' Slope, completely outfaced, returns home after further verbal fencing 'with a sad heart, troubled mind, and uneasy conscience' (1962: 236). Mr Slope has discovered that women can be dangerous. The beautiful Signora, invalided to a chaise-longue, exemplifies the power women can derive from the skilled exploitation of the rhetoric of love, a

■ *Theory, Culture & Society* 1998 (SAGE, London, Thousand Oaks and New Delhi),
  Vol. 15(3–4): 405–415
  [0263-2764(199808/11)15:3–4;405–415;006078]

central theme in Stephen Kern's cultural history of representations of heterosexual love in Victorian paintings 1840–1900.

The origins of his argument can be traced back to his first book, *Anatomy and Destiny* (1975) where, in a pioneering analysis of the cultural construction of the body, he first discussed love in the context of Victorian sexuality and marriage. In this work he drew attention to evidence of the emergence of an increasing tension between the demands of family morality and the claims of individuality in love:

> In response to the many social, economic, and cultural forces that held the Victorian family together as a sanctuary from the rest of the world, many attempted to break away. The literature reflects this dialectical process: a growing sense of the biological and psychological unity of the family and a mounting tension between the members who sought independence from it. (1975: 122)

In her novel *The Mill on The Floss* (1860) George Eliot deals with these issues in terms of gender. Maggie Tulliver, the central character in the novel, falls in love with Stephen Guest who is engaged to Lucy, her best friend. But Maggie and Stephen respond to this moral dilemma in totally different ways. Stephen passionately argues that love overrides conventional morality: the denial of true feelings is the greater wrong. Maggie initially resists with the argument that the more enduring value is faithfulness and memory. She pleads with Stephen to help her renounce him but he persists in asking for one kiss before they part. Although Maggie temporarily yields and compromises her moral stance, Eliot shows Stephen to be the weaker person. Stephen and Maggie cannot become a couple, not because they have infringed conventional morality, but because the gulf between their moral character is so wide: 'He ignores the more profound level of suffering and rejection which Maggie experiences; he is indicted for his superficiality' (Karl, 1995: 323–4). Although Maggie is temporarily diverted by her feelings, Eliot allows her an even greater depth of feeling, and a larger will to resist her personal impulses.

In *Eyes* Kern, like Eliot, examines love as an expression of the gendered morality characteristic of the Victorian period, *c.* 1840–1900. The power love gives to women is derived from the practice of a number of ethical constraints which include fidelity, long-term commitment and resistance to immediate sexual gratification. It is only when women and men come together in face-to-face encounters that this source of strength is so dramatically revealed. But, as he argued in his previous book, *The Culture of Love* (1992), an appreciation of the conflict of interests between women and men in these emotionally intense encounters must be contextualized within 'the mixed forms of being-with that constitute the history of love, interpreted as authentic and inauthentic ways of encountering others' (1992: 45). The Victorian period should be read, therefore, as a transitional stage in the emancipation of love from 'inauthentic' modes of experience and the gradual emergence of 'authentic' ways of becoming intimate with another individual.

In *Culture* Kern shows that love is not a universal constant but a process of the gradual self-realization of historical beings as they move towards modernity; a process which is uneven, inegalitarian and gendered. In *Eyes* he returns to the Victorian period to explore a moment in this process as it is recorded in popular paintings of love's gendered gaze. Representations of face-to-face interaction between men and women as they negotiate the rhetoric of romantic love are thus seen as part of a wider struggle for emancipation from the constraining collective structures of Victorian sexual morality. The quest by both women and men for the ideal of intersubjective and physical intimacy is enhanced by the gradual dissolution of 'the ties that bind' and the increasing expectation of individual autonomy. If the modern dilemma of love is how to retain an ideal of the social, the Victorian problem was how to realize the ideal of heterosexual love within the constraints of a gendered, inegalitarian, less individuated and sexually disembodied social order.

Love's Gendered Gaze

A study of representations of love's gendered gaze in Victorian art, Kern's main source of data is a critical selection of paintings of the period supported by readings from literature. His interest is in paintings depicting a man and a woman together where a relationship between the two is indicated in terms of the way they look at, or look away from, each other. His choice includes many familiar works of the day which makes it easy for the reader to compare the author's interpretation of art and gender with those of significant contributors to the art history of the 19th century (e.g. Dijkstra, 1988; Jenkyns, 1992; Kestner, 1989; Nead, 1992). Such a comparative exercise is also important because Kern's book offers an interpretation of representations of the gendered gaze which is in certain respects in critical opposition to these writers. As already implied, this most recent of Kern's books should be read in relation to his preceding work on sexuality and love, and in particular as a companion volume to *The Culture of Love* (1992). In the discussion that follows *Eyes* and *Love* will therefore be cited as interdependent texts.

In the introductory chapter of *Eyes* the focus of the theoretical critique is the concept of 'the male gaze'. Kern's main argument is that a preoccupation of art historians and critics with the feminist conception of the male gaze (the male dominates and objectifies) has neglected the subtle range of contradictory female looks and expressions evident in Victorian paintings and resulted in a misleadingly overdetermined analysis. He wishes, for example, to qualify Kestner's view of the concerted effort to maintain 'the dominant fiction of masculinity' (Kern, 1996: 254 n13) and draws on Sartre's *Being and Nothingness* (1943) for support for the view that freedom exists in the look; the observed is always free to look back. Dijkstra's magisterial analysis of the fear of female sexuality displayed by male artists in fin-de-siecle culture can be seen as an acknowledgement of feminine power in love and sexuality, of the emerging independence of women and their transition to 'authenticity'.

But Kern's quest for evidence of an alternative female gaze of love does not result in a simplistic rejection of the male gaze thesis. He acknowledges in *Culture* the impossibility of avoiding the artistic convention equating creativity with male desire and the relegation of women to a more passive inspirational role. He cites William Frith's *The Sleeping Model* (1853) as a classic example of the male gaze thesis: here an artist stands commandingly at his easel, his eyes focused directly on the young female model seated on the dais. Dressed in full outdoor clothing the girl has fallen asleep, presumably from exhaustion, and is completely unaware of the scrutiny to which she is exposed (1992: 113–14). Essentially Kern is arguing against 'wild' feminist criticism (1996: 266, n5) for a more complex representation and theorization of women's role in Victorian love. He challenges, for example, Griselda Pollock's statement that Renoir's painting *The Loge* (1874) is remarkable simply because it shows a woman 'actively looking' (1996: 76). In this famous painting a man and woman are shown occupying a box at the theatre, the woman to the forefront dominating the picture, her arm resting on the balcony and her gaze directed out towards the audience/viewer. Her male companion is very much in the background, his eyes fixed to a pair of binoculars focused away from the viewer and upwards to the right-hand side of the frame. For Kern there is 'nothing remarkable about a depiction of a woman actively looking at all sorts of things, more intriguingly and more imaginatively, if not more intently, than men whose gazes are repeatedly pinned on women. Women are just not shown actively looking at men with clear erotic purposes' (1996: 76–8). As Linda Williams has shown (1995), it is necessary to turn to Victorian photographic pornography for evidence of a directly erotic female gaze.

Whilst the male gaze in the paintings is more erotically direct, the female gaze expresses a greater tension between sexual desire and love as the desire for a reciprocal, enduring and moral union of two separate selves. In Kern's view Victorian art is replete with representations of the moral superiority of women. This moral superiority is revealed through the face, and especially the eyes. It is representations of the eyes of women that reflect the crucial distinction between active and passive involvement in a love relationship: 'Inauthentic eyes are seen; authentic eyes see' (1992: 68). The authentic eyes of love are the eyes of women who actively *see*; they are not painted emblems of a desirable aesthetic surface into which man can gaze in search of his own reflection. Paintings of the eyes are therefore evidence of a 'creative effort to restore balance to a world that was so imbalanced by male privilege and power' (1996: 239). In this sense, within the unifying thematic frame of Kern's existential history of love, pictorial images of the female gaze can be interpreted as an indication of the direction of future change in the experience and expression of love. These images of love's gendered gaze anticipate the possibility of modern authentic love which was denied by the encumbering frame of Victorian sexual morality. Kern finds compelling evidence in his collection of images of:

> ... a woman's eyes straining with moral anguish about whether to continue giving herself to a fancy man, to let a lover risk his life for religious faith, to take a gambling stake from a seducer, or to accept a proposal of marriage from someone she hardly knew. (1996: 24)

And even when eyes are closed in sleep or death the power of women is not necessarily diminished. Kern is critical of Dijkstra (1986) for interpreting fin-de-siecle representations of sleeping or dead women as essential passivity and vulnerability. Reiterating a comment in *Culture* (1992: 414 n3), he writes: 'I interpret sleeping women as at peace with themselves and the world, absorbed in their own dreams, not in fulfilling men's fantasies. The attitude of male artists is envy rather than the projection of patriarchal anxiety' (1996: 264, n7).

He also takes Dijkstra to task for a misreading of the fin-de-siecle tendency to portray belligerently erotic women (the *female fatale*): 'But if potent snake-kissing women brought new weaponry to the battle of the sexes, they were welcome in the battle men and women fought together against two millennia of sexual guilt' (1992: 112). Another example of Kern's alternative reading of the tendency to impute evil intent to women who take the sexual initiative is his reappraisal of a contemporary review of Burne-Jones' *The Depths of the Sea* (1887) where a siren has pulled a man down to the bottom of the sea. The critic of the *Athenaeum* described the expression on the face of the siren as that of a triumphant witch but to Kern this is an overblown reaction reflecting anxiety over a potent female figure. In Kern's eyes the siren's face does not resemble that of a witch and her eyes do not indicate evil but rather an 'inner strength' (1996: 177).

Similarly the famous painting *The Turkish Bath* by J.A.D. Ingres (1862) is described as 'a visual gauntlet for the male ego' (1996: 100). The nude women may be displayed to service a man, they may be unfree to leave the room, captured in a state of artistic undress, but the male Christian viewer of the 19th century would be unable to free himself of the anxiety created by his consciousness of so many female eyes upon him. Thus Kern argues against Parker and Pollock's assertion that the absence of men in this painting and others should be read as evidence of male superiority. The absence of the male figure is an admission of vulnerability.

In Victorian painting the female nude is not therefore necessarily stripped of the power of subjectivity. The sleeping nude, allegedly doubly vulnerable, can derive 'visual potency from the possibility of her waking, and an awake nude has the power to see, but a nude who could be asleep or awake is especially formidable for a male viewer, because he does not know if he can be seen' (1996: 102). The male gaze is therefore less than triumphant and may indicate a sense of impending disempowerment: there is a 'reciprocal seduction of artist and model' (1996: 104).

The women in Ingres' *Turkish Bath* are clearly waiting for a man. But if in Victorian paintings it is sexually available and marriageable women who typically wait for men and for love 'it must not be assumed that men drew authentic capital from women's passivity, because authenticity is incompatible with either side of passivity or oppression' (1992: 19). In its authentic mode love is not an experience to be passively awaited by either women or men but must be actively pursued. Authentic love is not a process of waiting for the 'one and only' but of shaping the future and making it one's own.

Even when eyes are read as 'vacant', as for example by Dijkstra (1986), Kern will argue for the alternative and more positive self-absorption of women in looking at their own bodies 'oblivious of the dimming male gaze' (1996: 123). And the male gaze 'is not always an act of possession; it can also be a frustrating reminder of what a man cannot have' (1996: 124). The gendered contrast between love (feminine) and seduction (masculine) is far too simple. When men are attempting to seduce women, women are shown to occupy the moral boundary, their eyes an indication of the complex moral decision they face. The eyes of male seducers 'were consistently relegated to the shadows and the margins' (1996: 180) while the frontally visible eyes of the women under siege were used to 'express the most intensely felt moral dilemmas of the age' (1996: 180).

The main ideological source of a distinctively independent female gaze was the prevailing assumption that women were endowed with a stronger moral sensibility. But Kern is in no doubt about the division of labour which confined the moral superiority of women to the domestic realm leaving men superior in the public sphere. Women who crossed the boundary into the male province could therefore expect to experience a state of emotional turmoil and this, too, is reflected in representations of the face and eyes. One example is the relatively rare depiction of women rescuing men from danger. Armoured knights rescuing partially clothed or naked damsels in distress were not uncommon but when a woman rescued a man the dominant code was reversed: 'women who rescued men had to make a code of their own that conflicted with traditional codes of womanly conduct, creating an inner turmoil that artists preferred to highlight' (1992: 206). Paintings of men being rescued by women can be seen in this sense as evidence of a transition: not of 'how powerful men were but how imperilled their powers were beginning to seem' (1992: 225). Because this art was produced by men 'we must assume that it was intended to assuage their fears about that loss' (1992: 225–6). For Kern this shift in the balance of power can be seen as a moment in the gradual emergence of more egalitarian relationships between men and women which is one of the hallmarks of modern authentic love.

Embodiment, Modernity and Authenticity

The romantic love depicted in respectable Victorian mainstream art was essentially disembodied, or more accurately, embodied in terms of the externals of a clothed appearance in which the face 'stuck out of its heavily clothed body like the head of a turtle' (Kern, 1992: 63). Because love was so closely associated with physical beauty, to 'fall in love' with a woman, or with a man, was to become enchanted by a physiognomically idealized surface appearance. That the efforts of authors such as Charlotte Bronte in *Jane Eyre* (1847) or Wilkie Collins in *The Woman in White* (1860) to give their heroines a 'plain' appearance were regarded by contemporary critics as deviant only serves to underline the primacy of constructions of feminine beauty in the culture of love. Victorian fiction, as Lefkovitz has observed, was 'rich in physical descriptions, and heroes and heroines, who are usually the most fully described characters in a novel, invariably develop into standards of beauty' (1987: 1).

Towards the end of the 19th century it gradually became more permissible to abandon the convention of the nude body as an idealized and de-natured construct and to look upon the naked form as a living embodiment of the self. There is a shift in the art record from the depiction of the naked body as the classical nude towards the naked body with sexual openings and the physical pleasures of love. The move is towards a greater authenticity in descriptions of the body, its imperfections, odours, sick-nesses, sexual inadequacies and ageing. 'Far from diminishing the possi-bilities of embodied love, these realities expanded them in the direction of greater authenticity, as men and women could include simply more of what they were and hence more awareness of themselves as human beings in love' (1992: 88). This cultural shift includes an increasing emphasis upon the value of privacy marked, for example, by the increasing salience of the honeymoon, a private affair where newlyweds were free to 'style their love in a uniquely personal way and reflect on its meaning' (1992: 326). This is reinforced by further developments in private housing which make it possible for the couple to return from their private honeymoon, a destination kept secret from the wedding guests, to the seclusion of their home.

In this interpretation Kern sees authentic love as an embodied ex-pression of the individual's consciousness of independent selfhood and his/her essential separateness from the other. While Victorian art displays a prioritization of the eye it is also a culturally blinkered inauthentic vision refusing an explicit acknowledgement of the sexual body and diverted into a (male) fantasy world of idealized union. Kern exemplifies this contradiction in the notorious example of John Ruskin, the most influential art critic of the 19th century, who 'was good at talking about sex, but ... was not so accomplished at seeing' (1992: 401). There is, then, an irony at the heart of Victorian culture: Ruskin, champion of the educated eye, simultaneously opened his eyes to the wonders of nature while averting them in disgust from the body of his young wife. Promoting a highly selective art of looking, he preferred to extol, as Robert Hewison has shown, 'the elements of nature framed by landscape, the human shaping of these elements into architecture, and human response to them expressed in sculpture and painting' (1976: 29). Ruskin, says Kern, was guilty of the Victorian sin of suppressing 'the sensory richness of vision' (1992: 402).

It is in the alternative images of love's female gaze that traces of a more authentic mode of self-understanding can be seen. Unlike the men, the women in the paintings of couples he describes are not eager for fusion or union with the body of a man but can be seen as mentally rehearsing the implications of love for the future of the self. Yet by and large they remained constrained within the Victorian family, the only sanctified social space for the sexual union of body and self. By the end of the 19th century, however, Kern detects in *Anatomy and Destiny* the early stages of a breakdown in Victorian attempts to integrate body and spirit in marriage: the 'tenuous solidity of the family' had already begun to disintegrate partly as a result of 'a growing awareness of the bodily determinants of human existence' (1975: 124).

An important element of authentic love is the active contemplation of the meaning of relationships between men and women which takes the desires of the body fully into account and accepts that a fusion of selves is impossible. The transition from the Victorian to the modern involves a move away from a form of love which was 'more patient, more polite, more self-sacrificing, and more Christian' (1992: 9) to modern love which is expressive of the reflective self striving with the other to realize authenticity. Authentic love includes the increasing enjoyment of sex and the extension of sexual interaction into a long drawn out but more reflective period of time. For the Victorians the post-coital phase was especially embarrassing 'because eyes opened, lights came on, and couples were obliged to look at one another or else away and begin to speak or else endure a nerve-wracking silence' (1992: 345). The transition is from love based upon gendered differences or blinkered concerns to extended interpersonal exchanges which expose vulnerabilities and the fragility of the self. The goal of modern lovers is 'a shared conquest of themselves together in love' (1992: 238).

But the passage, however commendable, is not an easy one because of the delicate balance that exists in love between fusion and autonomy. Authentic love rejects the ideal of love as fusion with another described by the poet Coleridge as 'you–me' (Jones, 1997: 153) because fusion seeks loss of self-awareness. The modern ideal of love expresses the wish to preserve the autonomy of the embodied self; the history of selfhood, claims Kern, reveals 'an increasingly favourable estimation of struggling to resist the lure of fusion and remain autonomous' (1992: 281). And yet, as a number of recent sociological analyses of modern love have shown (Duncombe and Marsden, 1998; Hochschild, 1985, 1994, 1998; Jackson, 1993; Wouters, 1998), the contradictions between fusion and autonomy continue to give the experience of love between men and women a quality which often eludes precise articulation in conventional social science discourse. Hochschild, for example, has recently addressed the issue of 'the modern paradox of love' (1998: 8), where love is located at the intersections of a number of contradictions and cross-pressures. On the one hand modern culture invites men and women to 'aspire to a richly communicative, intimate, playful, sexually fulfilling love' and on the other hand 'warns us against trusting such a love too much' (1998: 8).

Much of this research seems to me to suggest that the desire for fusion with another as the quintessential dream of 'falling in love' has by no means been entirely eclipsed. It is clear that the developments documented by Kern with such scholarly flair should not be regarded as linear or exclusive. The characteristics of modern love (self-reflection, privacy, the gradual elimination of gender imbalances) are not necessarily totally congruent with the desire for independent authenticity but might equally result in the desire for fusion with another. The desire for the confirmation of self by an other and the fear of the loss of a 'significant other' or 'partner' – what Coleridge described as the disintegration of the 'you–me' into the 'you and me' (Jones, 1997: 153) – continues to haunt the discourse of love. If, as Kern argues, many Victorian artists saw love as a moment of hope menaced by human deficiencies and frailties, there is still abundant evidence of the persistence of this romantic vision.

In this respect Kern's work offers insights from cultural history into the complexities of the negotiations involved in making sense of love. Love involves relationships between real people in which ideals with a long historical pedigree act as a cultural reference point as, for example, Hoggart (1958) showed in his pioneering analysis of the role of romantic fiction in the lives of working-class women. But, as Jackson (1993) shows, the ideology is confusing and ambiguous and, as Duncombe and Marsden (1998) indicate in their study of women's emotion work in marriage, efforts to 'sustain the image that "we're ever so happy really"' (1998: 211) are not necessarily evidence of a subjective sense of inauthenticity.

It seems to be the case that love exists in all societies and is a product of the existential impossibility of sustaining a coherent sense of self without a confirming other or, as the symbolic interactionists show, an image, memory or dream of another. In this sense love represents an ideal form of social bonding: it offers a golden opportunity to the individual to risk all, totally transform his/her life and legitimately sacrifice others for a greater good. Or, as Kern would perhaps argue, to engage in a complex moral calculation. As such it transcends everyday routine but paradoxically is the cause in which considerable routine effort has to be made to realize the ideal throughout an extending lifetime and possibly in loving relations with several others. In an individuated society love may be regarded as the ultimate moral contract: a celebration of intense emotion in an allegedly rational world. Love, Kern concludes in *Culture*, is not static and like many other commentators on love he is drawn in the end towards an expression of value: 'In trying to understand the history of love, which I have argued is a move toward greater authenticity, I have found it impossible not to valorise the direction of that movement' (1992: 400).

Bibliography

Bendelow, G. and S.J. Williams (eds) (1998) *Emotions in Social Life: Critical Theories and Contemporary Issues*. London and New York: Routledge.

Daly, G. (1990) *Pre-Raphaelites in Love*. Glasgow: Fontana/Collins.

Dijkstra, B. (1988) *Idols of Perversity: Fantasies of Feminine Evil in Fin-de-Siècle Culture*. New York and Oxford: Oxford University Press.

Duncombe, J. and D. Marsden (1998) ' "Stepford Wives" and "Hollow Men"? Doing Emotion Work, Doing Gender and "Authenticity" in Intimate Heterosexual Relationships', pp. 211–17 in G. Bendelow and S.J. Williams (eds) *Emotions in Social Life: Critical Theories and Contemporary Issues*. London and New York: Routledge.

Hewison, R. (1976) *John Ruskin: The Argument of the Eye*. London: Thames and Hudson.

Hochschild, A.R. (1985) *The Managed Heart: Commercialisation of Human Feeling*. Berkeley, Los Angeles, London: University of California Press.

Hochschild, A.R. (1994) 'The Commercial Spirit of Intimate Life and the Abduction of Feminism: Signs from Women's Advice Books', *Theory, Culture & Society* 11(2): 1–24.

Hochschild, A.R. (1998) 'The Sociology of Emotion as a Way of Seeing', pp. 3–15 in G. Bendelow and S.J. Williams (eds) *Emotions in Social Life: Critical Theories and Contemporary Issues*. London and New York: Routledge.

Hoggart, R. (1958) *The Uses of Literacy: Aspects of Working-Class Life with Special Reference to Publications and Entertainments*. Harmondsworth: Penguin.

Jackson, S. (1993) 'Even Sociologists Fall in Love: An Exploration in the Sociology of Emotions', *Sociology* 27(2): 201–20.

Jenkyns, R. (1992) *Dignity and Decadence: Victorian Art and the Classical Inheritance*. London: Fontana.

Jones, K. (1997) *A Passionate Sisterhood: The Sisters, Wives and Daughters of the Lake Poets*. London: Constable.

Karl, F. (1995) *George Eliot: A Biography*. London: HarperCollins.

Kern, S. (1975) *Anatomy and Destiny: A Cultural History of the Human Body*. Indianapolis, IN: Bobbs-Merrill.

Kern, S. (1992) *The Culture of Love: Victorians to Moderns*. Cambridge, MA and London: Harvard University Press.

Kern, S. (1996) *Eyes of Love: The Gaze in English and French Paintings and Novels 1840–1900*. London: Reaktion Books.

Kestner, J.A. (1989) *Mythology and Misogyny: The Social Discourse of Nineteenth-Century British Classical-Subject Painting*. Madison: University of Wisconsin Press.

Lefkovitz, L.H. (1987) *The Character of Beauty in the Victorian Novel*. Ann Arbor, MI: UMI Research Press.

Marsh, J. (1986) *Jane and May Morris: A Biographical Story 1839–1938*. London and New York: Pandora.

Marsh, J. (1992) *Pre-Raphaelite Sisterhood*. London: Quartet Books.

Nead, L. (1992) *The Female Nude: Art, Obscenity and Sexuality*. London and New York: Routledge.

Trollope, A. (1962) *Barchester Towers*. London: Dent. (Orig. 1857.)

Vaughan, D. (1988) *Uncoupling: How and Why Relationships Come Apart*. London: Methuen.

Williams, L. (1995) 'Corporealized Observers: Visual Pornographies and the "Carnal Density of Vision"', pp. 3–41 in P. Petro (ed.) *Fugitive Images: From Photography to Video*. Bloomington and Indianapolis: Indiana University Press.

Wouters, C. (1998) 'Changes in the "Lust Balance" of Sex and Love Since the Sexual Revolution: The Example of the Netherlands', pp. 228–49 in G. Bendelow and S.J. Williams (eds) *Emotions in Social Life: Critical Theories and Contemporary Issues*. London and New York: Routledge.

Mike Hepworth teaches Sociology at the University of Aberdeen. His research interests include the sociology of the emotions and representations of the body in painting and popular fiction.

Bodies, Sex and Death

Arthur W. Frank

He tells me not to worry or rush around so much. 'Everything you really need will come to you,' he insists. Perhaps only a creature that can't move, that has to trust and to wait, can say that with genuine persuasiveness. (Belden Lane, 1997: 981)

T WO SUCH DIFFERENT lives, different illnesses, different books, yet they speak to each other across those distances. Gillian Rose was academically brilliant, grew up privileged in at least an economic sense, and died of a colon cancer that was resistant to chemotherapy. Gary Fisher was considered to have great talent as a writer. At the time of his death he was technically a graduate student at Berkeley but had no real expectation of finishing his doctorate. Fisher grew up in a middle-class African American family. He was gay, engaged in unsafe sex, shared needles and died of AIDS. *Love's Work* is a kind of *summa* of Gillian Rose's productive career. *Gary in Your Pocket* is posthumously edited, introducing a writer who during his life was not known beyond his immediate circle of friends.

Both books talk about illness inter alia. In her study of first-person illness narratives, Anne Hunsaker Hawkins calls these books 'monothematic', dominated by 'the desire to get well' (1993: 32). Both Fisher and Rose struggle against the volition of illness to make their writing and their lives monothematic. Each works to keep illness out of centre stage. What takes the stage instead is sexuality. It's too simple an equation to say that in each book sexuality is an affirmation of life and illness leads inexorably to death, yet the oppositions are hard to avoid: sex and life, illness and death. At the centre of these oppositions is the body: pleasurable and dangerous.

But I am already constructing too symmetrical a framework. Eve Sedgwick writes in her afterword how she first imagined Gary Fisher 'in terms [that were] more or less concentric, consolidating selfhood and

• *Theory, Culture & Society* 1998 (SAGE, London, Thousand Oaks and New Delhi),
  Vol. 15(3–4): 417–425
  [0263-2764(199809/11)15:3–4;417–425;006084]

privacy – his passion as a writer, his sexual life, his complex understanding of racism, for example, along with his friendships and his relation to illness'. As she comes to know him better the concentric order falls away. She sees how these aspects of Fisher 'might coexist as far sharper, less integrated shards of personality, history, and desire' (p. 280). Gillian Rose's construction of her memoir seems intended as a refusal of any concentric order that a reader might wish to impose on her text or her life. She moves the reader, not randomly but inexplicably, between different places, different friendships, different moments in her life, leaving it to us to put these pieces together. We must constantly ask, why did she choose to include that, and what does it have to do with what she placed before and after? Fisher did not make these choices, his editor did. But he did choose to write notebooks, a genre that would eventually require editing. Both books are about putting the pieces together, and the two biggest pieces are sex and illness.

'Love is the submission of power', writes Gillian Rose (p. 61). For Gary Fisher submission and power were literal. He lived in what sociologists would call a subculture of a subculture: he was a masochist whose pleasure was in oral receptive sex. Fisher desired being degraded; Sedgwick observes that for him a sexual exchange was incomplete 'unless he can induce some white man to call him "nigger" and seem to mean it' (p. 282). Much of *Gary in Your Pocket* is descriptions of anonymous sex in public settings. I distance myself from these passages by reading them as clinical documents; I need to pathologize their author. Sedgwick anticipates my reaction when she writes about understanding masochism in psychoanalytic terms, formulating it as a result of some early trauma that has deformed the self. This view contains masochists as 'people too abject or damaged to stay out of harmful situations' (p. 283). Fisher's death is ample testimony to the harmful situations he put himself in. But Sedgwick argues, as well as I could imagine the argument being made, that far from S/M guaranteeing 'that no new meanings, feelings, or selves may ever emerge through its practice' (p. 283), Fisher did reinvent himself through S/M.

> One can view both trauma and mimesis less rigidly, though; there are people – Gary Fisher was one – for whom the only way out is through. Suppose, as Gary seems to suppose, the sadomasochistic scene to occur on a performative axis that extends from political theater to religious ritual; an axis that spans, as well, the scenes of psychotherapy and other dramaturgically abreactive healing traditions. According to this understanding, the S/M scene might offer a self-propelled, demotic way – independent of experts and institutions – to perform ... the detailed, phenomenologically rich reconstruction of the fragments of traumatic memory; claiming and exercise of the power to reexperience and transform that memory, and to take control of the time and rhythm of entering, exploring, and leaving the space of it; and having its power, and one's experience of it, acknowledged and witnessed by others. (p. 283)

The above quotation also describes the pedagogy of a writer, and if anything makes Sedgwick's rationale persuasive for me, it is that Fisher *wrote* about his sexual encounters. I hate reading about these encounters as much because of the purposive degradation in them as because of the death I see them leading to. But I can see in the act of writing about degradation a process of self-creation: an enacted poststructuralist separation of the 'I' who is acted upon in the writing (the 'slave') from the 'I' who exerts mastery (becomes an author) in writing. 'Love-making', writes Rose, 'is never simply pleasure' (p. 69). Fisher expresses pleasure in sexual acts that I interpret as antithetical to love-making, but he wants more than pleasure.

Perhaps Rose puts an even finer gloss on Fisher's masochism when she writes about the need of the mature human to learn the difference 'between fantasy and actuality'. If one searches for some rationale for Fisher's behaviour, and I admit I need a rationale to make this text readable, Rose provides a good one:

> The child who is able to explore that border will feel safe in experiencing violent, inner conflict, and will acquire compassion for other people. The child who is locked away from aggressive experiment and play will be left terrified and paralysed by its emotions, unable to release or face them, for they may destroy the world and himself or herself. (p. 126)

Rose helps me to understand Fisher not as 'abject' but as seeking 'aggressive experiment' in order to be less terrified in a terrifying world. His descriptions of 'torture' are written, not so curiously if we take Rose seriously, without any undercurrent of residual violent feelings toward the others involved. Rose's description rings true: at the end of these descriptions there is a sense of safety in the physical violence that has been experienced without emotional conflict. Fisher does express compassion for those whom he sought out to degrade him. But this line of argument remains a kind of apologetic: a way of reducing the otherness of Fisher and his world. What is striking about Fisher is the absence of apology or self-justification in his writing. He allowed himself to be, not simply, but without rationalization.

Gillian Rose was not a masochist in Fisher's sense, but she does describe herself as 'highly qualified in unhappy love affairs'. 'To be at someone's mercy', she writes of love, 'is dialectical damage: they may be merciful and they may be merciless' (p. 61). At the centre of her book is a love affair in which her partner seems merciless. Sedgwick, as editor, changed the names of Fisher's sexual partners. Rose names her lover, a priest who, I can only suppose, will suffer from the notoriety. She mentions without naming them two lovers with whom she had much longer, happier relationships and from whom she initiated a break, but she names this man who seems to have left her. Dialectical damage, certainly: 'Yet each party, woman, man, the child in each, and their child, is absolute power as well as absolute vulnerability' (p. 60). And so she demonstrates. In Fisher's world of physical violence power seems far less absolute.

But is any attempt to explain sexuality necessarily too concentric, revealing a desire – which I freely admit too – to reduce deeply troubling bodies to safer ideas? 'It was a project', writes Sedgwick on Fisher's masochism, 'not in the first place of *representing sex*, but of stretching every boundary of *what sex can represent*' (p. 282). In both books the authors' boundaries are stretched not by sex but by illness, the unwanted project that seizes them. Illness becomes the project of what disease can represent, even as disease represents nothing but simply is, a null point at which representation ends.

One of Rose's most provocative digressions occurs when she interrupts her chapter on colon cancer to discuss the researchers of Robert Jan van Pelt on the Holocaust. Van Pelt has demonstrated, controversially but to Rose's satisfaction, that in Auschwitz 'death was a by-product of the inclusion of individuals unsuited for work among the transports of potential workers' (p. 91). The point is contingency, and how difficult it is for us who come after to accept that an event of massive consequences happened without design. 'Van Pelt is keen, moreover, to emphasise the contingent nature of many of the features of the so-called "Holocaust"' (p. 92). Part of the demonstration of contingency rests on showing 'lack of foresight regarding sanitation', and this aspect of his argument – the disposal of shit – meets with most 'reluctance, embarrassment and loss of attention' among his audiences (p. 92). Rose then integrates her digression by seguing into the history of colostomies (first performed in 1797; first published on in 1805) and the disposal of shit, her preferred word.

But the discussion of Auschwitz would be mere cleverness, a scatological joke, if it only segued back to colostomies. As Rose makes the case that Auschwitz emerged contingently, and as she challenges our willingness to accept this contingency, she is challenging something deeper in our beliefs about life and causality.

> A lot of things were happening at once for Gary Fisher in the few years after he moved to San Francisco, and there's no easy way of tracing the feedback loops by which the transformations of his sexual practice, political consciousness, literary vocation, theoretical interests, and relation to illness and death were making one another happen. (Sedgwick, p. 281)

Both these books are about feedback loops: how real they are but how there's no easy way to trace them. The project of stretching the boundary of what disease can represent is ultimately about feedback loops, traces that cannot be traced.

At least materially the loops trace back to the body: 'I need to invent colostomy ethnography', writes Rose (p. 94). Here her project and Fisher's coincide most directly. Her descriptions of her colostomy *stoma* – the opening at which the colon is brought out through the abdomen to form 'a surrogate rectum and anus' (p. 93) – find their complement in Fisher's evocation of living with AIDS:

> And if it happens: the bowels stir, the muscles twitch, ache, threaten knots. And the shockjuice mixes explosively with the acid already burning a new hole in your stomach. You gleefully, yes almost that, jump onto the stool and unload a half gallon of brown water, then you thank your body sincerely like you've only just met it. But this is once in 36–48 hours, or in 24–36 runs to the toilet.
>
> *   *   *
>
> $36/36 = 1$ run per hour =
> no sleep = delirium by the third night,
> death (by suicide or homicide) by the fourth night. (p. 255)

'My interest is in the uncharted', Rose writes of her colostomy ethnography and Fisher might have written also; 'my difficulty that I will inevitably enlist, by connotation and implication, the power and grace of the symbol' (p. 94). Here we reach the complex question of writing, central to both Rose's and Fisher's identities. Compare these passages:

> I must continue to write for the same reason I am always compelled to write, in sickness and in health: for, otherwise, I die deadly, but this way, by this work, I may die forward into the intensified agon of living. (Rose, p. 77)

> Well, I've told her [i.e. told Eve Sedgwick that he has what he then knew as ARC] and now I'm freed up to write, to let loose on the wonder and ... words, words gone ... it's horrible, just horrible that I should find enjoyment here. Where's the rock? the stoic? I should have died. I should be the walking corpse, not this vivid dreamer. Who ever measured dreamers by their lifespan? ... (Fisher, pp. 213–14, ellipses in original)

Gillian Rose finds the means to 'die forward' in her writing, and Gary Fisher becomes a dreamer who cannot be measured by his life-span.

What do they write about? First their bodies, starting at the skin where internal organs and disease processes are now inscribed. 'Tight coils of concentric, flesh, blood-red flesh 25 millimeters (one inch) in diameter, protrude a few millimetres from the centre left of my abdomen, just below the waist. Blueness would be a symptom of distress' (Rose, p. 94). 'I'm looking at my arm and I don't trust what I just said. There is a geometry to this, a poetry too. If I didn't know it was cancer and AIDS I'd say my arm – my right arm – is interesting, attractive. The spots are grayish, purplish, a light eggplant, mauve – a combination' (Fisher, pp. 271–2). Their common experience is described by Fisher: 'I have a new skin. I have a new identity' (p. 271).

Conventionally the skin is imagined as a kind of boundary, but disease erodes its illusion of separating inside from outside; Rose's stoma effaces this distinction, as do the frequency of Fisher's trips to the toilet. Boundaries between self and other are more durable. Rose writes how judgement becomes the boundary between a person who has cancer and others who do not, for whom cancer means 'a judgment, a species of ineluctable condemnation' (p. 78). Yet she introduces cancer by the elliptical device of asking how the reader would react if she revealed she had AIDS, which is exactly Fisher's problem. Her metaphor of judgement is his reality.

At least in the writings we have, Fisher says little about AIDS in the abstract. AIDS is always his body: its pain, its skin, its survival. As noted above, the feedback loops between AIDS and the rest of his life are complex. Consider the following journal entry and how Fisher conveys the news that he has tested HIV+, as he suspected he would:

> I have a cold. I had a positive test. I still haven't finished the Chaucer paper; really haven't started writing it. But the greatest disappointment, at least as it sits with me right now, comes from an encounter at the I-Beam. That handsome, white, flat-topped man, I asked him to dance – after spending an hour looking at him (after Gurrile *told him* I was interested!) – and he said 'no'. How else was I supposed to break the ice? (p. 221)

Much ice is being broken here: the ice that the news of being seriopositive suddenly freezes over a life that then must go on. Fisher seems intent to exclude any reflective space to absorb his news, aligning himself instead with Rose's desire to 'die forward in the intensified agon of living'.

But Fisher's rapid movement from the HIV test to the dance club raises another troubling aspect of his life. Four years earlier, suspecting he was HIV+, Fisher wrote: 'But wait! What if *I've* killed somebody with this? What if Jason dies because of my carelessness and embarrassment on the subject. What if Roy dies because of me, or vice-versa?' (p. 185). Issues of contagion and death remain part of Fisher's descriptions of sexual scenes, but avoiding contagion does not enter into his journal. Risking death, his own and others', seems to have been inextricably linked to what sex was, and sex seems inextricably a part of living. In the persona Fisher creates, sex seems always to have led to death. He writes that when his mother is dying from breast cancer he prayed to take her place, 'because you didn't deserve this, you hadn't planned for it all your life, while I think I started studying it the very first time I brushed knees with Gord W. in Mr. Jackson's class' (p. 213).

Different as their diseases and their moral dilemmas are, Rose and Fisher live disease with complementary attitudes. In a passage that seems directed at her defected lover, she writes: 'what people now seem to find most daunting with me, I discover, is not my illness or possibly death, but my accentuated being; not my morbidity, but my renewed vitality' (p. 79). Fisher writes: 'Trying to stave off the need to sleep because I don't know for sure where life begins and ends – not like I need to – and I don't want to miss anything' (p. 266).

As complex as the poetics of skin and the dynamics of vitality are, more complex still is sadness. Both are very sad people, their sadness crystallized in their illnesses but antedating them. Rose writes how philosophy provided some antidote to 'the burgeoning sadness of the teenage soul' (p. 128). Her long description of the Arthurian legend, in the last chapter, is about sadness. Arthur's dilemma of how to respond to the love between Guinevere and Launcelot means 'one way or the other, the King must now be sad' (p. 123). Her critique of postmodernism is its failure to recognize that 'philosophy is born out of the sadness of the King, to whom it offers the consolation of reflection' (p. 125). Again the feedback loops are complex between Rose's childhood, her identification with the Holocaust, her love affairs, her friendships with people who are ill or dying, her philosophy and her cancer. Each recreates a sadness that pervades all.

If Rose displaces her sadness on to the King, Fisher confronts his directly. He writes about his journals and art work:

> They dwell on the dark hours spent staring at a candle trying to forget my pain, on the particulars of the pain itself, on the draining revelation that my medicines are killing me too.
>
>   *   *   *
>
> It's suffering specific pain specifically. Every day, day to day, a single pain remembered, singularly. Or pain to pain, each so clear it seems like a visual experience, particularly in the dark, particularly at night. And the collection of them act like rare jewelry in a box. I'm only hopeful that I will live to see the party where I can wear them strongly and honestly and not be driven home by the talk, never mind the pain itself. (p. 255)

The Gary Fisher who wrote that journal entry is the one I can love without qualification. In these words I discover the person about whom his friend, the poet and physician Rafael Campo, wrote:

> He wisely allowed himself the space of one forgiven of everything, for whom there are no expectations or attendant failures, whose only responsibility is to imagine a world without suffering, and then to suffer. (Campo, 1997: 149)

Campo knows Fisher the only way he can be known: as a projection of the knower. When I was struggling with all I find so difficult about Fisher, especially his obsession with sexual encounters, I wrote to Campo unleashing my least considered emotions. I trusted he would not judge me for them. By his allowing me to express those things I could let them recede and let Gary Fisher emerge. But the Gary Fisher who emerges is the one we each need. Campo's need is to become a physician who can know, not merely treat, his patients with AIDS, and my need is that I readily admit Gillian Rose's illness to my experience but hold Gary Fisher at a distance.

The eventual effect of reading Gary Fisher is that he does not seek forgiveness so much as he offers it. Here is a journal entry written in 1982, when he was 18 or 19 years old, possibly the time he was infected with HIV:

There's a disease going around that is killing gay males. It may be linked to drug abuse. What about the shroud of Christ. God, how could human beings be *so* cruel? Would I do that? I never want the chance, ever. We need to re-humanize. (p. 164)

Fisher's own re-humanizing never seems to have included being more than tacitly concerned about how he might be spreading the disease that he knew was 'going around'. But in the ethics being struggled for here, physical contagion seems a risk subordinated to other values. The issue is acceptance, without reservation, of all that is human.

Rose describes ethics as 'being at a loss yet exploring various routes, different ways towards the good enough justice, which recognizes the intrinsic and the contingent limitations in its exercise. Earthly, human sadness is the divine comedy – the ineluctable discrepancy between our worthy intentions and the ever-surprising outcome of our actions' (pp. 124–5). Fisher lived this comedy. The various routes he followed finally led him to be alone in his apartment in front of a mirror studying his KS lesions. Sedgwick describes these times:

> ... he would spend hours, sometimes whole days of months, paralyzed in front of his mirror, incredulous, unable – also to stop trying – to constitute there a recognizable self. Impaled by the stigma. (p. 281)

How, in a racist, violent world, can a person find what Campo calls the space of one forgiven? How can a boy growing up in this world assure himself that he will never be so cruel? How to explore all the different ways not only to justice but to love, and at the end of that exploration, 'constitute there a recognizable self'?

What are these books? Not at all what Hawkins (1993) calls 'pathographies', texts revolving around the monotheme of getting well. Fisher and Rose each hoped to live, but each transmutes getting well on to a different ethical plane: impaled by stigma, there to constitute a recognizable self. I find my own capacity to recognize selves expands as I puzzle over Gary Fisher's linkage of the 'new disease', the human cruelty exemplified in Christ's crucifixion, and the need not to be cruel. Others will read these books differently, finding in them different selves and different imperatives of being.

Finally, what of their deaths? Another of Gillian Rose's 'digressions' – a shard we must find a place for in the complex whole of her text and life – is her analysis of the film *Picnic at Hanging Rock*. 'Everything begins and ends at exactly the right time and place', the film tells us, announcing the doom of one of the school girls (p. 35). Can we believe that these vastly talented lives also began and ended at the right time and place? Sedgwick imagines the writer Gary Fisher could have become, and we imagine the books that Gillian Rose might have given us. But writing books, as valuable as it may be within a life, is not the point of a life.

'Hold me, Gary, set me free. I don't want to stay locked in this journal' (p. 159). Gary Fisher wrote that when he was 18 or 19; he died when he was 32. Gillian Rose died in her early 40s. Their lives were tragically shortened, but in no sense can I imagine these lives incomplete.

References

Campo, Rafael (1997) *The Poetry of Healing: A Doctor's Education in Empathy, Identity, and Desire.* New York: Norton.

Hawkins, Anne Hunsaker (1993) *Reconstructing Illness: Studies in Pathography.* West Lafayette, IN: Purdue University Press.

Lane, Belden C. (1997) 'Open the Kingdom for a Cottonwood Tree', *The Christian Century* 114(30): 979–83.

Rose, Gillian (1995) *Love's Work: A Reckoning with Life.* New York: Schoken Books.

Sedgwick, Eve Kosofsky (ed.) (1996) *Gary in Your Pocket: Stories and Notebooks of Gary Fisher.* Durham, NC and London: Duke University Press.

Arthur W. Frank teaches Sociology at the University of Calgary in Alberta, Canada. His publications include *The Wounded Storyteller: Body, Illness, and Ethics* and recent articles in *Body & Society* and *Health.*

Love and Eroticism
Index

Theory, Culture & Society

Theory, Culture & Society caters for the resurgence of interest in culture within contemporary social science and the humanities. Building on the heritage of classical social theory, the book series examines ways in which this tradition has been reshaped by a new generation of theorists. It also publishes theoretically informed analyses of everyday life, popular culture, and new intellectual movements.

EDITOR: Mike Featherstone, *Nottingham Trent University*

SERIES EDITORIAL BOARD
Roy Boyne, *University of Durham*
Mike Hepworth, *University of Aberdeen*
Scott Lash, *Goldsmiths College, University of London*
Roland Robertson, *University of Pittsburgh*
Bryan S. Turner, *University of Cambridge*

THE TCS CENTRE
The Theory, Culture & Society book series, the journals *Theory, Culture & Society* and *Body & Society*, and related conference, seminar and postgraduate programmes operate from the TCS Centre at Nottingham Trent University. For further details of the TCS Centre's activities please contact:

Centre Administrator
The TCS Centre, Room 175
Faculty of Humanities
Nottingham Trent University
Clifton Lane, Nottingham, NG11 8NS, UK
e-mail: tcs@ntu.ac.uk
web: http//tcs@ntu.ac.uk

LIVERPOOL
JOHN MOORES UNIVERSITY
AVRIL ROBARTS LRC
TITHEBARN STREET
LIVERPOOL L2 2ER
TEL. 0151 231 4022

Recent volumes include:

Georges Bataille – Essential Writings
edited by Michael Richardson

Digital Aesthetics
Sean Cubitt

Facing Modernity
Ambivalence, Reflexivity and Morality
Barry Smart

Culture as Praxis
Zygmunt Bauman

Radical Conservatism and the Future of Politics
Göran Dahl

Spaces of Culture
City, Nation, World
Mike Featherstone and Scott Lash